# Introduction to Microcomputers

CS 101

Ann Shaffer
Patrick Carey
June Jamrich Parsons
Dan Oja
Kathleen Finnegan
Katherine Pinard
Lisa Ruffolo
Robin Romer
Joseph Adamski

D1530728

CENGAGE
Learning·

Australia • Brazil • Japan • Korea • Mexico • Singapore • Spain • United Kingdom • United States

**Introduction to Microcomputers**
**CS 101**

Senior Manager, Student Engagement:
Linda deStefano

Manager, Student Engagement:
Julie Dierig

Manager, Student Engagement:
Janey Moeller

Senior Marketing Manager:
Heather Kramer

Manager, Production Editorial:
Kim Fry

Manager, Intellectual Property Project Manager:
Brian Methe

Senior Manager, Production and Manufacturing:
Donna M. Brown

Manager, Production:
Terri Daley

New Perspectives on Microsoft Office 2013
First Course
© 2014 Cengage Learning. All rights reserved.

New Perspectives on Microsoft Office 200
First Course
© 2011, 2010, 2008 Cengage Learning. All rights reserved.

For product information and technology assistance, contact us at
**Cengage Learning Customer & Sales Support, 1-800-354-9706**

For permission to use material from this text or product,
submit all requests online at **cengage.com/permissions**
Further permissions questions can be emailed to
**permissionrequest@cengage.com**

This book contains select works from existing Cengage Learning resources and was produced by Cengage Learning Custom Solutions for collegiate use. As such, those adopting and/or contributing to this work are responsible for editorial content accuracy, continuity and completeness.

**Compilation © 2014 Cengage Learning**

ISBN-13: 978-1-305-29193-5

ISBN-10: 1-305-29193-X

**WCN: 01-100-101**

**Cengage Learning**
5191 Natorp Boulevard
Mason, Ohio 45040
USA
Cengage Learning is a leading provider of customized learning solutions with office locations around the globe, including Singapore, the United Kingdom, Australia, Mexico, Brazil, and Japan. Locate your local office at:
**international.cengage.com/region.**

Cengage Learning products are represented in Canada by Nelson Education, Ltd.
For your lifelong learning solutions, visit **www.cengage.com/custom.**
Visit our corporate website at **www.cengage.com.**

Printed in the United States of America

# BRIEF CONTENTS

<br>

# Exploring the Basics of Windows 8

*Investigating the Windows 8 Operating System*

OBJECTIVES

- Start and turn off Windows 8
- Describe how to use Windows 8 with a touchscreen device
- Tour the Start screen and the desktop
- Start Windows 8 and desktop applications
- Switch between applications and close them
- Identify and use the controls in windows and dialog boxes
- Get help with Windows 8 tasks

## Case | *Behind the Scenes*

Behind the Scenes is a small but growing temporary employment agency in St. Louis, Missouri. The agency specializes in training and providing virtual assistants, high-quality support staff that work from home to perform office tasks and projects for clients. As the training manager at Behind the Scenes, Emma Garcia coordinates staff training sessions on a wide range of professional and computer skills.

Emma recently hired you as her assistant. She has asked you to lead the upcoming training sessions on the fundamentals of the Microsoft Windows 8 operating system. As you prepare for the sessions, she offers to help you identify the topics you should cover and the skills you should demonstrate while focusing on the new features in Windows 8.

In this tutorial, you will start Windows 8 and practice some fundamental computer skills. You will tour the Start screen, start applications, and then explore the desktop. You will also work with windows and their tools, use the Windows 8 Help system, and turn off Windows 8.

**STARTING DATA FILES**

There are no starting Data Files needed for this tutorial.

# Visual Overview:

The four corners of the Start screen are **hot corners**; point to one to display objects for interacting with Windows.

The **user icon** identifies the current user and provides access to your account settings.

The **Start screen** appears after you sign in to Windows; you use it to start applications.

Click the Desktop tile to display the Windows 8 desktop.

The name you use to sign in to Windows appears next to the user icon.

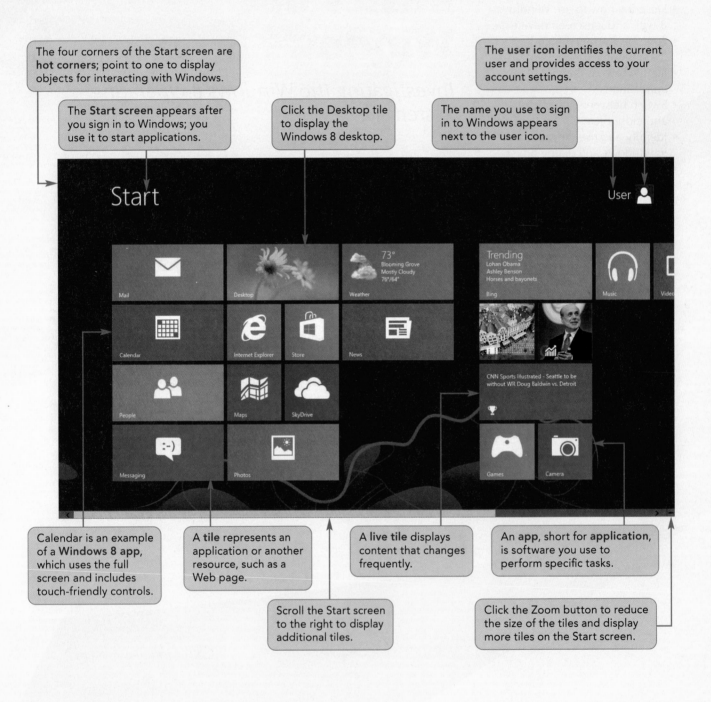

Calendar is an example of a **Windows 8 app**, which uses the full screen and includes touch-friendly controls.

A **tile** represents an application or another resource, such as a Web page.

A **live tile** displays content that changes frequently.

An **app**, short for **application**, is software you use to perform specific tasks.

Scroll the Start screen to the right to display additional tiles.

Click the Zoom button to reduce the size of the tiles and display more tiles on the Start screen.

# Windows 8 Start Screen & Desktop

The **desktop** is your work area for running many productivity applications and applications designed for previous versions of Windows.

This graphic is part of a **theme**, a set of coordinated desktop backgrounds, window colors, sounds, and screen savers.

The **Recycle Bin** holds deleted items until you remove them permanently.

Two applications are **pinned** to the taskbar, which means their buttons always appear on the left side of the taskbar.

The **taskbar** contains icons and buttons that give you quick access to common tools and running applications.

An **icon** is a small picture that represents a resource on your computer.

The **notification area** displays icons corresponding to services Windows provides, such as an Internet connection.

The **Date/time control** is an element that shows the current date and time and lets you set the clock.

# Introducing Windows 8

The **operating system** is software that manages and coordinates activities on the computer and helps the computer perform essential tasks, such as displaying information on the screen and saving data on disks. Your computer uses the **Microsoft Windows 8** operating system—**Windows 8** for short. Windows is the name of the operating system, and 8 indicates the version you are using.

Computers can run two types of software—system software and applications. **System software** is the software that runs a computer, including the operating system. An application (abbreviated as "app") is the software you use most directly to perform tasks such as writing a screenplay or viewing a webpage. In general, a computer runs system software to perform computer tasks, and you run applications to carry out your work or personal tasks. On Windows 8, you can run applications created specifically for the Windows 8 operating system and for earlier versions of Windows, such as Windows 7. With both versions of Windows, you can use more than one application at a time and switch seamlessly from one application to another to perform your work effectively.

Windows 8 is designed to run on computers that use a touchscreen, such as tablets, those that use a keyboard and mouse, such as a desktop computer, and those that use a touchpad, such as a laptop. A **touchscreen** is a display that lets you touch areas of the screen to interact with software. See Figure 1.

| Figure 1 | Windows 8 on different types of computers |
| --- | --- |

© 2014 Cengage Learning

## Using Windows 8 with Pointing Devices

As shown in the Visual Overview, when you work with Windows 8, you interact with objects such as tiles and icons to start applications, provide information to Windows, and perform other computer tasks. If you are using a laptop or desktop computer, you most likely use a **pointing device** to interact with the objects on the screen. Pointing devices come in many shapes and sizes. The most common one is called a **mouse**, so this book uses that term. If you are using a different pointing device, such as a trackball or touchpad, substitute that device whenever you see the term "mouse."

You use a mouse to move the pointer over locations and objects on the screen, or to **point** to them. The **pointer** is an on-screen object, often shaped like an arrow, though it changes shape depending on its location on the screen and the tasks you are performing. As you move the mouse on a surface, such as a table top, the pointer moves in a corresponding direction.

You also use the mouse to interact with specific objects on the screen. For example, you can use the mouse to click an object. **Clicking** refers to pressing a mouse button and immediately releasing it. Clicking sends a signal to your computer that you want to perform an action with the object you click. In Windows 8, you perform most actions with the left mouse button. If a step instructs you to click an on-screen object, such as a Start screen tile, position the pointer on that object and click the left mouse button. Another common mouse action is **double-clicking**, which means to click the left mouse button twice in quick succession. You can also press and release the right button on a mouse, which is called **right-clicking**. (If your mouse has only one button, you right-click by pressing the right side of the button.) Finally, you can point to an object, press and hold down the mouse button, and then move the mouse, which is called **dragging** the object.

## Using Windows 8 with Touchscreen Devices

If you are using a computer with a touchscreen, such as a tablet, you use your fingertips to interact with on-screen objects. The movements you make as you touch the screen with your fingertips are called **gestures**. The six basic gestures are tap, press, swipe, slide or drag, pinch, and rotate. For example, instead of clicking a tile on the Start screen, you tap the tile, which means you use your fingertip to touch the item briefly. Figure 2 illustrates the six gestures you use with touchscreen devices.

| Figure 2 | Gestures used with touchscreen devices |

| Touch Gesture | Description | Illustration |
|---|---|---|
| Tap | Touch an item with a fingertip |  Tap to start an application or select an object |
| Press | Touch and hold an item | 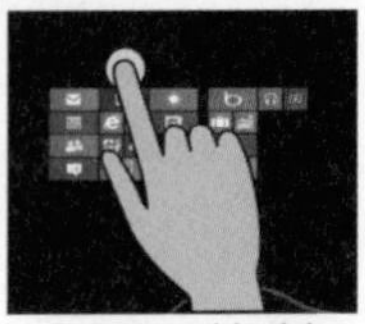 Press and hold to learn |
| Swipe | Drag a fingertip across the screen and then release | 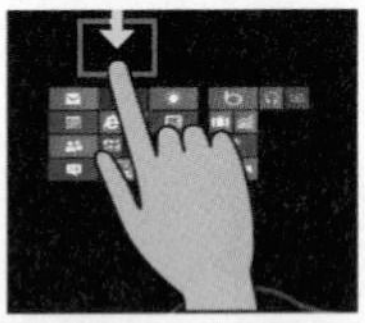 Swipe to display commands |
| Slide or drag | Drag a fingertip across the screen without releasing | 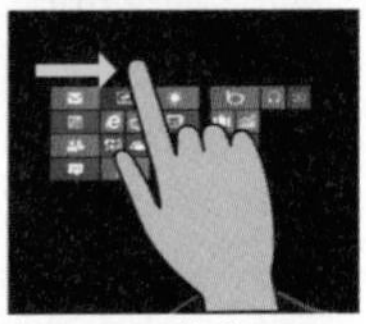 Slide to scroll the screen or move an object |
| Pinch | Touch the screen with two fingers and then drag your fingertips toward each other to zoom out, or drag your fingertips away from each other to zoom in |  Pinch and stretch to zoom |
| Rotate | Touch the screen with two fingers and then drag either clockwise or counterclockwise |  Turn to rotate |

© 2014 Cengage Learning

Many elements of Windows 8 are designed with touchscreen users in mind. For example, the Start screen includes large tiles instead of small icons because tiles are easier to tap. However, you are not required to use a touchscreen with Windows 8. In fact, this book assumes that you are using a computer with a keyboard and a mouse.

### The Windows 8 User Interface

The part of the operating system you use when you work with a computer is called the **user interface (UI)**. The UI includes everything that lets you interact with the computer, including the layout of the screen and the controls that the operating system provides so you can make selections and change settings. (**Controls** are graphical or textual objects you use to work with the operating system and applications.) On the Start screen, the Windows 8 UI uses a design that emphasizes large, clear graphical icons to identify screen objects. When you use a Windows 8 app, the focus is on the content, so the screen is not cluttered with tools and controls. The Windows 8 UI also uses animation and fluid motions to respond to your actions and selections, which make the system seem livelier than a collection of static objects. To take advantage of wide screens, multiple monitors, and touch-screen devices, the Windows 8 UI is more horizontally oriented than previous versions of Windows. For example, you scroll right and left to access content currently out of view.

## Starting Windows 8

Windows 8 starts automatically when you turn on your computer. After completing some necessary startup tasks, Windows 8 might display a **lock screen**, which includes a picture, the date, and the time. You clear the lock screen to display the Welcome screen, which lists all the users for the computer. Before you start working with Windows 8, you might also need to click your **username** (a unique name that identifies you to Windows 8) and type a **password** (a confidential series of characters). After you provide this information, the Windows 8 Start screen appears, as shown in the Visual Overview.

### Decision Making: Selecting a User Account Type

In order to use Windows 8, you must have a user account. A **user account** identifies you to the computer. You access your user account by selecting your username and typing your password, if required. You can create additional user accounts at any time. If you share a computer with other people, your user account allows you to keep your work and settings separate from the other users. When you create your user account, you must choose from one of the following types of accounts:

- Microsoft account—This is a user account that is associated with Microsoft's **SkyDrive**, a Microsoft server on the Internet on which you can store files and access some Microsoft programs. If you have a user account on more than one computer running Windows 8, you can access your applications, preferences, and other settings. In addition, you can use some Windows 8 applications only if you are signed in with a Microsoft account, including the Store app, which lets you add new applications to your computer, and the Music app, which you use to purchase songs and albums. You sign in to a Microsoft account using an email address. Any email address can be associated with a Microsoft account, and that email address then becomes the username for that account. You can also set up a Microsoft account when you create your user account in Windows 8.
- Local account—When you sign in with a local account, you are signed in to Windows 8 but you are not automatically connected to SkyDrive. This type of account accesses resources on your computer in the same way user accounts worked in earlier versions of Windows. You can, however, create a separate account on Microsoft SkyDrive to access SkyDrive features.

Make sure you understand the differences between these two types of user accounts so you can decide which one is the best type for you and your work habits.

To begin preparing for the Windows 8 training session you will deliver, Emma asks you to start Windows 8.

**To start Windows 8:**

▶ **1.** Turn on your computer. After a moment, Windows 8 starts and displays the Welcome screen.

**Trouble?** If you are asked to select an operating system, do not take action. Windows 8 should start automatically after a designated number of seconds. If it does not, ask your instructor or technical support person for help.

**Trouble?** If a lock screen appears before the Welcome screen does, press any key to clear the lock screen.

▶ **2.** If the Welcome screen is displayed for more than a few seconds, click your username, type your password, and then press the **Enter** key.

The Windows 8 Start screen appears, as shown in the Visual Overview. Your screen might look different.

**Trouble?** If your username does not appear on the Welcome screen, ask your instructor or technical support person for further assistance.

**Trouble?** If a blank screen or an animated design replaces the Start screen, your computer might be set to use a **screen saver**, a program that causes a monitor to go blank or to display an animated design after a specified amount of idle time. Press any key or move your mouse to restore the Start screen.

**Trouble?** If your computer is using a screen resolution other than 1366 x 768, the figures shown in this tutorial might not match exactly what you see in Windows 8 as you work through the steps. Take the screen resolution difference into account as you compare your screen to the figures.

# Touring the Start Screen

The screen that appears after you sign in to Windows 8 is called the Start screen because you start working on your computer from this screen. The Start screen includes multicolored rectangles called tiles, which represent applications and other resources your computer can access. See Figure 3.

**Figure 3**    Tiles on the Start screen

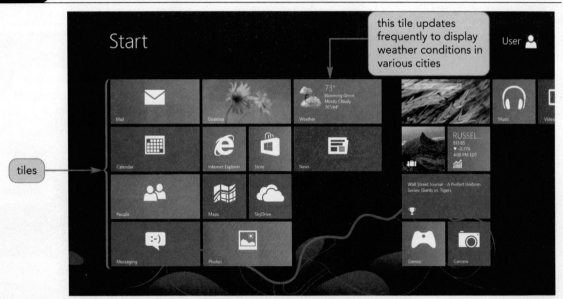

Some tiles display changing pictures or text that previews the contents of the tile. A tile that displays updated content is called a live tile. For example, the Weather tile is a live tile that displays current weather conditions in cities around the world. You click the Weather live tile to open the Weather app, a Windows 8 app that lets you check the current and forecasted weather in various locations.

The first time you start Windows 8, the computer uses **default settings**, which are preset by the operating system. The default Start screen you see after you first install Windows 8, for example, displays a number of tiles, including those for Internet Explorer (an application you use to access the Internet), Weather, and Photos. However, Microsoft designed Windows 8 so that you can easily change the appearance of the Start screen. You can, for example, move and add tiles and change the background color.

Emma suggests that during your class, you introduce Behind the Scenes employees to the Start screen by showing them how to scroll in case some tiles are out of view.

**To scroll the Start screen:**

**TIP**

Make sure you position the pointer on the very edge of the Start screen. You might also need to press and hold the mouse button as you scroll.

1. Use the mouse to point to the **right edge** of the Start screen. The screen scrolls to display additional tiles or those not shown on the main Start screen. See Figure 4.

   **Trouble?** If a bar of buttons appears on the right side of the screen, you pointed to the upper-right or lower-right corner. Point to the middle of the right edge of the screen to scroll.

   **Trouble?** If the screen does not scroll, your Start screen might not contain additional or half-shown tiles.

| Figure 4 | Scrolling the Start screen |
|---|---|

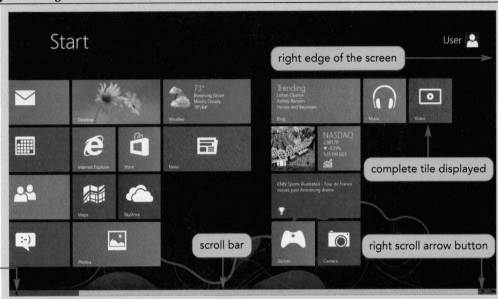

left scroll arrow button

When you move the pointer, a scroll bar appears at the bottom of the screen indicating that the screen includes content currently out of view. (Some screens display both vertical and horizontal scroll bars.) You can drag the scroll bar or click the arrow buttons to scroll.

2. Click the **left scroll arrow** button ◄ on the horizontal scroll bar at the bottom of the screen. The view shifts to display the left portion of the Start screen.

Besides scrolling the Start screen to display additional tiles, you can zoom the Start screen to make the tiles smaller (to display more tiles) or larger (to display fewer tiles).

**To zoom the Start screen:**

1. Move the pointer until the Zoom button ▬ appears in the lower-right corner of the Start screen. See Figure 5.

| Figure 5 | Displaying the Zoom button |
|---|---|

Zoom button

2. Click the **Zoom** button ▬ to reduce the size of the tiles. See Figure 6.

| Figure 6 | Zooming the Start screen |

tiles are smaller to
display more of them
on the Start screen

**3.** Click a blank area on the Start screen to return the tiles to their original size.

When you moved the pointer to the Zoom button to click it, a bar appeared on the right edge of the Start screen. This is called the **Charms bar**, and it contains buttons, also called **charms**, for interacting with Windows 8. The Charms bar appears when you point to the upper-right or lower-right corner of the screen. These locations are two of the four hot corners Windows 8 provides for mouse users. When you point to the Charms bar, it appears with a black background, indicating it is the **active object**. You can interact with active objects by clicking them. For example, when you click some charms, such as the Settings charm, a menu opens. A **menu** is a list, or group, of commands, and a **menu command** is an item on the list that you can click to perform a task. The **Settings menu** lets you access options and information for your current task and your system. Emma suggests you use the Settings charm on the Charms bar to open the Settings menu.

**To open the Settings menu:**

**1.** Point to the upper-right corner of the screen to display the Charms bar.

**2.** Point to the **Charms bar** to display it with a black background, indicating it is active. See Figure 7. When you activate the Charms bar, a status box appears on the screen displaying the date and time. It might also display other status information, such as the strength of your network connection or battery level.

TIP

You can also press and
hold the Windows key
and then press the C key
to display the Charms bar.

**Figure 7**   Active Charms bar

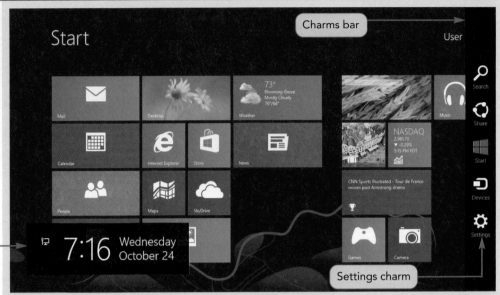

3. Click the **Settings** charm on the Charms bar to display the Settings menu, which is shown in Figure 8. Because you opened the Settings menu from the Start screen, some commands are specific to the Start screen. For example, you can use the Tiles command to change tile settings.

**Figure 8**   Settings menu

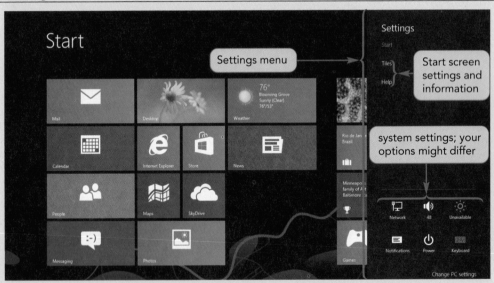

4. Click a blank area on the Start screen to close the Settings menu.

# Starting Applications

Windows 8 runs two types of applications. Windows 8 applications, as the name suggests, are designed to use the Windows 8 interface and work with touchscreen devices. They are often called apps. When you start a Windows 8 application, it takes up the entire screen and provides an uncluttered workspace for performing tasks. You can also use Windows 8 to run **desktop applications**, programs that open and run on the desktop, which is shown in the Visual Overview. For example, WordPad is a desktop application you use to create basic word-processing documents.

**REFERENCE**

*Starting an Application*

- Click the application's tile on the Start screen.

*or*

- Right-click a blank area on the Start screen, click the All apps button on the Apps bar at the bottom of the screen, and then click the application on the Apps screen.

*or*

- On the Start screen, type the name of the application until the application appears in the search results on the Apps screen.
- Click the application in the search results.

The easiest way to start an application is to click its tile on the Start screen. Emma suggests you use this technique to start the Weather app.

**To start the Weather app from the Start screen:**

▶ 1. Click the **Weather** tile on the Start screen to start the Weather app.

   **Trouble?** If a message appears asking if you want to allow Weather to use your location, click the Block button.

▶ 2. If an Enter Location box appears, type **St** to display a list of location names that start with "St," and then click **St Louis, Missouri, United States** in the list to display weather information for that location. See Figure 9. Your weather information will differ.

   **Trouble?** If an Enter Location box does not appear after you click the Weather tile, your Weather app is set to use a specific location and shows the weather for that location. Continue to Step 3.

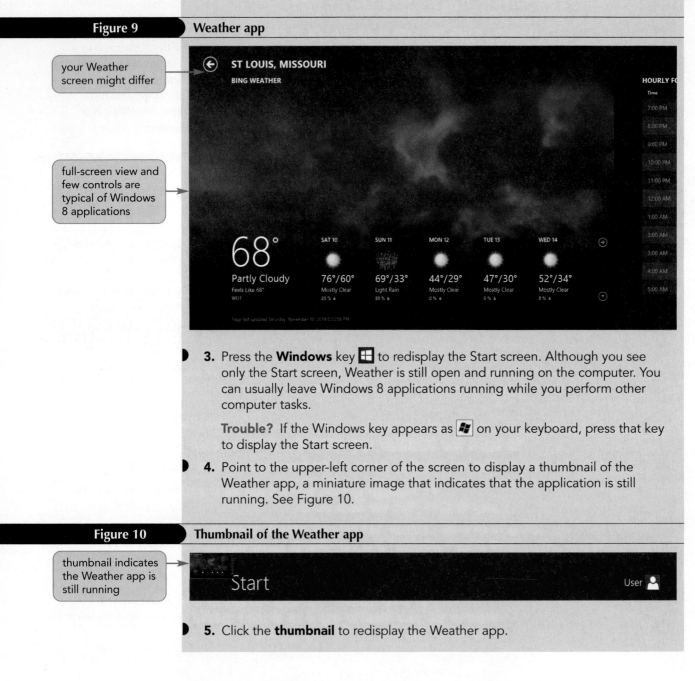

**Figure 9**  **Weather app**

your Weather screen might differ

full-screen view and few controls are typical of Windows 8 applications

3. Press the **Windows** key to redisplay the Start screen. Although you see only the Start screen, Weather is still open and running on the computer. You can usually leave Windows 8 applications running while you perform other computer tasks.

   **Trouble?** If the Windows key appears as on your keyboard, press that key to display the Start screen.

4. Point to the upper-left corner of the screen to display a thumbnail of the Weather app, a miniature image that indicates that the application is still running. See Figure 10.

**Figure 10**  **Thumbnail of the Weather app**

thumbnail indicates the Weather app is still running

5. Click the **thumbnail** to redisplay the Weather app.

## Using the Apps Screen to Start an Application

If an application's tile does not appear on the Start screen, you can open the application using the **Apps screen**, which lists all the applications installed on your computer. One way to display the Apps screen is to right-click a blank area of the Start screen to display the **Apps bar**, which includes buttons related to your current task, and then click the All apps button.

Emma wants you to demonstrate how to use more than one technique to start applications, so you will use the Apps screen to start Reader, a Windows 8 application that does not appear on the Start screen by default. Reader lets you view and navigate **PDF documents**, which are files in the Portable Document Format that usually include text and graphics and are readable on most computer systems. First, you must return to the Start screen so you can display the Apps bar with the All apps button.

### To start the Reader app from the Apps screen:

**1.** Press the **Windows** key  to display the Start screen.

**2.** Right-click a blank area on the Start screen to display the Apps bar at the bottom of the screen.

**3.** Click the **All apps** button on the right side of the Apps bar to display the Apps screen. See Figure 11. The Apps screen lists Windows 8 applications on the left and categories of desktop applications on the right.

| Figure 11 | Apps screen |

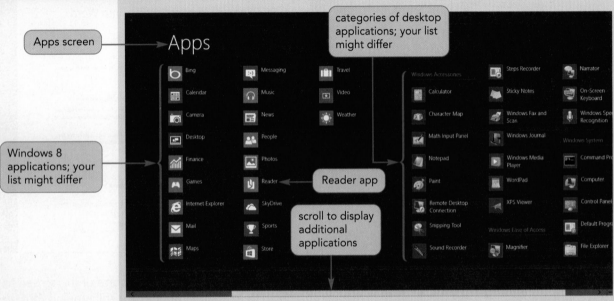

**4.** Click **Reader** to start the Reader app. A PDF document opens in Reader explaining how to edit PDF files using Microsoft Word.

**Trouble?** You might have a different PDF document that opens in Reader, or no document will open at all and you will see the Recent screen for Reader. This is not a problem.

Windows 8 applications start and run as full-screen programs so you can focus on your task and the content on the screen. Occasionally, you need to refer to information in one application while you are working in another application. For example, you might want to keep the Weather app open so you can check the weather while you are reading a document in the Reader app. If you are using a high screen resolution (at least 1366 × 768), you can **snap** an app, which means you display a Windows 8 application on the left or right side of the screen and leave it open as you work in another Windows 8 application. You can snap only Windows 8 applications, not desktop applications.

If a Windows 8 application appears on the screen, you snap it by dragging it to the left or right. If the application is open and running but does not appear on the screen, you can display its thumbnail, and then right-click the thumbnail to open a **shortcut menu**, which lists actions you can take with the application. The thumbnail shortcut menu includes commands for snapping the application to the left or right side of the screen.

**TIP**

You can right-click other objects on the Start screen and the desktop to view a shortcut menu of commands associated with that object.

**To snap the Weather app:**

1. Point to the upper-left hot corner to display the Weather thumbnail.

2. Right-click the **Weather** thumbnail, and then click **Snap left** on the shortcut menu to snap the Weather app to the left side of the screen while the Reader app is open on the right. See Figure 12.

| Figure 12 | Weather app snapped on the left |

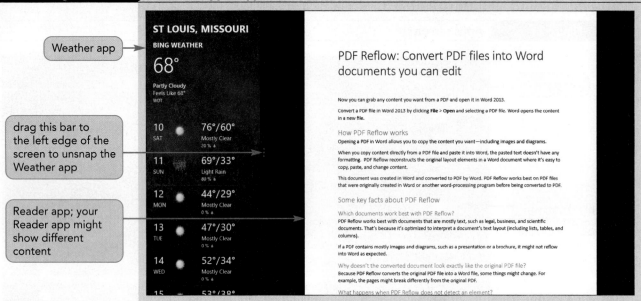

Weather app

drag this bar to the left edge of the screen to unsnap the Weather app

Reader app; your Reader app might show different content

**TIP**

You can also drag the bar between the applications to adjust the amount of screen space devoted to each one.

3. Drag the **bar** between the two applications to the left edge of the screen to unsnap the Weather app. Both Reader and Weather are still running, but the Weather app is no longer snapped to the screen.

## Using the Search Menu to Start an Application

Besides using the Apps screen to start Windows 8 applications, you can also use it to start desktop applications. When you first install Windows 8, the Apps screen lists so many applications that you need to scroll to the right at least once to display all of them. As you add other applications to your computer, you might need to scroll a few more times to find the application you want to start. Instead of scrolling the Apps screen, you can use the **Search menu** as a time-saving shortcut for starting applications. You open the Search menu from the Charms bar. When you do, it appears on top of the Apps screen by default. See Figure 13.

| Figure 13 | Apps screen and Search menu |

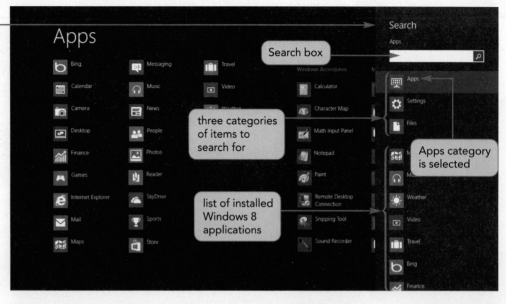

use the Search menu to search for applications, settings, and files

Search box

three categories of items to search for

Apps category is selected

list of installed Windows 8 applications

You use the **Search box** on the Search menu to quickly find anything stored on your computer including applications, documents, pictures, music, videos, and settings. Below the Search box, the Search menu lists three major categories of items you can search for—Apps, Settings, and Files. The Apps category is selected by default. Below the category list on the Search menu is a list of Windows 8 applications installed on your computer. To search for an application, click in the Search box and start typing the name of the application. As you type, the Apps screen displays the search results—applications containing words beginning with that text in their names. Another way to search for an application is to type some or all of the application name on the Start screen. (You don't need to click a particular part of the screen or open a box first.) When you start typing, the Search menu opens on the Apps screen and the text you typed appears in the Search box. The Apps screen displays the search results, which are the applications whose names start with the text in the Search box. You then click the application in the search results to start the application.

If you want to search for settings, you enter the text relating to the setting you are searching for, and then click Settings in the category list. Searching for files works the same way—in the Search box, type the text related to the file you are looking for, and then click Files in the category list.

Emma suggests you use the Search menu to locate and start the WordPad desktop application, which Behind the Scenes employees can use to write and open text documents.

**To start WordPad:**

1. Press the **Windows** key ⊞ to display the Start screen.

2. On the Start screen, type **wordp** to display the Search menu with "wordp" inserted in the Search box. The Apps screen lists the search results, which include the WordPad application. See Figure 14.

TIP

You can also display the Charms bar and then click the Search charm to open the Search menu.

| Figure 14 | WordPad in the search results |
| --- | --- |

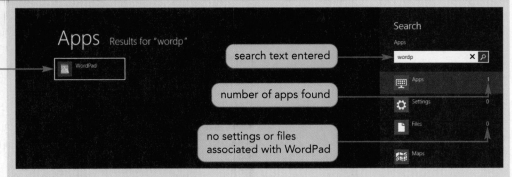

WordPad is listed in the search results

search text entered

number of apps found

no settings or files associated with WordPad

**Trouble?** If settings or files appear in the search results, click Apps in the category list, and then repeat Step 2 if necessary, making sure the search text is displayed in the Search box.

3. Click **WordPad** in the search results. WordPad opens on the desktop, as shown in Figure 15.

| Figure 15 | WordPad open on the desktop |
| --- | --- |

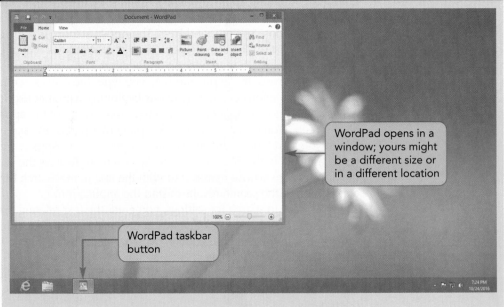

WordPad opens in a window; yours might be a different size or in a different location

WordPad taskbar button

When you open a desktop application such as WordPad, its **window**—a rectangular work area that contains tools for performing tasks in the application—is displayed on the desktop and a taskbar button for WordPad appears on the taskbar. You use **taskbar buttons** to identify and work with open desktop applications.

## Manipulating Windows

After you open a window, you can manipulate it to display as much or as little information as you need. In most windows, three buttons appear on the right side of the title bar. See Figure 16. The first button is the Minimize button, which you can use to **minimize** a window, or hide it so that only its button is visible on the taskbar. Depending on the status of the window, the middle button either maximizes the window or restores it to a predefined size. **Maximizing** means to enlarge a window so that it fills the entire screen. The last button is the Close button, which closes the window.

| Figure 16 | Window buttons |

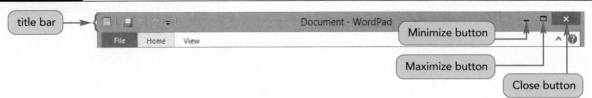

To make sure Behind the Scenes employees know how to manipulate windows, Emma suggests you show them how to use the WordPad taskbar button and the buttons on the WordPad title bar.

### To manipulate the WordPad window:

**1.** Click the **Minimize** button ⊟ on the WordPad title bar to minimize the WordPad window. The WordPad window shrinks so that only the WordPad button is visible on the taskbar. With the WordPad window hidden, you can view the entire desktop.

**2.** Click the **WordPad** button ▣ on the taskbar to redisplay the WordPad window.

**3.** Click the **Maximize** button ▢ on the WordPad title bar to maximize the WordPad window.

> **Trouble?** If the window is already maximized, it fills the entire screen and the Maximize button ▢ doesn't appear. Instead, you see the Restore Down button ▤. Skip Step 3.

**4.** Click the **Restore Down** button ▤ on the title bar to make the WordPad window smaller than the entire screen. After a window is restored, the Restore Down button ▤ changes to the Maximize button ▢.

**TIP**

You can also double-click a window's title bar to maximize the window. Double-click the title bar again to restore the window to its previous size.

You can also manipulate windows by moving and resizing them. To move a window, you drag the window by its title bar. You also drag to resize a window. When you point to an edge or a corner of a window, the pointer changes to a resize pointer, which is a double-headed arrow, similar to ⤢. You can use the resize pointer to drag an edge or a corner of the window and change the size of the window. If a window is maximized, you must click the Restore Down button before you can move or resize the window.

### To move and resize the WordPad window:

**1.** Position the mouse pointer on the title bar of the WordPad window.

**2.** Press and hold the mouse button, and then move the pointer up or down a little to drag the window. The window moves as you move the pointer.

**3.** Drag the window to the middle of the desktop so it does not cover any part of the Recycle Bin icon that appears on the desktop, and then release the mouse button. The WordPad window remains in the new location.

> **Trouble?** If the WordPad window becomes maximized when you drag it, click the Restore Down button ▤ before performing Step 4.

> **4.** Point to the lower-right corner of the WordPad window until the ⬉ pointer appears, and then drag down and to the right to enlarge the window.

> **5.** Drag up and to the left until the window is about its original size.

In addition to the window manipulation buttons, the WordPad window contains other tools common in desktop applications.

# Using Tools in Desktop Applications

In a desktop application, you use controls to manipulate the application window and perform your work in the application. Many desktop applications organize controls in two places—ribbons and dialog boxes.

## Using the Ribbon

Many desktop applications use a **ribbon** to consolidate the application's features and commands. The ribbon is located at the top of a desktop application window, immediately below the title bar, and is organized into tabs. Each **tab** contains commands that perform a variety of related tasks. For example, the **Home tab** has commands for tasks you perform frequently, such as changing the appearance of a document. You use the commands on the **View tab** to change your view of the WordPad window. You use the commands on the **File tab** to work with WordPad documents, such as to save or print them.

To select a command and perform an action, you click a button or another type of control on the ribbon. Controls for related actions are organized on a tab in **groups**. For example, on the Home tab in the Font group, you click the Bold button to enter bold text in a WordPad document. If a button displays only an icon and not the button name, you can point to the button to display a **ScreenTip**, which is text that identifies the name or purpose of the button.

Figure 17 shows examples of the types of controls on the ribbon.

| Figure 17 | Examples of ribbon controls |
| --- | --- |

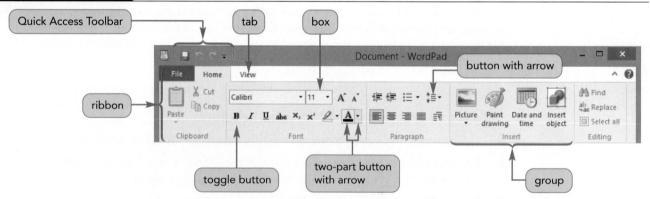

If a button includes an arrow, you click the button to display a menu of related commands. To use a box, you click the box and type an entry, such as numbers or other text, or you click the arrow button to select an item from the list. A toggle button is like a switch; you click the button to turn on or apply a setting, and then click the button again to turn off the setting. When a toggle button is turned on, it is highlighted. To use a two-part button with an arrow, you first point to the button. If an arrow is displayed on a separate part of the button, click the arrow to display a menu of commands. Click the button itself to apply the current selection.

Most desktop applications, including WordPad, include a **Quick Access Toolbar**, which is a row of buttons on the title bar that let you perform common tasks such as saving your work and undoing an action. You can display the name of each button on the Quick Access Toolbar in a ScreenTip by pointing to the button, just as you do for buttons on the ribbon.

Emma mentions that the WordPad application displays the controls you are likely to see in most desktop application windows, including the ribbon, which might be unfamiliar to Behind the Scenes employees. She suggests that you identify the controls on the WordPad ribbon and in WordPad dialog boxes during your first training session.

### To use buttons on the WordPad ribbon and the Quick Access Toolbar:

▶ **1.** On the Home tab, in the Font group, click the **Bold** button B. Now any text you type will appear as bold text.

▶ **2.** Type your full name in the WordPad window. See Figure 18.

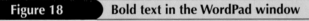

Figure 18 ▶ Bold text in the WordPad window

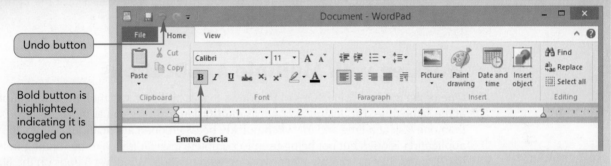

Undo button

Bold button is highlighted, indicating it is toggled on

Emma Garcia

▶ **3.** On the Quick Access Toolbar, click the **Undo** button. WordPad reverses your last action by removing your name from the WordPad window.

## Using Dialog Boxes

A **dialog box** is a special kind of window in which you enter or choose settings for performing a task. Dialog boxes can include tabs, option buttons, check boxes, and other controls to collect information about how you want to perform the task. Emma says a good way to learn how dialog box controls work is to open a typical WordPad dialog box, such as the Print dialog box, which you use to print a document.

### To work with a typical Windows 8 dialog box:

▶ **1.** On the ribbon, click the **File** tab, and then click **Print** on the menu to open the Print dialog box. See Figure 19.

| Figure 19 | Print dialog box |
| --- | --- |

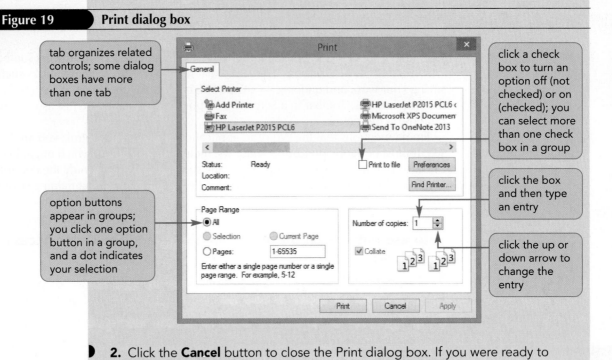

tab organizes related controls; some dialog boxes have more than one tab

click a check box to turn an option off (not checked) or on (checked); you can select more than one check box in a group

click the box and then type an entry

option buttons appear in groups; you click one option button in a group, and a dot indicates your selection

click the up or down arrow to change the entry

2. Click the **Cancel** button to close the Print dialog box. If you were ready to print a document with the settings you specified, you would click the Print button instead of the Cancel button.

## Working with Multiple Applications

One of the most useful features of Windows 8 is its ability to run multiple applications at the same time. This feature, known as **multitasking**, allows you to work on more than one task at a time and to switch quickly between open applications. When an application is open but not being used to complete tasks, it is said to be running in the **background**. Just as you saw when working with multiple Windows 8 apps on the Start screen, you can run multiple desktop applications and then switch from one to another so you can work efficiently. To demonstrate, Emma suggests that you open the Recycle Bin so that two applications are running on the desktop. (The Recycle Bin is part of an application that lets you explore the contents of your computer.)

**To open the Recycle Bin on the desktop:**

1. Point to the **Recycle Bin** icon on the desktop, and then double-click the **Recycle Bin** icon by pressing the left mouse button twice quickly. The Recycle Bin window opens on top of the WordPad window, as shown in Figure 20.

| Figure 20 | Recycle Bin and WordPad open on the desktop |

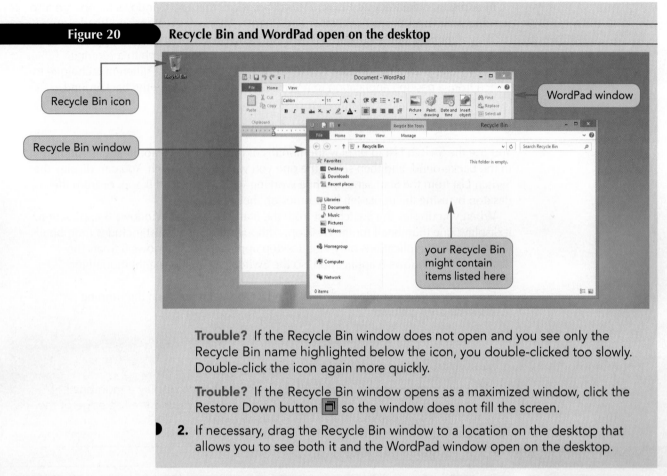

**Trouble?** If the Recycle Bin window does not open and you see only the Recycle Bin name highlighted below the icon, you double-clicked too slowly. Double-click the icon again more quickly.

**Trouble?** If the Recycle Bin window opens as a maximized window, click the Restore Down button 🗗 so the window does not fill the screen.

2. If necessary, drag the Recycle Bin window to a location on the desktop that allows you to see both it and the WordPad window open on the desktop.

Now that two application windows are open, Emma wants you to demonstrate how to switch from one to the other.

## Switching Between Desktop Applications

When two or more applications are open and their windows are displayed on the desktop, only one can be the **active window**, which is the application window in which you are currently working. When a window is active, any keystroke or command you select applies only to that window. The active window appears on top of all other open windows, and its title bar and window borders are blue; the title bar and window border of all other open windows are gray. Right now, the Recycle Bin is the active window. To switch to the WordPad window, you can click its button on the taskbar or you can click in the window itself. If you minimize an active window, it is no longer active, and the window directly under it becomes the active window.

### To switch between the Recycle Bin and WordPad:

1. Click the **WordPad** button 🖼 on the taskbar. The WordPad window now appears on top of the Recycle Bin window, and the color of its title bar and borders changes to blue, indicating that WordPad is the active window.

2. Click any part of the Recycle Bin window to make it the active window.

3. Click the **Minimize** button ➖ on the Recycle Bin title bar to minimize the Recycle Bin window and make WordPad the active window.

In addition to the Recycle Bin and WordPad, recall that two Windows 8 apps are also running in the background—Weather and Reader. Although Weather and Reader are running right now, neither one is visible from the desktop. Only desktop applications have buttons on the taskbar, so you cannot use the taskbar to switch to a running Windows 8 app from the desktop. Next, you'll learn how to use a different technique to switch from a desktop application to a Windows 8 app running in the background.

## Switching Between Windows 8 Applications

You use the **Switch List** to display thumbnails of the Windows 8 applications running in the background, and then select the one you want to work with. You can display the Switch List from the Start screen, while working with a Windows 8 app, or from the desktop by using the upper-left hot corner on the screen.

When you display the Switch List from the Start screen or a Windows 8 application, it displays one thumbnail for the desktop. Although the Switch List includes thumbnails for Windows 8 applications only, not desktop applications, Windows 8 treats the desktop as a Windows 8 application, so the Switch List includes a thumbnail for the desktop.

Emma encourages you to use the Switch List to switch between the running Windows 8 applications.

### To switch between Windows 8 applications:

1. Point to the upper-left hot corner of the desktop to display a thumbnail of the Reader app, and then move the pointer down along the left edge of the screen to display the Switch List. See Figure 21.

**Figure 21**    Switch List displayed on the desktop

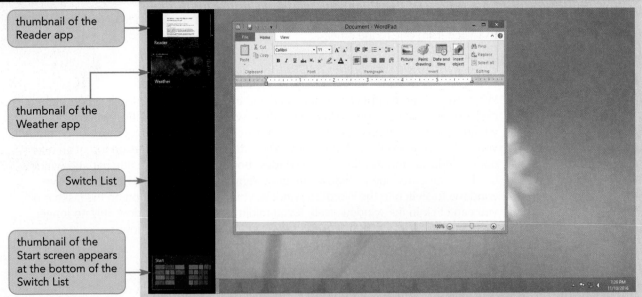

thumbnail of the Reader app

thumbnail of the Weather app

Switch List

thumbnail of the Start screen appears at the bottom of the Switch List

2. Click the **Weather** thumbnail to switch to the Weather app.

3. Point to the upper-left hot corner of the screen to display a thumbnail, and then move the pointer down along the left edge of the screen to display the Switch List, which now includes a thumbnail for the desktop.

4. Click the **Reader** thumbnail to switch to the Reader app.

**TIP**

You can also click the thumbnail that appears when you point to the upper-left hot corner to start the associated application without displaying the Switch List.

If you want to switch from the Start screen or a Windows 8 application to an inactive desktop application using the Switch List, you must click the Desktop thumbnail in the Switch List, and then activate the application's window on the desktop. A simpler way is to use a keyboard shortcut.

## Using Keyboard Shortcuts

Windows 8 provides many keyboard shortcuts for streamlining your work. A **keyboard shortcut** is one or more keys you press on the keyboard to perform an action. The keyboard shortcut for switching to any type of running application is Alt+Tab. To use this keyboard shortcut, you press and hold the Alt key and then press the Tab key to display thumbnails of all running applications. Continue pressing the Alt key as you press the Tab key to select a thumbnail, and then release the Alt key to make that application active.

You can use the Alt+Tab keyboard shortcut to switch to any running application, such as from a Windows 8 application to an inactive desktop application. Right now, the Recycle Bin is inactive on the desktop. Emma wants you to show Behind the Scenes employees how to use the Alt+Tab keyboard shortcut to switch to the inactive Recycle Bin window.

**To use the Alt+Tab keyboard shortcut:**

1. Press and hold the **Alt** key, and then press the **Tab** key to display thumbnails of the running applications, including Windows 8 and desktop applications. See Figure 22.

**Figure 22**   **Thumbnails of running applications**

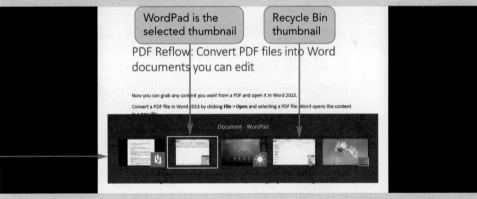

WordPad is the selected thumbnail

Recycle Bin thumbnail

PDF Reflow: Convert PDF files into Word documents you can edit

Now you can grab any content you want from a PDF and open it in Word 2013.

Convert a PDF file in Word 2013 by clicking **File > Open** and selecting a PDF file. Word opens the content

Document - WordPad

thumbnails of Reader, WordPad, Weather, Recycle Bin, and the desktop

2. While holding down the Alt key, press the **Tab** key as many times as necessary to select the Recycle Bin thumbnail, and then release the Alt key. You return to the desktop, where the Recycle Bin is no longer minimized but is now the active window.

Emma says you don't need to demonstrate any other skills with WordPad and the Recycle Bin. When you're finished working with an application, you can close it.

# Closing Applications

When you finish working with applications, you can close them to keep the desktop and the Switch List free of clutter, and to allow your computer to run more efficiently. To close a desktop application, you close its window. To close a Windows 8 application, you can use a shortcut menu or drag the application off the screen. You can also use a keyboard shortcut to close either type of application.

## Closing Desktop Applications

When you are finished working in a desktop application, you can close it. One way to close an application is to use the Close button on the window's title bar. Another way is to right-click the application window's taskbar button to display a shortcut menu that includes a command to close the window. The advantage of using the shortcut menu is that it lets you close active or inactive windows, even if they are minimized.

Emma suggests that you show Behind the Scenes employees two ways to close a desktop application. You'll start by using a shortcut menu to close the inactive WordPad window.

**To close desktop applications:**

 **1.** Right-click the **WordPad** button 🖼 on the taskbar. The shortcut menu for the WordPad taskbar button opens. See Figure 23.

| Figure 23 | Taskbar button shortcut menu |

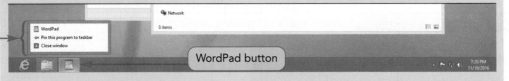

shortcut menu

WordPad button

 **2.** Click **Close window** on the shortcut menu.

 **3.** When a message appears asking if you want to save changes, click the **Don't Save** button. The WordPad window closes and its button no longer appears on the taskbar.

 **4.** Click the **Close** button ☒ in the title bar of the Recycle Bin window to close the application.

Now the WordPad and Recycle Bin windows are closed and only the desktop is displayed on the screen.

## Closing Windows 8 Applications

**TIP**

You can also point to the top of a Windows 8 application until a hand pointer appears, drag the application down until it shrinks to a thumb-nail, and then continue dragging to the bottom of the screen to close the application.

As you've seen, Windows 8 applications do not include a control such as a Close button that you can use to close the application. Instead, you close a Windows 8 application using its thumbnail when it appears on its own in the upper-left corner of the screen, or when it appears in the Switch List. You right-click the thumbnail and then click Close on the shortcut menu to close the application. You can also use the Alt+F4 keyboard shortcut to close any application. To do so, you press the Alt and F4 keys at the same time when the application is displayed on the screen.

To demonstrate how to close Windows 8 applications, Emma suggests that you use the shortcut menu and the keyboard shortcut to close the open Windows 8 applications.

**To close Windows 8 applications:**

▶ **1.** Point to the upper-left hot corner, and then click the **Reader** thumbnail to display the Reader app.

▶ **2.** Press the **Alt+F4** keys to close the Reader app and return to the Start screen.

▶ **3.** Point to the upper-left hot corner, and then move the mouse down to display the Switch List.

▶ **4.** Right-click the **Weather** thumbnail, and then click **Close** on the shortcut menu to close the Weather app.

▶ **5.** Click a blank area on the Start screen to close the Switch List.

Before you finish working with Windows 8, you should show Behind the Scenes employees how to get help when they need it.

# Getting Help

Windows 8 **Help and Support** provides on-screen information about Windows 8 and its applications. Help and Support gives you access to Help files stored on your computer as well as Help information stored on the Microsoft website. If you are not connected to the web, you have access to only the Help files stored on your computer.

**To start Windows 8 Help and Support:**

▶ **1.** On the Start screen, type **help** to display the Apps screen and Search menu, with "help" inserted in the Search box.

▶ **2.** Click **Help and Support** in the search results to open the Windows Help and Support window on the desktop. By default, this window displays the Help home page when you start Help and Support.

▶ **3.** Click the **Maximize** button 🔲 to maximize the Windows Help and Support window. See Figure 24. The contents of the home page differ depending on whether you are connected to the Internet.

**Trouble?** If the Help and Support window does not display the home page, click the Help home link near the top of the window.

| Figure 24 | Windows Help and Support window |
| --- | --- |

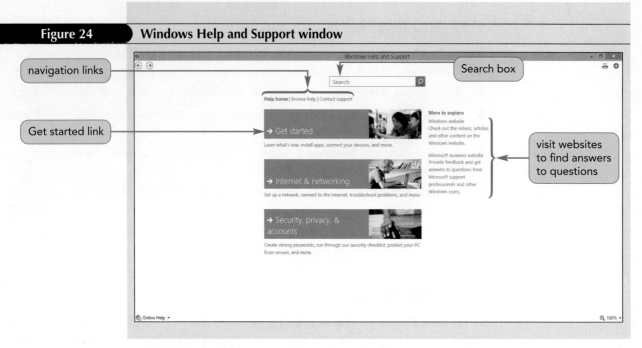

The Help home page provides tools for finding answers and other information about Windows 8. You can click links on the page to view information about popular topics, browse for a specific topic, or search to find an answer to a Windows 8 question.

## Viewing the Get Started Topics

Windows Help and Support includes instructions on the basics of using Windows 8. You can learn more about these basic topics by using the Get started link on the Windows Help and Support home page.

### To view Get started topics:

1. Click the **Get started** link. A list of topics related to using Windows 8 appears in the Windows Help and Support window.

2. Click the **Mouse and keyboard: What's new** topic. An article explaining how to use the mouse and keyboard appears.

3. Scroll down to the bottom of the page, and then click the **Get to know Windows** link. A page opens describing the new features in Windows 8.

4. Click the **Back** button ⊖ at the top of the window to return to the previous page you visited, which is the Mouse and keyboard page, and then click the **Back** button ⊖ to return to the Get started page.

## Selecting a Topic from the Browse Help List

The Browse help list organizes the information in Windows Help and Support into topics and categories. You can click a link to display the titles of related categories, and then click a topic in a specific category to get help with a particular task or feature. For example, you can use the Browse help list to learn more about personalizing your computer.

**To find a Help topic using the Browse help list:**

1. Click the **Browse help** link. A list of Windows Help topics appears in the Windows Help and Support window.

2. Click the **Personalization** topic to display a list of topics divided by categories related to personalizing your computer.

3. In the Customize your PC category, click the **Adding apps, websites, and more to Start** topic. The Windows Help and Support window displays information about that topic.

4. Scroll down to review the information on this page, and then scroll up to return to the top of the page.

## Searching the Help Pages

If you can't find the topic you need by clicking a link or browsing topics, or if you want to quickly find Help pages related to a particular topic, you can use the Search box. Suppose you want to know how to exit Windows 8, but you don't know if Windows refers to this as exiting, quitting, closing, or shutting down. Emma suggests you can search the Help pages to find just the right topic.

**To search the Help pages for information on exiting Windows 8:**

1. Click the **Help home** link to return to the home page.

2. Click the **Search** box, type **shut down**, and then press the **Enter** key. A list of Help pages containing the words "shut down" appears in the Windows Help and Support window. See Figure 25. (Your results might differ.)

| Figure 25 | Search Help results |

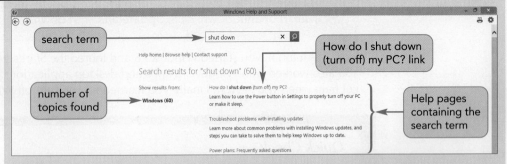

3. Click the **How do I shut down (turn off) my PC?** link. The instructions appear in the Windows Help and Support window.

   If this topic did not answer your question, you could click the Help home link and then click the Microsoft Answers website link. Doing so opens a webpage where you can search for answers to your questions.

4. Click the **Close** button ⬛✕ on the title bar to close the Windows Help and Support window.

Now that you know how Windows 8 Help works, Emma reminds you to use it when you need to perform a new task or want a reminder about how to complete a procedure.

## Turning Off Windows 8

When you're finished working in Windows 8, you should always turn it off properly. Doing so saves energy, preserves your data and settings, and makes sure your computer starts quickly the next time you use it.

<aside>
TIP

Shutting down does not automatically save your work, so be sure to save your files before selecting the Shut down or Restart option.
</aside>

You turn off Windows 8 using the Power button on the Settings menu. First, you use the Charms bar to display the Settings menu, and then you click the Power button to display a menu, which includes the Shut down option. Click Shut down to have Windows close all open programs, including Windows itself, and then completely turn off your computer.

The Power button menu might also include the Sleep option, which instructs Windows to save your work and then turn down the power to your monitor and computer, a condition called **sleep**. A light on the outside of your computer case blinks or changes color to indicate that the computer is sleeping. Because Windows saves your work, you do not need to close your programs or files before your computer goes to sleep. To wake a computer, you typically press the hardware power button on your computer case. Some computer manufacturers might set the computer to wake when you press a key or move the mouse. After you wake a computer, the screen looks exactly as it did when you put your computer to sleep.

### To turn off Windows 8:

▶ 1. Point to the upper-right hot corner on the desktop to display the Charms bar, and then click the **Settings** charm to display the Settings menu.

▶ 2. Click the **Power** button, and then click **Shut down**. Windows 8 turns off the computer.

   **Trouble?** If the Power button displays the Update and shut down option instead of Shut down, click Update and shut down.

In this tutorial, you started Windows 8 and toured the Start screen and the desktop. You also worked with Windows 8 apps and desktop applications, and learned how to get help when you need it. Finally you learned how to turn off Windows 8.

**REVIEW**

### Quick Check

1. What does the operating system do for your computer?
2. The Start screen includes multicolored rectangles called _____, which represent _____.
3. How can you display the Charms bar?
4. Explain the difference between the Start screen and the desktop.
5. Explain how to start a desktop application from the Start screen.
6. The keyboard shortcut for closing an application is _____.
7. What page opens by default when you start Windows Help and Support?
8. What option saves your work before turning off your computer?

## Review Assignments

**There are no Data Files needed for the Review Assignments.**

The day before your first Windows 8 training session for Behind the Scenes employees, Emma Garcia offers to observe your tour of the operating system and help you fine-tune your lesson. You'll start working on the Start screen, with no applications open. Complete the following steps, recording your answers to any questions according to your instructor's preferences:

1. Start Windows 8 and sign in, if necessary.
2. Use the mouse to scroll the Start screen. How many full tiles appear on the screen when you scroll?
3. Zoom the Start screen to reduce the size of the tiles. How many tiles appear on the screen now?
4. Display the desktop. List the major parts of the desktop, including any icons.
5. Start WordPad. Identify each object on the taskbar (not including the notification area). Minimize the WordPad window.
6. Open the Recycle Bin window and then maximize it. How do you know that the Recycle Bin window is active?
7. Redisplay the WordPad window. Which window is active now? How can you tell?
8. Start the Weather app, and then display the Switch List. Which thumbnails are displayed in the Switch List?
9. Display the Start screen, and then start the Reader app. How did you start the Reader app?
10. If possible, snap the Weather app to the left side of the screen, and then unsnap it. Explain how to snap a Windows 8 application to the left side of the screen and then unsnap it.
11. Use a keyboard shortcut to close the Reader app and then the Weather app. Which keyboard shortcut did you use?
12. Use a keyboard shortcut to switch back to the desktop. Which keyboard shortcut did you use?
13. Minimize the WordPad window. In the Recycle Bin window, click the Home tab. Which buttons are active (not gray)? Use any button on the Home tab to open a dialog box. What dialog box did you open? What do you think this dialog box is used for? Click the Cancel button to close the dialog box, and then close the Recycle Bin window.
14. Close the WordPad window from the taskbar. What command did you use?
15. Open Windows Help and Support. Use any link on the home page to learn something new about Windows 8. What did you learn? How did you find this topic?
16. Close Help and Support.
17. Turn off Windows 8 by using the Sleep option, shutting down, or signing out.

## Case Problem 1

**There are no Data Files needed for this Case Problem.**

***Up and Running***   Up and Running is a computer support firm located in major electronics stores throughout the Midwest. Ken Mathias is the manager of a store in Red Wing, Minnesota. He hired you to work with customers in their homes or businesses. You are preparing for a visit to a customer who is new to Windows 8 and wants to learn about the applications installed on his computer. Complete the following steps:

1. Start Windows 8 and sign in, if necessary.
2. Examine the tiles on the Start screen and use one to start an application that plays music or videos. Which application did you start?
3. Search for an application installed on your computer related to photos. What application did you find?
4. Start the application you found in Step 3. Is it a Windows 8 application or a desktop application? How can you tell?

5. Search for an application installed on your computer that lets you perform calculations. What application did you find?

6. Start the application you found in Step 5. Is it a Windows 8 application or a desktop application? How can you tell?

⊕ **Explore**  7. Use the Search menu to find settings related to music. (*Hint*: After you use the Search menu to search for "music," click the Settings category on the Search menu.) How many settings did you find?

8. Use the Apps screen to start the Paint application. Describe how you started this application.

⊕ **Explore**  9. Point to the buttons in the Paint window until you find one that displays a "Paint Help (F1)" ScreenTip. Click this button, and then describe what happens.

10. Close all open Windows 8 applications only. Describe how you closed the applications.

11. Use Windows Help and Support to find and read about topics that describe two Windows features that make your PC more secure. Which two features did you read about?

12. Close all open windows.

## Case Problem 2

**RESEARCH**

**There are no Data Files needed for this Case Problem.**

*Home Care Therapy*    After earning their certifications as physical and occupational therapists, Josh Cohen and Deborah Whiting decided to start a service called Home Care Therapy for people who need physical or occupational therapy in their homes. They have been using Windows 8 on laptops to schedule client appointments and track client progress, but recently purchased tablet computers to use when they are working with clients face to face. They hired you as a consultant to help them use and maintain their computers. Because Josh and Deborah learned to use Windows 8 on laptop computers, they anticipate that they might have trouble adapting to tablets. Josh asks you to research the skills and techniques they need to use Windows 8 on a tablet. Complete the following:

1. In Windows Help and Support, find information about how to perform the following tasks on a tablet computer:
   • Display the Charms bar.
   • Scroll the Start screen.
   • Zoom the Start screen.
   • Display the desktop.
   • Display app settings, such as Save and Edit.

2. Use the Windows website link to visit the Microsoft website to obtain more information about Windows 8 on a tablet computer. Watch a video that showcases Windows 8 touch features. Then, describe how to rearrange tiles on the Start screen.

3. Choose a topic that describes how to browse the web, and then watch the related video. Explain what's new and different in Internet Explorer for touchscreen devices.

4. Write one to two paragraphs for Josh and Deborah explaining the basics of using Windows 8 on a tablet with a touchscreen.

## OBJECTIVES

- Explore the differences between Windows 7 and Windows 8
- Plan the organization of files and folders
- Use File Explorer to view and manage libraries, folders, and files
- Open and save files
- Create folders
- Copy and move files and folders
- Compress and extract files

# Managing Your Files

*Organizing Files and Folders with Windows 8*

## Case | *Savvy Traveler*

After spending a summer traveling in Italy, Matt Marino started Savvy Traveler, a travel company that organizes small tours in Europe. To market his company, Matt created flyers, brochures, webpages, and other materials that describe the tours he offers. Matt uses the Savvy Traveler office computer to locate and store photos, illustrations, and text documents he can include in his marketing materials. He recently hired you to help manage the office. To keep Matt connected to the office while traveling, he just purchased a new laptop computer running Windows 8. He is familiar with Windows 7, so he needs an overview explaining how Windows 8 is different. Matt asks you to train him on using Windows 8 to organize his files and folders. Although he has only a few files, he knows it's a good idea to set up a logical organization now so he can find his work later as he stores more files and folders on the computer.

In this tutorial, you'll explore the differences between Windows 7 and Windows 8, especially those related to file management tools. You'll also work with Matt to devise a plan for managing his files. You'll learn how Windows 8 organizes files and folders, and then create files and folders yourself and organize them on Matt's computer. You'll also use techniques to display the information you need in folder windows, and explore options for working with compressed files.

## STARTING DATA FILES

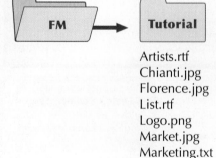

| FM → Tutorial | Review | Case1 | Case2 |
| --- | --- | --- | --- |
| Artists.rtf | Banner.png | Fall Classes.rtf | Budget1.xlsx |
| Chianti.jpg | Colosseum.jpg | Instructors.txt | Budget2.xlsx |
| Florence.jpg | Lectures.xlsx | Kings Canyon.jpg | Report1.xlsx |
| List.rtf | Rome.jpg | Mojave.jpg | Report2.xlsx |
| Logo.png | Rome.rtf | Redwoods.jpg | Report3.xlsx |
| Market.jpg | Schedule.rtf | Spring Classes.rtf | Report4.xlsx |
| Marketing.txt | Tours.rtf | Summer Classes.rtf | Tips1.rtf |
| Tour Rates.rtf | | Winter Classes.rtf | Tips1 – Copy.rtf |
| Tuscany.rtf | | Workshops.rtf | Tips2.rtf |
| | | Yosemite.jpg | Tips2 – Copy.rtf |

# Visual Overview:

You use the Change your view button to change the size of the icons in the window.

In Windows 7, you use **Windows Explorer** to navigate the contents of your computer.

Use the arrow buttons in the Address bar to navigate to other locations on your computer.

The **file path** is a notation that indicates a file's location on your computer.

Use the Search box to search for files in the current folder.

The Windows Explorer **toolbar** provides buttons for completing tasks.

Windows Explorer includes a **navigation pane**, which displays icons and links to resources and locations on your computer.

By default, Windows Explorer includes the **Details pane** at the bottom of the window, which displays the properties of the selected object.

Windows provides **libraries** so you can organize files by category—documents, music, pictures, and video.

A thumbnail image previews the file contents for certain types of files.

The zipped folder icon indicates a **compressed folder**, which stores files so they take up less disk space.

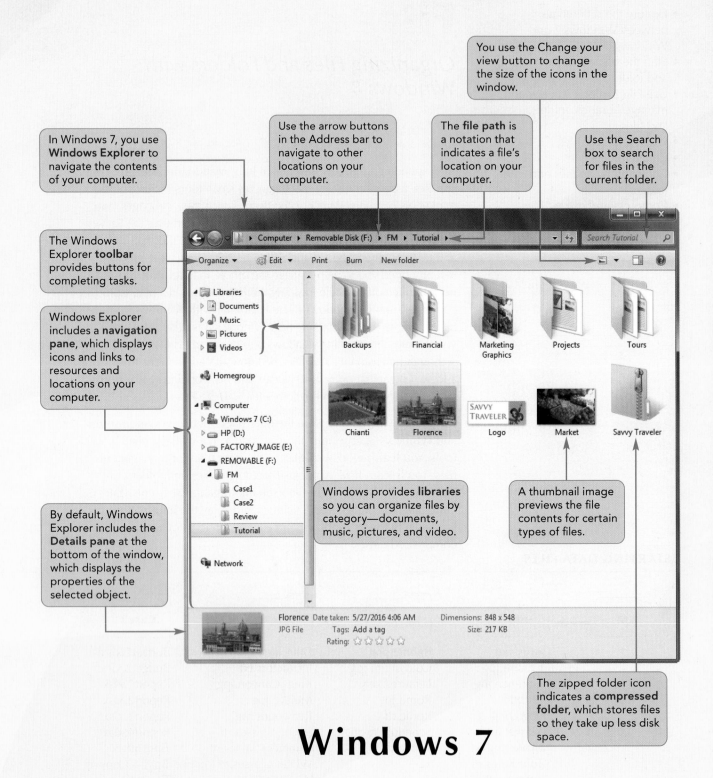

# Windows 7

# Comparing Windows 7 & Windows 8

The **View tab** on the ribbon contains options for specifying how the information displays in File Explorer.

Windows provides **libraries** so you can organize files by category—documents, music, pictures, and videos.

The **Quick Access toolbar** contains buttons for viewing properties and creating a folder.

Use the arrow buttons in the Address bar to navigate to other locations on your computer.

The **file path** in the Address bar shows a file's location on your computer.

In Windows 8, you use **File Explorer** to navigate the contents of your computer.

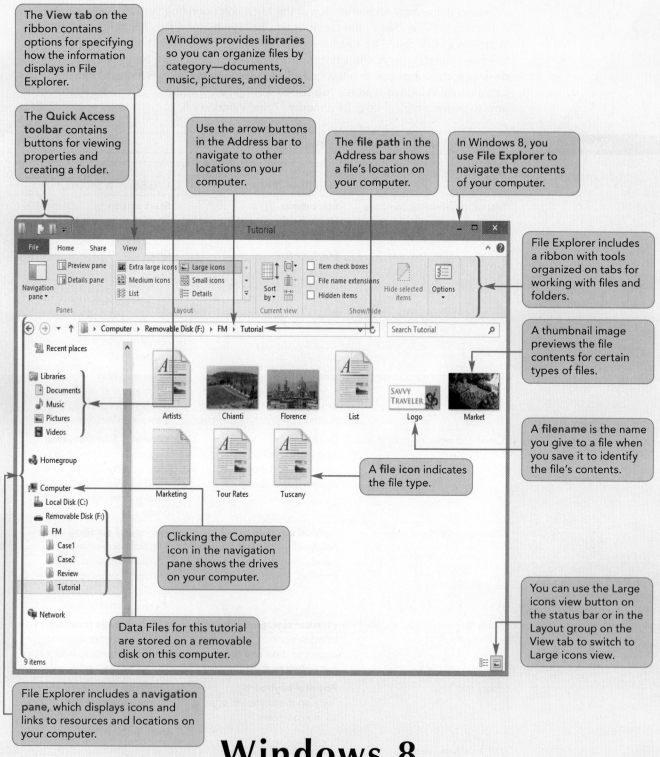

File Explorer includes a ribbon with tools organized on tabs for working with files and folders.

A thumbnail image previews the file contents for certain types of files.

A **filename** is the name you give to a file when you save it to identify the file's contents.

A **file icon** indicates the file type.

Clicking the Computer icon in the navigation pane shows the drives on your computer.

You can use the Large icons view button on the status bar or in the Layout group on the View tab to switch to Large icons view.

Data Files for this tutorial are stored on a removable disk on this computer.

File Explorer includes a **navigation pane**, which displays icons and links to resources and locations on your computer.

# Windows 8

# Exploring the Differences Between Windows 7 and Windows 8

Windows 8, the most recent version of the Microsoft operating system, is significantly different from Windows 7, the previous version. The major difference is that Windows 8 is designed for touchscreen computers such as tablets and laptops with touch-activated displays, though it runs on computers with more traditional pointing devices such as a mouse or a trackpad. This design change affects many of the fundamental Windows features you use to work on a computer. Figure 1 compares how to perform typical tasks in Windows 7 and Windows 8.

**Figure 1**    **Comparing Windows 7 and Windows 8**

| Task | Windows 7 Method | Windows 8 Method |
|------|------------------|------------------|
| Start applications (sometimes called apps) | **Start menu** Open the Start menu by clicking the Start button. | **Start screen** The Start screen appears when you start Windows. |
| Access applications, documents, settings, and other resources | **Start menu** Use the Start menu, All Programs list, and Search box. | **Charms bar** The Charms bar appears when you point to the upper-right or lower-right corner of the screen, and displays buttons, called charms, for interacting with Windows 8 and accessing applications. |
| Select objects and commands | **Icons** Icons are small and detailed, designed for interaction with mechanical pointing devices. | **Icons and tiles** Icons and tiles are large and simplified, designed for interaction with your fingertips. |
| Open and work in applications | **Desktop** Applications all use a single desktop interface featuring windows and dialog boxes. | **Windows 8 and desktop** Applications use one of two interfaces: the Windows 8 interface (featuring tiles and a full-screen layout) or the desktop. |
| Display content out of view | **Vertical scrolling** Applications allow more vertical scrolling than horizontal scrolling. | **Horizontal scrolling** The Start screen and applications allow more horizontal scrolling than vertical scrolling to take advantage of wide-screen monitors. |
| Store files | **Physical storage devices** Windows primarily provides access to disks physically connected to the computer. | **Cloud storage locations** A Microsoft user account provides access to information stored online. |
| Enter text | **Physical keyboard** Type on the keyboard attached to the computer. | **On-screen keyboard** If your computer does not have a physical keyboard, type using the on-screen keyboard. |

© 2014 Cengage Learning

Although Windows 7 introduced a few gestures for touchscreen users, Windows 8 expands the use of gestures and interactions. In Windows 8, you can use touch gestures to do nearly everything you can do with a pointing device. Figure 2 lists common Windows 8 interactions and their touch and mouse equivalents.

| Figure 2 | Windows 8 touch and mouse interactions |

| Interaction | Touch Gesture | Mouse Action |
| --- | --- | --- |
| Display a ScreenTip, text that identifies the name or purpose of the button | Touch and hold (or press) an object such as a button. | Point to an object such as a button. |
| Display an Apps bar, which displays options related to the current task and access to the Apps screen | Swipe from the top or bottom of the screen toward the center. | Right-click the bottom edge of the screen. |
| Display the Charms bar | Swipe from the right edge of the screen toward the center. | Point to the upper-right or lower-right corner of the screen. |
| Display thumbnails of open apps (the Switch List) | Swipe from the left edge of the screen toward the center. | Point to the upper-left corner of the screen, and then drag the pointer down. |
| Drag an object | Press and then drag. | Click, hold, and then drag. |
| Scroll the Start screen | Swipe from the right edge of the screen to the left. | Click the scroll arrows, or drag the scroll bar. |
| Select an object or perform an action such as starting an app | Tap the object. | Click the object. |
| Zoom | Pinch two fingers to zoom out or move the fingers apart to zoom in. | Click the Zoom button. |

© 2014 Cengage Learning

Despite the substantial differences between how you interact with Windows 7 and Windows 8, the steps you follow to perform work in either operating system are the same. In a typical computer session, you start an application and open a **file**, often referred to as a document, which is a collection of data that has a name and is stored on a computer. You view, add, or change the file contents, and then save and close the file. You can complete all of these steps using Windows 7 or Windows 8. Because most of your work involves files, you need to understand how to save and organize files so you can easily find and open them when necessary.

## Organizing Files and Folders

Knowing how to save, locate, and organize computer files makes you more productive when you are working with a computer. After you create a file, you can open it, edit its contents, print the file, and save it again—usually using the same application you used to create the file. You organize files by storing them in folders. A **folder** is a container for files. You need to organize files and folders so that you can find them easily and work efficiently.

A file cabinet is a common metaphor for computer file organization. As shown in Figure 3, a computer is like a file cabinet that has two or more drawers—each drawer is a storage device, or **disk**. Each disk contains folders that hold files. To make it easy to retrieve files, you arrange them logically into folders. For example, one folder might contain financial data, another might contain your creative work, and another could contain information you're gathering for an upcoming vacation.

| Figure 3 | Computer as a file cabinet |
|---|---|

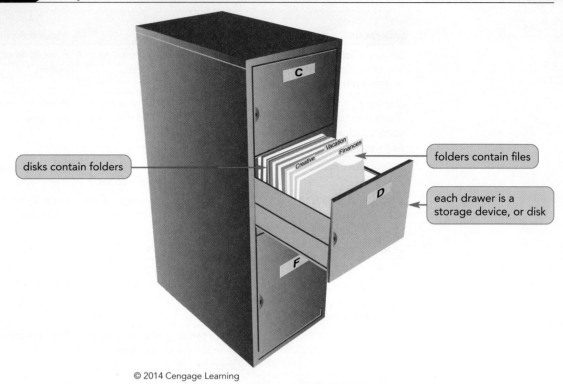

disks contain folders

folders contain files

each drawer is a storage device, or disk

© 2014 Cengage Learning

A computer can store folders and files on different types of disks, ranging from removable media—such as **USB drives** (also called USB flash drives) and digital video discs (DVDs)—to **hard disks**, or fixed disks, which are permanently housed in a computer. Hard disks are the most popular type of computer storage because they provide an economical way to store many gigabytes of data. (A **gigabyte**, or **GB**, is about 1 billion bytes, with each byte roughly equivalent to a character of data.)

To have your computer access a removable disk, you must insert the disk into a **drive**, which is a device that can retrieve and sometimes record data on a disk. A computer's hard disk is already contained in a drive inside the computer, so you don't need to insert it each time you use the computer.

A computer distinguishes one drive from another by assigning each a drive letter. The hard disk is assigned to drive C. The remaining drives can have any other letters, but are usually assigned in the order that the drives were installed on the computer—so your USB drive might be drive D or drive F.

## Understanding How to Organize Files and Folders

Windows stores thousands of files in many folders on the hard disk of your computer. These are system files that Windows needs to display the Start screen and desktop, use drives, and perform other operating system tasks. To keep the system stable and to find files quickly, Windows organizes the folders and files in a hierarchy, or **file system**. At the top of the hierarchy, Windows stores folders and important files that it needs when you turn on the computer. This location is called the **root directory** and is usually drive C (the hard disk). As Figure 4 shows, the root directory contains all the other folders and files on the computer. The figure also shows that folders can contain other folders. An effectively organized computer contains a few folders in the root directory, and those folders contain other folders, also called **subfolders**.

| Figure 4 | Organizing folders and files on a hard disk |

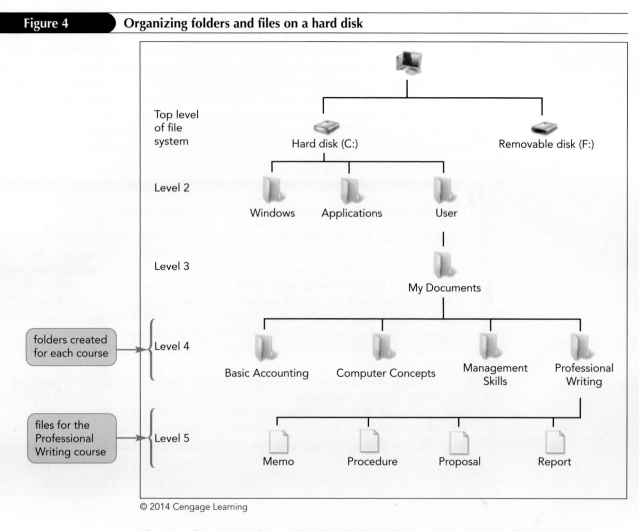

© 2014 Cengage Learning

The root directory is the top level of the hard disk and is for system files and folders only. You should not store your own work in the root directory because your files could interfere with Windows or an application. (If you are working in a computer lab, you might not be allowed to access the root directory.)

Do not delete or move any files or folders from the root directory of the hard disk; doing so could disrupt the system so that you can't start or run the computer. In fact, you should not reorganize or change any folder that contains installed software because Windows 8 expects to find the files for specific applications within certain folders. In Figure 4, folders containing software are stored at Level 2 of the file system. If you reorganize or change these folders, Windows 8 can't locate and start the applications stored in those folders. Likewise, you should not make changes to the folder (usually named Windows) that contains the Windows 8 operating system.

Level 2 of the file system also includes a folder for your user account, such as the User folder. This folder contains all of your system settings, preferences, and other user account information. It also contains subfolders, such as the My Documents folder, for your personal files. The folders in Level 3 of the file system are designed to contain subfolders for your personal files. You can create as many subfolders at Level 4 of the file system as you need to store other folders and files and keep them organized.

Figure 4 shows how you could organize your files on a hard disk if you were taking a full semester of business classes. To duplicate this organization, you would open the main folder for your documents, such as My Documents, create four folders—one each for the Basic Accounting, Computer Concepts, Management Skills, and Professional Writing courses—and then store the writing assignments you complete in the Professional Writing folder.

If you store your files on removable media, such as a USB drive, you can use a simpler organization because you do not have to account for system files. In general, the larger the storage medium, the more levels of folders you should use because large media can store more files and, therefore, need better organization. For example, if you were organizing your files on a 12 GB USB drive, you could create folders in the top level of the USB drive for each general category of documents you store—one each for Courses, Creative, Financials, and Vacation. The Courses folder could then include one folder for each course (Basic Accounting, Computer Concepts, Management Skills, and Professional Writing), and each of those folders could contain the appropriate files.

**PROSKILLS**

### Decision Making: Determining Where to Store Files

When you create and save files on your computer's hard disk, you should store them in subfolders. The top level of the hard disk is off-limits for your files because they could interfere with system files. If you are working on your own computer, store your files within the My Documents folder in the Documents library, which is where many applications save your files by default. When you use a computer on the job, your employer might assign a main folder to you for storing your work. In either case, if you simply store all your files in one folder, you will soon have trouble finding the files you want. Instead, you should create subfolders within a main folder to separate files in a way that makes sense for you.

Even if you store most of your files on removable media, such as USB drives, you still need to organize those files into folders and subfolders. Before you start creating folders, whether on a hard disk or removable disk, you need to plan the organization you will use. Following your plan increases your efficiency because you don't have to pause and decide which folder to use when you save your files. A file organization plan also makes you more productive in your computer work—the next time you need a particular file, you'll know where to find it.

## Exploring Files and Folders

As shown in the Visual Overview, you use File Explorer in Windows 8 to explore the files and folders on your computer. File Explorer displays the contents of your computer by using icons to represent drives, folders, and files. When you open File Explorer, it shows the contents of the Windows built-in libraries by default. Windows provides these libraries so you can organize files by category—documents, music, pictures, and video. A library can display these categories of files together, no matter where the files are actually stored. For example, you might keep some music files in a folder named Albums on your hard disk. You might also keep music files in a Songs folder on a USB drive. Although the Albums and Songs folders are physically stored in different locations, you can set up the Music library to display both folders in the same File Explorer window. You can then search and arrange the files as a single collection to quickly find the music you want to open and play. In this way, you use libraries to organize your files into categories so you can easily locate and work with files.

The File Explorer window is divided into two sections, called panes. The left pane is the navigation pane, which contains icons and links to locations on your computer. The right pane displays the contents of the location selected in the navigation pane. If the navigation pane showed all the contents on your computer at once, it could be a very long list. Instead, you open drives and folders only when you want to see what they contain. For example, to display the hierarchy of the folders and other locations on your computer, you select the Computer icon in the navigation pane, and then select the icon for a drive, such as Local Disk (C:) or Removable Disk (F:). You can then open and explore folders on that drive.

If a folder contains undisplayed subfolders, an expand icon appears to the left of the folder icon. (The same is true for drives.) To view the folders contained in an object, you click the expand icon. A collapse icon then appears next to the folder icon; click the collapse icon to hide the folder's subfolders. To view the files contained in a folder, you click the folder icon, and the files appear in the right pane. See Figure 5.

**Figure 5**    **Viewing files in File Explorer**

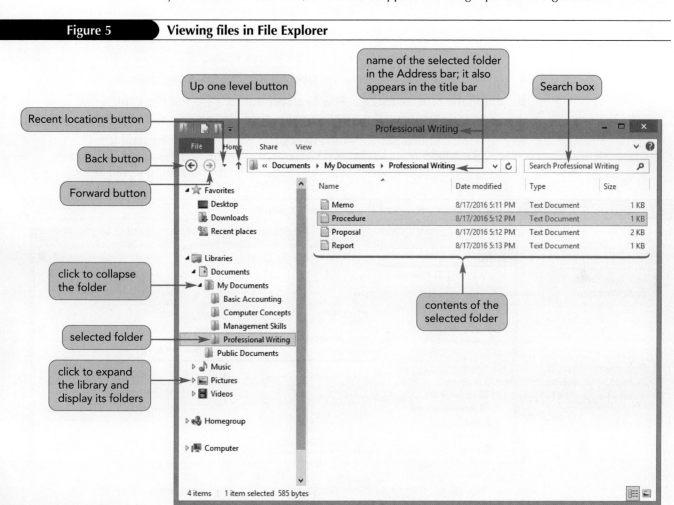

Using the navigation pane helps you explore your computer and orients you to your current location. As you move, copy, delete, and perform other tasks with the files and folders in the right pane of File Explorer, you can refer to the navigation pane to see how your changes affect the overall organization of the selected location.

In addition to using the navigation pane, you can explore your computer in File Explorer using the following navigation techniques:

- Opening drives and folders in the right pane—To view the contents of a drive or folder, double-click the drive or folder icon in the right pane of File Explorer.
- Using the Address bar—You can use the Address bar to navigate to a different folder. The Address bar displays the file path for your current folder. (Recall that a file path shows the location of a folder or file.) Click a folder name such as My Documents in the Address bar to navigate to that folder, or click an arrow button to navigate to a different location in the folder's hierarchy.
- Clicking the Back, Forward, Recent locations, and Up to buttons—Use the Back, Forward, and Recent locations buttons to navigate to other folders you have already opened. Use the Up to button to navigate up to the folder containing the current folder.
- Using the Search box—To find a file or folder stored in the current folder or its subfolders, type a word or phrase in the Search box. The search begins as soon as you

start typing. Windows finds files based on text in the filename, text within the file, and other properties of the file.

You'll practice using some of these navigation techniques later in the tutorial. Right now, you'll show Matt how to open File Explorer. Your computer should be turned on and displaying the Start screen.

**To open File Explorer:**

▶ **1.** On the Start screen, click the **Desktop** tile to display the desktop.

▶ **2.** On the taskbar, click the **File Explorer** button 📁. The File Explorer window opens, displaying the contents of the default libraries.

▶ **3.** In the Libraries section of the navigation pane, click the **expand** icon ▷ next to the Documents icon. The folders in the Documents library appear in the navigation pane; see Figure 6. The contents of your computer will differ.

| Figure 6 | Viewing the contents of the Documents library |

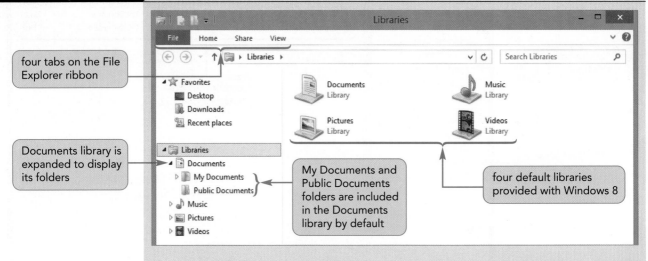

four tabs on the File Explorer ribbon

Documents library is expanded to display its folders

My Documents and Public Documents folders are included in the Documents library by default

four default libraries provided with Windows 8

**Trouble?** If your window displays icons in a size or arrangement different from the one shown in the figure, you can still explore files and folders. The same is true for all the figures in this tutorial.

**TIP**

When you are working in the navigation pane, you only need to click a folder to open it; you do not need to double-click it.

▶ **4.** In the navigation pane, click the **My Documents** folder to display its contents in the right pane.

As Figure 6 shows, the File Explorer window includes a ribbon, which is collapsed by default so it displays only tab names, such as File, Home, Share, and View. The Visual Overview shows the expanded ribbon, which displays the options for the selected tab. You'll work with the ribbon and learn how to expand it later in the tutorial.

## Navigating to Your Data Files

To navigate to the files you want, it helps to know the file path because the file path tells you exactly where the file is stored in the hierarchy of drives and folders on your computer. For example, Matt has a file named "Logo," which contains an image of the company's logo. If Matt stored the Logo file in a folder named "Marketing" and saved that folder in a folder named "Savvy Traveler" on drive F (a USB drive) on his computer, the Address bar would show the following file path for the Logo file:

**Computer ▸ Removable Disk (F:) ▸ Savvy Traveler ▸ Marketing ▸ Logo.png**

This path has five parts, with each part separated by an arrow button:

- Computer—The main container for the file, such as "Computer" or "Network"
- Removable Disk (F:)—The drive name, including the drive letter followed by a colon, which indicates a drive rather than a folder
- Savvy Traveler—The top-level folder on drive F
- Marketing—A subfolder in the Savvy Traveler folder
- Logo.png—The name of the file

Although File Explorer uses arrow buttons to separate locations in a file path, printed documents use backslashes ( \ ). For example, if you read an instruction to open the Logo file in the Savvy Traveler\Marketing folder on your USB drive, you know you must navigate to the USB drive attached to your computer, open the Savvy Traveler folder, and then open the Marketing folder to find the Logo file.

File Explorer displays the file path in the Address bar so you can keep track of your current location as you navigate between drives and folders. You can use File Explorer to navigate to the Data Files you need for this tutorial. Before you perform the following steps, you should know where you stored your Data Files, such as on a USB drive. The following steps assume that drive is Removable Disk (F:), a USB drive. If necessary, substitute the appropriate drive on your system when you perform the steps.

**To navigate to your Data Files:**

▸ **1.** Make sure your computer can access your Data Files for this tutorial. For example, if you are using a USB drive, insert the drive into the USB port.

   **Trouble?** If you don't have the starting Data Files, you need to get them before you can proceed. Your instructor will either give you the Data Files or ask you to obtain them from a specified location (such as a network drive). If you have any questions about the Data Files, see your instructor or technical support person for assistance.

▸ **2.** In the navigation pane of File Explorer, click the **expand** icon ▷ next to the Computer icon to display the drives on your computer, if necessary.

▸ **3.** Click the **expand** icon ▷ next to the drive containing your Data Files, such as Removable Disk (F:). A list of the folders on that drive appears below the drive name.

▸ **4.** If the list of folders does not include the FM folder, continue clicking the **expand** icon ▷ to navigate to the folder that contains the FM folder.

▸ **5.** Click the **expand** icon ▷ next to the FM folder to expand the folder, and then click the **FM** folder so that its contents appear in the navigation pane and in the right pane of the folder window. The FM folder contains the Case1, Case2, Review, and Tutorial folders, as shown in Figure 7. The other folders on your computer might vary.

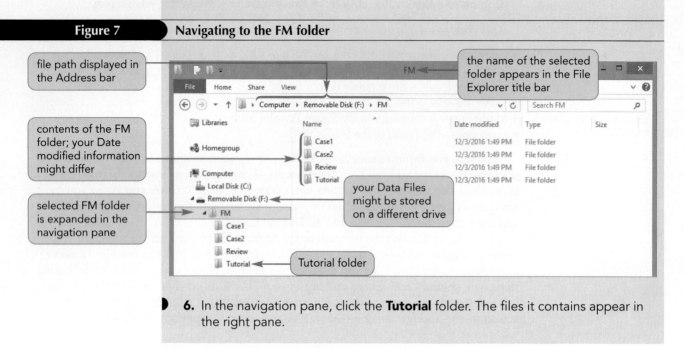

**Figure 7**　Navigating to the FM folder

file path displayed in the Address bar

the name of the selected folder appears in the File Explorer title bar

contents of the FM folder; your Date modified information might differ

your Data Files might be stored on a different drive

selected FM folder is expanded in the navigation pane

Tutorial folder

>  **6.** In the navigation pane, click the **Tutorial** folder. The files it contains appear in the right pane.

You can change the appearance of the File Explorer window to suit your preferences. You'll do so next so you can see more details about folders and files.

## Changing the View

File Explorer provides eight ways to view the contents of a folder: Extra large icons, Large icons, Medium icons, Small icons, List, Details, Tiles, and Content. For example, the files in the Tutorial folder are currently displayed in Details view, which is the default view for all folders except those stored in the Pictures library. Details view displays a small icon to identify each file's type and lists file details in columns, such as the date the file was last modified, the file type, and the size of the file. Although only Details view lists the file details, you can see these details in any other view by pointing to a file to display a ScreenTip.

To change the view of File Explorer to any of the eight views, you use the View tab on the ribbon. To switch to Details view or Large icons view, you can use the view buttons on the status bar.

**REFERENCE**

### Changing the View in File Explorer

- Click a view button on the status bar.

or

- Click the View tab on the ribbon.
- In the Layout group, click the view option; or click the More button, if necessary, and then click a view option.

You'll show Matt how to change the view of the Tutorial folder in the File Explorer window.

**To change the view of the Tutorial folder in File Explorer:**

1. On the ribbon, click the **View** tab.

2. In the Layout group, click **Medium icons**. The files appear in Medium icons view in File Explorer. See Figure 8.

**Figure 8**     **Files in the Tutorial folder in Medium icons view**

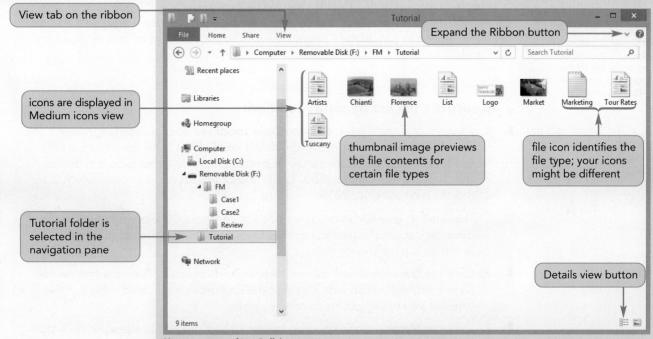

View tab on the ribbon

Expand the Ribbon button

icons are displayed in Medium icons view

thumbnail image previews the file contents for certain file types

file icon identifies the file type; your icons might be different

Tutorial folder is selected in the navigation pane

Details view button

Photos courtesy of Lisa Ruffolo

Because the icons used to identify types of files depend on the applications installed on your computer, the file icons that appear in your window might be different.

**TIP**

When you change the view, it only changes the view for the currently selected folder.

3. On the status bar, click the **Large icons view** button 🖼. The window shows the files with large icons and no file details.

When you clicked the View tab in the previous steps, the ribbon expanded so you could select an option and then collapsed after you clicked the Medium icons option. You can keep the ribbon expanded in the File Explorer window so you can easily access all of its options. You'll show Matt how to expand the ribbon and then use the View tab to switch to Details view.

**To expand the ribbon in File Explorer:**

1. Click the **Expand the Ribbon** button ⌄ to expand the ribbon. The Expand the Ribbon button changes to the Minimize the Ribbon button, which you could click if you wanted to collapse the ribbon.

2. On the View tab, in the Layout group, click **Details**. The window shows the files with small icons and lists the file details.

No matter which view you use, you can sort the file list by the name of the files or another detail, such as size, type, or date. When you **sort** files, you list them in ascending order (A to Z, 0 to 9, or earliest to latest date) or descending order (Z to A, 9 to 0, or latest to earliest date) by a file detail. If you're viewing music files, you can sort by details such as contributing artists or album title; and if you're viewing picture files, you can sort by details such as date taken or size. Sorting can help you find a particular file in a long file listing. For example, suppose you want to work on a document that you know you edited on June 4, 2016, but you can't remember the name of the file. You can sort the file list by date modified to find the file you want.

When you are working in Details view in File Explorer, you sort by clicking a column heading that appears at the top of the file list. In other views, you use the View tab on the ribbon to sort. In the Current view group, click the Sort by button, and then click a file detail.

**TIP**

To sort by a file detail that does not appear as a column heading, right-click any column heading and then select a file detail.

### To sort the file list by date modified:

1. At the top of the file list, click the **Date modified** column heading button. The down arrow that appears above the label of the Date modified button indicates that the files are sorted in descending (newest to oldest) order by the date the file was modified. At the top of the list is the List file, which was modified on June 18, 2016.

   **Trouble?** If your folder window does not contain a Date modified column, right-click any column heading, click Date modified on the shortcut menu, and then repeat Step 1.

2. Click the **Date modified** column heading button again. The up arrow on the Date modified button indicates that the sort order is reversed, with the files listed in ascending (oldest to newest) order.

3. Click the **Name** column heading button to sort the files in alphabetical order by name. The Artists file is now listed first.

Now that Matt is comfortable working in File Explorer, you're ready to show him how to manage his files and folders.

## Managing Files and Folders

As discussed earlier, you manage your personal files and folders by storing them according to a logical organization so that they are easy to find later. You can organize files as you create, edit, and save them, or you can do so later by creating folders, if necessary, and then moving and copying files into the folders.

To create a file-organization plan for Matt's files, you can review Figure 8 and look for files that logically belong together. In the Tutorial folder, Chianti, Florence, Logo, and Market are all graphics files that Matt uses for marketing and sales. He created the Artists and Tuscany files to describe Italian tours. The Marketing and Tour Rates files relate to business finances. Matt thinks the List file contains a task list for completing a project, but he isn't sure of its contents. He does recall creating the file using WordPad.

If the List file does contain a project task list, you can organize the files by creating four folders—one for graphics, one for tours, another for the financial files, and a fourth folder for projects. When you create a folder, you give it a name, preferably one that describes its contents. A folder name can have up to 255 characters, and any character is allowed, except / \ : * ? " < > and |. Considering these conventions, you could create four folders to contain Matt's files, as follows:

- Marketing Graphics folder—Chianti, Florence, Logo, and Market files
- Tours folder—Artists and Tuscany files
- Financial folder—Marketing and Tour Rates files
- Projects folder—List file

Before you start creating folders according to this plan, you need to verify the contents of the List file. You can do so by opening the file.

## Opening a File

**TIP**

To select the default application for opening a file, right-click the file in File Explorer, point to Open with, and then click Choose default application. Click an application in the list that opens, and then click OK.

You can open a file from a running application or from File Explorer. To open a file in a running application, you select the application's Open command to access the Open dialog box, which you use to navigate to the file you want, select the file, and then open it. In the Open dialog box, you use the same tools that are available in File Explorer to navigate to the file you want to open. If the application you want to use is not running, you can open a file by double-clicking it in the right pane of File Explorer. The file usually opens in the application that you used to create or edit it.

Occasionally, File Explorer will open the file in an application other than the one you want to use to work with the file. For example, double-clicking a digital picture file usually opens the picture in a picture viewer application. If you want to edit the picture, you must open the file in a graphics editing application. When you need to specify an application to open a file, you can right-click the file, point to Open with on the shortcut menu, and then click the name of the application that you want to use.

Matt says that he might want to edit the List file to add another task. You'll show him how to use File Explorer to open the file in WordPad, which he used to create the file, and then edit it.

**To open and edit the List file:**

1. In the right pane of File Explorer, right-click the **List** file, and then point to **Open with** on the shortcut menu to display a list of applications that can open the file. See Figure 9.

   **Trouble?** If a list does not appear when you point to Open with on the shortcut menu, click Open with to display a window asking how you want to open this file.

| Figure 9 | Shortcut menu for opening a file |

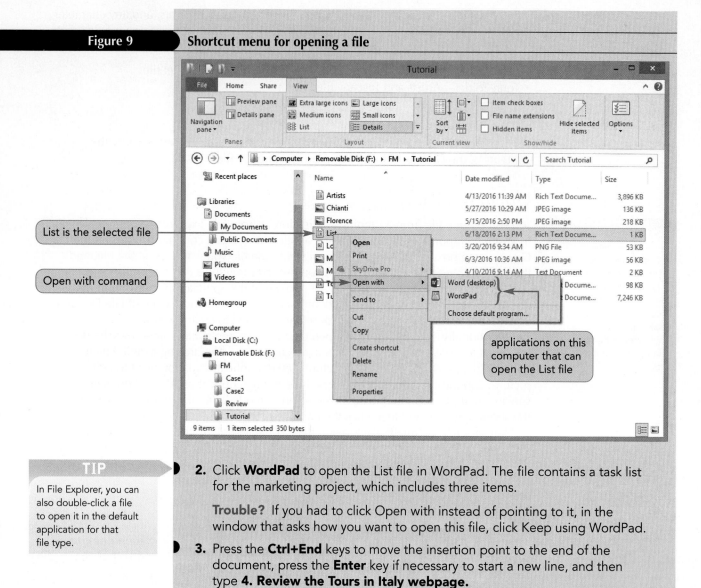

List is the selected file

Open with command

applications on this computer that can open the List file

TIP

In File Explorer, you can also double-click a file to open it in the default application for that file type.

2. Click **WordPad** to open the List file in WordPad. The file contains a task list for the marketing project, which includes three items.

   **Trouble?** If you had to click Open with instead of pointing to it, in the window that asks how you want to open this file, click Keep using WordPad.

3. Press the **Ctrl+End** keys to move the insertion point to the end of the document, press the **Enter** key if necessary to start a new line, and then type **4. Review the Tours in Italy webpage.**

Now that you've added text to the List file, you need to save it to preserve the changes you made.

## Saving a File

As you are creating or editing a file, you should save it frequently so you don't lose your work. When you save a file, you need to decide what name to use for the file and where to store it. Most applications provide a default location for saving a file, which makes it easy to find the file again later. However, you can select a different location depending on where you want to store the file.

Besides a storage location, every file must have a filename, which provides important information about the file, including its contents and purpose. A filename such as Italian Tours.docx has the following three parts:

- Main part of the filename—When you save a file, you need to provide only the main part of the filename, such as "Italian Tours."
- Dot—The dot ( . ) separates the main part of the filename from the extension.
- Extension—The **extension** includes the three or four characters that follow the dot in the filename and identify the file's type.

Similar to folder names, the main part of a filename can have up to 255 characters. This gives you plenty of room to name your file accurately enough so that you'll recognize the contents of the file just by looking at the filename. You can use spaces and certain punctuation symbols in your filenames. However, filenames cannot contain the symbols / \ : * ? " < > or | because these characters have special meanings in Windows 8.

Windows and other software add the dot and the extension to a filename, though File Explorer does not display them by default. Instead, File Explorer shows the file icon associated with the extension or a thumbnail for some types of files, such as graphics. For example, in a file named Italian Tours.docx, the docx extension identifies the file as one created in Microsoft Word, a word-processing application. File Explorer displays this file using a Microsoft Word icon and the main part of its filename. For a file named Italian Tours.png, the png extension identifies the file as one created in a graphics application such as Paint. In Details view or List view, File Explorer displays this file using a Paint icon and the main part of its filename. In other views, File Explorer does not use an icon, but displays the file contents in a thumbnail. File Explorer treats the Italian Tours.docx and Italian Tours.png files differently because their extensions distinguish them as different types of files, even though the main parts of their filenames are identical.

When you save a new file, you use the Save As dialog box to provide a filename and select a location for the file. You can create a folder for the new file at the same time you save the file. When you edit a file you saved previously, you can use the application's Save command to save your changes to the file, keeping the same name and location. If you want to save the edited file with a different name or in a different location, however, you need to use the Save As dialog box to specify the new name or location.

As with the Open dialog box, you specify the file location in the Save As dialog box using the same navigation techniques and tools that are available in File Explorer. You might need to click the Browse Folders button to expand the Save As dialog box so it displays these tools. In addition, the Save As dialog box always includes a File name box where you specify a filename.

## INSIGHT

### Saving Files on SkyDrive

Some Windows 8 applications, such as Microsoft Office, include SkyDrive as a location for saving and opening files. **SkyDrive** is a Microsoft service that provides up to 7 GB of online storage space for your files at no charge. You can purchase additional space if you need it. For example, if you create a document in Microsoft Word, your SkyDrive appears as a location for saving the document. (Your SkyDrive appears with your username, such as Matt's SkyDrive.) If you have a Microsoft account, you can select a folder on your SkyDrive to save the document online. (If you don't have a Microsoft account, you can sign up for one by visiting the SkyDrive website.) Because the file is stored online, it takes up no storage space on your computer and is available from any computer with an Internet connection. You access the document by opening it in Word or by visiting the SkyDrive website, and then signing in to your Microsoft account. To share the document with other people, you can send them a link to the document via email. They can use the link to access the document even if they do not have a Microsoft account.

One reason that Matt had trouble remembering the contents of the List file is that "List" is not a descriptive name. A better name for this file is Task List. You will save this document in the Tutorial subfolder of the FM folder provided with your Data Files. You will also use the Save As dialog box to specify a new name for the file as you save it.

### To save the List file with a new name:

▶ 1. On the ribbon in the WordPad window, click the **File** tab to display commands for working with files.

▶ 2. Click **Save as** to open the Save As dialog box, as shown in Figure 10. The Tutorial folder is selected as the storage location for this file because you opened the file from this folder.

| Figure 10 | Saving a file using the Save As dialog box |

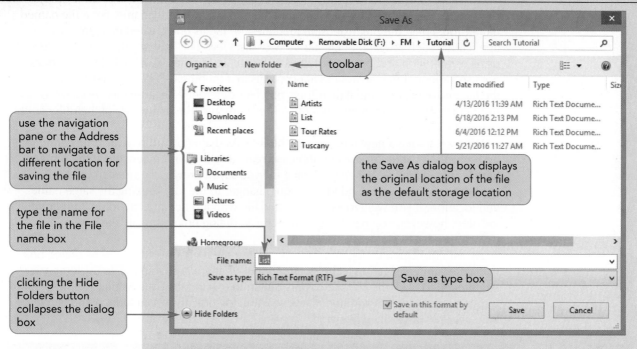

use the navigation pane or the Address bar to navigate to a different location for saving the file

type the name for the file in the File name box

clicking the Hide Folders button collapses the dialog box

the Save As dialog box displays the original location of the file as the default storage location

Save as type box

**Trouble?** If the navigation pane does not appear in the Save As dialog box, click the Browse Folders button. The Browse Folders button toggles to become the Hide Folders button.

▶ 3. With the current filename selected in the File name box, type **Task List**. The Save as type box shows that WordPad will save this file as a Rich Text Format (RTF) file, which is the default file type for WordPad files.

**Trouble?** If the current filename is not selected in the File name box, drag to select the text in the File name box and then type Task List.

▶ 4. Click the **Save** button. The Save As dialog box closes, WordPad saves the Task List file in the Tutorial folder, and the new filename appears in the WordPad title bar.

▶ 5. On the title bar, click the **Close** button ⊠ to close WordPad.

Now you're ready to start creating the folders you need to organize Matt's files.

## Creating Folders

You originally proposed creating four new folders for Matt's files: Marketing Graphics, Tours, Financial, and Projects. Matt asks you to create these folders now. After that, you'll move his files to the appropriate folders. You create folders in File Explorer using one of three methods: using the New folder button in the New group on the Home tab; using the New folder button on the Quick Access Toolbar; or right-clicking to display a shortcut menu that includes the New command.

### Guidelines for Creating Folders

**INSIGHT**

Consider the following guidelines as you create folders:

- Keep folder names short yet descriptive of the folder's contents. Long folder names can be more difficult to display in their entirety in folder windows, so use names that are short but clear. Choose names that will be meaningful later, such as project names or course numbers.
- Create subfolders to organize files. If a file list in File Explorer is so long that you must scroll the window, you should probably organize those files into subfolders.
- Develop standards for naming folders. Use a consistent naming scheme that is clear to you, such as one that uses a project name as the name of the main folder, and includes step numbers in each subfolder name (for example, 1-Outline, 2-First Draft, 3-Final Draft, and so on).

In the following steps, you will create the four folders for Matt in your Tutorial folder. Because it is easier to work with files using large file icons, you'll switch to Large icons view first.

### To create the folders:

1. On the status bar in the File Explorer window, click the **Large icons view** button 🖼 to switch to Large icons view.

2. Click the **Home** tab to display the Home tab on the ribbon.

3. In the New group, click the **New folder** button. A folder icon with the label "New folder" appears in the right pane of the File Explorer window. See Figure 11.

| Figure 11 | Creating a new folder in the Tutorial folder |

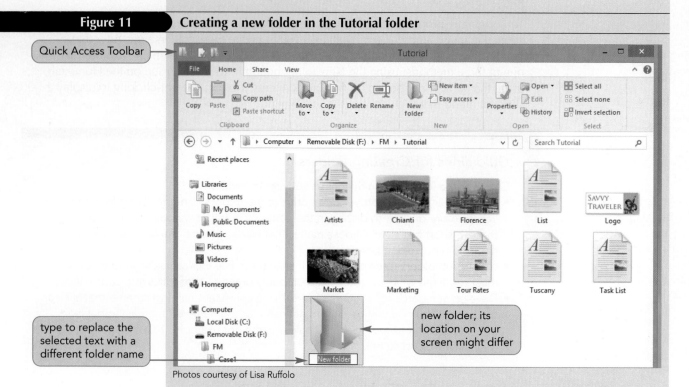

Quick Access Toolbar

type to replace the selected text with a different folder name

new folder; its location on your screen might differ

Photos courtesy of Lisa Ruffolo

> **Trouble?** If the "New folder" name is not selected, right-click the new folder, click Rename on the shortcut menu, and then continue with Step 4.

> Windows uses "New folder" as a placeholder, and selects the text so that you can replace it immediately by typing a new name. You do not need to press the Backspace or Delete key to delete the text.

> **4.** Type **Marketing Graphics** as the folder name, and then press the **Enter** key. The new folder is named Marketing Graphics and is the selected item in the right pane. To create a second folder, you can use a shortcut menu.

> **5.** In the right pane, right-click a blank area, point to **New** on the shortcut menu, and then click **Folder**. A folder icon appears in the right pane with the "New folder" text selected.

> **6.** Type **Tours** as the name of the new folder, and then press the **Enter** key. To create the third folder, you can use the Quick Access Toolbar.

> **7.** On the Quick Access Toolbar, click the **New folder** button 🗋, type **Financial**, and then press the **Enter** key to create and name the folder.

> **8.** Create a new folder in the Tutorial folder named **Projects**.

After creating four folders, you're ready to organize Matt's files by moving them into the appropriate folders.

## Moving and Copying Files and Folders

You can either move or copy a file from its current location to a new location. **Moving** a file removes it from its current location and places it in a new location that you specify. **Copying** a file places a duplicate version of the file in a new location that you specify, while leaving the original file intact in its current location. You can also move and copy folders. When you do, you move or copy all the files contained in the folder. (You'll practice copying folders in a Case Problem at the end of this tutorial.)

In File Explorer, you can move and copy files by using the Move to or Copy to buttons in the Organize group on the Home tab; using the Copy and Cut commands on a file's shortcut menu; or using keyboard shortcuts. When you copy or move files using these methods, you are using the **Clipboard**, a temporary storage area for files and information that you copy or move from one location to place in another.

You can also move files by dragging the files in the File Explorer window. You will now organize Matt's files by moving them to the appropriate folders you have created. You'll start by moving the Marketing file to the Financial folder by dragging the file.

**To move the Marketing file by dragging it:**

1. In File Explorer, point to the **Marketing** file in the right pane, and then press and hold the mouse button.

2. While still pressing the mouse button, drag the **Marketing** file to the **Financial** folder. See Figure 12.

**Figure 12** Dragging a file to move it to a folder

3. When the Move to Financial ScreenTip appears, release the mouse button. The Marketing file is removed from the main Tutorial folder and stored in the Financial subfolder.

   **Trouble?** If you released the mouse button before the Move to Financial ScreenTip appeared, press the Ctrl+Z keys to undo the move, and then repeat Steps 1–3.

   **Trouble?** If you moved the Market file instead of the Marketing file, press the Ctrl+Z keys to undo the move, and then repeat Steps 1–3.

4. In the right pane, double-click the **Financial** folder to verify that it contains the Marketing file.

**TIP**

If you drag a file or folder to a location on a different drive, the file is copied, not moved, to preserve the file in its original location.

**Trouble?** If the Marketing file does not appear in the Financial folder, you probably moved it to a different folder. Press the Ctrl+Z keys to undo the move, and then repeat Steps 1–3.

▶ 5. Click the **Back** button Ⓔ on the Address bar to return to the Tutorial folder.

You'll move the remaining files into the folders using the Clipboard.

### To move files using the Clipboard:

▶ 1. Right-click the **Artists** file, and then click **Cut** on the shortcut menu. Although the file icon still appears selected in the right pane of File Explorer, Windows removes the Artists file from the Tutorial folder and stores it on the Clipboard.

▶ 2. In the right pane, right-click the **Tours** folder, and then click **Paste** on the shortcut menu. Windows pastes the Artists file from the Clipboard to the Tours folder. The Artists file icon no longer appears in the File Explorer window, which is currently displaying the contents of the Tutorial folder.

▶ 3. In the navigation pane, click the **expand** icon ▷ next to the Tutorial folder, if necessary, to display its contents, and then click the **Tours** folder to view its contents in the right pane. The Tours folder now contains the Artists file. See Figure 13.

**Figure 13** | **Artists file in its new location**

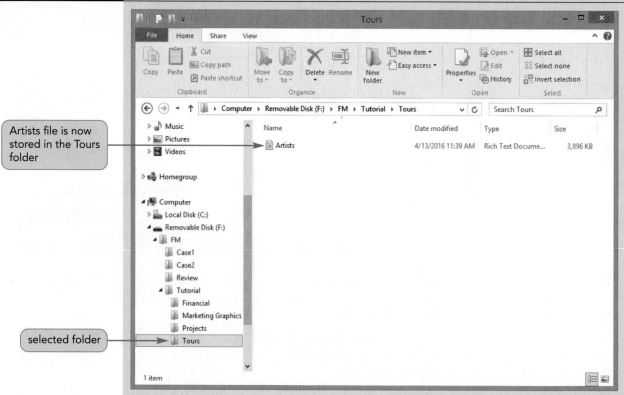

Artists file is now stored in the Tours folder

selected folder

Next, you'll use the Clipboard again to move the Tuscany file from the Tutorial folder to the Tours folder. But this time, you'll access the Clipboard using the ribbon.

4. On the Address bar, point to the **Up to** button ⬆ to display its ScreenTip (Up to "Tutorial"), click the **Up to** button ⬆ to return to the Tutorial folder, and then click the **Tuscany** file to select it.

5. On the Home tab, in the Clipboard group, click the **Cut** button to remove the Tuscany file from the Tutorial folder and temporarily store it on the Clipboard.

6. In the Address bar, click the **arrow** button ▶ to the right of "Tutorial" to display a list of subfolders in the Tutorial folder, and then click **Tours** to display the contents of the Tours folder in File Explorer.

7. In the Clipboard group, click the **Paste** button to paste the Tuscany file in the Tours folder. The Tours folder now contains the Artists and Tuscany files.

Finally, you'll move the Task List file from the Tutorial folder to the Projects folder using the Move to button in the Organize group on the Home tab. This button and the Copy to button are ideal when you want to move or copy files without leaving the current folder. When you select a file and then click the Move to or Copy to button, a list of locations appears, including all of the Windows libraries and one or more folders you open frequently. You can click a location in the list to move the selected file to that library or folder. You can also select the Choose location option to open the Move Items or Copy Items dialog box, and then select a location for the file, which you'll do in the following steps.

**To move the Task List file using the Move to button:**

1. In the Address bar, click **Tutorial** to return to the Tutorial folder, and then click the **Task List** file to select it.

2. On the Home tab, in the Organize group, click the **Move to** button to display a list of locations to which you can move the selected file. The Projects folder is not included on this list because you haven't opened it yet.

3. Click **Choose location** to open the Move Items dialog box. See Figure 14.

| Figure 14 | Move Items dialog box |
|---|---|

locations on your computer; yours might differ

4. If necessary, scroll the list of locations, and then click the **expand** icon ▷ next to the drive containing your Data Files, such as Removable Disk (F:).

> **5.** Navigate to the FM ▸ Tutorial folder, and then click the **Projects** folder to select it.

> **6.** Click the **Move** button to close the dialog box and move the Task List file to the Projects folder.

> **7.** Open the Projects folder to confirm that it contains the Task List file.

One way to save steps when moving or copying multiple files or folders is to select all the files and folders you want to move or copy, and then work with them as a group. You can use several techniques to select multiple files or folders at the same time, which are described in Figure 15.

**Figure 15**    **Selecting multiple files or folders**

| Items to Select in the Right Pane of File Explorer | Method |
| --- | --- |
| Files or folders listed together | Click the first item, press and hold the Shift key, click the last item, and then release the Shift key. |
| | or |
| | Drag the pointer to create a selection box around all the items you want to include. |
| Files or folders not listed together | Press and hold the Ctrl key, click each item you want to select, and then release the Ctrl key. |
| All files and folders | On the Home tab, in the Select group, click the Select all button. |

| Items to Deselect in the Right Pane of File Explorer | Method |
| --- | --- |
| Single file or folder in a selected group | Press and hold the Ctrl key, click each item you want to remove from the selection, and then release the Ctrl key. |
| All selected files and folders | Click a blank area of the File Explorer window. |

© 2014 Cengage Learning

Next, you'll copy the four graphics files from the Tutorial folder to the Marketing Graphics folder using the Clipboard. To do this efficiently, you will select multiple files at once.

### To copy multiple files at once using the Clipboard:

> **1.** Display the contents of the Tutorial folder in File Explorer.

> **2.** Click the **Chianti** file, press and hold the **Shift** key, click the **Market** file, and then release the **Shift** key.

> **3.** Press and hold the **Ctrl** key, click the **List** file to deselect it, and then release the **Ctrl** key. Four files—Chianti, Florence, Logo, and Market—are selected in the Tutorial folder window.

> **4.** Right-click a selected file, and then click **Copy** on the shortcut menu. Windows copies the selected files to the Clipboard.

> **5.** Right-click the **Marketing Graphics** folder, and then click **Paste** on the shortcut menu.

> **6.** Open the **Marketing Graphics** folder to verify it contains the four files you copied, and then return to the Tutorial folder.

7. Right-click the **Tour Rates** file, and then click **Copy** on the shortcut menu.

8. In the right pane, double-click the **Financial** folder to open it, right-click a blank area of the right pane, and then click **Paste** on the shortcut menu.

INSIGHT

### Duplicating Your Folder Organization

If you work on two computers, such as one computer at an office or school and another computer at home, you can duplicate the folders you use on both computers to simplify the process of transferring files from one computer to another. For example, if you have four folders in your My Documents folder on your work computer, create these same four folders on a USB drive and in the My Documents folder of your home computer. If you change a file on the hard disk of your home computer, you can copy the most recent version of the file to the corresponding folder on your USB drive so the file is available when you are at work. You also then have a **backup**, or duplicate copy, of important files. Having a backup of your files is invaluable if your computer has a fatal error.

All the files that originally appeared in the Tutorial folder are now stored in appropriate subfolders. You can streamline the organization of the Tutorial folder by deleting the duplicate files you no longer need.

## Deleting Files and Folders

TIP

In most cases, a file deleted from a USB drive does not go into the Recycle Bin. Instead, it is deleted when Windows 8 removes its icon, and the file cannot be recovered.

You should periodically delete files and folders you no longer need so that your main folders and disks don't get cluttered. In File Explorer, you delete a file or folder by deleting its icon. When you delete a file from a hard disk, Windows 8 removes the file from the folder but stores the file contents in the Recycle Bin. The Recycle Bin is an area on your hard disk that holds deleted files until you remove them permanently. When you delete a folder from the hard disk, the folder and all of its files are stored in the Recycle Bin. If you change your mind and want to retrieve a deleted file or folder, you can double-click the Recycle Bin on the desktop, right-click the file or folder you want to retrieve, and then click Restore. However, after you empty the Recycle Bin, you can no longer recover the files it contained.

Because you copied the Chianti, Florence, Logo, Market, and Tour Rates files to the subfolders in the Tutorial folder, you can safely delete the original files. You can also delete the List file because you no longer need it. You can delete a file or folder using various methods, including using a shortcut menu or selecting one or more files and then pressing the Delete key.

### To delete files in the Tutorial folder:

1. Display the Tutorial folder in the File Explorer window.

2. In the right pane, click **Chianti**, press and hold the **Shift** key, click **Tour Rates**, and then release the **Shift** key. All files in the Tutorial folder are now selected. None of the subfolders should be selected.

Make sure you have copied the selected files to the Marketing Graphics and Financial folders before completing this step.

3. Right-click the selected files, and then click **Delete** on the shortcut menu. A message box appears, asking if you're sure you want to permanently delete these files.

4. Click the **Yes** button to confirm that you want to delete the files.

## Renaming Files

After creating and naming a file or folder, you might realize that a different name would be more meaningful or descriptive. You can easily rename a file or folder by using the Rename command on the file's shortcut menu.

Now that you've organized Matt's files into folders, he reviews your work and notes that the Artists file was originally created to store text specifically about Florentine painters and sculptors. You can rename that file to give it a more descriptive filename.

**TIP**

To rename a file, you can also click the file, pause, click it again to select the filename, and then type to enter a new filename.

**To rename the Artists file:**

▶ **1.** In the right pane of the File Explorer window, double-click the **Tours** folder to display its contents.

▶ **2.** Right-click the **Artists** file, and then click **Rename** on the shortcut menu. The filename is highlighted and a box appears around it.

▶ **3.** Type **Florentine Artists**, and then press the **Enter** key. The file now appears with the new name.

**Trouble?** If you make a mistake while typing and you haven't pressed the Enter key yet, press the Backspace key until you delete the mistake and then complete Step 3. If you've already pressed the Enter key, repeat Steps 2 and 3 to rename the file again.

**Trouble?** If your computer is set to display filename extensions, a message might appear asking if you are sure you want to change the filename extension. Click the No button, and then repeat Steps 2 and 3.

# Working with Compressed Files

You compress a file or a folder of files so it occupies less space on the disk. It can be useful to compress files before transferring them from one location to another, such as from your hard disk to a removable disk or vice versa, or from one computer to another via email. You can then transfer the files more quickly. Also, if you or your email contacts can send and receive files only up to a certain size, compressing large files might make them small enough to send and receive. Compare two folders—a folder named Photos that contains files totaling about 8.6 MB, and a compressed folder containing the same files but requiring only 6.5 MB of disk space. In this case, the compressed files use about 25 percent less disk space than the uncompressed files.

You can compress one or more files in File Explorer using the Zip button, which is located in the Send group on the Share tab of the ribbon. Windows stores the compressed files in a special type of folder called an **archive**, or a compressed folder. File Explorer uses an icon of a folder with a zipper to represent a compressed folder. To compress additional files or folders, you drag them into the compressed folder. You can open a file directly from a compressed folder, although you cannot modify the file. To edit and save a compressed file, you must extract it first. When you **extract** a file, you create an uncompressed copy of the file in a folder you specify. The original file remains in the compressed folder.

Matt suggests that you compress the files and folders in the Tutorial folder so that you can more quickly transfer them to another location.

## To compress the folders and files in the Tutorial folder:

**TIP**

Another way to compress files is to select the files, right-click the selection, point to Send to on the shortcut menu, and then click Compressed (zipped) folder.

1. In File Explorer, navigate to the Tutorial folder, and then select all the folders in the Tutorial folder.

2. Click the **Share** tab on the ribbon.

3. In the Send group, click the **Zip** button. After a few moments, a new compressed folder appears in the Tutorial window with the filename selected. By default, File Explorer uses the name of the first selected item as the name of the compressed folder. You'll replace the name with a more descriptive one.

4. Type **Savvy Traveler**, and then press the **Enter** key to rename the compressed folder. See Figure 16.

---

**Figure 16**  **Compressing files and folders**

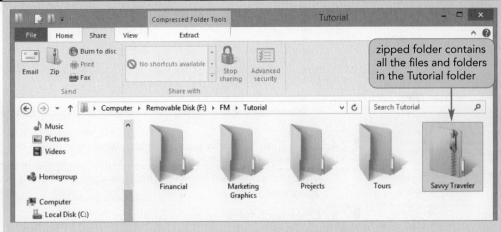

5. Double-click the **Savvy Traveler** compressed folder to open it, open the **Tours** folder, and then note the size of the compressed Tuscany file, which is 1,815 KB.

6. Navigate back to the Tutorial folder.

You can move and copy the files and folders from an opened compressed folder to other locations, although you cannot rename the files. More often, you extract all of the files from the compressed folder to a new location that you specify, preserving the files in their original folders as appropriate.

## To extract the compressed files:

1. Click the **Savvy Traveler** compressed folder to select it, and then click the **Compressed Folder Tools Extract** tab on the ribbon.

2. In the Extract all group, click the **Extract all** button. The Extract Compressed (Zipped) Folders Wizard starts and opens the Select a Destination and Extract Files dialog box.

3. Press the **End** key to deselect the path in the box and move the insertion point to the end of the path, press the **Backspace** key as many times as necessary to delete the Savvy Traveler text, and then type **Backups**. The final three parts of the path in the box should be \FM\Tutorial\Backups. See Figure 17.

| Figure 17 | **Extracting files from a compressed folder** |
|---|---|

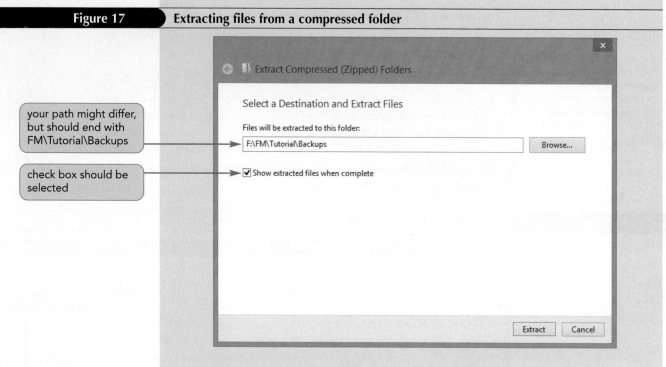

your path might differ, but should end with FM\Tutorial\Backups

check box should be selected

**4.** Make sure the Show extracted files when complete check box is checked, and then click the **Extract** button. Windows extracts the files and then opens the Backups folder, showing the Financial, Marketing Graphics, Projects, and Tours folders.

**5.** Open each folder to make sure it contains the files you worked with in this tutorial. When you open the Tours folder, note the uncompressed size of the Tuscany file, which is about four times as large as its compressed version.

**6.** Close all open windows.

In this tutorial, you examined the purpose of organizing files and folders, and you planned and created an organization for a set of related files and folders. You also explored your computer using File Explorer and learned how to navigate to your Data Files using the navigation pane. You used File Explorer to manage files and folders by opening and saving files; creating folders; and selecting, moving, and copying files. You also renamed and deleted files according to your organization plan. Finally, you compressed and extracted files.

## Quick Check

**REVIEW**

1. You organize files by storing them in _____.
2. What is the purpose of the Address bar in File Explorer?
3. A filename _____ identifies the file's type and indicates the application that created the file.
4. Explain how to use File Explorer to navigate to a file in the following location: E: ▶ Courses ▶ Computer Basics ▶ Operating Systems.txt.
5. One way to move files and folders is to use the _____, a temporary storage area for files and information that you copied or moved from one place and plan to use somewhere else.
6. What happens if you click the first file in a folder window, press the Shift key, click the last file, and then release the Shift key?
7. When you delete a file from a hard disk, Windows removes the file from the folder but stores the file contents in the _____.
8. Describe how to compress a file or folder.
9. What are the benefits of compressing files and folders?

PRACTICE

## Review Assignments

**Data Files needed for the Review Assignments: Banner.png, Colosseum.jpg, Lectures.xlsx, Rome.jpg, Rome.rtf, Schedule.rtf, Tours.rtf**

Matt has saved a few files from his old computer to a removable disk. He gives you these files in a single, unorganized folder, and asks you to organize them logically into subfolders. To do this, you will need to devise a plan for managing the files, and then create the subfolders you need. Next, you will rename, copy, move, and delete files, and then perform other management tasks to make it easy for Matt to work with these files and folders. Complete the following steps:

1. Use File Explorer to navigate to and open the FM ▸ Review folder provided with your Data Files. Examine the seven files in this folder and consider the best way to organize the files.
2. Open the **Rome** text file in WordPad, and then add the following tip to the end of the document: **Dine on the Italian schedule, with the main meal in the middle of the day.**
3. Save the document as **Rome Dining Tips** in the Review folder. Close the WordPad window.
4. In the Review folder, create three folders: **Business**, **Destinations**, and **Supplements**.
5. To organize the files into the correct folders, complete the following steps:
   - Move the Banner and Schedule files from the Review folder to the Business folder.
   - Move the Colosseum and Rome JPEG image files and the Rome Dining Tips and Tours text files to the Destinations folder.
   - Copy the Lectures file to the Supplements folder.
6. Copy the Tours file in the Destinations folder to the Business folder.
7. Rename the Schedule file in the Business folder as **2016 Schedule**. Rename the Lectures file in the Supplements folder as **On-site Lectures**.
8. Delete the Lectures file and the Rome text file from the Review folder.
9. Create a compressed (zipped) folder in the Review folder named **Rome** that contains all the files and folders in the Review folder.
10. Extract the contents of the Rome compressed folder to a new folder named **Rome Backups** in the Review folder. (*Hint:* The file path will end with \FM\Review\Rome Backups.)
11. Close the File Explorer window.

## Case Problem 1

APPLY

See the Starting Data Files section at the beginning of this tutorial for the list of Data Files needed for this Case Problem.

*Bay Shore Arts Center*   Casey Sullivan started the Bay Shore Arts Center in Monterey, California, to provide workshops and courses on art and photography. Attracting students from the San Francisco and San José areas, Casey's business has grown and she now holds classes five days a week. She recently started a course on fine art landscape photography, which has quickly become her most popular offering. Casey hired you to help her design new classes and manage other parts of her growing business, including maintaining electronic business files and communications. Your first task is to organize the files on her new Windows 8 computer. Complete the following steps:

1. Open File Explorer. In the FM ► Case1 folder provided with your Data Files, create three folders: **Classes**, **Landscapes**, and **Management**.
2. Move the Fall Classes, Spring Classes, Summer Classes, and Winter Classes files from the Case1 folder to the Classes folder.
3. Rename the four files in the Classes folder by deleting the word "Classes" from each filename.
4. Move the four JPEG image files from the Case1 folder to the Landscapes folder.
5. Copy the remaining two files to the Management folder.
6. Copy the Workshops file to the Classes folder.
7. Delete the Instructors and Workshops files from the Case1 folder.
8. Make a copy of the Landscapes folder in the Case1 folder. The name of the duplicate folder appears as Landscapes – Copy. Rename the Landscapes – Copy folder as **California Photos**.
9. Copy the Workshops file from the Classes folder to the California Photos folder. Rename this file **California Workshops**.
10. Compress the graphics files in the California Photos folder in a new compressed folder named **Photos**.
11. Move the compressed Photos folder to the Case1 folder.
12. Close File Explorer.

## Case Problem 2

**See the Starting Data Files section at the beginning of this tutorial for the list of Data Files needed for this Case Problem.**

*Charlotte Area Business Incubator*    Antoine Jackson is the director of the Charlotte Area Business Incubator, a service run by the University of North Carolina in Charlotte to consult with new and struggling small businesses. You work as an intern at the business incubator and spend part of your time organizing client files. Since Antoine started using Windows 8, he has been having trouble finding files on his computer. He sometimes creates duplicates of files and then doesn't know which copy is the most current. Complete the following steps:

1. Navigate to the FM ▸ Case2 folder provided with your Data Files, and then examine the files in this folder. Based on the filenames and file types, begin to create an organization plan for the files.

☼ **Troubleshoot** 2. Open the Tips1 and the Tips1 – Copy files and consider the problem these files could cause. Close the files and then fix the problem, renaming one or more files as necessary to reflect the contents.

☼ **Troubleshoot** 3. Open the Tips2 and the Tips2 – Copy files and compare their contents. Change the filenames to clarify the purpose and contents of the files.

4. Complete the organization plan for Antoine's files. In the FM ▸ Case2 folder, create the subfolders you need according to your plan.

5. Move the files in the Case2 folder to the subfolders you created. When you finish, the Case2 folder should contain at least two subfolders containing files.

6. Rename the spreadsheet files in each subfolder according to the following descriptions.
   - Budget1: **Website budget**
   - Budget2: **Marketing budget**
   - Report1: **Travel expense report**
   - Report2: **Project expense report**
   - Report3: **Balance sheet**
   - Report4: **Event budget**

☼ **Troubleshoot** 7. Make sure all files have descriptive names that accurately reflect their contents.

☼ **Troubleshoot** 8. Based on the work you did in Steps 6 and 7, move files as necessary to improve the file organization.

9. Close File Explorer.

# Internet Basics and Information Literacy

*Conducting Research on Energy Conservation*

## OBJECTIVES

- Learn about the Internet and the World Wide Web
- Start the Internet Explorer app and the Internet Explorer desktop application
- Develop search techniques for locating information on the web
- Use a search engine to conduct a search
- Find and evaluate information on the web
- Learn about copyright laws
- Document web resources

## Case | *Hinsdale University*

Martha Weiss is a graduate student studying environmental engineering at Hinsdale University. She is writing a paper on how large corporations in different industries are using natural resources, and ways that these organizations can improve their energy efficiency and use natural resources more effectively. She has gathered information in many areas related to energy, sustainability, and the environment, including upgrading computer systems to reduce energy consumption, making company facilities more energy-smart, using recycled resources whenever practical such as using recycled water from the city's waste center in the cooling systems, and using renewable energy resources such as wind, solar, and hydropower.

Now, Martha wants to feature a few case studies highlighting the efforts large companies like Microsoft Corporation are making to reduce their carbon footprint, which is the amount of greenhouse gases, such as carbon dioxide, that are released into the atmosphere during activities like air travel and commuting. She wants to find the most current information for her case studies, so she plans to use the Internet for her research. Martha recently bought a new computer running Windows 8 and Internet Explorer 10. She is not familiar with Internet Explorer 10, so she asks for your help in conducting her research.

**STARTING DATA FILES**

There are no starting Data Files needed for this tutorial.

# Visual Overview:

The Internet Explorer app opens from the Start screen. Internet Explorer is a **web browser**, a program that locates, retrieves, and displays webpages.

Most webpages have a **search box** that allows you to enter **keywords**, which are specific words and phrases that describe a topic of interest. You then click the search button and the browser displays a list of pages pertaining to your topic.

**Tabs** are used to open multiple webpages simultaneously in one browser window.

The Tabs bar appears at the top of the browser when you right-click the window.

The New Tab button opens a tab for displaying another webpage.

A **webpage** is a document created with a special programming language that displays in a web browser.

In the Internet Explorer app, the navigation bar appears at the bottom of the browser when you right-click the window.

A **hyperlink** (or **link**) is text or a graphic that, when clicked, connects to and displays another part of the webpage or a different webpage.

The Back button redisplays a previously viewed webpage.

The **Address bar** is where you enter the **URL** (**uniform resource locator**), the address of the webpage you want to view.

The Pin site button is used to pin or save a webpage on the Start screen or save it as a favorite.

The Forward button returns you to a previously viewed webpage.

# Internet Explorer App

# Microsoft Internet Explorer 10

The Back button redisplays a previously viewed webpage. The Forward button returns you to a previously viewed webpage.

The Internet Explorer desktop application opens from the desktop. Internet Explorer is a **web browser**, a program that locates, retrieves, and displays webpages.

The **Address bar** is where you enter the **URL (Uniform Resource Locator)**, the address of the webpage you want to view.

**Tabs** are used to open multiple webpages simultaneously in one browser window.

The New Tab button opens a tab for displaying another webpage.

The Favorites button opens the **Favorites Center**, which has tools for saving favorite webpages and viewing a history list of previously visited webpages.

A **webpage** is a document created with a special programming language that displays in a web browser. The **home page** is the webpage that appears when the browser starts. The main page of a website is also called the home page.

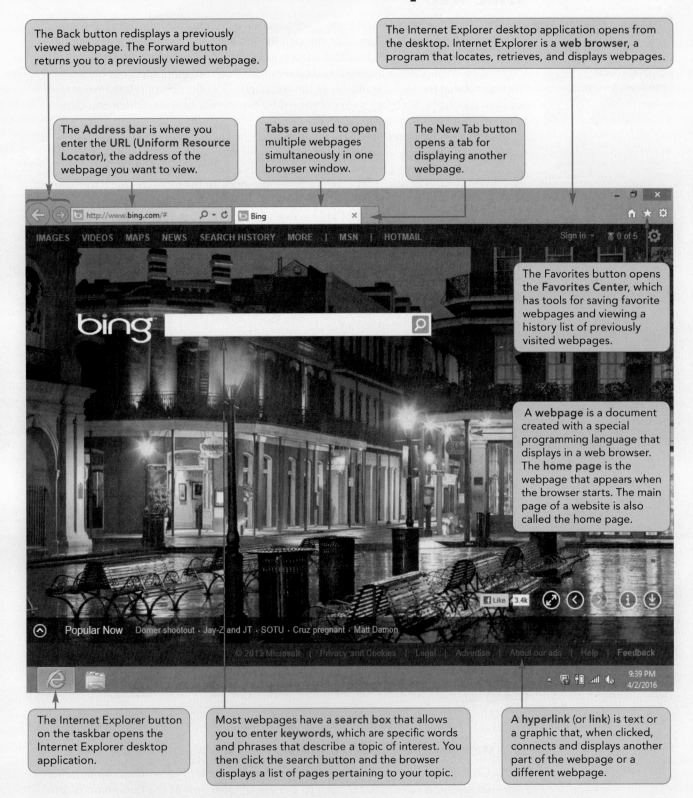

The Internet Explorer button on the taskbar opens the Internet Explorer desktop application.

Most webpages have a **search box** that allows you to enter **keywords**, which are specific words and phrases that describe a topic of interest. You then click the search button and the browser displays a list of pages pertaining to your topic.

A **hyperlink** (or **link**) is text or a graphic that, when clicked, connects and displays another part of the webpage or a different webpage.

# Internet Explorer Desktop Application

Flirt/Superstock

# Understanding the Internet and the World Wide Web

The **web** (short for **World Wide Web**) is a collection of electronic documents or files—called webpages—that are available through the Internet. The **Internet** is a worldwide collection of computer networks that allows people to communicate and exchange information. Webpages are stored on **web servers**, which are computers connected to the Internet that manage the display of the webpages. A collection of related webpages is called a **website**. Webpages are connected by hyperlinks, or links, which you click to move from one webpage to another.

You use a web browser to access, retrieve, and display webpages from a computer that is connected to the Internet. Common browsers include Microsoft Internet Explorer, Mozilla Firefox, Google Chrome, Apple Safari, and Opera. Internet Explorer 10, the current version of Microsoft's web browser, provides all the tools you need to communicate, access, and share information on the web. As shown in the Visual Overview, Internet Explorer is available in two versions—the Internet Explorer app that opens from the Start screen, and the Internet Explorer application that opens from the desktop. Both versions perform the same basic functions, but you access them differently.

**INSIGHT**

### Connecting to the Internet

To access information on the web, you must use a computer that is connected to the Internet. Common Internet connections include cable, DSL, dial-up, and wireless networks. A **wireless** network uses radio frequency signals to transmit data between computers and devices, such as routers, that are physically connected to a network. Home connections require an account with an **Internet service provider (ISP)**, a company that provides Internet access by connecting your computer to one of its servers via a telephone or cable modem. When you are logged on to your ISP account, you use a web browser to access, retrieve, and display webpages.

Martha can use either version of Internet Explorer to conduct her research into Microsoft's initiatives to reduce its carbon footprint. First, she needs your help to become familiar with the features of Internet Explorer and basic browsing skills. You will begin by starting the Internet Explorer app and visiting a website.

## Starting the Internet Explorer App

The Internet Explorer app hides the browser interface so that the focus is on the webpage content. Because the tools are hidden until you need them, the Internet Explorer app is a good choice for casual browsing or looking up information quickly. When you start Internet Explorer, the home page set for your browser appears in the browser window.

**To start the Internet Explorer app:**

1. On the Start screen, click the **Internet Explorer** tile. The home page appears and fills the screen. Refer back to the Visual Overview at the beginning of this tutorial. The home page on your screen might be different, or you might not see any home page at all.

**Trouble?** If a message bar appears at the bottom of the screen, indicating that Internet Explorer blocked content with security certificate errors, you can click the Show content button to display blocked content, click the Close button to hide the message bar, or do nothing and leave the message displayed. You will need to make this decision each time this message appears.

2. Compare the tools in the navigation bar at the bottom of your screen to the Visual Overview at the beginning of this tutorial.

## Entering a URL in the Address Bar

A Uniform Resource Locator (URL) identifies where a webpage is located on the Internet. For example, the URL for the Microsoft home page is http://www.microsoft.com/en-us/default.aspx. A URL consists of the following four parts:

**TIP**

Generally, organizations use URLs that include their name, making it easier to find their site.

- The first part of the URL, *http://*, is the **protocol**, which is a set of rules that computers use to exchange files. Hypertext Transfer Protocol (HTTP) and File Transfer Protocol (FTP) are two of the most common protocols used on the Internet. In this example, *http://* is the protocol.
- The second part of the URL, www.microsoft.com, specifies the location of the web server. The prefix is often *www,* indicating the server is a web server, but it can be something else or omitted entirely. The next part provides a unique name for the website, and the last part identifies the type of website. In this example, *microsoft* is the unique name and *.com* indicates that it is a commercial enterprise. Other categories include .edu (educational institutions), .gov (government agencies), .mil (U.S. military units or agencies), .net (network service providers or resources), .org (organizations, usually not-for-profit), and .biz (businesses).
- The third portion of the URL, */en-us/* in this example, provides the path for the folder in which the webpage file is located.
- The last part of the URL, *default.aspx,* is the filename of the webpage.

### INSIGHT

### IP Addresses and Domain Names

The web server address corresponds to an Internet Protocol (IP) address. An **IP address** is a unique number consisting of four sets of numbers from 0 to 255, separated by periods (such as 216.35.148.4), that identifies the server or computer connected to the Internet. Because IP addresses can be difficult to remember, web addresses use a **domain name**, which is a unique string of letters and/or numbers that are easy to remember, such as *microsoft.com* in the previous example. Some URLs include a filename after the domain name. If a URL does not include a filename, many web browsers will load the file that contains the website's home page—for example, index.htm or default.aspx.

To display a specific webpage, you can enter its URL in the Address bar. As you type, the names or URLs of other webpages you have visited that start with the same characters appear in a list above the Address bar. URLs are not case sensitive, so you can type them in all lowercase letters even though some longer URLs use a mix of uppercase and lowercase letters to distinguish the different words in the address.

You will begin your research into Microsoft's environmental sustainable business practices by visiting the Microsoft website. You can type the URL for the website into the Address bar of the Internet Explorer app.

### To visit the Microsoft website by entering its URL:

1. Click in the **Address bar** to select the URL of the currently displayed webpage. The navigation bar expands, and it might show tiles for webpages you visited recently or have saved as favorites.

2. Type **http://www.microsoft.com**. As you type, URLs of other websites you have visited that begin with the same letters you are typing appear above the Address bar.

3. Press the **Enter** key. The home page of the Microsoft website appears in the browser window. See Figure 1. The content you see might differ because webpages are dynamic and their content is updated frequently.

**Figure 1**    **Microsoft's home page in the Internet Explorer app**

a Microsoft link appears in the upper-left corner of each page on the site and links back to this home page

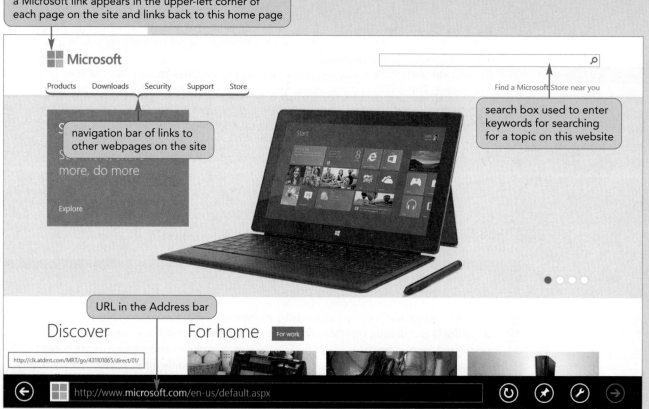

navigation bar of links to other webpages on the site

search box used to enter keywords for searching for a topic on this website

URL in the Address bar

**Trouble?** If a message bar appears at the bottom of the screen, indicating that Internet Explorer blocked content with security certificate errors, click the Close button to hide the message bar.

Although there are millions of websites that are designed for a multitude of purposes and audiences, most websites are organized similarly. The home page provides basic information about the individual or organization and includes a navigation bar with links to other pages of information. The number of additional pages depends on how much information the person or organization wants to share. Common pages include a Contact page that contains information about how to get in touch with the company; an About page that contains information about the company such as its history, mission, and staff; and a Products or Services page that contains information about the items the company sells or the services it provides. Depending on the amount of information that is included, each top-level page could be linked to additional pages with more details or related information. In addition, each page usually includes a link to return to the site's home page.

**INSIGHT**

### Information Bar Messages

Webpages are designed for different audiences and purposes. Some pages contain elements that require the Internet Explorer desktop application. Others might have blocked content for security purposes. If an issue arises when you try to load a webpage, a message bar with details about the issue appears near the bottom of the browser window. It includes buttons for resolving the issue, such as showing blocked content, opening a page in the desktop application, ignoring the issue for the current site, and closing the information bar without making a change. You can also do nothing and just leave the message bar displayed. You'll need to decide on a course of action whenever you see a message bar.

## Clicking Links

Each time you click a link, a new webpage appears in the browser window, replacing the previous page. Likewise, the URL in the Address box changes to correspond to the new webpage.

You can use links to navigate the site and locate information. The Microsoft home page has many links to a variety of resources. The navigation bar includes links to the following categories—Products, Downloads, Security, Support, and Store. In addition, you can use other links on the page to find a Microsoft store near you, to visit other Microsoft sites, and to get information about Microsoft products.

Martha is interested in finding basic information about Microsoft Corporation to use in her case study. You will begin to navigate the site to find out more about Microsoft.

**TIP**

To scroll the page, move the pointer to the right edge of the screen to display the scroll bar, and then click and drag the scroll bar to see more of the webpage.

### To use links to navigate webpages on the Microsoft site:

1. On the Microsoft home page, scroll down to the bottom of the page. A list of links appears.

2. In the About list, point to the **Microsoft** link, as shown in Figure 2. The pointer changes to 🖑 and a ScreenTip lists the URL of the page that the link will open.

| Figure 2 | Links on a webpage |
| --- | --- |

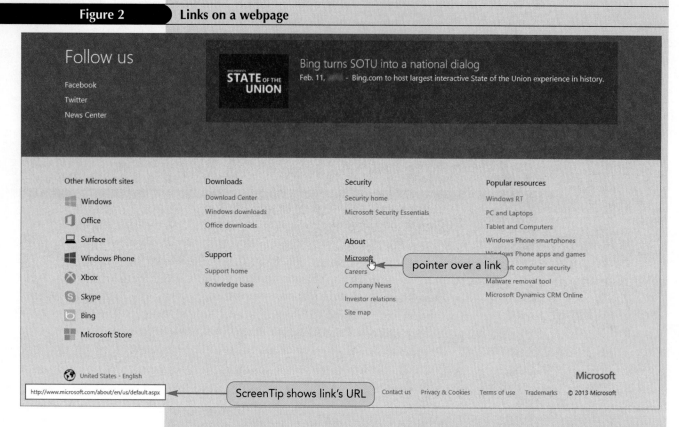

3. Click the **Microsoft** link. The About Microsoft page loads. It includes some information about the company, such as its mission, company information, corporate citizenship, and customer and partner experience, as well as a variety of links to additional information.

   **Trouble?** If a message bar appears above the Address bar indicating the site uses add-ons that require Internet Explorer on the desktop, click the Close button.

4. Click the **Company Information** link to open the corresponding webpage, and then read the information that appears.

5. Click the **Our Businesses** link to load Microsoft's Business page, and then read the information about the various business divisions at Microsoft.

## Moving Between Viewed Pages

In Internet Explorer, you can move back and forth between the different webpages you have viewed during a browsing session. As shown in the Visual Overview, the Back button appears to the left of the navigation bar and the Forward button appears to the right of the navigation bar in the Internet Explorer app. Clicking the Back button redisplays the previous webpage you visited. You can continue backward through the visited pages until you reach the first page that opened when you started Internet Explorer. Once you navigate back a page, the Forward button becomes available so you can return to the more recent pages you visited. In the Internet Explorer app, you can also click the arrow buttons that appear when you move the pointer to the left or right side of the screen to move between the pages you have viewed.

You will go back to a previous page.

**To navigate between visited pages:**

▶ **1.** If the navigation bar is hidden, right-click the webpage to redisplay it. The Tabs bar also opens at the top of the window.

▶ **2.** On the left side of the navigation bar, click the **Back** button ⬅. The Company Information page reappears in the browser window.

▶ **3.** Move the pointer to the left side of the webpage. An arrow button appears.

▶ **4.** Click the **Back arrow** button ⟨. The About Microsoft page reappears in the browser window.

▶ **5.** Point to the right side of the webpage, and then click the **Forward arrow** button ⟩. The Company Information page reappears.

The web provides a vast amount of information. As you can see from visiting the Microsoft website, some information can be easy to find by going directly to a known website and using the navigation tools provided on the site to locate specific information—in this case, basic information about Microsoft Corporation and its business divisions. You also could have used the search box on the Microsoft website to enter keywords to search for more specific information on the site, such as the company's mission statement.

Sometimes information you are looking for on the web might be more difficult to track down. In those instances, when the information could be available on a variety of websites or it isn't related to a specific person or organization that has a website, you will need to search the web to find the sites that have the relevant information. To do that, you can use a search engine.

## Understanding Search Engines

If you don't know the URL of the site you want to visit or which site contains the information you want, you can use a **search engine** to locate webpages related to the keywords you enter. Popular search engines include Google, Bing, and Yahoo!

Search engines use a program called a spider or bot to compile databases of webpages that are indexed by keywords. When you enter keywords in a search engine, it searches its database to find webpages that include those keywords, and shows the results as a list of links to those webpages. Because each search engine creates its own database, collecting different information or different levels of detail, the results delivered by each search engine can be different.

Each search engine has its own website. From the search engine's home page, you can enter keywords for your topic in a search box and then click the search button or press the Enter key to conduct the search. The results page that appears includes a list of links to pages that contain your search words. The links are arranged in descending order by relevancy—the pages that seem more related to your search term appear at the top of the list. Other webpages at the search engine site let you search for images, videos, news, and so forth.

**TIP**

Internet Explorer can differentiate between a URL and keywords for a search engine because a URL includes a domain name and keywords do not.

Because search engines are the most effective way to locate information on the web, the Address bar in Internet Explorer also provides access to a search engine. Instead of entering a URL, you can enter keywords that relate to your search topic in the Address bar, and then press the Enter key. The search engine's results page, which contains links to other webpages, appears—the same as if you entered the keywords in the search box on the search engine site's home page. Although the default search engine for Internet Explorer is Bing, you can change this to another search engine if you prefer.

## Other Web Search Tools

Although search engines are a great place to start your research, there are other, more specialized search tools that can be useful. Some of these search tools are:

- **Metasearch engines** explore multiple search engines and show the combined results, which include a list of links to webpages that match your keywords. Some common metasearch engines are www.dogpile.com and www.webcrawler.com.
- The **deep web** (also called the **invisible web**) refers to information that is stored in databases rather than on webpages. Most search engines do not include deep web resources in their results. To find these resources, you usually have to search a specific website, such as infomine.ucr.edu, www.lii.org, and www.wolframalpha.com.
- **Web directories** list websites organized by categories. These directories are compiled by people, so the results can be more refined than those generated by search engines. If you want general information on a topic, you might find better results with a web directory.
- **Blogs**, short for web logs, are personal commentaries that present the writer's opinion, but they can also provide innovative ideas or breaking news. Bloggers sometimes include links to other resources to support their views, providing additional resources for you to review about your topic. You can search for blogs with a blog search engine, such as technorati.com and Google Blog Search at www.google.com/blogsearch.

While visiting the Microsoft website, you did not see information on how Microsoft is working to reduce its carbon footprint. To help Martha find the information for her case study, you need to broaden your search by using a search engine to locate more resources on this topic.

# Finding Information on the Web

Organizations and individuals use the web for a variety of reasons. Businesses use websites to sell or advertise their products, and to communicate information to customers or employees. Individuals use the web to find a wide variety of information, to communicate and share information with others, and to purchase products and services. Because so much information is available, you need a way to sift through and find the information that is relevant to your needs. To do this, you first must develop a search strategy.

## Formulating a Search Strategy

When you are looking for information on the web, it is important to figure out exactly what you want to find and how to find it before you start. This means developing a search strategy so you can find the information you need efficiently and effectively. Otherwise, you will find a lot of information, but not necessarily the information you need or want. Before beginning your search, develop a search strategy by doing the following:

- **Identify your topic.** You want to pinpoint the main concept, subject, or issue that you want to research. You can do this by formulating a question. For example, Martha might formulate the question "What are Microsoft's sustainable business practices?" or "How is Microsoft reducing its carbon footprint?"
- **List keywords that represent your topic.** Keywords should be specific words and phrases that are connected to your main topic, such as unique words, names, abbreviations, or organizations associated with your topic. At this point, you should jot down any keywords you think might be relevant. For Martha's research, keywords might include "Microsoft," "carbon footprint," "sustainable," and "environment."

- **Refine your keywords list.** Once you have a list of potential keywords, you need to review them to determine which are most relevant, identify synonyms that might provide better results, and consider if the keywords provide a complete representation of your topic. Add, remove, and modify the list as needed. You want to use keywords that are most likely to be on the webpages you want to find. For example, Martha might refine her list to the keywords "Microsoft" and "carbon footprint."

- **Develop your search query.** A **search query** is the translation of your original question into a form that a search engine can understand. A search query is built from the keywords you identified as most related to your topic. Be descriptive and specific, and combine keywords to pare the search results to the most relevant. The more descriptive and complete your search query is, the better and more accurate the results. For example, Martha might find that "carbon footprint" will return many results, as will "Microsoft." But, "Microsoft carbon footprint" will return fewer but more specific results.

- **Refine your search query.** As you review the initial results from your search query, you might not find the exact information you were looking for. However, you might discover related information that will help you refine your search query. For example, you might find additional keywords you could add to your query to locate more specific information related to your topic. Conversely, you might need to remove a keyword because it's leading to incorrect or misleading results. Likewise, you might need to change some of the keywords to synonyms to obtain better results. You might need to adjust your search query several times to refine the results to locate the specific information you wanted to find.

You will use a search engine to implement Martha's search strategy for finding information on how Microsoft is reducing its carbon footprint. When conducting more in-depth research on the web, it is often more efficient to use the Internet Explorer desktop application. Because you are working on the desktop, you can use other desktop applications to compile your research as you go. For example, you might want to use Microsoft WordPad to record some of the information you gathered and to begin outlining a report.

# Starting the Internet Explorer Desktop Application

The Internet Explorer desktop application functions similarly to the Internet Explorer app; however, the Address bar and navigation bar appear at the top of the browser window and remain displayed. Having these tools easily and consistently available will be helpful as you conduct your research. You will start the Internet Explorer desktop application now.

**To start the Internet Explorer desktop application:**

1. Return to the **Start** screen, and then click the **Desktop** tile. The Desktop application opens.

2. On the taskbar, click the **Internet Explorer** button ![e]. The Internet Explorer desktop application opens, as shown in the Visual Overview at the beginning of this tutorial. Your home page might differ.

   **Trouble?** If a message bar appears at the bottom of the screen, indicating that Internet Explorer blocked content with security certificate errors, click the Close button in the upper-right corner of the message bar to hide the message bar.

As stated earlier, you can use the Address bar to access a search engine, or you can go directly to a search engine's home page to access all of its features and functionality. Either way, the search results appear in the browser window. At the top of the results page, the search box shows the current search words. You can enter new keywords to start a new search at any time. The number of results indicates the number of **hits**, which are pages containing content that matches your search words. Hits are generally organized in order of relevancy. The first line contains a link with a headline of the page, the second line shows the URL, and the next lines display a more detailed summary or description of what you will find on the page. Also, website owners can purchase a paid placement, or ad, to get a hit to appear in the first page of search results that include a specific keyword—even if it is not the most relevant. Ads appear in the right column of the page and sometimes at the top of the page.

You will use the Bing search engine to implement Martha's search strategy for finding details on how Microsoft is working to reduce its carbon footprint.

### To use the Bing search engine from the Address bar:

▶ **1.** Click in the Address bar to select the URL of your home page, type **microsoft carbon footprint** as the search query, and then press the **Enter** key. The search query is sent to Bing. After a moment, the search results appear in the browser window. See Figure 3.

| Figure 3 | Search results in Bing |
|---|---|

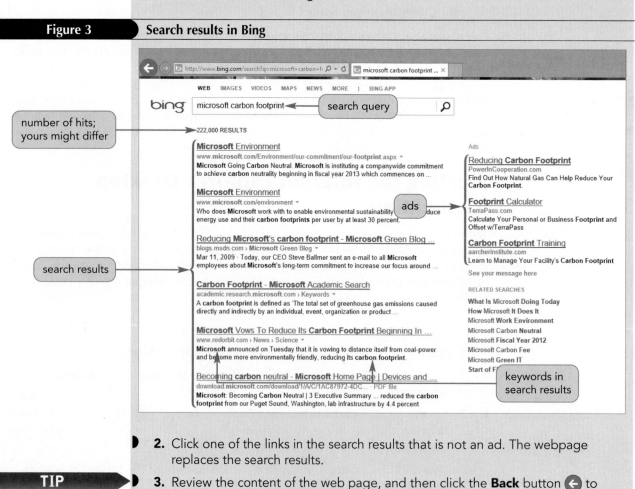

▶ **2.** Click one of the links in the search results that is not an ad. The webpage replaces the search results.

**TIP**

You can also press the Backspace key to return to a previously viewed page.

▶ **3.** Review the content of the web page, and then click the **Back** button ← to return to the search results page.

You should review the links that appear in the search results, looking for ones that seem to have the information most related to the topic you are researching. The description following each search result highlights the keywords from your search, giving you some indication of how relevant that search result might be to your topic.

It is also a good idea to conduct your search using multiple search engines. Different search engines can return different results depending on which part of the web the search engine's spider accesses. Also, each search engine uses a unique ranking system when listing search results. Tabbed browsing can make it convenient to compare search results from multiple search engines.

## Using Page Tabs

**Tabbed browsing** displays multiple webpages in the same browser window. With tabbed browsing, you can open a tab for each webpage you visit that you might want to return to quickly. Opening multiple pages in tabs lets you easily compare the content of different pages, or follow a pathway of information without losing your starting point.

When multiple pages are open in different tabs, the tab with the Close Tab button is the active tab. You click a tab to display that page. You can close a tab for a webpage that no longer interests you by clicking its Close Tab button.

When you point to the Internet Explorer button on the taskbar, **thumbnail** images (which are miniature pictures) of all open tabs are displayed. You can click a thumbnail to display its related page in the browser. You can also close a tab by pointing to the thumbnail and then clicking the Close button that appears in the upper-right corner of the thumbnail.

---

**REFERENCE**

### Opening Tabs for Browsing

- Click the New Tab button, which appears to the right of the open tabs.
- In the Address box, enter the URL for the webpage you want to visit, and then press the Enter key.

*or*

- Press and hold the Ctrl key as you click a link on a webpage to open a new webpage in a new tab.
- Right-click a link on a webpage, and then on the shortcut menu, click Open in new tab.

---

You will open a new tab so that you can perform the same search with a different search engine–Google.

---

**To open, switch between, and close page tabs in the Internet Explorer desktop application:**

1. To the right of the open page tab, point to the **New Tab** button ▢. The New Tab button changes to ▢.

2. Click ▢. A new tab opens with the insertion point blinking in the Address bar. The tab displays links to sites that you have recently or regularly visited, and you can click a link to open one of the sites in the tab. See Figure 4.

**Figure 4**    **Tabbed browsing**

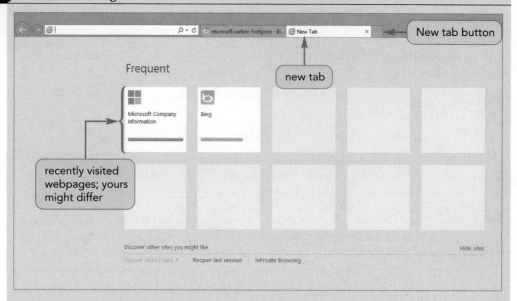

3. Click in the **Address bar**, if necessary, type **www.google.com**, and then press the **Enter** key. The Google home page opens with the insertion point blinking in the search box.

4. In the search box, type **microsoft carbon footprint**, and then press the **Enter** key. The search query is sent to Google. After a moment, the search results appear on the screen.

5. Review the search results. Notice the number of hits and the first three websites listed in the results. You will return to the Bing search results so you can compare them with the Google search results.

6. Click the **Bing** tab to redisplay the Bing search results, and then look for differences in the search results. For example, the number of hits on Bing will differ from the number of hits on Google, and the list of results might have different hits at the top, or the same hits but in a different order.

   You will open pages from the search results in different tabs so you can leave the search results open in the original tab.

7. Press and hold the **Ctrl** key as you click a promising link in the Bing search results, and then release the **Ctrl** key. The linked webpage opens in a new tab, but the Bing search results tab remains active.

8. In the Bing search results, right-click the link for another page with promising information, and then click **Open in new tab** on the shortcut menu. The page opens in another tab.

9. Point to the **Google** tab. A Close Tab button ☒ appears in the upper-right corner of the tab. You don't need these search results any longer, so you can close the page.

10. Click the **Close Tab** button ☒. The page with the Google search results closes, leaving the other tabs available.

The Internet Explorer app also offers tabbed browsing. As described in the Visual Overview, the tabs don't appear until you right-click in the browser window, which displays the Tabs bar at the top of the screen and the navigation bar at the bottom of the screen. From the Tabs bar, you can create new tabs by clicking the New Tabs button, switch between open tabs by clicking each page tab, and closing tabs by clicking the Close Tab button.

## Using the History List

The **History list** tracks the webpages you visit over a certain time period, not just during one browsing session. The History list contains the URLs for the websites and pages that you have visited using both versions of Internet Explorer; however, you can only access the complete History list from the desktop application. By default, the entries in the History list are organized into date folders (Today, Yesterday, Two Weeks ago, and so on). Each date folder contains a folder for every website you visited. Within each site folder, the webpages you visited appear in alphabetical order.

You will use the History list to open the Microsoft home page you viewed earlier in the Internet Explorer app.

**To use the History list:**

1. In the upper-right corner of the window, click the **View favorites, feeds, and history** button 🌟. The Favorites Center opens on the right side of the screen.

2. Click the **History** tab. The list of visited sites is displayed by date.

   **Trouble?** If the History list is not organized by date, you need to change the setting. Click the View by button just below the History tab, and then click View By Date.

3. Click **Today**. The Today list expands so you can see a list of the sites you viewed today.

4. Click the **microsoft** folder to display the pages you viewed at the Microsoft site today. See Figure 5.

**Figure 5**     History list

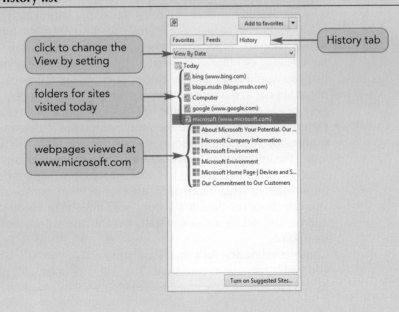

click to change the View by setting

folders for sites visited today

webpages viewed at www.microsoft.com

History tab

> **5.** Click **Microsoft Home Page | Devices and Services** to open the same Microsoft home page you viewed in the Internet Explorer app.

Now that you have implemented your search strategy, you need to determine if the results meet your needs.

# Evaluating the Search Results

You should review and evaluate all of the information you find on the web to identify its author, source, and accuracy, and to evaluate the usefulness of the information. The cost of publishing on the web is low, and anyone who has access to a computer connected to the Internet can publish content. The content of webpages is not regulated or verified. Although information can be and is updated regularly, there is plenty of outdated information on the web. As you gather facts, be sure to read the information you find to determine whether it is relevant, useful, accurate, balanced, and objective. The following list provides the basic steps for evaluating your search results:

- **Identify the author.** Determine who wrote the information and check whether the author has the credentials or expertise to write about the topic. Some credentials to consider are the author's background, education, professional experience, and affiliations. Often, the site includes a link to more information about the author—either on the site or at the author's site.
- **Check for objectivity/bias.** Think about the author's purpose for writing—conveying information, persuading others, creating controversy, and so forth. Determine whether the information is fact, opinion, or speculation. Consider whether other viewpoints might provide differing or conflicting information. One way to determine bias is to read articles from a variety of different sources and compare the information they present. Sources can include periodicals (magazines, newspapers, and other publications), blogs (websites on which people post commentaries and readers respond), wikis (websites that many people contribute to and edit but whose content is not necessarily validated for accuracy), online references (dictionaries, thesauri, encyclopedias, atlases, quotations, and grammar checkers), government sites, business sites, and personal sites.
- **Verify currency.** Try to find out when the information was last updated. Consider whether timeliness affects the reliability of the information. Most webpages include a last revision date somewhere on the page (usually at the top or the bottom).
- **Assess accuracy.** Evaluate the content for correctness—take note of glaring errors, misspellings, or other sloppy errors. Confirm the information with a second source, like you would with other research materials. On the web, the same information might appear in multiple places; but when you dig deeper, you might find that everyone is repeating the same information from a single source.
- **Determine validity.** Look at the source of the site to determine whether this is a trustworthy information resource. Consider who owns the website on which you found the information—a recognized, legitimate publication or an individual. Check whether the website has a stated goal that might influence how it presents information or what information it presents. From the About and Contact pages, you can check out the site's history, read mission or vision statements, and find the address and details about key staff. You can also search the web to find reviews of the source.
- **Consider relevancy.** As a final step, you need to consider whether the information you find is relevant to your topic. You will encounter a lot of interesting information as you go, and it's easy to get lost in tangential information.

Based on your evaluation, you can determine whether the information is useful. For example, Figure 6 shows how Martha evaluated one webpage from the search results. Although this webpage provides information on her topic, given her evaluation, she might want to continue looking for more information.

**Figure 6** ▸ **Webpage evaluated for usefulness to search topic**

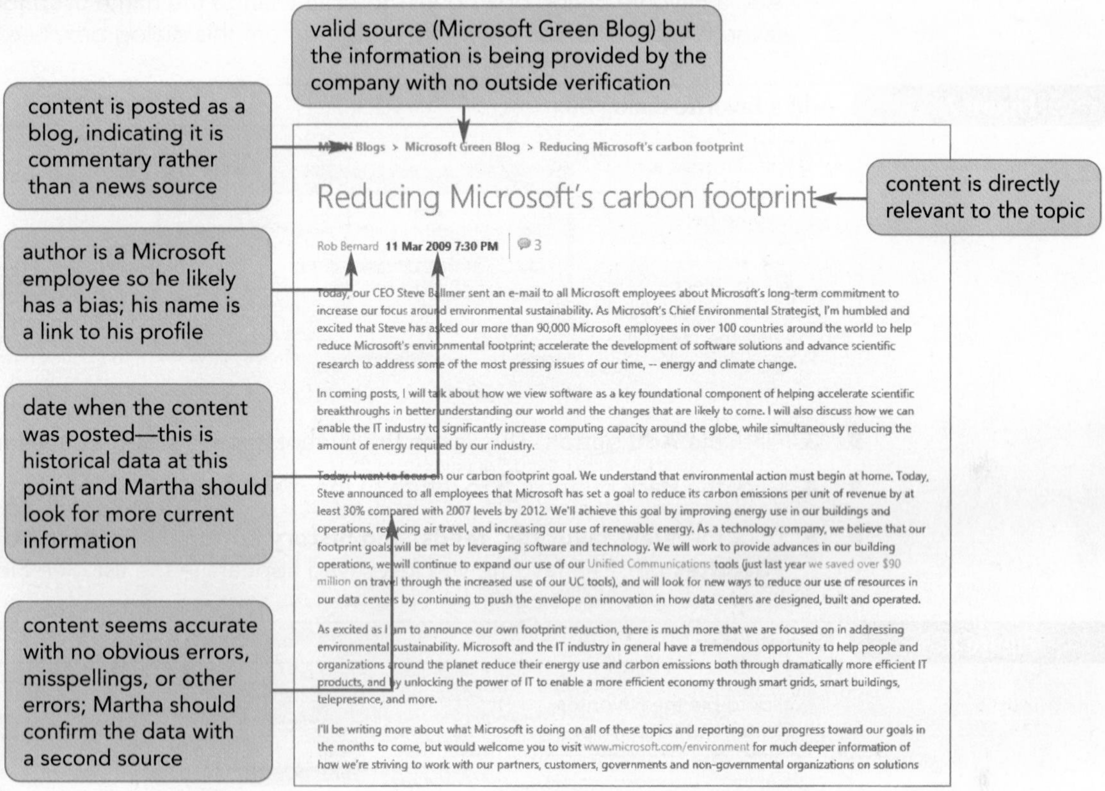

If the information does meet your needs, Internet Explorer provides several ways to save the information so you can access it later as you compile your research results.

## Saving Webpages as Favorites

Web addresses can be very long and, as a result, difficult to remember. In Internet Explorer, you can save the URL of a website as a favorite in the **Favorites list**, a feature that you can use to store and organize a list of webpages you want to revisit.

You can save a webpage as a favorite from both versions of Internet Explorer. From the Internet Explorer desktop application, you open the Favorites Center, and then click the Add to favorites button. The Add a Favorite dialog box opens, allowing you to specify a name for the favorite and select a folder in which to save the favorite in the Favorites list. Using folders to organize your Favorites list makes it easier to find a favorite when you need it. From the Internet Explorer app, you click the Pin site button in the navigation bar, and then click Add to favorites. The page is added to the Favorites list using the title of the webpage.

Martha will want to refer back to the Microsoft home page as she completes her case study. You will save the Microsoft home page as a favorite.

**To save the Microsoft home page as a favorite:**

▶ **1.** With the Microsoft home page displayed in the browser window, click the **View favorites, feeds, and history** button ⭐.

▶ **2.** At the top of the Favorites Center, click the **Add to favorites** button. The Add a Favorite dialog box opens. You can change the name used for the favorite and the folder in which it is stored from this dialog box. See Figure 7.

**Figure 7**    **Add a Favorite dialog box**

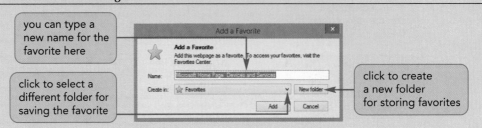

you can type a new name for the favorite here

click to select a different folder for saving the favorite

click to create a new folder for storing favorites

▶ **3.** Click the **Add** button. The link to the current page is saved as a favorite.

▶ **4.** Click the **Back** button ⬅ to return to the previous page.

▶ **5.** Click the **View favorites, feeds, and history** button ⭐, and then click the **Favorites** tab. The favorite you just saved appears in the list. See Figure 8.

**Figure 8**    **Favorites tab**

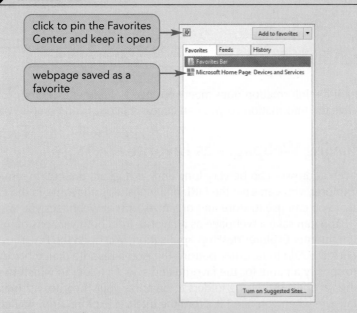

click to pin the Favorites Center and keep it open

webpage saved as a favorite

▶ **6.** Click the **Microsoft Home  Page Devices and Services** favorite. The page is displayed again in the browser window.

When you no longer need to save a page as a favorite, you should delete it to keep your Favorites list current and streamlined. You will delete the Microsoft home page favorite.

**To delete the Microsoft home page favorite:**

1. Click the **View favorites, feeds, and history** button ⭐.

2. On the Favorites tab, right-click the **Microsoft Home Page  Devices and Services** favorite. A shortcut menu opens with options for working with favorites.

3. On the shortcut menu, click **Delete**. The Microsoft Home Page Devices and Services favorite is deleted from the Favorites Center.

## Pinning Webpages

You can pin a page to the taskbar so you can open the webpage directly from the desktop without first starting Internet Explorer. To pin a webpage to the taskbar, drag the tab of the webpage from the Internet Explorer window to the taskbar, and then release the mouse button when the ScreenTip "Pin to Taskbar" appears. The button on the taskbar is a shortcut to the webpage. When you click the button for the pinned page, the page opens in a new browser window.

You can also pin a page to the right side of the Start screen. In the Internet Explorer desktop application, click the Tools button, and then click Add site to Start Screen. A dialog box opens asking you to confirm the name and URL for the tile. In the Internet Explorer app, you pin a page to the Start screen by clicking the Pin site button on the navigation bar, and then clicking Pin to Start. A dialog box opens so you can change the name that will appear on the tile.

You will pin the Microsoft home page to the Start screen for Martha.

**To pin the Microsoft home page to the Start screen:**

1. Click the **Tools** button ⚙ to open the Tools menu, and then click **Add site to Start Screen**. A dialog box opens in which you can confirm the name for the tile and the URL for the website. See Figure 9.

**Figure 9**    Dialog box to pin site to Start screen

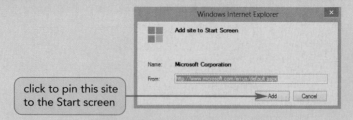

click to pin this site to the Start screen

2. Click the **Add** button. The tile is added to the Start screen.

3. Display the **Start** screen, and then scroll to the far right until you see the Microsoft Corporation tile you added to the Start screen. See Figure 10.

**Figure 10**    **Tile for pinned site on the Start screen**

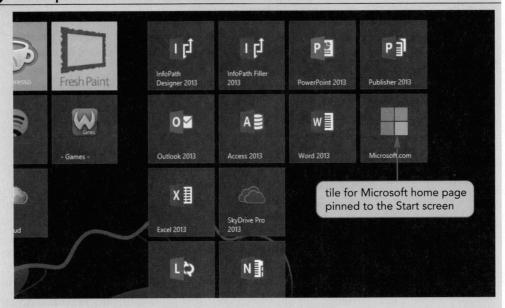

4. Click the **Microsoft.com** tile. The Microsoft home page opens in the Internet Explorer desktop application in a new browser window.

5. Click the **Close Tab** button ☒ to close the tab and the browser window displaying the Microsoft home page. The other browser window remains open.

As with favorites, you should delete the tiles for pinned pages you no longer need to avoid unwanted clutter on your Start screen. You unpin a page directly from the Start screen. You will unpin the tile for the Microsoft home page from the Start screen.

### To unpin the tile for the Microsoft home page:

1. Display the **Start** screen, and then scroll to the far right until you see the Microsoft.com tile you added to the Start screen.

2. Right-click the **Microsoft.com** tile. On the navigation bar at the bottom of the screen, you have options to unpin the page from the Start screen, pin the page to the taskbar, or open the file location.

3. Click the **Unpin from Start** button. The Microsoft.com tile is removed from the Start screen.

Before Martha compiles and uses information in her case study on Microsoft's efforts to reduce its carbon footprint, she needs to understand the rules of copyright and fair use. This knowledge will help her determine what information she can use for her own purposes and how to properly cite its source.

# Using the Information You Find

The content you find on the web is a form of **intellectual property**, which includes all creations of the human mind, such as original ideas and creative works presented in a form that can be shared or that others can recreate, emulate, or manufacture. On a webpage, intellectual property includes the text, images, and videos on the page, as well as the design of the page itself. Intellectual property as a tangible expression of an idea is protected just like other tangible forms of property, such as houses and cars. Each country has its own rules and laws governing intellectual property rights and protection. In the United States, intellectual property is protected through patents, trademarks, trade secrets, and copyrights.

A **copyright** is a protection granted by law to the author or creator of an original work who creates a tangible expression of that work or creation. Creations that can be copyrighted include virtually all forms of artistic or intellectual expression, such as books, music, artwork, audio and video recordings, architectural drawings, choreographic works, product packaging, and computer software. The tangible form of the work can be words, numbers, notes, sounds, pictures, and so forth. A collection of facts can be copyrighted, but only if the collection is arranged, coordinated, or selected in a way that causes the resulting work to rise to the level of an original work. Copyright protection exists whether the work is published or unpublished.

The copyright is in effect for the length of time specified in the copyright law and gives the author or creator the exclusive right to reproduce, adapt, distribute, publicly perform, publicly display, or sell the work. In the United States, under the 1976 Copyright Act, works created after 1977 are protected for the life of the author (or the last surviving author in the case of a "joint work" with multiple authors) plus another 70 years. Works made for hire and anonymous or pseudonymous works are protected for 95 years from the date of publication or 120 years from the date of creation, whichever is earlier. The copyright holder can transfer, license, sell, donate, or leave the copyright to his or her heirs. Works created before 1978 are protected under the 1909 Copyright Act and have more complex and variable terms of copyright.

## Determining Fair Use

U.S. copyright law allows people to use portions of copyrighted works without obtaining permission from the copyright holder if that use is a fair use. Section 107 of the 1976 Copyright Act lists criticism, comment, news reporting, teaching, scholarship, and research as examples of uses that may be eligible for fair use. However, the circumstances surrounding a particular use determine whether that use is considered fair. Keep in mind that the legal definition of fair use is intentionally broad and can be difficult to interpret. As a result, many disputes about whether a use is fair have landed in court. Courts generally consider the following four factors when determining fair use:

- **The purpose and character of the new work**—This factor considers such issues as whether the use adds something new to the body of knowledge and arts or just reproduces the work, and whether the use is commercial or for nonprofit educational purposes.

- **The nature of the copyrighted work**—In general, more creative works have stronger protection than factual works. Keep in mind that an unpublished work has the same copyright protections for fair use as a published work.
- **The amount and substantiality of the portion used in relation to the copyrighted work as a whole** (in other words, how much of the copyrighted work was used)—The less work that is used, the more likely it falls under fair use. However, using even a small amount of the work can be copyright infringement if it is the heart of the work.
- **The effect of the use on the potential market, or value, of the copyrighted work**—For example, does the use of the copyrighted material hurt the market for the original work, and does it impair or limit the ability of the copyright owner to earn income or otherwise benefit from the work?

Again, no hard-and-fast rule determines fair use. If you are unsure whether your use is indeed fair use, the safest course of action is to contact the copyright owner and ask for permission to use the work.

## Identifying Works in the Public Domain

Once the term of the copyright has expired, the work moves into the **public domain**, which means that anyone is free to copy the work without requesting permission from the last copyright holder. Older literary works, such as *A Tale of Two Cities* by Charles Dickens, which was published in 1859, are in the public domain and can be reproduced freely. Songs or musical works published earlier than 1922, such as the *Star-Spangled Banner,* written by Francis Scott Key in 1814, are also in the public domain in the United States. However, if a publisher creates a new print edition of the public domain literary work or an orchestra makes an audio recording of the public domain musical work, the book or performance is a separate work that can be copyrighted and protected under current copyright laws.

Authors or creators can place their work into the public domain voluntarily at any time. For example, some websites provide graphics files that visitors can use free of charge. You can include public domain content on a webpage, in a paper, or in any other form of creative expression. However, you should still acknowledge the source of the public domain material and not represent the work as your own, which is plagiarism.

## Avoiding Plagiarism

The web makes it very easy to copy someone else's work. If you use someone else's work, whether the work is in the public domain or protected by copyright, you must cite the source of the material. Failure to cite the source of material that you use is called **plagiarism**. Claiming someone else's work as your own is a serious legal violation that can lead to a failing grade, being expelled from school, being fired from a job, or being subjected to a hefty fine or prosecution.

Plagiarism can be as simple as including a sentence or two from someone else's work without using quotation marks or attribution. It can be as blatant as duplicating substantial parts of someone else's work and claiming them as your own. It can be more subtle, such as paraphrasing someone else's content without the proper citation of the source. Another form of plagiarism is when students purchase essays, term papers, and even theses or dissertations from commercial services and then pass them off as their own.

To ensure that you don't unintentionally plagiarize someone else's work, be sure to properly reference the sources of works that you use. Keep in mind that just including a source citation is not enough if you plan to use the finished product commercially. You must also obtain the copyright holder's permission if you want to use the work in a way that falls outside of fair use.

> **TIP**
>
> For more information about current U.S. copyright law, you can visit the United States Copyright Office website at www.copyright.gov.

## Documenting Web Resources

To avoid charges of plagiarism, all works you reference—whether they are protected by copyright, in the public domain, or considered fair use—need to be documented. This gives proper credit to the original authors as well as provides readers with the information they need to find and review the works you used.

However, documentation can become a challenge when you are referencing a webpage. Because the web is a dynamic medium, the content of any given page can change in an instant. Also, its URL can change or disappear from day to day. Unlike published books and journals, which have a physical existence, a webpage exists only in an HTML document on a web server computer. If the file's name or location changes, or if the web server is disconnected from the Internet, the page is no longer accessible.

For academic research, the two most widely followed standards for citations are those of the American Psychological Association (APA) and the Modern Language Association (MLA). The APA and MLA formats for webpage citations are similar. Figure 11 shows both APA and MLA citations for a specific webpage, and how the citation information is obtained from the webpage.

| Figure 11 | Webpage citations |
|---|---|

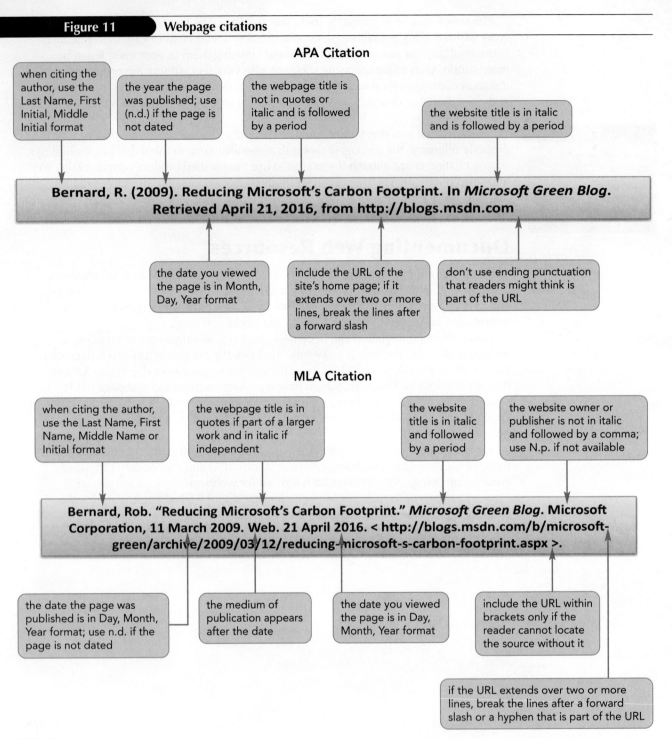

## APA Citation

when citing the author, use the Last Name, First Initial, Middle Initial format

the year the page was published; use (n.d.) if the page is not dated

the webpage title is not in quotes or italic and is followed by a period

the website title is in italic and is followed by a period

**Bernard, R. (2009). Reducing Microsoft's Carbon Footprint. In *Microsoft Green Blog*. Retrieved April 21, 2016, from http://blogs.msdn.com**

the date you viewed the page is in Month, Day, Year format

include the URL of the site's home page; if it extends over two or more lines, break the lines after a forward slash

don't use ending punctuation that readers might think is part of the URL

## MLA Citation

when citing the author, use the Last Name, First Name, Middle Name or Initial format

the webpage title is in quotes if part of a larger work and in italic if independent

the website title is in italic and followed by a period

the website owner or publisher is not in italic and followed by a comma; use N.p. if not available

**Bernard, Rob. "Reducing Microsoft's Carbon Footprint." *Microsoft Green Blog*. Microsoft Corporation, 11 March 2009. Web. 21 April 2016. < http://blogs.msdn.com/b/microsoft-green/archive/2009/03/12/reducing-microsoft-s-carbon-footprint.aspx >.**

the date the page was published is in Day, Month, Year format; use n.d. if the page is not dated

the medium of publication appears after the date

the date you viewed the page is in Day, Month, Year format

include the URL within brackets only if the reader cannot locate the source without it

if the URL extends over two or more lines, break the lines after a forward slash or a hyphen that is part of the URL

Be aware, however, that both the APA and MLA standards change from time to time. Consult these organizations' websites as well as the APA and MLA style guides for the latest rules and updates to these styles before using them. Also, always check to see if your instructor or editor (for work you are submitting for publication) has established other guidelines.

## Printing a Webpage

The web is a dynamic medium, so pages can be removed or changed without warning. When doing research, you might want to print or save copies of pages that you have used during your research to document the information.

**INSIGHT**

### Printing Webpages

Webpages are not necessarily designed with printing in mind. Before you print a webpage, it is a good idea to preview it to ensure that the text and graphics fit well on the page. If necessary, you can change the settings to adjust the webpage to fit better on the paper. In both versions of Internet Explorer, you can change the orientation from portrait to landscape to better accommodate the text and graphics on the page. The Internet Explorer desktop application provides more options, including changing the print size to shrink the webpage to fit onto a certain number of pages and adjusting the margins.

Also, many webpages provide a link to a separate printer-friendly version of the page. This option controls what is printed, including only essential information and ensuring that it will print in an appropriate format.

The Print dialog box lets you review the print settings and select a different printer, the pages to print, and the number of copies. It is a good idea to preview the page before you print so that you can see how it will fit on the page. The Print Preview window lets you change the page orientation between portrait (where the page is taller than it is wide) and landscape (where the page is wider than it is tall), and change the print size to force the content to fit on a specific number of pages.

You will preview and print one of the pages with promising information that you reviewed.

### To preview and print a webpage:

1. Return to the Internet Explorer desktop application.

2. Display one of the pages you opened.

3. Click the **Tools** button ⚙, point to **Print** on the menu, and then click **Print preview** on the submenu. The Print Preview window opens. See Figure 12.

**TIP**

To open the Print dialog box without displaying the Print Preview window, click the Tools button, point to Print, and then click **Print**.

**Figure 12** **Print Preview window**

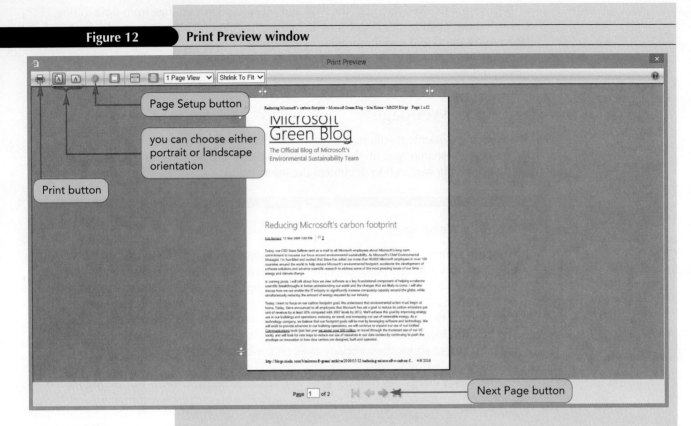

Page Setup button

you can choose either portrait or landscape orientation

Print button

Next Page button

4. If the page you are viewing has two or more pages, click the **Next Page** button ➡ to view the subsequent pages.

5. On the toolbar, click the **Print Document** button 🖨. The Print dialog box opens. See Figure 13.

**Figure 13** **Print dialog box**

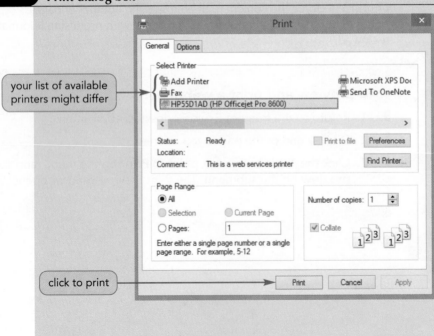

your list of available printers might differ

click to print

▶ **6.** In the Select Printer section, click the printer you want to use, if necessary.

▶ **7.** If you are instructed to print, click the **Print** button. Otherwise, click the **Cancel** button.

▶ **8.** In the title bar of the Print Preview window, click the **Close** button ┃ × ┃.

## Saving a Webpage

Saving a webpage is a good option if you want to keep a version of a webpage with the content it contained when you accessed it, but you don't want to use the resources to print. You have several options for saving a webpage, depending on what portion of the webpage you want to save. The "Webpage, complete (*.htm,*.html)" option in the Save Webpage dialog box saves the entire webpage, including its graphics and other elements that make up the page. This option creates a folder with all of the site's related files, including page elements, such as images and sounds. The "Web Archive, single file (*.mht)" option saves a "picture" of the current webpage, without any of the page elements. The two other options—"Webpage, HTML only (*.htm,*.html)" and "Text File (*.txt)"—let you save just the HTML code or the text from the webpage, respectively, without saving the graphics, frames, or styles on the webpage.

Martha asks you to save the page you found for future reference.

**To save the webpage:**

▶ **1.** Click the **Tools** button ⚙, point to **File** on the menu, and then click **Save as** on the submenu. The Save Webpage dialog box opens. See Figure 14.

| Figure 14 | Save Webpage dialog box |

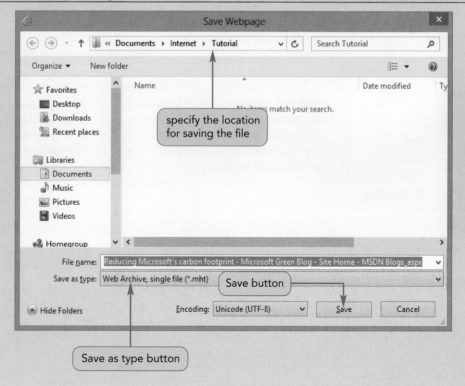

2. Navigate to the location where you are saving your files.

3. If necessary, click the **Save as type** button, and then click **Webpage, complete (\*.htm,\*.html)**. You can leave the default filename.

4. Click the **Save** button. After a few moments, a folder with all of the files needed for the webpage is saved in the location you specified.

Martha will keep the saved webpage on file with the rest of her research.

**PROSKILLS**

### Written Communication: Organizing Your Research

Research is the first step toward conveying information and facts in a written report. When you summarize your research results, how you organize the information and write the report is just as important as the quality of the research that you have done. If you do an excellent job gathering the facts, be sure to deliver a report that is clear and easy to understand. This ensures that your audience benefits from your hard work and gets the information it needs. A lack of clarity can introduce noise into the communication and prevent readers from getting the message you intend to convey.

As you research a topic, be sure to take accurate notes about what you learn. Remember to include complete information about your sources so you can cite them as needed in your report. After you finish your research, you should organize your notes into a logical order so that you can present the information clearly and logically. This is also a good way to check whether you need to locate additional information.

As you begin writing, make sure it is apparent why you are writing in the first place. Are you writing to inform, to entertain, or to express your opinion? When writing a factual report, your opinions are not relevant and should not be included. Next, determine the appropriate writing style—formal or informal. If you are writing for a professor or supervisor, you usually use a more formal tone than you would in a casual email to a colleague, friend, or family member.

When you have finished your report, be sure to read it carefully, keeping the recipient's viewpoint in mind. Make sure your points are clear and are presented in a logical order. Also, check your spelling and grammar, and correct any errors that you find. However, do not rely only on spelling and grammar checkers because they do not always find all errors. You might find it helpful to read what you have written out loud to determine whether your intended message and tone are coming through clearly. As a final step, you could ask a friend or colleague to read your final report and provide feedback.

Martha feels comfortable continuing to use Internet Explorer to research Microsoft's methods for reducing its carbon footprint. She is confident she can find relevant information, and that she can compile and document her sources appropriately.

## Quick Check

**REVIEW**

1. How do you open the two versions of Internet Explorer 10?
2. What are the two functions of the Address bar?
3. What are the basic steps for developing a search strategy?
4. Why should you conduct a search using multiple search engines?
5. Why would you want to use tabbed browsing?
6. What is the difference between the History list and the Favorites list?
7. Why should you review and evaluate information you find on the web?
8. What is plagiarism and how can you avoid it?

PRACTICE

## Review Assignments

**There are no Data Files needed for the Review Assignments.**

Martha wants to gather information about how another large company is reducing its impact on the environment. Sprint, with 40,000 employees, provides another good case study. Martha has already gathered information on some of the programs that Sprint has implemented, including moving toward renewable energy sources, reducing its electricity use, reducing its use of paper, and collecting customer phones for reuse and recycling. Now Martha wants to research how the company is reducing its greenhouse gas emissions. Complete the following:

1. Start the Internet Explorer app, and then visit the Sprint website by entering its URL **www.sprint.com** in the Address bar.
2. Click links on the page to navigate the site, looking for basic information about Sprint.
3. Formulate a search strategy for finding the information Martha wants to gather for her case study.
4. Start the Internet Explorer desktop application, and then use the Address bar to implement the search strategy you developed.
5. Open a new tab, visit the website for a different search engine (such as Google, Bing, or Yahoo!), and then implement the same search strategy using that search engine.
6. Compare the results of the two search engines, and then open three promising pages on new tabs.
7. Evaluate one of the pages you opened to determine whether it is relevant, useful, accurate, balanced, and objective.
8. Preview and then print the page you evaluated. Record your evaluation notes on the printout.
9. Include a complete citation for the webpage on the printout.
10. Save the webpage using its default name as a Web Archive, single file in the location specified by your instructor.

## Case Problem 1

APPLY

**There are no Data Files needed for this Case Problem.**

*Chicken Coops*   Mable Chong is planning to raise chickens in her backyard so she can enjoy fresh eggs. She has already researched the local regulations, how to care for chickens, and the pros and cons of different types of chickens. Before she purchases the chicks, she needs to build a chicken coop. She plans to have four chicks. She asks you to research the backyard coops and find one that will meet her needs and be simple to build. Complete the following steps:

1. Formulate a search strategy for finding the information Mable wants to gather about chicken coops.
2. Start Internet Explorer, and then implement the search strategy you developed using the default search engine.
3. On a new tab, repeat the search strategy using a different search engine.
4. Compare the results of the two search engines, and then open three promising pages on new tabs.
5. Evaluate the pages you opened to find one that is relevant, useful, accurate, balanced, and objective.
6. Preview and then print the page you evaluated. Record your evaluation notes on the printout.
7. Include a complete citation for the webpage on the printout.
8. Save the webpage using its default name as a Web Archive, single file in the location specified by your instructor.

**RESEARCH**

## Case Problem 2

**There are no Data Files needed for this Case Problem.**

*Great Espresso*    Ira Moss is planning to open Great Espresso, a coffee cart that will provide top-quality espresso and coffee drinks as well as some pastries and cookies. He has all of his business licenses in place, has purchased most of his equipment and supplies, and has set up orders with local bakeries for the snacks. The last thing he needs to do is determine what kind of coffee grinder he should purchase. He knows that there are blade grinders and burr grinders, and he asks you to research the differences between them. He also asks you to recommend a type of grinder and suggest two different models that he might purchase. Complete the following steps:

1. Formulate a search strategy for finding the information Ira wants to gather about coffee grinders.
2. Start Internet Explorer, and then implement the search strategy you developed. Repeat your strategy on a different search engine.
3. Open as many pages as needed to find information about the differences between the two grinders.
4. Start WordPad, and then record the information you found. Be sure to document your sources.
5. Evaluate the pages you opened to find one that is relevant, useful, accurate, balanced, and objective.
6. Preview and then print the page you evaluated. Record your evaluation notes on the printout.
7. Include a complete citation for the webpage on the printout.
8. Save the webpage using its default name as a Web Archive, single file in the location specified by your instructor.

# Creating and Editing a Document

*Writing a Business Letter and Formatting a Flyer*

## OBJECTIVES

**Session 1.1**
- Create and save a document
- Enter text and correct errors as you type
- Use AutoComplete and AutoCorrect
- Select text and move the insertion point
- Undo and redo actions
- Adjust paragraph spacing, line spacing, and margins
- Preview and print a document
- Create an envelope

**Session 1.2**
- Open an existing document
- Use the Spelling and Grammar task panes
- Change page orientation, font, font color, and font size
- Apply text effects and align text
- Copy formatting with the Format Painter
- Insert a paragraph border and shading
- Delete, insert, and edit a photo
- Use Word Help

## Case | *Sandy Hill Portrait Studio*

Sandy Hill Portrait Studio in Baltimore, Maryland, specializes in wedding photography and family portraits. It also offers weekend and evening classes for new and experienced photographers. The sales manager, Tim Bartolutti, has asked you to create a cover letter to accompany a set of prints that he needs to send to a client, and an envelope for sending a class schedule to another client. He also wants your help creating a flyer announcing a class that focuses on photographing pets.

You will create the letter and flyer using **Microsoft Office Word 2013** (or simply **Word**), a word-processing program. You'll start by opening Word and saving a new document. Then you'll type the text of the cover letter and print it. In the process of entering the text, you'll learn several ways to correct typing errors and how to adjust paragraph and line spacing. When you create the envelope, you'll learn how to save it as part of a document for later use. As you work on the flyer, you will learn how to open an existing document, change the way text is laid out on the page, format text, and insert and resize a photo. Finally, you'll learn how to use Word's Help system.

## STARTING DATA FILES

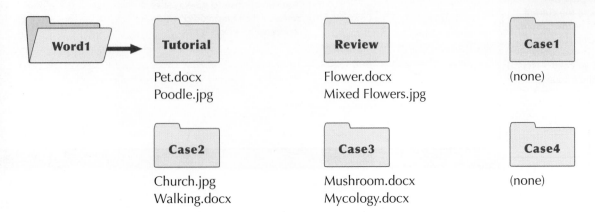

**Word1** → **Tutorial**

Pet.docx
Poodle.jpg

**Review**

Flower.docx
Mixed Flowers.jpg

**Case1**

(none)

**Case2**

Church.jpg
Walking.docx

**Case3**

Mushroom.docx
Mycology.docx

**Case4**

(none)

# Session 1.1 Visual Overview:

The **Quick Access Toolbar** is a collection of buttons that provides one-click access to commonly used commands, such as Save, Undo, and Repeat.

Each **tab** includes commands related to particular activities or tasks. The HOME tab includes options for formatting and editing text.

The **title bar** displays the name of the open file and the program.

The **ribbon** is the main set of buttons and other tools you can use to complete tasks. It is organized into tabs and groups.

The dark gray areas on the ruler represent the document's margins. **Margins** are the blank spaces around the edges of a document's content.

The **insertion point** shows where characters will appear when you start typing.

The **paragraph mark** indicates the end of a paragraph. It is only visible if nonprinting characters are turned on. **Nonprinting characters** appear on the screen but not on the printed page.

Buttons for related commands are organized on a tab in **groups**. The buttons in this group can be used to change the appearance of a paragraph.

The **status bar** provides information about the current document, such as the current page and number of words in the document; it also contains buttons and other controls for working with the document.

You can choose to display the rulers, which help you position elements in a document.

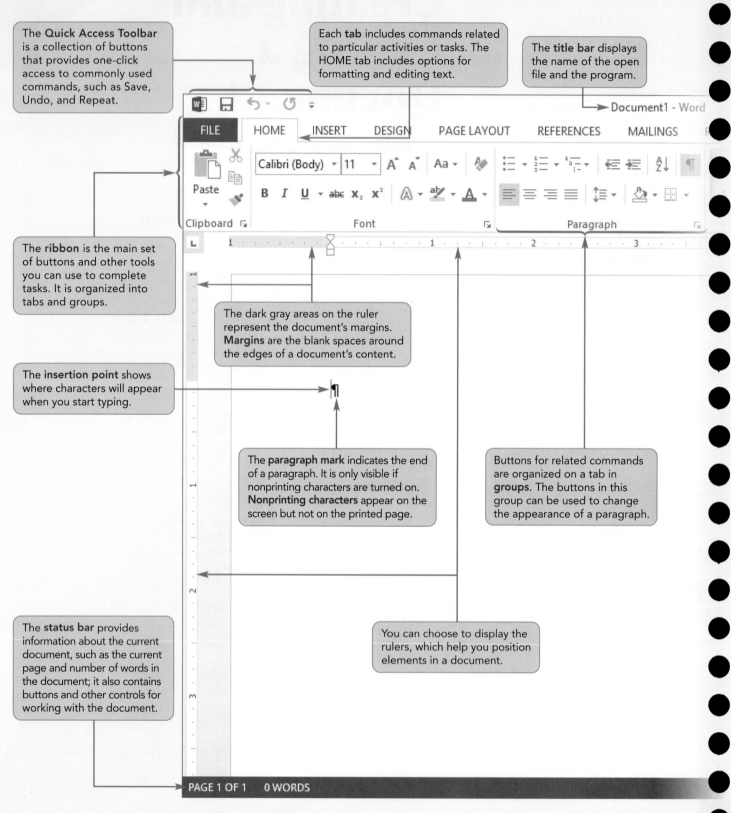

# The Word Window

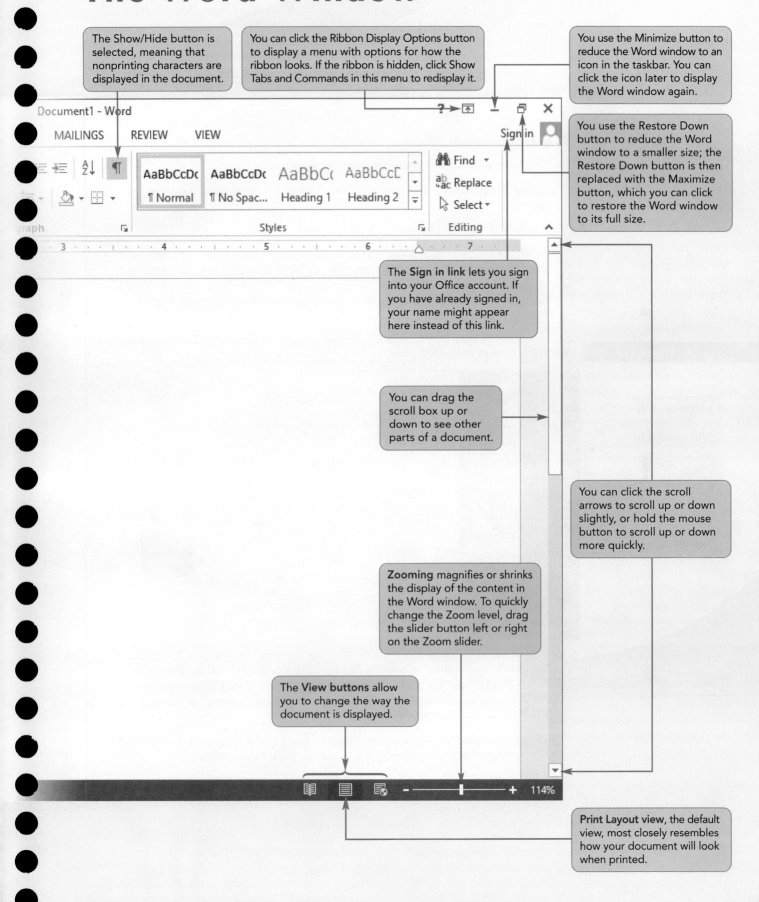

The Show/Hide button is selected, meaning that nonprinting characters are displayed in the document.

You can click the Ribbon Display Options button to display a menu with options for how the ribbon looks. If the ribbon is hidden, click Show Tabs and Commands in this menu to redisplay it.

You use the Minimize button to reduce the Word window to an icon in the taskbar. You can click the icon later to display the Word window again.

You use the Restore Down button to reduce the Word window to a smaller size; the Restore Down button is then replaced with the Maximize button, which you can click to restore the Word window to its full size.

The **Sign in link** lets you sign into your Office account. If you have already signed in, your name might appear here instead of this link.

You can drag the scroll box up or down to see other parts of a document.

You can click the scroll arrows to scroll up or down slightly, or hold the mouse button to scroll up or down more quickly.

**Zooming** magnifies or shrinks the display of the content in the Word window. To quickly change the Zoom level, drag the slider button left or right on the Zoom slider.

The **View buttons** allow you to change the way the document is displayed.

**Print Layout view**, the default view, most closely resembles how your document will look when printed.

Document1 - Word

MAILINGS    REVIEW    VIEW

Sign in

AaBbCcDc    AaBbCcDc    AaBbCc    AaBbCcD

¶ Normal    ¶ No Spac...    Heading 1    Heading 2

Styles

Editing

Find
Replace
Select

graph

3        4        5        6        7

114%

# Starting Word

With Word, you can quickly create polished, professional documents. You can type a document, adjust margins and spacing, create columns and tables, add graphics, and then easily make revisions and corrections. In this session, you will create one of the most common types of documents—a block style business letter.

To begin creating the letter, you first need to start Word and then set up the Word window.

### To start Microsoft Word:

▶ **1.** Display the Windows Start screen, if necessary.

**Using Windows 7?** To complete Step 1, click the Start button on the taskbar.

▶ **2.** Click the **Word 2013** tile.

Word starts and displays the Recent screen in Backstage view, with template options for new documents on the right. A list of recently opened documents might appear on the left. **Backstage view** provides access to various screens with commands that allow you to manage files and Word options. See Figure 1-1.

**Figure 1-1**      **Recent screen in Backstage view**

- a list of recently opened documents might appear here
- click to open a new, blank document
- your list of available templates may differ

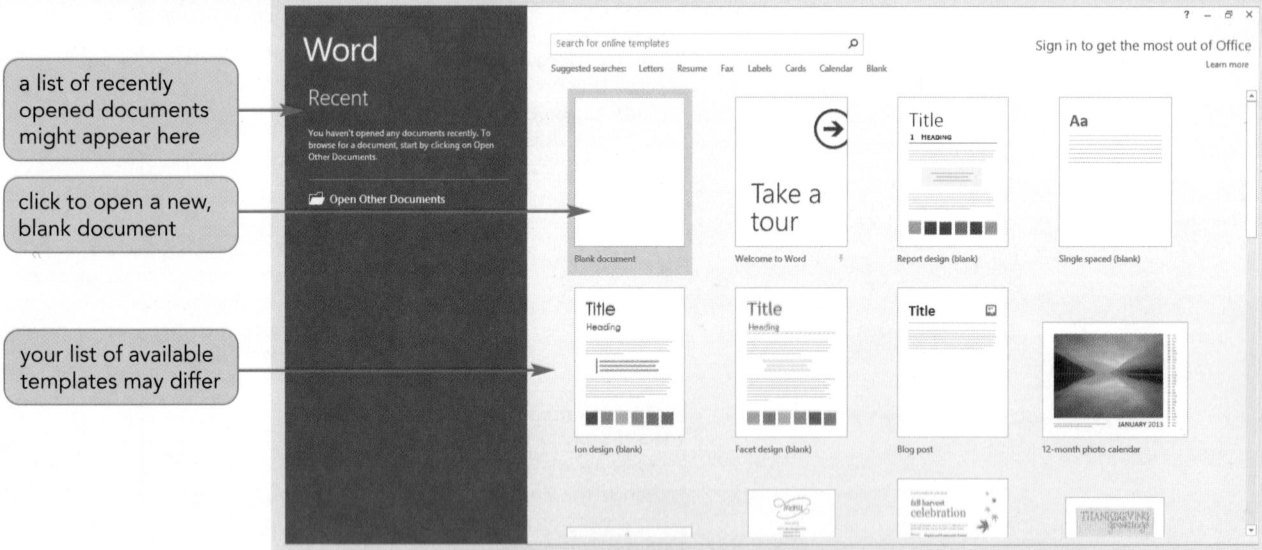

**Trouble?** If you don't see Word 2013 on the Windows Start screen, type Word 2013 to display the Apps screen with the Word 2013 tile highlighted, and then click the tile. If you still can't find Word 2013, ask your instructor or technical support person for help.

**Using Windows 7?** To complete Step 2, point to All Programs on the Start menu, click Microsoft Office 2013, and then click Word 2013.

3. Click **Blank document**. The Word window opens, with the ribbon displayed.

   **Trouble?** If you don't see the ribbon, click the Ribbon Display Options button 🔲, as shown in the Session 1.1 Visual Overview, and then click Show Tabs and Commands.

   Don't be concerned if your Word window doesn't match the Session 1.1 Visual Overview exactly. You'll have a chance to adjust its appearance shortly.

## Working in Touch Mode

You can interact with the Word screen using a mouse, or, if you have a touch screen, you can work in Touch Mode, using a finger instead of the mouse pointer. In **Touch Mode**, extra space around the buttons on the ribbon allows your finger to tap the specific button you need. The figures in this text show the screen with Mouse Mode on, but it's helpful to learn how to switch back and forth between Touch Mode and Mouse Mode.

**Note:** The following steps assume that you are using a mouse. If you are instead using a touch device, please read these steps but don't complete them so that you remain working in Touch Mode.

### To switch between Touch and Mouse Mode:

1. On the Quick Access Toolbar, click the **Customize Quick Access Toolbar** button ▾ to open the menu. The Touch/Mouse Mode command near the bottom of the menu does not have a checkmark next to it, indicating that it is currently not selected.

   **Trouble?** If the Touch/Mouse Mode command has a checkmark next to it, press the Esc key to close the menu, and then skip to Step 3.

2. On the menu, click **Touch/Mouse Mode**. The menu closes, and the Touch/Mouse Mode button 👆 appears on the Quick Access Toolbar.

3. On the Quick Access Toolbar, click the **Touch/Mouse Mode** button 👆. A menu opens with two options—Mouse and Touch. The icon next to Mouse is shaded blue to indicate it is selected.

   **Trouble?** If the icon next to Touch is shaded blue, press the Esc key to close the menu and skip to Step 5.

4. On the menu, click **Touch**. The menu closes, and the ribbon increases in height so that there is more space around each button on the ribbon. See Figure 1-2.

**Figure 1-2**    **Word window in Touch Mode**

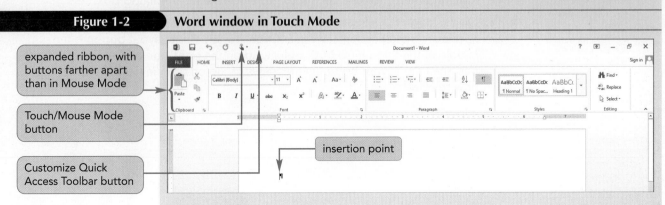

expanded ribbon, with buttons farther apart than in Mouse Mode

Touch/Mouse Mode button

Customize Quick Access Toolbar button

insertion point

**Trouble?** If you are working with a touch screen and want to use Touch Mode, skip Steps 5 and 6.

▶  **5.** On the Quick Access Toolbar, click the **Touch/Mouse Mode** button 👆, and then click **Mouse**. The ribbon changes back to its Mouse Mode appearance, as shown in the Session 1-1 Visual Overview.

▶  **6.** On the Quick Access Toolbar, click the **Customize Quick Access Toolbar** button ▼, and then click **Touch/Mouse Mode** to deselect it. The Touch/Mouse Mode button is removed from the Quick Access Toolbar.

# Setting Up the Word Window

Before you start using Word, you should make sure you can locate and identify the different elements of the Word window, as shown in the Session 1.1 Visual Overview. In the following steps, you'll make sure your screen matches the Visual Overview.

**To set up your Word window to match the figures in this book:**

▶  **1.** If the Word window does not fill the entire screen, click the **Maximize** button ▢ in the upper-right corner of the Word window.

The insertion point on your computer should be positioned about an inch from the top of the document, as shown in Figure 1-2, with the top margin visible.

**Trouble?** If the insertion point appears at the top of the document, with no white space above it, position the mouse pointer between the top of the document and the horizontal ruler, until it changes to ⬍, double-click, and then scroll up to top of the document.

▶  **2.** On the ribbon, click the **VIEW** tab. The ribbon changes to display options for changing the appearance of the Word window.

▶  **3.** In the Show group, click the **Ruler** check box to insert a checkmark, if necessary. If the rulers were not displayed, they are displayed now.

Next, you'll change the Zoom level to a setting that ensures that your Word window will match the figures in this book. To increase or decrease the screen's magnification, you could drag the slider button on the Zoom slider in the lower-right corner of the Word window. But to choose a specific Zoom level, it's easier to use the Zoom dialog box.

**TIP**

Changing the Zoom level affects only the way the document is displayed on the screen; it does not affect the document itself.

▶  **4.** In the Zoom group, click the **Zoom** button to open the Zoom dialog box. Double-click the **Percent** box to select the current zoom percentage, type **120**, and then click the **OK** button to close the Zoom dialog box.

▶  **5.** On the status bar, click the **Print Layout** button 🗐 to select it, if necessary. As shown in the Session 1.1 Visual Overview, the Print Layout button is the middle of the three View buttons located on the right side of the status bar. The Print Layout button in the Views group on the View tab is also now selected.

Before typing a document, you should make sure nonprinting characters are displayed. Nonprinting characters provide a visual representation of details you might otherwise miss. For example, the (¶) character marks the end of a paragraph, and the (•) character marks the space between words.

**To verify that nonprinting characters are displayed:**

 **1.** On the ribbon, click the **HOME** tab.

 **2.** In the blank Word document, look for the paragraph mark (¶) in the first line of the document, just to the right of the blinking insertion point.

   **Trouble?** If you don't see the paragraph mark, click the Show/Hide ¶ button ¶ in the Paragraph group.

   In the Paragraph group, the Show/Hide ¶ button should be highlighted in blue, indicating that it is selected, and the paragraph mark (¶) should appear in the first line of the document, just to the right of the insertion point.

# Saving a Document

Before you begin working on a document, you should save it with a new name. When you use the Save button on the Quick Access Toolbar to save a document for the first time, Word displays the Save As screen in Backstage view. In the Save As screen, you can select the location where you want to store your document. After that, when you click the Save button, Word saves your document to the same location you specified earlier, and with the same name.

**To save the document:**

 **1.** On the Quick Access Toolbar, click the **Save** button 🖫. Word switches to the Save As screen in Backstage view, as shown in Figure 1-3.

| Figure 1-3 | Save As screen in Backstage view |
| --- | --- |

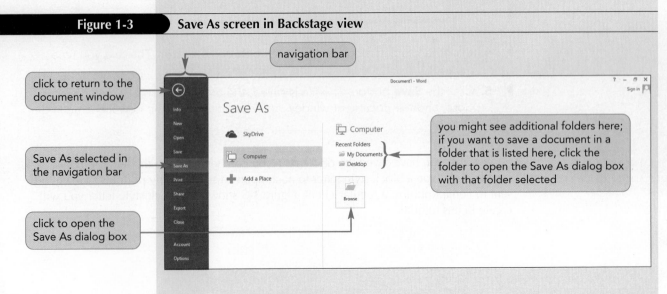

Because a document is now open, more commands are available in Backstage view than when you started Word. The **navigation bar** on the left contains commands for working with the open document and for changing settings that control how Word works.

2. Click **Computer**, if necessary, and then click the **Browse** button. The Save As dialog box opens.

   **Trouble?** If your instructor wants you to save your files to your SkyDrive account, click SkyDrive, log in to your account, if necessary, and then click the Browse button.

3. Navigate to the location specified by your instructor. The default filename, "Doc1," appears in the File name box. You will change that to something more descriptive. See Figure 1-4.

**Figure 1-4**    **Save As dialog box**

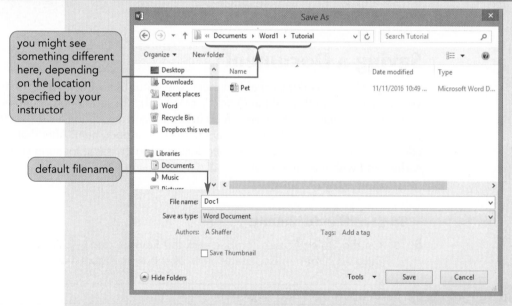

4. Click the File name box, and then type **Robbins Letter**. The text you type replaces the selected text in the File name box.

5. Click the **Save** button. The file is saved, the dialog box and Backstage view close, and the document window appears again, with the new filename in the title bar.

Now that you have saved the document, you can begin typing the letter. Tim has asked you to type a block style letter to accompany a set of family portraits that will be sent to Sonia Robbins, a regular client. Figure 1-5 shows the block style letter you will create in this tutorial.

| **Figure 1-5** | **Completed block style letter** |

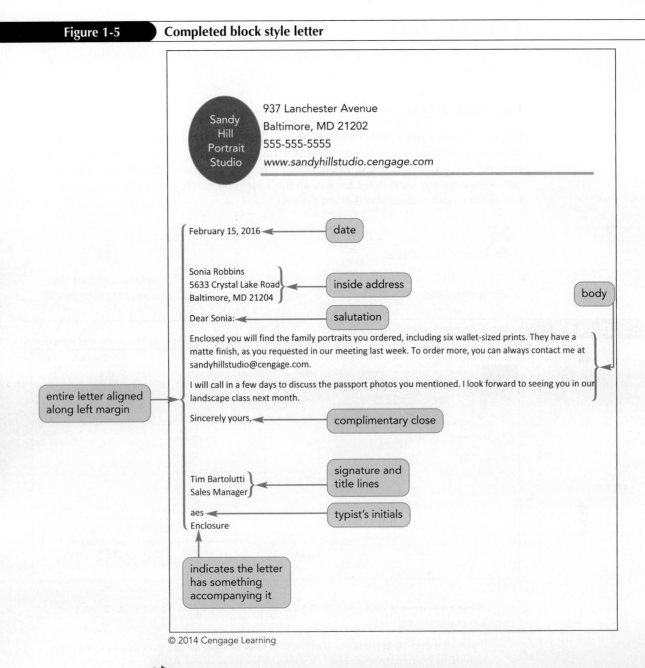

© 2014 Cengage Learning

## Written Communication: Creating a Business Letter

Several styles are considered acceptable for business letters. The main differences among the styles have to do with how parts of the letter are indented from the left margin. In the block style, which you will use in this tutorial, each line of text starts at the left margin. In other words, nothing is indented. Another style is to indent the first line of each paragraph. The choice of style is largely a matter of personal preference, or it can be determined by the standards used in a particular business or organization. To further enhance your skills in writing business correspondence, you should consult an authoritative book on business writing that provides guidelines for creating a variety of business documents, such as *Business Communication: Process & Product,* by Mary Ellen Guffey.

PROSKILLS

# Entering Text

The letters you type in a Word document appear at the current location of the blinking insertion point.

## Inserting a Date with AutoComplete

The first item in a block style business letter is the date. Tim plans to send the letter to Sonia on February 15, so you need to insert that date into the document. To do so, you can take advantage of **AutoComplete**, a Word feature that automatically inserts dates and other regularly used items for you. In this case, you can type the first few characters of the month and let Word insert the rest.

### To insert the date:

1. Type **Febr** (the first four letters of February). A ScreenTip appears above the letters, as shown in Figure 1-6, suggesting "February" as the complete word.

| Figure 1-6 | AutoComplete suggestion |
|---|---|

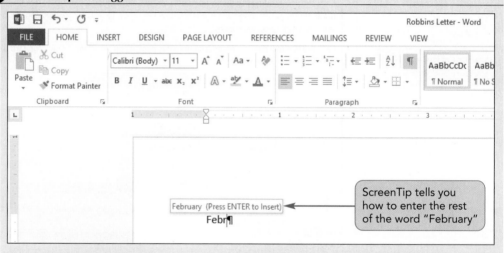

A **ScreenTip** is a box with descriptive text about an object or button you are pointing to.

If you wanted to type something other than "February," you could continue typing to complete the word. You want to accept the AutoComplete suggestion.

2. Press the **Enter** key. The rest of the word "February" is inserted in the document. Note that AutoComplete works for long month names like February but not shorter ones like May, because "Ma" could be the beginning of many words besides "May."

3. Press the **spacebar,** type **15, 2016** and then press the **Enter** key twice, leaving a blank paragraph between the date and the line where you will begin typing the inside address, which contains the recipient's name and address. Notice the nonprinting character (•) after the word "February" and before the number "15," which indicates a space. Word inserts this nonprinting character every time you press the spacebar.

**Trouble?** If February happens to be the current month, you will see a second AutoComplete suggestion displaying the current date after you press the spacebar. To ignore that AutoComplete suggestion, continue typing the rest of the date as instructed in Step 3.

## Continuing to Type the Block Style Letter

In a block style business letter, the inside address appears below the date, with one blank paragraph in between. Some style guides recommend including even more space between the date and the inside address. But in the short letter you are typing, more space would make the document look out of balance.

### To insert the inside address:

1. Type the following information, pressing the **Enter** key after each item:

   **Sonia Robbins**

   **5633 Crystal Lake Road**

   **Baltimore, MD 21204**

   Remember to press the Enter key after you type the zip code. Your screen should look like Figure 1-7. Don't be concerned if the lines of the inside address seem too far apart. You'll use the default spacing for now, and then adjust it after you finish typing the letter.

**Figure 1-7** Letter with inside address

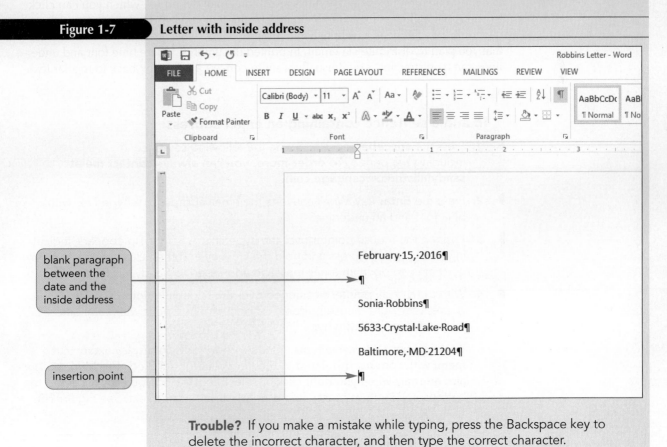

blank paragraph between the date and the inside address

insertion point

**Trouble?** If you make a mistake while typing, press the Backspace key to delete the incorrect character, and then type the correct character.

Now you can move on to the salutation and the body of the letter. As you type the body of the letter, notice that Word automatically moves the insertion point to a new line when the current line is full.

---

**To type the salutation and the body of the letter:**

1. Type **Dear Sonia:** and then press the **Enter** key to start a new paragraph for the body of the letter.

2. Type the following sentence, including the period: **Enclosed you will find the family portraits you ordered, including six wallet-sized prints.**

3. Press the **spacebar**. Note that you should only include one space between sentences.

4. Type the following sentence, including the period: **They have a matte finish, as you requested in our conversation last week.**

5. On the Quick Access Toolbar, click the **Save** button 💾. Word saves the document as Robbins Letter to the same location you specified earlier.

---

**TIP**

The obsolete practice of pressing the spacebar twice at the end of a sentence dates back to the age of typewriters, when the extra space made it easier to see where one sentence ended and another began.

The next sentence you need to type includes Tim's email address.

## Typing a Hyperlink

When you type an email address and then press the spacebar or the Enter key, Word converts it to a hyperlink, with blue font and an underline. A **hyperlink** is text or a graphic you can click to jump to another file or to somewhere else in the same file. The two most common types of hyperlinks are: 1) an email hyperlink, which you can click to open an email message to the recipient specified by the hyperlink; and 2) a web hyperlink, which opens a webpage in a browser. Hyperlinks are useful in documents that you plan to distribute via email. In printed documents, where blue font and underlines can be distracting, you'll usually want to convert a hyperlink back to regular text.

---

**To add a sentence containing an email address:**

1. Press the **spacebar**, and then type the following sentence, including the period: **To order more, you can always contact me at sandyhillstudio@cengage.com.**

2. Press the **Enter** key. Word converts the email address to a hyperlink, with blue font and an underline.

3. Position the mouse pointer over the hyperlink. A ScreenTip appears, indicating that you could press and hold the Ctrl key and then click the link to follow it—that is, to open an email message addressed to Sandy Hill Portrait Studio.

4. With the mouse pointer positioned over the hyperlink, right-click—that is, press the right mouse button. A shortcut menu opens with commands related to working with hyperlinks.

You can right-click many items in the Word window to display a **shortcut menu** with commands related to the item you right-clicked. The **Mini toolbar** also appears when you right-click or select text, giving you easy access to the buttons and settings most often used when formatting text. See Figure 1-8.

**Figure 1-8**    Shortcut menu

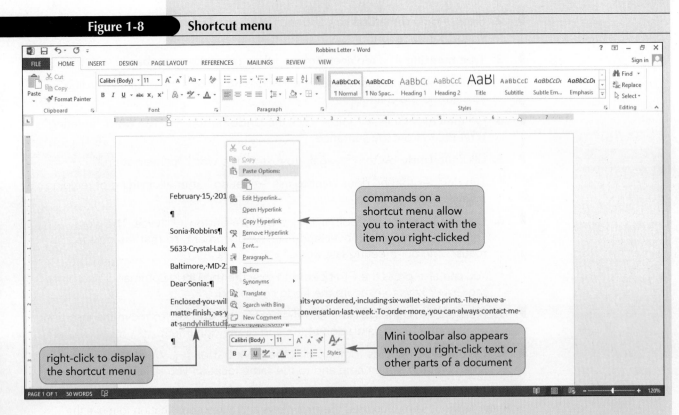

commands on a shortcut menu allow you to interact with the item you right-clicked

right-click to display the shortcut menu

Mini toolbar also appears when you right-click text or other parts of a document

**5.** Click **Remove Hyperlink** in the shortcut menu. The shortcut menu and the Mini toolbar are no longer visible. The email address is now formatted in black, like the rest of the document text.

**6.** On the Quick Access Toolbar, click the **Save** button 🖫.

# Using the Undo and Redo Buttons

To undo (or reverse) the last thing you did in a document, click the Undo button on the Quick Access Toolbar. To restore your original change, click the Redo button, which reverses the action of the Undo button (or redoes the undo). To undo more than your last action, you can continue to click the Undo button, or you can click the Undo button arrow on the Quick Access Toolbar to open a list of your most recent actions. When you click an action in the list, Word undoes every action in the list up to and including the action you clicked.

Tim asks you to change the word "conversation" to "meeting" in the second-to-last sentence you typed. You'll make the change now. If Tim decides he doesn't like it after all, you can always undo it. To delete a character, space, or blank paragraph to the right of the insertion point, you use the Delete key; or to delete an entire word, you can use the Ctrl+Delete key combination. To delete a character, space, or blank paragraph to the left of the insertion point, you use the Backspace key; or to delete an entire word, you can use the Ctrl+Backspace key combination.

### To change the word "conversation":

**1.** Press the ↑ key once and then press the → key as necessary to move the insertion point to the left of the "c" in the word "conversation."

▶ 2. Press and hold the **Ctrl** key, and then press the **Delete** key to delete the word "conversation."

▶ 3. Type **meeting** as a replacement, and then press the **spacebar**.

   After reviewing the sentence, Tim decides he prefers the original wording, so you'll undo the change.

▶ 4. On the Quick Access Toolbar, click the **Undo** button ↶. The word "meeting" is removed from the sentence.

▶ 5. Click the **Undo** button ↶ again to restore the word "conversation."

   Tim decides that he does want to use "meeting" after all. Instead of retyping it, you'll redo the undo.

▶ 6. On the Quick Access Toolbar, click the **Redo** button ↷ twice. The word "meeting" replaces "conversation" in the document, so that the phrase reads "…in our meeting last week."

   You can also press the Ctrl+Z keys to execute the Undo command, and press the Ctrl+Y keys to execute the Redo command.

▶ 7. Press and hold the **Ctrl** key, and then press the **End** key to move the insertion point to the blank paragraph at the end of the document.

▶ 8. On the Quick Access Toolbar, click the **Save** button 💾. Word saves your letter with the same name and to the same location you specified earlier.

In the previous steps, you used the arrow keys and a key combination to move the insertion point to specific locations in the document. For your reference, Figure 1-9 summarizes the most common keystrokes for moving the insertion point in a document.

**Figure 1-9**    **Keystrokes for moving the insertion point**

| To Move the Insertion Point | Press |
| --- | --- |
| Left or right one character at a time | ← or → |
| Up or down one line at a time | ↑ or ↓ |
| Left or right one word at a time | Ctrl+← or Ctrl+→ |
| Up or down one paragraph at a time | Ctrl+↑ or Ctrl+↓ |
| To the beginning or to the end of the current line | Home or End |
| To the beginning or to the end of the document | Ctrl+Home or Ctrl+End |
| To the previous screen or to the next screen | Page Up or Page Down |
| To the top or to the bottom of the document window | Alt+Ctrl+Page Up or Alt+Ctrl+Page Down |

© 2014 Cengage Learning

# Correcting Errors as You Type

As you have seen, you can use the Backspace or Delete keys to remove an error, and then you can type a correction. In many cases, however, Word's AutoCorrect feature will do the work for you. Among other things, **AutoCorrect** automatically corrects common typing errors, such as typing "adn" instead of "and." For example, you might have noticed AutoCorrect at work if you forgot to capitalize the first letter in a sentence as you typed the letter. After you type this kind of error, AutoCorrect automatically corrects it when you press the spacebar, the Tab key, or the Enter key.

Word draws your attention to other potential errors by marking them with wavy underlines. If you type a word that doesn't match the correct spelling in Word's dictionary, or if a word is not in the dictionary at all, a wavy red line appears beneath it. A wavy red underline also appears if you mistakenly type the same word twice in a row. Misused words (for example, "your" instead of "you're") are underlined with a wavy blue line. Likewise, punctuation errors, problems with possessives and plurals, and grammatical errors are marked with a wavy blue underline.

You'll see how this works as you continue typing the letter and make some intentional typing errors.

**To learn more about correcting errors as you type:**

▶ **1.** Type the following sentence, including the errors shown here: **i will call in a few few days to disuss teh pasport photos you mentioned.**

As you type, AutoCorrect changes the lowercase "i" at the beginning of the sentence to uppercase. It also changes "teh" to "the" and "pasport" to "passport." The spelling error "disuss" and the second "few" are marked with wavy red underlines. You will correct these errors after you finish typing the rest of the paragraph.

▶ **2.** Press the **spacebar**, and then type the following sentence, including the extra period and the other errors: **I look forward too seeing you in our landscape class next month..** The word "too" is underlined with a wavy blue line, indicating a misused word. The sentence also contains a punctuation error, but Word won't identify it until you start a new sentence or press the Enter key to begin a new paragraph.

▶ **3.** Press the **Enter** key to begin a new paragraph. As shown in Figure 1-10, the two periods at the end of the sentence are now underlined in blue.

| **Figure 1-10** | **Errors marked in the document** |

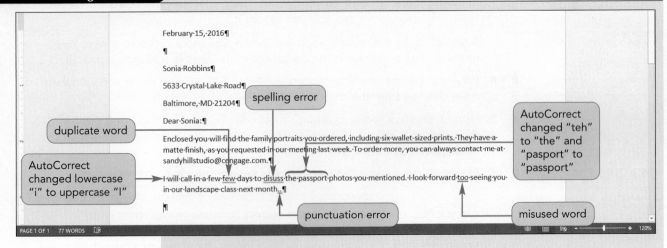

To correct an error marked with a wavy underline, you can right-click the error, and then click a replacement in the shortcut menu. If you don't see the correct word in the shortcut menu, click anywhere in the document to close the menu, and then type the correction yourself. You can also bypass the shortcut menu entirely, and simply delete the error and type a correction.

### To correct the spelling and grammar errors:

▶ **1.** Right-click **disuss** to display the shortcut menu shown in Figure 1-11.

| Figure 1-11 | Shortcut menu with suggested spellings |
|---|---|

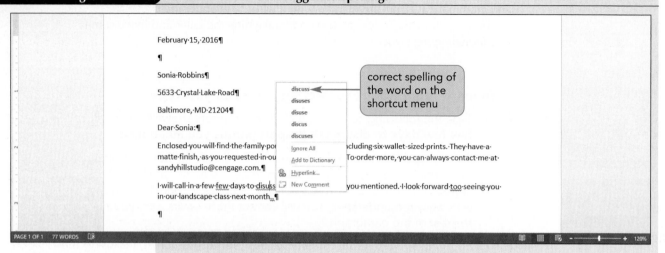

**Trouble?** If you see a shortcut menu other than the one shown in Figure 1-11, you didn't right-click exactly on the word "disuss." Press the Esc key to close the menu, and then repeat Step 1.

▶ **2.** On the shortcut menu, click **discuss**. The correct word is inserted into the sentence, and the shortcut menu closes. You could use a shortcut menu to remove the second instance of "few," but in the next step you'll try a different method—selecting the word and deleting it.

▶ **3.** Double-click anywhere in the underlined word **few**. The word and the space following it are highlighted in gray, indicating that they are selected. The Mini toolbar is also visible, but you can ignore it.

**Trouble?** If the entire paragraph is selected, you triple-clicked the word by mistake. Click anywhere in the document to deselect it, and then repeat Step 3.

▶ **4.** Press the **Delete** key. The second instance of "few" and the space following it are deleted from the sentence.

▶ **5.** Use the shortcut menu to replace the underlined word "too" with "to," and then click to the right of the second period after "month" and press the **Backspace** key to delete it.

▶ **6.** On the Quick Access Toolbar, click the **Save** button 🖫.

You can see how quick and easy it is to correct common typing errors with AutoCorrect and the wavy red and blue underlines, especially in a short document that you are typing yourself. If you are working on a longer document or a document typed by someone else, you'll also want to have Word check the entire document for errors. You'll learn how to do this in Session 1.2.

Next, you'll finish typing the letter.

**To finish typing the letter:**

1. Press the **Ctrl+End** keys. The insertion point moves to the end of the document.

2. Type **Sincerely yours,** (including the comma).

3. Press the **Enter** key three times to leave space for the signature.

4. Type **Tim Bartolutti** and then press the **Enter** key. Because Tim's last name is not in Word's dictionary, a wavy red line appears below it. You can ignore this for now.

5. Type your first, middle, and last initials in lowercase, and then press the **Enter** key. AutoCorrect wrongly assumes your first initial is the first letter of a new sentence, and changes it to uppercase.

6. On the Quick Access Toolbar, click the **Undo** button 🔄. Word reverses the change, replacing the uppercase initial with a lowercase one.

7. Type **Enclosure**. At this point, your screen should look similar to Figure 1-12. Notice that as you continue to add lines to the letter, the top part of the letter scrolls off the screen. For example, in Figure 1-12, you can no longer see the date.

> **TIP**
>
> You only need to include your initials in a letter if you are typing it for someone else.

**Figure 1-12** ▶ **Robbins Letter**

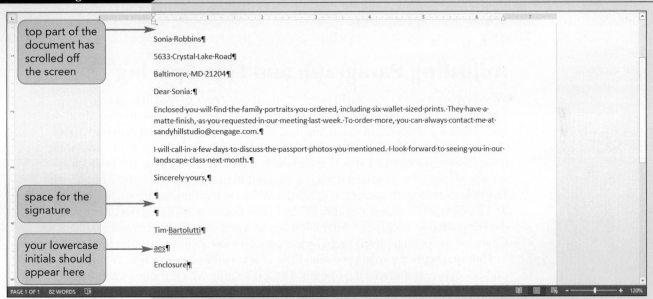

8. Save the document.

Now that you have finished typing the letter, you need to proofread it.

# Proofreading a Document

After you finish typing a document, you need to proofread it carefully from start to finish. Part of proofreading a document in Word is removing all wavy underlines, either by correcting the text or by telling Word to ignore the underlined text because it isn't really an error. For example, Tim's last name is marked as an error, when in fact it is spelled correctly. You need to tell Word to ignore "Bartolutti" wherever it occurs in the letter. You need to do the same for your initials.

**To proofread and correct the remaining marked errors in the letter:**

▶ 1. Right-click **Bartolutti**. A shortcut menu opens.

▶ 2. On the shortcut menu, click **Ignore All** to indicate that Word should ignore the word "Bartolutti" each time it occurs in this document. (The Ignore All option can be particularly helpful in a longer document.) The wavy red underline disappears from below Tim's last name. If your initials do not form a word, a red wavy underline appears beneath them; otherwise, a blue wavy underline appears there.

▶ 3. If you see a wavy red underline below your initials, right-click your initials. On the shortcut menu, click **Ignore All** to remove the red wavy underline. If you didn't see a wavy blue underline below your initials before, you should see one now.

▶ 4. Right-click your initials again. On the shortcut menu, click **Ignore Once** to remove the blue underline.

▶ 5. Read the entire letter to proofread it for typing errors. Correct any errors using the techniques you have just learned.

▶ 6. Save the document.

The text of the letter is finished. Now you need to think about how it looks—that is, you need to think about the document's **formatting**. First, you need to adjust the spacing in the inside address.

# Adjusting Paragraph and Line Spacing

When typing a letter, you might need to adjust two types of spacing—paragraph spacing and line spacing. **Paragraph spacing** is the space that appears directly above and below a paragraph. In Word, any text that ends with a paragraph mark symbol (¶) is a paragraph. So, a **paragraph** can be a group of words that is many lines long, a single word, or even a blank line, in which case you see a paragraph mark alone on a single line. Paragraph spacing is measured in points; a **point** is 1/72 of an inch. The default setting for paragraph spacing in Word is 0 points before each paragraph and 8 points after each paragraph. When laying out a complicated document, resist the temptation to simply press the Enter key to insert extra space between paragraphs. Changing the paragraph spacing gives you much more control over the final result.

**Line spacing** is the space between lines of text within a paragraph. Word offers a number of preset line spacing options. The 1.0 setting, which is often called **single-spacing**, allows the least amount of space between lines. All other line spacing options are measured as multiples of 1.0 spacing. For example, 2.0 spacing (sometimes called **double-spacing**) allows for twice the space of single-spacing. The default line spacing setting is 1.08, which allows a little more space between lines than 1.0 spacing.

Now consider the line and paragraph spacing in the Robbins letter. The three lines of the inside address are too far apart. That's because each line of the inside address is actually a separate paragraph. Word inserted the default 8 points of paragraph spacing after each of these separate paragraphs. See Figure 1-13.

**Figure 1-13**    Line and paragraph spacing in the letter to Sonia Robbins

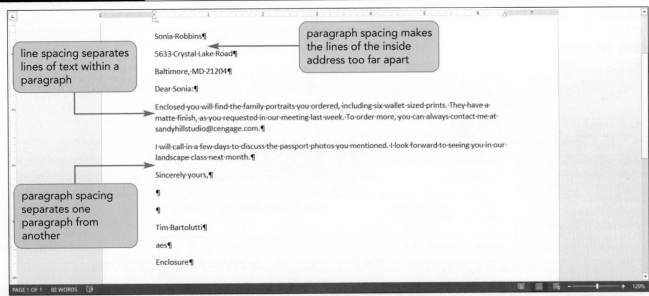

To follow the conventions of a block style business letter, the three paragraphs that make up the inside address should have the same spacing as the lines of text within a single paragraph—that is, they need to be closer together. You can accomplish this by removing the 8 points of paragraph spacing after the first two paragraphs in the inside address. To conform to the block style business letter format, you also need to close up the spacing between your initials and the word "Enclosure" at the end of the letter.

To adjust paragraph and line spacing in Word, you use the Line and Paragraph Spacing button in the Paragraph group on the HOME tab. Clicking this button displays a menu of preset line spacing options (1.0, 1.15, 2.0, and so on). The menu also includes two paragraph spacing options, which allow you to add 12 points before a paragraph or remove the default 8 points of space after a paragraph.

Next you'll adjust the paragraph spacing in the inside address and after your initials. In the process, you'll also learn some techniques for selecting text in a document.

**TIP**

The white space in the left margin is sometimes referred to as the selection bar because you click it to select text.

## To adjust the paragraph spacing in the inside address and after your initials:

1. Move the pointer to the white space just to the left of "Sonia Robbins" until it changes to a right-facing arrow.

2. Click the mouse button. The entire name, including the paragraph symbol after it, is selected.

3. Press and hold the mouse button, drag the pointer down to select the next paragraph of the inside address as well, and then release the mouse button.

   The name and street address are selected as well as the paragraph marks at the end of each paragraph. You did not select the paragraph containing the city, state, and zip code because you do not need to change its paragraph spacing. See Figure 1-14.

**Figure 1-14**    Inside address selected

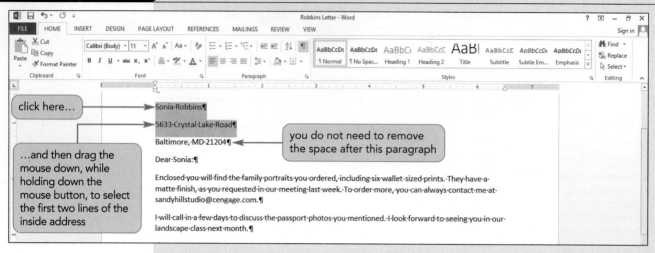

4. Make sure the HOME tab is selected on the ribbon.

5. In the Paragraph group on the HOME tab, click the **Line and Paragraph Spacing** button. A menu of line spacing options appears, with two paragraph spacing options at the bottom. See Figure 1-15. At the moment, you are only interested in the paragraph spacing options. Your goal is to remove the default 8 points of space after the first two paragraphs in the inside address.

**Figure 1-15**    Line and paragraph spacing options

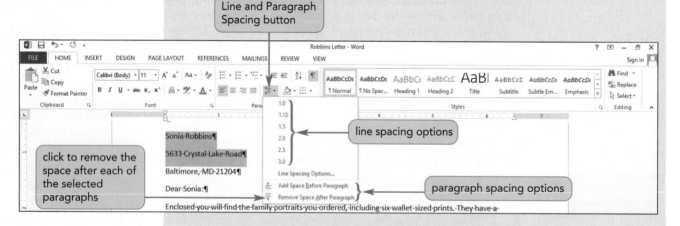

6. Click **Remove Space After Paragraph**. The menu closes, and the paragraphs are now closer together.

7. Double-click your initials to select them and the paragraph symbol after them.

8. In the Paragraph group, click the **Line and Paragraph Spacing** button, click **Remove Space After Paragraph**, and then click anywhere in the document to deselect your initials.

Another way to compress lines of text is to press the Shift+Enter keys at the end of a line. This inserts a **manual line break**, also called a **soft return**, which moves the insertion point to a new line without starting a new paragraph. You will use this technique now as you add Tim's title below his name in the signature line.

---

**To use a manual line break to move the insertion point to a new line without starting a new paragraph:**

▶ **1.** Click to the right of the "i" in "Bartolutti."

▶ **2.** Press the **Shift+Enter** keys. Word inserts a small arrow symbol ↵ , indicating a manual line break, and the insertion point moves to the line below Tim's name.

▶ **3.** Type **Sales Manager**. Tim's title now appears directly below his name with no intervening paragraph spacing, just like the lines of the inside address.

▶ **4.** Save the document.

---

INSIGHT

*Understanding Spacing Between Paragraphs*

When discussing the correct format for letters, many business style guides talk about single-spacing and double-spacing between paragraphs. In these style guides, to single-space between paragraphs means to press the Enter key once after each paragraph. Likewise, to double-space between paragraphs means to press the Enter key twice after each paragraph. With the default paragraph spacing in Word 2013, however, you only need to press the Enter key once after a paragraph. The space Word adds after a paragraph is not quite the equivalent of double-spacing, but it is enough to make it easy to see where one paragraph ends and another begins. Keep this in mind if you're accustomed to pressing the Enter key twice; otherwise, you could end up with more space than you want between paragraphs.

As you corrected line and paragraph spacing in the previous set of steps, you used the mouse to select text. Word provides multiple ways to select, or highlight, text as you work. Figure 1-16 summarizes these methods and explains when to use them most effectively.

| Figure 1-16 | Methods for selecting text |
|---|---|

| To Select | Mouse | Keyboard | Mouse and Keyboard |
|---|---|---|---|
| A word | Double-click the word | Move the insertion point to the beginning of the word, press and hold Ctrl+Shift, and then press → | |
| A line | Click in the white space to the left of the line | Move the insertion point to the beginning of the line, press and hold Shift, and then press ↓ | |
| A sentence | Click at the beginning of the sentence, then drag the pointer until the sentence is selected | | Press and hold Ctrl, then click any location within the sentence |
| Multiple lines | Click and drag in the white space to the left of the lines | Move the insertion point to the beginning of the first line, press and hold Shift, and then press ↓ until all the lines are selected | |
| A paragraph | Double-click in the white space to the left of the paragraph, or triple-click at any location within the paragraph | Move the insertion point to the beginning of the paragraph, press and hold Ctrl+Shift, and then press ↓ | |
| Multiple paragraphs | Click in the white space to the left of the first paragraph you want to select, and then drag to select the remaining paragraphs | Move the insertion point to the beginning of the first paragraph, press and hold Ctrl+Shift, and then press ↓ until all the paragraphs are selected | |
| An entire document | Triple-click in the white space to the left of the document text | Press Ctrl+A | Press and hold Ctrl, and click in the white space to the left of the document text |
| A block of text | Click at the beginning of the block, then drag the pointer until the entire block is selected | | Click at the beginning of the block, press and hold Shift, and then click at the end of the block |
| Nonadjacent blocks of text | | | Press and hold Ctrl, then drag the mouse pointer to select multiple blocks of nonadjacent text |

© 2014 Cengage Learning

# Adjusting the Margins

Another important aspect of document formatting is the amount of margin space between the document text and the edge of the page. You can check the document's margins by changing the Zoom level to display the entire page.

**To change the Zoom level to display the entire page:**

▶ **1.** On the ribbon, click the **VIEW** tab.

▶ **2.** In the Zoom group, click the **One Page** button. The entire document is now visible in the Word window. See Figure 1-17.

**Figure 1-17**    **Document zoomed to show entire page**

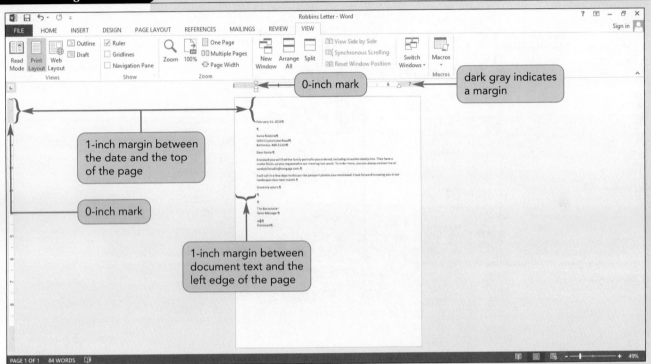

**Trouble?** If the wavy blue underline reappears under your initials, you can ignore it.

On the rulers, the margins appear dark gray. By default, Word documents include 1-inch margins on all sides of the document. By looking at the vertical ruler, you can see that the date in the letter, the first line in the document, is located 1 inch from the top of the page. Likewise, the horizontal ruler indicates the document text begins 1 inch from the left edge of the page.

Reading the measurements on the rulers can be tricky at first. On the horizontal ruler, the 0-inch mark is like the origin on a number line. You measure from the 0-inch mark to the left or to the right. On the vertical ruler, you measure up or down from the 0-inch mark.

Tim plans to print the letter on Sandy Hill Portrait Studio letterhead, which includes a graphic and the company's address. To allow more blank space for the letterhead, and to move the text down so it doesn't look so crowded at the top of the page, you need to increase the top margin. The settings for changing the page margins are located on the PAGE LAYOUT tab on the ribbon.

**To change the page margins:**

▶ **1.** On the ribbon, click the **PAGE LAYOUT** tab. The PAGE LAYOUT tab displays options for adjusting the layout of your document.

**2.** In the Page Setup group, click the **Margins** button. The Margins gallery opens, as shown in Figure 1-18.

**Figure 1-18** **Margins gallery**

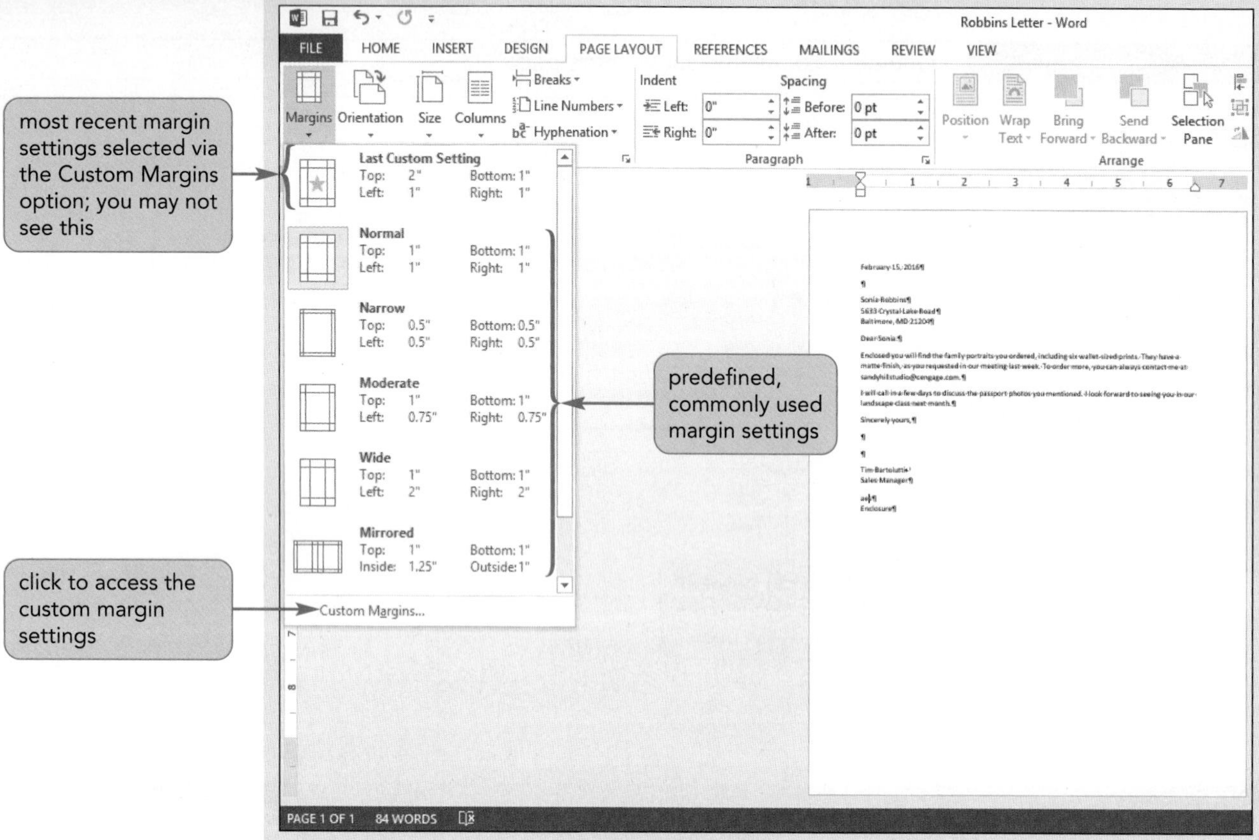

most recent margin settings selected via the Custom Margins option; you may not see this

predefined, commonly used margin settings

click to access the custom margin settings

In the Margins gallery, you can choose from a number of predefined margin options, or you can click the Custom Margins command to select your own settings. After you create custom margin settings, the most recent set appears as an option at the top of the menu. For the Robbins letter, you will create custom margins.

**3.** Click **Custom Margins**. The Page Setup dialog box opens with the Margins tab displayed. The default margin settings are displayed in the boxes at the top of the Margins tab. The top margin of 1" is already selected, ready for you to type a new margin setting.

**4.** In the Top box in the Margins section, type **2.5**. You do not need to type an inch mark ("). See Figure 1-19.

**Figure 1-19**    **Creating custom margins in the Page Setup dialog box**

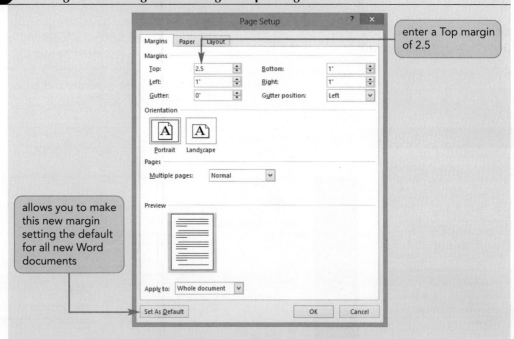

enter a Top margin of 2.5

allows you to make this new margin setting the default for all new Word documents

**5.** Click the **OK** button. The text of the letter is now lower on the page. The page looks less crowded, with room for the company's letterhead.

**6.** Change the Zoom level back to **120%**, and then save the document.

For most documents, the Word default of 1-inch margins is fine. In some professional settings, however, you might need to use a particular custom margin setting for all your documents. In that case, define the custom margins using the Margins tab in the Page Setup dialog box, and then click the Set As Default button to make your settings the default for all new documents. Keep in mind that most printers can't print to the edge of the page; if you select custom margins that are too narrow for your printer's specifications, Word alerts you to change your margin settings.

# Previewing and Printing a Document

To make sure the document is ready to print, and to avoid wasting paper and time, you should first review it in Backstage view to make sure it will look right when printed. Like the One Page zoom setting you used earlier, the Print option in Backstage view displays a full-page preview of the document, allowing you to see how it will fit on the printed page. However, you cannot actually edit this preview. It simply provides one last opportunity to look at the document before printing.

### To preview the document:

**1.** Proofread the document one last time and correct any remaining errors.

**2.** Click the **FILE** tab to display Backstage view.

**3.** In the navigation bar, click **Print**.

The Print screen displays a full-page version of your document, showing how the letter will fit on the printed page. The Print settings to the left of the preview allow you to control a variety of print options. For example, you can change the number of copies from the default setting of "1." The 1 Page Per Sheet button opens a menu where you can choose to print multiple pages on a single sheet of paper, or to scale the printed page to a particular paper size. You can also use the navigation controls at the bottom of the screen to display other pages in a document. See Figure 1-20.

**Figure 1-20**    **Print settings in Backstage view**

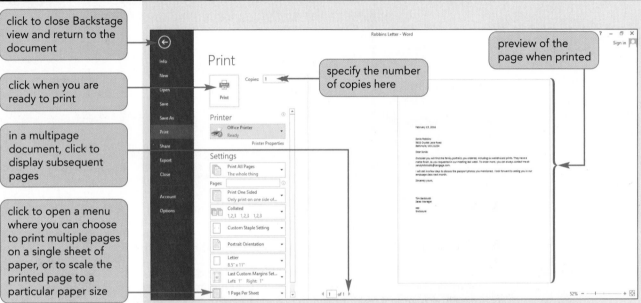

click to close Backstage view and return to the document

click when you are ready to print

in a multipage document, click to display subsequent pages

click to open a menu where you can choose to print multiple pages on a single sheet of paper, or to scale the printed page to a particular paper size

specify the number of copies here

preview of the page when printed

   **4.** Review your document and make sure its overall layout matches that of the document in Figure 1-20. If you notice a problem with paragraph breaks or spacing, click the **Back** button 🔙 at the top of the navigation bar to return to the document, make any necessary changes, and then start again at Step 2.

At this point, you can print the document or you can leave Backstage view and return to the document in Print Layout view. In the following steps, you should only print the document if your instructor asks you to. If you will be printing the document, make sure your printer is turned on and contains paper.

### To leave Backstage view or to print the document:

   **1.** Click the **Back** button 🔙 at the top of the navigation bar to leave Backstage view and return to the document in Print Layout view, or click the **Print** button. Backstage view closes, and the letter prints if you clicked the Print button.

   **2.** Click the **FILE** tab, and then click **Close** in the navigation bar to close the document without closing Word.

Next, Tim asks you to create an envelope he can use to send a class schedule to another client.

# Creating an Envelope

Before you can create the envelope, you need to open a new, blank document. To create a new document, you can start with a blank document—as you did with the letter to Sonia Robbins—or you can start with one that already contains formatting and generic text commonly used in a variety of professional documents, such as a fax cover sheet or a memo. These preformatted files are called **templates**. You could use a template to create a formatted envelope, but first you'll learn how to create one on your own in a new, blank document. You'll have a chance to try out a template in the Case Problems at the end of this tutorial.

### To create a new document for the envelope:

▶ 1. Click the **FILE** tab, and then click **New** in the navigation bar. The New screen is similar to the one you saw when you first started Word, with a blank document in the upper-left corner, along with a variety of templates. See Figure 1-21.

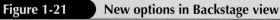

| Figure 1-21 | New options in Backstage view |

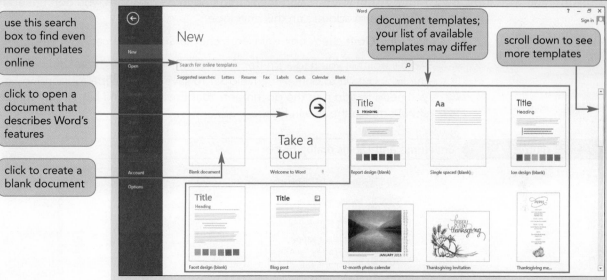

▶ 2. Click **Blank document**. A new document named Document2 opens in the document window, with the HOME tab selected on the ribbon.

▶ 3. If necessary, change the Zoom level to **120%**, and display nonprinting characters and the rulers.

▶ 4. Save the new document as **Keating Envelope** in the location specified by your instructor.

### To create the envelope:

▶ **1.** On the ribbon, click the **MAILINGS** tab. The ribbon changes to display the various Mailings options.

▶ **2.** In the Create group, click the **Envelopes** button. The Envelopes and Labels dialog box opens, with the Envelopes tab displayed. The insertion point appears in the Delivery address box, ready for you to type the recipient's address. Depending on how your computer is set up, and whether you are working on your own computer or a school computer, you might see an address in the Return address box.

▶ **3.** In the Delivery address box, type the following address, pressing the Enter key to start each new line:

**Lakeisha Keating**

**2245 Farley Lane**

**Baltimore, MD 21206**

Because Tim will be using the studio's printed envelopes, you don't need to print a return address on this envelope.

▶ **4.** Click the **Omit** check box to insert a checkmark, if necessary.

At this point, if you had a printer stocked with envelopes, you could click the Print button to print the envelope. To save an envelope for printing later, you need to add it to the document. Your Envelopes and Labels dialog box should match the one in Figure 1-22.

**Figure 1-22**   Envelopes and Labels dialog box

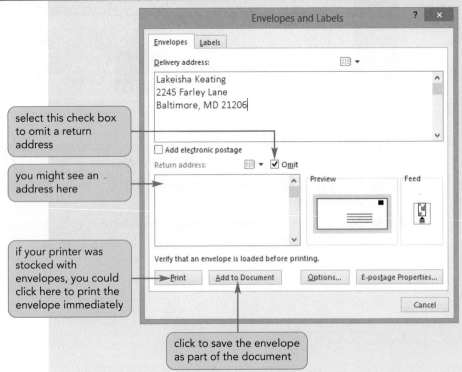

5. Click the **Add to Document** button. The dialog box closes, and you return to the document window. The envelope is inserted at the top of your document, with 1.0 line spacing. The double line with the words "Section Break (Next Page)" is related to how the envelope is formatted, and will not be visible when you print the envelope. The envelope will print in the standard business envelope format.

6. Save the document. Tim will print the envelope later, so you can close the document now.

7. Click the **FILE** tab and then click **Close** in the navigation bar. The document closes, but Word remains open.

## INSIGHT

### Creating Documents with Templates

Microsoft offers predesigned templates for all kinds of documents, including calendars, reports, and thank you cards. You can use the scroll bar on the right of the New screen (shown earlier in Figure 1-21) to scroll down to see more templates, or you can use the Search for online templates box in the New screen to search among hundreds of other options available at Office.com. When you open a template, you actually open a new document containing the formatting and text stored in the template, leaving the original template untouched. A typical template includes placeholder text that you replace with your own information.

Templates allow you to create stylish, professional-looking documents quickly and easily. To use them effectively, however, you need to be knowledgeable about Word and its many options for manipulating text, graphics, and page layouts. Otherwise, the complicated formatting of some Word templates can be more frustrating than helpful. As you become a more experienced Word user, you'll learn how to create your own templates.

You're finished creating the cover letter and the envelope. In the next session, you will modify a flyer that announces an upcoming class by formatting the text and adding a photo.

## REVIEW

### Session 1.1 Quick Check

1. In a block style letter, does each line of text start at the left or right margin? *left margin*
2. What do you call the recipient's address, which appears below the date in a block style letter?
3. Explain how to use a hyperlink in a Word document to open a new email message.
4. Explain how to display nonprinting characters. *Use the Show/Hide button*
5. Define the term "paragraph spacing." *The space directly above or below a paragraph.*
6. How does Word indicate a potential spelling error? *a red wavy line under the word*

# Session 1.2 Visual Overview:

Alignment buttons control the text's **alignment**—that is, the way it lines up between the left and right margins. Here, the Center button is selected because the text containing the insertion point is center-aligned.

You can click the Clear All Formatting button to restore selected text to the default font, font size, and color.

Clicking the Format Painter button displays the Format Painter pointer, which you can use to copy formatting from the selected text to other text in the document.

The Font group on the HOME tab includes the Font box and the Font size box for setting the text's font and the font size, respectively. A **font** is a set of characters that uses the same typeface.

This document has a landscape orientation, meaning it is wider than it is tall.

You can insert a photo or another type of picture in a document by using the **Pictures button** located on the INSERT tab of the ribbon. After you insert a photo or another picture, you can format it with a style that adds a border or a shadow, or changes its shape.

You click the Shading button arrow to apply a colored background to a selected paragraph.

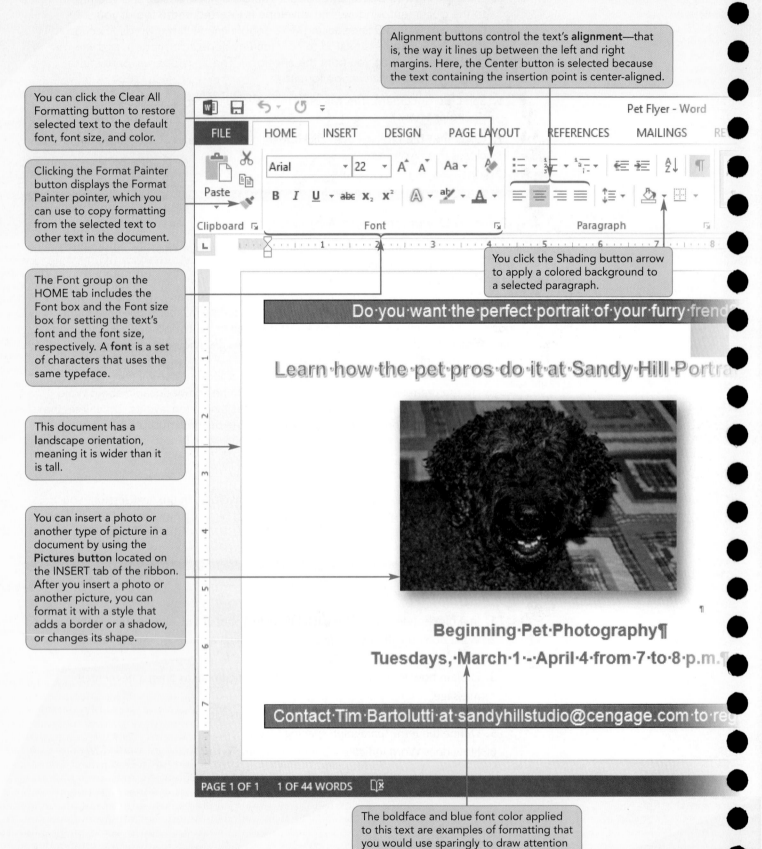

The boldface and blue font color applied to this text are examples of formatting that you would use sparingly to draw attention to a specific part of a document.

# Formatting a Document

The black border and dark orange shading around this paragraph are examples of **paragraph formatting** because they affect the entire paragraph.

The Microsoft Word Help button opens the **Word Help** window, where you can find information about Word commands and features, as well as instructions for using them.

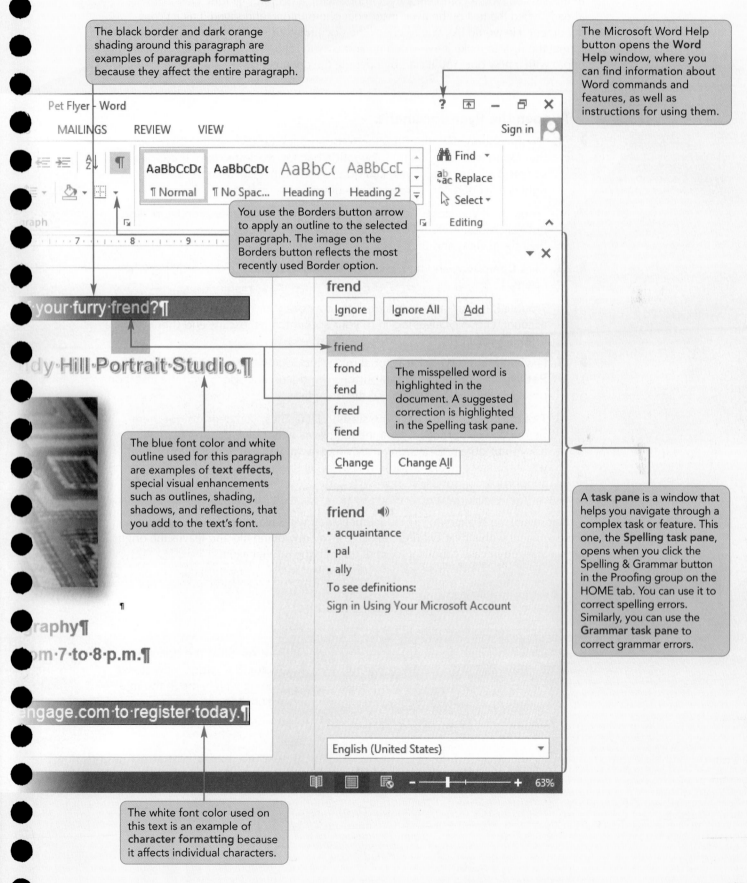

Pet Flyer - Word

MAILINGS    REVIEW    VIEW    Sign in

AaBbCcDc    AaBbCcDc    AaBbC    AaBbCcE

¶ Normal    ¶ No Spac...    Heading 1    Heading 2

Find
Replace
Select

Editing

You use the Borders button arrow to apply an outline to the selected paragraph. The image on the Borders button reflects the most recently used Border option.

your·furry·frend?¶

frend

Ignore    Ignore All    Add

friend
frond
fend
freed
fiend

dy·Hill·Portrait·Studio.¶

The misspelled word is highlighted in the document. A suggested correction is highlighted in the Spelling task pane.

Change    Change All

The blue font color and white outline used for this paragraph are examples of **text effects**, special visual enhancements such as outlines, shading, shadows, and reflections, that you add to the text's font.

friend

- acquaintance
- pal
- ally

To see definitions:
Sign in Using Your Microsoft Account

A **task pane** is a window that helps you navigate through a complex task or feature. This one, the **Spelling task pane**, opens when you click the Spelling & Grammar button in the Proofing group on the HOME tab. You can use it to correct spelling errors. Similarly, you can use the **Grammar task pane** to correct grammar errors.

¶

raphy¶

m·7·to·8·p.m.¶

English (United States)

engage.com·to·register·today.¶

63%

The white font color used on this text is an example of **character formatting** because it affects individual characters.

# Opening an Existing Document

In this session, you'll complete a flyer announcing a pet photography class. Tim has already typed the text of the flyer, inserted a photo into it, and saved it as a Word document. He would like you to check the document for spelling and grammar errors, format the flyer to make it eye-catching and easy to read, and then replace the current photo with a new one. You'll start by opening the document.

### To open the flyer document:

▶ 1. On the ribbon, click the **FILE** tab to open Backstage view, and then verify that **Open** is selected in the navigation bar. On the left side of the Open screen is a list of places you can go to locate other documents, and on the right is a list of recently opened documents.

   **Trouble?** If you closed Word at the end of the previous session, start Word now, click Open Other Documents at the bottom of the navigation bar in Backstage view, and then begin with Step 2.

▶ 2. Click **Computer**, and then click the **Browse** button. The Open dialog box opens.

   **Trouble?** If your instructor asked you to store your files to your SkyDrive account, click SkyDrive, log in to your account, if necessary, and then click the Browse button.

▶ 3. Navigate to the Word1 ▶ Tutorial folder included with your Data Files, click **Pet**, and then click the **Open** button. The document opens with the insertion point blinking in the first line of the document.

   **Trouble?** If you don't have the starting Data Files, you need to get them before you can proceed. Your instructor will either give you the Data Files or ask you to obtain them from a specified location (such as a network drive). If you have any questions about the Data Files, see your instructor or technical support person for assistance.

Before making changes to Tim's document, you will save it with a new name. Saving the document with a different filename creates a copy of the file and leaves the original file unchanged in case you want to work through the tutorial again.

### To save the document with a new name:

▶ 1. On the ribbon, click the **FILE** tab.

▶ 2. In the navigation bar in Backstage view, click **Save As**. Save the document as **Pet Flyer** in the location specified by your instructor. Backstage view closes, and the document window appears again with the new filename in the title bar. The original Pet document closes, remaining unchanged.

**PROSKILLS**

### Decision Making: Creating Effective Documents

Before you create a new document or revise an existing document, take a moment to think about your audience. Ask yourself these questions:

- Who is your audience?
- What do they know?
- What do they need to know?
- How can the document you are creating change your audience's behavior or opinions?

Every decision you make about your document should be based on your answers to these questions. To take a simple example, if you are creating a flyer to announce an upcoming seminar on college financial aid, your audience would be students and their parents. They probably all know what the term "financial aid" means, so you don't need to explain that in your flyer. Instead, you can focus on telling them what they need to know—the date, time, and location of the seminar. The behavior you want to affect, in this case, is whether or not your audience will show up for the seminar. By making the flyer professional looking and easy to read, you increase the chance that they will.

You might find it more challenging to answer these questions about your audience when creating more complicated documents, such as corporate reports. But the focus remains the same—connecting with the audience. As you are deciding what information to include in your document, remember that the goal of a professional document is to convey the information as effectively as possible to your target audience.

Before revising a document for someone else, it's a good idea to familiarize yourself with its overall structure.

### To review the document:

1. Verify that the document is displayed in Print Layout view and that nonprinting characters are displayed. For now, you can ignore the wavy underlines that appear in the document.

2. Change the Zoom level to **120%**, if necessary.

   At this point, the document is very simple. By the time you are finished, it will look like the document shown in the Session 1.2 Visual Overview, with the spelling and grammar errors corrected. Figure 1-23 summarizes the tasks you will perform.

Figure 1-23  **Formatting changes requested by Tim**

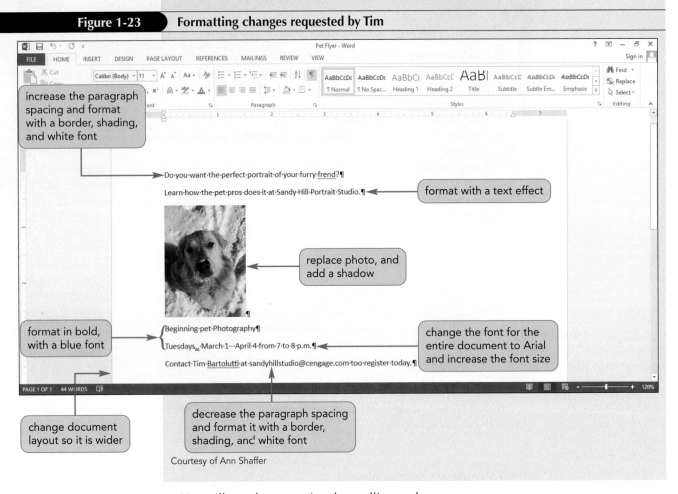

increase the paragraph spacing and format with a border, shading, and white font

format with a text effect

replace photo, and add a shadow

format in bold, with a blue font

change the font for the entire document to Arial and increase the font size

change document layout so it is wider

decrease the paragraph spacing and format it with a border, shading, and white font

Courtesy of Ann Shaffer

You will start by correcting the spelling and grammar errors.

# Using the Spelling and Grammar Task Panes

As you learned in Tutorial 1, Word marks possible spelling and grammatical errors with wavy underlines as you type so you can quickly go back and correct those errors. A more thorough way of checking the spelling in a document is to use the Spelling and Grammar task panes to check a document word by word for a variety of errors. You can customize the spelling and grammar settings to add or ignore certain types of errors.

Tim asks you to use the Spelling and Grammar task panes to check the flyer for mistakes. Before you do, you'll configure the grammar settings to look for subject/verb agreement, in addition to other types of errors.

### To customize the grammar settings:

 1. On the ribbon, click the **FILE** tab, and then click **Options** in the navigation bar. The Word Options dialog box opens. You can use this dialog box to change a variety of settings related to how Word looks and works.

 2. In the left pane, click **Proofing**, and then, in the "When correcting spelling and grammar in Word" section, click the **Settings** button. The Grammar Settings dialog box opens.

**3.** If necessary, scroll down in the Grammar Settings dialog box to display all the check boxes under "Grammar," and then click the **Subject-verb agreement** check box to insert a checkmark. See Figure 1-24.

| Figure 1-24 | Grammar Settings dialog box |
| --- | --- |

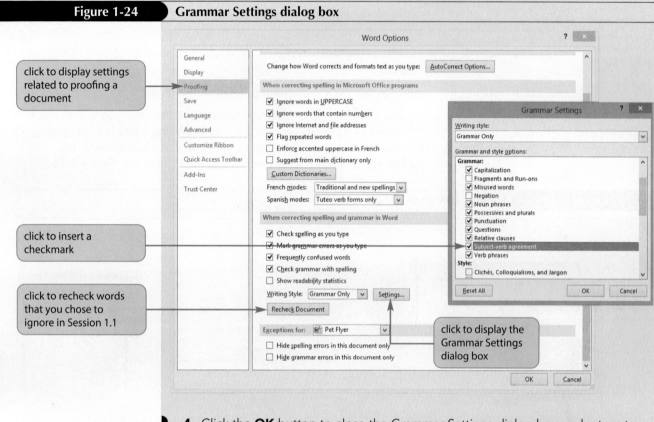

click to display settings related to proofing a document

click to insert a checkmark

click to recheck words that you chose to ignore in Session 1.1

click to display the Grammar Settings dialog box

**4.** Click the **OK** button to close the Grammar Settings dialog box and return to the Word Options dialog box.

To ensure that Word checks the entire Pet Flyer document, and doesn't skip any words that you chose to ignore when you checked the Robbins Letter in Session 1.1, you can click the Recheck Document button.

**5.** Click the **Recheck Document** button, and then click **Yes** in the warning dialog box.

**6.** In the Word Options dialog box, click the **OK** button to close the dialog box.

You return to the Pet Flyer document, where three errors are now marked with wavy blue underlines. The two new errors are related to subject-verb agreement. You should also see two words marked with wavy red underlines, including Tim's last name in the final paragraph.

Now you are ready to check the document's spelling and grammar. All errors marked with red underlines are considered spelling errors, while all errors marked with blue underlines are considered grammatical errors.

**To check the Pet Flyer document for spelling and grammatical errors:**

1. Press the **Ctrl+Home** keys, if necessary, to move the insertion point to the beginning of the document, to the left of the "D" in "Do." By placing the insertion point at the beginning of the document, you ensure that Word will check the entire document from start to finish without having to go back and check an earlier part.

2. On the ribbon, click the **REVIEW** tab. The ribbon changes to display reviewing options.

3. In the Proofing group, click the **Spelling & Grammar** button.

   The Spelling task pane opens on the right side of the Word window, with the word "frend" listed as a possible spelling error. The same word is highlighted in gray in the document. In the task pane's list of possible corrections, the correctly spelled word "friend" is highlighted in light blue. See Figure 1-25.

| Figure 1-25 | Spelling task pane |

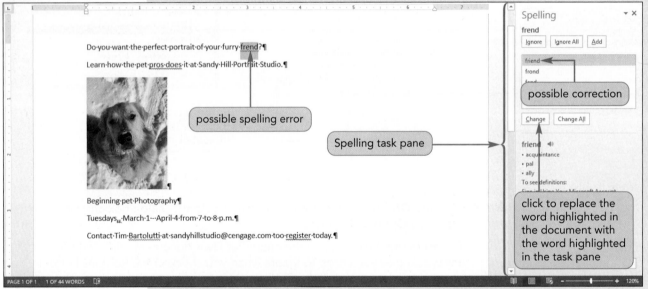

Courtesy of Ann Shaffer

4. In the task pane, click the **Change** button. The misspelled word "frend" is replaced with "friend."

   Next, Word highlights the entire second sentence, indicating another possible error. The Spelling task pane changes to the Grammar task pane, and the information at the bottom of the task pane explains that the error is related to subject-verb agreement.

5. Verify that "pros do" is selected in the Grammar task pane, and then click the **Change** button. The second to last paragraph of text is now highlighted in the document. The explanation at the bottom of the task pane indicates that the error is related to punctuation.

6. Verify that the comma is selected in the Grammar task pane, and then click the **Change** button.

   Tim's last name is now highlighted in the document, and the Grammar task pane changes to the Spelling task pane. Although the Spelling task pane doesn't recognize "Bartolutti" as a word, it is spelled correctly, so you can ignore it.

7. Click the **Ignore** button in the Spelling task pane.

   The last paragraph in the document is highlighted, and the Grammar task pane indicates a possible subject-verb agreement problem related to the word "register." However, the real problem is the word "too," just before "register." It should be replaced with "to." You can fix this problem by typing directly in the document.

8. In the document, click to the right of the word "too," delete the second letter "o," and then click the **Resume** button in the task pane. The task pane closes and a dialog box opens indicating that the spelling and grammar check is complete.

9. Click the **OK** button to close the dialog box.

   Finally, you'll restore the grammar settings to their original configuration.

10. Click the **FILE** tab, and then click **Options**.

11. In the Word Options dialog box, click **Proofing**, and then click the **Settings** button.

12. Scroll down, and then click the **Subject-verb agreement** check box to remove the checkmark.

13. Click the **OK** button to close the Grammar Settings dialog box, and then click the **OK** button to close the Word Options dialog box.

**PROSKILLS**

### Written Communication: Proofreading Your Document

Although the Spelling and Grammar task panes are useful tools, they won't always catch every error in a document, and they sometimes flag "errors" that are actually correct. This means there is no substitute for careful proofreading. Always take the time to read through your document to check for errors the Spelling and Grammar task panes might have missed. Keep in mind that the Spelling and Grammar task panes cannot pinpoint inaccurate phrases or poorly chosen words. You'll have to find those yourself. To produce a professional document, you must read it carefully several times. It's a good idea to ask one or two other people to read your documents as well; they might catch something you missed.

You still need to proofread the Pet Flyer document. You'll do that next.

### To proofread the Pet Flyer document:

1. Review the document text for any remaining errors. In the third paragraph of text, change the lowercase "p" in "pet" to an uppercase "P."

2. In the last line of text, replace "Tim Bartolutti" with your first and last name, and then save the document. Including your name in the document will make it easier for you to find your copy later if you print it on a shared printer.

Now you're ready to begin formatting the document. You will start by turning the page so it is wider than it is tall. In other words, you will change the document's **orientation**.

# Changing Page Orientation

**Portrait orientation**, with the page taller than it is wide, is the default page orientation for Word documents because it is the orientation most commonly used for letters, reports, and other formal documents. However, Tim wants you to format the pet flyer in **landscape orientation**—that is, with the page turned so it is wider than it is tall to better accommodate the photo. You can accomplish this task by using the Orientation button located on the PAGE LAYOUT tab on the ribbon. After you change the page orientation, you will select narrower margins so you can maximize the amount of color on the page.

### To change the page orientation:

1. Change the document zoom setting to **One Page** so that you can see the entire document.

2. On the ribbon, click the **PAGE LAYOUT** tab. The ribbon changes to display options for formatting the overall layout of text and images in the document.

3. In the Page Setup group, click the **Orientation** button, and then click **Landscape** on the menu. The document changes to landscape orientation.

4. In the Page Setup group, click the **Margins** button, and then click the **Narrow** option on the menu. The margins shrink from 1 inch to .5 inch on all four sides. See Figure 1-26.

**Figure 1-26**    Document in landscape orientation with narrow margins

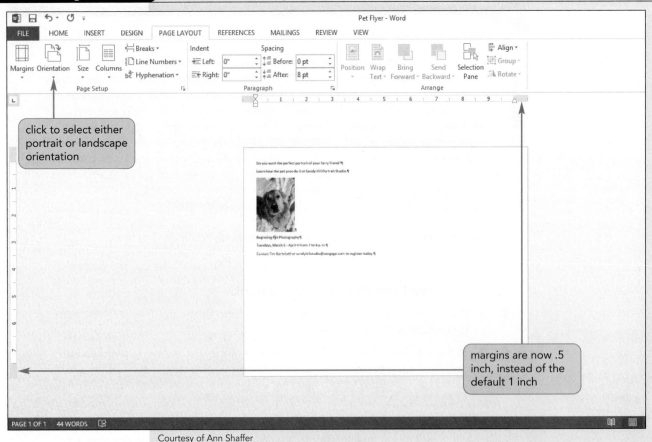

click to select either portrait or landscape orientation

margins are now .5 inch, instead of the default 1 inch

Courtesy of Ann Shaffer

# Changing the Font and Font Size

Tim typed the document in the default font size, 11 point, and the default font, Calibri, but he would like to switch to the Arial font instead. Also, he wants to increase the size of all five paragraphs of the document text. To apply these changes, you start by selecting the text you want to format. Then you select the options you want in the Font group on the HOME tab.

## To change the font and font size:

1. On the ribbon, click the HOME tab.

2. Change the document Zoom level to **120%**.

3. To verify that the insertion point is located at the beginning of the document, press the **Ctrl+HOME** keys.

4. Press and hold the **Shift** key, and then click to the right of the second paragraph marker, at the end of the second paragraph of text. The first two paragraphs of text are selected, as shown in Figure 1-27.

**Figure 1-27**     Selected text, with default font displayed in Font box

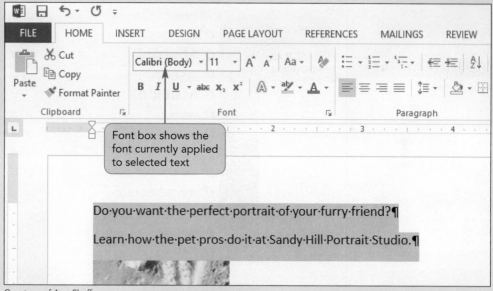

Courtesy of Ann Shaffer

The Font box in the Font group displays the name of the font applied to the selected text, which in this case is Calibri. The word "Body" next to the font name indicates that the Calibri font is intended for formatting body text. **Body text** is ordinary text, as opposed to titles or headings.

5. In the Font group on the HOME tab, click the **Font** arrow. A list of available fonts appears, with Calibri Light and Calibri at the top of the list. Calibri is highlighted in blue, indicating that this font is currently applied to the selected text. The word "Headings" next to the font name "Calibri Light" indicates that Calibri Light is intended for formatting headings.

Below Calibri Light and Calibri, you might see a list of fonts that have been used recently on your computer, followed by a complete alphabetical list of all available fonts. (You won't see the list of recently used fonts if you just installed Word.) You need to scroll the list to see all the available fonts. Each name in the list is formatted with the relevant font. For example, the name "Arial" appears in the Arial font. See Figure 1-28.

**Figure 1-28**   **Font list**

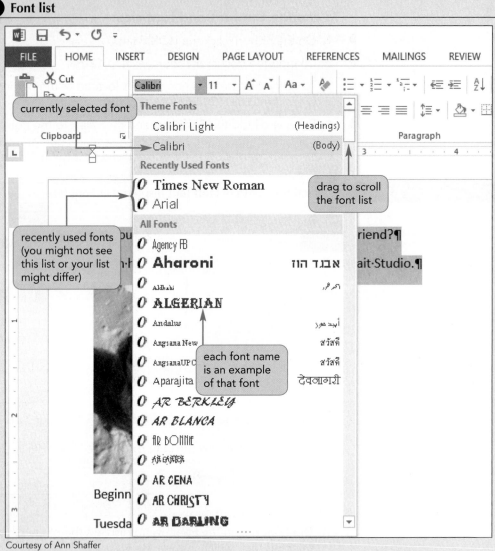

Courtesy of Ann Shaffer

6. Without clicking, move the pointer over a dramatic-looking font in the font list, such as Algerian or Arial Black, and then move the pointer over another font.

   The selected text in the document changes to show a Live Preview of the font the pointer is resting on. **Live Preview** shows the results that would occur in your document if you clicked the option you are pointing to.

7. When you are finished reviewing the Font list, click **Arial**. The Font menu closes, and the selected text is formatted in Arial.

   Next, you will make the text more eye-catching by increasing the font size. The Font Size box currently displays the number "11," indicating that the selected text is formatted in 11-point font.

8. Verify that the two paragraphs are still selected, and then click the **Font Size** arrow in the Font group to display a menu of font sizes. As with the Font menu, you can move the pointer over options in the Font Size menu to see a Live Preview of that option.

9. On the Font Size menu, click **22**. The selected text increases significantly in size and the Font Size menu closes.

10. Select the three paragraphs of text below the photo, format them in the Arial font, and then increase the paragraphs' font size to 22 points.

11. Click a blank area of the document to deselect the text, and then save the document.

Tim examines the flyer and decides he would like to apply more character formatting, which affects the appearance of individual characters, in the middle three paragraphs. After that, you can turn your attention to paragraph formatting, which affects the appearance of the entire paragraph.

## Applying Text Effects, Font Colors, and Font Styles

To really make text stand out, you can use text effects. You access these options by clicking the Text Effects button in the Font group on the HOME tab. Keep in mind that text effects can be very dramatic. For formal, professional documents, you probably only need to use **bold** or *italic* to make a word or paragraph stand out.

Tim suggests applying text effects to the second paragraph.

### To apply text effects to the second paragraph:

1. Scroll up, if necessary, to display the beginning of the document, and then click in the selection bar to the left of the second paragraph. The entire second paragraph is selected.

2. In the Font group on the HOME tab, click the **Text Effects and Typography** button [A].

   A gallery of text effects appears. Options that allow you to fine-tune a particular text effect, perhaps by changing the color or adding an even more pronounced shadow, are listed below the gallery. A **gallery** is a menu or grid that shows a visual representation of the options available when you click a button.

3. In the middle of the bottom row of the gallery, place the pointer over the blue letter "A." This displays a ScreenTip with the text effect's full name, which is "Fill - Blue, Accent 1, Outline - Background 1, Hard Shadow - Accent 1." A Live Preview of the effect appears in the document. See Figure 1-29.

| Figure 1-29 | Live Preview of a text effect |
|---|---|

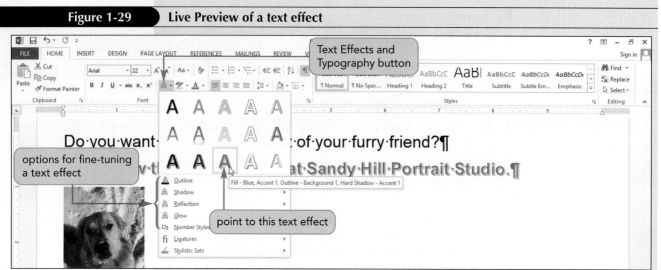

Courtesy of Ann Shaffer

▶ **4.** In the bottom row of the gallery, click the blue letter "A." The text effect is applied to the selected paragraph and the Text Effects gallery closes. The second paragraph is formatted in blue, as shown in the Session 1.2 Visual Overview. The Bold button in the Font group is now highlighted because bold formatting is part of this text effect.

Next, to make the text stand out a bit more, you'll increase the font size. This time, instead of using the Font Size button, you'll use a different method.

▶ **5.** In the Font group, click the **Increase Font Size** button A⁺. The font size increases from 22 points to 24 points.

▶ **6.** Click the **Increase Font Size** button A⁺ again. The font size increases to 26 points. If you need to decrease the font size of selected text, you can use the Decrease Font Size button.

Tim asks you to emphasize the third and fourth paragraphs by adding bold and a blue font color.

### To apply a font color and bold:

▶ **1.** Select the third and fourth paragraphs of text, which contain the class name as well as the dates and times.

▶ **2.** In the Font group on the Home tab, click the **Font Color button arrow** A▾. A gallery of font colors appears. Black is the default font color and appears at the top of the Font Color gallery, with the word "Automatic" next to it.

The options in the Theme Colors section of the menu are complementary colors that work well when used together in a document. The options in the Standard Colors section are more limited. For more advanced color options, you could use the More Colors or Gradient options. Tim prefers a simple blue.

**Trouble?** If the class name turned red, you clicked the Font Color button A instead of the arrow next to it. On the Quick Access Toolbar, click the Undo button ↺, and then repeat Step 2.

**3.** In the Theme Colors section, place the mouse pointer over the square that's second from the right in the top row. A ScreenTip with the color's name, "Blue, Accent 5," appears. A Live Preview of the color appears in the document, where the text you selected in Step 1 now appears formatted in blue. See Figure 1-30.

| Figure 1-30 | Font Color gallery showing a Live Preview |

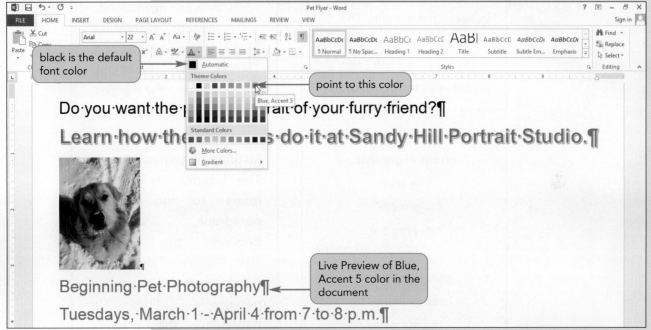

Courtesy of Ann Shaffer

**4.** Click the **Blue, Accent 5** square. The Font color gallery closes, and the selected text is formatted in blue. On the Font Color button, the bar below the letter "A" is now blue, indicating that if you select text and click the Font Color button, the text will automatically change to blue.

**TIP**

You can use other buttons in the Font group on the HOME tab to apply other character attributes, such as underline, italic, or superscript.

**5.** In the Font group, click the **Bold** button B. The selected text is now formatted in bold, with thicker, darker lettering.

Next, you will complete some paragraph formatting, starting with paragraph alignment.

## Aligning Text

Alignment refers to how text and graphics line up between the page margins. By default, Word aligns text along the left margin, with the text along the right margin **ragged**, or uneven. This is called **left alignment**. With **right alignment**, the text is aligned along the right margin and is ragged along the left margin. With **center alignment**, text is centered between the left and right margins and is ragged along both the left and right margins. With **justified alignment**, full lines of text are spaced between both the left and the right margins, and no text is ragged. Text in newspaper columns is often justified. See Figure 1-31.

| Figure 1-31 | Varieties of text alignment |

**left alignment**

The term "alignment" refers to the way a paragraph lines up between the margins. The term "alignment" refers to the way a paragraph lines up between the margins.

**right alignment**

The term "alignment" refers to the way a paragraph lines up between the margins. The term "alignment" refers to the way a paragraph lines up between the margins.

**center alignment**

The term "alignment" refers to the way a paragraph lines up between the margins.

**justified alignment**

The term "alignment" refers to the way a paragraph lines up between the margins. The term "alignment" refers to the way a paragraph lines up between the margins.

© 2014 Cengage Learning

The Paragraph group on the HOME tab includes a button for each of the four major types of alignment described in Figure 1-31: the Align Left button, the Center button, the Align Right button, and the Justify button. To align a single paragraph, click anywhere in that paragraph, and then click the appropriate alignment button. To align multiple paragraphs, select the paragraphs first, and then click an alignment button.

You need to center all the text in the flyer now. You can center the photo at the same time.

**To center-align the text:**

Use the Ctrl+A keys to select the entire document, instead of dragging the mouse pointer. It's easy to miss part of the document when you drag the mouse pointer.

1. Press the **Ctrl+A** keys to select the entire document, and make sure the HOME tab is still selected.

2. In the Paragraph group, click the **Center** button ≡, and then click a blank area of the document to deselect the selected paragraphs. The text and photo are now centered on the page, similar to the centered text shown earlier in the Session 1.2 Visual Overview.

3. Save the document.

# Adding a Paragraph Border and Shading

A **paragraph border** is an outline that appears around one or more paragraphs in a document. You can choose to apply only a partial border—for example, a bottom border that appears as an underline under the last line of text in the paragraph—or an entire box around a paragraph. You can select different colors and line weights for the border as well, making it more prominent or less prominent as needed. You apply paragraph borders using the Borders button in the Paragraph group on the HOME tab. **Shading** is background color that you can apply to one or more paragraphs and can be used in conjunction with a border for a more defined effect. You apply shading using the Shading button in the Paragraph group on the HOME tab.

Now you will apply a border and shading to the first paragraph, as shown earlier in the Session 1.2 Visual Overview. Then you will use the Format Painter to copy this formatting to the last paragraph in the document.

### To add shading and a paragraph border:

1. Select the first paragraph. Be sure to select the paragraph mark at the end of the paragraph.

2. On the HOME tab, in the Paragraph group, click the **Borders button arrow** ⊞ ▾. A gallery of border options appears, as shown in Figure 1-32. To apply a complete outline around the selected text, you use the Outside Borders option.

| Figure 1-32 | Border gallery |
|---|---|

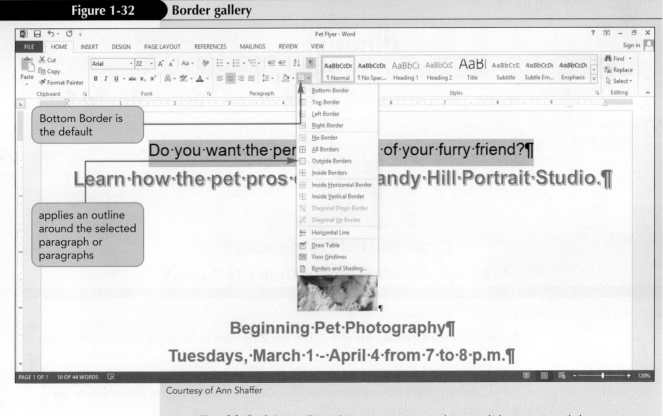

Courtesy of Ann Shaffer

**Trouble?** If the gallery does not open, and instead the paragraph becomes underlined with a single underline, you clicked the Borders button ⊞ instead of the arrow next to it. On the Quick Access Toolbar, click the Undo button ↺, and then repeat Step 2.

3. In the Border gallery, click **Outside Borders**. The menu closes and a black border appears around the selected paragraph, spanning the width of the page. In the Paragraph group, the Borders button ⊞ changes to show the Outside Borders option.

   **Trouble?** If the border around the first paragraph doesn't extend all the way to the left and right margins, and instead only encloses the text, you didn't select the paragraph mark as directed in Step 1. Click the Undo button ↶ repeatedly to remove the border, and begin again with Step 1.

4. In the Paragraph group, click the **Shading button arrow** ◌▾. A gallery of shading options opens, divided into Theme Colors and Standard Colors. You will use a shade of orange in the sixth column from the left.

5. In the second row from the bottom in the Theme Colors section, move the pointer over the square in the sixth column from the left to display a ScreenTip that reads "Orange, Accent 2, Darker 25%." A Live Preview of the color appears in the document. See Figure 1-33.

**Figure 1-33**    **Shading gallery with a Live Preview displayed**

Courtesy of Ann Shaffer

6. Click the **Orange, Accent 2, Darker 25%** square to apply the shading to the selected text.

   On a dark background like the one you just applied, a white font creates a striking effect. Tim asks you to change the font color for this paragraph to white.

7. Make sure the HOME tab is still selected.

8. In the Font group, click the **Font Color button arrow** A▾ to open the Font Color gallery, and then click the **white** square in the top row of the Theme Colors. The Font Color gallery closes and the paragraph is now formatted with white font.

**9.** Click a blank area of the document to deselect the text, review the change, and then save the document. See Figure 1-34.

**Figure 1-34**    **Paragraph formatted with dark orange shading, a black border, and white font**

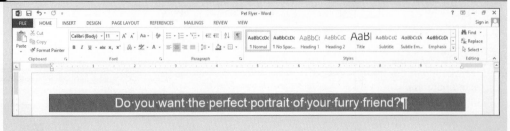

To add balance to the flyer, Tim suggests formatting the last paragraph in the document with the same shading, border, and font color as the first paragraph. You'll do that next.

# Copying Formatting with the Format Painter

You could select the last paragraph and then apply the border, shading, and font color one step at a time. But it's easier to copy all the formatting from the first paragraph to the last paragraph using the Format Painter button in the Clipboard group on the HOME tab.

*Using the Format Painter*

- Select the text whose formatting you want to copy.
- On the HOME tab, in the Clipboard group, click the Format Painter button; or to copy formatting to multiple sections of nonadjacent text, double-click the Format Painter button.
- The mouse pointer changes to the Format Painter pointer, the I-beam pointer with a paintbrush.
- Click the words you want to format, or drag to select and format entire paragraphs.
- When you are finished formatting the text, click the Format Painter button again to turn off the Format Painter.

You'll use the Format Painter now.

**To use the Format Painter:**

**1.** Change the document Zoom level to **One Page** so you can easily see both the first and last paragraphs.

**2.** Select the first paragraph, which is formatted with the dark orange shading, the border, and the white font color.

**3.** On the ribbon, click the HOME tab.

**4.** In the Clipboard group, click the **Format Painter** button to activate, or turn on, the Format Painter.

**5.** Move the pointer over the document. The pointer changes to the Format Painter pointer ▲[ when you move the mouse pointer near an item that can be formatted. See Figure 1-35.

**Figure 1-35** | **Format Painter**

Format Painter is turned on

Format Painter copies the formatting of the selected paragraph

paintbrush pointer

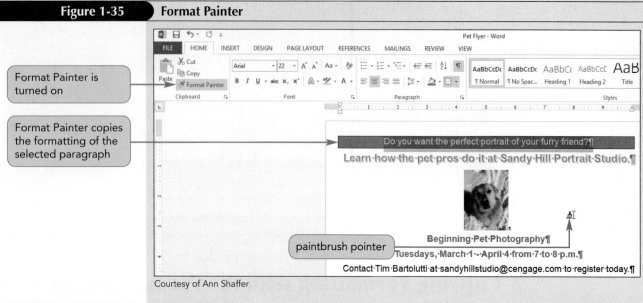

Courtesy of Ann Shaffer

6. Click and drag the Format Painter pointer 🖌I to select the last paragraph in the document. The paragraph is now formatted with dark orange shading, a black border, and white font. The mouse pointer returns to its original I-beam shape I.

   **Trouble?** If the text in the newly formatted paragraph wrapped to a second line, replace your full name with your first name, or, if necessary, use only your initials so the paragraph is only one line long.

7. Click anywhere in the document to deselect the text, review the change, and then save the document.

You're almost finished working on the document's paragraph formatting. Your last step is to increase the paragraph spacing below the first paragraph and above the last paragraph. This will give the shaded text even more weight on the page. To complete this task, you will use the settings on the PAGE LAYOUT tab, which offer more options than the Line and Paragraph Spacing button on the HOME tab.

**To increase the paragraph spacing below the first paragraph and above the last paragraph:**

1. Click anywhere in the first paragraph, and then click the **PAGE LAYOUT** tab. On this tab, the Paragraph group contains settings that control paragraph spacing. Currently, the paragraph spacing for the first paragraph is set to the default 0 points before the paragraph and 8 points after.

2. In the Paragraph group, click the **After** box to select the current setting, type **42**, and then press the **Enter** key. The added space causes the second paragraph to move down 42 points.

3. Click anywhere in the last paragraph.

4. On the PAGE LAYOUT tab, in the Paragraph group, click the **Before** box to select the current setting, type **42**, and then press the **Enter** key. The added space causes the last paragraph to move down 42 points.

*Formatting Professional Documents*

In more formal documents, use color and special effects sparingly. The goal of letters, reports, and many other types of documents is to convey important information, not to dazzle the reader with fancy fonts and colors. Such elements only serve to distract the reader from your main point. In formal documents, it's a good idea to limit the number of colors to two and to stick with left alignment for text. In a document like the flyer you're currently working on, you have a little more leeway because the goal of the document is to attract attention. However, you still want it to look professional.

Finally, Tim wants you to replace the photo of the golden retriever with one that will look better in the document's new landscape orientation. You'll replace the photo, and then you'll resize it so the flyer fills the entire page.

# Working with Pictures

A **picture** is a photo or another type of image that you insert into a document. To work with a picture, you first need to select it. Once a picture is selected, a contextual tab— the PICTURE TOOLS FORMAT tab—appears on the ribbon, with options for editing the picture and adding effects such as a border, a shadow, a reflection, or a new shape. A **contextual tab** appears on the ribbon only when an object is selected. It contains commands related to the selected object so you can manipulate, edit, and format the selected object. You can also use the mouse to resize or move a selected picture. To insert a new picture, you use the Pictures button in the Illustrations group on the INSERT tab.

### To delete the current photo and insert a new one:

**1.** Click the photo to select it.

The squares, called **handles**, around the edge of the photo indicate the photo is selected. The Layout Options button, to the right of the photo, gives you access to options that control how the document text flows around the photo. You don't need to worry about these options now. Finally, note that the PICTURE TOOLS FORMAT tab appeared on the ribbon when you selected the photo. See Figure 1-36.

**Figure 1-36**     Selected photo

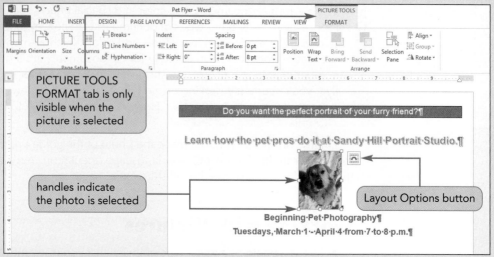

Courtesy of Ann Shaffer

2. Press the **Delete** key. The photo is deleted from the document. The insertion point blinks next to the paragraph symbol. You will insert the new photo in that paragraph.

3. On the ribbon, click the **INSERT** tab. The ribbon changes to display the Insert options.

4. In the Illustrations group, click the **Pictures** button. The Insert Picture dialog box opens.

5. Navigate to the Word1 ▸ Tutorial folder included with your Data Files, and then click **Poodle** to select the file. The name of the selected file appears in the File name box.

6. Click the **Insert** button to close the Insert Picture dialog box and insert the photo. An image of a black poodle appears in the document, below the text. The photo is selected, as indicated by the handles that appear on its border.

Now you need to enlarge the photo to fit the available space on the page. You could do so by clicking one of the picture's corner handles, holding down the mouse button, and then dragging the handle to resize the picture. But using the Shape Height and Shape Width boxes on the PICTURE TOOLS FORMAT tab gives you more precise results.

**To resize the photo:**

1. Make sure the PICTURE TOOLS FORMAT tab is still selected on the ribbon.

2. In the Size group on the far right edge of the ribbon, locate the Shape Height box, which tells you that the height of the selected picture is currently 2.46". The Shape Width box tells you that the width of the picture is 3.69". As you'll see in the next step, when you change one of these measurements, the other changes accordingly, keeping the overall shape of the picture the same. See Figure 1-37.

**Figure 1-37**    Shape Height and Shape Width boxes

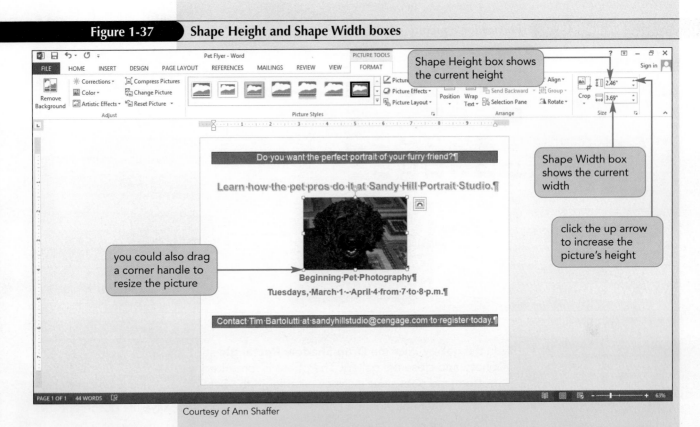

Courtesy of Ann Shaffer

**3.** Click the **up arrow** in the Shape Height box in the Size group. The photo increases in size slightly. The measurement in the Shape Height box increases to 2.5" and the measurement in the Shape Width box increases to 3.75".

**4.** Click the **up arrow** in the Shape Height box repeatedly until the picture is 3.3" tall and 4.95" wide.

Finally, to make the photo more noticeable, you can add a **picture style**, which is a collection of formatting options, such as a frame, a rounded shape, and a shadow. You can apply a picture style to a selected picture by clicking the style you want in the Picture Styles gallery on the PICTURE TOOLS FORMAT tab. In the following steps, you'll start by displaying the gallery.

### To add a style to the photo:

**1.** Make sure the PICTURE TOOLS FORMAT tab is still selected on the ribbon.

**2.** In the Picture Styles group, click the **More** button to the right of the Picture Styles gallery to open the gallery and display more picture styles. Some of the picture styles simply add a border, while others change the picture's shape. Other styles combine these options with effects such as a shadow or a reflection.

**3.** Place the mouse pointer over various styles to observe the Live Previews in the document, and then place the mouse pointer over the Drop Shadow Rectangle style, which is the middle style in the top row. See Figure 1-38.

| Figure 1-38 | Previewing a picture style |
| --- | --- |

Courtesy of Ann Shaffer

4. In the gallery, click the **Drop Shadow Rectangle** style to apply it to the photo and close the gallery. The photo is formatted with a shadow on the bottom and right sides, as shown earlier in the Session 1.2 Visual Overview.

5. Click anywhere outside the photo to deselect it, and then, save the document.

6. Click the **FILE** tab, and then click **Close** in the navigation bar to close the document without closing Word.

## INSIGHT

### Working with Inline Pictures

By default, when you insert a picture in a document, it is treated as an inline object, which means its position changes in the document as you add or delete text. Also, because it is an inline object, you can align the picture just as you would align text, using the alignment buttons in the Paragraph group on the HOME tab. Essentially, you can treat an inline picture as just another paragraph.

When you become a more advanced Word user, you'll learn how to wrap text around a picture so that the text flows around the picture—with the picture maintaining its position on the page no matter how much text you add to or delete from the document. The alignment buttons don't work on pictures that have text wrapped around them. Instead, you can drag the picture to the desired position on the page.

The flyer is complete and ready for Tim to print later. Because Tim is considering creating a promotional brochure that would include numerous photographs, he asks you to look up information about other ways to format a picture. You can do that using Word's Help system.

# Getting Help

To get the most out of Help, your computer must be connected to the Internet so it can access the reference information stored at Office.com.

### To look up information in Help:

1. Verify that your computer is connected to the Internet, and then, on the title bar, click the **Microsoft Word Help** button [?]. The Word Help window opens, with its Home page displayed. You might see the topics shown in Figure 1-39, or you might see other topics. You can click the various options in the Word Help window to browse among topics, or you can use the Search online help box to look up information on a particular topic.

**Figure 1-39**     Word Help window

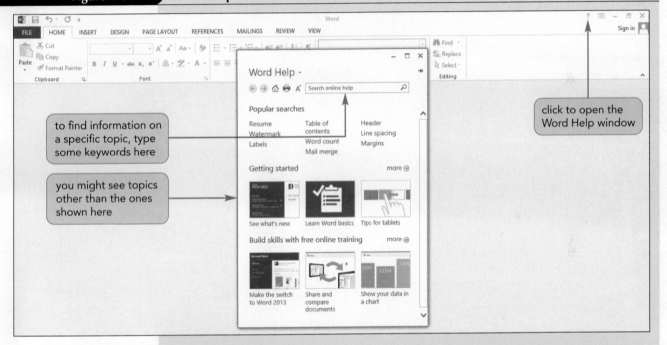

to find information on a specific topic, type some keywords here

you might see topics other than the ones shown here

click to open the Word Help window

2. Click in the **Search online help** box, type **format picture**, and then press the **Enter** key. The Word Help window displays a list of articles related to inserting pictures in a document.

3. Click the first topic listed, and then read the article to see if it contains any information about formatting pictures that might be useful to Tim. Note that to print information about a topic, you can click the Print button near the top of the Word Help window.

4. When are you finished reading the article, click the **Back** button ⊕ near the top of the Word Help window to return to the previous list of topics.

5. Click the **Home** button to return to the Home page.

6. Click the **Close** button ✖ in the upper-right corner to close the Word Help window.

Word Help is a great way to learn more about Word's many features. Articles on basic skills provide step-by-step guides for completing tasks, while more elaborate, online tutorials walk you through more complicated tasks. Be sure to take some time on your own to explore Word Help so you can find the information you want when you need it.

**REVIEW**

### Session 1.2 Quick Check

1. Explain how to open the Spelling and Grammar task panes.
2. What is the default page orientation for Word documents?
3. What is the default font size?
4. Explain how to use the Format Painter button.
5. What button do you use to insert a photo in a document?
6. Explain how to open the Help window.

**ASSESS**

## SAM Projects

Put your skills into practice with SAM Projects! SAM Projects for this tutorial can be found online. If you have a SAM account, go to www.cengage.com/sam2013 to download the most recent Project Instructions and Start Files.

**PRACTICE**

## Review Assignments

**Data Files needed for the Review Assignments: Flower.docx, Mixed Flowers.jpg**

Tim asks you to write a cover letter to accompany a wedding photography contract. After that, he wants you to create an envelope for the letter, and to format a flyer announcing a class about photographing flowers. Change the Zoom level as necessary while you are working. Complete the following steps:

1. Open a new, blank document and then save the document as **Sommer Letter** in the location specified by your instructor.
2. Type the date **February 16, 2016** using AutoComplete for "February."
3. Press the Enter key twice, and then type the following inside address, using the default paragraph spacing and pressing the Enter key once after each line:
   **Kiley Sommer**
   **2355 Greenwillow Drive**
   **Baltimore, MD 21204**
4. Type **Dear Ms. Sommer:** as the salutation, press the Enter key, and then type the following as the body of the letter:
   **Enclosed you will find the contract summarizing our plans for your wedding. Please return your signed copy to me by next Monday, along with the down payment specified in the contract.**
   **As you'll see, the second page of the contract lists the specific shots we've already agreed on. For more ideas about possible group shots, please see our website at www.sandyhillstudio. cengage.com. Of course, the photographer will be taking candid shots throughout the day.**
5. Press the Enter key, type **Sincerely yours,** as the complimentary closing, press the Enter key three times, type **Tim Bartolutti** as the signature line, insert a manual line break, and type **Sales Manager** as his title.
6. Press the Enter key, type your initials, insert a manual line break, and then use the Undo button to make your initials all lowercase, if necessary.
7. Type **Enclosure** and save the document.
8. Scroll to the beginning of the document and proofread your work. Remove any wavy underlines by using a shortcut menu or by typing a correction yourself. Remove the hyperlink formatting from the web address.
9. Remove the paragraph spacing from the first two lines of the inside address.
10. Change the top margin to 2.75 inches. Leave the other margins at their default settings.
11. Save your changes to the letter, preview it, print it if your instructor asks you to, and then close it.
12. Create a new, blank document, and then create an envelope. Use Kiley Sommer's address (from Step 3) as the delivery address. Use your school's name and address for the return address. Add the envelope to the document. If you are asked if you want to save the return address as the new return address, click No.

13. Save the document as **Sommer Envelope** in the location specified by your instructor, and then close the document.

14. Open the file **Flower**, located in the Word1 ▸ Review folder included with your Data Files, and then check your screen to make sure your settings match those in the tutorial.

15. Save the document as **Flower Flyer** in the location specified by your instructor.

16. Configure the grammar settings to check for subject-verb agreement errors, and then use the Spelling and Grammar task panes to correct any errors marked with wavy underlines. When you are finished, return the grammar settings to their original configuration.

17. Proofread the document and correct any other errors. Be sure to change "gardens" to "garden's" in the first paragraph.

18. Change the page orientation to Landscape and the margins to Narrow.

19. Format the document text in 22-point Times New Roman font.

20. Center the text and the photo.

21. Format the first paragraph with an outside border, and then add green shading, using the Green, Accent 6, Darker 25% color in the Theme Colors section of the Shading gallery. Format the paragraph text in white.

22. Format the last paragraph in the document using the same formatting you applied to the first paragraph.

23. Increase the paragraph spacing after the first paragraph to 42 points. Increase the paragraph spacing before the last paragraph in the document to 42 points.

24. Format the second paragraph with the Fill - Orange, Accent 2, Outline - Accent 2 text effect. Increase the paragraph's font size to 26 points.

25. Format the third and fourth paragraphs (containing the class name, date, and time) in green, using the Green, Accent 6, Darker 50% font color, and then add bold and italic.

26. Delete the photo and replace it with the **Mixed Flowers.jpg** photo, located in the Word1 ▸ Review folder included with your Data Files.

27. Resize the new photo so that it is 3.8" tall, and then add the Soft Edge Rectangle style in the Pictures Styles gallery.

28. Save your changes to the flyer, preview it, and then close it.

29. Start Word Help and look up the topic "work with pictures." Read the article, return to the Help home page, and then close Help.

## Case Problem 1

**There are no Data Files needed for this Case Problem.**

APPLY

***Prairie Public Health Consultants***   You are a program administrator at Prairie Public Health Consultants. Over the past few months, you have collected handwritten surveys from high school students about their exercise habits. Now you need to send the surveys to the researcher in charge of compiling the data. Create a cover letter to accompany the surveys by completing the following steps. Because your office is currently out of letterhead, you'll start the letter by typing a return address. As you type the letter, remember to include the appropriate number of blank paragraphs between the various parts of the letter. Complete the following steps:

1. Open a new, blank document, and then save the document as **Prairie Letter** in the location specified by your instructor. If necessary, change the Zoom level to 120%.

2. Type the following return address, using the default paragraph spacing, and replacing [Your Name] with your first and last names:

**[Your Name]**

**Prairie Public Health Consultants**

**6833 Erickson Lane**

**Des Moines, IA 50301**

3. Type **November 7, 2016** as the date, leaving a blank paragraph between the last line of the return address and the date.

4. Type the following inside address, using the default paragraph spacing and leaving the appropriate number of blank paragraphs after the date:

**Dr. Anna Witinski**

**4643 University Circle**

**Ames, IA 50010**

5. Type **Dear Dr. Witinski:** as the salutation.

6. To begin the body of the letter, type the following paragraph:

**Enclosed please find the surveys I have collected so far. I hope to have another 200 for you in a week, but I thought you would like to get started on these now. After you've had a chance to review the surveys, please call or email me with your answers to these questions:**

7. Add the following questions as separate paragraphs, using the default paragraph spacing:

**Do you need help tabulating the survey responses?**

**Should we consider expanding the survey to additional schools?**

**Should we rephrase any of the survey questions?**

8. Insert a new paragraph before the second question, and then add the following as the new second question in the list:

**Have you hired a student to help you with your analysis?**

9. Insert a new paragraph after the last question, and then type the complimentary closing **Sincerely,** (including the comma).

10. Leave the appropriate amount of space for your signature, type your full name, insert a manual line break, and then type **Program Administrator**.

11. Type **Enclosure** in the appropriate place.

12. Use the Spelling and Grammar task panes to correct any errors. Instruct the Spelling task pane to ignore the recipient's name.

13. Italicize the four paragraphs containing the questions.

14. Remove the paragraph spacing from the first three lines of the return address. Do the same for the first two paragraphs of the inside address.

15. Center the four paragraphs containing the return address, format them in 16-point font, and then add the Fill - Black, Text 1, Shadow text effect.

16. Save the document, preview it, and then close it.

17. Create a new, blank document, and create an envelope. Use Dr. Witinski's address (from Step 4) as the delivery address. Use the return address shown in Step 2. Add the envelope to the document. If you are asked if you want to save the return address as the new return address, click No.

18. Save the document as **Witinski Envelope** in the location specified by your instructor, and then close the document.

CREATE

## Case Problem 2

**Data Files needed for this Case Problem: Church.jpg, Walking.docx**

***Walking Tours of Old San Juan***    You work as the guest services coordinator at Hotel Azul, a luxury resort hotel in San Juan, Puerto Rico. You need to create a flyer promoting a daily walking tour of Old San Juan, the historic Colonial section of Puerto Rico's capital city. Complete the following steps:

1. Open the file **Walking** located in the Word1 ▸ Case2 folder included with your Data Files, and then save the document as **Walking Tour Flyer** in the location specified by your instructor.

2. In the document, replace "Student Name" with your first and last names.

3. Use the Spelling and Grammar task panes to correct any errors, including problems with subject-verb agreement. Instruct the Spelling task pane to ignore the Spanish church names, as well as your name if Word marks it with a wavy underline.

4. Change the page margins to Narrow.

5. Complete the flyer as shown in Figure 1-40. Use the file **Church.jpg** located in the Word1 ▸ Case2 folder included with your Data Files. Use the default line spacing and paragraph spacing unless otherwise specified in Figure 1-40.

**Figure 1-40**    Formatted Walking Tour flyer

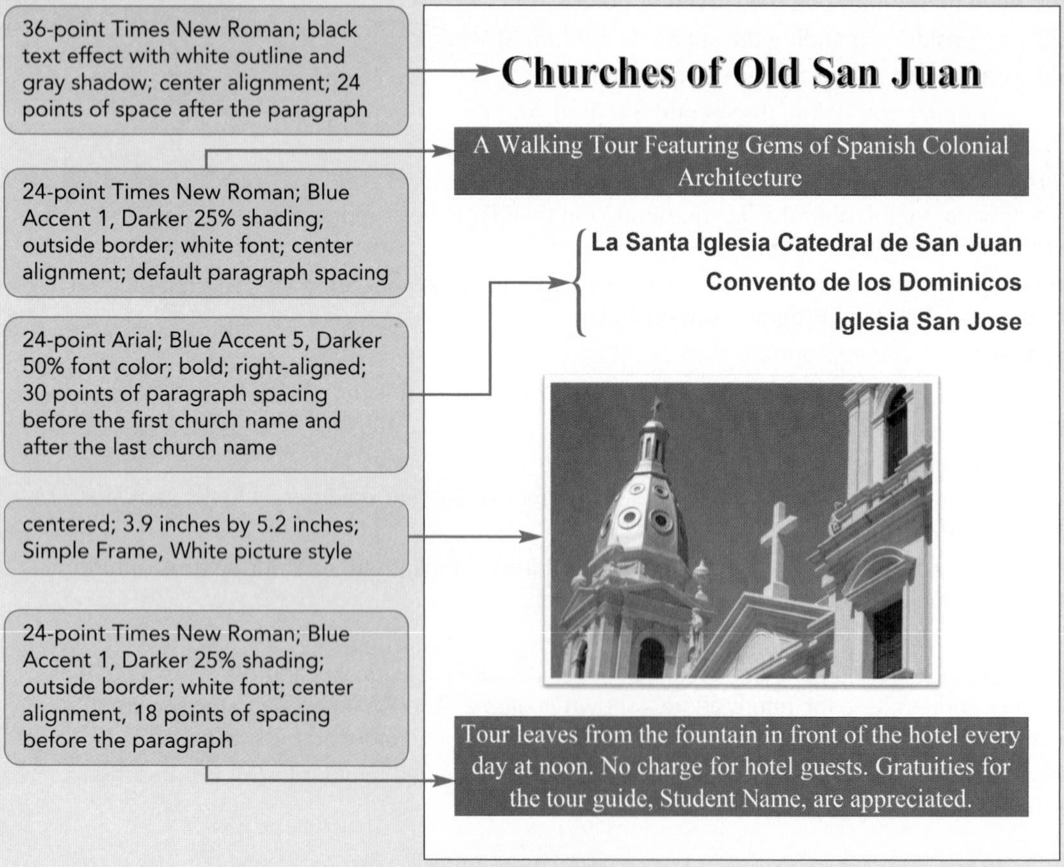

36-point Times New Roman; black text effect with white outline and gray shadow; center alignment; 24 points of space after the paragraph

24-point Times New Roman; Blue Accent 1, Darker 25% shading; outside border; white font; center alignment; default paragraph spacing

24-point Arial; Blue Accent 5, Darker 50% font color; bold; right-aligned; 30 points of paragraph spacing before the first church name and after the last church name

centered; 3.9 inches by 5.2 inches; Simple Frame, White picture style

24-point Times New Roman; Blue Accent 1, Darker 25% shading; outside border; white font; center alignment, 18 points of spacing before the paragraph

### Churches of Old San Juan

A Walking Tour Featuring Gems of Spanish Colonial Architecture

La Santa Iglesia Catedral de San Juan

Convento de los Dominicos

Iglesia San Jose

Tour leaves from the fountain in front of the hotel every day at noon. No charge for hotel guests. Gratuities for the tour guide, Student Name, are appreciated.

Courtesy of Ann Shaffer

6. Save the document, preview it, and then close it.

## Case Problem 3

**Data Files needed for this Case Problem: Mushroom.docx, Mycology.docx**

*Green Valley Arborists*   You work as the office manager for Green Valley Arborists, a tree care service in Billings, Montana. One of the company's arborists noticed a bright orange fungus growing on a tree stump in a client's backyard. She has started writing a letter to a mycologist at the local community college to ask if he can identify the fungus. The letter is almost finished, but the arborist needs help correcting errors and formatting the text to match the block style. The photo itself is stored in a separate document. The arborist mistakenly applied a picture style to the photo that is inappropriate for professional correspondence. She asks you to remove the picture style and then format the page. Complete the following steps:

1. Open the file **Mycology** located in the Word1 ► Case3 folder included with your Data Files, and then save the document as **Mycology Letter** in the location specified by your instructor.
2. Use the Spelling and Grammar task panes to correct any errors, including subject-verb errors. When you are finished, return the Grammar settings to their original configuration.

⚙ **Troubleshoot** 3. Make any necessary changes to ensure that the letter matches the formatting of a block style business letter, including the appropriate paragraph spacing. Keep in mind that the letter will include an enclosure. Include your initials where appropriate.

⚙ **Troubleshoot** 4. The letterhead for Green Valley Arborists requires a top margin of 2.5 inches. Determine if the layout of the letter will work with the letterhead, make any necessary changes, and then save the letter.

5. Save the document and preview it.
6. With the letter still open, create an envelope. Use the delivery address taken from the letter, but edit the delivery address. Click the Omit check box to deselect it (if necessary), and then, for the return address, type your school's name and address. Add the envelope to the document. If you are asked if you want to save the return address as the new default return address, answer No.
7. Save the document, preview it, and then close it.
8. Open the file **Mushroom** located in the Word1 ► Case3 folder included with your Data Files, and then save the document as **Mushroom Photo** in the location specified by your instructor.

⚙ **Troubleshoot** 9. Reset the picture to its original appearance, before the arborist mistakenly added the style with the reflection.

⚙ **Troubleshoot** 10. Modify the page layout and adjust the size of the photo so the photo fills as much of the page as possible without overlapping the page margins.

11. Save the document, preview it, and then close it.

## Case Problem 4

There are no Data Files needed for this Case Problem.

*Hapsburg Interior Design*    As a design assistant at Hapsburg Interior Design, you are responsible for distributing manufacturer samples throughout the office so the firm's designers can stay up to date on newly available paint colors, wallpaper patterns, and fabrics. Along with each sample, you need to include an explanatory memo. Complete the following steps:

⊕ **Explore** 1. Open a new document—but instead of selecting the Blank document option, search for a memo template online. In the list of search results, click the Memo (Simple design) template, and then click the Create button. A memo template opens in the Word window. Above the memo template is the Document Properties panel, where you could enter information about the document that might be useful later. You don't need the panel for this project, so you can ignore it, as well as any entries in the text boxes in the panel.

2. Save the document as **Samples Memo** in the location specified by your instructor. If you see a dialog box indicating that the document will be upgraded to the newest file format, click the OK button. Note that of the hundreds of templates available online, only a small portion have been created in the most recent version of Word, so you will often see this dialog box when working with templates.

⊕ **Explore** 3. In the document, click the text "[Company name]." The placeholder text appears in a box with gray highlighting. The box containing the highlighted text (with the small rectangle attached) is called a document control. You can enter text in a document control just as you enter text in a dialog box. Type **Hapsburg Interior Design**, and then press the Tab key. The "[Recipient names]" placeholder text now appears in a document control next to the word "To." (*Hint*: As you work on the memo in the following steps, keep in mind that if you accidentally double-click the word "memo" at the top of the document, you will access the header portion of the document, which is normally closed to editing. In that case, press the Esc key to return to the main document.)

4. Type **All Designers** and then press the Tab key twice. A document control is now visible to the right of the word "From." Depending on how your computer is set up, you might see your name or another name here, or the document control might be empty. Delete the name, if necessary, and then type your first and last names.

⊕ **Explore** 5. Continue using the Tab key to edit the remaining document controls as indicated below. If you press the Tab key too many times and accidentally skip a document control, you can click the document control to select it.

   - In the CC: document control, delete the placeholder text.
   - In the Date document control, click the down arrow, and then click the current date in the calendar.
   - In the Re: document control, type **Rowley Fabrics**.
   - In the Comments document control, type **Here are the latest offerings from Rowley Fabrics. After you have reviewed the collection, please write your initials at the bottom of this memo and pass the collection on to another designer. If you are the last of the group to review the samples, please return them to my desk. Thank you.**

6. Use the Spelling and Grammar task panes to correct any underlined errors, and then proofread the document to look for any additional errors.

7. Save the document, preview it, and then close it.

## OBJECTIVES

**Session 2.1**
- Read, reply to, delete, and add comments
- Create bulleted and numbered lists
- Move text using drag and drop
- Cut and paste text
- Copy and paste text
- Navigate through a document using the Navigation pane
- Find and replace text
- Format text with styles
- Apply a theme to a document

**Session 2.2**
- Review the MLA style for research papers
- Indent paragraphs
- Insert and modify page numbers
- Create citations
- Create and update a bibliography
- Modify a source

# Navigating and Formatting a Document

*Editing an Academic Document According to MLA Style*

## Case | *Rivas-Garcia College*

Kaya Cho, a student at Rivas-Garcia College, works part-time in the college's Media Studies department. She has written a handout describing the requirements for a Media Studies major, and asks you to help her finish it. The text of the handout needs some reorganization and other editing. It also needs formatting so the finished document looks professional and is easy to read.

Kaya is also taking a Media Studies class this semester, and is writing a research paper on the history of newspapers. To complete the paper, she needs to follow a set of very specific formatting and style guidelines for academic documents.

Kaya has asked you to help her edit these two very different documents. In Session 2.1, you will review and respond to some comments in the handout, and then revise and format that document. In Session 2.2, you will review the MLA style for research papers, and then format Kaya's research paper to match the MLA specifications.

## STARTING DATA FILES

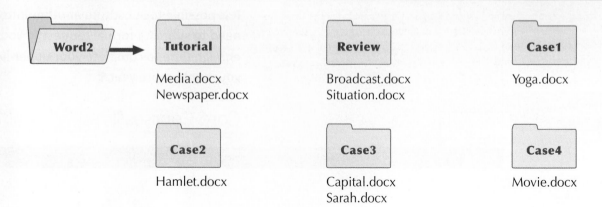

Word2 → Tutorial
Media.docx
Newspaper.docx

Review
Broadcast.docx
Situation.docx

Case1
Yoga.docx

Case2
Hamlet.docx

Case3
Capital.docx
Sarah.docx

Case4
Movie.docx

# Session 2.1 Visual Overview:

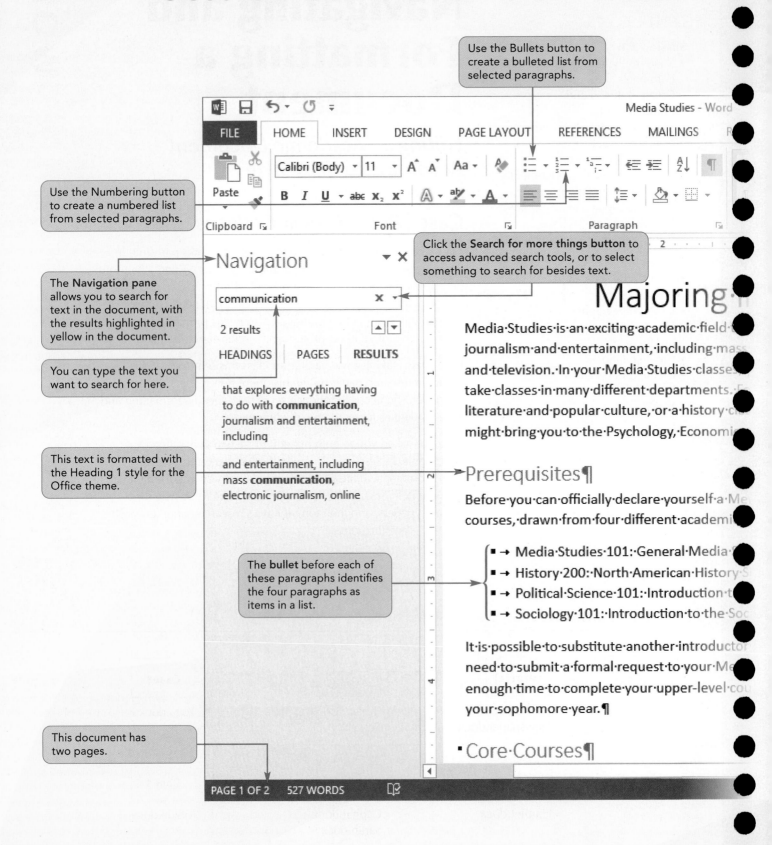

Use the Bullets button to create a bulleted list from selected paragraphs.

Use the Numbering button to create a numbered list from selected paragraphs.

Click the **Search for more things button** to access advanced search tools, or to select something to search for besides text.

The **Navigation pane** allows you to search for text in the document, with the results highlighted in yellow in the document.

You can type the text you want to search for here.

This text is formatted with the Heading 1 style for the Office theme.

The **bullet** before each of these paragraphs identifies the four paragraphs as items in a list.

This document has two pages.

# Working with Lists and Styles

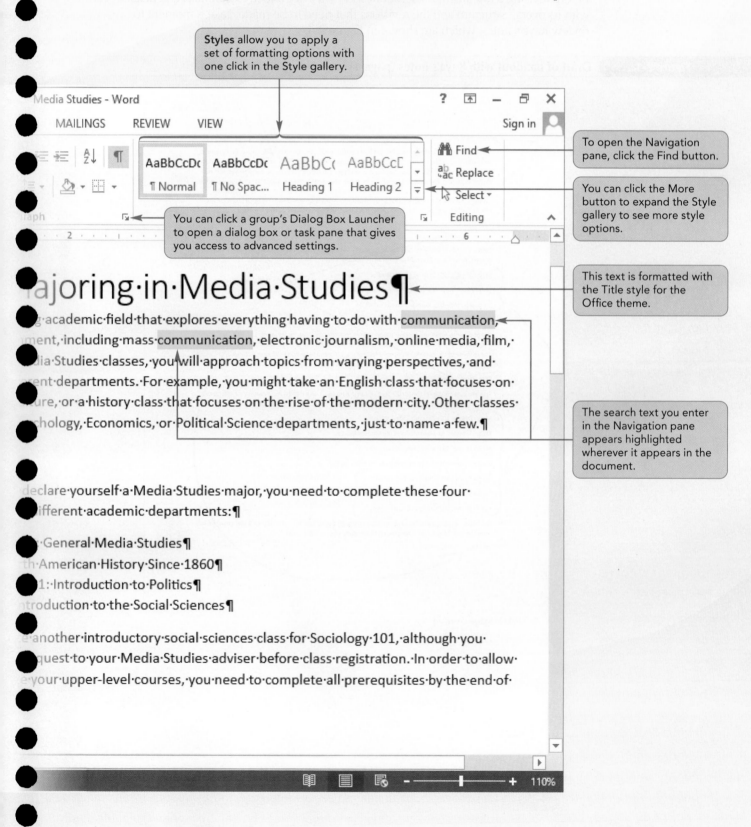

**Styles** allow you to apply a set of formatting options with one click in the Style gallery.

To open the Navigation pane, click the Find button.

You can click the More button to expand the Style gallery to see more style options.

You can click a group's Dialog Box Launcher to open a dialog box or task pane that gives you access to advanced settings.

This text is formatted with the Title style for the Office theme.

The search text you enter in the Navigation pane appears highlighted wherever it appears in the document.

# Reviewing the Document

Before revising a document for someone else, it's a good idea to familiarize yourself with its overall structure and the revisions that need to be made. Take a moment to review Kaya's notes, which are shown in Figure 2-1.

**Figure 2-1**     **Draft of handout with Kaya's notes (page 1)**

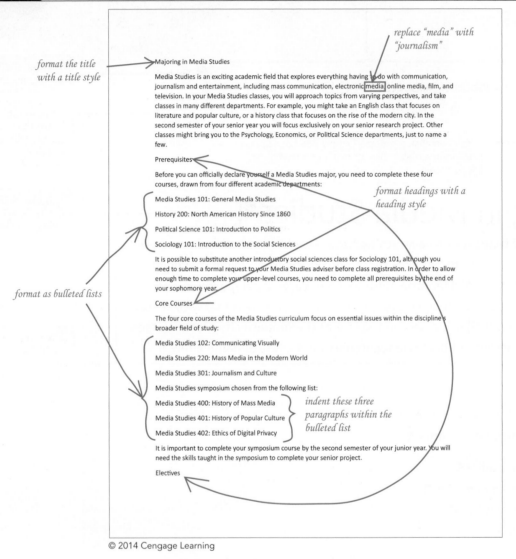

© 2014 Cengage Learning

**Figure 2-1** Draft of handout with Kaya's notes (page 2)

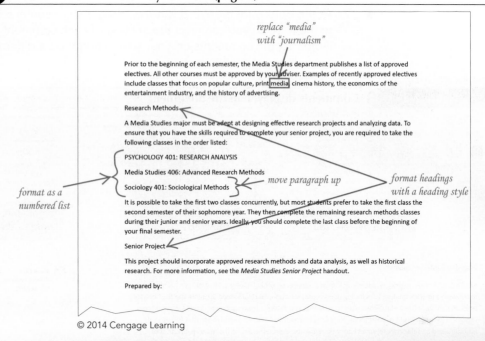

© 2014 Cengage Learning

Kaya also included additional guidance in some comments she added to the document file. A **comment** is like an electronic sticky note attached to a word, phrase, or paragraph in a document. Comments appear in the margin, along with the name of the person who added them. Within a single document, you can add new comments, reply to existing comments, and delete comments.

You will open the document now, save it with a new name, and then review Kaya's comments in Word.

**To open and rename the document:**

1. Open the document named **Media** located in the Word2 ▸ Tutorial folder included with your Data Files.

2. Save the document as **Media Studies** in the location specified by your instructor.

3. Verify that the document is displayed in Print Layout view, that the zoom is set to **120%**, and that the rulers and nonprinting characters are displayed.

4. On the ribbon, click the **REVIEW** tab to display the tools used for working with comments. Comments can be displayed in several different ways, so your first step is to make sure the comments in the Media Studies document are displayed to match the figures in this book—using Simple Markup view.

5. In the Tracking group, click the **Display for Review** arrow, and then click **Simple Markup** to select it, if necessary. At this point, you might see comment icons to the right of the document text, or you might see the full text of each comment.

6. In the Comments group, click the **Show Comments** button several times to practice displaying and hiding the comments, and then, when you are finished, make sure the Show Comments button is selected so the full text of each comment is displayed.

**7.** At the bottom of the Word window, drag the horizontal scroll bar all the way to the right so you can read the full text of each comment. See Figure 2-2. Note that the comments on your screen might be a different color than the ones shown in the figure.

**Figure 2-2**  **Comments displayed in the document**

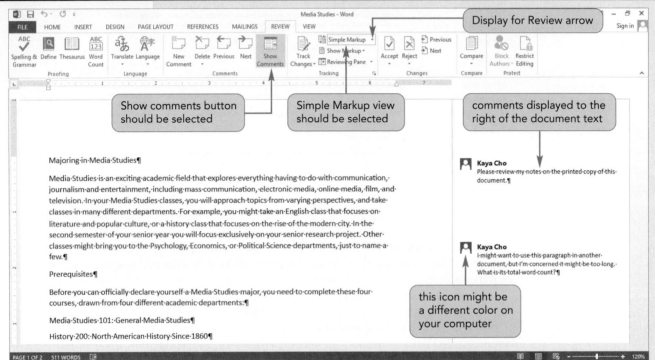

Note that when working on a small monitor, it can be helpful to switch the document Zoom level to Page Width, in which case Word automatically reduces the width of the document to accommodate the comments on the right.

**8.** Read the document, including the comments. The handout includes the title "Majoring in Media Studies" at the top, as well as headings (such as "Prerequisites" and "Core Courses") that divide the document into parts. Right now the headings are hard to spot because they don't look different from the surrounding text. Kaya used the default font size, 11-point, and the default font, Calibri (Body), for all the text in the document. Note, too, that the document includes some short paragraphs that would work better as bulleted or numbered lists.

**9.** Scroll down until you can see the first line on page 2, which begins "Prior to the beginning of each semester…." and then click anywhere in that sentence. The message "PAGE 2 OF 2" in the status bar, in the lower-left corner of the Word window, tells you that the insertion point is currently located on page 2 of the two-page document. The shaded space between the first and second pages of the document indicates a page break. To hide the top and bottom margins in a document, as well as the space between pages, you can double-click the shaded space between any two pages.

**10.** Position the mouse pointer over the shaded space between page 1 and page 2 until the pointer changes to ⊟, and then double-click. The shaded space disappears. Instead, the two pages are now separated by a gray, horizontal line.

> **Trouble?** If the HEADER & FOOTER TOOLS DESIGN tab appears on the ribbon, you double-clicked the top or bottom of one of the pages, instead of in the space between them. Click the Close Header and Footer button on the DESIGN tab, and then repeat Step 10.

▶ **11.** Use the ⬍ pointer to double-click the gray horizontal line between pages 1 and 2. The shaded space between the two pages is redisplayed.

# Working with Comments

Now that you are familiar with the Media Studies document, you can review and respond to Kaya's comments. The Comment group on the REVIEW tab includes helpful tools for working with comments.

**REFERENCE**

### Working with Comments

- On the ribbon, click the REVIEW tab.
- To display comments in an easy-to-read view, in the Tracking group, click the Display for Review button, and then click Simple Markup.
- To see the text of each comment in Simple Markup view, click the Show Comments button in the Comments group.
- To move the insertion point to the next or previous comment in the document, click the Next button or the Previous button in the Comments group.
- To delete a comment, click anywhere in the comment, and then click the Delete button in the Comments group.
- To delete all the comments in a document, click the Delete button arrow in the Comments group, and then click Delete All Comments in Document.
- To add a new comment, select the document text you want to comment on, click the New Comment button in the Comments group, and then type the comment text.
- To reply to a comment, click the Reply button to the right of the comment, and then type your reply.
- To indicate that a comment or an individual reply to a comment is no longer a concern, right-click the comment or reply, and then click Mark Comment Done in the shortcut menu. To mark a comment and all of the replies attached to it as done, right-click the original comment and then click Mark Comment Done.

### To review and respond to the comments in the document:

▶ **1.** Press the **Ctrl+Home** keys to move the insertion point to the beginning of the document.

▶ **2.** On the REVIEW tab, in the Comments group, click the **Next** button. The first comment now has an outline, indicating that it is selected. See Figure 2-3.

In the document, the word "Majoring" is highlighted. A line connects the comment to the word "Majoring," indicating that the comment is attached to that word. Because Kaya created the comment, her name appears at the beginning of the comment, followed by the date on which she created it. The insertion point blinks at the beginning of the comment, and is ready for you to edit the comment if you want.

**Figure 2-3** **Comment attached to document text**

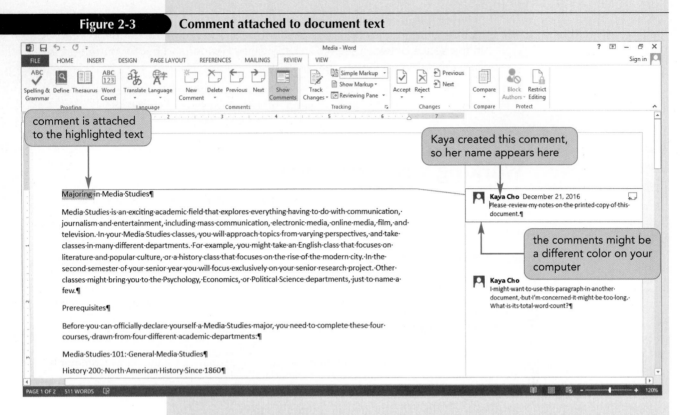

3. Read the comment, and then in the Comments group, click the **Next** button to select the next comment. According to this comment, Kaya wants to know the total word count of the paragraph the comment is attached to. You can get this information by selecting the entire paragraph and locating the word count in the status bar.

4. Triple-click anywhere in the second paragraph of the document (which begins "Media studies is an exciting academic field…") to select the paragraph. In the status bar, the message "110 of 511" tells you that 110 of the document's 511 words are currently selected. So the answer to Kaya's question is 110.

5. Point to the second comment to select it again, click the **Reply** button 🔲, and then type **110**. Your reply appears below Kaya's original comment.

**Trouble?** If you do not see the Reply button in the comment box, drag the horizontal scroll bar at the bottom of the Word window to the right until you can see it.

The name that appears in your reply comment is taken from the User name box in the General tab of the Word Options dialog box. If your name is the username for your computer, your name appears attached to the comment. If you are working on a shared computer at school, or on a computer owned by someone else, another name will appear in the comment.

You can quickly open the General tab of the Word Options dialog box by clicking the Dialog Box Launcher in the Tracking group on the REVIEW tab, and then clicking Change User Name. From there, you can change the username and the initials associated with your copy of Word. However, there is no need to change these settings for this tutorial, and you should never change them on a shared computer at school unless specifically instructed to do so by your instructor.

6. In the Comments group, click the **Next** button to move the insertion point to the next comment, which asks you to insert your name after "Prepared by:" at the end of the document.

7. Click after the colon in "Prepared by:", press the **spacebar**, and then type your first and last name. To indicate that you have complied with Kaya's request by adding your name, you could right-click the comment, and then click Mark Comment Done. However, in this case, you'll simply delete the comment. Kaya also asks you to delete the first comment in the document.

8. Click anywhere in the final comment, and then in the Comments group, click the **Delete** button.

9. In the Comments group, click the **Previous** button three times to select the comment at the beginning of the document, and then click the **Delete** button to delete the comment.

As you reviewed the document, you might have noticed that, on page 2, one of the class names in the Research Methods section appears in all uppercase letters. This is probably just a typing mistake. You can correct it, and then add a comment that points out the change to Kaya.

### To correct the mistake and add a comment:

1. Scroll down to page 2, and then select the fourth paragraph on the page, which contains the text "PSYCHOLOGY 401: RESEARCH ANALYSIS."

2. On the ribbon, click the **HOME** tab.

3. In the Font group, click the **Change Case** button Aa ▾, and then click **Capitalize Each Word**. The text changes to read "Psychology 401: Research Analysis."

4. Verify that the paragraph is still selected, and then click the **REVIEW** tab on the ribbon.

5. In the Comments group, click the **New Comment** button. A new comment appears, with the insertion point ready for you to begin typing.

6. In the new comment, type **I assumed you didn't want this all uppercase, so I changed it.** and then save the document.

   You can now hide the text of the comments because you are finished working with them.

7. In the Comments group, click the **Show Comments** button. You now see a comment icon in the document margin rather than on the right side of the Word screen. A comment icon alerts you to the presence of a comment without taking up all the space required to display the comment text. You can click a comment icon to read a particular comment without displaying the text of all the comments.

8. Click the comment icon 🗩. The comment icon is highlighted, and the full comment is displayed, as shown in Figure 2-4.

**Figure 2-4**    **Document with the comment icon**

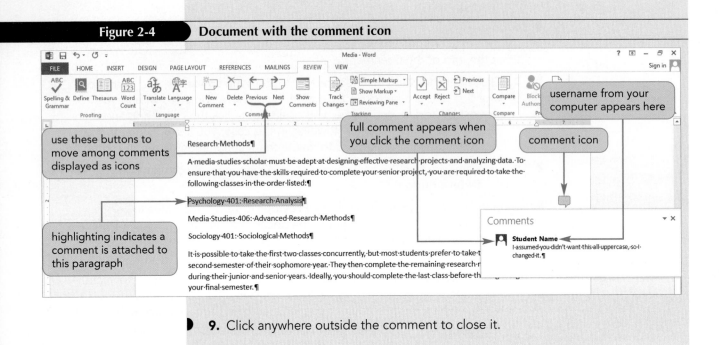

> **9.** Click anywhere outside the comment to close it.

# Creating Bulleted and Numbered Lists

A **bulleted list** is a group of related paragraphs with a black circle or other character to the left of each paragraph. For a group of related paragraphs that have a particular order (such as steps in a procedure), you can use consecutive numbers instead of bullets to create a **numbered list**. If you insert a new paragraph, delete a paragraph, or reorder the paragraphs in a numbered list, Word adjusts the numbers to make sure they remain consecutive.

**PROSKILLS**

### Written Communication: Organizing Information in Lists

Bulleted and numbered lists are both great ways to draw the reader's attention to information. But it's important to know how to use them. Use numbers when your list contains items that are arranged by priority in a specific order. For example, in a document reviewing the procedure for performing CPR, it makes sense to use numbers for the sequential steps. Use bullets when the items in the list are of equal importance, or when they can be accomplished in any order. For example, in a resume, you could use bullets for a list of professional certifications.

To add bullets to a series of paragraphs, you use the Bullets button in the Paragraph group on the HOME tab. To create a numbered list, you use the Numbering button in the Paragraph group instead. Both the Bullets button and the Numbering button have arrows you can click to open a gallery of bullet or numbering styles.

Kaya asks you to format the list of prerequisites on page 1 as a bulleted list. She also asks you to format the list of core courses on page 1 as a separate bulleted list. Finally, you need to format the list of research methods classes on page 2 as a numbered list.

**To apply bullets to paragraphs:**

1. Scroll up until you see the paragraphs containing the list of prerequisites, which begins with "Media Studies 101: General Media Studies," and then select this paragraph and the three that follow it.

2. On the ribbon, click the **HOME** tab.

**TIP**

The Bullets button is a toggle button which means you can click it to add or remove bullets from selected text.

3. In the Paragraph group, click the **Bullets** button ☰. Black circles appear as bullets before each item in the list. Also, the bulleted list is indented and the paragraph spacing between the items is reduced.

   After reviewing the default, round bullet in the document, Kaya decides she would prefer square bullets.

4. In the Paragraph group, click the **Bullets button arrow** ☰▾. A gallery of bullet styles opens. See Figure 2-5.

**Figure 2-5**    **Bullets gallery**

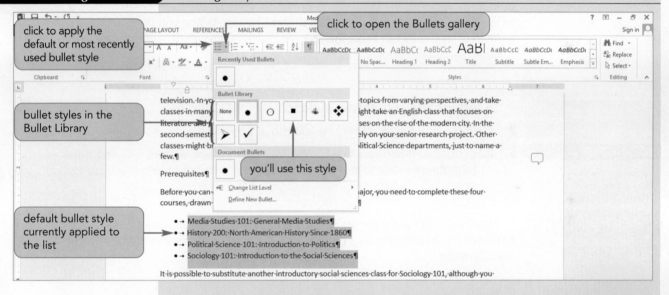

The Recently Used Bullets section appears at the top of the gallery of bullet styles; it displays the bullet styles that have been used since you started Word, which, in this case, is just the round black bullet style that was applied by default when you clicked the Bullets button. The **Bullet Library**, which offers a variety of bullet styles, is shown below the Recently Used Bullets. To create your own bullets from a picture file or from a set of predesigned symbols including diamonds, hearts, or Greek letters, click Define New Bullet, and then click the Symbol button or the Picture button in the Define New Bullet dialog box.

5. Move the mouse pointer over the bullet styles in the Bullet Library to see a Live Preview of the bullet styles in the document. Kaya prefers the black square style.

6. In the Bullet Library, click the **black square**. The round bullets are replaced with square bullets.

Next, you need to format the list of core courses on page 1 with square bullets. When you first start Word, the Bullets button applies the default, round bullets you saw earlier. But after you select a new bullet style, the Bullets button applies the last bullet style you used. So, to add square bullets to the decorating styles list, you just have to select the list and click the Bullets button.

### To add bullets to the list of core courses:

▶ **1.** Scroll down in the document and select the paragraphs listing the core courses, starting with "Media Studies 102: Communicating Visually" and ending with "Media Studies 402: Ethics of Digital Privacy."

▶ **2.** In the Paragraph group, click the **Bullets** button ⊞. The list is now formatted with square black bullets.

The list is finished except for one issue. A Media Studies major only needs to take one of the last three classes in the list, but that's not clear because of the way the list is currently formatted. To clarify this information, you can use the Increase Indent button in the Paragraph group to indent the last three bullets. When you do this, Word inserts a different style bullet to make the indented paragraphs visually subordinate to the bulleted paragraphs above.

### To indent the last three bullets:

▶ **1.** In the list of core courses, select the last three paragraphs.

▶ **2.** In the Paragraph group, click the **Increase Indent** button ⊞. The three paragraphs move to the right, and the black square bullets are replaced with open circle bullets.

**TIP**

To remove the indent from selected text, click the Decrease Indent button in the Paragraph group.

Next, you will format the list of research methods classes on page 2. Kaya wants you to format this information as a numbered list because the classes must be taken in a specific order.

### To apply numbers to the list of research methods classes:

▶ **1.** Scroll down to page 2 until you see the "Psychology 401: Research Analysis" paragraph. You added a comment to this paragraph earlier, but that will have no effect on the process of creating the numbered list.

▶ **2.** Select the three paragraphs containing the list of research methods classes, starting with "Psychology 401: Research Analysis" and ending with "Sociology 401: Sociological Methods."

▶ **3.** In the Paragraph group, click the **Numbering** button ⊞. Consecutive numbers appear in front of each item in the list. See Figure 2-6.

**Figure 2-6**    Numbered list

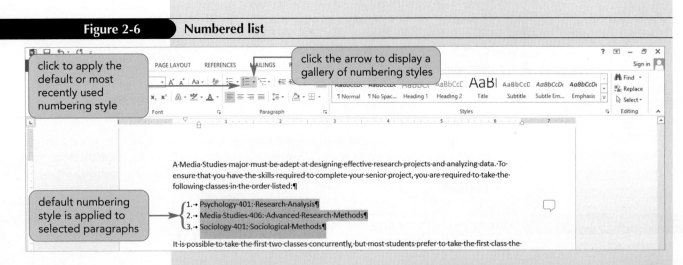

click to apply the default or most recently used numbering style

click the arrow to display a gallery of numbering styles

default numbering style is applied to selected paragraphs

A·Media·Studies·major·must·be·adept·at·designing·effective·research·projects·and·analyzing·data.·To·ensure·that·you·have·the·skills·required·to·complete·your·senior·project,·you·are·required·to·take·the·following·classes·in·the·order·listed:¶

1.→ Psychology·401:·Research·Analysis¶
2.→ Media·Studies·406:·Advanced·Research·Methods¶
3.→ Sociology·401:·Sociological·Methods¶

It·is·possible·to·take·the·first·two·classes·concurrently,·but·most·students·prefer·to·take·the·first·class·the·

**4.** Click anywhere in the document to deselect the numbered list, and then save the document.

**TIP**

The Numbering button is a toggle button, which means you can click it to add or remove numbering from selected text.

As with the Bullets button arrow, you can click the Numbering button arrow and then select from a library of numbering styles. You can also indent paragraphs in a numbered list to create an outline, in which case the indented paragraphs will be preceded by lowercase letters instead of numbers. To apply a different list style to the outline (for example, with Roman numerals and uppercase letters), select the list, click the Multilevel List button in the Paragraph group, and then click a multilevel list style.

# Moving Text in a Document

One of the most useful features of a word-processing program is the ability to move text easily. For example, Kaya wants to reorder the information in the numbered list. You could do this by deleting a paragraph and then retyping it at a new location. However, it's easier to select and then move the text. Word provides several ways to move text—drag and drop, cut and paste, and copy and paste.

## Dragging and Dropping Text

To move text with **drag and drop**, you select the text you want to move, press and hold the mouse button while you drag the selected text to a new location, and then release the mouse button.

In the numbered list you just created, Kaya wants you to move the paragraph that reads "Sociology 401 Sociological Methods" up so it is the first item in the list.

**To move text using drag and drop:**

**1.** Select the third paragraph in the numbered list, "Sociology 401: Sociological Methods," being sure to include the paragraph marker at the end. The number 3 remains unselected because it's not actually part of the paragraph text.

**2.** Position the pointer over the selected text. The pointer changes to a left-facing arrow.

3. Press and hold the mouse button until the drag-and-drop pointer appears. A dark black insertion point appears within the selected text.

4. Without releasing the mouse button, drag the pointer to the beginning of the list until the insertion point is positioned to the left of the "P" in "Psychology 401: Research Analysis." Use the insertion point, rather than the mouse pointer, to guide the text to its new location. See Figure 2-7.

   **Trouble?** If the numbers in the numbered list appear highlighted in gray, you moved the mouse pointer too close to the numbers. Ignore the highlighting and position the insertion point just to the left of the "P" in "Psychology 401: Research Analysis."

**Figure 2-7**   Moving text with the drag-and-drop pointer

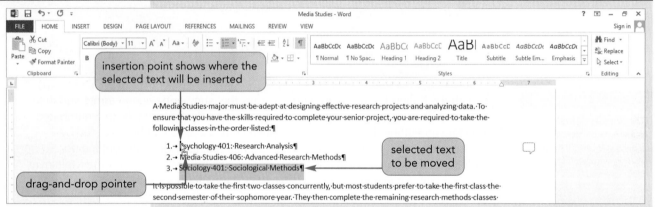

5. Release the mouse button, and then click a blank area of the document to deselect the text. The text "Sociology 401: Sociological Methods" is now the first item in the list, and the remaining paragraphs have been renumbered as paragraphs 2 and 3. See Figure 2-8.

**Figure 2-8**   Text in new location

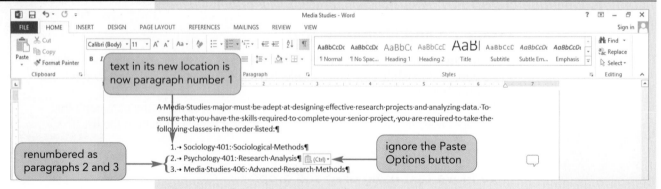

The Paste Options button appears near the newly inserted text, providing access to more advanced options related to pasting text. You don't need to use the Paste Options button right now; it will disappear when you start performing another task.

**Trouble?** If the selected text moves to the wrong location, click the Undo button ⟲ on the Quick Access Toolbar, and then repeat Steps 2 through 5.

**6.** Save the document.

Dragging and dropping works well when you are moving text a short distance. When you are moving text from one page to another, it's easier to cut, copy, and paste text using the Clipboard.

## Cutting or Copying and Pasting Text Using the Clipboard

The **Office Clipboard** is a temporary storage area on your computer that holds objects such as text or graphics until you need them. To **cut** means to remove text or another item from a document and place it on the Clipboard. Once you've cut something, you can paste it somewhere else. To **copy** means to copy a selected item to the Clipboard, leaving the item in its original location. To **paste** means to insert a copy of whatever is on the Clipboard into the document, at the insertion point. When you paste an item from the Clipboard into a document, the item remains on the Clipboard so you can paste it again somewhere else if you want. The buttons for cutting, copying, and pasting are located in the Clipboard group on the HOME tab.

By default, Word pastes text in a new location in a document with the same formatting it had in its old location. To select other ways to paste text, you can use the Paste Options button, which appears next to newly pasted text, or the Paste button arrow in the Clipboard group. Both buttons display a menu of paste options. Two particularly useful paste options are Merge Formatting, which combines the formatting of the copied text with the formatting of the text in the new location, and Keep Text Only, which inserts the text using the formatting of the surrounding text in the new location.

When you need to keep track of multiple pieces of cut or copied text, it's helpful to open the **Clipboard task pane**, which displays the contents of the Clipboard. You open the Clipboard task pane by clicking the Dialog Box Launcher in the Clipboard group on the HOME tab. When the Clipboard task pane is displayed, the Clipboard can store up to 24 text items. When the Clipboard task pane is *not* displayed, the Clipboard can hold only the most recently copied item.

Kaya would like to move the second-to-last sentence under the heading "Majoring in Media Studies" on page 1. You'll use cut and paste to move this sentence to a new location.

**To move text using cut and paste:**

**1.** Make sure the HOME tab is selected on the ribbon.

**2.** Scroll up until you can see the second paragraph in the document, just below the heading "Majoring in Media Studies."

**3.** Press and hold the **Ctrl** key, and then click anywhere in the sentence near the end of the second paragraph, which begins "In the second semester of your senior year...." The entire sentence and the space following it are selected.

**TIP**

You can also press the Ctrl+X keys to cut selected text. Press the Ctrl+V keys to paste the most recently copied item.

4. In the Clipboard group, click the **Cut** button. The selected text is removed from the document and copied to the Clipboard.

5. Scroll down to page 2, and then click at the beginning of the second-to-last paragraph in the document, just to the left of the "T" in "This project should…."

6. In the Clipboard group, click the **Paste** button. The sentence and the space following it are displayed in the new location. The Paste Options button appears near the newly inserted sentence.

   **Trouble?** If a menu opens below the Paste button, you clicked the Paste button arrow instead of the Paste button. Press the Esc key to close the menu, and then repeat Step 6, taking care not to click the arrow below the Paste button.

7. Save the document.

Kaya explains that she'll be using some text from the Media Studies document as the basis for another department handout. She asks you to copy that information and paste it into a new document. You can do this using the Clipboard task pane.

### To copy text to paste into a new document:

1. In the Clipboard group, click the **Dialog Box Launcher**. The Clipboard task pane opens on the left side of the document window, as shown in Figure 2-9.

**Figure 2-9**   **Clipboard task pane**

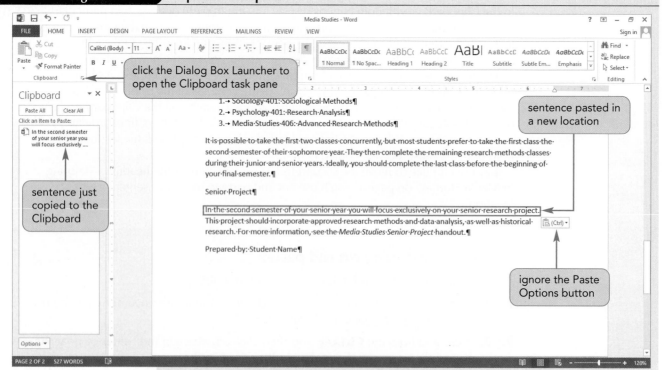

Notice the Clipboard contains the sentence you copied in the last set of steps, although you can only see the first part of the sentence. You'll copy the last two sentences in the current paragraph for use in Kaya's other document.

2. Select the text **This project should incorporate approved research methods and data analysis, as well as historical research. For more information, see the *Media Studies Senior Project* handout.** Do not select the paragraph mark.

**TIP**

You can also copy selected text by pressing the Ctrl+C keys.

3. In the Clipboard group, click the **Copy** button. The first few words of the text appear at the top of the Clipboard task pane, but in fact the entire two sentences are now stored on the Clipboard.

4. Click anywhere in the document to deselect the text, scroll up, if necessary, and then locate the first sentence on page 2.

5. Press and hold the **Ctrl** key, and then click anywhere in the first sentence on page 2, which begins "A Media Studies major must be adept…." The sentence and the space following it are selected.

6. In the Clipboard group, click the **Copy** button. The first part of the sentence appears at the top of the Clipboard task pane, as shown in Figure 2-10.

**Figure 2-10**    **Items in the Clipboard task pane**

click to close the Clipboard task pane

text you copied second

text you copied first

text you cut earlier, before you opened the Clipboard task pane

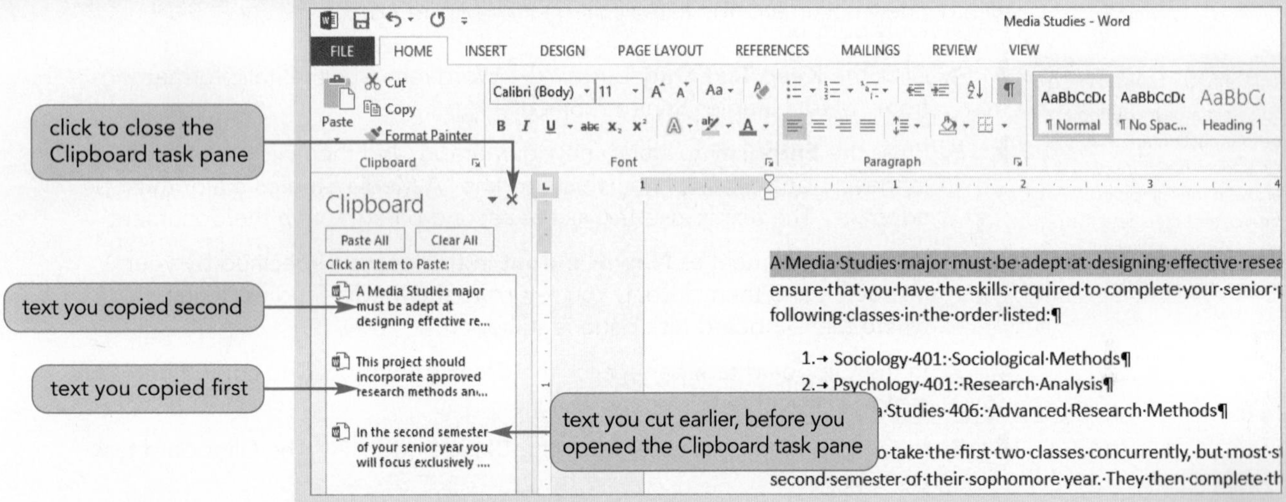

Now you can use the Clipboard task pane to insert the copied text into a new document.

## To insert the copied text into a new document:

1. Open a new, blank document. If necessary, open the Clipboard task pane.

2. In the Clipboard task pane, click the second item in the list of copied items, which begins "This project should incorporate…." The text is inserted in the document and the "*Media Studies Senior Project*" title retains its italic formatting.

Kaya doesn't want to keep the italic formatting in the newly pasted text. You can remove this formatting by using the Paste Options button, which is visible just below the pasted text.

3. Click the **Paste Options** button in the document. The Paste Options menu opens, as shown in Figure 2-11.

**Figure 2-11**     Paste Options menu

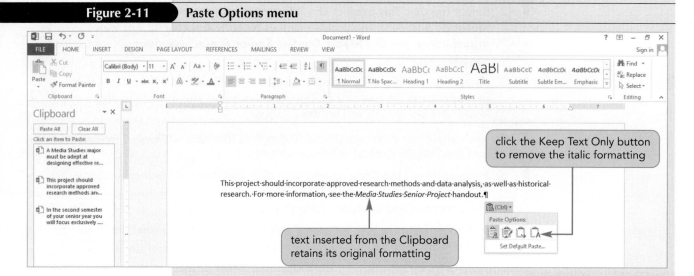

click the Keep Text Only button
to remove the italic formatting

This·project·should·incorporate·approved·research·methods·and·data·analysis,·as·well·as·historical·
research.·For·more·information,·see·the·*Media·Studies·Senior·Project*·handout.¶

text inserted from the Clipboard
retains its original formatting

To paste the text without the italic formatting, you can click the Keep Text Only button.

**TIP**

To select a paste option
before pasting an item,
click the Paste button
arrow in the Clipboard
group, and then click the
paste option you want.

4. Click the **Keep Text Only** button. Word removes the italic formatting from "Media Studies Senior Project."

5. Press the **Enter** key to start a new paragraph, and then click the first item in the Clipboard task pane, which begins "A Media Studies major must be adept...." The text is inserted as the second paragraph in the document.

6. Save the document as **New Handout** in the location specified by your instructor, and then close it. You return to the Media Studies document, where the Clipboard task pane is still open.

7. In the Clipboard task pane, click the **Clear All** button. The copied items are removed from the Clipboard.

8. In the Clipboard task pane, click the **Close** button. The Clipboard task pane closes.

9. Click anywhere in the document to deselect the paragraph, and then save the document.

# Using the Navigation Pane

The Navigation pane simplifies the process of moving through a document page by page. You can also use the Navigation pane to locate a particular word or phrase. You start by typing the text you're searching for—the **search text**—in the Search box at the top of the Navigation pane. As shown in the Session 2.1 Visual Overview, Word highlights every instance of the search text in the document. At the same time, a list of the **search results** appears in the Navigation pane. You can click a search result to go immediately to that location in the document.

To become familiar with the Navigation pane, you'll use it to navigate through the Media Studies document page by page. You'll start by moving the insertion point to the beginning of the document.

### To navigate through the document page by page:

1. Press the **Ctrl+Home** keys to move the insertion point to the beginning of the document, making sure the HOME tab is still selected on the ribbon.

2. In the Editing group, click the **Find** button. The Navigation pane opens on the left side of the Word window.

   In the Search document box at the top, you can type the text you want to find. The three links below the Search document box—HEADINGS, PAGES, and RESULTS—allow you to navigate through the document in different ways. As you become a more experienced Word user, you'll learn how to use the HEADINGS link; for now, you'll ignore it. To move quickly among the pages of a document, you can use the PAGES link.

3. In the Navigation pane, click the **PAGES** link. The Navigation pane displays thumbnail icons of the document's two pages, as shown in Figure 2-12. You can click a page in the Navigation pane to display that page in the document window.

| Figure 2-12 | Document pages displayed in the Navigation pane |
| --- | --- |

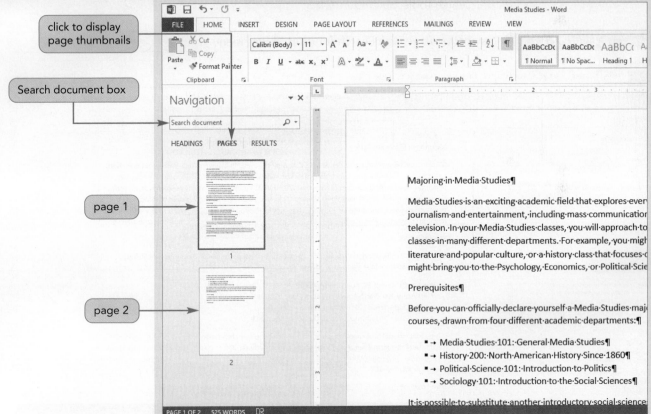

4. In the Navigation pane, click the **page 2** thumbnail. Page 2 is displayed in the document window, with the insertion point blinking at the beginning of the page.

5. In the Navigation pane, click the **page 1** thumbnail to move the insertion point back to the beginning of the document.

Kaya thinks she might have mistakenly used the word "media" when she actually meant to use "journalism" in certain parts of the document. She asks you to use the Navigation pane to find all instances of "media."

### To search for the word "media" in the document:

1. In the Navigation pane, click the **RESULTS** link, click the **Search document** box, and then type **media**. You do not have to press the Enter key.

   Every instance of the word "media" is highlighted in yellow in the document. The yellow highlight is only temporary; it will disappear as soon as you begin to perform any other task in the document. A full list of the 24 search results is displayed in the Navigation pane. Some of the search results contain the word "Media" (with an uppercase "M") while others contain the word "media" (with a lowercase "m"). To narrow the search results, you need to tell Word to match the case of the search text.

2. In the Navigation pane, click the **Search for more things** button ▼. This displays a two-part menu. In the bottom part, you can select other items to search for, such as graphics or tables. The top part provides more advanced search tools. See Figure 2-13.

| Figure 2-13 | Navigation pane with Search for more things menu |
| --- | --- |

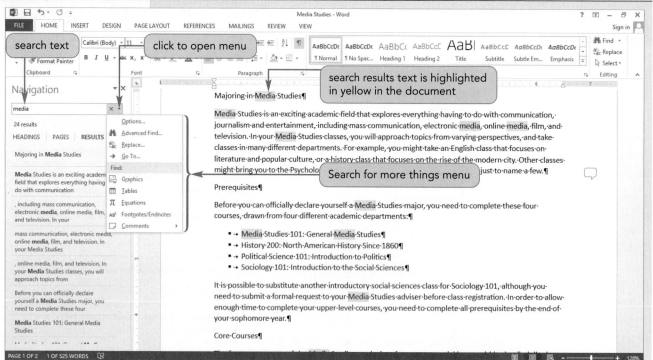

3. At the top of the Search for more things menu, click **Options** to open the Find Options dialog box.

The check boxes in this dialog box allow you to fine-tune your search. For example, to ensure that Word finds the search text only when it appears as a separate word, and not when it appears as part of another word, you could select the Find whole words only check box. Right now, you are only concerned with making sure the search results have the same case as the search text.

4. Click the **Match case** check box to select it, and then click the **OK** button to close the Find Options dialog box. Now you can search the document again.

5. Press the **Ctrl+Home** keys to move the insertion point to the beginning of the document, click the **Search document** box in the Navigation pane, and then type **media**. This time, there are only three search results in the Navigation pane, and they all start with a lowercase "m."

To move among the search results, you can use the up and down arrows in the Navigation pane.

6. In the Navigation pane, click the **down arrow** button ▼. Word selects the first instance of "media" in the Navigation pane, as indicated by a blue outline. Also, in the document, the first instance has a gray selection highlight over the yellow highlight. See Figure 2-14.

**Figure 2-14** | **Navigation pane with the first search result selected**

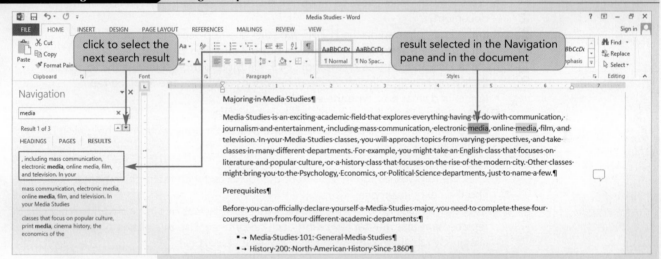

**Trouble?** If the second instance of "media" is selected in the Navigation pane, then you pressed the Enter key after typing "media" in Step 5. Click the up arrow button ▲ to select the first instance.

7. In the Navigation pane, click the **down arrow** button ▼. Word selects the second instance of "media" in the document and in the Navigation pane.

8. Click the **down arrow** button ▼ again to select the third search result, in the paragraph after "Electives," and then click the **up arrow** button ▲ to select the second search result again.

You can also select a search result in the document by clicking a search result in the Navigation pane.

9. In the Navigation pane, click the third search result, which begins "classes that focus on popular culture...." The third search result is selected in the document and in the Navigation pane.

After reviewing the search results, Kaya decides she would like to replace two of the three instances of "media" with the word "journalism." You can do that by using the Find and Replace dialog box.

# Finding and Replacing Text

To open the Find and Replace dialog box from the Navigation pane, click the Find more things button, and then click Replace. This opens the **Find and Replace dialog box**, with the Replace tab displayed by default. The Replace tab provides options for finding a specific word or phrase in the document and replacing it with another word or phrase. To use the Replace tab, type the search text in the Find what box, and then type the text you want to substitute in the Replace with box. You can also click the More button on the Replace tab to display the Search Options section, which includes the same options you saw earlier in the Find Options dialog box, including the Find whole words only check box and the Match case check box.

After you have typed the search text and selected any search options, you can click the Find Next button to select the first occurrence of the search text; you can then decide whether or not to substitute the search text with the replacement text.

**REFERENCE**

*Finding and Replacing Text*

- Press the Ctrl+Home keys to move the insertion point to the beginning of the document.
- In the Editing group on the HOME tab, click the Replace button; or, in the Navigation pane, click the Search for more things button, and then click Replace.
- In the Find and Replace dialog box, click the More button, if necessary, to expand the dialog box and display the Search Options section of the Replace tab.
- In the Find what box, type the search text.
- In the Replace with box, type the replacement text.
- Select the appropriate check boxes in the Search Options section of the dialog box to narrow your search.
- Click the Find Next button.
- Click the Replace button to substitute the found text with the replacement text and find the next occurrence.
- Click the Replace All button to substitute all occurrences of the found text with the replacement text without reviewing each occurrence. Use this option only if you are absolutely certain that the results will be what you expect.

You'll use the Find and Replace dialog box now to replace two instances of "media" with "journalism."

## To replace two instances of "media" with "journalism":

1. Press the **Ctrl+Home** keys to move the insertion point to the beginning of the document.

2. In the Navigation pane, click the **Search for more things** button ▼ to open the menu, and then click **Replace**. The Find and Replace dialog box opens with the Replace tab on top.

   The search text you entered earlier in the Navigation pane, "media," appears in the Find what box. If you hadn't already conducted a search, you would need to type your search text now. Because you selected the Match case check box earlier in the Find Options dialog box, "Match Case" appears below the Find what box.

3. In the lower-left corner of the dialog box, click the **More** button to display the search options. Because you selected the Match case check box earlier in the Find Options dialog box, it is selected here.

   **Trouble?** If you see the Less button instead of the More button, the search options are already displayed.

4. Click the **Replace with** box, and then type **journalism**.

5. Click the **Find Next** button. Word highlights the first instance of "media" in the document. See Figure 2-15.

| Figure 2-15 | Find and Replace dialog box |

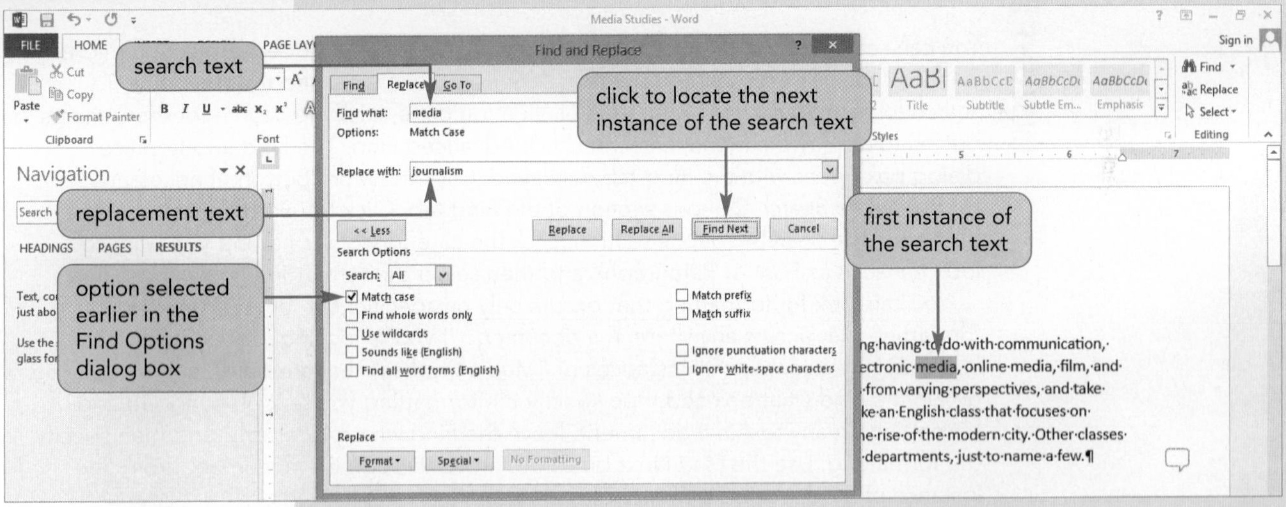

6. Click the **Replace** button. Word replaces "media" with "journalism," so the text reads "electronic journalism." Then, Word selects the next instance of "media," which happens to be in the same sentence. Kaya does not want to replace this instance, so you can find the next one.

7. Click the **Find Next** button. Word selects the last instance of "media," located in the sentence just before the "Research Methods" heading.

▶ 8. Click the **Replace** button. Word makes the substitution, so the text reads "print journalism," and then displays a message box telling you that Word has finished searching the document.

▶ 9. Click the **OK** button to close the message box, and then in the Find and Replace dialog box, click the **Close** button.

You are finished with the Navigation pane, so you can close it. But first you need to restore the search options to their original settings. It's a good practice to restore the original search settings so that future searches are not affected by any settings that might not apply.

**To restore the search options to their original settings:**

▶ 1. In the Navigation pane, open the Find Options dialog box, deselect the Match case check box, and then click the **OK** button to close the Find Options dialog box.

▶ 2. Click the **Close** button ✖ in the upper-right corner of the Navigation pane.

▶ 3. Save the document.

## INSIGHT

### Searching for Formatting

You can search for formatting just as you can search for text. For example, you might want to check a document to look for text formatted in bold and the Arial font. To search for formatting from within the Navigation pane, click the Search for more things button to display the menu, and then click Advanced Find. The Find and Replace dialog box opens with the Find tab displayed. Click the More button, if necessary, to display the Search Options section of the Find tab. Click the Format button at the bottom of the Search Options section, click the category of formatting you want to look for (such as Font or Paragraph), and then select the formatting you want to find.

You can look for formatting that occurs only on specific text, or you can look for formatting that occurs anywhere in a document. If you're looking for text formatted in a certain way (such as all instances of "Media Studies" that are bold), enter the text in the Find what box and then specify the formatting you're looking for. To find formatting on any text in a document, leave the Find what box empty, and then specify the formatting. Use the Find Next button to move through the document, from one instance of the specified formatting to another.

You can follow the same basic steps on the Replace tab to replace one type of formatting with another. First, click the Find what box and select the desired formatting. Then click the Replace with box and select the desired formatting. If you want, type search text and replacement text in the appropriate boxes. Then proceed as with any Find and Replace operation.

Now that the text in the Media Studies document is final, you will turn your attention to styles and themes, which affect the look of the entire document.

# Working with Styles

A style is a set of formatting options that you can apply by clicking an icon in the Style gallery on the HOME tab. Each style is designed for a particular use. For example, the Title style is intended for formatting the title at the beginning of a document.

All the text you type into a document has a style applied to it. By default, text is formatted in the Normal style, which applies 11-point Calibri font, left alignment, 1.08 line spacing, and a small amount of extra space between paragraphs. In other words, the Normal style applies the default formatting you learned about when you first began typing a Word document.

Note that some styles apply **paragraph-level formatting**—that is, they are set up to format an entire paragraph, including the paragraph and line spacing. The Normal, Heading, and Title styles all apply paragraph-level formatting. Other styles apply **character-level formatting**—that is, they are set up to format only individual characters or words (for example, emphasizing a phrase by adding italic formatting and changing the font color).

One row of the Style gallery is always visible on the HOME tab. To display the entire Style gallery, click the More button in the Styles group. After you begin applying styles in a document, the visible row of the Style gallery changes to show the most recently used styles.

You are ready to use the Style gallery to format the document title.

**To display the entire Style gallery and then format the document title with a style:**

▶ 1. Press the **Ctrl+Home** keys to move the insertion point to the beginning of the document, if necessary.

▶ 2. Make sure the HOME tab is still selected and locate the More button in the Styles group, as shown earlier in the Session 2.1 Visual Overview.

▶ 3. In the Styles group, click the **More** button. The Style gallery opens, displaying a total of 16 styles arranged in two rows, as shown in Figure 2-16. If your screen is set at a lower resolution than the screenshots in this book, the Style gallery on your screen might contain more than two rows.

Figure 2-16    Displaying the Style gallery

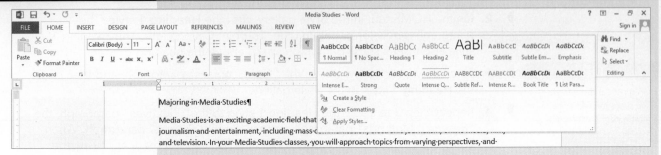

You don't actually need any of the styles in the bottom row now, so you can close the Style gallery.

▶ 4. Press the **Esc** key to close the Style gallery.

5. Click anywhere in the first paragraph, "Majoring in Media Studies," and then point to (but don't click) the **Title** style, which is the fifth style from the left in the top row of the gallery. The ScreenTip "Title" is displayed, and a Live Preview of the style appears in the paragraph containing the insertion point, as shown in Figure 2-17. The Title style changes the font to 28-point Calibri Light.

**Figure 2-17**    **Title style in the Style gallery**

6. Click the **Title** style. The style is applied to the paragraph. To finish the title, you need to center it.

7. In the Paragraph group, click the **Center** button. The title is centered in the document.

Next, you will format the document headings using the heading styles, which have different levels. The highest level, Heading 1, is used for the major headings in a document, and it applies the most noticeable formatting with a larger font than the other heading styles. (In heading styles, the highest, or most important, level has the lowest number.) The Heading 2 style is used for headings that are subordinate to the highest level headings; it applies slightly less dramatic formatting than the Heading 1 style.

The Media Studies handout only has one level of headings, so you will only apply the Heading 1 style.

**To format text with the Heading 1 style:**

1. Click anywhere in the "Prerequisites" paragraph.

2. On the HOME tab, in the Style gallery, click the **Heading 1** style. The paragraph is now formatted in blue, 16-point Calibri Light. The Heading 1 style also inserts some paragraph space above the heading.

**TIP**

On most computers, you can press the F4 key to repeat your most recent action.

3. Scroll down, click anywhere in the "Core Courses" paragraph, and then click the **Heading 1** style in the Style gallery.

4. Repeat Step 3 to apply the Heading 1 style to the "Electives" paragraph, the "Research Methods" paragraph and the "Senior Project" paragraph. When you are finished, scroll up to the beginning of the document to review the new formatting. See Figure 2-18.

**Figure 2-18**    Document with Title and Heading 1 styles

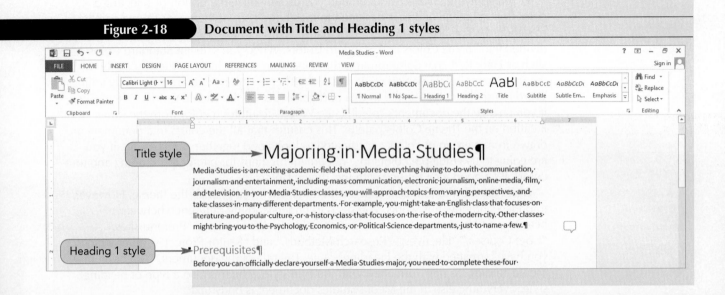

## Understanding the Benefits of Heading Styles

By default, the Style gallery offers 16 styles, each designed for a specific purpose. As you gain more experience with Word, you will learn how to use a wider array of styles. You'll also learn how to create your own styles. Styles allow you to change a document's formatting in an instant. But the benefits of heading styles go far beyond attractive formatting. Heading styles allow you to reorganize a document or generate a table of contents with a click of the mouse. Also, the heading styles are set up to keep a heading and the body text that follows it together, so a heading is never separated from its body text by a page break. Each Word document includes nine levels of heading styles, although only the Heading 1 and Heading 2 styles are available by default in the Style gallery. Whenever you use the lowest heading style in the Style gallery, the next-lowest level is added to the Style gallery. For example, after you use the Heading 2 style, the Heading 3 style appears in the Styles group in the Style gallery.

After you format a document with a variety of styles, you can alter the look of the document by changing the document's theme.

## Working with Themes

A **theme** is a coordinated collection of fonts, colors, and other visual effects designed to give a document a cohesive, polished look. A variety of themes are installed with Word, with more available online at Office.com. When you open a new blank document in Word, the Office theme is applied by default. To change a document's theme, you click the Themes button, which is located in the Document Formatting group on the DESIGN tab, and then click the theme you want. Pointing to the Themes button displays a ScreenTip that tells you what theme is currently applied to the document.

When applying color to a document, you usually have the option of selecting a color from a palette of colors designed to match the current theme, or from a palette of standard colors. For instance, recall that the colors in the Font Color gallery are divided into Theme Colors and Standard Colors. When you select a Standard Color, such as Dark Red, that color remains the same no matter which theme you apply to the document. But when you click one of the Theme Colors, you are essentially telling Word to use the color located in that particular spot on the Theme Colors palette. Then, if you change the document's theme later, Word substitutes a color from the same location on the Theme Colors palette. This ensures that all the colors in a document are drawn from a group of colors coordinated to look good together. So as a rule, if you are going to use multiple colors in a document (perhaps for paragraph shading and font color), it's a good idea to stick with the Theme Colors.

A similar substitution takes place with fonts when you change the theme. However, to understand how this works, you need to understand the difference between headings and body text. Kaya's document includes the headings "Prerequisites," "Core Courses," "Electives," "Research Methods," and "Senior Project"—all of which you have formatted with the Heading1 style. The title of the document, "Majoring in Media Studies," is now formatted with the Title style, which is also a type of heading style. Everything else in the Media Studies document is body text.

To ensure that your documents have a harmonious look, each theme assigns a font for headings and a font for body text. Typically, in a given theme, the same font is used for both headings and body text, but not always. In the Office theme, for instance, they are slightly different; the heading font is Calibri Light, and the body font is Calibri. These two fonts appear at the top of the Font list as "Calibri Light (Headings)" and "Calibri (Body)" when you click the Font box arrow in the Font group on the HOME tab. When you begin typing text in a new document with the Office theme, the text is formatted as body text with the Calibri font by default.

When applying a font to selected text, you can choose one of the two theme fonts at the top of the Font list, or you can choose one of the other fonts in the Font list. If you choose one of the other fonts and then change the document theme, that font remains the same. But if you use one of the theme fonts and then change the document theme, Word substitutes the appropriate font from the new theme. When you paste text into a document that has a different theme, Word applies the theme fonts and colors of the new document. To retain the original formatting, use the Keep Source Formatting option in the Paste Options menu.

Figure 2-19 compares elements of the default Office theme with the Integral theme. The Integral theme was chosen for this example because, like the Office theme, its heading and body fonts are different.

**Figure 2-19**    Comparing the Office theme to the Integral theme

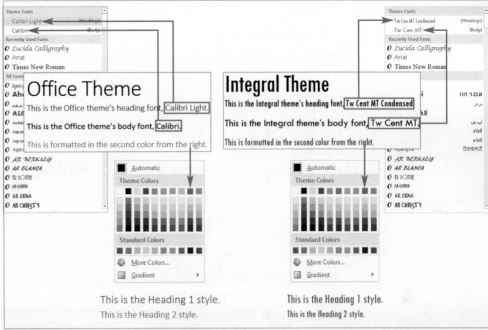

© 2014 Cengage Learning

Each document theme is designed to convey a specific look and feel. The Office theme is designed to be appropriate for standard business documents. Other themes are designed to give documents a flashier look. Because Kaya has not yet selected a new theme, the Office theme is currently applied to the Media Studies document. However, she thinks the Facet theme might be more appropriate for the Media Studies document. She asks you to apply it now.

**To change the document's theme:**

1. If necessary, press the **Ctrl+Home** keys to move the insertion point to the beginning of the document. With the title and first heading visible, you will more easily see what happens when you change the document's theme.

2. On the ribbon, click the **DESIGN** tab.

3. In the Document Formatting group, point to the **Themes** button. A ScreenTip appears containing the text "Current: Office Theme" as well as general information about themes.

4. In the Document Formatting group, click the **Themes** button. The Themes gallery opens. See Figure 2-20.

**Figure 2-20**    **Themes gallery displayed**

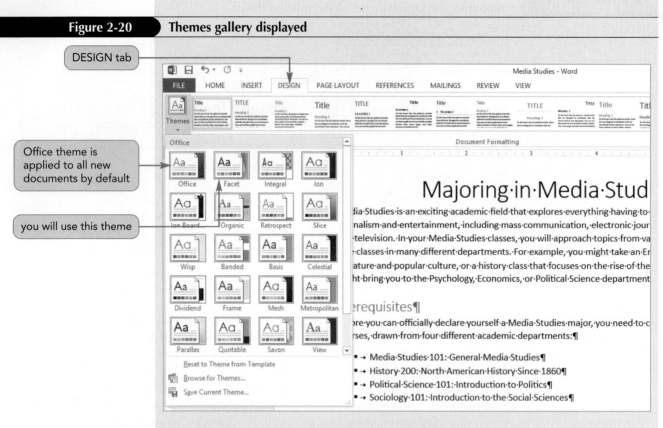

5. Move the mouse pointer (without clicking it) over the various themes in the gallery to see a Live Preview of each theme in the document. The heading and body fonts as well as the heading colors change to reflect the fonts associated with the various themes.

6. In the Themes gallery, click the **Facet** theme. The text in the Media Studies document changes to the body and heading fonts of the Facet theme, with the headings formatted in green. To see exactly what the Facet theme fonts are, you can point to the Fonts button in the Document Formatting group.

7. In the Document Formatting group, point to the **Fonts** button. A ScreenTip appears, listing the currently selected theme (Facet), the heading font (Trebuchet MS), and the body font (Trebuchet MS). See Figure 2-21.

| Figure 2-21 | Fonts for the Facet theme |

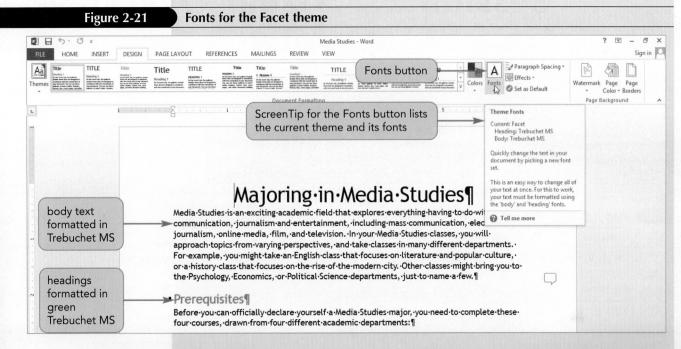

**Trouble?** If a menu appears, you clicked the Fonts button instead of pointing to it. Press the Esc key, and then repeat Step 7.

8. Save your changes and then close the document.

Kaya's Media Studies document is ready to be handed in to her supervisor. The use of styles, bulleted and numbered lists, and a new theme gives the document a professional look appropriate for use in a department handout.

## Session 2.1 Quick Check

REVIEW

1. Explain how to display comments to the right of the document text in Simple Markup view.
2. What term refers to the process of using the mouse to drag text to a new location?
3. How can you ensure that the Navigation pane will find "ZIP code" instead of "zip code"?
4. What is a style?
5. What style is applied to all text in a new document by default?
6. Explain the relationship between a document's theme and styles.

# Session 2.2 Visual Overview:

Use an easy-to-read font, such as the default Calibri, set to 12 point.

An MLA-style research paper does not require a separate title page; instead, type your name, your instructor's name, the course number, and the date in the upper-left corner of the first page.

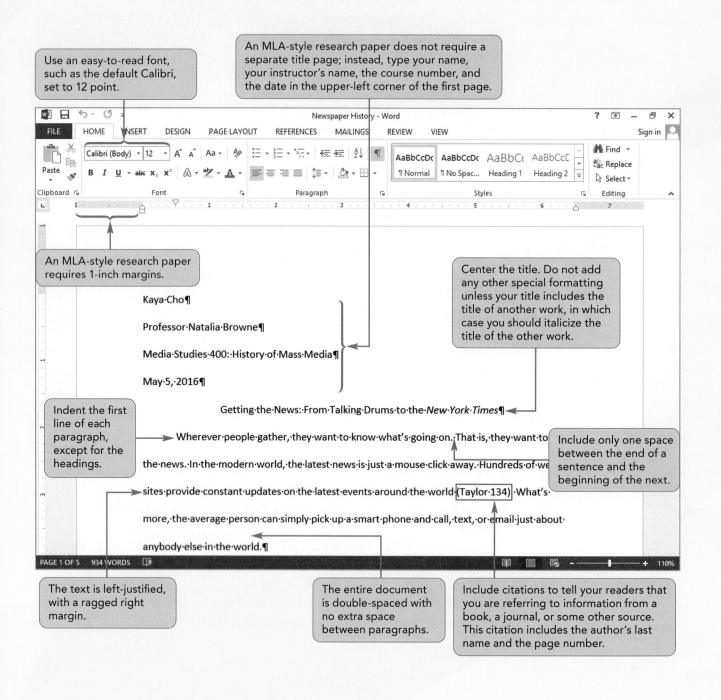

An MLA-style research paper requires 1-inch margins.

Kaya·Cho¶

Professor·Natalia·Browne¶

Media·Studies·400:·History·of·Mass·Media¶

May·5,·2016¶

Center the title. Do not add any other special formatting unless your title includes the title of another work, in which case you should italicize the title of the other work.

Getting·the·News:·From·Talking·Drums·to·the *New·York·Times*¶

Indent the first line of each paragraph, except for the headings.

Wherever·people·gather,·they·want·to·know·what's·going·on.·That·is,·they·want·to

the·news.·In·the·modern·world,·the·latest·news·is·just·a·mouse·click·away.·Hundreds·of·we

sites·provide·constant·updates·on·the·latest·events·around·the·world.·(Taylor·134)··What's

more,·the·average·person·can·simply·pick·up·a·smart·phone·and·call,·text,·or·email·just·about·

anybody·else·in·the·world.¶

Include only one space between the end of a sentence and the beginning of the next.

Newspaper History - Word

FILE    HOME    INSERT    DESIGN    PAGE LAYOUT    REFERENCES    MAILINGS    REVIEW    VIEW    Sign in

Calibri (Body)  12

B  I  U  abe  x₂  x²

¶ Normal    ¶ No Spac...    Heading 1    Heading 2

Find
Replace
Select

Clipboard    Font    Paragraph    Styles    Editing

PAGE 1 OF 5    934 WORDS    110%

The text is left-justified, with a ragged right margin.

The entire document is double-spaced with no extra space between paragraphs.

Include citations to tell your readers that you are referring to information from a book, a journal, or some other source. This citation includes the author's last name and the page number.

# MLA Formatting Guidelines

The REFERENCES tab includes options that help you create a research paper.

In the Style box, specify the style of research paper you are creating. For college research papers, the MLA style is commonly used.

After you create all the citations, click the Bibliography button to create a list of all the sources mentioned in your citations. This list is known as a **bibliography** or, in the MLA style, a **works cited list**.

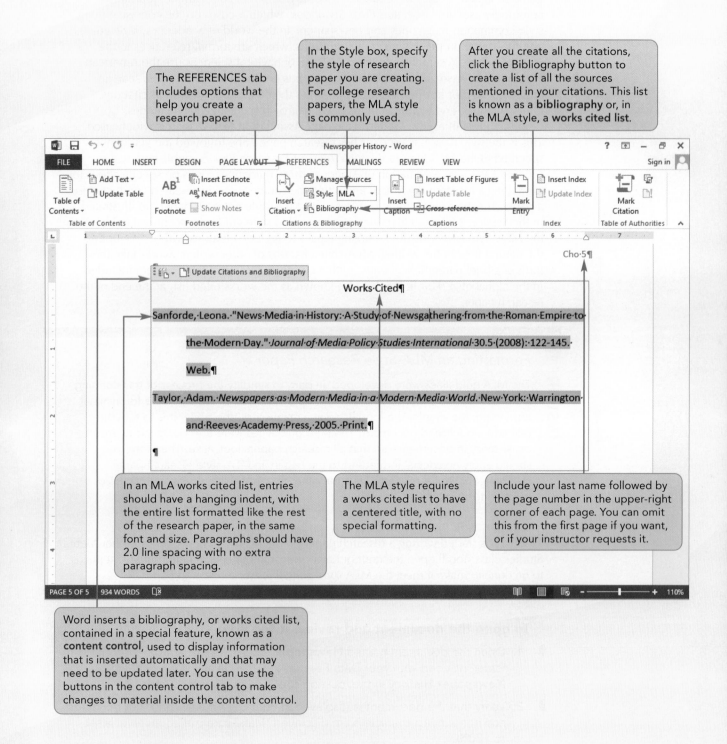

In an MLA works cited list, entries should have a hanging indent, with the entire list formatted like the rest of the research paper, in the same font and size. Paragraphs should have 2.0 line spacing with no extra paragraph spacing.

The MLA style requires a works cited list to have a centered title, with no special formatting.

Include your last name followed by the page number in the upper-right corner of each page. You can omit this from the first page if you want, or if your instructor requests it.

Word inserts a bibliography, or works cited list, contained in a special feature, known as a **content control**, used to display information that is inserted automatically and that may need to be updated later. You can use the buttons in the content control tab to make changes to material inside the content control.

# Reviewing the MLA Style

A **style guide** is a set of rules that describe the preferred format and style for a certain type of writing. People in different fields use different style guides, with each style guide designed to suit the needs of a specific discipline. For example, journalists commonly use the *Associated Press Stylebook*, which focuses on the concise writing style common in magazines and newspapers. In the world of academics, style guides emphasize the proper way to create **citations**, which are formal references to the work of others. Researchers in the social and behavioral sciences use the **American Psychological Association (APA) style**, which is designed to help readers scan an article quickly for key points and emphasizes the date of publication in citations. Other scientific and technical fields have their own specialized style guides.

In the humanities, the **Modern Language Association (MLA) style** is widely used. This is the style Kaya has used for her research paper. She followed the guidelines specified in the *MLA Handbook for Writers of Research Papers*, published by the Modern Language Association of America. These guidelines focus on specifications for formatting a research document and citing the sources used in research conducted for a paper. The major formatting features of an MLA-style research paper are illustrated in the Session 2.2 Visual Overview. Compared to style guides for technical fields, the MLA style is very flexible, making it easy to include citations without disrupting the natural flow of the writing. MLA-style citations of other writers' works take the form of a brief parenthetical entry, with a complete reference to each item included in the alphabetized bibliography, also known as the works cited list, at the end of the research paper.

**INSIGHT**

## Formatting an MLA-Style Research Paper

The MLA guidelines were developed, in part, to simplify the process of transforming a manuscript into a journal article or a chapter of a book. The style calls for minimal formatting; the simpler the formatting in a manuscript, the easier it is to turn the text into a published document. The MLA guidelines were also designed to ensure consistency in documents, so that all research papers look alike. Therefore, you should apply no special formatting to the text in an MLA-style research paper. Headings should be formatted like the other text in the document, with no bold or heading styles.

Kaya has started writing a research paper on the history of newspapers for her Media Studies class. You'll open the draft of Kaya's research paper and determine what needs to be done to make it meet the MLA style guidelines for a research paper.

### To open the document and review it for MLA style:

1. Open the document named **Newspaper** located in the Word2 ▸ Tutorial folder included with your Data Files, and then save the document as **Newspaper History** in the location specified by your instructor.

2. Verify that the document is displayed in Print Layout view, and that the rulers and nonprinting characters are displayed. Make sure the Zoom level is set to **120%**.

**3.** Review the document to familiarize yourself with its structure. First, notice the parts of the document that already match the MLA style. Kaya included a block of information in the upper-left corner of the first page, giving her name, her instructor's name, the course name, and the date. The title at the top of the first page also meets the MLA guidelines in that it is centered and does not have any special formatting except for "*New York Times*," which is italicized because it is the name of a newspaper. The headings ("Early News Media," "Merchant Newsletters," "Modern American Newspapers," and "Looking to the Future") have no special formatting; but unlike the title, they are left-aligned. Finally, the body text is left-aligned with a ragged right margin, and the entire document is formatted in the same font, Calibri, which is easy to read.

What needs to be changed in order to make Kaya's paper consistent with the MLA style? Currently, the entire document is formatted using the default settings, which are the Normal style for the Office theme. To transform the document into an MLA-style research paper, you need to complete the checklist shown in Figure 2-22.

**Figure 2-22**    **Checklist for formatting a default Word document to match the MLA style**

✓ Double-space the entire document.

✓ Remove paragraph spacing from the entire document.

✓ Increase the font size for the entire document to 12 points.

✓ Indent the first line of each body paragraph .5 inch from the left margin.

✓ Add the page number (preceded by your last name) in the upper-right corner of each page. If you prefer, you can omit this from the first page.

© 2014 Cengage Learning

You'll take care of the first three items in the checklist now.

**To begin applying MLA formatting to the document:**

**1.** Press the **Ctrl+A** keys to select the entire document.

**2.** Make sure the HOME tab is selected on the ribbon.

**3.** In the Paragraph group, click the **Line and Paragraph Spacing** button, and then click **2.0**.

**4.** Click the **Line and Spacing** button again, and then click **Remove Space After Paragraph**. The entire document is now double-spaced, with no paragraph spacing, and the entire document is still selected.

**5.** In the Font group, click the **Font Size** arrow, and then click **12**. The entire document is formatted in 12-point font.

**6.** Click anywhere in the document to deselect the text.

**7.** In the first paragraph of the document, replace Kaya's name with your first and last name, and then save the document.

Now you need to indent the first line of each body paragraph.

# Indenting a Paragraph

Word offers a number of options for indenting a paragraph. You can move an entire paragraph to the right, or you can create specialized indents, such as a **hanging indent**, where all lines except the first line of the paragraph are indented from the left margin. As you saw in the Session 2.2 Visual Overview, all the body paragraphs (that is, all the paragraphs except the information in the upper-left corner of the first page, the title, and the headings) have a first-line indent in MLA research papers. Figure 2-23 shows some examples of other common paragraph indents.

| Figure 2-23 | Common paragraph indents |
| --- | --- |

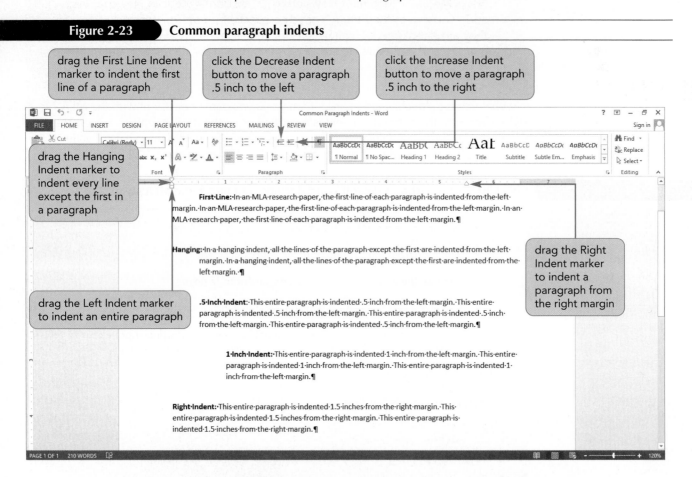

To quickly indent an entire paragraph .5 inch from the left, position the insertion point in the paragraph you want to indent and then click the Increase Indent button in the Paragraph group on the HOME tab. You can continue to indent the paragraph in increments of .5 inch by repeatedly clicking the Increase Indent button. To move an indented paragraph back to the left .5 inch, click the Decrease Indent button.

To create first line, hanging, or right indents, you can use the indent markers on the ruler. First, click in the paragraph you want to indent, or select multiple paragraphs. Then drag the appropriate indent marker to the left or right on the horizontal ruler. The indent markers are small and can be hard to see. As shown in Figure 2-23, the **First Line Indent marker** looks like the top half of an hourglass; the **Hanging Indent marker** looks like the bottom half. The rectangle below the Hanging Indent marker is the **Left Indent marker**. The **Right Indent Marker** looks just like the Hanging Indent marker except that it is located on the far-right side of the horizontal ruler.

Note that when you indent an entire paragraph using the Increase Indent button, the three indent markers, shown stacked on top of one another in Figure 2-23, move as a unit along with the paragraphs you are indenting.

In Kaya's paper, you will indent the first lines of the body paragraphs .5 inch from the left margin, as specified by the MLA style.

**To indent the first line of each paragraph:**

1. On the first page of the document, just below the title, click anywhere in the first main paragraph, which begins "Wherever people gather...."

2. On the horizontal ruler, position the mouse pointer over the First Line Indent marker ⬇. When you see the ScreenTip that reads "First Line Indent," you know the mouse is positioned correctly.

3. Press and hold the mouse button as you drag the **First Line Indent** marker ⬇ to the right, to the .5-inch mark on the horizontal ruler. As you drag, a vertical guide line appears over the document, and the first line of the paragraph moves right. See Figure 2-24.

| Figure 2-24 | Dragging the First Line Indent marker |

First Line Indent marker

.5-inch mark

as you drag the indent marker, a guide line appears and the first line of the paragraph moves right

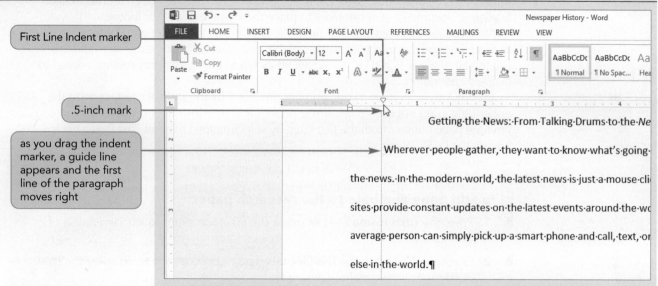

**TIP**

You can also click in the paragraph you want to indent, or select multiple paragraphs. Click the Dialog Box Launcher in the Paragraph group, and then adjust the Indentation settings.

4. When the First Line Indent marker ⬇ is positioned at the .5-inch mark on the ruler, release the mouse button. The first line of the paragraph containing the insertion point indents .5 inch and the vertical guide line disappears.

5. Scroll down, if necessary, click anywhere in the next paragraph in the document, which begins "These days, it's not hard to know...," and then drag the **First Line Indent** marker ⬇ to the right, to the .5-inch mark on the horizontal ruler. As you move the indent marker, you can use the vertical guide line to ensure that you match the first line indent of the preceding paragraph.

   You could continue to drag the indent marker to indent the first line of the remaining body paragraphs, but it's faster to use the Repeat button on the Quick Access Toolbar.

6. Scroll down and click in the paragraph below the heading "Early News Media," and then on the Quick Access Toolbar, click the **Repeat** button ↻.

7. Click in the next paragraph, at the top of page 2, which begins "Early news media took many forms," and then click the **Repeat** button ↻.

8. Continue using the **Repeat** button ↻ to indent the first line of all of the remaining body paragraphs. Take care not to indent the headings, which in this document are formatted just like the body text.

> **9.** Scroll to the top of the document, verify that you have correctly indented the first line of each body paragraph, and then save the document.

Next, you need to insert page numbers.

# Inserting and Modifying Page Numbers

When you insert page numbers in a document, you don't have to type a page number on each page. Instead, you insert a **page number field**, which is an instruction that tells Word to insert a page number on each page, no matter how many pages you eventually add to the document. Word inserts page number fields above the top margin, in the blank area known as the **header**, or below the bottom margin, in the area known as the **footer**. You can also insert page numbers in the side margins, although for business or academic documents, it's customary to place them in the header or footer.

After you insert a page number field, Word switches to Header and Footer view. In this view, you can add your name or other text next to the page number field, or use the HEADER & FOOTER TOOLS DESIGN tab to change various settings related to headers and footers.

The MLA style requires a page number preceded by the student's last name in the upper-right corner of each page. If you prefer (or if your instructor requests it), you can omit the page number from the first page by selecting the Different First Page check box on the DESIGN tab.

**To add page numbers to the research paper:**

> **1.** Press the **Ctrl+Home** keys to move the insertion point to the beginning of the document.

> **2.** On the ribbon, click the **INSERT** tab. The ribbon changes to display the Insert options, including options for inserting page numbers.

**TIP**

To remove page numbers from a document, click the Remove Page Numbers command on the Page Number menu.

> **3.** In the Header & Footer group, click the **Page Number** button to open the Page Number menu. Here you can choose where you want to position the page numbers in your document—at the top of the page, at the bottom of the page, in the side margins, or at the current location of the insertion point.

> **4.** Point to **Top of Page**. A gallery of page number styles opens. You can scroll the list to review the many styles of page numbers. Because the MLA style calls for a simple page number in the upper-right corner, you will use the Plain Number 3 style. See Figure 2-25.

**Figure 2-25**    Gallery of page number styles

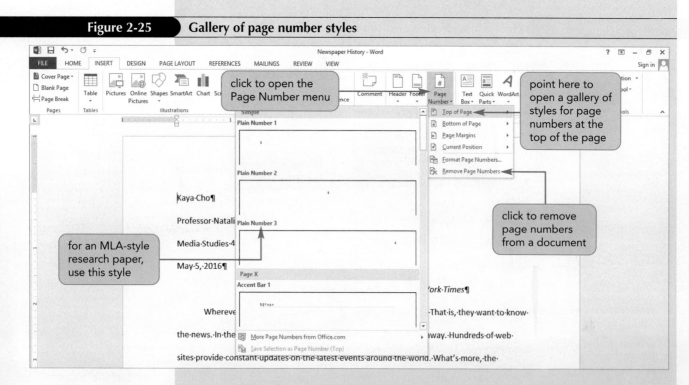

5. In the gallery, click the **Plain Number 3** style. The Word window switches to Header and Footer view, with the page number for the first page in the upper-right corner. The page number has a gray background, indicating that it is actually a page number field and not simply a number that you typed.

   The HEADER & FOOTER TOOLS DESIGN tab is displayed on the ribbon, giving you access to a variety of formatting options. The insertion point blinks to the left of the page number field, ready for you to add text to the header if you wish. Note that in Header and Footer view, you can only type in the header or footer areas. The text in the main document area is a lighter shade of gray, indicating that it cannot be edited in this view.

6. Type your last name, and then press the **spacebar**. If you see a wavy red line below your last name, right-click your name, and then click **Ignore** on the Shortcut menu. See Figure 2-26.

**Figure 2-26** **Last name inserted next to the page number field**

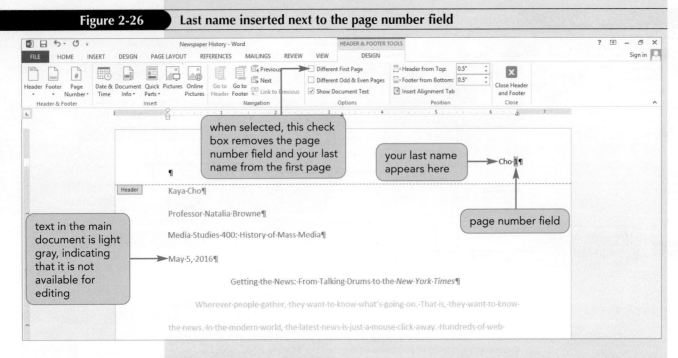

> **7.** Scroll down and observe the page number (with your last name) at the top of pages 2, 3, and 4. As you can see, whatever you insert in the header on one page appears on every page of the document by default.

> **8.** Press the **Ctrl+Home** keys to return to the header on the first page.

> **9.** On the HEADER & FOOTER TOOLS DESIGN tab, in the Options group, click the **Different First Page** check box to insert a check. The page number field and your last name are removed from the first page header. The insertion point blinks at the header's left margin in case you want to insert something else for the first page header. In this case, you don't.

> **10.** In the Close group, click the **Close Header and Footer** button. You return to Print Layout view, and the HEADER & FOOTER TOOLS DESIGN tab is no longer displayed on the ribbon.

> **11.** Scroll down to review your last name and the page number in the headers for pages 2, 3, and 4. In Print Layout view, the text in the header is light gray, indicating that it is not currently available for editing.

**TIP**

After you insert page numbers, you can reopen Header and Footer view by double-clicking a page number in Print Layout view.

You have finished all the tasks related to formatting the MLA-style research paper. Now Kaya wants your help with creating the essential parts of any research paper—the citations and the bibliography.

# Creating Citations and a Bibliography

A bibliography (or, as it is called in the MLA style, the works cited list) is an alphabetical list of all the books, magazine articles, websites, movies, and other works referred to in a research paper. The items listed in a bibliography are known as **sources**. The entry for each source includes information such as the author, the title of the work, the publication date, and the publisher.

Within the research paper itself, you include a parenthetical reference, or citation, every time you quote or refer to a source. Every source included in your citations then has a corresponding entry in the works cited list. A citation should include enough information to identify the quote or referenced material so the reader can easily locate the source in the accompanying works cited list. The exact form for a citation varies depending on the style guide you are using and the type of material you are referencing.

Some style guides are very rigid about the form and location of citations, but the MLA style offers quite a bit of flexibility. Typically, though, you insert an MLA citation at the end of a sentence in which you quote or refer to material from a source. For books or journals, the citation itself usually includes the author's last name and a page number. However, if the sentence containing the citation already includes the author's name, you only need to include the page number in the citation. Figure 2-27 provides some sample MLA citations for books and journals. For detailed guidelines, you can consult the *MLA Handbook for Writers of Research Papers, Seventh Edition*, which includes many examples.

**Figure 2-27**    **MLA guidelines for citing a book or journal**

| Citation Rule | Example |
|---|---|
| If the sentence includes the author's name, the citation should only include the page number. | Peterson compares the opening scene of the movie to a scene from Shakespeare (188). |
| If the sentence does not include the author's name, the citation should include the author's name and the page number. | The opening scene of the movie has been compared to a scene from Shakespeare (Peterson 188). |

© 2014 Cengage Learning

Word greatly simplifies the process of creating citations and a bibliography. You specify the style you want to use, and then Word takes care of setting up the citation and the works cited list appropriately. Every time you create a citation for a new source, Word prompts you to enter the information needed to create the corresponding entry in the works cited list. If you don't have all of your source information available, Word also allows you to insert a temporary, placeholder citation, which you can replace later with a complete citation. When you are finished creating your citations, Word generates the bibliography automatically. Note that placeholder citations are not included in the bibliography.

PROSKILLS

*Written Communication: Acknowledging Your Sources*

A research paper is a means for you to explore the available information about a subject and then present this information, along with your own understanding of the subject, in an organized and interesting way. Acknowledging all the sources of the information presented in your research paper is essential. If you fail to do this, you might be subject to charges of plagiarism, or trying to pass off someone else's thoughts as your own. Plagiarism is an extremely serious accusation for which you could suffer academic consequences ranging from failing an assignment to being expelled from school.

To ensure that you don't forget to cite a source, you should be careful about creating citations in your document as you type. It's very easy to forget to go back and cite all your sources correctly after you've finished typing a research paper. Failing to cite a source could lead to accusations of plagiarism and all the consequences that entails. If you don't have the complete information about a source, you should at least insert a placeholder citation. But take care to go back later and substitute complete citations for any placeholders.

## Creating Citations

Before you create citations, you need to select the style you want to use, which in the case of Kaya's paper is the MLA style. Then, to insert a citation, you click the Insert Citation button in the Citations & Bibliography group on the REFERENCES tab. If you are citing a source for the first time, Word prompts you to enter all the information required for the source's entry in the bibliography or works cited list. If you are citing an existing source, you simply select the source from the Insert Citation menu.

By default, an MLA citation includes only the author's name in parentheses. However, you can use the Edit Citation dialog box to add a page number. You can also use the Edit Citation dialog box to remove, or suppress, the author's name, so only the page number appears in the citation. However, in an MLA citation, Word will replace the suppressed author name with the title of the source, so you need to suppress the title as well, by selecting the Title check box in the Edit Citation dialog box.

REFERENCE

## Creating Citations

- On the ribbon, click the REFERENCES tab. In the Citations & Bibliography group, click the Style button arrow, and then select the style you want.
- Click in the document where you want to insert the citation. Typically, a citation goes at the end of a sentence, before the ending punctuation.
- To add a citation for a new source, click the Insert Citation button in the Citations & Bibliography group, click Add New Source, enter information in the Create Source dialog box, and then click the OK button.
- To add a citation for an existing source, click the Insert Citation button, and then click the source.
- To add a placeholder citation, click the Insert Citation button, click Add New Placeholder, and then, in the content control, type placeholder text, such as the author's last name, that will serve as a reminder about which source you need to cite. Note that a placeholder citation cannot contain any spaces.
- To add a page number to a citation, click the citation in the document, click the Citation Options button, click Edit Citation, type the page number, and then click the OK button.
- To display only the page number in a citation, click the citation in the document, click the Citation Options button, and then click Edit Citation. In the Edit Citation dialog box, select the Author and Title check boxes to suppress this information, and then click the OK button.

So far, Kaya has referenced information from two different sources in her research paper. You'll select a style and then begin adding the appropriate citations.

### To select a style for the citation and bibliography:

1. On the ribbon, click the **REFERENCES** tab. The ribbon changes to display references options.

2. In the Citations & Bibliography group, click the **Style button arrow**, and then click **MLA Seventh Edition** if it is not already selected.

3. Press the **Ctrl+F** keys to open the Navigation pane.

4. Use the Navigation pane to find the phrase "As at least one historian has observed," which appears on page 1, and then click in the document at the end of that sentence (between the end of the word "medium" and the closing period).

5. Close the Navigation pane, and then click the **REFERENCES** tab on the ribbon, if necessary. You need to add a citation that informs the reader that historian Adam Taylor made the observation described in the sentence. See Figure 2-28.

**Figure 2-28** MLA style selected and insertion point positioned for new citation

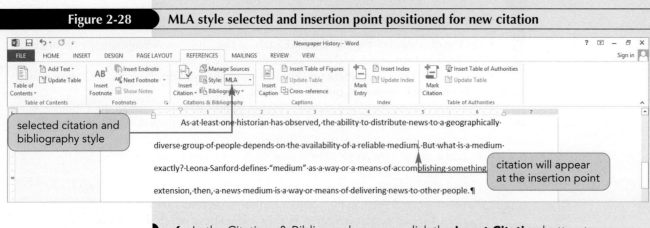

6. In the Citations & Bibliography group, click the **Insert Citation** button to open the menu. At this point, you could click Add New Placeholder on the menu to insert a temporary, placeholder citation. However, because you have all the necessary source information, you can go ahead and create a complete citation.

7. On the menu, click **Add New Source**. The Create Source dialog box opens, ready for you to add the information required to create a bibliography entry for Adam Taylor's book.

8. If necessary, click the **Type of Source** arrow, scroll up or down in the list, and then click **Book**.

9. In the Author box, type **Adam Taylor**.

10. Click in the **Title** box, and then type **Newspapers as Modern Media in a Modern Media World**.

11. Click in the **Year** box, and then type **2005**. This is the year the book was published. Next, you need to enter the name and location of the publisher.

12. Click the **City** box, type **New York**, click the **Publisher** box, and then type **Warrington and Reeves Academy Press**.

Finally, you need to indicate the medium used to publish the book. In this case, Kaya used a printed copy, so the medium is "Print." For books or journals published online, the correct medium would be "Web."

13. Click the **Medium** box, and then type **Print**. See Figure 2-29.

> **TIP**
> When entering information in a dialog box, you can press the Tab key to move the insertion point from one box to another.

**Figure 2-29** Create Source dialog box with information for the first source

Create Source

| | |
|---|---|
| Type of Source | Book |

Bibliography Fields for MLA

| | |
|---|---|
| Author | Adam Taylor [Edit] |
| | ☐ Corporate Author |
| Title | Newspapers as Modern Media in a Modern Media World |
| Year | 2005 |
| City | New York |
| Publisher | Warrington and Reeves Academy Press |
| Medium | Print |

☐ Show All Bibliography Fields

Tag name     Example: Document

Ada05          [OK]  [Cancel]

**14.** Click the **OK** button. Word inserts the parenthetical "(Taylor)" at the end of the sentence in the document.

Although the citation looks like ordinary text, it is actually contained inside a content control, a special feature used to display information that is inserted automatically and that may need to be updated later. You can only see the content control itself when it is selected. When it is unselected, you simply see the citation. In the next set of steps, you will select the content control, and then edit the citation to add a page number.

### To edit the citation:

**TIP**

To delete a citation, click the citation to display the content control, click the tab on the left side of the content control, and then press the Delete key.

**1.** In the document, click the citation **(Taylor)**. The citation appears in a content control, which is a box with a tab on the left and an arrow button on the right. The arrow button is called the Citation Options button.

**2.** Click the **Citation Options** button ⬚. A menu of options related to editing a citation opens, as shown in Figure 2-30. To edit the information about the source, you click Edit Source. To change the information that is displayed in the citation itself, you use the Edit Citation option.

**Figure 2-30**     **Citation Options menu**

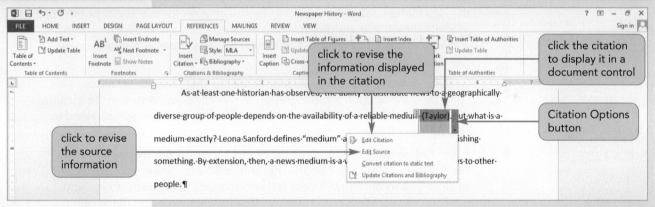

click to revise the information displayed in the citation

click the citation to display it in a document control

click to revise the source information

Citation Options button

**3.** On the Citation Options menu, click **Edit Citation**. The Edit Citation dialog box opens, as shown in Figure 2-31.

**Figure 2-31**     **Edit Citation dialog box**

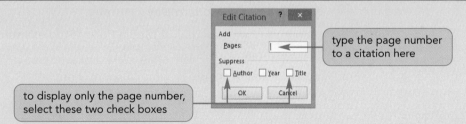

type the page number to a citation here

to display only the page number, select these two check boxes

To add a page number for the citation, you type the page number in the Pages box. If you want to display only the page number in the citation (which would be necessary if you already mentioned the author's name in the same sentence in the text), then you would also select the Author and Title check boxes in this dialog box to suppress this information.

**4.** Type **45** to insert the page number in the Pages box, click the **OK** button to close the dialog box, and then click anywhere in the document outside the citation content control. The revised citation now reads "(Taylor 45)."

Next, you will add two more citations, both for the same journal article.

### To insert two more citations:

**1.** Click at the end of the second-to-last sentence of the current paragraph (which begins "Leona Sanford defines..."), between the word "something" and the period. This sentence mentions historian Leona Sanford; you need to add a citation to one of her journal articles.

**2.** In the Citations & Bibliography group, click the **Insert Citation** button to open the Insert Citation menu. Notice that Adam Taylor's book is now listed as a source on this menu. You could click Taylor's book on the menu to add a citation to it, but right now you need to add a new source.

**3.** Click **Add New Source** to open the Create Source dialog box, click the **Type of Source** arrow, and then click **Journal Article**.

The Create Source dialog box displays the boxes, or fields, appropriate for a journal article. The information required to cite a journal article differs from the information you entered earlier for the citation for the Taylor book. For journal articles, you are prompted to enter the page numbers for the entire article. If you want to display a particular page number in the citation, you can add it later.

By default, Word displays boxes, or fields, for the information most commonly included in a bibliography. In this case, you also want to include the volume and issue numbers for Leona Sanford's article, so you need to display more fields.

**4.** In the Create Source dialog box, click the **Show All Bibliography Fields** check box to select this option. The Create Source dialog box expands to allow you to enter more detailed information. Red asterisks highlight the fields that are recommended, but these recommended fields don't necessarily apply to every source.

**5.** Enter the following information, scrolling down to display the necessary boxes:

Author: **Leona Sanford**

Title: **News Media in History: A Study of Newsgathering from the Roman Empire to the Modern Day**

Journal Name: **Journal of Media Policy Studies International**

Year: **2008**

Pages: **122–145**

Volume: **30**

Issue: **5**

Medium: **Web**

When you are finished, your Create Source dialog box should look like the one shown in Figure 2-32.

**Figure 2-32** | Create Source dialog box with information for the journal article

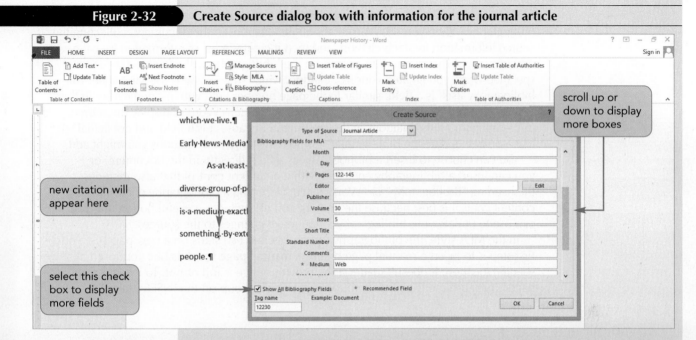

6. Click the **OK** button. The Create Source dialog box closes, and the citation "(Sanford)" is inserted in the text. Because the sentence containing the citation already includes the author's name, you will edit the citation to include the page number and suppress the author's name.

7. Click the **(Sanford)** citation to display the content control, click the **Citation Options** button , and then click **Edit Citation** to open the Edit Citation dialog box.

8. In the Pages box, type **142**, and then click the **Author** and **Title** check boxes to select them. You need to suppress both the author's name and the title because otherwise Word will replace the suppressed author name with the title. When using the MLA style, you don't ever have to suppress the year because the year is never included as part of an MLA citation. When working in other styles, however, you might need to suppress the year.

9. Click the **OK** button to close the Edit Citation dialog box, and then click anywhere outside the content control to deselect it. The end of the sentence now reads "…accomplishing something (142)."

10. Use the Navigation pane to find the sentence that begins "Throughout history…" on the second page. Click at the end of the sentence, to the left of the period after "news," and then close the Navigation pane.

11. On the REFERENCES tab, in the Citations & Bibliography group, click the **Insert Citation** button, and then click the **Sanford, Leona** source at the top of the menu. You want the citation to refer to the entire article instead of just one page, so you will not edit the citation to add a specific page number.

12. Save the document.

You have entered the source information for two sources.

## Generating a Bibliography

Once you have created a citation for a source in a document, you can generate a bibliography. When you do, Word scans all the citations in the document, collecting the source information for each citation, and then it creates a list of information for each unique source. The format of the entries in the bibliography will reflect the style you specified when you created your first citation, which in this case is the MLA style. The bibliography itself is a **field**, similar to the page number field you inserted earlier in this session. In other words, it is really an instruction that tells Word to display the source information for all the citations in the document. Because it is a field and not actual text, you can update the bibliography later to reflect any new citations you might add.

You can choose to insert a bibliography as a field directly in the document, or you can insert a bibliography enclosed within a content control that also includes the heading "Bibliography" or "Works Cited." Inserting a bibliography enclosed in a content control is best because the content control includes a useful button that you can use to update your bibliography if you make changes to the sources.

In the MLA style, the bibliography (or works cited list) starts on a new page. So your first step is to insert a manual page break. A **manual page break** is one you insert at a specific location; it doesn't matter if the previous page is full or not. To insert a manual page break, use the Page Break button in the Pages group on the INSERT tab.

### To insert a manual page break:

1. Press the **Ctrl+End** keys to move the insertion point to the end of the document.

2. On the ribbon, click the **INSERT** tab.

**TIP**

Use the Blank Page button to insert a new, blank page in the middle of a document.

3. In the Pages group, click the **Page Break** button. Word inserts a new, blank page at the end of the document, with the insertion point blinking at the top. Note that you could also use the Ctrl+Enter keyboard shortcut to insert a manual page break.

4. Scroll up to see the dotted line with the words "Page Break" at the bottom of the text on page 4. See Figure 2-33.

**Figure 2-33**   **Manual page break inserted into the document**

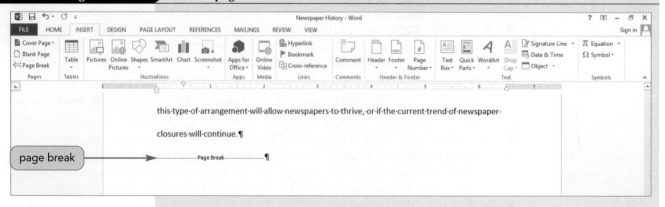

Now you can insert the bibliography on the new page 5.

### To insert the bibliography:

1. Scroll down so you can see the insertion point at the top of page 5.

2. On the ribbon, click the **REFERENCES** tab.

3. In the Citations & Bibliography group, click the **Bibliography** button. The Bibliography menu opens, displaying three styles with preformatted headings—"Bibliography," "References," and "Works Cited." The Insert Bibliography command at the bottom inserts a bibliography without a preformatted heading. See Figure 2-34.

| **Figure 2-34** | **Bibliography menu** |

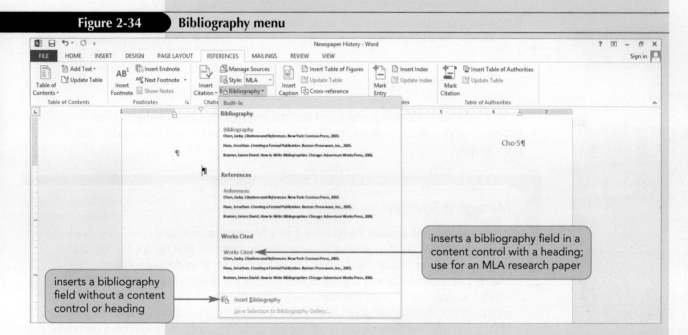

inserts a bibliography field without a content control or heading

inserts a bibliography field in a content control with a heading; use for an MLA research paper

4. Click **Works Cited**. Word inserts the bibliography, with two entries, below the "Works Cited" heading.

   The bibliography text is formatted in Calibri, the default font for the Office theme. The "Works Cited" heading is formatted with the Heading 1 style. To see the content control that contains the bibliography, you need to select it.

5. Click anywhere in the bibliography. Inside the content control, the bibliography is highlighted in gray, indicating that it is a field and not regular text. The content control containing the bibliography is also now visible in the form of a rectangular border and a tab with two buttons. See Figure 2-35.

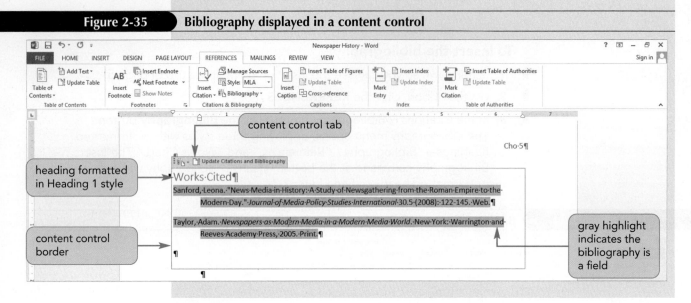

**Figure 2-35**   Bibliography displayed in a content control

As Kaya looks over the works cited list, she realizes that she misspelled the last name of one of the authors. You'll correct the error now, and then update the bibliography.

## INSIGHT

### Managing Sources

When you create a source, Word adds it to a Master List of sources, which is available to any document created using the same user account on that computer. Word also adds each new source to the Current List of sources for that document. Both the Master List and the Current List are accessible via the Source Manager dialog box, which you open by clicking the Manage Sources button in the Citations & Bibliography group on the REFERENCES tab. Using this dialog box, you can copy sources from the Master List into the Current List, and vice versa. As you begin to focus on a particular academic field and turn repeatedly to important works in your chosen field, you'll find this ability to reuse sources very helpful.

## Modifying an Existing Source

To modify information about a source, you click a citation to that source in the document, click the Citation Options button on the content control, and then click Edit Source. After you are finished editing the source, Word prompts you to update the master list and the source information in the current document. In almost all cases, you should click Yes to ensure that the source information is correct in all the places it is stored on your computer.

### To edit a source in the research paper:

1. Click in the blank paragraph below the bibliography content control to deselect the bibliography.

2. Scroll up to display the last paragraph on page 2, and then click the **(Sanford)** citation you entered earlier in the first line of the paragraph. The content control appears around the citation.

3. Click the **Citation Options** button ⫿, and then click **Edit Source**. The Edit Source dialog box opens. Note that Word displays the author's last name first in the Author box, just as it would appear in a bibliography.

4. Click the **Author** box, and then add an "e" to the last name "Sanford" to change it to "Sanforde."

5. Click the **OK** button. A message dialog box opens, asking if you want to update the master source list and the current document.

6. Click the **Yes** button, and then click anywhere on the second page to deselect the citation content control. The revised author name in the citation now reads "Sanforde."

7. Scroll up to the last paragraph on page 1, locate "Sanford" in the last paragraph on the page, and then change "Sanford" to "Sanforde."

8. Save the document.

You've edited the document text and the citation to include the correct spelling of "Sanforde," but now you need to update the bibliography to correct the spelling.

## Updating and Finalizing a Bibliography

The bibliography does not automatically change to reflect edits you make to existing citations or to show new citations. To incorporate the latest information stored in the citations, you need to update the bibliography. To update a bibliography in a content control, click the bibliography, and then, in the content control tab, click Update Citations and Bibliography. To update a bibliography field that is not contained in a content control, right-click the bibliography, and then click Update Field on the shortcut menu.

**To update the bibliography:**

1. Scroll down to page 5 and click anywhere in the works cited list to display the content control.

2. In the content control tab, click **Update Citations and Bibliography**. The works cited list is updated, with "Sanford" changed to "Sanforde" in the first entry.

Kaya still has a fair amount of work to do on her research paper. After she finishes writing it and adding all the citations, she will update the bibliography again to include all her cited sources. At that point, you might think the bibliography would be finished. However, a few steps remain to ensure that the works cited list matches the MLA style. To finalize Kaya's works cited list to match the MLA style, you need to make the changes shown in Figure 2-36.

| Figure 2-36 | Steps for finalizing a bibliography to match MLA guidelines for a Works Cited list |

1. Format the "Works Cited" heading to match the formatting of the rest of the text in the document.

2. Center the "Works Cited" heading.

3. Double-space the entire works cited list, including the heading, and remove extra space after the paragraphs.

4. Change the font size for the entire works cited list to 12 points.

© 2014 Cengage Learning

**To format the bibliography as an MLA style works cited list:**

1. Click in the **Works Cited** heading, and then click the **HOME** tab on the ribbon.

2. In the Styles group, click the **Normal** style. The "Works Cited" heading is now formatted in Calibri body font like the rest of the document. The MLA style for a works cited list requires this heading to be centered.

3. In the Paragraph group, click the **Center** button.

4. Select the entire works cited list, including the heading. Change the font size to **12** points, change the line spacing to **2.0**, and then remove the paragraph spacing after each paragraph.

5. Click below the content control to deselect the works cited list, and then review your work. See Figure 2-37.

**Figure 2-37** | **MLA-style Works Cited list**

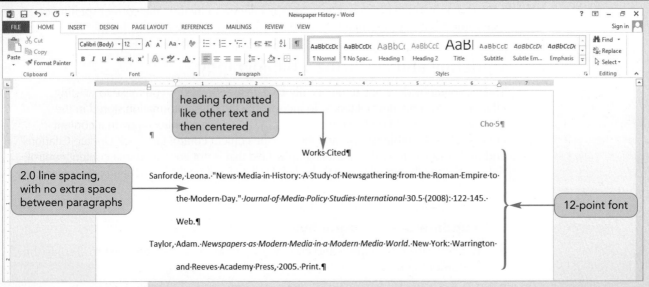

6. Save the document and close it.

Kaya's research paper now meets the MLA style guidelines.

### Session 2.2 Quick Check

**REVIEW**

1. List the five tasks you need to perform to make a default Word document match the MLA style.
2. How do you indent a paragraph one inch from the left margin using an option on the ribbon?
3. Explain how to remove a page number from the first page of a document.
4. What is a bibliography called according to the MLA style?
5. Explain how to create a citation for a new source.
6. Explain how to edit a citation to display only the page number.

ASSESS

## SAM Projects

Put your skills into practice with SAM Projects! SAM Projects for this tutorial can be found online. If you have a SAM account, go to www.cengage.com/sam2013 to download the most recent Project Instructions and Start Files.

PRACTICE

## Review Assignments

**Data Files needed for the Review Assignments: Broadcast.docx, Situation.docx**

Because the Media Studies document turned out so well, Kaya has been asked to help a student assistant in the Journalism department create a handout describing the classes required for a major in Broadcast Journalism. Kaya asks you to help her revise and format the document. She also asks you to create a document listing the prerequisites and core courses. Finally, as part of her Media Studies class, Kaya is working on a research paper on the history of situation comedy. She asks you to help her format the paper according to the MLA style, and to create some citations and a bibliography. She has inserted the uppercase word "CITATION" wherever she needs to insert a citation. Complete the following steps:

1. Open the file **Broadcast** located in the Word2 ▸ Review folder included with your Data Files, and then save the document as **Broadcast Journalism** in the location specified by your instructor.
2. Read the first comment, which provides an overview of the changes you will be making to the document in the following steps. Perform the task described in the second comment, and then delete both comments.
3. On page 2, in the second paragraph, revise the name of the first public speaking class so that only the first letter of each word is capitalized. Attach a comment to this paragraph that explains the change.
4. On page 2, move the "Senior Project" heading up to position it before the paragraph that begins "This project should incorporate…."
5. Replace the first instance of "journalism" with "media," being sure to match the case.
6. On page 1, format the list of four prerequisite classes as a bulleted list with square bullets. Do the same for the list of core courses, and then indent the three symposium names so they are formatted with an open circle bullet.
7. At the top of page 2, format the list of three public speaking classes as a numbered list, using the "1), 2), 3)" numbering style.
8. In the numbered list, move paragraph 3 ("Broadcast Journalism 220: Video Reporting") up to make it paragraph 2.
9. Format the title "Majoring in Broadcast Journalism" using the Title style. Format the following headings with the Heading 1 style: "Prerequisites," "Core Courses," "Electives," "Public Speaking," and "Senior Project."
10. Change the document theme to the Integral theme.
11. Display the Clipboard task pane. Copy the bulleted list of prerequisites to the Clipboard, and then copy the heading "Prerequisites" to the Clipboard. To ensure that you copy the heading formatting, be sure to select the paragraph mark after "Prerequisites" before you click the Copy button.
12. Open a new, blank document, and then save the document as **Prerequisite List** in the location specified by your instructor.
13. At the beginning of the document, paste the heading "Prerequisites," and then, from the Paste Options menu, apply the Keep Source Formatting option. Below the heading, paste the list of prerequisites, which begins with the text "Journalism 101…."

14. At the end of the document, insert a new paragraph, and then type **Prepared by:** followed by your first and last names.

15. Save the Prerequisite List document and close it.

16. In the Broadcast Journalism document, clear the contents of the Clipboard task pane, close the Clipboard task pane, save the document, and then close it.

17. Open the file **Situation** located in the Word2 ▸ Review folder included with your Data Files.

18. Save the document as **Situation Comedy** in the location specified by your instructor.

19. In the first paragraph, replace Kaya's name with your own.

20. Adjust the font size, line spacing, paragraph spacing, and paragraph indents to match the MLA style.

21. Insert your last name and a page number on every page except the first.

22. If necessary, select MLA Seventh Edition as the citations and bibliography style.

23. Use the Navigation pane to highlight all instances of the uppercase word "CITATION." Keep the Navigation pane open so you can continue to use it to find the locations where you need to insert citations in Steps 24–28.

24. Delete the first instance of "CITATION" and the space before it, and then create a new source with the following information:
    Type of Source: **Book**
    Author: **Cecile Webster**
    Title: **The Comedy of Situations: A History in Words and Pictures**
    Year: **2008**
    City: **Boston**
    Publisher: **Boston Valley Press**
    Medium: **Print**

25. Edit the citation to add **203** as the page number. Display only the page number in the citation.

26. Delete the second instance of "CITATION" and the space before it, and then create a new source with the following information:
    Type of Source: **Journal Article**
    Author: **Oliver Bernault**
    Title: **How Slapstick Conquered the World**
    Journal Name: **Pacific Film Quarterly: Criticism and Comment**
    Year: **2011**
    Pages: **68–91**
    Volume: **11**
    Issue: **2**
    Medium: **Web**

27. Edit the citation to add "80" as the page number.

28. Delete the third instance of "CITATION" and the space before it, and then insert a citation for the book by Cecile Webster.

29. At the end of the document, start a new page and insert a bibliography in a content control with the heading "Works Cited."

30. In the second source you created, add an "e" to change the last name "Bernault" to "Bernaulte," and then update the bibliography.

31. Finalize the bibliography to create an MLA-style Works Cited list.

32. Save the **Situation Comedy** document and close it.

33. Close any other open documents.

APPLY

## Case Problem 1

Data File needed for this Case Problem: Yoga.docx

***Green Willow Yoga Studio and Spa*** Karl Boccio, the manager of Green Willow Yoga Studio and Spa, created a flyer to inform clients of the studio's move to a new location. The flyer also lists classes for the summer session and explains the registration process. It's your job to format the flyer to make it look professional and easy to read. Karl included comments in the document explaining what he wants you to do. Complete the following steps:

1. Open the file **Yoga** located in the Word2 ▸ Case1 folder included with your Data Files, and then save the file as **Yoga Flyer** in the location specified by your instructor.
2. Format the document as directed in the comments. After you complete a task, delete the relevant comment. Respond "Yes" to the comment asking if twenty is the correct number of years. When you are finished with the formatting, the comment with the question and the comment with your reply should be the only remaining comments.
3. Move the third bulleted item (which begins "Yoga for Relaxation...") up to make it the first bulleted item in the list.
4. Change the theme to the Ion theme, and then attach a comment to the title listing the heading and body fonts applied by the Ion theme.
5. Save the document and then close it.

## Case Problem 2

Data File needed for this Case Problem: Hamlet.docx

***South Valley Community College*** Jaleel Reynolds is a student at South Valley Community College. He's working on a research paper about Shakespeare's tragic masterpiece, *Hamlet*. The research paper is only partly finished, with notes in brackets indicating the material Jaleel still plans to write. He also inserted the uppercase word "CITATION" wherever he needs to insert a citation. Jaleel asks you to help him format this early draft to match the MLA style. He also asks you to help him create some citations and a first attempt at a bibliography. He will update the bibliography later, after he finishes writing the research paper. Complete the following steps:

1. Open the file **Hamlet** located in the Word2 ▸ Case2 folder included with your Data Files, and then save the document as **Hamlet Paper** in the location specified by your instructor.
2. In the first paragraph, replace "Jaleel Reynolds" with your name, and then adjust the font size, line spacing, paragraph spacing, and paragraph indents to match the MLA style.
3. Insert your last name and a page number in the upper-right corner of every page except the first page in the document.
4. If necessary, select MLA Seventh Edition as the citations and bibliography style.
5. Use the Navigation pane to find three instances of the uppercase word "CITATION."
6. Delete the first instance of "CITATION" and the space before it, and then create a new source with the following information:
   Type of Source: **Book**
   Author: **Andre Kahn**
   Title: **Tragic Drama in a Tragic Age**
   Year: **2000**
   City: **Chicago**
   Publisher: **Houghton University Press**
   Medium: **Print**
7. Edit the citation to add **127** as the page number.

8. Delete the second instance of "CITATION" and the space before it, and then create a new source with the following information:

Type of Source: **Sound Recording**

Performer: **Avery Pohlman**

Title: **Live From New York's Golden Arch Theater**

Production Company: **Prescott**

Year: **1995**

Medium: **CD**

City: **New York**

9. Edit the citation to suppress the Author and the Year, so that it displays only the title.

10. Delete the third instance of "CITATION" and the space before it, and then insert a second reference to the book by Andre Kahn.

11. Edit the citation to add **35** as the page number.

12. At the end of the document, start a new page, and then insert a bibliography with the preformatted heading "Works Cited."

13. Edit the first source you created, changing the last name from "Kahn" to **Klann.**

14. Update the bibliography so it shows the revised name "Klann."

15. Finalize the bibliography so that it matches the MLA style.

16. Save the Hamlet Paper document and close it.

## Case Problem 3

**CREATE**

**Data Files needed for this Case Problem: Capital.docx, Sarah.docx**

*Sports Training*    Sarah Vang has more than a decade of experience as an athletic trainer in several different settings. After moving to a new city, she is looking for a job as a trainer in a hospital. She has asked you to edit and format her resume. As part of the application process, she will have to upload her resume to the hospitals' employee recruitment websites. Because these sites typically request a simple page design, Sarah plans to rely primarily on heading styles and bullets to organize her information. When the resume is complete, she wants you to remove any color applied by the heading styles. She also needs help formatting a document she created for a public health organization for which she volunteers. Complete the following steps:

1. Open the file **Sarah** located in the Word2 ▸ Case3 folder included with your Data Files, and then save the file as **Sarah Resume** in the location specified by your instructor.

2. Read the comment included in the document, and then perform the task it specifies.

3. Respond to the comment with the response **I think that's a good choice for the theme.**, and then mark Sarah's comment as done.

4. Replace all occurrences of "Mesacrest" with **Mesa Crest**.

5. Format the resume as shown in Figure 2-38. To ensure that the resume fits on one page, pay special attention to the paragraph spacing settings specified in Figure 2-38.

**Figure 2-38** **Formatting for Sarah Vang's resume**

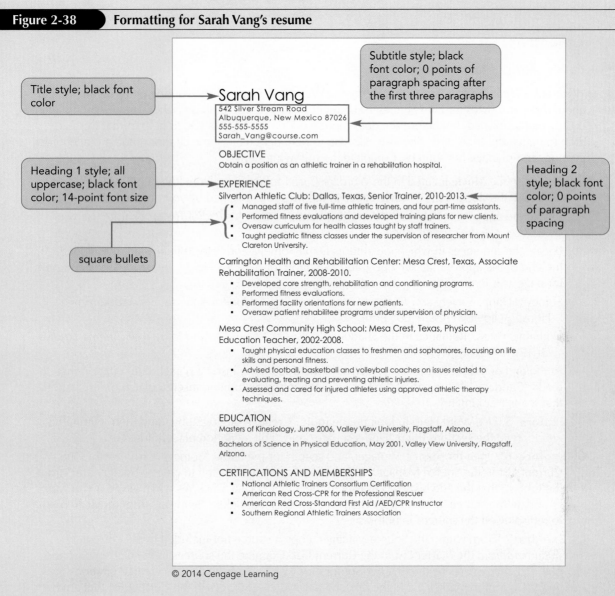

© 2014 Cengage Learning

6. In the email address, replace "Sarah_Vang" with your first and last names, separated by an underscore, and then save the document and close it.

7. Open the file **Capital** located in the Word2 ▸ Case4 folder included with your Data Files, and then save the file as **Capital Campaign** in the location specified by your instructor. Search for the text "Your Name", and then replace it with your first and last names.

8. Select the three paragraphs below your name, and then decrease the indent for the selected paragraphs so that they align at the left margin. Create a .5-inch hanging indent for the selected paragraphs instead.

9. Change the document theme to Ion, and then add a comment to the first word in the document that reads "I changed the theme to Ion."

10. Use the Advanced Find dialog box to search for bold formatting. Remove the bold formatting from the fourth bold element in the document, and then add a comment to that element that reads "I assumed bold here was a mistake, so I removed it."

11. Save and close the document.

CHALLENGE

## Case Problem 4

Data File needed for this Case Problem: Movie.docx

***Winona College***    Tristan Giroux is a student at Winona College. She's working on a research paper about disaster movies for Film Studies 105, taught by Professor Douglas Fischer. The research paper is only partly finished, but before she does more work on it, she asks you to help format this early draft to match the MLA style. She also asks you to help her create some citations, add a placeholder citation, and manage her sources. Complete the following steps:

1. Open the file **Movie** located in the Word2 ▸ Case4 folder included with your Data Files, and then save the document as **Movie Paper** in the location specified by your instructor.

2. Revise the paper to match the MLA style, seventh edition. Instead of Tristan's name, use your own. Also, use the current date.

3. Locate the sentences in which the authors Dana Someya and Peter Williams are mentioned. At the end of the appropriate sentence, add a citation for page 135 in the following book and one for page 152 in the following journal article:

   Someya, Dana. *Society and Disaster in the Silent Era: A Modern Analysis*. New York: Movie House Academy Press, 1997. Print.

   Williams, Peter. "Romance in the Shadow of Disaster." *New England Journal of Cinema Studies* (2012): 133–155. Web.

4. At the end of the second-to-last sentence in the document, insert a placeholder citation that reads "Candela." At the end of the last sentence in the document, insert a placeholder citation that reads "Goldman."

⊕ **Explore** 5. Use Word Help to look up the topic "Create a bibliography," and then, within that article, read the sections titled "Find a source" and "Edit a citation placeholder."

⊕ **Explore** 6. Open the Source Manager, and search for the name "Someya." From within the Current List in the Source Manager, edit the Dana Someya citation to delete "Society and" from the title, so that the title begins "Disaster in the Silent Era…." Click Yes when asked if you want to update the source in both lists. When you are finished, delete "Someya" from the Search box to redisplay all the sources in both lists.

⊕ **Explore** 7. From within the Source Manager, copy a source not included in the current document from the Master List to the Current List. Examine the sources in the Current List and note the checkmarks next to the two sources for which you have already created citations, and the question marks next to the placeholder sources. Sources in the Current list that are not actually cited in the text have no symbol next to them in the Current List. For example, if you copied a source from the Master List into your Current List, that source has no symbol next to it in the Current List.

8. Close the Source Manager, create a bibliography in the MLA style, and note which works appear in it.

⊕ **Explore** 9. Open the Source Manager, and then edit the Goldman placeholder source to include the following information about a journal article:

   Goldman, Simon. "Attack of the Killer Disaster Movie." *Cinema International Journal* (2009): 72–89. Web.

10. Update the bibliography.

⊕ **Explore** 11. Open Internet Explorer and use the Web to research the difference between a works cited list and a works consulted list. If necessary, open the Source Manager, and then delete any uncited sources from the Current List to ensure that your document contains a true works cited list, as specified by the MLA style, and not a works consulted list. (Tristan will create a full citation for the "Candela" placeholder later.)

12. Update the bibliography, finalize it so it matches the MLA style, save the document and close it.

TUTORIAL **3**

# Creating Tables and a Multipage Report

*Writing a Recommendation*

## OBJECTIVES

**Session 3.1**
- Review document headings in the Navigation pane
- Reorganize document text using the Navigation pane
- Collapse and expand body text in a document
- Create and edit a table
- Sort rows in a table
- Modify a table's structure
- Format a table

**Session 3.2**
- Set tab stops
- Turn on automatic hyphenation
- Create footnotes and endnotes
- Divide a document into sections
- Create a SmartArt graphic
- Create headers and footers
- Insert a cover page
- Change the document's theme
- Review a document in Read Mode

## Case | *Orchard Street Art Center*

Katherine Hua is the facilities director for Orchard Street Art Center, a nonprofit organization that provides performance, rehearsal, and classroom space for arts organizations in St. Louis, Missouri. The center's facilities include a 300-seat indoor theater, a 200-seat outdoor theater, public terraces and lobbies, five classrooms, 20 rehearsal rooms, and several offices. Katherine hopes to improve the wireless network that serves the center's staff and patrons through a process known as a wireless site survey. She has written a multiple-page report for the center's board of directors summarizing basic information about wireless site surveys. She has asked you to finish formatting the report. Katherine also needs your help with adding a table and a diagram to the end of the report.

In this tutorial, you'll use the Navigation pane to review the document headings and reorganize the document. You will also insert a table, modify it by changing the structure and formatting, set tab stops, create footnotes and endnotes, hyphenate the document, and insert a section break. In addition, you'll create a SmartArt graphic and add headers and footers. Finally, you will insert a cover page and review the document in Read Mode.

## STARTING DATA FILES

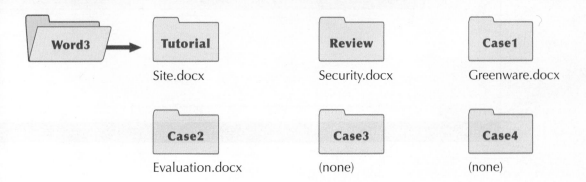

| Word3 | → | Tutorial | Review | Case1 |
|---|---|---|---|---|
| | | Site.docx | Security.docx | Greenware.docx |
| | | Case2 | Case3 | Case4 |
| | | Evaluation.docx | (none) | (none) |

# Session 3.1 Visual Overview:

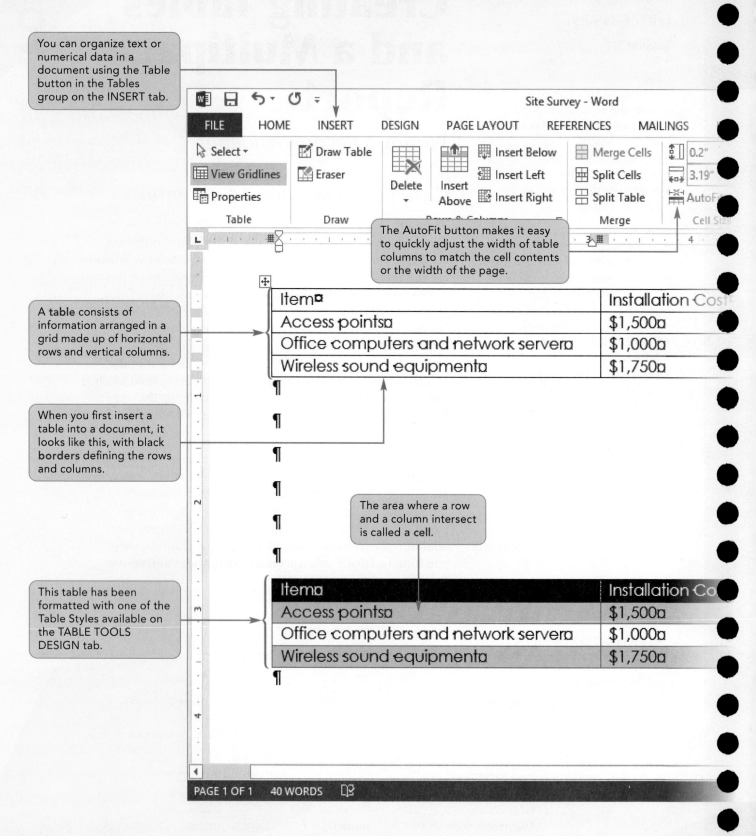

You can organize text or numerical data in a document using the Table button in the Tables group on the INSERT tab.

The AutoFit button makes it easy to quickly adjust the width of table columns to match the cell contents or the width of the page.

A table consists of information arranged in a grid made up of horizontal rows and vertical columns.

When you first insert a table into a document, it looks like this, with black borders defining the rows and columns.

The area where a row and a column intersect is called a cell.

This table has been formatted with one of the Table Styles available on the TABLE TOOLS DESIGN tab.

Site Survey - Word

FILE    HOME    INSERT    DESIGN    PAGE LAYOUT    REFERENCES    MAILINGS

Select ·    Draw Table    Delete    Insert Above    Insert Below    Insert Left    Insert Right    Merge Cells    Split Cells    Split Table    0.2"    3.19"    AutoFit

View Gridlines    Eraser

Properties

Table      Draw      Merge      Cell Size

| Item¤ | Installation Cost |
|---|---|
| Access points¤ | $1,500¤ |
| Office computers and network server¤ | $1,000¤ |
| Wireless sound equipment¤ | $1,750¤ |

| Item¤ | Installation Co |
|---|---|
| Access points¤ | $1,500¤ |
| Office computers and network server¤ | $1,000¤ |
| Wireless sound equipment¤ | $1,750¤ |

PAGE 1 OF 1    40 WORDS

# Organizing Information in Tables

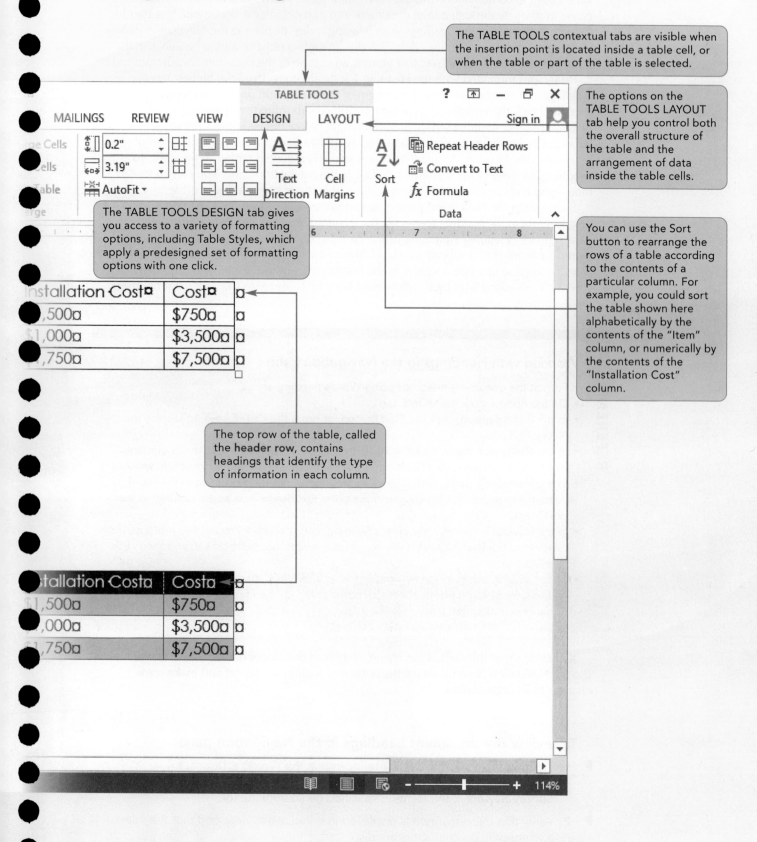

The TABLE TOOLS contextual tabs are visible when the insertion point is located inside a table cell, or when the table or part of the table is selected.

The options on the TABLE TOOLS LAYOUT tab help you control both the overall structure of the table and the arrangement of data inside the table cells.

The TABLE TOOLS DESIGN tab gives you access to a variety of formatting options, including Table Styles, which apply a predesigned set of formatting options with one click.

You can use the Sort button to rearrange the rows of a table according to the contents of a particular column. For example, you could sort the table shown here alphabetically by the contents of the "Item" column, or numerically by the contents of the "Installation Cost" column.

The top row of the table, called the **header row**, contains headings that identify the type of information in each column.

# Working with Headings in the Navigation Pane

When used in combination with the Navigation pane, Word's heading styles make it easier to navigate through a long document and to reorganize a document. You start by formatting the document headings with heading styles, displaying the Navigation pane, and then clicking the Headings link. This displays a hierarchy of all the headings in the document, allowing you to see, at a glance, an outline of the document headings.

Paragraphs formatted with the Heading 1 style are considered the highest level headings and are aligned at the left margin of the Navigation pane. Paragraphs formatted with the Heading 2 style are considered **subordinate** to Heading 1 paragraphs, and are indented slightly to the right below the Heading 1 paragraphs. Subordinate headings are often referred to as **subheadings**. Each successive level of heading styles (Heading 3, Heading 4, and so on) is indented farther to the right. To simplify your view of the document outline in the Navigation pane, you can choose to hide lower-level headings from view, leaving only the major headings visible.

From within the Navigation pane, you can **promote** a subordinate heading to the next level up in the heading hierarchy. For example, you can promote a Heading 2 paragraph to a Heading 1 paragraph. You can also do the opposite—that is, you can **demote** a heading to a subordinate level. You can also click and drag a heading in the Navigation pane to a new location in the document's outline. When you do so, any subheadings—along with their subordinate body text—move to the new location in the document.

**REFERENCE**

## Working with Headings in the Navigation Pane

- Format the document headings using Word's heading styles.
- On the ribbon, click the HOME tab.
- In the Editing group, click the Find button, or press the Ctrl+F keys, to display the Navigation pane.
- In the Navigation pane, click the HEADINGS link to display a list of the document headings, and then click a heading to display that heading in the document window.
- In the Navigation pane, click a heading, and then drag it up or down in the list of headings to move that heading and the body text below it to a new location in the document.
- In the Navigation pane, right-click a heading, and then click Promote to promote the heading to the next-highest level. To demote a heading, right-click it, and then click Demote.
- To hide subheadings in the Navigation pane, click the Collapse arrow next to the higher level heading above them. To redisplay the subheadings, click the Expand arrow next to the higher level heading.

Katherine saved the draft of her report as a Word document named Site. You will use the Navigation pane to review the outline of Katherine's report and make some changes to its organization.

**To review the document headings in the Navigation pane:**

1. Open the document named **Site** located in the Word3 ► Tutorial folder included with your Data Files, and then save the file with the name **Site Survey Report** in the location specified by your instructor.

2. Verify that the document is displayed in Print Layout view, and that the rulers and nonprinting characters are displayed.

3. Make sure the Zoom level is set to **120%**, and that the HOME tab is selected on the ribbon.

4. Press the **Ctrl+F** keys. The Navigation pane opens to the left of the document.

5. In the Navigation pane, click the **HEADINGS** link. The document headings are displayed in the Navigation pane, as shown in Figure 3-1. The blue highlighted heading ("Summary") indicates which part of the document currently contains the insertion point.

| Figure 3-1 | Headings displayed in the Navigation pane |

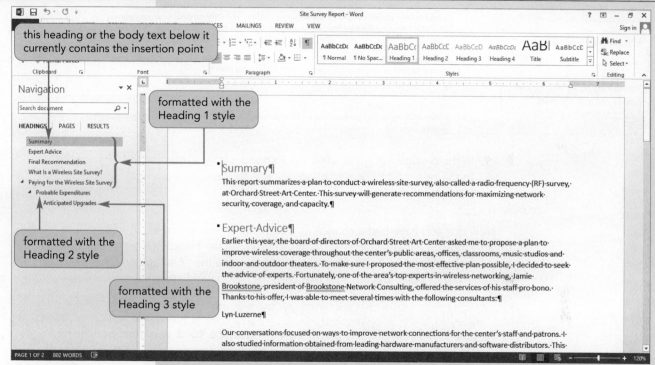

6. In the Navigation pane, click the **What Is a Wireless Site Survey?** heading. Word displays the heading in the document window, with the insertion point at the beginning of the heading. "The What Is a Wireless Site Survey?" heading is highlighted in blue in the Navigation pane.

7. In the Navigation pane, click the **Paying for the Wireless Site Survey** heading. Word displays the heading in the document window. In the Navigation pane, you can see that there are subheadings below this heading.

8. In the Navigation pane, click the **Collapse** arrow ◢ next to the "Paying for the Wireless Site Survey" heading. The subheadings below this heading are no longer visible in the Navigation pane. This has no effect on the text in the actual document. See Figure 3-2.

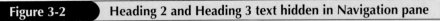

Figure 3-2 **Heading 2 and Heading 3 text hidden in Navigation pane**

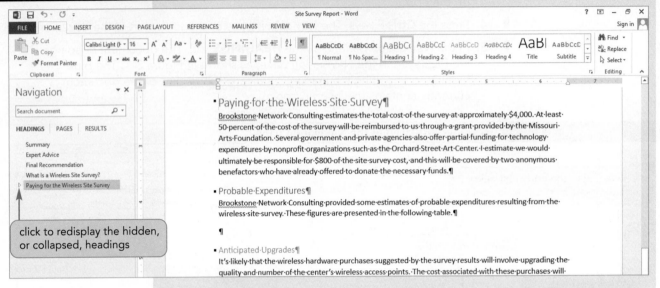

**9.** In the Navigation pane, click the **Expand** arrow ▷ next to the "Paying for the Wireless Site Survey" heading. The subheadings are again visible in the Navigation pane.

Now that you have had a chance to review the report, you need to make a few organizational changes. Katherine wants to promote the Heading 3 text "Anticipated Upgrades" to Heading 2 text. Then she wants to move the "Anticipated Upgrades" heading and its body text up, so it precedes the "Probable Expenditures" section.

**To use the Navigation pane to reorganize text in the document:**

**1.** In the Navigation pane, right-click the **Anticipated Upgrades** heading to display the shortcut menu.

**2.** Click **Promote**. The heading moves to the left in the Navigation pane, aligning below the "Probable Expenditures" heading. In the document window, the text is now formatted with the Heading 2 style, with its slightly larger font.

**3.** In the Navigation pane, click and drag the **Anticipated Upgrades** heading up. As you drag the heading, the pointer changes to ⬚, and a blue guideline is displayed. You can use the guideline to position the heading in its new location.

**4.** Position the guideline directly below the "Paying for the Wireless Site Survey" heading, as shown in Figure 3-3.

| Figure 3-3 | Moving a heading in the Navigation pane |
| --- | --- |

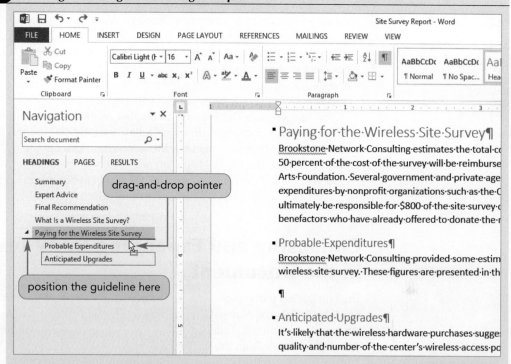

5. Release the mouse button. The "Anticipated Upgrades" heading is displayed in its new position in the Navigation pane, as the second-to-last heading in the outline. The heading and its body text are displayed in their new location in the document, before the "Probable Expenditures" heading. See Figure 3-4.

| Figure 3-4 | Heading and body text in new location |
| --- | --- |

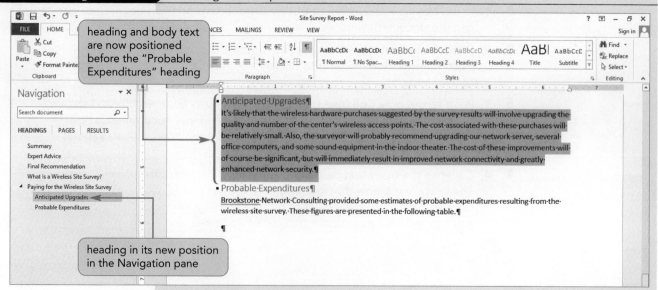

6. Click anywhere in the document to deselect the text, and then save the document.

Katherine also wants you to move the "Final Recommendation" heading and its accompanying body text. You'll do that in the next section, using a different method.

INSIGHT

*Promoting and Demoting Headings*

When you promote or demote a heading, Word applies the next higher or lower level heading style to the heading paragraph. You could accomplish the same thing by using the Style gallery to apply the next higher or lower level heading style, but it's easy to lose track of the overall organization of the document that way. By promoting and demoting headings from within the Navigation pane, you ensure that the overall document outline is right in front of you as you work.

You can also use Outline view to display, promote, and demote headings, and to reorganize a document. Turn on Outline view by clicking the VIEW tab, and then clicking the Outline button in the Views group to display the OUTLINING tab on the ribbon. To hide the OUTLINING tab and return to Print Layout view, click the Close Outline View button on the ribbon or the Print Layout button in the status bar.

# Collapsing and Expanding Body Text in the Document

The Navigation pane gives you an overview of the entire document, and dragging headings within the Navigation pane is the best way to reorganize a document. However, you can also hide, or collapse, the body text below a heading in a document. You do this from within the document window, without using the Navigation pane. After you collapse the body text below a heading, you can drag the heading to a new location in the document. When you do, the body text moves along with the heading, just as if you had dragged the heading in the Navigation pane. You'll use this technique now to move the "Final Recommendation" heading and its body text.

**To collapse and move a heading in the document:**

1. In the Navigation pane, click the **Final Recommendation** heading to display it in the document window.

2. In the document window, place the mouse pointer over the **Final Recommendation** heading to display the gray Collapse button ◢ to the left of the heading.

3. Point to the gray **Collapse** button ◢ until it turns blue, and then click the **Collapse** button ◢. The body text below the "Final Recommendation" heading is now hidden. The Collapse button is replaced with an Expand button.

4. Collapse the body text below the "What Is a Wireless Site Survey?" heading. The body text below that heading is no longer visible. Collapsing body text can be helpful when you want to hide details in a document temporarily, so you can focus on a particular part. See Figure 3-5.

**Figure 3-5**    **Body text collapsed in the document**

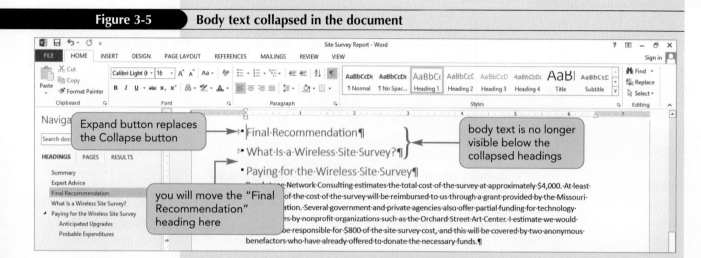

5. Select the **Final Recommendation** heading.

6. Click and drag the heading down. As you drag, a dark black insertion point moves along with the mouse pointer.

7. Position the dark black insertion point to the left of the "P" in the "Paying for the Wireless Site Survey" heading, and then release the mouse button. The "Final Recommendation" heading and its body text move to the new location, before the "Paying for the Wireless Site Survey" heading.

   Finally, you need to expand the body text below the two collapsed headings.

8. Click anywhere in the document to deselect the text.

9. Point to the **Expand** button ▷ to the left of the "Final Recommendation" heading until it turns blue, and then click the **Expand** button ▶ to redisplay the body text below the heading.

10. Point to the **Expand** button ▷ to the left of the "What Is a Wireless Site Survey?" heading until it turns blue, and then click the **Expand** button ▶ to redisplay the body text below the heading.

11. Save the document.

The document is now organized the way Katherine wants it. Next, you need to create a table summarizing her data on probable expenditures.

## Inserting a Blank Table

**TIP**

The terms "table," "field," and "record" are also used to discuss information stored in database programs, such as Microsoft Access.

A table is a useful way to present information that is organized into categories, or **fields**. For example, you could use a table to organize contact information for a list of clients. For each client, you could include information in the following fields: first name, last name, street address, city, state, and zip code. The complete set of information about a particular client is called a **record**. In a typical table, each column is a separate field, and each row is a record. A header row at the top contains the names of each field.

The sketch in Figure 3-6 shows what Katherine wants the table in her report to look like.

**Figure 3-6**    Table sketch

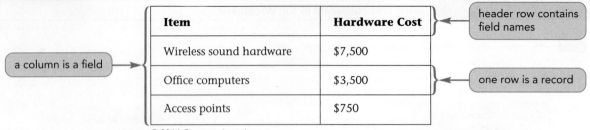

| Item | Hardware Cost |
|---|---|
| Wireless sound hardware | $7,500 |
| Office computers | $3,500 |
| Access points | $750 |

a column is a field → header row contains field names
one row is a record

© 2014 Cengage Learning

Katherine's table includes two columns, or fields—"Item" and "Hardware Cost." The header row contains the names of these two fields. The three rows below contain the records.

Creating a table in Word is a three-step process. First, you use the Table button on the INSERT tab to insert a blank table structure. Then you enter information into the table. Finally, you format the table to make it easy to read.

Before you begin creating the table, you'll insert a page break before the "Probable Expenditures" heading. This will move the heading and its body text to a new page, with plenty of room below for the new table. As a general rule, you should not use page breaks to position a particular part of a document at the top of a page. If you add or remove text from the document later, you might forget that you inserted a manual page break, and you might end up with a document layout you didn't expect. By default, Word heading styles are set up to ensure that a heading always appears on the same page as the body text paragraph below it, so you'll never need to insert a page break just to move a heading to the same page as its body text. However, in this case, a page break is appropriate because you need the "Probable Expenditures" heading to appear at the top of a page with room for the table below.

### To insert a page break and insert a blank table:

1. In the Navigation pane, click **Probable Expenditures** to display the heading in the document, with the insertion point to the left of the "P" in "Probable."

2. Close the Navigation pane, and then press the **Ctrl+Enter** keys to insert a page break. The "Probable Expenditures" heading and the body text following it move to a new, third page.

3. Scroll to position the "Probable Expenditures" heading at the top of the Word window, and then press the **Ctrl+End** keys to move the insertion point to the blank paragraph at the end of the document.

4. On the ribbon, click the **INSERT** tab.

5. In the Tables group, click the **Table** button. A table grid opens, with a menu at the bottom.

6. Use the mouse pointer to point to the upper-left cell of the grid, and then move the mouse pointer down and across the grid to highlight **two columns** and **four rows**. (The outline of a cell turns orange when it is highlighted.) As you move the pointer across the grid, Word indicates the size of the table (columns by rows) at the top of the grid. A Live Preview of the table structure is displayed in the document. See Figure 3-7.

**TIP**

You can use the Quick Tables option to choose from preformatted tables that contain placeholder text.

| Figure 3-7 | Inserting a blank table |

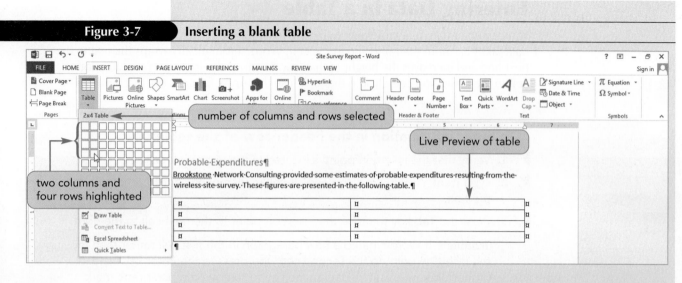

number of columns and rows selected

Live Preview of table

two columns and four rows highlighted

**7.** When the table size is 2×4, click the lower-right cell in the block of selected cells. An empty table consisting of two columns and four rows is inserted in the document, with the insertion point in the upper-left cell. See Figure 3-8.

| Figure 3-8 | Blank table inserted in document |

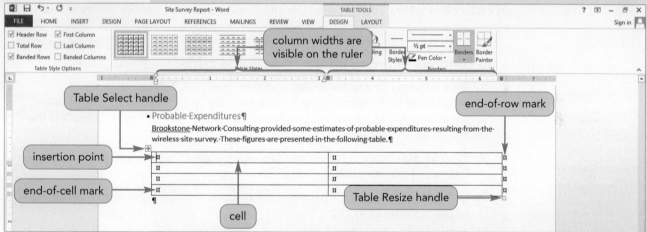

column widths are visible on the ruler

Table Select handle

end-of-row mark

insertion point

end-of-cell mark

Table Resize handle

cell

The two columns are of equal width. Because nonprinting characters are displayed in the document, each cell contains an end-of-cell mark, and each row contains an end-of-row mark, which are important for selecting parts of a table. The Table Select handle ⊞ is displayed at the table's upper-left corner. You can click the Table Select handle ⊞ to select the entire table, or you can drag it to move the table. You can drag the Table Resize handle ☐, which is displayed at the lower-right corner, to change the size of the table. The TABLE TOOLS DESIGN and LAYOUT contextual tabs appear on the ribbon.

**Trouble?** If you inserted a table with the wrong number of rows or columns, click the Undo button ↺ on the Quick Access Toolbar to remove the table, and then repeat Steps 4 through 7.

The blank table is ready for you to begin entering information.

# Entering Data in a Table

You can enter data in a table by moving the insertion point to a cell and typing. If the data takes up more than one line in the cell, Word automatically wraps the text to the next line and increases the height of that row. To move the insertion point to another cell in the table, you can click in that cell, use the arrow keys, or use the Tab key.

### To enter information in the header row of the table:

▶ **1.** Verify that the insertion point is located in the upper-left cell.

▶ **2.** Type **Item**. As you type, the end-of-cell mark moves right to accommodate the text.

▶ **3.** Press the **Tab** key to move the insertion point to the next cell to the right.

   **Trouble?** If Word created a new paragraph in the first cell rather than moving the insertion point to the second cell, you pressed the Enter key instead of the Tab key. Press the Backspace key to remove the paragraph mark, and then press the Tab key to move to the second cell in the first row.

▶ **4.** Type **Hardware Cost** and then press the **Tab** key to move to the first cell in the second row.

You have finished entering the header row—the row that identifies the information in each column. Now you can enter the information about the various expenditures.

### To continue entering information in the table:

▶ **1.** Type **wireless sound hardware** and then press the **Tab** key to move to the second cell in the second row. Notice that the "w" in "wireless" is capitalized, even though you typed it in lowercase. By default, AutoCorrect capitalizes the first letter in a cell entry.

▶ **2.** Type **$7,500** and then press the **Tab** key to move the insertion point to the first cell in the third row.

▶ **3.** Enter the following information in the bottom two rows, pressing the **Tab** key to move from cell to cell:

   **Office computers**; **$3,500**

   **Access points**; **$750**

At this point, the table consists of a header row and three records. Katherine realizes that she needs to add one more row to the table. You can add a new row to the bottom of a table by pressing the Tab key when the insertion point is in the rightmost cell in the bottom row.

### To add a row to the table:

▶ **1.** Verify that the insertion point is in the lower-right cell (which contains the value "$750") and then press the **Tab** key. A new, blank row is added to the bottom of the table.

▶ **2.** Type **Network server**, press the **Tab** key, and then type **$2,200**. When you are finished, your table should look like the one shown in Figure 3-9.

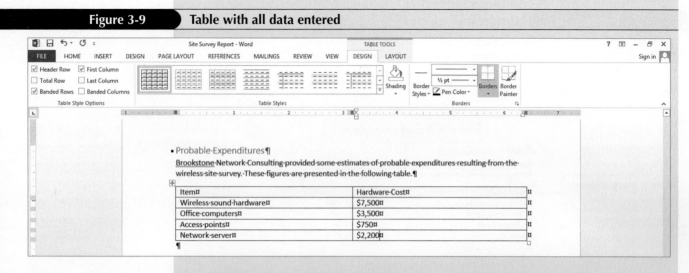

**Figure 3-9**     **Table with all data entered**

**Trouble?** If a new row is added to the bottom of your table, you pressed the Tab key after entering "$2,200". Click the Undo button ⤺ on the Quick Access Toolbar to remove the extra row from the table.

The table you've just created presents information about expenditures in an easy-to-read format. To make it even easier to read, you can format the header row in bold so it stands out from the rest of the table. To do that, you need to first select the header row.

## Selecting Part of a Table

**TIP**

To merge multiple cells into one cell, select the cells you want to merge, and then click the Merge Cells button in the Merge group on the TABLE TOOLS LAYOUT tab.

When selecting part of a table, you need to make sure you select the end-of-cell mark in a cell or the end-of-row mark at the end of a row. If you don't, the formatting changes you make next might not have the effect you expect. The foolproof way to select part of a table is to click in the cell, row, or column you want to select; click the Select button on the TABLE TOOLS LAYOUT contextual tab; and then click the appropriate command—Select Cell, Select Column, or Select Row. (You can also click Select Table to select the entire table.) To select a row, you can also click in the left margin next to the row. Similarly, you can click just above a column to select it. After you've selected an entire row, column, or cell, you can drag the mouse to select adjacent rows, columns, or cells.

Note that in the following steps, you'll position the mouse pointer until it takes on a particular shape so that you can then perform the task associated with that type of pointer. Pointer shapes are especially important when working with tables and graphics; in many cases, you can't perform a task until the pointer is the right shape. It takes some patience to get accustomed to positioning the pointer until it takes on the correct shape, but with practice you'll grow to rely on the pointer shapes as a quick visual cue to the options currently available to you.

### To select and format the header row:

1. Position the mouse pointer in the selection bar, to the left of the header row. The pointer changes to a right-facing arrow ⤤.

2. Click the mouse button. The entire header row, including the end-of-cell mark in each cell and the end-of-row mark, is selected. See Figure 3-10.

**Figure 3-10**    **Header row selected**

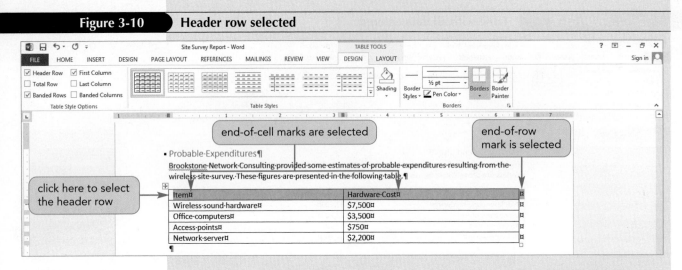

3.  Press the **Ctrl+B** keys to apply bold to the text in the header row. You can also use the formatting options on the HOME tab to format selected text in a table, including adding italics, changing the font, aligning text within cells, or applying a style.

4.  Click anywhere in the table to deselect the header row, and then save the document.

**INSIGHT**

### Formatting a Multipage Table

In some documents, you might have a long table that extends across multiple pages. To make a multipage table easier to read, you can format the table header row to appear at the top of every page. To do so, click in the header row, click the TABLE TOOLS LAYOUT tab, and then click the Properties button in the Table group. In the Table Properties dialog box, click the Row tab, and then select the "Repeat as header row at the top of each page" check box.

Now that you have created a very basic table, you can sort the information in it and improve its appearance.

## Sorting Rows in a Table

The term **sort** refers to the process of rearranging information in alphabetical, numerical, or chronological order. You can sort a series of paragraphs, including the contents of a bulleted list, or you can sort the rows of a table.

When you sort a table, you arrange the rows based on the contents of one of the columns. For example, you could sort the table you just created based on the contents of the "Item" column—either in ascending alphabetical order (from *A* to *Z*) or in descending alphabetical order (from *Z* to *A*). Alternatively, you could sort the table based on the contents of the "Hardware Cost" column—either in ascending numerical order (lowest to highest) or in descending numerical order (highest to lowest).

Clicking the Sort button in the Data group on the TABLE TOOLS LAYOUT tab opens the Sort dialog box, which provides a number of options for fine-tuning the sort, including options for sorting a table by the contents of more than one column. This is useful if, for example, you want to organize the table rows by last name, and then by first name within each last name. By default, Word assumes your table includes a header row that should remain at the top of the table—excluded from the sort.

**REFERENCE**

### Sorting the Rows of a Table

- Click anywhere within the table.
- On the ribbon, click the TABLE TOOLS LAYOUT tab.
- In the Data group, click the Sort button.
- In the Sort dialog box, click the Sort by arrow, and then select the header for the column you want to sort by.
- In the Type box located to the right of the Sort by box, select the type of information stored in the column you want to sort by; you can choose Text, Number, or Date.
- To sort in alphabetical, chronological, or numerical order, verify that the Ascending option button is selected. To sort in reverse order, click the Descending option button.
- To sort by a second column, click the Then by arrow, and then click a column header. If necessary, specify the type of information stored in the Then by column, and the sort order.
- At the bottom of the Sort dialog box, make sure the Header row option button is selected. This indicates that the table includes a header row that should not be included in the sort.
- Click the OK button.

Katherine would like you to sort the contents of the table in ascending numerical order based on the contents of the "Hardware Cost" column.

### To sort the information in the table:

1. Make sure the insertion point is located somewhere in the table.

2. On the ribbon, click the **TABLE TOOLS LAYOUT** tab.

3. In the Data group, click the **Sort** button. The Sort dialog box opens. Take a moment to review its default settings. The leftmost column in the table, the "Item" column, is selected in the Sort by box, indicating the sort will be based on the contents in this column. Because the "Item" column contains text, "Text" is selected in the Type box. The Ascending option button is selected by default, indicating that Word will sort the contents of the "Item" column from A to Z. The Header row option button is selected in the lower-left corner of the dialog box, ensuring the header row will not be included in the sort. You want to sort the column by the contents of the "Hardware Cost" column, so you need to change the Sort by setting.

4. Click the **Sort by** button arrow, and then click **Hardware Cost**. Because the "Hardware Cost" column contains numbers, the Type box now displays "Number". The Ascending button is still selected, indicating that Word will sort the numbers in the "Hardware Cost" column from lowest to highest. See Figure 3-11.

**Figure 3-11** **Sort dialog box**

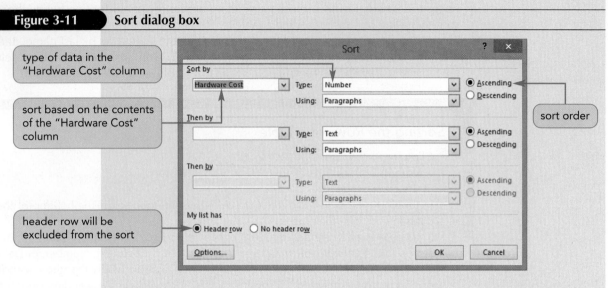

5. Click the **OK** button to close the Sort dialog box, and then click anywhere in the table to deselect it. Rows 2 through 5 are now arranged numerically, according to the numbers in the "Hardware Cost" column, with the "Wireless sound hardware" row at the bottom. See Figure 3-12.

**Figure 3-12** **Table after being sorted**

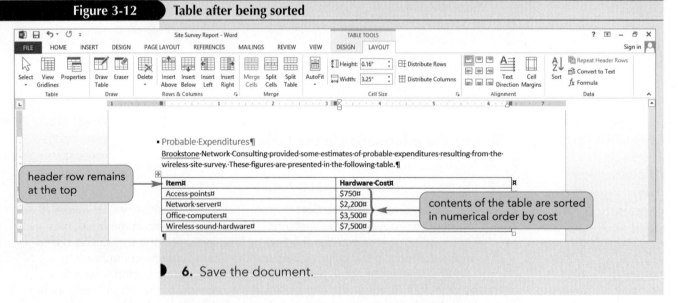

6. Save the document.

Katherine decides that the table should also include the installation cost for each item. She asks you to insert an "Installation Cost" column.

# Inserting Rows and Columns in a Table

To add a column to a table, you can use the tools in the Rows & Columns group on the TABLE TOOLS LAYOUT tab, or you can use the Add Column button in the document window. To use the Add Column button, make sure the insertion point is located somewhere within the table. When you position the mouse pointer at the top of the table, pointing to the border between two columns, the Add Column button appears. When you click that button, a new column is inserted between the two existing columns.

### To insert a column in the table:

1. Verify that the insertion point is located anywhere in the table.

2. Position the mouse pointer at the top of the table, so that it points to the border between the two columns. The Add Column button ⊕ appears at the top of the border. A blue guideline shows where the new column will be inserted. See Figure 3-13.

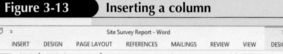

Figure 3-13 | Inserting a column

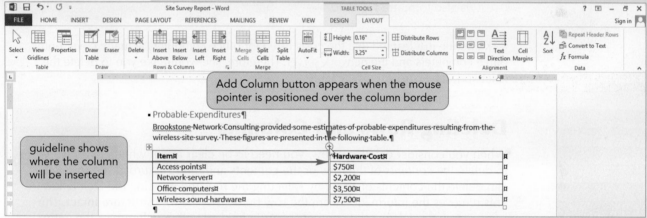

3. Click the **Add Column** button ⊕. A new, blank column is inserted between the "Item" and "Hardware Cost" columns. The three columns in the table are narrower than the original two columns, but the overall width of the table remains the same.

4. Click in the top cell of the new column, and then enter the following header and data. Use the ↓ key to move the insertion point down through the column.

**Installation Cost**

**$1,500**

**$850**

**$1,000**

**$1,750**

Your table should now look like the one in Figure 3-14.

**Figure 3-14** New "Installation Cost" column

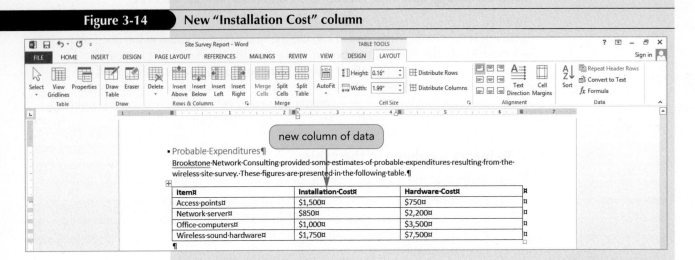

Because you selected the entire header row when you formatted the original headers in bold, the newly inserted header, "Installation Cost," is also formatted in bold.

Katherine just learned that the costs listed for office computers actually cover both office computers and the network server. Therefore, she would like you to delete the "Network server" row from the table.

# Deleting Rows and Columns

When you consider deleting a row, you need to be clear about whether you want to delete the *contents* of the row, or the contents and the *structure* of the row. You can delete the contents of a row by selecting the row and pressing the Delete key. This removes the information from the row but leaves the row structure intact. The same is true for deleting the contents of an individual cell, a column, or the entire table. To delete the structure of a row, a column, or the entire table—including its contents—you select the row (or column or the entire table) and then use the Delete button in the Rows & Columns group, or on the Mini toolbar. To delete multiple rows or columns, start by selecting all the rows or columns you want to delete.

Before you delete the Network server row, you need to edit the contents in the last cell in the first column to indicate that the items in that row are for office computers and a server.

**To delete the Network server row:**

1. In the cell containing the text "Office computers," click to the right of the "s," press the **spacebar**, and then type **and network server**. The cell now reads "Office computers and network server." Part of the text wraps to a second line within the cell. Next, you can delete the Network server row, which is no longer necessary.

2. Click in the selection bar to the left of the **Network server** row. The row is selected, with the Mini toolbar displayed on top of the selected row.

3.  On the Mini toolbar, click the **Delete** button. The Delete menu opens, displaying options for deleting cells, columns, rows, or the entire table. See Figure 3-15.

| **Figure 3-15** | **Deleting a row** |

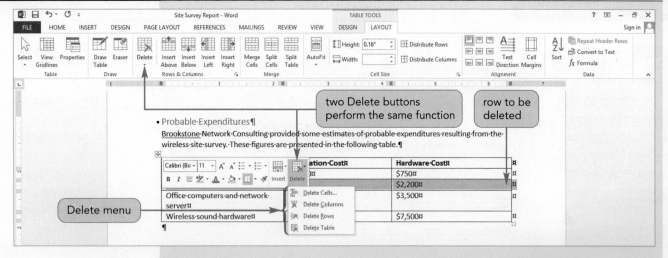

4.  Click **Delete Rows**. The "Network server" row is removed from the table, and the Mini toolbar disappears.

5.  Save your work.

The table now contains all the information Katherine wants to include. Next, you'll adjust the widths of the three columns.

# Changing Column Widths

Columns that are too wide for the material they contain can make a table hard to read. You can change a column's width by dragging the column's right border to a new position. Or, if you prefer, you can double-click a column border to make the column width adjust automatically to accommodate the widest entry in the column. To adjust the width of all the columns to match their widest entries, click anywhere in the table, click the AutoFit button in the Cell Size group on the TABLE TOOLS LAYOUT tab, and then click AutoFit Contents. To adjust the width of the entire table to span the width of the page, click the AutoFit Contents button and then click AutoFit Window.

You'll adjust the columns in Katherine's table by double-clicking the right column border. You need to start by making sure that no part of the table is selected. Otherwise, when you double-click the border, only the width of the selected part of the table will change.

When resizing a column, be sure that no part of the table is selected. Otherwise, you'll resize just the selected part.

### To change the width of the columns in the table:

1. Verify that no part of the table is selected, and then position the mouse pointer over the right border of the "Installation Cost" column until the pointer changes to ◄‖►. See Figure 3-16.

**Figure 3-16**   Adjusting the column width

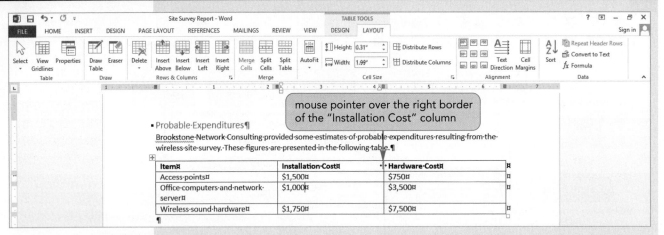

**TIP**

To change the height of a row, position the mouse pointer over the bottom row border and drag the border up or down.

2. Double-click the mouse button. The right column border moves left so that the "Installation Cost" column is just wide enough to accommodate the widest entry in the column.

3. Verify that no part of the table is selected, and that the insertion point is located in any cell in the table.

4. Make sure the TABLE TOOLS LAYOUT tab is selected on the ribbon.

5. In the Cell Size group, click the **AutoFit** button, and then click **AutoFit Contents**. All of the table columns adjust so that each is just wide enough to accommodate its widest entry. The text "Office computers and network server" in the lower-left cell no longer wraps to a second line.

To finish the table, you will add some formatting to improve the table's appearance.

## Formatting Tables with Styles

To adjust a table's appearance, you can use any of the formatting options available on the HOME tab. To change a table's appearance more dramatically, you can use table styles, which allow you to apply a collection of formatting options, including shading, color, borders, and other design elements, with a single click.

By default, a table is formatted with the Table Grid style, which includes only black borders between the rows and columns, no paragraph spacing, no shading, and the default black font color. You can select a more colorful table style from the Table Styles group on the TABLE TOOLS DESIGN tab. Whatever table style you choose, you'll give your document a more polished look if you use the same style consistently in all the tables in a single document.

Some table styles format rows in alternating colors, called **banded rows**, while others format the columns in alternating colors, called **banded columns**. You can choose a style that includes different formatting for the header row than for the rest of the table. Or, if the first column in your table is a header column—that is, if it contains headers identifying the type of information in each row—you can choose a style that instead applies different formatting to the first column.

### Formatting a Table with a Table Style

- Click in the table you want to format.
- On the ribbon, click the TABLE TOOLS DESIGN tab.
- In the Table Styles group, click the More button to display the Table Styles gallery.
- Position the mouse pointer over a style in the Table Styles gallery to see a Live Preview of the table style in the document.
- In the Table Styles gallery, click the style you want.
- To apply or remove style elements (such as special formatting for the header row, banded rows, or banded columns), select or deselect check boxes as necessary in the Table Style Options group.

Katherine wants to use a table style that emphasizes the header row with special formatting, does not include column borders, and uses color to separate the rows.

### To apply a table style to the Probable Expenditures table:

1. Click anywhere in the table, and then scroll to position the table at the very bottom of the Word window. This will make it easier to see the Live Preview in the next few steps.

2. On the ribbon, click the **TABLE TOOLS DESIGN** tab. In the Table Styles group, the plain Table Grid style is highlighted, indicating that it is the table's current style.

3. In the Table Styles group, click the **More** button. The Table Styles gallery opens. The default Table Grid style now appears under the heading "Plain Tables." The more elaborate styles appear below, in the "Grid Tables" section of the gallery.

4. Use the gallery's vertical scroll bar to view the complete collection of table styles. When you are finished, scroll up until you can see the "Grid Tables" heading again.

5. Move the mouse pointer over the style located in the fourth row of the Grid Tables section, second column from the right. See Figure 3-17.

**Figure 3-17**   **Table Styles gallery**

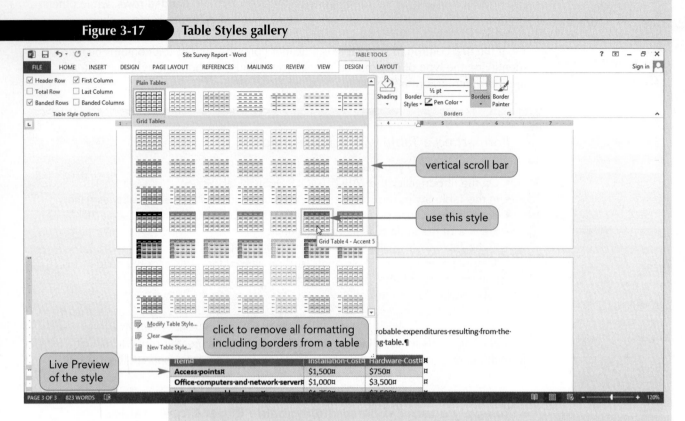

A ScreenTip displays the style's name, "Grid Table 4 - Accent 5." The style consists of a dark blue heading row, with alternating rows of light blue and white below. A Live Preview of the style is visible in the document.

6. Click the **Grid Table 4 - Accent 5** style. The Table Styles gallery closes.

7. Scroll to position the table at the top of the Word window, so you can review it more easily. The table's header row is formatted with dark blue shading and white text. The rows below appear in alternating colors of light blue and white.

The only problem with the newly formatted table is that the text in the first column is formatted in bold. In tables where the first column contains headers, bold would be appropriate—but this isn't the case with Katherine's table. You'll fix this by deselecting the First Column check box in the Table Style Options group.

### To remove the bold formatting from the first column:

1. In the Table Style Options group, click the **First Column** check box to deselect this option. The bold formatting is removed from the entries in the Item column. Note that the Header Row check box is selected. This indicates that the table's header row is emphasized with special formatting (dark blue shading with white text). The Banded Rows check box is also selected because the table is formatted with banded rows of blue and white. Figure 3-18 shows the finished table.

**Figure 3-18**   Completed table

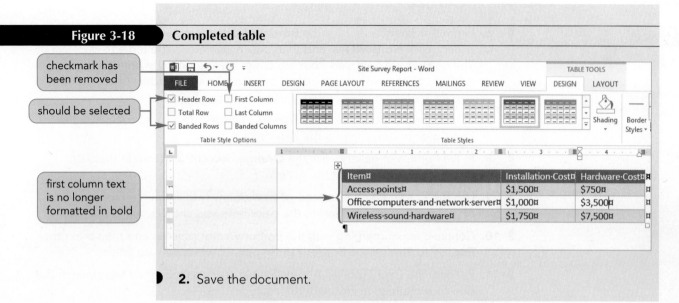

checkmark has been removed

should be selected

first column text is no longer formatted in bold

**2.** Save the document.

After you apply a table style, it's helpful to know how to remove it in case you want to start over from scratch. The Clear option on the menu below the Table styles gallery removes the current style from a table, including the borders between cells. When a table has no borders, the rows and columns are defined by **gridlines**, which are useful as guidelines but do not appear when you print the table.

In the following steps, you'll experiment with clearing the table's style, displaying and hiding the gridlines, and removing the table's borders.

**To experiment with table styles, gridlines, and borders:**

**1.** In the Table Styles group, click the **More** button, and then click **Clear** in the menu below the gallery. Next, you need to make sure the table gridlines are displayed.

**2.** On the ribbon, click the **TABLE TOOLS LAYOUT** tab.

**3.** In the View group, click the **View Gridlines** button, if necessary, to select it. The table now looks much simpler, with no shading or font colors. Instead of the table borders, dotted gridlines separate the rows and columns. The text in the table is spaced farther apart because removing the table style restored the default paragraph and line spacing of the Normal style. The bold formatting that you applied earlier, which is not part of a table style, is visible again.

It is helpful to clear a table's style and view only the gridlines if you want to use a table to lay out text and graphics on a page, but you want no visible indication of the table itself. You'll have a chance to try this technique in the Case Problems at the end of this tutorial.

Another option is to remove only the table borders, leaving the rest of the table style applied to the table. To do this, you have to select the entire table. But first you need to undo the style change.

**4.** On the Quick Access Toolbar, click the **Undo** button 🔄 to restore the Grid Table 4 - Accent 5 style, so that your table looks like the one in Figure 3-18.

**5.** In the upper-left corner of the table, click the **Table Select** handle ⊞ to select the entire table, and then click the **TABLE TOOLS DESIGN** tab.

▶ **6.** In the Borders group, click the **Borders button arrow** to open the Borders gallery, click **No Borders**, and then click anywhere in the table to deselect it. The borders are removed from the table, leaving only the nonprinting gridlines to separate the rows and columns. To add borders of any color to specific parts of a table, you can use the Border Painter.

▶ **7.** In the Borders group, click the **Border Painter** button, and then click the **Pen Color** button to open the Pen Color gallery.

▶ **8.** In the Pen Color gallery, click the **Orange, Accent 2** square in the sixth column of the first row of the gallery.

▶ **9.** Use the Border Painter pointer ✐ to click any gridline in the table. An orange border is added to the cell where you clicked.

▶ **10.** Continue experimenting with the Border Painter pointer, and then press the **Esc** key to turn off the Border Painter pointer when you are finished.

▶ **11.** Reapply the Grid Table 4 - Accent 5 table style to make your table match the one shown earlier in Figure 3-18.

▶ **12.** Save the document and then close it.

**PROSKILLS**

## Problem Solving: Fine-Tuning Table Styles

After you apply a table style to a table, you might like the look of the table but find that it no longer effectively conveys your information or is not quite as easy to read. To solve this problem, you might be inclined to go back to the Table Styles gallery to find another style that might work better. Another method to correct problems with a table style is to identify the table elements with problematic formatting, and then manually make formatting adjustments to only those elements using the options on the TABLE TOOLS DESIGN tab. For example, you can change the thickness and color of the table borders using the options in the Borders group, and you can add shading using the Shading button in the Table Styles group. Also, if you don't like the appearance of table styles in your document, consider changing the document's theme and previewing the table styles again. The table styles have a different appearance in each theme. When applying table styles, remember there are many options for attractively formatting the table without compromising the information being conveyed.

In the next session, you'll complete the rest of the report by organizing information using tab stops, creating footnotes and endnotes, dividing the document into sections, inserting headers and footers, and finally inserting a cover page.

**REVIEW**

## Session 3.1 Quick Check

1. What must you do before you can display document headings in the Navigation pane?
2. Explain how to insert a table in a document.
3. After you enter data in the last cell in the last row in a table, how can you insert a new row?
4. Explain how to insert a new column in a table.
5. What button do you use to sort a table?
6. To adjust the width of a table's column to fit its widest entry, would you use the AutoFit Contents option or the AutoFit Window option?
7. How can you adjust a table style so that the first column in the table is formatted like all the others?

# Session 3.2 Visual Overview:

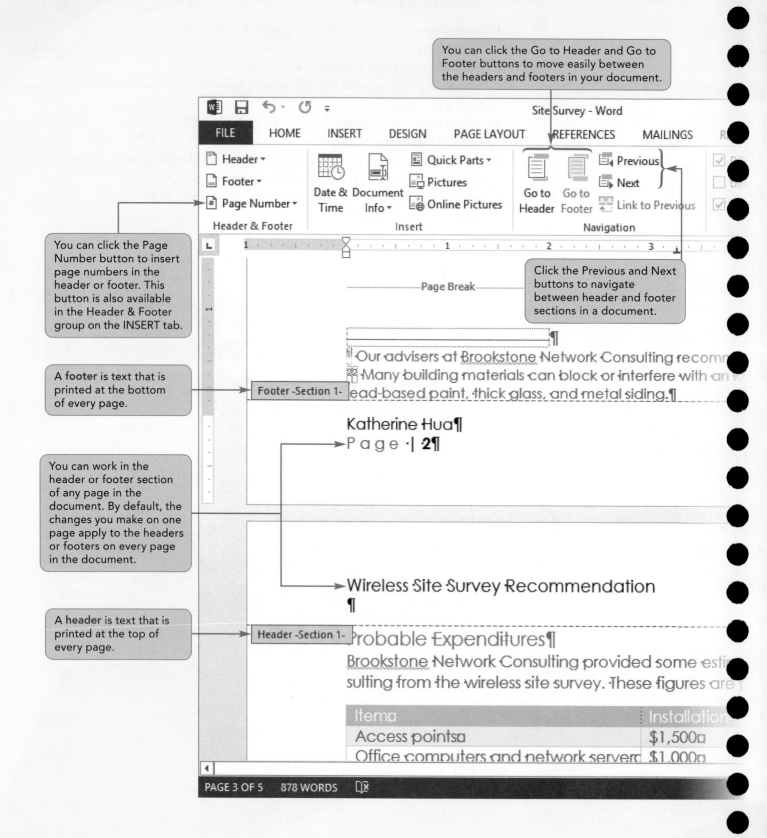

You can click the Go to Header and Go to Footer buttons to move easily between the headers and footers in your document.

You can click the Page Number button to insert page numbers in the header or footer. This button is also available in the Header & Footer group on the INSERT tab.

Click the Previous and Next buttons to navigate between header and footer sections in a document.

A **footer** is text that is printed at the bottom of every page.

You can work in the header or footer section of any page in the document. By default, the changes you make on one page apply to the headers or footers on every page in the document.

A header is text that is printed at the top of every page.

# Working with Headers and Footers

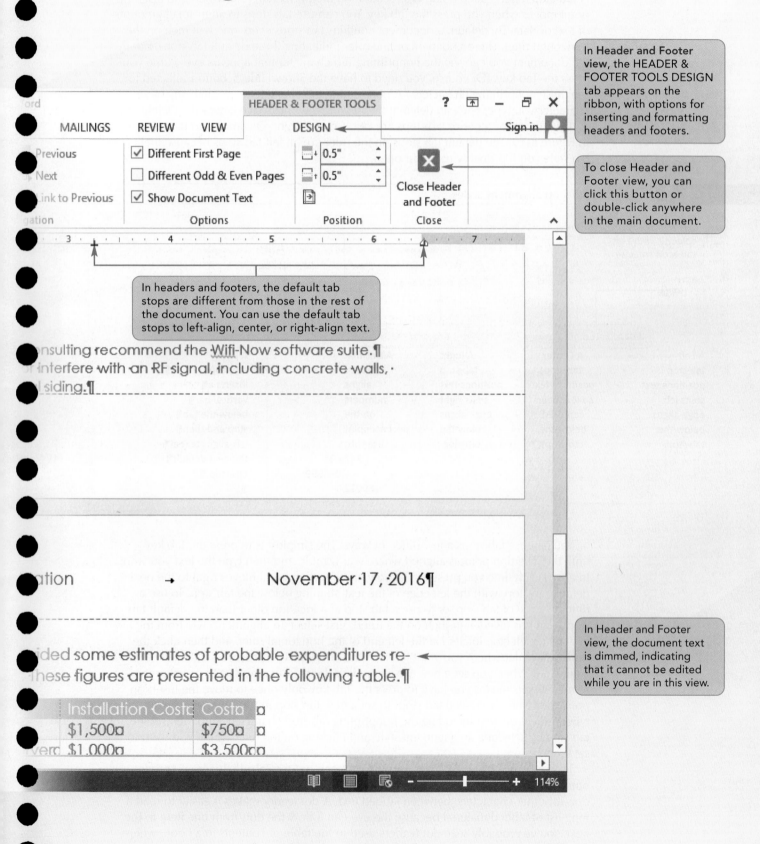

In **Header and Footer** view, the HEADER & FOOTER TOOLS DESIGN tab appears on the ribbon, with options for inserting and formatting headers and footers.

To close Header and Footer view, you can click this button or double-click anywhere in the main document.

In headers and footers, the default tab stops are different from those in the rest of the document. You can use the default tab stops to left-align, center, or right-align text.

In Header and Footer view, the document text is dimmed, indicating that it cannot be edited while you are in this view.

# Setting Tab Stops

A **tab stop** (often called a **tab**) is a location on the horizontal ruler where the insertion point moves when you press the Tab key. You can use tab stops to align small amounts of text or data. By default, a document contains tab stops every one-half inch on the horizontal ruler. There's no mark on the ruler indicating these default tab stops, but in the document you can see the nonprinting Tab character that appears every time you press the Tab key. (Of course, you need to have the Show/Hide ¶ button selected to see these nonprinting characters.) A nonprinting tab character is just like any other character you type; you can delete it by pressing the Backspace key or the Delete key.

The five major types of tab stops are Left, Center, Right, Decimal, and Bar, as shown in Figure 3-19. The default tab stops on the ruler are all left tab stops because that is the tab style you'll probably use most often.

**Figure 3-19** **Tab stop alignment styles**

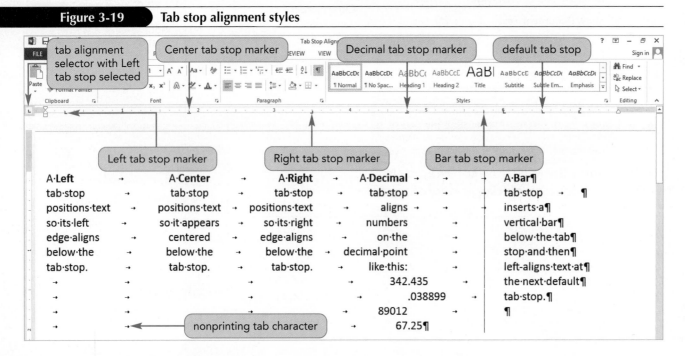

You can use tab stops a few different ways. The simplest is to press the Tab key until the insertion point is aligned where you want it, and then type the text you want to align. Each time you press the Tab key, the insertion point moves right to the next default tab stop, with the left edge of the text aligning below the tab stop. To use a different type of tab stop, or to use a tab stop at a location other than the default tab stop locations (every half-inch on the ruler), first select an alignment style from the tab alignment selector, located at the left end of the horizontal ruler, and then click the horizontal ruler where you want to insert the tab stop. This process is called setting a tab stop. When you set a new tab stop, all of the default tab stops to its left are removed. This means you have to press the Tab key only once to move the insertion point to the newly created tab stop. To set a new tab stop in text you have already typed, select the text including the nonprinting tab stop characters, and then set the tab stop by selecting an alignment style and clicking on the ruler where you want to set the tab stop.

To create more complicated tab stops, you can use the Tabs dialog box. Among other things, the Tabs dialog box allows you to insert a **dot leader**, which is a row of dots (or other characters) between tabbed text. A dot leader makes it easier to read a long list of tabbed material because the eye can follow the dots from one item to the next. You've probably seen dot leaders used in the table of contents in a book, where the dots separate the chapter titles from the page numbers.

To create a left tab stop with a dot leader, click the Dialog Box Launcher in the Paragraph group on the HOME tab, click the Indents and Spacing tab, if necessary, and then click the Tabs button at the bottom of the dialog box. In the Tab stop position box in the Tabs dialog box, type the location on the ruler where you want to insert the tab. For example, to insert a tab stop at the 4-inch mark, type 4. Verify that the Left option button is selected in the Alignment section, and then, in the Leader section, click the option button for the type of leader you want. Click the Set button and then click the OK button.

**REFERENCE**

### Setting, Moving, and Clearing Tab Stops

- To set a tab stop, click the tab alignment selector on the horizontal ruler until the appropriate tab stop alignment style is displayed, and then click the horizontal ruler where you want to position the tab stop.
- To move a tab stop, drag it to a new location on the ruler. If you have already typed text that is aligned by the tab stop, select the text before dragging the tab stop to a new location.
- To clear a tab stop, drag it off the ruler.

In the Site Survey Report document you have been working on, you need to type the list of consultants and their titles. You can use tab stops to quickly format this small amount of information in two columns. As you type, you'll discover whether Word's default tab stops are appropriate for this document or whether you need to set a new tab stop. Before you get started working with tabs, you'll take a moment to explore Word's Resume Reading feature.

### To enter the list of consultants using tabs:

**1.** Open the **Site Survey Report** document. The document opens with the "Summary" heading at the top of the Word window. In the lower-right corner, a "Welcome back!" message is displayed briefly, and is then replaced with the Resume Reading button ⌐.

**2.** Point to the **Resume Reading** button ⌐ to expand its "Welcome back!" message. See Figure 3-20.

| Figure 3-20 | "Welcome back!" message displayed in reopened document |

indoor·and·outdoor·theaters.·To·make·sure·I·proposed·the·most·effective·plan·possible,·I·decided·to·seek·
the·advice·of·experts.·Fortunately,·one·of·the·area's·top·experts·in·wireless·networking,·Jamie·
Brookstone,·president·of·Brookstone·Network·Consulting,·offered·the·services·of·his·staff·pro·bono.·
Thanks·to·his·offer,·I·was·able·to·meet·several·times·with·the·foll

click to display the part of the document you were working on before

Welcome back!
Pick up where you left off:
Probable Expenditures
8 minutes ago

Lyn·Luzerne¶

Our·conversations·focused·on·ways·to·improve·network·connect
also·studied·information·obtained·from·leading·hardware·manufacturers·and·software·distributors.·This·

PAGE 1 OF 3    823 WORDS

**3.** Click the **Welcome back!** message. The document window scrolls down to display the table, which you were working on just before you closed the document.

**4.** Scroll up to display the "Expert Advice" heading on page 1.

**5.** Confirm that the ruler and nonprinting characters are displayed, and that the document is displayed in Print Layout view, zoomed to 120%.

**6.** Click to the right of the last "e" in "Lyn Luzerne."

**7.** Press the **Tab** key. An arrow-shaped tab character appears, and the insertion point moves to the first tab stop after the last "e" in "Luzerne." This tab stop is the default tab located at the 1-inch mark on the horizontal ruler. See Figure 3-21.

**Figure 3-21** | **Tab character**

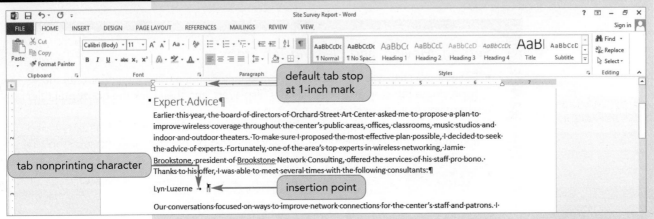

**8.** Type **Associate Engineer**, and then press the **Enter** key to move the insertion point to the next line.

**9.** Type **Dean Armstrong**, and then press the **Tab** key. The insertion point moves to the next available tab stop, this time located at the 1.5-inch mark on the rule.

**10.** Type **Senior Engineer**, and then press the **Enter** key to move to the next line. Notice that Dean Armstrong's title does not align with Lyn Luzerne's title on the line above it. You'll fix this after you type the last name in the list.

**11.** Type **Suzanne J. Sheffield-Harper**, press the **Tab** key, and then type **Project Manager**. See Figure 3-22.

**Figure 3-22** | **List of consultants**

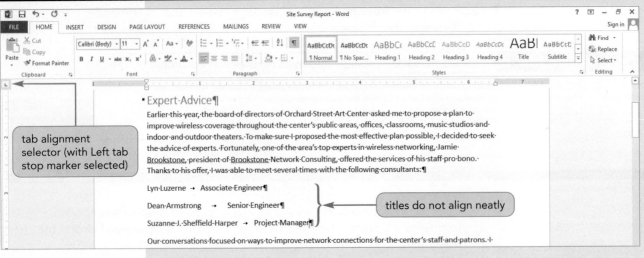

The list of names and titles is not aligned properly. You can fix this by inserting a new tab stop.

**To add a new tab stop to the horizontal ruler:**

1. Make sure the HOME tab is displayed on the ribbon, and then select the list of consultants and their titles.

2. On the horizontal ruler, click at the 2.5-inch mark. Because the current tab stop alignment style is Left tab, Word inserts a left tab stop at that location. Remember that when you set a new tab stop, all the default tab stops to its left are removed. The column of titles shifts to the new tab stop. See Figure 3-23.

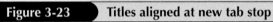

Figure 3-23    **Titles aligned at new tab stop**

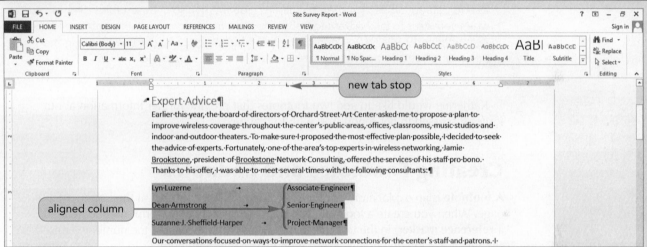

To complete the list, you need to remove the paragraph spacing after the first two paragraphs in the list, so the list looks like it's all one paragraph. You can quickly reduce paragraph and line spacing to 0 points by clicking the No Spacing style in the Styles group. In this case, you want to reduce only the paragraph spacing to 0 points, so you'll use the Line and Paragraph Spacing button instead.

3. Select the first two paragraphs in the list, which contain the names and titles for Lyn and Dean.

4. In the Paragraph group, click the **Line and Paragraph Spacing** button , and then click **Remove Space After Paragraph**.

5. Click anywhere in the document to deselect the list, and then save your work.

PROSKILLS

*Decision Making: Choosing Between Tabs and Tables*

When you have information that you want to align in columns in your document, you need to decide whether to use tabs or tables. Whatever you do, don't try to align columns of data by adding extra spaces with the spacebar. Although the text might seem precisely aligned on the screen, it probably won't be aligned when you print the document. Furthermore, if you edit the text, the spaces you inserted to align your columns will be affected by your edits; they get moved just like regular text, ruining your alignment.

So what is the most efficient way to align text in columns? It depends. Inserting tabs works well for aligning small amounts of information in just a few columns and rows, such as two columns with three rows, but tabs become cumbersome when you need to organize a lot of data over multiple columns and rows. In this case, using a table to organize columns of information is better. Unlike with tabbed columns of data, it's easy to add data to tables by inserting columns. You might also choose tables over tab stops when you want to take advantage of the formatting options available with table styles. As mentioned earlier, if you don't want the table structure itself to be visible in the document, you can clear its table style and then hide its gridlines.

Katherine would like to add two footnotes that provide further information about topics discussed in her report. You will do that next.

# Creating Footnotes and Endnotes

A **footnote** is an explanatory comment or reference that appears at the bottom of a page. When you create a footnote, Word inserts a small, superscript number (called a **reference marker**) in the text. The term **superscript** means that the number is raised slightly above the line of text. Word then inserts the same number in the page's bottom margin and positions the insertion point next to it so you can type the text of the footnote. **Endnotes** are similar, except that the text of an endnote appears at the end of a section or, in the case of a document without sections, at the end of the document. (You'll learn about dividing a document into sections later in this tutorial.) By default, the reference marker for an endnote is a lowercase Roman numeral.

Word automatically manages the reference markers for you, keeping them sequential from the beginning of the document to the end, no matter how many times you add, delete, or move footnotes or endnotes. For example, if you move a paragraph containing footnote 4 so that it falls before the paragraph containing footnote 1, Word renumbers all the footnotes in the document to keep them sequential.

REFERENCE

*Inserting a Footnote or an Endnote*

- Click the location in the document where you want to insert a footnote or an endnote.
- On the ribbon, click the REFERENCES tab.
- In the Footnotes group, click the Insert Footnote button or the Insert Endnote button.
- Type the text of the footnote in the bottom margin of the page, or type the text of the endnote at the end of the document.
- When you are finished typing the text of a footnote or an endnote, click in the body of the document to continue working on the document.

Katherine asks you to insert a footnote that explains the phrase "barriers to RF signal propagation."

### To add a footnote to the report:

1. Use the Navigation pane to find the phrase "barriers to RF signal propagation" near the bottom of page 1, and then click to the right of the period after "propagation."

2. Close the Navigation pane.

3. On the ribbon, click the **REFERENCES** tab.

4. In the Footnotes group, click the **Insert Footnote** button. A superscript "1" is inserted to the right of the period after "propagation." Word also inserts the number "1" in the bottom margin below a separator line. The insertion point is now located next to the number in the bottom margin, ready for you to type the text of the footnote.

5. Type **Many building materials can block or interfere with an RF signal, including concrete walls, lead-based paint, thick glass, and metal siding.** See Figure 3-24.

| Figure 3-24 | Inserting a footnote |
|---|---|

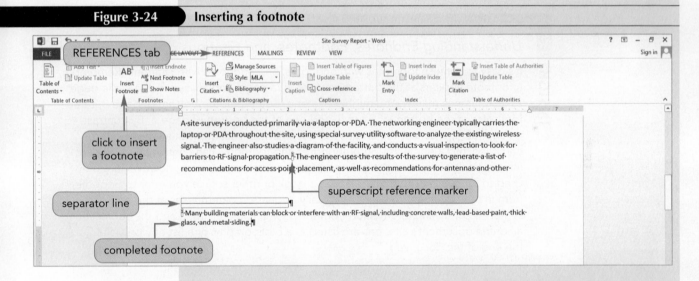

Now, Katherine would like you to insert a second footnote.

### To insert a second footnote:

1. In the third line of the same paragraph, click at the end of the second sentence to position the insertion point to the right of the period after "signal."

2. In the Footnotes group, click the **Insert Footnote** button, and then type **Our advisers at Brookstone Network Consulting recommend the Wifi-Now software suite.** Because this footnote is placed earlier in the document than the one you just created, Word inserts a superscript "1" for this footnote, and then renumbers the other footnote as "2." See Figure 3-25.

**Figure 3-25** | **Inserting a second footnote**

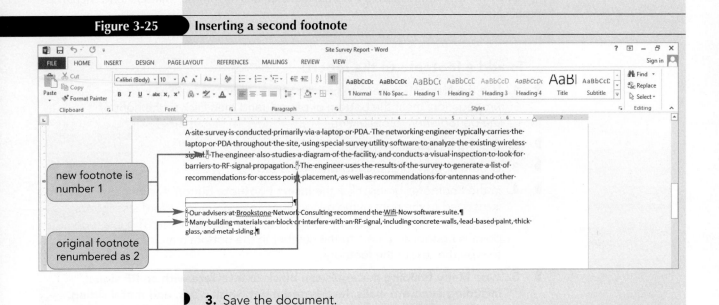

**3.** Save the document.

### Understanding Endnotes, Footnotes, and Citations

It's easy to confuse footnotes with endnotes, and endnotes with citations. Remember, a footnote appears at the bottom, or foot, of a page, and always on the same page as its reference marker. You might have one footnote at the bottom of page 3, three footnotes at the bottom of page 5, and one at the bottom of page 6. By contrast, an endnote appears at the end of the document or section, with all the endnotes compiled into a single list. Both endnotes and footnotes can contain any kind of information you think might be useful to your readers. Citations, however, are only used to list specific information about a book or other source you refer to or quote from in the document. A citation typically appears in parentheses at the end of the sentence containing information from the source you are citing, and the sources for all of the document's citations are listed in a bibliography, or a list of works cited, at the end of the document.

Now you're ready to address some other issues with the document. First, Katherine has noticed that the right edges of most of the paragraphs in the document are uneven, and she'd like you to try to smooth them out. You'll correct this problem in the next section.

## Hyphenating a Document

By default, hyphenation is turned off in Word documents. That means if you are in the middle of typing a word and you reach the end of a line, Word moves the entire word to the next line instead of inserting a hyphen and breaking the word into two parts. This can result in ragged text on the right margin. To ensure a smoother right margin, you can turn on automatic hyphenation—in which case, any word that ends within the last .25 inch of a line will be hyphenated.

**To turn on automatic hyphenation in the document:**

▶ **1.** Review the paragraph above the footnotes on page 1. The text on the right side of this paragraph is uneven. Keeping an eye on this paragraph will help you see the benefits of hyphenation.

▶ **2.** On the ribbon, click the **PAGE LAYOUT** tab.

▶ **3.** In the Page Setup group, click the **Hyphenation** button to open the Hyphenation menu, and then click **Automatic**. The Hyphenation menu closes. Throughout the document, the text layout shifts to account for the insertion of hyphens in words that break near the end of a line. For example, in the last paragraph on page 1, the word "recommendations" is now hyphenated. See Figure 3-26.

| Figure 3-26 | Hyphenated document |
|---|---|

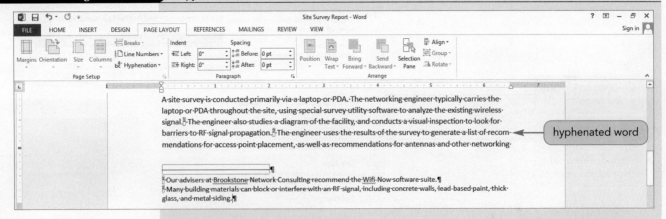

▶ **4.** Save the document.

Katherine plans to post a handout on the bulletin board at the art center to help inform the staff about the upcoming site survey, and she wants to include a sample handout in the report. Before you can add the sample of the handout, you need to divide the document into sections.

# Formatting a Document into Sections

A **section** is a part of a document that can have its own page orientation, margins, headers, footers, and so on. In other words, each section is like a document within a document. To divide a document into sections, you insert a **section break**. You can select from a few different kinds of section breaks. One of the most useful is a Next page section break, which inserts a page break and starts the new section on the next page. Another commonly used kind of section break, a Continuous section break, starts the section at the location of the insertion point without changing the page flow. To insert a section break, you click the Breaks button in the Page Setup group on the PAGE LAYOUT tab and then select the type of section break you want to insert.

Katherine wants to format the handout in landscape orientation, but the report is currently formatted in portrait orientation. To format part of a document in an orientation different from the rest of the document, you need to divide the document into sections.

### To insert a section break below the table:

▶ **1.** Press the **Ctrl+End** keys to move the insertion point to the end of the document, just below the table.

▶ **2.** In the Page Setup group, click the **Breaks** button. The Breaks gallery opens, as shown in Figure 3-27.

| Figure 3-27 | **Breaks gallery** |
| --- | --- |

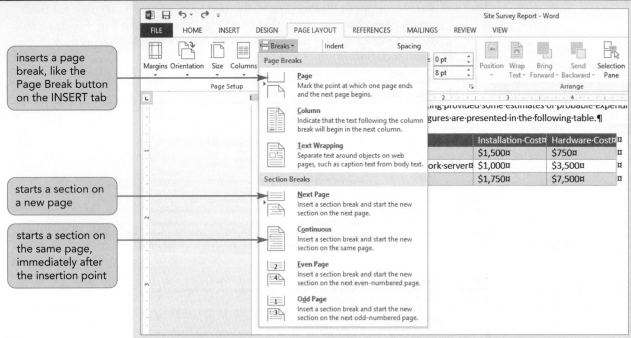

inserts a page break, like the Page Break button on the INSERT tab

starts a section on a new page

starts a section on the same page, immediately after the insertion point

The Page Breaks section of the gallery includes options for controlling how the text flows from page to page. The first option, Page, inserts a page break. It has the same effect as pressing the Page Break button on the INSERT tab or pressing the Ctrl+Enter keys. The Section Breaks section of the gallery includes four types of section breaks. The two you'll use most often are Next Page and Continuous.

▶ **3.** Under "Section Breaks," click **Next Page**. A section break is inserted, and the insertion point moves to the top of the new page 4.

▶ **4.** Scroll up until you can see the double-dotted line and the words "Section Break (Next Page)" below the table on page 3. This line indicates that a new section begins on the next page.

▶ **5.** Save the document.

**TIP**

To delete a section break, click to the left of the line representing the break, and then press the Delete key.

You've created a new page that is a separate section from the rest of the report. The sections are numbered consecutively. The first part of the document is section 1, and the new page is section 2. Now you can format section 2 in landscape orientation without affecting the rest of the document.

**To format section 2 in landscape orientation:**

1. Scroll down and verify that the insertion point is positioned at the top of the new page 4.

2. Change the Zoom level to **30%** so you can see all four pages of the document displayed side-by-side.

3. On the ribbon, click the **PAGE LAYOUT** tab.

4. In the Page Setup group, click the **Orientation** button, and then click **Landscape**. Section 2, which consists solely of page 4, changes to landscape orientation, as shown in Figure 3-28. Section 1, which consists of pages 1–3, remains in portrait orientation.

| Figure 3-28 | Page 4 formatted in landscape orientation |

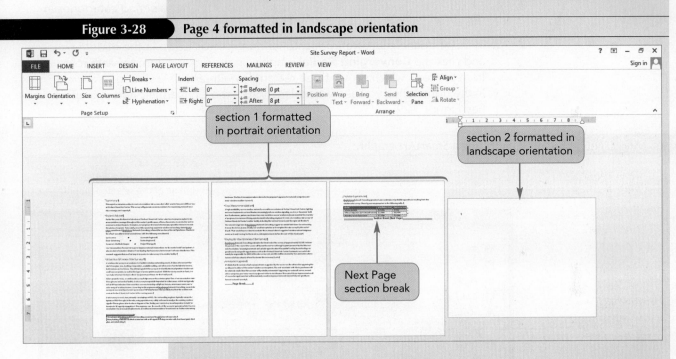

5. Change the Zoom level back to **120%**, and then save the document.

Page 4 is now formatted in landscape orientation, ready for you to create Katherine's handout, which will consist of a graphic that shows the benefits of a site survey. You'll use Word's SmartArt feature to create the graphic.

# Creating SmartArt

A **SmartArt** graphic is a diagram of shapes, such as circles, squares, or arrows. A well-designed SmartArt graphic can illustrate concepts that might otherwise require several paragraphs of explanation. To create a SmartArt graphic, you switch to the INSERT tab and then, in the Illustrations group, click the SmartArt button. This opens the Choose a SmartArt Graphic dialog box, where you can select from eight categories of graphics, including graphics designed to illustrate relationships, processes, and hierarchies. Within each category, you can choose from numerous designs. Once inserted into your document, a SmartArt graphic contains placeholder text that you replace with your own text. When a SmartArt graphic is selected, the SMARTART TOOLS DESIGN AND FORMAT tabs appear on the ribbon.

**To create a SmartArt graphic:**

▸ **1.** Verify that the insertion point is located at the top of page 4, which is blank.

▸ **2.** On the ribbon, click the **INSERT** tab.

▸ **3.** In the Illustrations group, click the **SmartArt** button. The Choose a SmartArt Graphic dialog box opens, with categories of SmartArt graphics in the left panel. The middle panel displays the graphics associated with the category currently selected in the left panel. The right panel displays a larger image of the graphic that is currently selected in the middle panel, along with an explanation of the graphic's purpose. By default, All is selected in the left panel.

▸ **4.** Explore the Choose a SmartArt Graphic dialog box by selecting categories in the left panel and viewing the graphics displayed in the middle panel.

▸ **5.** In the left panel, click **Relationship**, and then scroll down in the middle panel and click the **Converging Radial** graphic (in the first column, seventh row from the top), which shows three rectangles with arrows pointing to a circle. In the right panel, you see an explanation of the Converging Radial graphic. See Figure 3-29.

| Figure 3-29 | Selecting a SmartArt graphic |
| --- | --- |

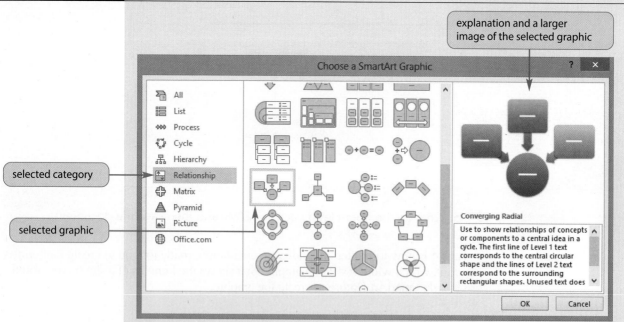

**6.** Click the **OK** button. The Converging Radial graphic, with placeholder text, is inserted at the top of page 4. The graphic is surrounded by a rectangular border, indicating that it is selected. The SMARTART TOOLS contextual tabs appear on the ribbon. To the left or right of the graphic, you also see the Text pane, a small window with a title bar that contains the text "Type your text here." See Figure 3-30.

| **Figure 3-30** | **SmartArt graphic with Text pane displayed** |

**Trouble?** If you do *not* see the Text pane, click the Text Pane button in the Create Graphic group on the SMARTART TOOLS DESIGN tab to select it.

The insertion point is blinking next to the first bullet in the Text pane, which is selected with an orange rectangle. The circle at the bottom of the SmartArt graphic is also selected, as indicated by the border with handles. At this point, anything you type next to the selected bullet in the Text pane will also appear in the selected circle in the SmartArt graphic.

**Trouble?** If you see the Text pane but the first bullet is not selected as shown in Figure 3-30, click next to the first bullet in the Text pane to select it.

Now you are ready to add text to the graphic.

### To add text to the SmartArt graphic:

1. Type **Better Wireless Network**. The new text is displayed in the Text pane and in the circle in the SmartArt graphic. Now you need to insert text in the three rectangles.

2. Press the ↓ key to move the insertion point down to the next placeholder bullet in the Text pane, and then type **Site Survey**. The new text is displayed in the Text pane and in the blue rectangle on the left. See Figure 3-31.

**Figure 3-31**   New text in Text pane and in SmartArt graphic

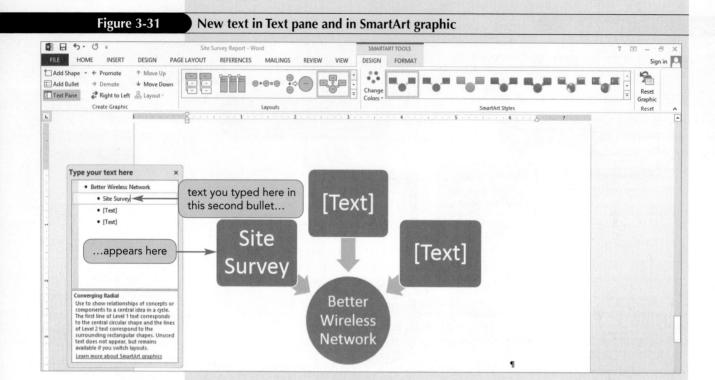

3. Press the ↓ key to move the insertion point down to the next placeholder bullet in the Text pane, and then type **Network Upgrades**. The new text appears in the middle rectangle and in the Text pane. You don't need the third rectangle, so you'll delete it.

4. Press the ↓ key to move the insertion point down to the next placeholder bullet in the Text pane, and then press the **Backspace** key. The rectangle on the right is deleted from the SmartArt graphic. The two remaining rectangles and the circle enlarge and shift position.

5. Make sure the SMARTART TOOLS DESIGN tab is still selected on the ribbon.

6. In the Create Graphic group, click the **Text Pane** button to deselect it. The Text pane closes.

7. Click in the white area inside the SmartArt border.

Next, you need to resize the SmartArt graphic so it fills the page.

**TIP**

To add a shape to a SmartArt graphic, click a shape in the SmartArt graphic, click the Add Shape arrow in the Create Graphic group on the DESIGN tab, and then click a placement option.

### To adjust the size of the SmartArt graphic:

1. Zoom out so you can see the entire page. As you can see on the ruler, the SmartArt is currently six inches wide. You could drag the SmartArt border to resize it, just as you can with any graphic, but you will get more precise results using the Size button on the SMARTART TOOLS FORMAT tab.

2. On the ribbon, click the **SMARTART TOOLS FORMAT** tab.

**3.** On the right side of the SMARTART TOOLS FORMAT tab, click the **Size** button to display the Height and Width boxes.

**4.** Click the **Height** box, type **6.5**, click the **Width** box, type **9**, and then press the **Enter** key. The SmartArt graphic resizes, so that it is now 9 inches wide and 6.5 inches high, taking up most of the page. See Figure 3-32.

| Figure 3-32 | **Resized SmartArt** |

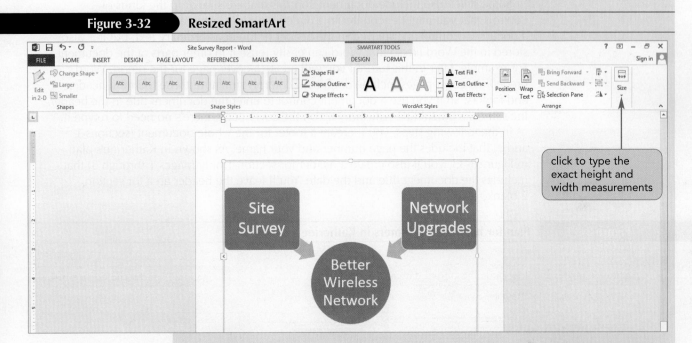

**Trouble?** If one of the shapes in the SmartArt graphic was resized, rather than the entire SmartArt graphic, the insertion point was located within the shape rather than in the white space. On the Quick Access Toolbar, click the Undo button ⟲, click in the white area inside the SmartArt border, and then repeat Steps 3 and 4.

**5.** Click outside the SmartArt border to deselect it, and then review the graphic centered on the page.

Next, you need to insert a header at the top of each page in the report and a footer at the bottom of each page in the report.

# Adding Headers and Footers

The first step to working with headers and footers is to open Header and Footer view. You can do that in three ways: (1) insert a page number using the Page Number button in the Header & Footer group on the INSERT tab; (2) double-click in the header area (in a page's top margin) or in the footer area (in a page's bottom margin); or (3) click the Header button or the Footer button on the INSERT tab.

By default, Word assumes that when you add something to the header or footer on any page of a document, you want the same text to appear on every page of the document. To create a different header or footer for the first page, you select the Different First Page check box in the Options group on the HEADER & FOOTER TOOLS DESIGN tab. When a document is divided into sections, like the Site Survey Report document, you can create a different header or footer for each section.

For a simple header or footer, double-click the header or footer area, and then type the text you want directly in the header or footer area, formatting the text as you would any other text in a document. To choose from a selection of predesigned header or footer styles, use the Header and Footer buttons on the HEADER & FOOTER TOOLS DESIGN tab (or on the INSERT tab). These buttons open galleries that you can use to select from a number of header and footer styles, some of which include page numbers and graphic elements such as horizontal lines or shaded boxes.

Some styles also include document controls that are similar to the kinds of controls that you might encounter in a dialog box. Any information that you enter in a document control is displayed in the header or footer as ordinary text, but it is also stored in the Word file so that Word can easily reuse it in other parts of the document. For example, later in this tutorial you will create a cover page for the report. Word's predefined cover pages include document controls similar to those found in headers and footers. So if you use a document control to enter the document title in the header, the same document title will show up on the cover page; there's no need to retype it.

In the following steps, you'll create a footer for the whole document (sections 1 and 2) that includes the page number and your name. As shown in Katherine's plan in Figure 3-33, you'll also create a header for section 1 only (pages 1 through 3) that includes the document title and the date. You'll leave the header area for section 2 blank.

**Figure 3-33**    **Plan for headers and footers in Katherine's report**

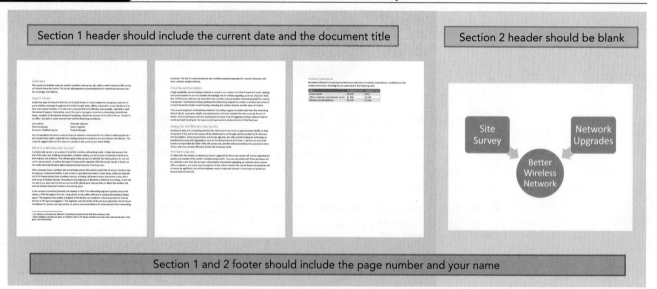

© 2014 Cengage Learning

First you will create the footer on page 1, so you can see how the footer fits below the footnotes at the bottom of the page.

### To create a footer for the entire document:

1. Change the Zoom level to **120%**, and then scroll up until you can see the bottom of page 1 and the top of page 2.

2. Double-click in the white space below the footnotes on page 1. The document switches to Header and Footer view. The HEADER & FOOTER TOOLS DESIGN tab is displayed on the ribbon. The insertion point is positioned on the left side of the footer area, ready for you to begin typing. The label "Footer -Section 1-" tells you that the insertion point is located in the footer for section 1. The document text (including the footnotes) is gray,

indicating that you cannot edit it in Header and Footer view. The header area for section 1 is also visible on top of page 2. The default footer tab stops (which are different from the default tab stops in the main document) are visible on the ruler. See Figure 3-34.

**Figure 3-34** Creating a footer

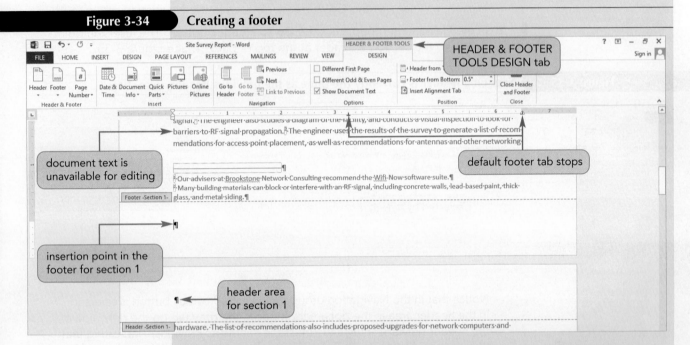

3. Type your first and last name, and then press the **Enter** key. The insertion point moves to the second line in the footer, aligned along the left margin. This is where you will insert the page number.

4. In the Header & Footer group, click the **Page Number** button. The Page Number menu opens. Because the insertion point is already located where you want to insert the page number, you'll use the Current Position option.

5. Point to **Current Position**. A gallery of page number styles opens. Katherine wants to use the Accent Bar 2 style.

6. Click the **Accent Bar 2** style (the third style from the top). The word "Page," a vertical bar, and the page number are inserted in the footer.

Next, you'll check to make sure that the footer you just created for section 1 also appears in section 2. To move between headers or footers in separate sections, you can use the buttons in the Navigation group on the HEADER & FOOTER TOOLS DESIGN tab.

7. In the Navigation group, click the **Next** button. Word displays the footer for the next section in the document—that is, the footer for section 2, which appears at the bottom of page 4. The label at the top of the footer area reads "Footer -Section 2-" and it contains the same text (your name and the page number) in this footer as in section 1. Word assumes, by default, that when you type text in one footer, you want it to appear in all the footers in the document.

**TIP**

To change the numbering style or to specify a number to use as the first page number, click the Page Number button in the Header & Footer group, and then click Format Page Numbers.

Now you need to create a header for section 1. Katherine does not want to include a header in section 2 because it would distract attention from the SmartArt graphic. So you will first separate the header for section 1 from the header for section 2.

**To separate the headers for section 1 and section 2:**

▶ **1.** Verify that the insertion point is located in the section 2 footer area at the bottom of page 4, and that the HEADER & FOOTER TOOLS DESIGN tab is selected on the ribbon. To switch from the footer to the header in the current section, you can use the Go to Header button in the Navigation group.

▶ **2.** In the Navigation group, click the **Go to Header** button. The insertion point moves to the section 2 header at the top of page 4. See Figure 3-35.

| Figure 3-35 | Section 2 header is currently the same as the previous header, in section 1 |

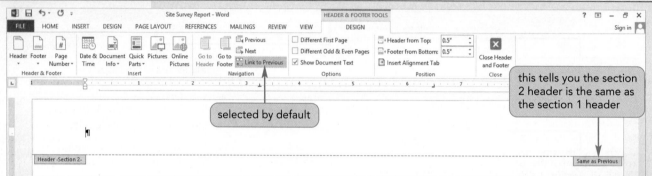

this tells you the section 2 header is the same as the section 1 header

selected by default

Notice that in the Navigation group, the Link to Previous button is selected. In the header area in the document window, the gray tab on the right side of the header border contains the message "Same as Previous," indicating that the section 2 header is set up to display the same text as the header in the previous section, which is section 1. To make the section 2 header a separate entity, you need to break the link between the section 1 and section 2 headers.

**TIP**

When you create a header for a section, it doesn't matter what page you're working on as long as the insertion point is located in a header in that section.

▶ **3.** In the Navigation group, click the **Link to Previous** button to deselect it. The Same as Previous tab is removed from the right side of the section 2 header border.

▶ **4.** In the Navigation group, click the **Previous** button. The insertion point moves up to the nearest header in the previous section, which is the section 1 header at the top of page 3. The label "Header -Section 1-" identifies this as a section 1 header.

▶ **5.** In the Header & Footer group, click the **Header** button. A gallery of header styles opens.

▶ **6.** Scroll down and review the various header styles, and then click the **Grid** style (eighth style from the top). The placeholder text "[Document title]" is aligned at the left margin. The placeholder text "[Date]" is aligned at the right margin.

▶ **7.** Click the **[Document title]** placeholder text. The placeholder text is now selected within a document control. See Figure 3-36.

**Figure 3-36** Adding a header to section 1

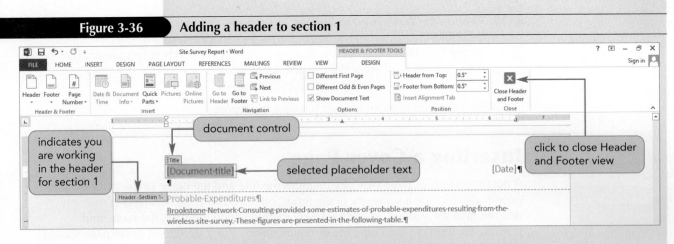

8. Type **Wireless Site Survey Recommendation**. The text you just typed is displayed in the document control instead of the placeholder text. Next, you need to add the date. The header style you selected includes a date picker document control, which allows you to select the date from a calendar.

9. Click the **[Date]** placeholder text to display an arrow in the document control, and then click the arrow. A calendar for the current month appears, as shown in Figure 3-37. In the calendar, the current date is outlined in dark blue.

**Figure 3-37** Adding a date to the section 1 header

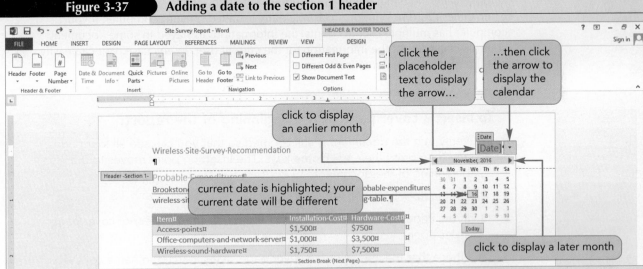

10. Click the current date. The current date, including the year, is inserted in the document control.

11. Scroll up slightly and click anywhere in the Section 1 footer (on the preceding page) to deselect the date document control. You are finished creating the header and footer for Katherine's report, so you can close Header and Footer view and return to Print Layout view.

12. In the Close group, click the **Close Header and Footer** button, or double-click anywhere in the main document, and then save your work.

▶ **13.** Change the Zoom level to **30%** so you can see all four pages of the document, including the header at the top of pages 1–3 and the footer at the bottom of pages 1–4. Take a moment to compare your completed headers and footers with Katherine's plan for the headers and footers shown earlier in Figure 3-33.

Finally, you need to insert a cover page for the report.

# Inserting a Cover Page

A document's cover page typically includes the title and the name of the author. Some people also include a summary of the report on the cover page, which is commonly referred to as an abstract. In addition, you might include the date, the name and possibly the logo of your company or organization, and a subtitle. A cover page should not include the document header or footer.

To insert a preformatted cover page at the beginning of the document, you use the Cover Page button on the INSERT tab. You can choose from a variety of cover page styles, all of which include document controls in which you can enter the document title, the document's author, the date, and so on. These document controls are linked to any other document controls in the document. For example, you already entered "Wireless Site Survey Recommendation" into a document control in the header of Katherine's report. So if you use a cover page that contains a similar document control, "Wireless Site Survey Recommendation" will be displayed on the cover page automatically. Note that document controls sometimes display information entered when either Word or Windows was originally installed on your computer. If your computer has multiple user accounts, the information displayed in some document controls might reflect the information for the current user. In any case, you can easily edit the contents of a document control.

### To insert a cover page at the beginning of the report:

▶ **1.** Verify that the document is still zoomed so that you can see all four pages, and then press the **Ctrl+Home** keys. The insertion point moves to the beginning of the document.

▶ **2.** On the ribbon, click the **INSERT** tab.

▶ **3.** In the Pages group, click the **Cover Page** button. A gallery of cover page styles opens.

Notice that the names of the cover page styles match the names of the preformatted header styles you saw earlier. For example, the list includes a Grid cover page, which is designed to match the Grid header used in this document. To give a document a uniform look, it's helpful to use elements with the same style throughout.

▶ **4.** Scroll down the gallery to see the cover page styles, and then locate the Grid cover page style.

▶ **5.** Click the **Grid** cover page style. The new cover page is inserted at the beginning of the document.

> **TIP**
>
> To delete a cover page that you inserted from the Cover Page gallery, click the Cover Page button in the Pages group, and then click Remove Current Cover Page.

▶ **6.** Change the Zoom level to **120%**, and then scroll down to display the report title in the middle of the cover page. The only difference between the title "Wireless Site Survey Recommendation" here and the title you entered in the document header is that here the title is displayed in all uppercase. The cover page also includes document controls for a subtitle and an abstract. See Figure 3-38.

**Figure 3-38**    Newly inserted cover page

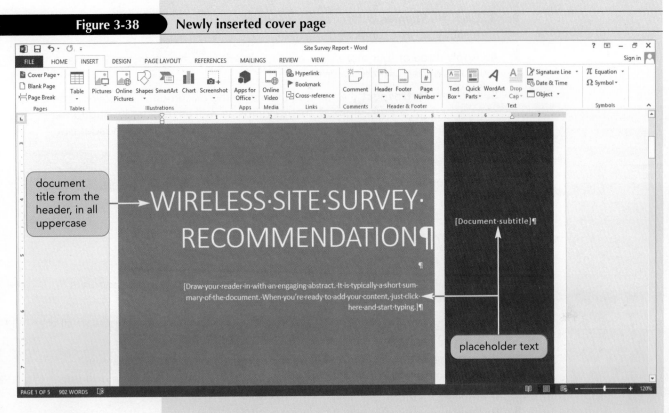

You need to type a subtitle in the subtitle document control on the right side of the page.

7. Click the **[Document subtitle]** placeholder text, and then type **Orchard Street Art Center**. Next, you will remove the abstract document control because you do not need an abstract for this report.

8. Below the document title, right-click the placeholder text that begins **[Draw your reader in...** to display the shortcut menu, and then click **Remove Content Control**. The content control is removed from the cover page.

9. Save the document.

## Changing the Theme

The report now contains several formatting elements that are controlled by the document's theme, so changing the theme will affect the document's overall appearance. Katherine suggests that you apply a different theme to the document.

### To change the document's theme:

1. Change the Zoom level to **40%** so you can see the first four pages side-by-side, with part of the fifth page visible on the bottom.

2. On the ribbon, click the **DESIGN** tab.

> **3.** Click the **Themes** button, select any theme you want, and then review the results in the document.

> **4.** Apply three or four more different themes of your choice and review the results of each in the document.

> **5.** Click the **Retrospect** theme, and then save the document. The cover page is now orange and olive green, the headings as well as the header and footer text are orange, and the table is formatted with an olive green header row and gray shading.

Your work on the report is finished. You should preview the report before closing it.

### To preview the report:

> **1.** On the ribbon, click the **FILE** tab.

> **2.** In the navigation bar, click the **Print** tab. The cover page of the report is displayed in the document preview in the right pane.

> **3.** Examine the document preview, using the arrow buttons at the bottom of the pane to display each page.

> **4.** If you need to make any changes to the report, return to Print Layout view, edit the document, preview the document again, and then save the document.

> **5.** Display the document in Print Layout view.

> **6.** Change the Zoom level back to **120%**, and then press the **Ctrl+Home** keys to make sure the insertion point is located on the first page.

## Reviewing a Document in Read Mode

The members of the board of directors might choose to print the report, but some might prefer to read it on their computers instead. In that case, they can take advantage of **Read Mode**, a document view designed to make reading on a screen as easy as possible. Unlike Print Layout view, which mimics the look of the printed page with its margins and page breaks, Read Mode focuses on the document's content. Read Mode displays as much content as possible on the screen at a time, with buttons that allow you to display more. Note that you can't edit text in Read Mode. To do that, you need to switch back to Page Layout view.

### To display the Site Survey document in Read Mode:

> **1.** In the status bar, click the **Read Mode** button 📖. The document switches to Read Mode, with a reduced version of the cover page on the left and the first part of the document text on the right. On the left edge of the status bar, the message "SCREENS 1-2 OF 8" explains that you are currently viewing the first two screens out of a total of 8.

> **Trouble?** If your status bar indicates that you have a different number of screens, change the Zoom level as needed so that the document is split into 8 screens.

The title page on the left is screen 1. The text on the right is screen 2. To display more of the document, you can click the arrow button on the right. See Figure 3-39.

| **Figure 3-39** | **Document displayed in Read Mode** |

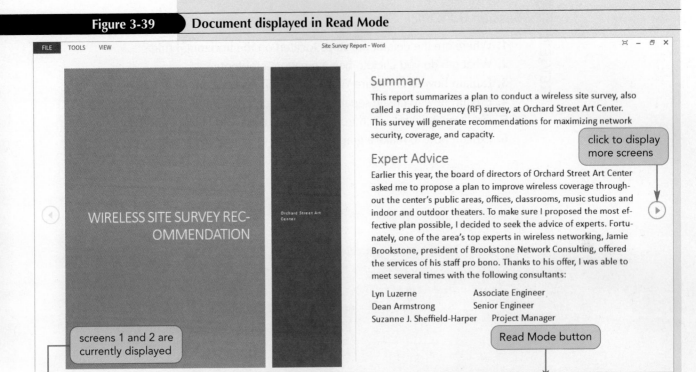

2. Click the **right arrow** button ⊙ on the right to display screens 3 and 4. A left arrow button now appears on the left side of the screen. You could click it to move back to the previous screens.

3. Click the **right arrow** button ⊙ to display screens 5 and 6, and then click the **right arrow** button ⊙ again to display the final two screens. To zoom in on the SmartArt graphic, you can double-click it.

4. Double-click the SmartArt graphic. An object zoom window opens, with the SmartArt graphic displayed. You can display an object zoom window like this for any graphic.

5. In the upper-right corner of the object zoom window, click the **magnifying glass** button ⊡ to zoom in on the SmartArt graphic even more.

6. Click the **magnifying glass** button ⊡ to return to the previous zoom level.

7. Click anywhere outside the object zoom window to return to screens 7 and 8 in Read Mode.

8. Click the **left arrow** button ⊙ on the left as necessary to return to screens 1 and 2, and then click the **Print Layout** button ⊟ in the status bar to return to Page Layout view.

9. Close the document.

You now have a draft of the Site Survey Report document, including a cover page, the report text, a nicely formatted table, and the SmartArt graphic (in landscape orientation).

REVIEW

## Session 3.2 Quick Check

1. Where are the default tab stops located on the horizontal ruler?
2. What tab do you click to begin creating a footnote?
3. Explain how to configure Word to hyphenate a document automatically.
4. Explain how to create separate headers for a document with two sections.
5. List three ways to switch from Page Layout view to Header and Footer view.
6. Explain how to make a graphic easier to view in Read Mode.

ASSESS

## SAM Projects

Put your skills into practice with SAM Projects! SAM Projects for this tutorial can be found online. If you have a SAM account, go to www.cengage.com/sam2013 to download the most recent Project Instructions and Start Files.

PRACTICE

## Review Assignments

**Data File needed for the Review Assignments: Security.docx**

The wireless site survey has been completed, and the Orchard Street Art Center has upgraded its network. Now, Katherine Hua is organizing a series of network security training classes for the art center staff. She has begun working on a report for the board that outlines basic information about the training. You need to format the report, add a table at the end containing a preliminary schedule, and create a sample graphic that Katherine could use in a handout announcing the training. Complete the following steps:

1. Open the file **Security** located in the Word3 ▸ Review folder included with your Data Files, and then save it as **Security Training Report** in the location specified by your instructor.
2. Promote the "Training Schedule" and "Level 1 Equipment Needs" headings from Heading 2 text to Heading 1 text, and then move the "Level 1 Equipment Needs" heading and its body text up above the "Training Schedule" heading.
3. Insert a page break before the "Training Schedule" heading. Insert a blank paragraph at the end of the new page 2, and then insert a table using the information shown in Figure 3-40. Format the header row in bold.

---

**Figure 3-40**     Information for training schedule table

| Date | Topic |
|------|-------|
| April 21 | Applications |
| March 16 | User account permissions |
| April 28 | Firewall procedures |
| April 6 | Wireless devices |
| March 3 | Password security |

© 2014 Cengage Learning

4. Sort the table by the contents of the "Date" column in ascending order.
5. In the appropriate location in the table, insert a new row for a **User privacy** class on **March 23**.
6. Delete the "Applications" row from the table.
7. Modify the widths of both columns to accommodate the widest entry in each.
8. Apply the Grid Table 4 - Accent 2 style to the table.
9. On page 1, replace the text "[instructor names]" with a tabbed list of instructors and their specialties, using the following information: **Jackie Fuhrman-Dunaway, Wireless security; Marcolo Jimenez, Multimedia wireless security; Surila Jin, Web privacy; Elizabeth Lawson, User support**. Insert a tab after each name, and don't include any punctuation in the list.
10. Use a left tab stop to align the instructors' specialities 2.5 inches from the left margin, and then adjust the list's paragraph spacing so it appears to be a single paragraph.

11. Locate the first sentence below the "Level 1 Equipment Needs" heading. At the end of that sentence, insert a footnote that reads **Some board members mentioned the possibility of holding classes in the concert hall, but the instructors prefer the smaller lecture hall, where microphones are unnecessary**.

12. Hyphenate the document using the default settings.

13. After the training schedule table on page 2, insert a section break that starts a new, third page, and then format the new page in landscape orientation. Insert a SmartArt graphic that illustrates the advantages of computer classes. Use the Equation graphic from the Process category, and, from left to right, include the following text in the SmartArt diagram: **User Education**, **Good Network Management**, and **Secure Wireless Network**. Do not include any punctuation in the SmartArt. Size the SmartArt graphic to fill the page.

14. Create a footer for sections 1 and 2 that aligns your first and last names at the left margin. Insert the page number, without any design elements and without the word "Page," below your name.

15. Separate the section 1 header from the section 2 header, and then create a header for section 1 using the Retrospect header style. Enter **SECURITY TRAINING** as the document title, and select the current date. Note that the document title will be displayed in all uppercase no matter how you type it.

16. Insert a cover page using the Retrospect style. If you typed the document title in all uppercase in the header, it will be displayed in all uppercase here. If you used a mix of uppercase and lowercase in the header, you'll see a mix here. Revise the document title as necessary to make it all uppercase, and then add the following subtitle: **A REPORT FOR THE ORCHARD STREET ART CENTER BOARD OF DIRECTORS**. Enter your name in the Author document control (you might have to replace a default name inserted by Word), and then delete the Company Name and Company Address document controls.

17. Change the document theme to Integral, save and preview the report, and then close it.

## Case Problem 1

APPLY

**Data File needed for this Case Problem: Greenware.docx**

***Greenware Consortium***   You are the assistant business manager of Greenware Consortium, a professional organization for LEED contractors in Seattle, Washington and the surrounding area. LEED, which is short for Leadership in Energy and Environmental Design, is a certification system designed to encourage environmentally friendly building construction and maintenance. Contractors join the Greenware Consortium to make professional contacts with like-minded vendors and customers. You have been asked to help prepare an annual report for the board of directors. The current draft is not complete, but it contains enough for you to get started. Complete the following steps:

1. Open the file **Greenware** located in the Word3 ▶ Case1 folder included with your Data Files, and then save it as **Greenware Report** in the location specified by your instructor.

2. Adjust the heading levels so that the "Greenware Faire" and "Green Tech Fest" headings are formatted with the Heading 2 style.

3. Move the "Membership Forecast" heading and its body text down to the end of the report.

4. Format the Board of Directors list using a left tab stop with a dot leader at the 2.2-inch mark. (*Hint*: Use the Dialog Box Launcher in the Paragraph group on the PAGE LAYOUT tab to open the Paragraph dialog box, and then click the Tabs button at the bottom of the Indents and Spacing tab to open the Tabs dialog box.)

5. At the end of the first paragraph below the "Going Green Walking Tours" heading, insert the following footnote: **The Going Green walking tours are sponsored by the Seattle Public Works Department in association with the Seattle Green for Life Foundation**.

6. Locate the "Purpose" heading on page 1. At the end of the body text below that heading, insert the following footnote: **We recently signed a ten-year contract renewal with our website host, NetMind Solutions**.

7. Insert a page break that moves the "Membership Forecast" heading to the top of a new page, and then, below the body text on the new page, insert a table consisting of three columns and four rows.

8. In the table, enter the information shown in Figure 3-41. Format the column headings in bold.

**Figure 3-41**     Information for membership forecast table

| Membership Type | 2016 | Projected 2017 |
|---|---|---|
| Contractor | 260 | 285 |
| Vendor | 543 | 670 |
| Building Owner/Operator | 350 | 400 |

© 2014 Cengage Learning

9. Sort the table in ascending order by membership type.

10. In the appropriate location in the table, insert a row for a **Student/Apprentice** membership type, with **250** members in 2016, and **300** projected members in 2017.

11. Adjust the column widths so each column accommodates the widest entry.

12. Format the table using the Grid Table 4 - Accent 1 table style without banded rows or a first column.

13. Hyphenate the document using the default settings.

14. Insert a Blank footer, and then type your name to replace the selected placeholder text in the footer's left margin. In the right margin, insert a page number using the Accent Bar 3 style. (*Hint:* Press the Tab key twice to move the insertion point to the right margin before inserting the page number, and then insert the page number at the current location.)

15. Insert a cover page using the Sideline style. Enter the company name, **Greenware Consortium**, and the title, **Annual Report**, in the appropriate document controls. In the subtitle document control, enter **Prepared by [Your Name]** (but replace "[Your Name]" with your first and last names). Delete the Author document control, which might contain a default name inserted by Word, and then insert the current date in the Date document control.

16. Change the document theme to Ion.

17. Save, preview, and then close the document.

## Case Problem 2

**TROUBLESHOOT**

Data File needed for this Case Problem: Evaluation.docx

*Customer Evaluation Report*   Academy Art Tours specializes in European tours emphasizing art and architecture. After managing this year's Masters of Architecture tour, Lisa Marisca has begun writing a report summarizing the customer evaluation forms. She asks you to review her incomplete draft and fix some problems. Complete the following steps:

1. Open the file named **Evaluation** located in the Word3 ▸ Case2 folder included with your Data Files, and then save it as **Evaluation Report** in the location specified by your instructor.

⚙ **Troubleshoot** 2. Adjust the document so that the following are true:
- The heading "Problems Acquiring Updated Passports," its body text, and the SmartArt graphic appear on the last page in landscape orientation, with the rest of the report in portrait orientation.
- In section 1, the heading "Summary" is displayed at the top of page 2.
- The document header contains your first and last names but not a content control for the document title.
- Neither the header nor the footer is displayed on page 1.
- The footer is not displayed on the last page of the document. (*Hint:* After you break the link between sections, you'll need to delete the contents of the footer in one section.)

⚙ **Troubleshoot** 3. On pages 2 and 3, promote headings as necessary so all the headings are on the same level.

4. Increase the paragraph spacing before the first paragraph, "Masters of Architecture," on page 1 as much as necessary so that the paragraph is located at about the 2-inch mark on the vertical ruler. When you're finished, the text should be centered vertically on the page, so it looks like a cover page.

⚙ **Troubleshoot** 5. On page 2, remove any extra rows and columns in the table, and sort the information in a logical way. When you are finished, format it with a style that applies green (Accent 6) shading to the header row, with banded rows below, and remove any bold formatting as necessary.

6. Add a fourth shape to the SmartArt Graphic with the text **Submit completed form, photo, and fee to post office clerk**. Resize the graphic to fill the white space below the document text.

7. Save the document, review it in Read Mode, preview it, and then close it.

## Case Problem 3

**There are no Data Files needed for this Case Problem.**

*"Aiden Eats" Blog and Newsletter*    Aiden Malloy publishes his reviews of Minneapolis restaurants both in his blog, Aiden Eats, and in a printed newsletter of the same name. These publications have become so popular that Aiden has decided to try selling advertising space in both venues to local businesses. A colleague has just emailed him a list of potential advertisers. Aiden asks you to create and format a table containing the list of advertisers. When you're finished with that project, you'll create a table detailing some of his recent expenses. Complete the following steps:

1. Open a new, blank document, and then save it as **Advertiser Table** in the location specified by your instructor.

2. Create the table shown in Figure 3-42.

**Figure 3-42    Advertiser table**

| Business | Contact | Phone |
|---|---|---|
| Allenton Knife Sharpening | Peter Allenton | 555-5555 |
| Bizmark Restaurant Supply | Nolan Everdeen | 555-5555 |
| Spices Boutique | Sigrid Larson | 555-5555 |
| WestMark Kitchen Design | Sheryl Wu | 555-5555 |

© 2014 Cengage Learning

For the table style, start with the Grid Table 4 - Accent 1 table style, and then make any necessary changes. Use the Blue, Accent 1 color for the borders. The final table should be about 6.5 inches wide and 2.5 inches tall, as measured on the horizontal and vertical rulers. (*Hint:* Remember that you can drag the Table Resize handle to increase the table's overall size.)

3. Replace "Peter Allenton" with your first and last names.

4. Save, preview, and then close the Advertiser Table document.

5. Open a new, blank document, and then save it as **Expense Table** in the location specified by your instructor.

6. Create the table shown in Figure 3-43.

**Figure 3-43**    **Expense table**

| Restaurant | Date | Expense |
|---|---|---|
| Beverly Coffee and Bake Shoppe | 2/3/16 | $13.50 |
| Vietnam Noodle House | 2/10/16 | $23.00 |
| The Everett Club | 2/23/16 | $45.50 |
| | Total | $82.00 |

© 2014 Cengage Learning

For the table style, start with the Grid Table 4 - Accent 1 table style, and then make any necessary changes. Use the Blue, Accent 1 color for the borders. Note that in the bottom row, you'll need to merge two cells and right-align text within the new, merged cell.

7. For the total, use a formula instead of simply typing the amount. (*Hint:* Click in the cell where you want to insert a formula to sum the values, click the TABLE TOOLS LAYOUT tab, and then click the Formula button in the Data group to open the Formula dialog box, and then click the OK button.)

8. Save, preview, and then close the Expense Table document.

## Case Problem 4

There are no Data Files needed for this Case Problem.

***Friends of Triangle Beach***    Kate Chomsky coordinates volunteers who monitor and protect native plant species on Triangle Beach, a nature preserve on the eastern coast of Florida. She needs a flyer to hand out at an upcoming neighborhood festival, where she hopes to recruit more volunteers. You can use Word's table features to lay out the flyer as shown in Kate's sketch in Figure 3-44. At the very end, you'll remove the table borders.

**CHALLENGE**

**Figure 3-44**    **Sketch for Triangle Beach flyer**

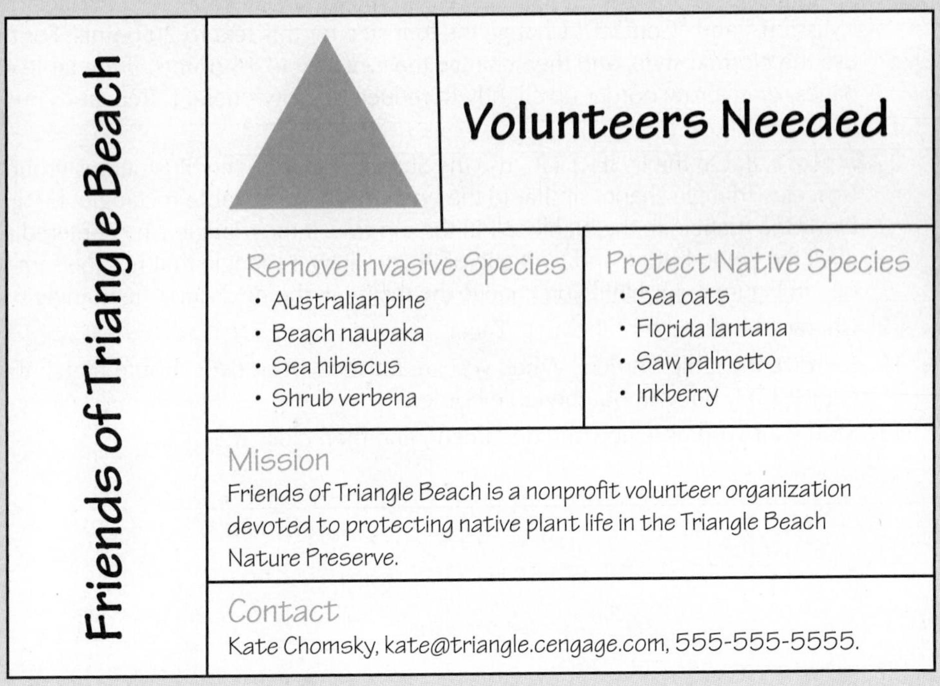

**Friends of Triangle Beach**

**Volunteers Needed**

**Remove Invasive Species**
- Australian pine
- Beach naupaka
- Sea hibiscus
- Shrub verbena

**Protect Native Species**
- Sea oats
- Florida lantana
- Saw palmetto
- Inkberry

**Mission**
Friends of Triangle Beach is a nonprofit volunteer organization devoted to protecting native plant life in the Triangle Beach Nature Preserve.

**Contact**
Kate Chomsky, kate@triangle.cengage.com, 555-555-5555.

© 2014 Cengage Learning

Complete the following steps:

1. Open a new, blank document, and then save it as **Triangle Beach** in the location specified by your instructor.

2. Change the document's orientation to landscape.

⊕ **Explore** 3. Use the Table button on the INSERT tab, to access the Insert Table menu, and then click Draw Table at the bottom of the menu to activate the Draw Table pointer (which looks like a pencil). Click in the upper-left corner of the document (near the paragraph mark), and, using the rulers as guides, drag down and to the right to draw a rectangle that is 9 inches wide and 6 inches high. After you draw the rectangle, you can adjust its height and width using the Height and Width boxes in the Cell Size group on the TABLE TOOLS LAYOUT tab, if necessary. (*Hint*: If the Draw Table pointer disappears after you change the table's height and width, you can turn it back on by clicking the Draw Table button in the Draw group on the TABLE TOOLS LAYOUT tab.)

⊕ **Explore** 4. Use the Draw Table pointer to draw the columns and rows shown in Figure 3-44. For example, to draw the column border for the "Friends of Triangle Beach" column, click the top of the rectangle at the point where you want the right column border to be located, and then drag down to the bottom of the rectangle. Use the same technique to draw rows. (*Hint:* To delete a border, click the Eraser button in the Draw group on the TABLE TOOLS LAYOUT tab, click anywhere on the border you want to erase, and then click the Eraser button again to turn it off.)

5. When you are finished drawing the table, press the Esc key to turn off the Draw Table pointer.

⊕ **Explore** 6. In the left column, type the text **Friends of Triangle Beach**. With the pointer still in that cell, click the TABLE TOOLS LAYOUT tab, and then in the Alignment group, click the Text Direction button twice to position the text vertically so that it reads from bottom to top. Using the formatting options on the HOME tab, format the text in 36-point font. Use the Align Center button in the Alignment group to center the text in the cell. (*Hint:* You will probably have to adjust and readjust the row and column borders throughout these steps until all the elements of the table are positioned properly.)

7. Type the remaining text as shown in Figure 3-44. Replace "Kate Chomsky" with your own name, remove the hyperlink formatting from the email address, and format it in bold. Change the font size for "Volunteers Needed" to 36 points, and center align the text in that cell. Use the Heading 1 style for the following text—"Remove Invasive Species," "Protect Native Species," "Mission," and "Contact." Change the font size for this text to 20 points. For the remaining text, use the Normal style, and then change the font size to 16 points. If the table expands to two pages, drag a row border up slightly to reduce the row's height. Repeat as necessary until the table fits on one page.

⊕ **Explore** 8. On the INSERT tab, use the Shapes button in the Illustrations group to draw the Isosceles Triangle shape, similar to the way you drew the table rectangle, by dragging the pointer. Draw the triangle in the blank cell in the top row. If the triangle isn't centered neatly in the cell, click the Undo button and try again until you draw a triangle that has the same proportions as the one in Figure 3-44. Until you change the theme in the next step, the triangle will be blue.

9. Change the document theme to Facet.

10. Remove the table borders. When you are finished, your flyer should match the table shown in Figure 3-44, but without the table borders.

11. Save your work, preview the document, and then close it.

## OBJECTIVES

**Session 1.1**
- Open and close a workbook
- Navigate through a workbook and worksheet
- Select cells and ranges
- Plan and create a workbook
- Insert, rename, and move worksheets
- Enter text, dates, and numbers
- Undo and redo actions
- Resize columns and rows

**Session 1.2**
- Enter formulas and the SUM and COUNT functions
- Copy and paste formulas
- Move or copy cells and ranges
- Insert and delete rows, columns, and ranges
- Create patterned text with Flash Fill
- Add cell borders and change font size
- Change worksheet views
- Prepare a workbook for printing
- Save a workbook with a new filename

# Getting Started with Excel

*Creating a Customer Order Report*

## Case | *Sparrow & Pond*

Sally Hughes is part owner of Sparrow & Pond, a small bookstore in Hudson, New Hampshire. Among her many tasks is to purchase new books from publishers. She also purchases rare and first edition books from online auctions as well as local library, estate, and garage sales.

Sally needs to quickly track sales data, compile customer profiles, and generate financial reports. She can perform all of these tasks with **Microsoft Excel 2013** (or **Excel**), an application used to enter, analyze, and present quantitative data. Sally asks you to use Excel to record a recent book order from a regular Sparrow & Pond customer.

**EXCEL**

## STARTING DATA FILES

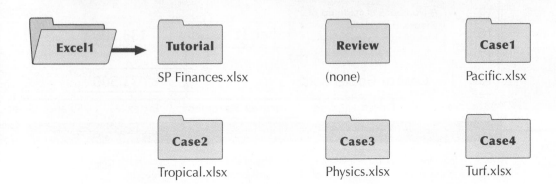

| Excel1 → Tutorial | Review | Case1 |
|---|---|---|
| SP Finances.xlsx | (none) | Pacific.xlsx |

| Case2 | Case3 | Case4 |
|---|---|---|
| Tropical.xlsx | Physics.xlsx | Turf.xlsx |

# Session 1.1 Visual Overview:

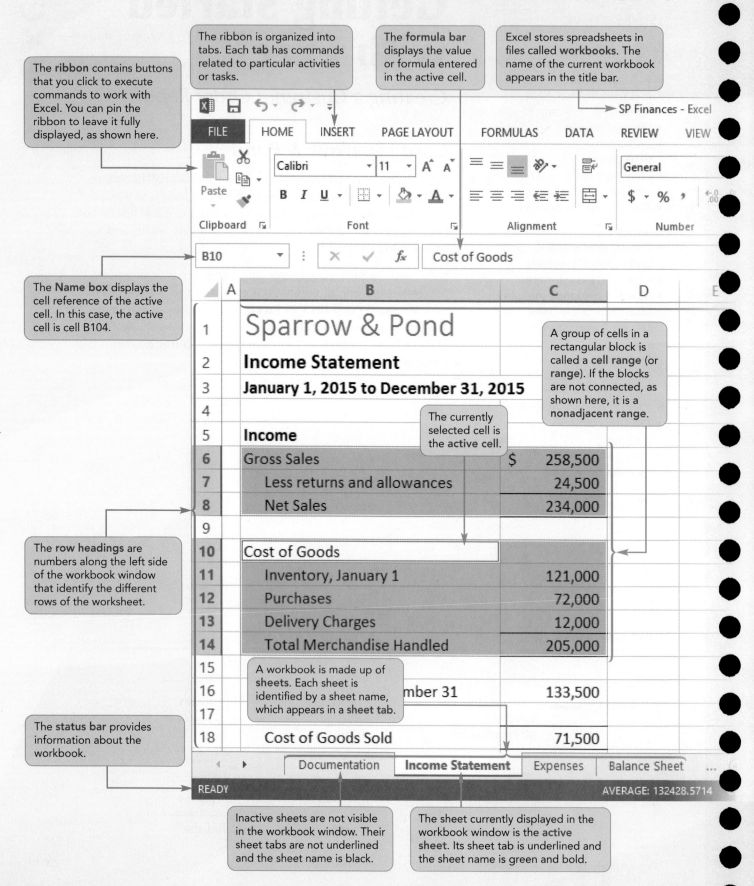

The **ribbon** is organized into tabs. Each **tab** has commands related to particular activities or tasks.

The **formula bar** displays the value or formula entered in the active cell.

Excel stores spreadsheets in files called **workbooks**. The name of the current workbook appears in the title bar.

The **ribbon** contains buttons that you click to execute commands to work with Excel. You can pin the ribbon to leave it fully displayed, as shown here.

The **Name box** displays the cell reference of the active cell. In this case, the active cell is cell B104.

A group of cells in a rectangular block is called a **cell range** (or **range**). If the blocks are not connected, as shown here, it is a **nonadjacent range**.

The currently selected cell is the **active cell**.

The **row headings** are numbers along the left side of the workbook window that identify the different rows of the worksheet.

A workbook is made up of **sheets**. Each sheet is identified by a sheet name, which appears in a **sheet tab**.

The **status bar** provides information about the workbook.

Inactive sheets are not visible in the workbook window. Their sheet tabs are not underlined and the sheet name is black.

The sheet currently displayed in the workbook window is the **active sheet**. Its sheet tab is underlined and the sheet name is green and bold.

SP Finances - Excel

FILE    HOME    INSERT    PAGE LAYOUT    FORMULAS    DATA    REVIEW    VIEW

Calibri    11    A  A

B  I  U

General

Clipboard    Font    Alignment    Number

B10    fx    Cost of Goods

| | A | B | C | D | E |
|---|---|---|---|---|---|
| 1 | | Sparrow & Pond | | | |
| 2 | | **Income Statement** | | | |
| 3 | | **January 1, 2015 to December 31, 2015** | | | |
| 4 | | | | | |
| 5 | | **Income** | | | |
| 6 | | Gross Sales | $ 258,500 | | |
| 7 | | Less returns and allowances | 24,500 | | |
| 8 | | Net Sales | 234,000 | | |
| 9 | | | | | |
| 10 | | Cost of Goods | | | |
| 11 | | Inventory, January 1 | 121,000 | | |
| 12 | | Purchases | 72,000 | | |
| 13 | | Delivery Charges | 12,000 | | |
| 14 | | Total Merchandise Handled | 205,000 | | |
| 15 | | | | | |
| 16 | | mber 31 | 133,500 | | |
| 17 | | | | | |
| 18 | | Cost of Goods Sold | 71,500 | | |

Documentation    **Income Statement**    Expenses    Balance Sheet

READY    AVERAGE: 132428.5714

# The Excel Window

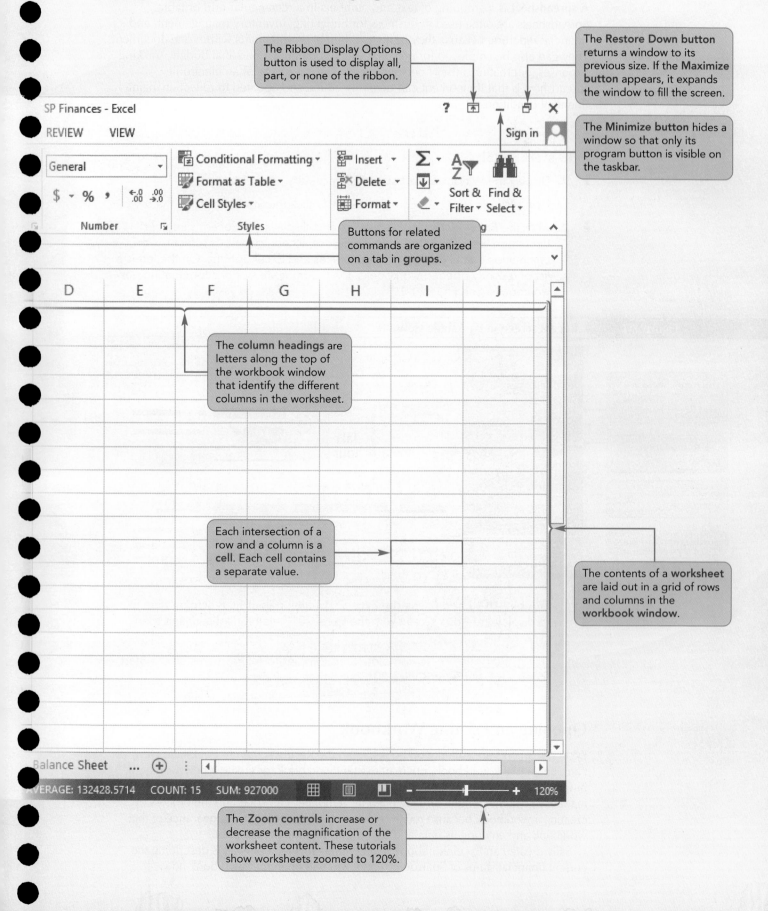

The Ribbon Display Options button is used to display all, part, or none of the ribbon.

The **Restore Down button** returns a window to its previous size. If the **Maximize button** appears, it expands the window to fill the screen.

The **Minimize button** hides a window so that only its program button is visible on the taskbar.

Buttons for related commands are organized on a tab in **groups**.

The **column headings** are letters along the top of the workbook window that identify the different columns in the worksheet.

Each intersection of a row and a column is a **cell**. Each cell contains a separate value.

The contents of a **worksheet** are laid out in a grid of rows and columns in the **workbook window**.

The **Zoom controls** increase or decrease the magnification of the worksheet content. These tutorials show worksheets zoomed to 120%.

SP Finances - Excel

REVIEW    VIEW

General

$ · % ·

Conditional Formatting ·
Format as Table ·
Cell Styles ·

Number    Styles

Insert ·
Delete ·
Format ·

Σ
A Z
Sort & Find &
Filter · Select ·

Sign in

D    E    F    G    H    I    J

Balance Sheet    ...

AVERAGE: 132428.5714    COUNT: 15    SUM: 927000    120%

# Introducing Excel and Spreadsheets

A **spreadsheet** is a grouping of text and numbers in a rectangular grid or table. Spreadsheets are often used in business for budgeting, inventory management, and financial reporting because they unite text, numbers, and charts within one document. They can also be employed for personal use for planning a personal budget, tracking expenses, or creating a list of personal items. The advantage of an electronic spreadsheet is that the content can be easily edited and updated to reflect changing financial conditions.

### To start Excel:

1. Display the Windows Start screen, if necessary.

   **Using Windows 7?** To complete Step 1, click the Start button on the taskbar.

2. Click the **Excel 2013** tile. Excel starts and displays the Recent screen in Backstage view. **Backstage view** provides access to various screens with commands that allow you to manage files and Excel options. On the left is a list of recently opened workbooks. On the right are options for creating new workbooks. See Figure 1-1.

| Figure 1-1 | Recent screen in Backstage view |
| --- | --- |

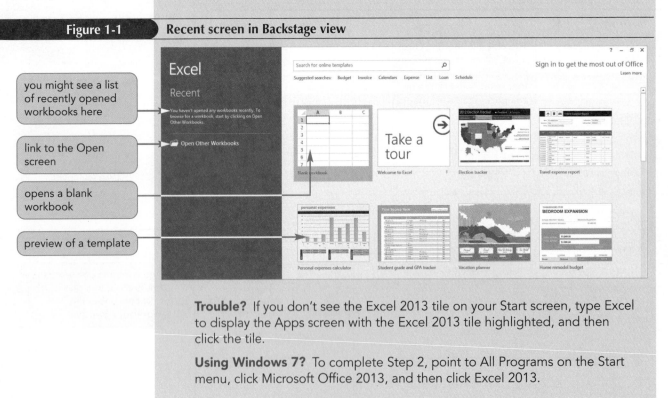

you might see a list of recently opened workbooks here

link to the Open screen

opens a blank workbook

preview of a template

**Trouble?** If you don't see the Excel 2013 tile on your Start screen, type Excel to display the Apps screen with the Excel 2013 tile highlighted, and then click the tile.

**Using Windows 7?** To complete Step 2, point to All Programs on the Start menu, click Microsoft Office 2013, and then click Excel 2013.

## Opening an Existing Workbook

Excel documents are called workbooks. From the Recent screen in Backstage view, you can open a blank workbook, open an existing workbook, or create a new workbook based on a template. A **template** is a preformatted workbook with many design features and some content already filled in. Templates can speed up the process of creating a workbook because much of the work in designing the appearance of the workbook and entering its data and formulas is already done for you.

Sally created an Excel workbook that contains several worksheets describing the current financial status of Sparrow & Pond. You will open that workbook now.

## To open Sally's workbook:

1. In the navigation bar on the Recent screen, click the **Open Other Workbooks** link. The Open screen is displayed and provides access to different locations where you might store files. The Recent Workbooks list shows the workbooks that were most recently opened on your computer.

2. Click **Computer**. The list of recently opened workbooks is replaced with a list of recently accessed folders on your computer and a Browse button.

   **Trouble?** If you are storing your files on your SkyDrive, click SkyDrive, and then log in if necessary.

3. Click the **Browse** button. The Open dialog box appears.

4. Navigate to the **Excel1 ▸ Tutorial** folder included with your Data Files.

   **Trouble?** If you don't have the starting Data Files, you need to get them before you can proceed. Your instructor will either give you the Data Files or ask you to obtain them from a specified location (such as a network drive). If you have any questions about the Data Files, see your instructor or technical support person for assistance.

5. Click **SP Finances** in the file list to select it.

6. Click the **Open** button. The SP Finances workbook opens in Excel.

   **Trouble?** If you don't see the full ribbon as shown in the Session 1.1 Visual Overview, the ribbon may be partially or fully hidden. To pin the ribbon so that the tabs and groups are fully displayed and remain visible, click the Ribbon Display Options button ⬆, and then click Show Tabs and Commands.

7. If the Excel window doesn't fill the screen, click the **Maximize** button ⬜ in the upper-right corner of the title bar. See Figure 1-2.

**Figure 1-2**          **SP Finances workbook**

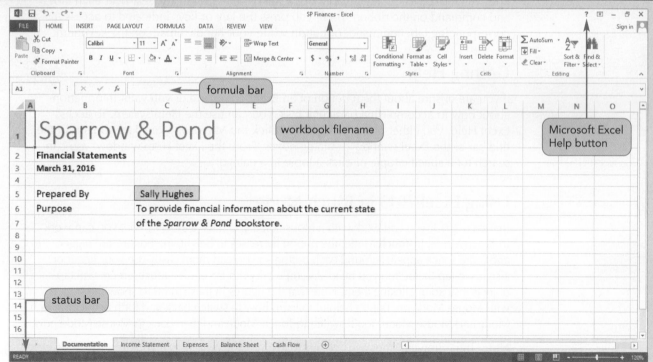

## Using Keyboard Shortcuts to Work Faster

Keyboard shortcuts can help you work faster and more efficiently because you can keep your hands on the keyboard. A **keyboard shortcut** is a key or combination of keys that you press to access a feature or perform a command. Excel provides keyboard shortcuts for many commonly used commands. For example, Ctrl+S is the keyboard shortcut for the Save command, which means you hold down the Ctrl key while you press the S key to save the workbook. (Note that the plus sign is not pressed; it is used to indicate that an additional key is pressed.) When available, a keyboard shortcut is listed next to the command's name in a ScreenTip. A **ScreenTip** is a box with descriptive text about a command that appears when you point to a button on the ribbon. Figure 1-3 lists some of the keyboard shortcuts commonly used in Excel. The tutorials in this text show the corresponding keyboard shortcuts for accomplishing an action when available.

**Figure 1-3**    **Excel keyboard shortcuts**

| Press | To | Press | To |
|---|---|---|---|
| Alt | Display the Key Tips for the commands and tools on the ribbon | Ctrl+V | Paste content that was cut or copied |
| Ctrl+A | Select all objects in a range | Ctrl+W | Close the current workbook |
| Ctrl+C | Copy the selected object(s) | Ctrl+X | Cut the selected object(s) |
| Ctrl+G | Go to a location in the workbook | Ctrl+Y | Repeat the last command |
| Ctrl+N | Open a new blank workbook | Ctrl+Z | Undo the last command |
| Ctrl+O | Open a saved workbook file | F1 | Display the Excel Help window |
| Ctrl+P | Print the current workbook | F5 | Go to a location in the workbook |
| Ctrl+S | Save the current workbook | F12 | Save the current workbook with a new name or to a new location |

© 2014 Cengage Learning

You can also use the keyboard to quickly select commands on the ribbon. First, you press the Alt key to display the **Key Tips**, which are labels that appear over each tab and command on the ribbon. Then, you press the key or keys indicated to access the corresponding tab, command, or button while your hands remain on the keyboard.

## Getting Help

If you are unsure about the function of an Excel command or you want information about how to accomplish a particular task, you can use the Help system. To access Excel Help, you either press the F1 key or click the Microsoft Excel Help button in the title bar of the Excel window or dialog boxes. From the Excel Help window, you can search for a specific topic or click a topic in a category.

## Using Excel 2013 in Touch Mode

In Office 2013, you can work with a mouse or, if you have a touchscreen, you can work in Touch Mode. In **Touch Mode**, the ribbon increases in height, the buttons are bigger, and more space appears around each button so you can more easily use your finger or a stylus to tap the button you need. As you work with Excel on a touchscreen, you tap objects instead of clicking them. Note that the figures in these tutorials show the screen with Mouse Mode on, but it's helpful to learn how to switch back and forth between Touch Mode and Mouse Mode. You'll switch to Touch Mode and then back to Mouse Mode now.

**Note:** The following steps assume that you are using a mouse. If you are instead using a touch device, please read these steps but don't complete them, so that you remain working in Touch Mode.

## To switch between Touch Mode and Mouse Mode:

▶ 1. On the Quick Access Toolbar, click the **Customize Quick Access Toolbar** button ⏷. A menu opens listing buttons you can add to the Quick Access Toolbar as well as other options for customizing the toolbar.

**Trouble?** If the Touch/Mouse Mode command on the menu has a checkmark next to it, press the Esc key to close the menu, and then skip Step 2.

▶ 2. Click **Touch/Mouse Mode**. The Quick Access Toolbar now contains the Touch/Mouse Mode button 👆, which you can use to switch between Mouse Mode, the default display, and Touch Mode.

▶ 3. On the Quick Access Toolbar, click the **Touch/Mouse Mode** button 👆. A menu opens listing Mouse and Touch, and the icon next to Mouse is shaded to indicate it is selected.

**Trouble?** If the icon next to Touch is shaded, press the Esc key to close the menu and skip Step 4.

▶ 4. Click **Touch**. The display switches to Touch Mode with more space between the commands and buttons on the ribbon. See Figure 1-4.

| Figure 1-4 | Ribbon displayed in Touch Mode |
|---|---|

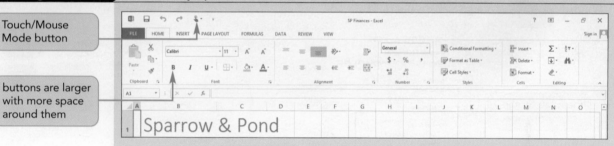

Touch/Mouse Mode button

buttons are larger with more space around them

Now you'll return to Mouse Mode.

**Trouble?** If you are working with a touchscreen and want to use Touch Mode, skip Steps 5 and 6.

▶ 5. On the Quick Access Toolbar, click the **Touch/Mouse Mode** button 👆, and then click **Mouse**. The ribbon returns to the Mouse Mode display shown in Figure 1-2.

▶ 6. On the Quick Access Toolbar, click the **Customize Quick Access Toolbar** button ⏷, and then click **Touch/Mouse Mode** to deselect it. The Touch/Mouse Mode button is removed from the Quick Access Toolbar.

## Exploring a Workbook

Workbooks are organized into separate pages called sheets. Excel supports two types of sheets: worksheets and chart sheets. A worksheet contains a grid of rows and columns into which you can enter text, numbers, dates, and formulas, and display charts. A **chart sheet** contains a chart that provides a visual representation of worksheet data. The contents of a workbook are shown in the workbook window.

## Changing the Active Sheet

The sheets in a workbook are identified in the sheet tabs at the bottom of the workbook window. The SP Finances workbook includes five sheets labeled Documentation, Income Statement, Expenses, Balance Sheet, and Cash Flow. The sheet currently displayed in the workbook window is the active sheet, which in this case is the Documentation sheet. To make a different sheet active and visible, you click its sheet tab. You can tell which sheet is active because its name appears in bold green.

If a workbook includes so many sheets that not all of the sheet tabs can be displayed at the same time in the workbook window, you can use the sheet tab scrolling buttons to scroll through the list of tabs. Scrolling the sheet tabs does not change the active sheet; it only changes which sheet tabs are visible.

You will view the different sheets in the SP Finances workbook.

### To change the active sheet:

1. Click the **Income Statement** sheet tab. The Income Statement worksheet becomes the active sheet, and its name is in bold green type. See Figure 1-5.

**Figure 1-5**    **Income Statement worksheet**

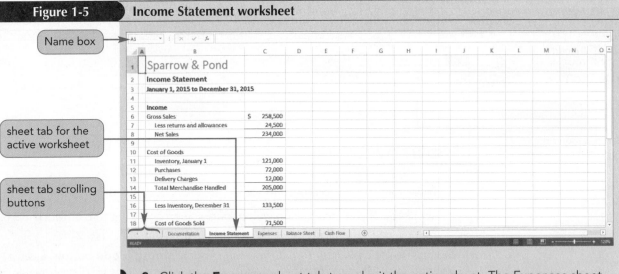

2. Click the **Expenses** sheet tab to make it the active sheet. The Expenses sheet is an example of a chart sheet containing only an Excel chart. See Figure 1-6.

**Figure 1-6**    **Expenses chart sheet**

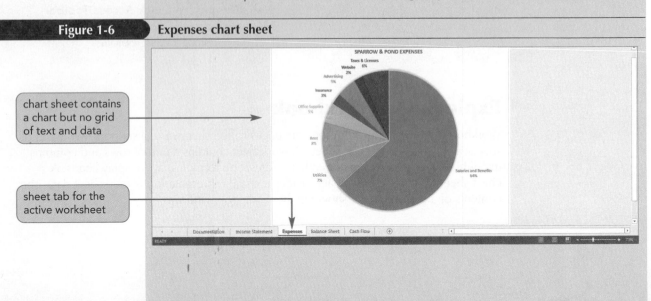

**TIP**

You can move to the previous or next sheet in the workbook by pressing the Ctrl+PgUp or Ctrl+PgDn keys.

3. Click the **Balance Sheet** sheet tab to make it the active sheet. Note that this sheet contains a chart embedded into the grid of data values. A worksheet can contain data values, charts, pictures, and other design elements.

4. Click the **Cash Flow** sheet tab. The worksheet with information about the company's cash flow is now active.

5. Click the **Income Statement** sheet tab to make the Income Statement worksheet the active sheet.

## Navigating Within a Worksheet

The worksheet is organized into individual cells. Each cell is identified by a **cell reference**, which is based on the cell's column and row location. For example, in Figure 1-5, the company name, Sparrow & Pond, is in cell B1, which is the intersection of column B and row 1. The column letter always appears before the row number in any cell reference. The cell that is currently selected in the worksheet is referred to as the active cell. The active cell is highlighted with a thick green border, its cell reference appears in the Name box, and the corresponding column and row headings are highlighted. The active cell in Figure 1-5 is cell A1.

Row numbers range from 1 to 1,048,576, and column labels are letters in alphabetical order. The first 26 column headings range from A to Z. After Z, the next column headings are labeled AA, AB, AC, and so forth. Excel allows a maximum of 16,384 columns in a worksheet (the last column has the heading XFD). This means that you can create large worksheets whose content extends well beyond what is visible in the workbook window.

To move different parts of the worksheet into view, you can use the horizontal and vertical scroll bars located at the bottom and right edges of the workbook window, respectively. A scroll bar has arrow buttons that you can click to shift the worksheet one column or row in the specified direction, and a scroll box that you can drag to shift the worksheet in the direction you drag.

You will scroll the active worksheet so you can review the rest of the Sparrow & Pond income statement.

### To scroll through the Income Statement worksheet:

1. On the vertical scroll bar, click the down arrow button ▼ to scroll down the Income Statement worksheet until you see cell C36, which displays the company's net income value of $4,600.

2. On the horizontal scroll bar, click the right arrow button ▶ three times. The worksheet scrolls three columns to the right, moving columns A through C out of view.

3. On the horizontal scroll bar, drag the scroll box to the left until you see column A.

4. On the vertical scroll bar, drag the scroll box up until you see the top of the worksheet and cell A1.

Scrolling the worksheet does not change the location of the active cell. Although the active cell might shift out of view, you can always see the location of the active cell in the Name box. To make a different cell active, you can either click a new cell or use the keyboard to move between cells, as described in Figure 1-7.

| Figure 1-7 | Excel navigation keys |

| Press | To move the active cell |
|---|---|
| ↑ ↓ ← → | Up, down, left, or right one cell |
| Home | To column A of the current row |
| Ctrl+Home | To cell A1 |
| Ctrl+End | To the last cell in the worksheet that contains data |
| Enter | Down one row or to the start of the next row of data |
| Shift+Enter | Up one row |
| Tab | One column to the right |
| Shift+Tab | One column to the left |
| PgUp, PgDn | Up or down one screen |
| Ctrl+PgUp, Ctrl+PgDn | To the previous or next sheet in the workbook |

© 2014 Cengage Learning

You will use both your mouse and your keyboard to change the location of the active cell in the Income Statement worksheet.

### To change the active cell:

1. Move your pointer over cell **B5**, and then click the mouse button. The active cell moves from cell A1 to cell B5. A green border appears around cell B5, the column heading for column B and the row heading for row 5 are both highlighted, and the cell reference in the Name box changes from A1 to B5.

2. Press the → key. The active cell moves one cell to the right to cell C5.

3. Press the **PgDn** key. The active cell moves down one full screen.

4. Press the **PgUp** key. The active cell moves up one full screen, returning to cell C5.

5. Press the **Ctrl+Home** keys. The active cell returns to the first cell in the worksheet, cell A1.

The mouse and keyboard provide quick ways to navigate the active worksheet. For larger worksheets that span several screens, you can move directly to a specific cell using the Go To command or by typing a cell reference in the Name box. You will try both of these methods.

### To use the Go To dialog box and the Name box:

1. On the HOME tab, in the Editing group, click the **Find & Select** button, and then click **Go To** on the menu that opens (or press the **F5** key). The Go To dialog box opens.

2. Type **C36** in the Reference box. See Figure 1-8.

**Figure 1-8**    Go To dialog box

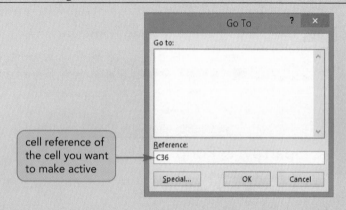

cell reference of
the cell you want
to make active

3. Click the **OK** button. Cell C36 becomes the active cell, displaying $4,600, which is Sparrow & Pond's net income for the year. Because cell C36 is the active cell, its cell reference appears in the Name box.

4. Click in the Name box, type **A1**, and then press the **Enter** key. Cell A1 is again the active cell.

## Selecting a Cell Range

Many tasks in Excel require you to work with a group of cells. You can use your mouse or keyboard to select those cells. A group of cells in a rectangular block is called a cell range (or simply a range). Each range is identified with a **range reference** that includes the cell reference of the upper-left cell of the rectangular block and the cell reference of the lower-right cell separated by a colon. For example, the range reference A1:G5 refers to all of the cells in the rectangular block from cell A1 through cell G5.

As with individual cells, you can select cell ranges using your mouse, the keyboard, or commands. You will select a range in the Income Statement worksheet.

### To select a cell range:

1. Click cell **B5** to select it, and without releasing the mouse button, drag down to cell **C8**.

2. Release the mouse button. The range B5:C8 is selected. See Figure 1-9. The selected cells are highlighted and surrounded by a green border. The first cell you selected in the range, cell B5, is the active cell in the worksheet. The active cell in a selected range is white. The Quick Analysis button appears, providing options for working with the range; you will use this button in another tutorial.

**TIP**

You can also select a range by clicking the upper-left cell of the range, holding down the Shift key as you click the lower-right cell in the range, and then releasing the Shift key.

| Figure 1-9 | Range B5:C8 selected |

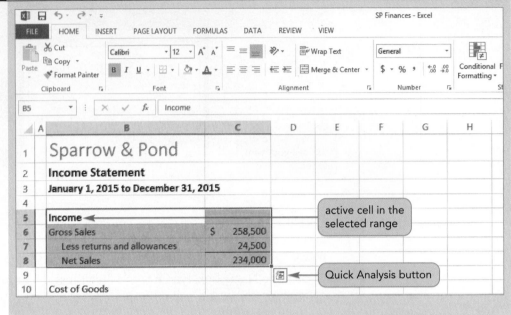

**3.** Click cell **A1** to deselect the range.

A nonadjacent range is a collection of separate ranges. The range reference for a nonadjacent range includes the range reference to each range separated by a semicolon. For example, the range reference A1:G5;A10:G15 includes two ranges—the first range is the rectangular block of cells from cell A1 to cell G5, and the second range is the rectangular block of cells from cell A10 to cell G15.

You will select a nonadjacent range in the Income Statement worksheet.

**To select a nonadjacent range in the Income Statement worksheet:**

**1.** Click cell **B5**, hold down the **Shift** key as you click cell **C8**, and then release the **Shift** key to select the range B5:C8.

**2.** Hold down the **Ctrl** key as you select the range **B10:C14**, and then release the **Ctrl** key. The two separate blocks of cells in the nonadjacent range B5:C8;B10:C14 are selected. See Figure 1-10.

**Figure 1-10** | **Nonadjacent range B5:C8;B10:C14 selected**

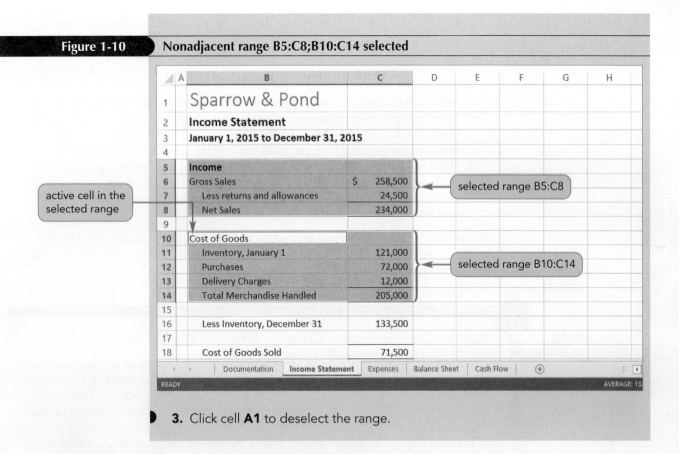

3. Click cell **A1** to deselect the range.

# Closing a Workbook

When you close a workbook, a dialog box might open, asking whether you want to save the workbook. If you have made changes that you want to keep, you should save the workbook. You have finished reviewing the SP Finances workbook, so you will close it. You will not save the workbook because you want the original version to remain unchanged.

**To close the SP Finances workbook:**

1. On the ribbon, click the **FILE** tab to display Backstage view, and then click **Close** in the navigation bar (or press the **Ctrl+W** keys).

2. If a dialog box opens asking whether you want to save your changes to the workbook, click the **Don't Save** button. The workbook closes without saving any changes. Excel remains opens, ready for you to create or open another workbook.

# Planning a Workbook

Before you begin creating a new workbook, you should develop a plan. You can do this by using a **planning analysis sheet**, which includes the following questions that help you think about the workbook's purpose and how to achieve your desired results:

1. **What problems do I want to solve?** The answer identifies the goal or purpose of the workbook. For example, Sally needs an easy way to record customer orders and analyze details from these orders.

2. **What data do I need?** The answer identifies the type of data that you need to collect and enter into the workbook. For example, Sally needs customer contact information, an order ID number, the date the order shipped, the shipping method, a list of books ordered, the quantity of each book ordered, and the price of each book.
3. **What calculations do I need to enter?** The answer identifies the formulas you need to apply to the data you have collected and entered. For example, Sally needs to calculate the charge for each book ordered, the number of books ordered, the shipping cost, the sales tax, and the total cost of the order.
4. **What form should my solution take?** The answer describes the appearance of the workbook content and how it should be presented to others. For example, Sally wants the information stored in a single worksheet that is easy to read and prints clearly.

Based on Sally's plan, you will create a workbook containing the details of a recent customer order. Sally will use this workbook as a model for future workbooks detailing other customer orders.

**PROSKILLS**

### Written Communication: Creating Effective Workbooks

Workbooks convey information in written form. As with any type of writing, the final product creates an impression and provides an indicator of your interest, knowledge, and attention to detail. To create the best impression, all workbooks—especially those you intend to share with others such as coworkers and clients—should be well planned, well organized, and well written.

A well-designed workbook should clearly identify its overall goal and present information in an organized format. The data it includes—both the entered values and the calculated values—should be accurate. The process of developing an effective workbook includes the following steps:

- Determine the workbook's purpose, content, and organization before you start.
- Create a list of the sheets used in the workbook, noting each sheet's purpose.
- Insert a documentation sheet that describes the workbook's purpose and organization. Include the name of the workbook author, the date the workbook was created, and any additional information that will help others to track the workbook to its source.
- Enter all of the data in the workbook. Add labels to indicate what the values represent and, if possible, where they originated so others can view the source of your data.
- Enter formulas for calculated items rather than entering the calculated values into the workbook. For more complicated calculations, provide documentation explaining them.
- Test the workbook with a variety of values; edit the data and formulas to correct errors.
- Save the workbook and create a backup copy when the project is completed. Print the workbook's contents if you need to provide a hard-copy version to others or for your files.
- Maintain a history of your workbook as it goes through different versions, so that you and others can quickly see how the workbook has changed during revisions.

By including clearly written documentation, explanatory text, a logical organization, and accurate data and formulas, you will create effective workbooks that others can use easily.

# Creating a New Workbook

You create new workbooks from the New screen in Backstage view. Similar to the Recent screen that opened when you started Excel, the New screen include templates for a variety of workbook types. You can see a preview of what the different workbooks will look like. You will create a new workbook from the Blank workbook template, in which you can add all of the content and design Sally wants for the Sparrow & Pond customer order worksheet.

**TIP**

You can also create a new, blank workbook by pressing the Ctrl+N keys.

**To start a new, blank workbook:**

1. On the ribbon, click the **FILE** tab to display Backstage view.

2. Click **New** in the navigation bar to display the New screen, which includes access to templates for a variety of workbooks.

3. Click the **Blank workbook** tile. A blank workbook opens. See Figure 1-11.

| Figure 1-11 | Blank workbook |
| --- | --- |

Save button on the Quick Access Toolbar

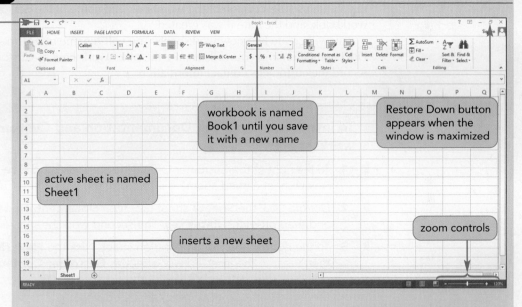

- workbook is named Book1 until you save it with a new name
- Restore Down button appears when the window is maximized
- active sheet is named Sheet1
- inserts a new sheet
- zoom controls

In these tutorials, the workbook window is zoomed to 120% for better readability. If you want to zoom your workbook window to match the figures, complete Step 4. If you prefer to work in the default zoom of 100% or at another zoom level, read but do not complete Step 4; you might see more or less of the worksheet on your screen, but this will not affect your work in the tutorials.

4. If you want your workbook window zoomed to 120% to match the figures, click the **Zoom In** button ➕ on the status bar twice to increase the zoom level to 120%. The 120% magnification increases the size of each cell, but reduces the number of worksheet cells visible in the workbook window.

The name of the active workbook, Book1, appears in the title bar. If you open multiple blank workbooks, they are named Book1, Book2, Book3, and so forth until you save them with a more descriptive name.

## Renaming and Inserting Worksheets

Blank workbooks open with a single blank sheet named Sheet1. You can give sheets more descriptive and meaningful names. This is a good practice so that you and others can easily tell what a sheet contains. Sheet names cannot exceed 31 characters, but they can contain blank spaces and include upper- and lowercase letters.

Because Sheet1 is not a very descriptive name, Sally wants you to rename the worksheet as Customer Order.

### To rename the Sheet1 worksheet:

▶ 1. Double-click the **Sheet1** tab. The Sheet1 label in the tab is selected.

▶ 2. Type **Customer Order** as the new name, and then press the **Enter** key. The width of the sheet tab expands to fit the longer sheet name.

Many workbooks include multiple sheets so that data can be organized in logical groups. A common business practice is to include a worksheet named Documentation that contains a description of the workbook, the name of the person who prepared the workbook, and the date it was created.

You will create two new worksheets. You will rename one worksheet as Documentation and you will rename the other worksheet as Customer Contact to record the customer's contact information.

### To insert and name the Documentation and Customer Contact worksheets:

▶ 1. To the right of the Customer Order sheet tab, click the **New sheet** button ⊕. A new sheet named Sheet2 is inserted to the right of the Customer Order sheet.

▶ 2. Double-click the **Sheet2** sheet tab, type **Documentation** as the new name, and then press the **Enter** key. The second worksheet is renamed.

▶ 3. To the right of the Documentation sheet, click the **New sheet** button ⊕, and then rename the inserted worksheet as **Customer Contact**.

## Moving Worksheets

A good practice is to place the most important sheets at the beginning of the workbook (the leftmost sheet tabs) and less important sheets at the end (the rightmost sheet tabs). To change the placement of sheets in a workbook, you drag them by their sheet tabs to the new location.

Sally wants you to move the Documentation worksheet to the front of the workbook, so that it appears before the Customer Order sheet.

### To move the Documentation worksheet:

▶ 1. Point to the **Documentation** sheet tab.

**TIP**

To copy a sheet, hold down the Ctrl key as you drag and drop its sheet tab.

▶ 2. Press and hold the mouse button. The pointer changes to ▧, and a small arrow appears in the upper-left corner of the tab.

▶ 3. Drag to the left until the small arrow appears in the upper-left corner of the Customer Order sheet tab, and then release the mouse button. The Documentation worksheet is now the first sheet in the workbook.

## Deleting Worksheets

In some workbooks, you will want to delete an existing sheet. The easiest way to delete a sheet is by using a **shortcut menu**, which is a list of commands related to a selection that opens when you click the right mouse button. Sally asks you to include the customer's contact information on the Customer Order worksheet so all of the information is on one sheet.

**To delete the Customer Contact worksheet from the workbook:**

1. Right-click the **Customer Contact** sheet tab. A shortcut menu opens.
2. Click **Delete**. The Customer Contact worksheet is removed from the workbook.

## Saving a Workbook

As you modify a workbook, you should save it regularly—every 10 minutes or so is a good practice. The first time you save a workbook, the Save As dialog box opens so you can name the file and choose where to save it. You can save the workbook on your computer or network, or to your account on SkyDrive.

**To save your workbook for the first time:**

1. On the Quick Access Toolbar, click the **Save** button 🖫 (or press the **Ctrl+S** keys). The Save As screen in Backstage view opens.
2. Click **Computer** in the Places list, and then click the **Browse** button. The Save As dialog box opens.

   **Trouble?** If your instructor wants you to save your files to your SkyDrive account, click SkyDrive, and then log in to your account, if necessary.

3. Navigate to the location specified by your instructor.
4. In the File name box, select **Book1** (the suggested name) if it is not already selected, and then type **SP Customer Order**.
5. Verify that **Excel Workbook** appears in the Save as type box.
6. Click the **Save** button. The workbook is saved, the dialog box closes, and the workbook window reappears with the new filename in the title bar.

As you modify the workbook, you will need to resave the file. Because you already saved the workbook with a filename, the next time you save, the Save command saves the changes you made to the workbook without opening the Save As dialog box.

# Entering Text, Dates, and Numbers

Workbook content is entered into worksheet cells. Those cells can contain text, numbers, or dates and times. **Text data** is any combination of letters, numbers, and symbols. Text data is often referred to as a **text string** because it contains a series, or string, of text characters. **Numeric data** is any number that can be used in a mathematical calculation. **Date** and **time data** are commonly recognized formats for date and time values. For example, Excel interprets the cell entry April 15, 2016 as a date and not as text. New data is placed into the active cell of the current worksheet. As you enter data, the entry appears in both the active cell and the formula bar. By default, text is left-aligned in cells, and numbers, dates, and times are right-aligned.

## Entering Text

Text is often used in worksheets to label other data and to identify areas of a sheet. Sally wants you to enter some of the information from the planning analysis sheet into the Documentation sheet.

**To enter the text for the Documentation sheet:**

1. Press the **Ctrl+Home** keys to make sure cell A1 is the active cell on the Documentation sheet.

2. Type **Sparrow and Pond** in cell A1. As you type, the text appears in cell A1 and in the formula bar.

3. Press the **Enter** key twice. The text is entered into cell A1 and the active cell moves down two rows to cell A3.

4. Type **Author** in cell A3, and then press the **Tab** key. The text is entered and the active cell moves one column to the right to cell B3.

5. Type your name in cell B3, and then press the **Enter** key. The text is entered and the active cell moves one cell down and to the left to cell A4.

6. Type **Date** in cell A4, and then press the **Tab** key. The text is entered and the active cell moves one column to the right to cell B4, where you would enter the date you created the worksheet. For now, you will leave the cell for the date blank.

7. Click cell **A5** to make it the active cell, type **Purpose** in the cell, and then press the **Tab** key. The active cell moves one column to the right to cell B5.

8. Type **To record customer book orders.** in cell B5, and then press the **Enter** key. Figure 1-12 shows the text entered in the Documentation sheet.

**Figure 1-12**   **Documentation sheet**

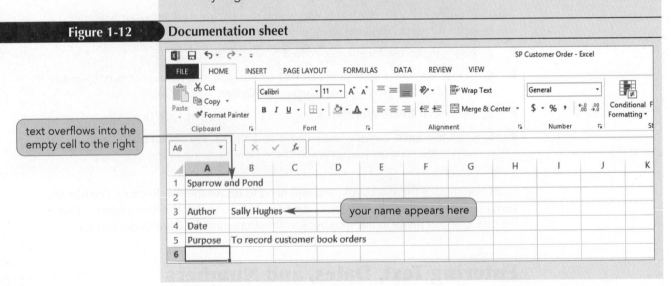

The text you entered in cell A1 is so long that it appears to overflow into cell B1. The same is true for the text you entered in cells B3 and B5. Any text you enter in a cell that doesn't fit within that cell will cover the adjacent cells to the right as long as they are empty. If the adjacent cells contain data, only the text that fits into the cell is displayed. The rest of the text entry is hidden from view. The text itself is not affected. The complete text is still entered in the cell; it is just not displayed. (You will learn how to display all text in a cell in the next session.)

## Undoing and Redoing an Action

As you enter data in a workbook, you might need to undo a previous action. Excel maintains a list of the actions you performed in the workbook during the current session, so you can undo most of your actions. You can use the Undo button on the Quick Access Toolbar or press the Ctrl+Z keys to reverse your most recent actions one at a time. If you want to undo more than one action, you can click the Undo button arrow and then select the earliest action you want to undo—all of the actions after the earliest action you selected are also undone.

You will undo the most recent change you made to the Documentation sheet— the text you entered into cell B5. Then you will enter more descriptive and accurate description of the worksheet's purpose.

**To undo the text entry in cell B5:**

▶  1. On the Quick Access Toolbar, click the **Undo** button ⤺ (or press the **Ctrl+Z** keys). The last action is reversed, removing the text you entered in cell B5.

▶  2. In cell B5, type **To record book orders from a Sparrow & Pond customer.** and then press the **Enter** key.

If you want to restore actions you have undone, you can redo them. To redo one action at a time, you can click the Redo button ⤻ on the Quick Access Toolbar or press the Ctrl+Y keys. To redo multiple actions at once, you can click the Redo button arrow and then click the earliest action you want to redo. After you undo or redo an action, Excel continues the action list starting from any new changes you make to the workbook.

## Editing Cell Content

As you work, you might find mistakes you need to correct or entries that you want to change. If you want to replace all of the content in a cell, you simply select the cell and then type the new entry to overwrite the previous entry. However, if you need to replace only part of a cell's content, you can work in **Edit mode**. To switch to Edit mode, you double-click the cell. A blinking insertion point indicates where the new content you type will be inserted. In the cell or formula bar, the pointer changes to an I-beam, which you can use to select text in the cell. Anything you type replaces the selected content.

You need to edit the text in cell A1 to Sparrow & Pond. You will switch to Edit mode to correct the text.

**To edit the text in cell A1:**

▶  1. Double-click cell **A1** to select the cell and switch to Edit mode. A blinking insertion point appears within the text of cell A1. The status bar displays EDIT instead of READY to indicate that the cell is in Edit mode.

▶  2. Press the arrow keys to move the insertion point directly to the right of the word "and" in the company name.

▶  3. Press the **Backspace** key three times to delete the word "and."

▶  4. Type **&** to enter the new text, and then press the **Enter** key. The cell text changes to Sparrow & Pond. See Figure 1-13.

Figure 1-13    **Revised Documentation sheet**

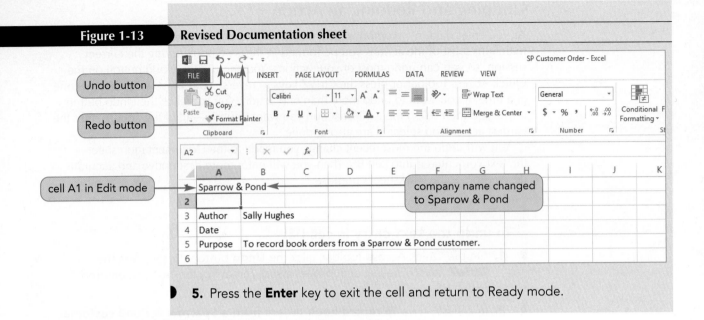

5. Press the **Enter** key to exit the cell and return to Ready mode.

## Understanding AutoComplete

As you type text in the active cell, Excel tries to anticipate the remaining characters by displaying text that begins with the same letters as a previous entry in the same column. This feature, known as **AutoComplete**, helps make entering repetitive text easier. To accept the suggested text, press the Tab or Enter key. To override the suggested text, continue to type the text you want to enter in the cell. AutoComplete does not work with dates or numbers, or when a blank cell is between the previous entry and the text you are typing.

Next, you will enter the contact information for Tobias Gregson, a customer who recently placed an order with Sparrow & Pond. You will enter the contact information on the Customer Order worksheet.

### To enter Tobias Gregson's contact information:

1. Click the **Customer Order** sheet tab to make it the active sheet.

2. In cell A1, type **Customer Order** as the worksheet title, and then press the **Enter** key twice. The worksheet title is entered in cell A1, and the active cell is cell A3.

3. Type **Ship To** in cell A3, and then press the **Enter** key. The label is entered in the cell, and the active cell is now cell A4.

4. In the range A4:A10, enter the following labels, pressing the **Enter** key after each entry and ignoring any AutoComplete suggestions: **First Name, Last Name, Address, City, State, Postal Code**, and **Phone**.

5. Click cell **B4** to make that cell the active cell.

**6.** In the range B4:B10, enter the following contact information, pressing the **Enter** key after each entry and ignoring any AutoComplete suggestions: **Tobias, Gregson, 412 Apple Grove St., Nashua, NH, 03061**, and **(603) 555-4128**. See Figure 1-14.

| Figure 1-14 | Text entered in the Customer Order worksheet |

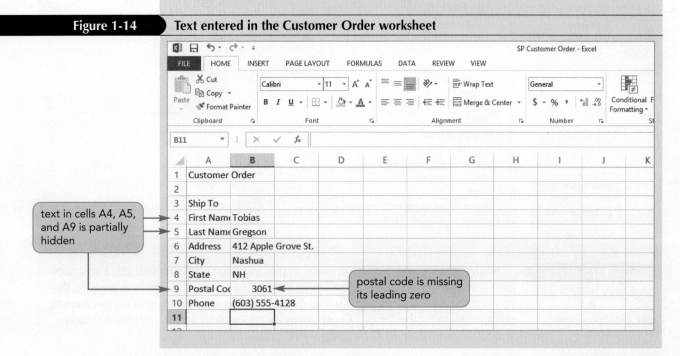

text in cells A4, A5, and A9 is partially hidden

postal code is missing its leading zero

## Displaying Numbers as Text

When you type numbers in the active cell, Excel treats the entry as a number and ignores any leading zero. For example, in cell B9, the first digit of the postal code 03061 is missing; Excel displays 3061 because the numbers 3061 and 03061 have the same value. To specify that a number entry should be considered text and all digits should be displayed, you include an apostrophe (') before the numbers.

You will make this change in cell B9 so that Excel treats the postal code as text and displays all of the digits you type.

**To enter the postal code as text:**

**1.** Click cell **B9** to select it. Notice that the postal code is right-aligned in the cell, unlike the other text entries, which are left-aligned—another indication that the entry is being treated as a number.

**2.** Type **'03061** in cell B9, and then press the **Enter** key. The text 03061 appears in cell B9 and is left-aligned in the cell, matching all of the other text entries. See Figure 1-15.

**Figure 1-15**    **Number displayed as text**

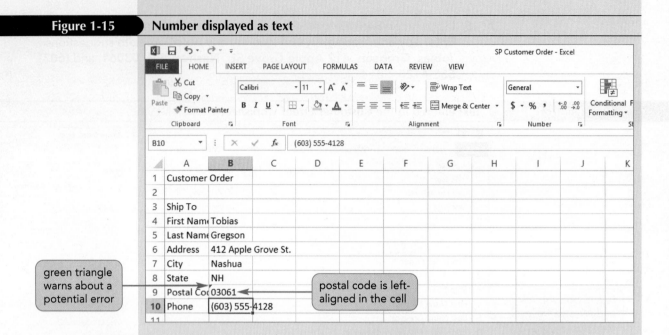

green triangle warns about a potential error

postal code is left-aligned in the cell

**TIP**

To remove a green triangle, click the cell, click the yellow caution icon that appears to the left of the cell, and then click Ignore Error.

Notice that a green triangle appears in the upper-left corner of cell B9. Excel uses green triangles to flag potential errors in cells. In this case, it is simply a warning that you entered a number as a text string. Because this is intentional, you do not have to edit the cell to fix the "error." Green triangles appear only in the workbook window and not in any printouts of the worksheet.

## Entering Dates

You can enter dates in any of the standard date formats. For example, all of the following entries are recognized by Excel as the same date:

- 4/6/2016
- 4/6/16
- 4-6-2016
- April 6, 2016
- 6-Apr-16

Even though you enter a date as text, Excel stores the date as a number equal to the number of days between the specified date and January 0, 1900. Times are also entered as text and stored as fractions of a 24-hour day. For example, the date and time April 4, 2016 @ 6:00 PM is stored by Excel as 42,464.75. Dates and times are stored as numbers so that Excel can easily perform date and time calculations, such as determining the elapsed time between one date and another.

Based on the default date format your computer uses, Excel might alter the format of a date after you type it. For example, if you enter the date 4/6/16 into the active cell, Excel might display the date with the four-digit year value, 4/6/2016; if you enter the text April 6, 2016, Excel might convert the date format to 6-Apr-16. Changing the date or time format does not affect the underlying date or time value.

## International Date Formats

As business transactions become more international in scope, you may need to adopt international standards for expressing dates, times, and currency values in your workbooks. For example, a worksheet cell might contain 06/05/16. This format could represent any of the following dates: the 5th of June, 2016; the 6th of May, 2016; and the 16th of May, 2006.

The date depends on which country the workbook has been designed for. You can avoid this problem by entering the full date, as in June 5, 2016. However, this might not work with documents written in foreign languages, such as Japanese, that use different character symbols.

To solve this problem, many international businesses adopt ISO (International Organization for Standardization) dates in the format *yyyy-mm-dd*, where *yyyy* is the four-digit year value, *mm* is the two-digit month value, and *dd* is the two-digit day value. So, a date such as June 5, 2016 is entered as 2016/06/05. If you choose to use this international date format, make sure that people using your workbook understand this format so they do not misinterpret the dates. You can include information about the date format in the Documentation sheet.

For the SP Customer Order workbook, you will enter dates in the format *mm/dd/yyyy*, where *mm* is the 2-digit month number, *dd* is the 2-digit day number, and *yyyy* is the 4-digit year number.

**To enter the current date into the Documentation sheet:**

1. Click the **Documentation** sheet tab to make the Documentation sheet the active worksheet.

2. Click cell **B4** to make it active, type the current date in the *mm/dd/yyyy* format, and then press the **Enter** key. The date is entered in the cell.

   **Trouble?** Depending on your system configuration, Excel might change the date to the date format *dd-mmm-yy*. This difference will not affect your work.

3. Make the **Customer Order** worksheet the active sheet.

The next part of the Customer Order worksheet will list the books the customer purchased from Sparrow & Pond. As shown in Figure 1-16, the list includes identifying information about each book, its price, and the quantity ordered.

**Figure 1-16**    **Book order from Tobias Gregson**

| ISBN | CATEGORY | BINDING | TITLE | AUTHOR(S) | PRICE | QTY |
|---|---|---|---|---|---|---|
| 0-374-25385-4 | Used | Hardcover | Samurai William: The Englishman Who Opened Japan | Milton, Giles | $5.95 | 2 |
| 4-889-96213-1 | New | Softcover | Floral Origami Globes | Fuse, Tomoko | $24.95 | 3 |
| 0-500-27062-7 | New | Hardcover | Tao Magic: The Secret Language of Diagrams and Calligraphy | Legeza, Laszlo | $8.95 | 1 |
| 0-785-82169-4 | Used | Hardcover | The Holy Grail | Morgan, Giles | $3.75 | 1 |
| 0-854-56516-7 | New | Softcover | Murder on the Links | Christie, Agatha | $7.50 | 2 |

© 2014 Cengage Learning

You will enter the first five columns of the book order into the worksheet.

### To enter the first part of the book order:

1. In the Customer Order worksheet, click cell **A12** to make it the active cell, type **ISBN** as the column label, and then press the **Tab** key to move to cell B12.

2. In the range B12:E12, type the following labels, pressing the **Tab** key to move to the next cell: **CATEGORY**, **BINDING**, **TITLE**, and **AUTHOR(S)**.

3. Press the **Enter** key to go to the next row of the worksheet, making cell A13 the active cell.

4. In the range A13:E17, enter the ISBN, category, binding, title, and author text for the five books listed in Figure 1-16, pressing the **Tab** key to move from one cell to the next, and pressing the **Enter** key to move to a new row. See Figure 1-17. The text in some cells will be partially hidden; you will fix that problem shortly.

| Figure 1-17 | Tobias Gregson's partial book order |
| --- | --- |

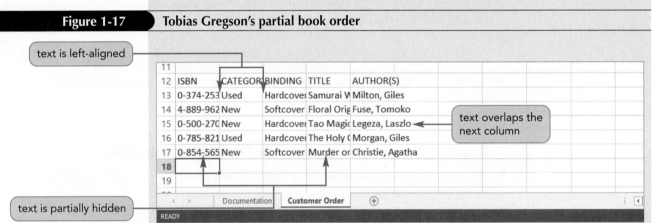

### Entering Numbers

**TIP**

If a number exceeds its cell size, you see ###### instead of the number. You can display the entire number by increasing the column width.

In Excel, numbers can be integers such as 378, decimals such as 1.95, or negatives such as −5.2. In the case of currency and percentages, you can include the currency symbol and percent sign when you enter the value. Excel treats a currency value such as $87.25 as the number 87.25, and a percentage such as 95% as the decimal 0.95. Much like dates, currency and percentages are formatted in a convenient way for you to read, but only the number is stored within the cell. This makes it easier to perform calculations with currency and percentage values.

You will complete the information for Tobias Gregson's order by entering the price for each title and the quantity of each title he ordered.

### To enter the price and quantity of books ordered:

1. In the range F12:G12, enter **PRICE** and **QTY** as the labels.

2. In cell F13, enter **$5.95** as the price of the first book. The book price is stored as a number but displayed with the $ symbol.

3. In cell G13, enter **2** as the quantity of books ordered.

4. In the range F14:G17, enter the remaining prices and quantities shown in Figure 1-16. See Figure 1-18.

**Figure 1-18**    **Price and quantity data**

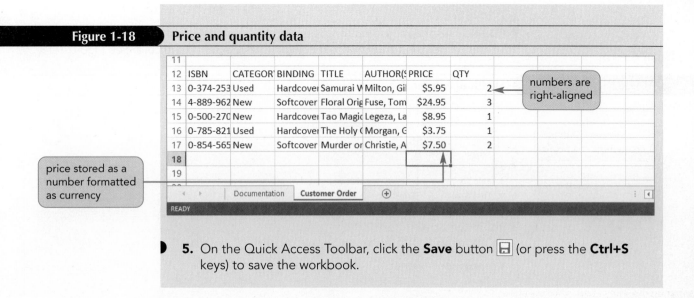

price stored as a number formatted as currency

numbers are right-aligned

**5.** On the Quick Access Toolbar, click the **Save** button 🔲 (or press the **Ctrl+S** keys) to save the workbook.

# Resizing Columns and Rows

Much of the information in the Customer Order worksheet is difficult to read because of the hidden text. You can make the cell content easier to read by changing the size of the columns and rows in the worksheet.

## Changing Column Widths

Column widths are expressed as the number of characters the column can contain. The default column width is 8.43 standard-sized characters. In general, this means that you can type eight characters in a cell; any additional text is hidden or overlaps the adjacent cell. Column widths are also expressed in terms of pixels. A **pixel** is a single point on a computer monitor or printout. A column width of 8.43 characters is equivalent to 64 pixels.

**INSIGHT**

### Setting Column Widths

On a computer monitor, pixel size is based on screen resolution. As a result, cell contents that look fine on one screen might appear very different when viewed on a screen with a different resolution. If you work on multiple computers or share your workbooks with others, you should set column widths based on the maximum number of characters you want displayed in the cells rather than pixel size. This ensures that everyone sees the cell contents the way you intended.

You will increase the width of column A so that the contact information labels in cells A4 and A5 and the ISBN numbers in the range A13:A17 are completely displayed.

### To increase the width of column A:

**1.** Move the pointer over the right border of the column A heading until the pointer changes to ↔.

**2.** Click and drag to the right until the width of the column heading reaches **15** characters, but do not release the mouse button. The ScreenTip that appears as you resize the column shows the new column width in characters and in pixels.

> **3.** Release the mouse button. The width of column A expands to 15 characters, and all of the text within that column is visible within the cells. See Figure 1-19.

**Figure 1-19**     **Width of column A increased**

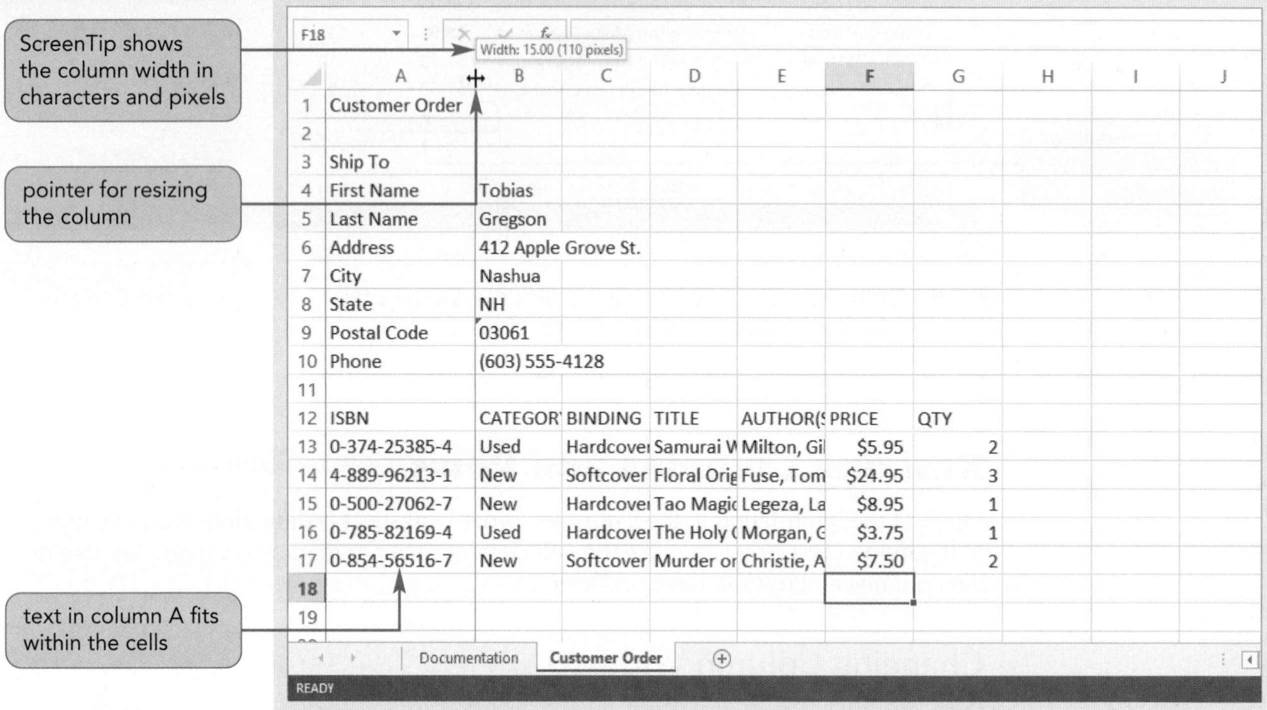

ScreenTip shows the column width in characters and pixels

pointer for resizing the column

text in column A fits within the cells

You will increase the widths of columns B and C to 18 characters so that their complete entries are visible. Rather than resizing each column separately, you can select both columns and adjust their widths at the same time.

### To increase the widths of columns B and C:

> **1.** Click the **column B** heading. The entire column is selected.
>
> **2.** Hold down the **Ctrl** key, click the **column C** heading, and then release the **Ctrl** key. Both columns B and C are selected.
>
> **3.** Move the pointer to the right border of the column C heading until the pointer changes to ✛.
>
> **4.** Drag to the right until the column width changes to **18** characters, and then release the mouse button. Both column widths increase to 18 characters and display all of the entered text.

**TIP**

To select multiple columns, you can also click and drag the pointer over multiple column headings.

The book titles in column D are partially hidden. You will increase the width of this column to 30 characters. Rather than using your mouse, you can set the column width using the Format command on the HOME tab. The Format command gives you precise control over setting column widths and row heights.

## To set the width of column D with the Format command:

1. Click the **column D** heading. The entire column is selected.

2. On the HOME tab, in the Cells group, click the **Format** button, and then click **Column Width**. The Column Width dialog box opens.

3. Type **30** in the Column width box to specify the new column width.

4. Click the **OK** button. The width of column D changes to 30 characters.

5. Change the width of column E to **15** characters.

6. Click cell **A1**. The revised column widths are shown in Figure 1-20.

**Figure 1-20**    Resized columns

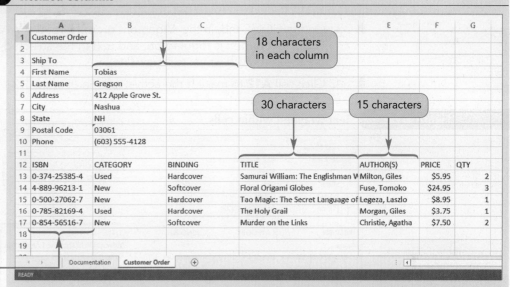

Even with the width of column D increased, some of the book titles still don't fit within the allotted space. Instead of manually changing the column width to display all of the text, you can autofit the column. **AutoFit** changes the column width or row height to display the longest or tallest entry within the column or row. You autofit a column or a row by double-clicking the right border of the column heading or the bottom border of the row heading.

**TIP**

If the row or column is blank, autofitting restores its default height or width.

## To autofit the contents of column D:

1. Move the pointer over the right border of column D until the pointer changes to ↔.

2. Double-click the right border of the column D heading. The width of column D increases to about 54 characters so that the longest book title is completely visible.

# Wrapping Text Within a Cell

Sometimes, resizing a column width to display all of the text entered in the cells makes the worksheet more difficult to read. This is the case with column D in the Customer Order worksheet. Another way to display long text entries is to wrap text to a new line when it extends beyond the column width. When text wraps within a cell, the row height increases so that all of the text within the cell is displayed.

You will resize column D, and then wrap the text entries in the column.

**To wrap text in column D:**

▶ **1.** Resize the width of column D to **30** characters.

▶ **2.** Select the range **D13:D17**. These cells include the titles that extend beyond the new cell width.

▶ **3.** On the HOME tab, in the Alignment group, click the **Wrap Text** button. The Wrap Text button is toggled on, and text in the selected cells that exceeds the column width wraps to a new line.

▶ **4.** Click cell **A12** to make it the active cell. See Figure 1-21.

| Figure 1-21 | Text wrapped within cells |

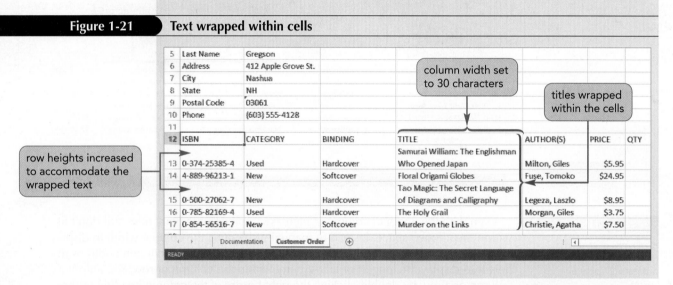

If you want to create a new line within a cell, press the Alt+Enter keys to move the insertion point to the next line within the cell. Whatever you type next will appear on the new line in the cell.

## Changing Row Heights

The height of a row is measured in points or pixels. A **point** is approximately 1/72 of an inch. The default row height is 15 points or 20 pixels. Row heights are set in the same way as column widths. You can drag the bottom border of the row heading to a new row height, specify a row height using the Format command, or autofit the row's height to match its content.

Sanjit wants you add more space above the labels in the book list by resizing row 12.

---

### To increase the height of row 12:

1. Move the pointer over the bottom border of the row 12 heading until the pointer changes to ⊹.

2. Drag the bottom border down until the height of the row is equal to **30** points (or **40** pixels), and then release the mouse button. The height of row 12 is set to 30 points.

3. Press the **Ctrl+S** keys to save the workbook.

---

**TIP**

You can also set the row height by clicking the Format button in the Cells group on the HOME tab and then using the Row Height command.

You have entered most of the data for Tobias Gregson's order at Sparrow & Pond. In the next session, you will calculate the total charge for the order and print the worksheet.

---

**REVIEW**

### Session 1.1 Quick Check

1. What are the two types of sheets used in a workbook?
2. What is the cell reference for the cell located in the fourth column and third row of a worksheet?
3. What is the range reference for the block of cells B10 through C15?
4. What is the reference for the nonadjacent block of cells B10 through C15 and cells B20 through D25?
5. What keyboard shortcut changes the active cell to cell A1?
6. What is text data?
7. Cell A4 contains *May 3, 2016*; why doesn't Excel consider this entry a text string?
8. How do you resize a column or row?

# Session 1.2 Visual Overview:

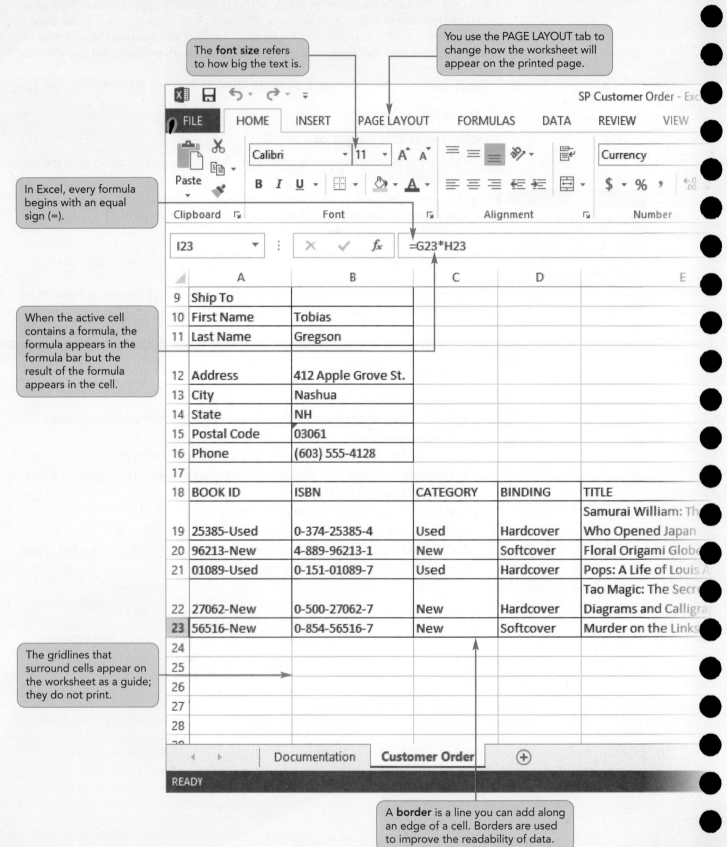

The **font size** refers to how big the text is.

You use the PAGE LAYOUT tab to change how the worksheet will appear on the printed page.

In Excel, every formula begins with an equal sign (=).

When the active cell contains a formula, the formula appears in the formula bar but the result of the formula appears in the cell.

The gridlines that surround cells appear on the worksheet as a guide; they do not print.

A **border** is a line you can add along an edge of a cell. Borders are used to improve the readability of data.

SP Customer Order - Exc

FILE    HOME    INSERT    PAGE LAYOUT    FORMULAS    DATA    REVIEW    VIEW

Calibri    11    A A    Currency

Paste    B I U

Clipboard    Font    Alignment    Number

I23    fx    =G23*H23

| | A | B | C | D | E |
|---|---|---|---|---|---|
| 9 | Ship To | | | | |
| 10 | First Name | Tobias | | | |
| 11 | Last Name | Gregson | | | |
| 12 | Address | 412 Apple Grove St. | | | |
| 13 | City | Nashua | | | |
| 14 | State | NH | | | |
| 15 | Postal Code | 03061 | | | |
| 16 | Phone | (603) 555-4128 | | | |
| 17 | | | | | |
| 18 | BOOK ID | ISBN | CATEGORY | BINDING | TITLE |
| 19 | 25385-Used | 0-374-25385-4 | Used | Hardcover | Samurai William: The Who Opened Japan |
| 20 | 96213-New | 4-889-96213-1 | New | Softcover | Floral Origami Globe |
| 21 | 01089-Used | 0-151-01089-7 | Used | Hardcover | Pops: A Life of Louis |
| 22 | 27062-New | 0-500-27062-7 | New | Hardcover | Tao Magic: The Secre Diagrams and Calligra |
| 23 | 56516-New | 0-854-56516-7 | New | Softcover | Murder on the Links |
| 24 | | | | | |
| 25 | | | | | |
| 26 | | | | | |
| 27 | | | | | |
| 28 | | | | | |

Documentation    **Customer Order**    ⊕

READY

# Formulas and Functions

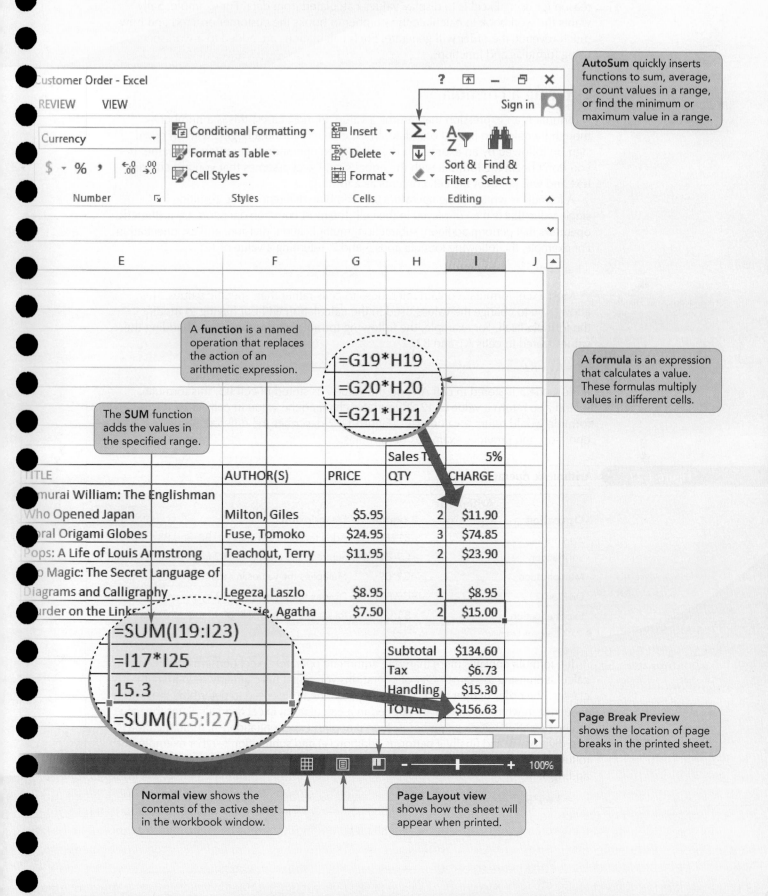

**AutoSum** quickly inserts functions to sum, average, or count values in a range, or find the minimum or maximum value in a range.

A **function** is a named operation that replaces the action of an arithmetic expression.

=G19*H19
=G20*H20
=G21*H21

A **formula** is an expression that calculates a value. These formulas multiply values in different cells.

The **SUM** function adds the values in the specified range.

=SUM(I19:I23)
=I17*I25
15.3
=SUM(I25:I27)

| TITLE | AUTHOR(S) | PRICE | QTY | CHARGE |
|---|---|---|---|---|
| | | | Sales T... | 5% |
| Samurai William: The Englishman Who Opened Japan | Milton, Giles | $5.95 | 2 | $11.90 |
| ...ral Origami Globes | Fuse, Tomoko | $24.95 | 3 | $74.85 |
| Pops: A Life of Louis Armstrong | Teachout, Terry | $11.95 | 2 | $23.90 |
| ...o Magic: The Secret Language of Diagrams and Calligraphy | Legeza, Laszlo | $8.95 | 1 | $8.95 |
| ...urder on the Links | ...ie, Agatha | $7.50 | 2 | $15.00 |
| | | | Subtotal | $134.60 |
| | | | Tax | $6.73 |
| | | | Handling | $15.30 |
| | | | TOTAL | $156.63 |

**Page Break Preview** shows the location of page breaks in the printed sheet.

**Normal view** shows the contents of the active sheet in the workbook window.

**Page Layout view** shows how the sheet will appear when printed.

Customer Order - Excel

REVIEW    VIEW

Sign in

Currency

$ - % , ←.0 .00
          .00 →.0

Number    Styles    Cells    Editing

Conditional Formatting ▾
Format as Table ▾
Cell Styles ▾

Insert ▾
Delete ▾
Format ▾

Sort & Filter ▾    Find & Select ▾

100%

# Adding Formulas to a Worksheet

So far you have entered text, numbers, and dates in the worksheet. However, the main reason for using Excel is to display values calculated from data. For example, Sally wants the workbook to calculate the number of books the customer ordered and how much revenue the order will generate. Such calculations are added to a worksheet using formulas and functions.

## Entering a Formula

A formula is an expression that returns a value. In most cases, this is a number—though it could also be text or a date. In Excel, every formula begins with an equal sign (=) followed by an expression describing the operation that returns the value. If you don't begin the formula with the equal sign, Excel assumes that you are entering text and will not treat the cell contents as a formula.

A formula is written using **operators** that combine different values, resulting in a single value that is then displayed in the cell. The most common operators are **arithmetic operators** that perform addition, subtraction, multiplication, division, and exponentiation. For example, the following formula adds 5 and 7, returning a value of 12:

=5+7

Most Excel formulas contain references to cells rather than specific values. This allows you to change the values used in the calculation without having to modify the formula itself. For example, the following formula returns the result of adding the values stored in cells A1 and B2:

=A1+B2

If the value 5 is stored in cell A1 and the value 7 is stored in cell B2, this formula would also return a value of 12. If you later changed the value in cell A1 to 10, the formula would return a value of 17. Figure 1-22 describes the different arithmetic operators and provides examples of formulas.

**Figure 1-22** **Arithmetic operators**

| Operation | Arithmetic Operator | Example | Description |
|---|---|---|---|
| Addition | + | =B1+B2+B3 | Adds the values in cells B1, B2, and B3 |
| Subtraction | – | =C9–B2 | Subtracts the value in cell B2 from the value in cell C9 |
| Multiplication | * | =C9*B9 | Multiplies the values in cells C9 and B9 |
| Division | / | =C9/B9 | Divides the value in cell C9 by the value in cell B9 |
| Exponentiation | ^ | =B5^3 | Raises the value of cell B5 to the third power |

© 2014 Cengage Learning

If a formula contains more than one arithmetic operator, Excel performs the calculation using the same order of operations you might have already seen in math classes. The **order of operations** is a set of predefined rules used to determine the sequence in which operators are applied in a calculation. Excel first calculates the value of any operation within parentheses, then it applies exponentiation (^), multiplication (*), and division (/), and finally it performs addition (+) and subtraction (–). For example, the following formula returns the value 23 because multiplying 4 by 5 takes precedence over adding 3:

=3+4*5

If a formula contains two or more operators with the same level of priority, the operators are applied in order from left to right. In the following formula, Excel first multiplies 4 by 10 and then divides that result by 8 to return the value 5:

=4*10/8

When parentheses are used, the value inside them is calculated first. In the following formula, Excel calculates (3+4) first, and then multiplies that result by 5 to return the value 35:

=(3+4)*5

Figure 1-23 shows how slight changes in a formula affect the order of operations and the result of the formula.

**Figure 1-23**    **Order of operations applied to Excel formulas**

| Formula | Application of the Order of Operations | Result |
|---|---|---|
| =50+10*5 | 10*5 calculated first and then 50 is added | 100 |
| =(50+10)*5 | (50+10) calculated first and then 60 is multiplied by 5 | 300 |
| =50/10–5 | 50/10 calculated first and then 5 is subtracted | 0 |
| =50/(10–5) | (10–5) calculated first and then 50 is divided by that value | 10 |
| =50/10*5 | Two operators at same precedence level, so the calculation is done left to right in the expression | 25 |
| =50/(10*5) | (10*5) is calculated first and then 50 is divided by that value | 1 |

© 2014 Cengage Learning

Sally wants the Customer Order worksheet to include the total amount charged for each book. The charge is equal to the number of books ordered multiplied by the book's price. You already entered this information in columns F and G. Now you will enter a formula to calculate the charge for books ordered in column H.

**To enter the formula to calculate the charge for the first book order:**

1. Make cell **H12** the active cell, type **CHARGE** as the column label, and then press the **Enter** key. The label text is entered in cell H12, and cell H13 is now the active cell.

2. Type **=F13*G13** (the price of the book multiplied by the quantity of books ordered). As you type the formula, a list of Excel function names appears in a ScreenTip, which provides a quick method for entering functions. The list will close when you complete the formula. You will learn more about Excel functions shortly. Also, as you type each cell reference, Excel color codes the cell reference with the cell. See Figure 1-24.

**Figure 1-24**    **Formula being entered in a cell**

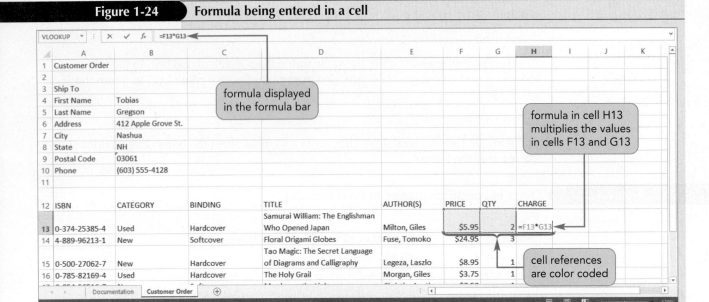

3. Press the **Enter** key. The formula is entered in cell H13, which displays the value $11.90. The result is displayed as currency because cell F13, which is referenced in the formula, contains a currency value.

4. Click cell **H13** to make it the active cell. The cell displays the result of the formula, and the formula bar displays the formula you entered.

For the first book, you entered the formula by typing each cell reference in the expression. You can also insert a cell reference by clicking the cell as you type the formula. This technique reduces the possibility of error caused by typing an incorrect cell reference. You will use this method to enter the formula to calculate the charge for the second book.

**To enter the cell references in the formula using the mouse:**

1. Click cell **H14** to make it the active cell.

2. Type **=**. The equal sign indicates that you are entering a formula. Any cell you click from now on inserts the cell reference of the selected cell into the formula until you complete the formula by pressing the Enter or Tab key.

Be sure to type = as the first part of the entry; otherwise, Excel will not interpret the entry as a formula.

3. Click cell **F14**. The cell reference is inserted into the formula in the formula bar. At this point, any cell you click changes the cell reference used in the formula. The cell reference isn't locked until you type an operator.

4. Type **\*** to enter the multiplication operator. The cell reference for cell F14 is locked in the formula, and the next cell you click will be inserted after the operator.

5. Click cell **G14** to enter its cell reference in the formula. The formula is complete.

6. Press the **Enter** key. Cell H14 displays the value $74.85, which is the total charge for the second book.

## Copying and Pasting Formulas

Sometimes you will need to repeat the same formula throughout a worksheet. Rather than retyping the formula, you can copy a formula from one cell and paste it into another cell. When you copy a formula, Excel places the formula into the **Clipboard**, which is a temporary storage location for text and graphics. When you paste, Excel takes the formula from the Clipboard and inserts it into the selected cell or range. Excel adjusts the cell references in the formula to reflect the formula's new location in the worksheet. This occurs because you usually want to copy the actions of a formula rather than the specific value the formula generates. In this case, the formula's action is to multiply the price of the book by the quantity. By copying and pasting the formula, you can quickly repeat that action for every book listed in the worksheet.

You will copy the formula you entered in cell H14 to the range H15:H17 to calculate the charges on the remaining three books in Tobias Gregson's order. By copying and pasting the formula, you will save time and avoid potential mistakes from retyping the formula.

### To copy and paste the formula:

1. Click cell **H14** to select the cell that contains the formula you want to copy.

2. On the HOME tab, in the Clipboard group, click the **Copy** button (or press the **Ctrl+C** keys). Excel copies the formula to the Clipboard.

3. Select the range **H15:H17**. You want to paste the formula into these cells.

4. In the Clipboard group, click the **Paste** button (or press the **Ctrl+V** keys). Excel pastes the formula into the selected cells, adjusting each formula so that the total charges calculated for the books are based on the corresponding values within each row. A button appears below the selected range, providing options for pasting formulas and values. See Figure 1-25.

| Figure 1-25 | Copied and pasted formula |

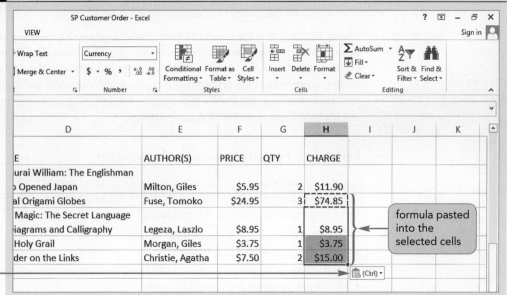

▶ **5.** Click cell **H15** and verify that the formula =F15*G15 appears in the formula bar. The formula was updated to reflect the cell references in the corresponding row.

▶ **6.** Click the other cells in column H and verify that the corresponding formulas are entered in those cells.

# Simplifying Formulas with Functions

In addition to cell references and operators, formulas can also contain functions. A function is a named operation that replaces the arithmetic expression in a formula. Functions are used to simplify long or complex formulas. For example, to add the values from cells A1 through A10, you could enter the following long formula:

=A1+A2+A3+A4+A5+A6+A7+A8+A9+A10

Or, you could use the SUM function to calculate the sum of those cell values by entering the following formula:

=SUM(A1:A10)

In both instances, Excel adds the values in cells A1 through A10, but the SUM function is faster and simpler to enter and less prone to a typing error. You should always use a function, if one is available, in place of a long, complex formula. Excel supports more than 300 different functions from the fields of finance, business, science, and engineering. Excel provides functions that work with numbers, text, and dates.

## Introducing Function Syntax

Every function follows a set of rules, or **syntax**, which specifies how the function should be written. The general syntax of all Excel functions is

FUNCTION (argument1, argument2, …)

where FUNCTION is the function name, and argument1, argument2, and so forth are values used by that function. For example, the SUM function shown above uses a single argument, A1:A10, which is the range reference of the cells whose values will be added. Some functions do not require any arguments and are entered as FUNCTION(). Functions without arguments still require the opening and closing parentheses, but do not include a value within the parentheses.

## Entering Functions with AutoSum

A fast and convenient way to enter commonly used functions is with AutoSum. The AutoSum button includes options to insert the SUM, AVERAGE, COUNT, MIN, and MAX functions to generate the following:

- Sum of the values in the specified range
- Average value in the specified range
- Total count of numeric values in the specified range
- Minimum value in the specified range
- Maximum value in the specified range

After you select one of the AutoSum options, Excel determines the most appropriate range from the available data and enters it as the function's argument. You should always verify that the range included in the AutoSum function matches the range that you want to use.

You will use AutoSum to enter the SUM function to add the total charges for Tobias Gregson's order.

## To use AutoSum to enter the SUM function:

▶ 1. Click cell **G18** to make it the active cell, type **Subtotal** as the label, and then press the **Tab** key to make cell H18 the active cell.

▶ 2. On the HOME tab, in the Editing group, click the **AutoSum button arrow**. The button's menu opens and displays five common summary functions: Sum, Average, Count Numbers, Max (for maximum), and Min (for minimum).

**TIP**

You can quickly insert the SUM function by pressing the Alt+= keys.

▶ 3. Click **Sum** to enter the SUM function. The formula =SUM(H13:H17) is entered in cell H18. The cells involved in calculating the sum are selected and highlighted on the worksheet so you can quickly confirm that Excel selected the most appropriate range from the available data. A ScreenTip appears below the formula describing the function's syntax. See Figure 1-26.

| Figure 1-26 | SUM function being entered with the AutoSum button |

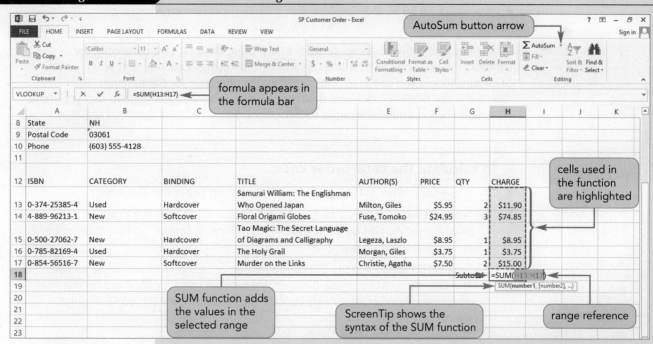

▶ 4. Press the **Enter** key to accept the formula. The subtotal of the book charges returned by the SUM function is $114.45.

AutoSum makes entering a commonly used formula such as the SUM function fast and easy. However, AutoSum can determine the appropriate range reference to include only when the function is adjacent to the cells containing the values you want to summarize. If you need to use a function elsewhere in the worksheet, you will have to select the range reference to include or type the function yourself.

Each sale made by Sparrow & Pond is subject to a 5 percent sales tax and a $15.30 handling fee. You will add these to the Customer Order worksheet so you can calculate the total charge for the order.

### To add the sales tax and handling fee to the worksheet:

▶ **1.** Click cell **G11**, type **Sales Tax** as the label, and then press the **Tab** key to make cell H11 the active cell.

▶ **2.** In cell H11, type **5%** as the sales tax rate, and then press the **Enter** key. The sales tax rate is entered in the cell, and can be used in other calculations. The value is displayed with the % symbol, but is stored as the equivalent decimal value 0.05.

▶ **3.** Click cell **G19** to make it the active cell, type **Tax** as the label, and then press the **Tab** key to make cell H19 the active cell.

▶ **4.** Type **=H11*H18** as the formula to calculate the sales tax on the book order, and then press the **Enter** key. The formula multiples the sales tax value in cell H11 by the order subtotal value in cell H18. The value $5.72 is displayed in cell H19, which is 5 percent of the book order subtotal of $114.45.

▶ **5.** In cell G20, type **Handling** as the label, and then press the **Tab** key to make cell H20 the active cell. You will enter the handling fee in this cell.

▶ **6.** Type **$15.30** as the handling fee, and then press the **Enter** key.

The last part of the customer order is to calculate the total cost by adding the subtotal, the tax, and the handling fee. Rather than using AutoSum, you will type the SUM function so you can enter the correct range reference for the function. You can type the range reference or select the range in the worksheet. Remember, that you must type parentheses around the range reference.

### To calculate the total order cost:

▶ **1.** In cell G21, type **TOTAL** as the label, and then press the **Tab** key.

▶ **2.** Type **=SUM(** in cell H21 to enter the function name and the opening parenthesis. As you begin to type the function, a ScreenTip lists the names of all functions that start with S.

Make sure the cell reference in the function matches the range you want to calculate.

▶ **3.** Type **H18:H20** to specify the range reference of the cells you want to add. The cells referenced in the function are selected and highlighted on the worksheet so you can quickly confirm that you entered the correct range reference.

**4.** Type **)** to complete the function, and then press the **Enter** key. The value of the SUM function appears in cell H21, indicating that the total charge for the order is $135.47. See Figure 1-27.

| Figure 1-27 | Total charge for the customer order |
| --- | --- |

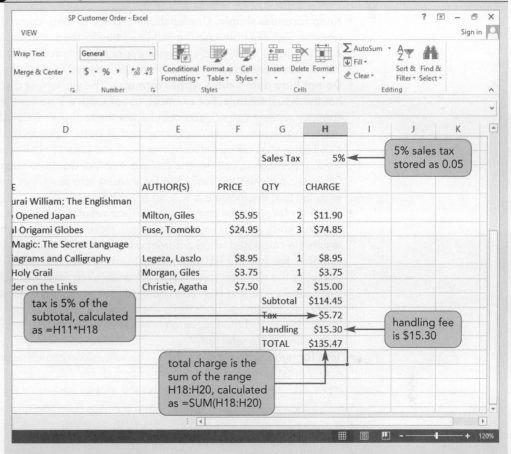

The SUM function makes it simple to quickly add the values in a group of cells.

**PROSKILLS**

*Problem Solving: Writing Effective Formulas*

You can use formulas to quickly perform calculations and solve problems. First, identify the problem you need to solve. Then, gather the data needed to solve the problem. Finally, create accurate and effective formulas that use the data to answer or resolve the problem. Follow these guidelines:

- **Keep formulas simple.** Use functions in place of long, complex formulas whenever possible. For example, use the SUM function instead of entering a formula that adds individual cells, which makes it easier to confirm that the formula is making an accurate calculation as it provides answers needed to evaluate the problem.

- **Do not hide data values within formulas.** The worksheet displays formula results, not the actual formula. For example, to calculate a 5 percent interest rate on a currency value in cell A5, you could enter the formula =0.05*A5. However, this doesn't show how the value is calculated. A better approach places the value 0.05 in a cell accompanied by a descriptive label and uses the cell reference in the formula. If you place 0.05 in cell A6, the formula =A6*A5 would calculate the interest value. Other people can then easily see the interest rate as well as the resulting interest, ensuring that the formula is solving the right problem.

- **Break up formulas to show intermediate results.** When a worksheet contains complex computations, other people can more easily comprehend how the formula results are calculated when different parts of the formula are distinguished. For example, the formula =SUM(A1:A10)/SUM(B1:B10) calculates the ratio of two sums, but hides the two sum values. Instead, enter each SUM function in a separate cell, such as cells A11 and B11, and use the formula =A11/B11 to calculate the ratio. Other people can see both sums and the value of their ratio in the worksheet and better understand the final result, which makes it more likely that the best problem resolution will be selected.

- **Test formulas with simple values.** Use values you can calculate in your head to confirm that your formula works as intended. For example, using 1s or 10s as the input values lets you easily figure out the answer and verify the formula.

Finding a solution to a problem requires accurate data and analysis. With workbooks, this means using formulas that are easy to understand, clearly show the data being used in the calculations, and demonstrate how the results are calculated. Only then can you be confident that you are choosing the best problem resolution.

# Modifying a Worksheet

As you develop a worksheet, you might need to modify its content and structure to create a more logical organization. Some ways you can modify a worksheet include moving cells and ranges, inserting rows and columns, deleting rows and columns, and inserting and deleting cells.

## Moving and Copying a Cell or Range

One way to move a cell or range is to select it, position the pointer over the bottom border of the selection, drag the selection to a new location, and then release the mouse button. This technique is called **drag and drop** because you are dragging the range and dropping it in a new location. If the drop location is not visible, drag the selection to the edge of the workbook window to scroll the worksheet, and then drop the selection.

You can also use the drag-and-drop technique to copy cells by pressing the Ctrl key as you drag the selected range to its new location. A copy of the original range is placed in the new location without removing the original range from the worksheet.

## Moving or Copying a Cell or Range

- Select the cell or range you want to move or copy.
- Move the pointer over the border of the selection until the pointer changes shape.
- To move the range, click the border and drag the selection to a new location (or to copy the range, hold down the Ctrl key and drag the selection to a new location).

*or*

- Select the cell or range you want to move or copy.
- On the HOME tab, in the Clipboard group, click the Cut or Copy button (or right-click the selection, and then click Cut or Copy on the shortcut menu, or press the Ctrl+X or Ctrl+C keys).
- Select the cell or the upper-left cell of the range where you want to paste the content.
- In the Clipboard group, click the Paste button (or right-click the selection and then click Paste on the shortcut menu, or press the Ctrl+V keys).

Sally wants the subtotal, tax, handling, and total values in the range G18:H21 moved down one row to the range G19:H22 to provide more space from the book orders. You will use the drag-and-drop method to move the range.

### To drag and drop the range G18:H21:

1. Select the range **G18:H21**. These are the cells you want to move.

2. Move the pointer over the bottom border of the selected range so that the pointer changes to.

3. Press and hold the mouse button to change the pointer to, and then drag the selection down one row. Do not release the mouse button. A ScreenTip appears, indicating that the new range of the selected cells will be G19:H22. A darker border also appears around the new range. See Figure 1-28.

**Figure 1-28**    **Range G18:H21 being moved to range G19:H22**

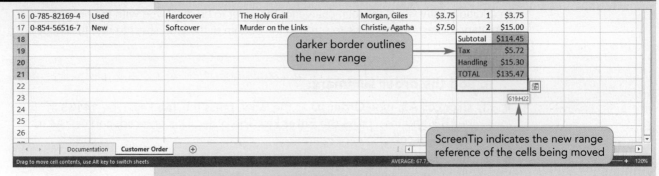

4. Make sure the ScreenTip displays the range **G19:H22**, and then release the mouse button. The selected cells move to their new location.

Some people find dragging and dropping a difficult and awkward way to move a selection, particularly if the selected range is large or needs to move a long distance in the worksheet. In those situations, it is often more efficient to cut or copy and paste the cell contents. Cutting moves the selected content, whereas copying duplicates the selected content. Pasting places the selected content in the new location.

Sally wants the worksheet to include a summary of the customer order starting in row 3. You will cut the customer contact information and the book listing from range A3:A22 and paste it into range A9:H23, freeing up space for the order information.

### To cut and paste the customer contact information and book listing:

▶ **1.** Click cell **A3** to select it.

▶ **2.** Press the **Ctrl+Shift+End** keys to extend the selection to the last cell in the lower-right corner of the worksheet (cell H22).

▶ **3.** On the HOME tab, in the Clipboard group, click the **Cut** button (or press the **Ctrl+X** keys). The range is surrounded by a moving border, indicating that it has been cut.

▶ **4.** Click cell **A9** to select it. This is the upper-left corner of the range where you want to paste the range that you cut.

▶ **5.** In the Clipboard group, click the **Paste** button (or press the **Ctrl+V** keys). The range A3:H22 is pasted into the range A9:H28. All of the formulas in the moved range were automatically updated to reflect their new locations.

## Using the COUNT Function

Sometimes you will want to know how many unique items are included in a range, such as the number of different books in the customer order. To calculate that value, you use the COUNT function, which has the syntax

`=COUNT(range)`

where *range* is the range of cells containing numeric values to be counted. Note that any cell in the range containing a non-numeric value is not counted in the final tally.

You will include the count of the number of different books for the order in the summary information. The summary will also display the order ID (a unique number assigned by Sparrow & Pond to the order), the shipping date, and the type of delivery (overnight, two-day, or standard) in the freed-up space at the top of the worksheet. In addition, Sally wants the total charge for the order to be displayed with the order summary so she does not have to scroll to the bottom of the worksheet to find that value.

### To add the order summary:

▶ **1.** Click cell **A3**, type **Order ID** as the label, press the **Tab** key, type **14123** in cell B3, and then press the **Enter** key. The order ID is entered, and cell A4 is the active cell.

▶ **2.** Type **Shipping Date** as the label in cell A4, press the **Tab** key, type **4/3/2016** in cell B4, and then press the **Enter** key. The shipping date is entered, and cell A5 is the active cell.

▶ **3.** Type **Delivery** as the label in cell A5, press the **Tab** key, type **Overnight** in cell B5, and then press the **Enter** key. The delivery type is entered, and cell A6 is the active cell.

▶ **4.** Type **Items Ordered** as the label in cell A6, and then press the **Tab** key. Cell B6 is the active cell. You will enter the COUNT function to determine the number of different books ordered.

▶ **5.** In cell B6, type **=COUNT(** to begin the function.

6. With the insertion point still blinking in cell B6, select the range **G19:G23**. The range reference is entered as the argument for the COUNT function.

7. Type **)** to complete the function, and then press the **Enter** key. Cell B6 displays the value 5, indicating that five items were ordered by Tobias Gregson. Cell A7 is the active cell.

8. Type **Total Charge** as the label in cell A7, and then press the **Tab** key to make cell B7 the active cell.

9. Type **=** to start the formula, and then click cell **H28** to enter its cell reference in the formula in cell B7. The formula =H28 tells Excel to display the contents of cell H28 in the current cell.

10. Press the **Enter** key to complete the formula. See Figure 1-29.

| Figure 1-29 | Customer order summary |
| --- | --- |

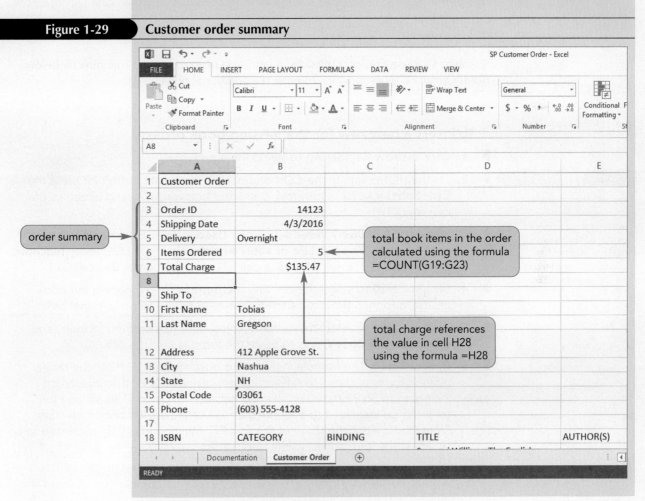

order summary

total book items in the order calculated using the formula =COUNT(G19:G23)

total charge references the value in cell H28 using the formula =H28

## Inserting a Column or Row

You can insert a new column or row anywhere within a worksheet. When you insert a new column, the existing columns are shifted to the right and the new column has the same width as the column directly to its left. When you insert a new row, the existing rows are shifted down and the new row has the same height as the row above it. Because inserting a new row or column moves the location of the other cells in the worksheet, any cell references in a formula or function are updated to reflect the new layout.

## Inserting or Deleting a Column or Row

**To insert a column or row:**
- Select the column(s) or row(s) where you want to insert the new column(s) or row(s). Excel will insert the same number of columns or rows as you select to the *left* of the selected columns or *above* the selected rows.
- On the HOME tab, in the Cells group, click the Insert button (or right-click a column or row heading or selected column and row headings, and then click Insert on the shortcut menu; or press the Ctrl+Shift+= keys).

**To delete a column or row:**
- Select the column(s) or row(s) you want to delete.
- On the HOME tab, in the Cells group, click the Delete button (or right-click a column or row heading or selected column and row headings, and then click Delete on the shortcut menu; or press the Ctrl+− keys).

Tobias Gregson's order is missing an item. You need to insert a row directly below *Floral Origami Globes* in which to enter the additional book.

**To insert a new row for the missing book order:**

1. Click the **row 21** heading to select the entire row.

2. On the HOME tab, in the Cells group, click the **Insert** button (or press the **Ctrl+Shift+=** keys). A new row is inserted below row 20 and becomes the new row 21.

3. Enter **0-151-01089-7** in cell A21, enter **Used** in cell B21, enter **Hardcover** in cell C21, enter **Pops: A Life of Louis Armstrong** in cell D21, enter **Teachout, Terry** in cell E21, enter **$11.95** in cell F21, and then enter **2** in cell G21.

4. Click cell **H20** to select the cell with the formula for calculating the book charge, and then press the **Ctrl+C** keys to copy the formula in that cell.

5. Click cell **H21** to select the cell where you want to insert the formula, and then press the **Ctrl+V** keys to paste the formula into the cell.

6. Click cell **H26**. The formula in this cell is now =SUM(H19:H24); the range reference was updated to reflect the inserted row. Also, the tax amount increased to $6.92 based on the new subtotal value of $138.35, and the total charge increased to $160.57 because of the added book order. See Figure 1-30. Also, the result of the COUNT function in cell B6 increased to 6 to reflect the item added to the book order.

**TIP**

You can insert multiple columns or rows by selecting that number of column or row headings, and then clicking the Insert button or pressing the Ctrl+Shift+= keys.

Figure 1-30     **New row inserted**

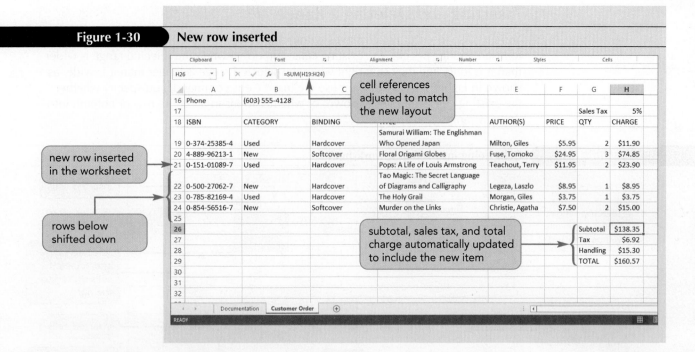

**Deleting a Row or Column**

You can delete rows or columns from a worksheet. **Deleting** removes the data from the row or column as well as the row or column itself. The rows below the deleted row shift up to fill the vacated space. Likewise, the columns to the right of the deleted column shift left to fill the vacated space. Also, all cell references in the worksheet are adjusted to reflect the change. You click the Delete button in the Cells group on the HOME tab to delete selected rows or columns.

Deleting a column or row is not the same as clearing a column or row. **Clearing** removes the data from the selected row or column but leaves the blank row or column in the worksheet. You press the Delete key to clear the contents of the selected row or column, which leaves the worksheet structure unchanged.

Tobias Gregson did not order *The Holy Grail* by Giles Morgan, so that book needs to be removed from the order. You will delete the row containing that book.

**To delete the *The Holy Grail* row from the book order:**

1. Click the **row 23** heading to select the entire row.

2. On the HOME tab, in the Cells group, click the **Delete** button (or press the **Ctrl+–** keys). Row 23 is deleted, and the rows below it shift up to fill the space.

All of the cell references in the worksheet are again updated automatically to reflect the impact of deleting row 23. The subtotal value in cell H25 now returns a value of $134.60 based on the sum of the cells in the range H19:H23. The sales tax amount in cell H26 decreases to $6.73. The total cost of the order decreases to $156.63. Also, the result of the COUNT function in cell B6 decreases to 5 to reflect the item deleted from the book order. As you can see, one of the great advantages of using Excel is that it modifies the formulas to reflect the additions and deletions you make to the worksheet.

## Inserting and Deleting a Range

You can also insert or delete ranges within a worksheet. When you use the Insert button to insert a range of cells, the existing cells shift down when the selected range is wider than it is long, and they shift right when the selected range is longer than it is wide, as shown in Figure 1-31. When you use the Insert Cells command, you specify whether the existing cells shift right or down, or whether to insert an entire row or column into the new range.

**Figure 1-31**    **Cells being inserted in a worksheet**
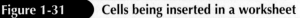

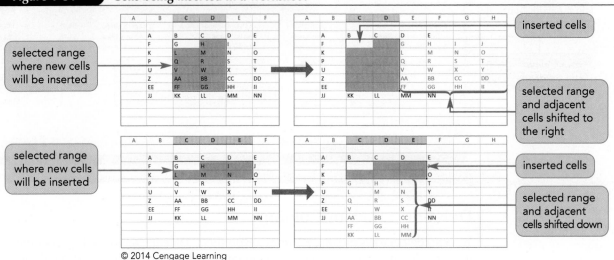

© 2014 Cengage Learning

The process works in reverse when you delete a range. As with deleting a row or column, the cells adjacent to the deleted range either move up or left to fill in the space vacated by the deleted cells. The Delete Cells command lets you specify whether you want to shift the adjacent cells left or up, or whether you want to delete the entire column or row.

When you insert or delete a range, cells that shift to a new location adopt the width of the columns they move into. As a result, you might need to resize columns and rows in the worksheet.

---

**REFERENCE**

### *Inserting or Deleting a Range*

- Select a range that matches the range you want to insert or delete.
- On the HOME tab, in the Cells group, click the Insert button or the Delete button.

*or*

- Select the range that matches the range you want to insert or delete.
- On the HOME tab, in the Cells group, click the Insert button arrow and then click Insert Cells, or click the Delete button arrow and then click Delete Cells (or right-click the selected range, and then click Insert or Delete on the shortcut menu).
- Click the option button for the direction to shift the cells, columns, or rows.
- Click the OK button.

---

Sally wants you to insert cells in the book list that will contain the Sparrow & Pond book ID for each book. You will insert these new cells into the range A17:A28, shifting the adjacent cells to the right.

### To insert a range in the book list:

1. Select the range **A17:A28**. You want to insert cells in this range.
2. On the HOME tab, in the Cells group, click the **Insert button arrow**. A menu of insert options appears.
3. Click **Insert Cells**. The Insert dialog box opens.
4. Verify that the **Shift cells right** option button is selected.
5. Click the **OK** button. New cells are inserted into the selected range, and the adjacent cells move to the right. The cell contents do not fit well in the columns and rows they shifted into, so you will resize the columns and rows.
6. Resize columns C and D to **12** characters, resize column E to **30** characters, and then resize column F to **15** characters. The text is easier to read in the resized columns.
7. Select the row **19** through row **23** headings.
8. In the Cells group, click the **Format** button, and then click **AutoFit Row Height**. The selected rows autofit to their contents.

**TIP**
You can also autofit by double-clicking the bottom border of row 23.

9. Click cell **A18**, type **BOOK ID** as the label, and then press the **Enter** key. See Figure 1-32.

**Figure 1-32**   Range added to the worksheet

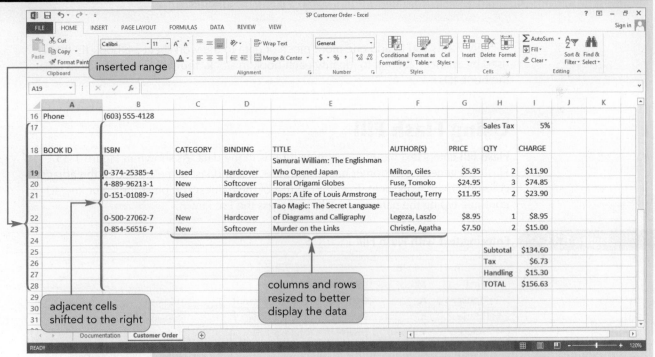

Why did you insert cells in the range A17:A28 even though the book ID values will be entered only in the range A18:A23? You did this to retain the layout of the page design. Selecting the additional rows ensures that the sales tax and summary values still line up with the QTY and CHARGE columns. Whenever you insert a new range, be sure to consider its impact on the layout of the entire worksheet.

### Hiding and Unhiding Rows, Columns, and Worksheets

Workbooks can become long and complicated, filled with formulas and data that are important for performing calculations but are of little interest to readers. In those situations, you can simplify these workbooks for readers by **hiding** rows, columns, and even worksheets. Although the contents of hidden cells cannot be seen, the data in those cells is still available for use in formulas and functions throughout the workbook.

Hiding a row or column essentially decreases that row height or column width to 0 pixels. To a hide a row or column, select the row or column heading, click the Format button in the Cells group on the HOME tab, point to Hide & Unhide on the menu that appears, and then click Hide Rows or Hide Columns. The border of the row or column heading is doubled to mark the location of hidden rows or columns.

A worksheet often is hidden when the entire worksheet contains data that is not of interest to the reader and is better summarized elsewhere in the document. To hide a worksheet, make that worksheet active, click the Format button in the Cells group on the HOME tab, point to Hide & Unhide, and then click Hide Sheet.

**Unhiding** redisplays the hidden content in the workbook. To unhide a row or column, click in a cell below the hidden row or to the right of the hidden column, click the Format button, point to Hide & Unhide, and then click Unhide Rows or Unhide Columns. To unhide a worksheet, click the Format button, point to Hide & Unhide, and then click Unhide Sheet. The Unhide dialog box opens. Click the sheet you want to unhide, and then click the OK button. The hidden content is redisplayed in the workbook.

Although hiding data can make a worksheet and workbook easier to read, be sure never to hide information that is important to the reader.

Sally wants you to add one more piece of data to the worksheet—a book ID that is used by Sparrow & Pond to identify each book in stock. You will use Flash Fill to create the book IDs.

## Using Flash Fill

**Flash Fill** enters text based on patterns it finds in the data. As shown in Figure 1-33, Flash Fill generates customer names from the first and last names stored in the adjacent columns in the worksheet. To enter the rest of the names, you press the Enter key; to continue typing the names yourself, you press the Esc key.

**Figure 1-33** Entering text with Flash Fill

| | A | B | C | D | E |
|---|---|---|---|---|---|
| 1 | First | M.I. | Last | Full Name | |
| 2 | Tobias | A. | Gregson | Tobias Gregson | |
| 3 | Maria | R. | Sanchez | Maria Sanchez | |
| 4 | Andrew | T. | Lewis | Andrew Lewis | |
| 5 | Brett | K. | Carls | Brett Carls | |
| 6 | Carmen | A. | Hzu | Carmen Hzu | |
| 7 | Karen | M. | Schultz | Karen Schultz | |
| 8 | Howard | P. | Gary | Howard Gary | |
| 9 | Natalia | N. | Shapiro | Natalia Shapiro | |
| 10 | Paul | O. | Douglas | Paul Douglas | |
| 11 | | | | | |

you enter the full name twice to begin the pattern

Flash Fill generates the remaining full names based on the pattern in the first two cells

Flash Fill works best when the pattern is clearly recognized from the values in the data. Be sure to enter the data pattern in the column or row right next to the related data. The data used to generate the pattern must be in a rectangular grid and cannot have blank columns or rows. Also, Flash Fill enters text, not formulas. If you edit or replace an entry originally used by Flash Fill, the content generated by Flash Fill will not be updated.

The Sparrow & Pond book ID combines five digits of the book's ISBN and its category (used or new). For example, *Floral Origami Globes* has the ISBN 4-889-96213-1 and is new, so its book ID is 96213-New. The book IDs follow a consistent and logical pattern. Rather than typing every book ID, you will use Flash Fill to enter the book IDs into the worksheet.

**To enter the book IDs using Flash Fill:**

▶ **1.** Make sure that cell **A19** is the active cell.

▶ **2.** Type **25385-Used** as the ID for the first book in the list, and then press the **Enter** key.

▶ **3.** Type **9** in cell A20. As soon as you start typing, Flash Fill generates the remaining entries in the column based on the pattern you entered. See Figure 1-34.

| Figure 1-34 | Book IDs generated by Flash Fill |

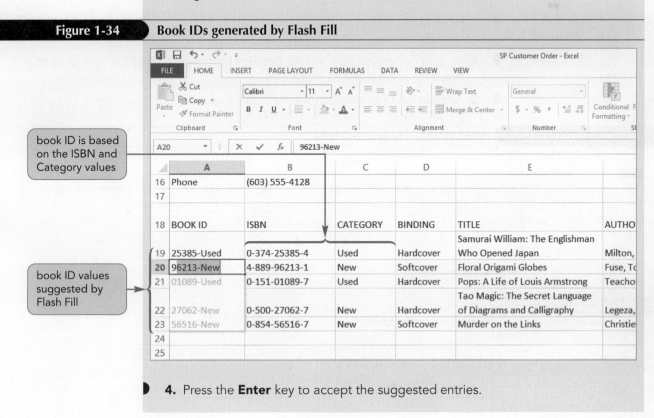

book ID is based on the ISBN and Category values

book ID values suggested by Flash Fill

▶ **4.** Press the **Enter** key to accept the suggested entries.

# Formatting a Worksheet

**Formatting** changes a workbook's appearance to make the content of a worksheet easier to read. Two common formatting changes are adding borders to cells and changing the font size of text.

## Adding Cell Borders

Sometimes you want to include lines along the edges of cells to enhance the readability of rows and columns of data. You can do this by adding borders to the left, top, right, or bottom edge of a cell or range. You can also specify the thickness of and the number of lines in the border. This is especially helpful when a worksheet is printed because the gridlines that surround the cells are not printed by default; they appear on the worksheet only as a guide.

Sally wants add borders around the cells that contain content in the Customer Order worksheet to make the content easier to read.

### To add borders around the worksheet cells:

1. Select the range **A3:B7**. You will add borders around all of the cells in the selected range.

2. On the HOME tab, in the Font group, click the **Borders button arrow** , and then click **All Borders**. Borders are added around each cell in the range. The Borders button changes to reflect the last selected border option, which in this case is All Borders. The name of the selected border option appears in the button's ScreenTip.

3. Select the nonadjacent range **A9:B16;H17:I17**. You will add borders around each cell in the selected range.

4. In the Font group, click the **All Borders** button to add borders to all of the cells in the selected range.

5. Click cell **A17** to deselect the cells. See Figure 1-35.

**Figure 1-35**    **Borders added to selected cells**

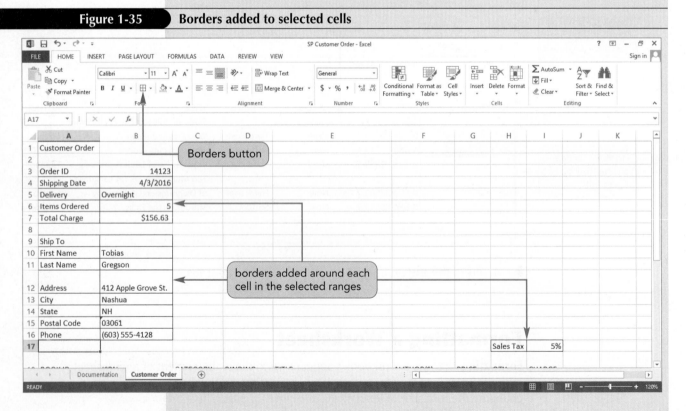

6. Select the nonadjacent range **A18:I23;H25:I28**, and then click the **All Borders** button to add borders to all of the cells in the selected range.

## Changing the Font Size

Changing the size of text in a sheet provides a way to identify different parts of a worksheet, such as distinguishing a title or section heading from data. The size of the text is referred to as the font size and is measured in points. The default font size for worksheets is 11 points, but it can be made larger or smaller as needed. You can resize text in selected cells using the Font Size button in the Font group on the HOME tab. You can also use the Increase Font Size and Decrease Font Size buttons to resize cell content to the next higher or lower standard font size.

Sally wants you to increase the size of the worksheet title to 26 points to make it stand out more.

### To change the font size of the worksheet title:

1. Click cell **A1** to select it. The worksheet title is in this cell.

2. On the HOME tab, in the Font group, click the **Font Size button arrow** to display a list of font sizes, and then click **28**. The worksheet title changes to 28 points. See Figure 1-36.

| Figure 1-36 | Font size of cell content increased |

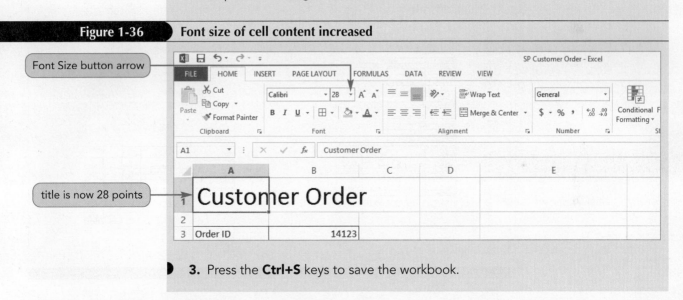

Font Size button arrow

title is now 28 points

3. Press the **Ctrl+S** keys to save the workbook.

# Printing a Workbook

Now that you have finished the workbook, Sally wants you to print a copy of the book order. Before you print a workbook, you should preview it to ensure that it will print correctly.

## Changing Worksheet Views

You can view a worksheet in three ways. Normal view, which you have been using throughout this tutorial, shows the contents of the worksheet. Page Layout view shows how the worksheet will appear when printed. Page Break Preview displays the location of the different page breaks within the worksheet. This is useful when a worksheet will span several printed pages and you need to control what content appears on each page.

Sally wants you to see how the Customer Order worksheet will appear on printed pages. You will do this by switching between views.

## To switch the Customer Order worksheet to different views:

▶ 1. Click the **Page Layout** button 🔲 on the status bar. The page layout of the worksheet appears in the workbook window.

▶ 2. Drag the **Zoom slider** to reduce the zoom level to 50%. The reduced magnification makes it clear that the worksheet will spread over two pages when printed. See Figure 1-37.

| Figure 1-37 | Worksheet in Page Layout view |
| --- | --- |

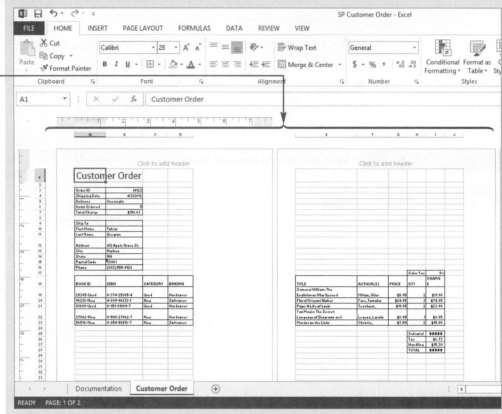

worksheet will span two printed pages

---

**TIP**

You can relocate a page break by dragging the dotted blue border in the Page Break Preview window.

▶ 3. Click the **Page Break Preview** button 🔲 on the status bar. The view switches to Page Break Preview, which shows only those parts of the current worksheet that will print. A dotted blue border separates one page from another.

▶ 4. Zoom the worksheet to **70%** so that you can more easily read the contents of the worksheet. See Figure 1-38.

**Figure 1-38**    Worksheet in Page Break Preview

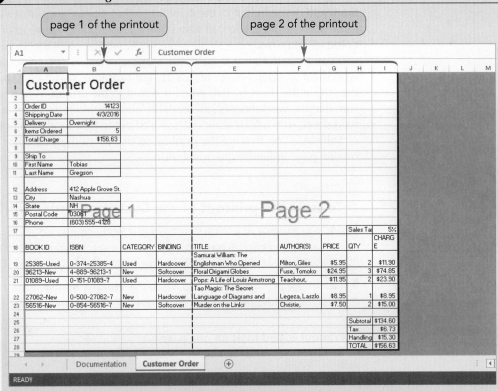

5. Click the **Normal** button ⊞ on the status bar. The worksheet returns to Normal view. A dotted black line indicates where the page break will occur.

## Changing the Page Orientation

Page orientation specifies in which direction content is printed on the page. In **portrait orientation**, the page is taller than it is wide. In **landscape orientation**, the page is wider than it is tall. By default, Excel displays pages in portrait orientation. Changing the page orientation affects only the active sheet.

As you saw in Page Layout view and Page Break Preview, the Customer Order worksheet will print on two pages—columns A through D will print on the first page, and columns E through I will print on the second page, although the columns that print on each page may differ slightly depending on the printer. Sally wants the entire worksheet to print on a single page, so you'll change the page orientation from portrait to landscape.

### To change the page orientation of the Customer Order worksheet:

1. On the ribbon, click the **PAGE LAYOUT** tab. The tab includes options for changing how the worksheet is arranged.

2. In the Page Setup group, click the **Orientation** button, and then click **Landscape**. The worksheet switches to landscape orientation.

3. Click the **Page Layout** button 📖 on the status bar to switch to Page Layout view. The worksheet will still print on two pages.

## Setting the Scaling Options

You change the size of the worksheet on the printed page by **scaling** it. You can scale the width or the height of the printout so that all of the columns or all of the rows fit on a single page. You can also scale the printout to fit the entire worksheet (both columns and rows) on a single page. If the worksheet is too large to fit on one page, you can scale the print to fit on the number of pages you select. You can also scale the worksheet to a percentage of its size. For example, scaling a worksheet to 50% reduces the size of the sheet by half when it is sent to the printer. When scaling a printout, make sure that the worksheet is still readable after shrinking. Scaling affects only the active worksheet, so you can scale each worksheet to best fit its contents.

Sally asks you to scale the printout so that all of the Customer Order worksheet fits on one page in landscape orientation.

### To scale the printout of the Customer Order worksheet:

1. On the PAGE LAYOUT tab, in the Scale to Fit group, click the **Width arrow**, and then click **1 page** on the menu that appears. All of the columns in the worksheet now fit on one page.

2. In the Scale to Fit group, click the **Height arrow**, and then click **1 page**. All of the rows in the worksheet now fit on one page. See Figure 1-39.

**Figure 1-39**    Printout scaled to fit on one page

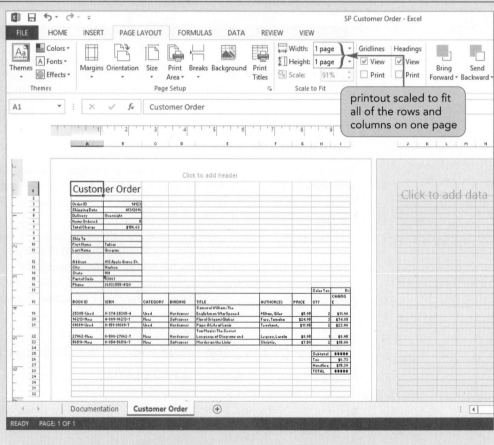

## Setting the Print Options

**TIP**

To print the gridlines or the column and row headings, click the corresponding Print check box in the Sheet Options group on the PAGE LAYOUT tab.

You can print the contents of a workbook by using the Print screen in Backstage view. The Print screen provides options for choosing where to print, what to print, and how to print. For example, you can specify the number of copies to print, which printer to use, and what to print. You can choose to print only the selected cells, only the active sheets, or all of the worksheets in the workbook that contain data. The printout will include only the data in the worksheet. The other elements in the worksheet, such as the row and column headings and the gridlines around the worksheet cells, will not print by default. The preview shows you exactly how the printed pages will look with the current settings. You should always preview before printing to ensure that the printout looks exactly as you intended and avoid unnecessary reprinting.

Sally asks you to preview and print the Sparrow & Pond workbook now.

**Note:** Check with your instructor first to make sure you should complete the steps for printing the workbook.

**To preview and print the workbook:**

▶ 1. On the ribbon, click the **FILE** tab to display Backstage view.

▶ 2. Click **Print** in the navigation bar. The Print screen appears with the print options and a preview of the Customer Order worksheet printout. See Figure 1-40.

**Figure 1-40**    **Print screen in Backstage view**

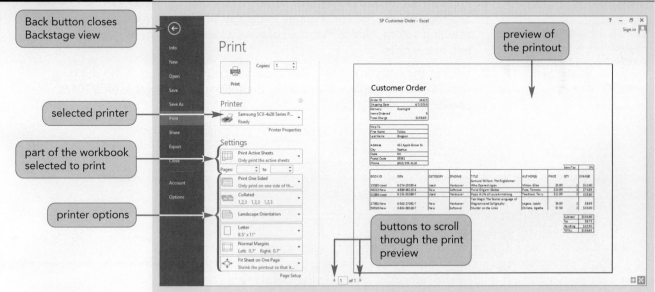

- Back button closes Backstage view
- selected printer
- part of the workbook selected to print
- printer options
- preview of the printout
- buttons to scroll through the print preview

▶ 3. Click the **Printer** button, and then click the printer to which you want to print, if it is not already selected. By default, Excel will print only the active sheet.

▶ 4. In the Settings options, click the top button, and then click **Print Entire Workbook** to print all of the sheets in the workbook—in this case, both the Documentation and the Customer Order worksheets. The preview shows the first sheet in the workbook—the Documentation worksheet. Note that this sheet is still in the default portrait orientation.

▶ 5. Below the preview, click the **Next Page** button ▶ to view the Customer Order worksheet. As you can see, the Customer Order worksheet will print on a single page in landscape orientation.

> **6.** If you are instructed to print, click the **Print** button to send the contents of the workbook to the specified printer. If you are not instructed to print, click the **Back** button ◉ in the navigation bar to exit Backstage view.

# Viewing Worksheet Formulas

Most of the time, you will be interested in only the final results of a worksheet, not the formulas used to calculate those results. However, in some cases, you might want to view the formulas used to develop the workbook. This is particularly useful when you encounter unexpected results and you want to examine the underlying formulas, or you want to discuss your formulas with a colleague. You can display the formulas instead of the resulting values in cells.

If you print the worksheet while the formulas are displayed, the printout shows the formulas instead of the values. To make the printout easier to read, you should print the worksheet gridlines as well as the row and column headings so that cell references in the formulas are easy to find in the printed version of the worksheet.

You will look at the Customer Order worksheet with the formulas displayed.

**To display the formulas in cells in the Customer Order worksheet:**

> **1.** Make sure the Customer Order worksheet is in Page Layout view.

> **2.** Press the **Ctrl+`** keys (the grave accent symbol ` is usually located above the Tab key). The worksheet changes to display all of the formulas instead of the resulting values. Notice that the columns widen to display all of the formula text in the cells.

> **3.** Look at the entry in cell B4. The underlying numeric value of the shipping date (42463) is displayed instead of the formatted date value (4/3/2016). See Figure 1-41.

| TIP |
| --- |
| You can also display formulas in a worksheet by clicking the Show Formulas button in the Formula Auditing group on the FORMULAS tab. |

**Figure 1-41**        Worksheet with formulas displayed

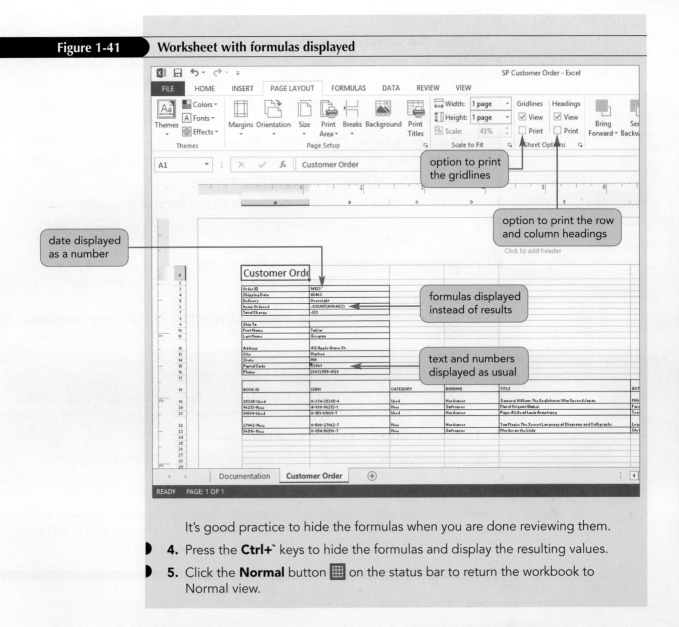

It's good practice to hide the formulas when you are done reviewing them.

▶ **4.** Press the **Ctrl+`** keys to hide the formulas and display the resulting values.

▶ **5.** Click the **Normal** button ⊞ on the status bar to return the workbook to Normal view.

# Saving a Workbook with a New Filename

Whenever you click the Save button on the Quick Access Toolbar or press the Ctrl+S keys, the workbook file is updated to reflect the latest content. If you want to save a copy of the workbook with a new filename or to a different location, you need to use the Save As command. When you save a workbook with a new filename or to a different location, the previous version of the workbook remains stored as well.

You have completed the SP Customer Order workbook. Sally wants to use the workbook as a model for other customer order reports. You will save the workbook with a new filename to avoid overwriting the Tobias Gregson book order. Then you'll clear the information related to Tobias Gregson, leaving the formulas intact. This new, revised workbook will then be ready for a new customer order.

### To save the workbook with a new filename:

1. Press the **Ctrl+S** keys to save the workbook. This ensures that the final copy of the SP Customer Order workbook contains the latest content.

2. On the ribbon, click the **FILE** tab to display Backstage view, and then click **Save As** on the navigation bar. The Save As screen is displayed.

3. Click **Computer**, and then click the **Browse** button. The Save As dialog box opens so you can save the workbook with a new filename or to a new location.

4. Navigate to the location specified by your instructor.

> **TIP**
>
> Save the workbook with the new name *before* making your changes to avoid inadvertently saving your edits to the wrong file.

5. In the File name box, type **SP Customer Order Form** as the new filename.

6. Click the **Save** button. The workbook is saved with the new filename and is open in Excel.

7. Select the range **B3:B5**, right-click the selected range to open the shortcut menu, and then click **Clear Contents** to clear the contents of the order ID, shipping date, and delivery type cells.

8. Select the nonadjacent range **B10:B16;A19:H23**, and then press the **Delete** key to clear the contact information for Tobias Gregson and the list of books he ordered from those cells.

9. Select cell **I27**, and then clear the handling fee.

10. Click cell **A3** to make that cell the active cell. The next time someone opens this workbook, cell A3 will still be the active cell.

11. Press the **Ctrl+S** keys to save the workbook.

12. Click the **Close** button ☒ on the title bar (or press the **Ctrl+W** keys). The workbook closes, and the Excel program closes.

Sally is pleased with the workbook you created. With the calculations already in place in the new workbook, she will be able to quickly enter new customer orders and see the calculated book charges without having to recreate the worksheet.

## Session 1.2 Quick Check

REVIEW

1. What formula would you enter to add the values in cells B4, B5, and B6? What function would you enter to achieve the same result?

2. What formula would you enter to count the number of numeric values in the range B2:B100?

3. What formula would you enter to find the maximum value of the cells in the range B2:B100?

4. If you insert cells into the range C1:D10 shifting the cells to the right, what is the new location of the data that was previously in cell E5?

5. Cell E11 contains the formula =SUM(E1:E10). How does this formula change if a new row is inserted above row 5?

6. Describe four ways of viewing the content of a workbook in Excel.

7. How are page breaks indicated in Page Break Preview?

8. How do you display the formulas used in a worksheet instead of the formula results?

## SAM Projects

Put your skills into practice with SAM Projects! SAM Projects for this tutorial can be found online. If you have a SAM account, go to www.cengage.com/sam2013 to download the most recent Project Instructions and Start Files.

**ASSESS**

## Review Assignments

**PRACTICE**

**There are no Data Files needed for the Review Assignments.**

Sally wants you to create a workbook to record the recent book purchases made by Sparrow & Pond. The workbook should list the recent acquisitions from private sellers, libraries, and other vendors; include a description of each book; and calculate the total number of books acquired and the total amount spent by Sparrow & Pond. Complete the following:

1. Create a new, blank workbook, and then save the workbook as **Book List** in the location specified by your instructor.
2. Rename the Sheet1 worksheet as **Documentation**, and then enter the data shown in Figure 1-42 in the specified cells.

**Figure 1-42**    **Documentation sheet data**

| Cell | Data |
| --- | --- |
| A1 | Sparrow & Pond |
| A3 | Author |
| A4 | Date |
| A5 | Purpose |
| B3 | *your name* |
| B4 | *current date* |
| B5 | To record book acquisitions by Sparrow & Pond |

© 2014 Cengage Learning

3. Set the font size of the title text in cell A1 to 26 points.
4. Add a new worksheet after the Documentation sheet, and then rename the sheet as **Books**.
5. In cell A1, enter the text **Book Acquisitions**. Set the font size of this text to 26 points.
6. In cell A2, enter the text **DATE** as the label. In cell B2, enter the date **4/3/2016**.
7. In the range A4:G9, enter the data shown in Figure 1-43.

**Figure 1-43**　Book list

| ISBN | STATUS | BINDING | TITLE | AUTHOR | CONDITION | PRICE |
|------|--------|---------|-------|--------|-----------|-------|
| 0-670-02103-2 | New | Softcover | Rocket Men: The Epic Story of the First Men on the Moon | Nelson, Craig | Excellent | $12.95 |
| 0-195-09076-4 | Used | Hardcover | Buildings of Colorado | Noel, Thomas J. | Good | $22.50 |
| 0-375-70365-9 | New | Softcover | American Visions: The Epic History of Art in America | Hughes, Robert | Excellent | $22.50 |
| 1-564-77848-7 | New | Softcover | Simple Comforts: 12 Cozy Lap Quilts | Diehl, Kim | Very Good | $9.25 |
| 1-851-70006-4 | Used | Hardcover | Beautiful Stories About Children | Dickens, Charles | Good | $33.50 |

© 2014 Cengage Learning

8. Insert cells into the range A4:A9, shifting the other cells to the right.

9. Enter the label **BOOK ID** in cell A4, type **02103-New** in cell A5, and then type **09076-Used** in cell A6.

10. Use Flash Fill to fill in the remaining book IDs.

11. Set the width of columns A through D to 15 characters each. Set the width of column E to 30 characters. Set the width of column F to 20 characters. Set the width of column G to 15 characters.

12. Set the book titles in the range E4:E9 to wrap to a new line.

13. Autofit the heights of rows 4 through 9.

14. Move the book list in the range A4:H9 to the range A8:H13.

15. In cell G15, enter the text **TOTAL**. In cell H15, enter a function to add the prices in the range H9:H13.

16. In cell A4, enter the text **TOTAL BOOKS**. In cell B4, enter a function to count the number of numeric values in the range H9:H13.

17. In cell A5, enter the text **TOTAL PRICE**. In cell B5, display the value from cell H15.

18. In cell A6, enter the text **AVERAGE PRICE**. In cell B6, enter a formula to calculate the total price paid for the books (listed in cell B5) divided by the number of books purchased (listed in cell B4).

19. Add borders around each cell in the nonadjacent range A4:B6;A8:H13;G15:H15.

20. For the Books worksheet, change the page orientation to landscape and scale the worksheet to print on a single page for both the width and the height. If you are instructed to print, print the entire workbook.

21. Display the formulas in the Books worksheet, and set the gridlines and row/column headings to print. If you are instructed to print, print the entire worksheet.

22. Save and close the workbook.

## Case Problem 1

**APPLY**

**Data File needed for this Case Problem: Pacific.xlsx**

***American Wheel Tours***   Kevin Bennett is a tours manager at American Wheel Tours, a bicycle touring company located in Philadelphia, Pennsylvania, that specializes in one- and two-week supported tours in destinations across the United States. Kevin wants you to create a workbook that details the itinerary of the company's Pacific Coast tour. The workbook will list the tour itinerary shown in Figure 1-44 and calculate the total number of riding days, total mileage, and average mileage per ride.

**Figure 1-44**   **Pacific Tour itinerary**

| DATE | START | FINISH | CAMPSITE | MILES | DESCRIPTION |
|---|---|---|---|---|---|
| 10-Oct-16 | Eugene | Eugene | Richardson Park | | Orientation day. Meet at Richardson Park, located at the Fern Ridge Reservoir. |
| 11-Oct-16 | Eugene | Florence | Honeyman State Park | 66 | Cycle over Low Pass to Honeyman State Park. |
| 12-Oct-16 | Florence | Charleston | Sunset Bay State Park | 56 | Cycle through Oregon Dunes National Recreation Area to Sunset Bay State Park. |
| 13-Oct-16 | Charleston | Port Orford | Humbug Mountain State Park | 60 | Cycle around Bullards Beach State Park and camp at Humbug Mountain State Park. |
| 14-Oct-16 | Port Orford | Brookings | Harris Beach State Park | 52 | Cycle past the mouth of the Rogue River to Harris Beach State Park. |
| 15-Oct-16 | Brookings | Crescent City | Jedediah State Park | 48 | Pass into California and camp at Jedediah State Park. |
| 16-Oct-16 | Crescent City | Eureka | Eureka Fairgrounds | 72 | A long day through Del Norte Coast Redwoods State Park to Eureka. |

© 2014 Cengage Learning

Complete the following:

1. Open the **Pacific** workbook located in the Excel1 ▶ Case1 folder included with your Data Files, and then save the workbook as **Pacific Coast** in the location specified by your instructor.
2. In the Documentation worksheet, enter your name in cell B3 and the date in cell B4.
3. Add a new sheet to the end of the workbook and rename it as **Itinerary**.
4. In cell A1, enter the text **Pacific Coast Tour** and set the font size to 28 points.
5. In the range A3:A8, enter the following labels: **Start Date**, **End Date**, **Total Days**, **Riding Days**, **Total Miles**, and **Miles per Day**.
6. Enter the date **October 10, 2016** in cell B3, and then enter the date **October 16, 2016** in cell B4.
7. In the range D3:D8, enter the labels **Type**, **Surface**, **Difficulty**, **Tour Leader**, **Cost**, and **Deposit**.
8. In the range E3:E8, enter **Van Supported**, **Paved**, **Intermediate**, **Kevin Bennett**, **$1,250**, and **$350**.
9. In the range A11:F18, enter the data shown in Figure 1-44, including the column labels. Leave the mileage value for October 10th blank.
10. In cell B5, enter a formula to calculate the total number of days in the tour by subtracting the starting date (cell B3) from the ending date (cell B4) and adding 1.

11. In cell B6, enter a function to count the total number of riding days based on the numbers in the range E12:E18.

12. In cell B7, enter a function to add the total number of miles in the range E12:E18.

13. In cell B8, enter a formula to calculate the average miles per day by dividing the total miles by the number of riding days.

14. Insert cells in the range A11:A18, shifting the cells to the right. In cell A11, enter **DAY**. In the range A12:A18, enter the numbers 1 through 7 to number each day of the tour.

15. Set the column widths so that column A is 12 characters, columns B through E are 14 characters each, column F is 6 characters, and column G is 50 characters.

16. Wrap text in the range A11:G18 as needed so that any hidden entries are displayed on multiple lines within the cell.

17. Autofit the height of rows 11 through 18.

18. Add borders around the ranges A3:B8, D3:E8, and A11:G18.

19. Format the Itinerary worksheet so that it prints on a single page in landscape orientation. If you are instructed to print, print the entire workbook.

20. Display the formulas in the Itinerary worksheet, and set the gridlines and column/row headings to print. If you are instructed to print, print the worksheet.

21. Return the Itinerary worksheet to Normal view, hide the formulas, set the gridlines and column/row headings so that they won't print, and then save the workbook.

22. Save the workbook as **Pacific Coast Revised** in the location specified by your instructor.

23. Determine what the total mileage and average mileage per day of the tour would be if Kevin adds a 10-mile warm-up ride on October 10th but decreases the length of the October 15th ride to 41 miles. Save the workbook.

## Case Problem 2

**APPLY**

Data File needed for this Case Problem: Tropical.xlsx

*Tropical Foods*   Tropical Foods is a health food grocery store located in Keizer, Oregon. Monica Li is working on the store's annual financial report. One part of the financial report will be the company's balance sheet for the previous two years. Monica already entered the labels for the balance sheet. You will enter the numeric data and formulas to perform the financial calculations. Complete the following:

1. Open the **Tropical** workbook located in the Excel1 ▸ Case2 folder included with your Data Files, and then save the workbook as **Tropical Foods Balance Sheet** in the location specified by your instructor.

2. In cells B3 and B4 of the Documentation sheet, enter your name and the date. In cell A1, increase the font size of the title to 28 points.

3. Go to the Balance Sheet worksheet. Increase the font size of the title in cell A1 to 28 points, and then increase the font size of the subtitle in cell A2 to 20 points.

4. In the corresponding cells of columns C and D, enter the numbers shown in Figure 1-45 for the company's assets and liabilities.

**Figure 1-45**    **Tropical Foods assets and liabilities**

|  |  | 2015 | 2014 |
|---|---|---|---|
| Assets | Cash | $645,785 | $627,858 |
|  | Accounts Receivable | 431,982 | 405,811 |
|  | Inventories | 417,615 | 395,648 |
|  | Prepaid Expenses | 2,152 | 4,151 |
|  |  |  |  |
|  | Other Assets | 31,252 | 26,298 |
|  |  |  |  |
|  | Fixed Assets @ Cost | 1,800,000 | 1,750,000 |
|  | Accumulated Depreciation | 82,164 | $77,939 |
|  |  |  |  |
| Liabilities | Accounts Payable | $241,191 | $193,644 |
|  | Accrued Expenses | 31,115 | 32,151 |
|  | Current Portion of Debt | 120,000 | 100,000 |
|  | Income Taxes Payable | 144,135 | 126,524 |
|  |  |  |  |
|  | Long-Term Debt | 815,000 | 850,000 |
|  |  |  |  |
|  | Capital Stock | 1,560,000 | 1,525,000 |
|  | Retain Earnings | 335,181 | 304,508 |

© 2014 Cengage Learning

5. Set the width of column A to 12 characters, column B to 28 characters, columns C and D to 14 characters each, column E to 2 characters, and column F to 10 characters.

6. In cells C8 and D8, enter formulas to calculate the current assets value for 2014 and 2015, which is equal to the sum of the cash, accounts receivable, inventories, and prepaid expenses values.

7. In cells C14 and D14, enter formulas to calculate the net fixed assets value for 2014 and 2015, which is equal to the difference between the fixed assets value and the accumulated depreciation value.

8. In cells C16 and D16, enter formulas to calculate the total assets value for 2014 and 2015, which is equal to the sum of the current assets, other assets, and net fixed assets value.

9. In cells C23 and D23, enter formulas to calculate the sum of the accounts payable, accrued expenses, current portion of debt, and income taxes payable values for 2014 and 2015.

10. In cells C29 and D29, enter formulas to calculate the shareholders' equity value for 2014 and 2015, which is equal to the sum of the capital stock and retained earnings.

11. In cells C31 and D31, enter formulas to calculate the total liabilities & equity value for 2014 and 2015, which is equal to the sum of the current liabilities, long-term debt, and shareholders' equity.

12. In a balance sheet, the total assets should equal the total liabilities & equity. Compare the values in cells C16 and C31, and then compare the values in cells D16 and D31 to confirm that this is the case for the Tropical Foods balance sheet in 2014 and 2015. If the account doesn't balance, check your worksheet for errors in either values or formulas.

13. In cell F4, enter a formula to calculate the percentage change in cash from 2014 to 2015, which is equal to (C4–D4)/D4.

14. Copy the formula in cell F4 and paste it in the nonadjacent range F5:F8;F10;F12:F14;F16; F19:F23;F25;F27:F29;F31 to show the percentage change in all values of the balance sheet.

15. Add borders around the cells in columns B, C, D, and F of the balance sheet, excluding the cells in rows 9, 11, 15, 17, 18, 24, 26, and 30.

16. Set the page layout of the Balance Sheet worksheet to portrait orientation and scaled to print on a single page. If you are instructed to print, print the entire workbook.

17. Display the formulas in the Balance Sheet worksheet, and then set the gridlines and row/column headings to print. If you are instructed to print, print the worksheet.

18. Display the Balance Sheet worksheet in Normal view, hide the formulas, set the gridlines and column/row headings so that they won't print, and then save the workbook.

## Case Problem 3

**CHALLENGE**

Data File needed for this Case Problem: Physics.xlsx

***Gladstone Country Day School*** Beatrix Melendez teaches Introduction to Physics at Gladstone Country Day School in Gladstone, Missouri. She wants to record students' quiz scores, and then calculate each student's total and average scores. She also wants to calculate the class average, high score, and low score for each quiz in her records. Beatrix has entered scores from 10 quizzes for 20 students in a worksheet. You will summarize these grades by student and by quiz using the functions listed in Figure 1-46.

**Figure 1-46** **Excel summary functions**

| Function | Description |
|----------|-------------|
| =AVERAGE (*range*) | Calculates the average of the values from the specified *range* |
| =MEDIAN (*range*) | Calculates the median or midpoint of the values from the specified *range* |
| =MIN (*range*) | Calculates the minimum of the values from the specified *range* |
| =MAX (*range*) | Calculates the maximum of the values from the specified *range* |

© 2014 Cengage Learning

Complete the following:

1. Open the **Physics** workbook located in the Excel1 ▶ Case3 folder included with your Data Files, and then save the workbook as **Physics Grading Sheet** in the location specified by your instructor.

2. In the Documentation sheet, enter your name in cell B3 and the date in cell B4. Increase the font size of the title in cell A1 to 28 points.

3. Go to the Grades worksheet. Increase the font size of cell A1 to 28 points, and then increase the font size of cell A2 to 22 points.

✦ **Explore** 4. In cell M5, enter a formula to calculate the median or midpoint of the quiz scores for Debra Alt. In cell N5, enter a formula to calculate the average of Debra Alt's quiz scores.

5. Copy the formulas in the range M5:N5 to the range M6:N24 to summarize the scores for the remaining students.

✦ **Explore** 6. In cell B26, enter a formula to calculate the minimum class score from the first quiz. In cell B27, enter a formula to calculate the median class score.

✦ **Explore** 7. In cell B28, use the MAX function to calculate the high score from the first quiz.

8. In cell B30, enter a formula to calculate the average score from the first quiz.

9. Copy the formulas in the range B26:B30 to the range C26:K30 to calculate the summary statistics for the rest of the quizzes.

10. Insert 10 new rows above row 4, shifting the student grade table and summary from the range A4:N30 to the range A14:N40. You will enter a summary of all of the students from all of the quizzes at the top of the worksheet.

11. In cell A4, enter the text **Class Size**. In cell B4, enter a formula to calculate the count of scores from the range N15:N34.

12. In the range A6:A9, enter the labels **Overall Scores**, **Lowest Average**, **Median Average**, and **Highest Average**. In cell A11, enter **Class Average**.

13. Using the average scores in the range N15:N34, enter formulas to calculate the overall lowest average score in cell B7, the median of the class averages in cell B8, the overall highest average in cell B9, and the average overall class score in cell B11.

14. Add cell borders around the ranges A4:B4, A7:B9, A11:B11, A14:K34, M14:N34, A36:K38, and A40:K40.

15. Set the page layout of the Grades worksheet to landscape orientation and scaled to print on a single page. If you are instructed to print, print the entire workbook.

16. Display the formulas in the Grades worksheet. Set the gridlines and the row/column headings to print. If you are instructed to print, print the worksheet.

17. Display the Grades worksheet in Normal view, hide the formulas, set the gridlines and column/row headings so that they won't print, and then save the workbook.

18. Determine the effect of raising each student's score on the first quiz by 10 points to curve the results. Report what impact this has on the overall class average from all 10 quizzes.

19. Save the workbook as **Physics Grading Sheet Revised**. If you are instructed to print, print the Grades worksheet.

## Case Problem 4

Data File needed for this Case Problem: Turf.xlsx

**TROUBLESHOOT**

*Turf Toughs*    Tim Gables is the owner and operator of Turf Toughs, a lawn and tree removal service located in Chicopee, Massachusetts. He created a workbook to record and analyze the service calls made by his company. So far, the workbook calculates the cost of each service call, the total charges for all of the calls, and the total number of billable hours. Unfortunately, the workbook contains several errors. You will fix these errors and then complete the workbook. Complete the following:

1. Open the **Turf** workbook located in the Excel1 ▸ Case4 folder included with your Data Files, and then save the workbook as **Turf Toughs Service Calls** in the location specified by your instructor.

2. In the Documentation sheet, enter your name in cell B3 and the date in cell B4.

3. Go to the Service Log worksheet. The log lists the contact information and the service calls for each customer.

   Tim wants you to insert a column of IDs for each customer. The customer ID is in the form *last-phone*, where *last* is the customer's last name and *phone* is the last four digits of the customer's phone number.

4. Insert cells in the range A4:A34, shifting the other cells to the right. Type **Cust ID** in cell A4, and then enter **Morris-4380** as the customer ID for Michael Morris. Use Flash Fill to fill in the remaining customer IDs in the column.

5. Add borders around the cells in the range A4:A32.

⚙ **Troubleshoot** 6. There is a problem with the all of the customer zip codes. Each zip code should begin with zero. Make the necessary changes to fix this problem.

7. Resize the columns of the worksheet so that all of the column labels in the service calls list are displayed entirely.

⚙ **Troubleshoot** 8. The formula in cell L5 is not correctly calculating the number of hours for each service call. Fix the formula so that it multiplies the difference between the starting and ending time by 24.

9. Copy the formula you created for cell L5 to the range L6:L32, replacing the previous calculated values.

10. Calculate the service charge for each service call so that it equals the base fee added to the hourly rate times the number of hours worked.

⚙ **Troubleshoot**  11. Cell N34 contains a formula to calculate the total service charges for all customer visits. Is it calculating the value correctly? If not, edit the formula to fix any errors you find.

12. Above row 4, insert six new rows, shifting the range A4:N34 down to the range A10:N40.

13. In the range A4:A8, enter the labels **From**, **To**, **Total Service Calls**, **Billable Hours**, and **Total Charges**.

14. In cell B4, calculate the starting date of the service calls by entering a formula that finds the minimum value of the dates in the Date column.

15. In cell B5, calculate the ending date of the service calls by entering a formula that finds the maximum value of the dates in the Date column.

16. In cell B6, enter a formula that counts the total number of service calls using the values in the Date column.

17. In cell B7, enter a formula that calculates the sum of hours from the Hours column.

18. In cell B8, enter a formula that references the value of cell N40.

19. Add borders around each cell in the range A4:B8.

20. Set the page layout of the Service Log worksheet so that it prints on a single page in landscape orientation. If you are instructed to print, print the entire workbook.

21. Display the formulas in the Service Log worksheet, scale the worksheet to fit on a single page, and then set the gridlines and row/column headings to print. If you are instructed to print, print the Service Log worksheet.

22. Return the Service Log worksheet to Normal view, hide the formulas, set the gridlines and column/row headings so that they won't print, and then save the workbook.

## OBJECTIVES

**Session 2.1**
- Change fonts, font style, and font color
- Add fill colors and a background image
- Create formulas to calculate sales data
- Apply Currency and Accounting formats and the Percent style
- Format dates and times
- Align, indent, and rotate cell contents
- Merge a group of cells

**Session 2.2**
- Use the AVERAGE function
- Apply cell styles
- Copy and paste formats with the Format Painter
- Find and replace text and formatting
- Change workbook themes
- Highlight cells with conditional formats
- Format a worksheet for printing
- Set the print area, insert page breaks, add print titles, create headers and footers, and set margins

# Formatting Workbook Text and Data

*Designing a Sales Report*

## Case | *Big Red Wraps*

Sanjit Chandra is a sales manager for Big Red Wraps, a growing restaurant chain that specializes in preparing made-to-order sandwich wraps, seasonal soups, and fresh salads. The first Big Red Wraps opened in Madison, Wisconsin, and has since expanded to 20 restaurants across six states. Four of these restaurants were opened this year. Each spring, the company has a sales conference where the restaurant managers meet to discuss sales concerns and review marketing plans for the upcoming year. Sanjit created a workbook that summarizes the sales data for the previous year and is part of a sales report that will be given to all conference attendees. He wants you to calculate some summary statistics and format the workbook.

## STARTING DATA FILES

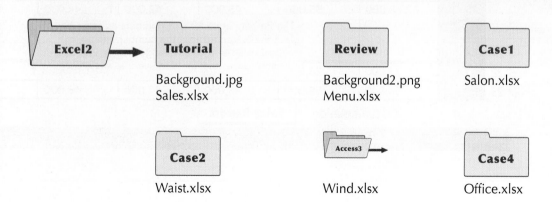

Excel2 → Tutorial
Background.jpg
Sales.xlsx

Review
Background2.png
Menu.xlsx

Case1
Salon.xlsx

Case2
Waist.xlsx

Access3 → Wind.xlsx

Case4
Office.xlsx

# Session 2.1 Visual Overview:

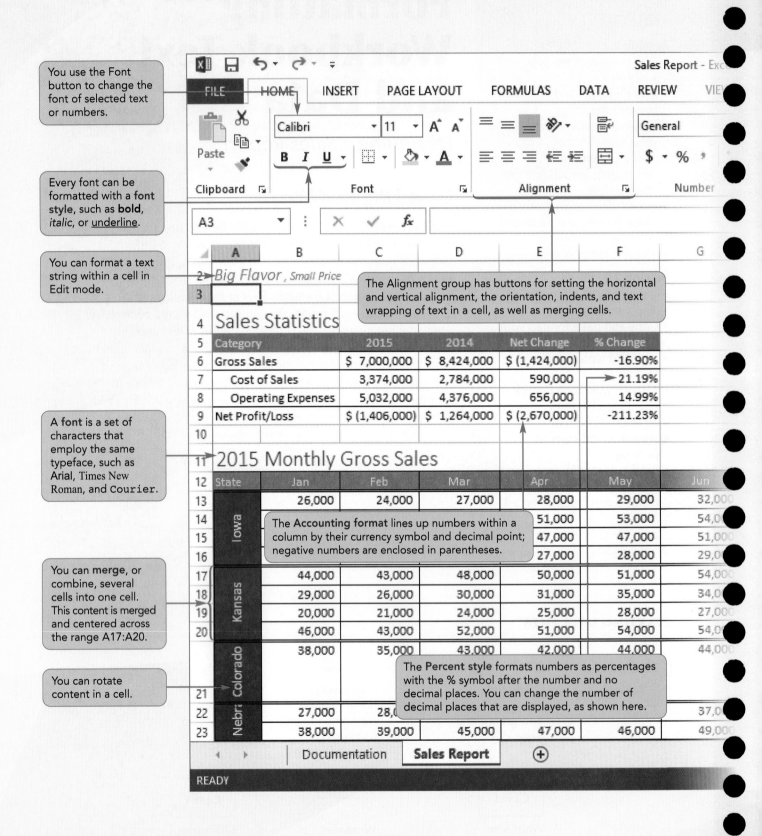

You use the Font button to change the font of selected text or numbers.

Every font can be formatted with a **font style**, such as **bold**, *italic*, or underline.

You can format a text string within a cell in Edit mode.

A **font** is a set of characters that employ the same typeface, such as Arial, Times New Roman, and Courier.

You can **merge**, or combine, several cells into one cell. This content is merged and centered across the range A17:A20.

You can rotate content in a cell.

Sales Report - Exc

The **Alignment group** has buttons for setting the horizontal and vertical alignment, the orientation, indents, and text wrapping of text in a cell, as well as merging cells.

The **Accounting format** lines up numbers within a column by their currency symbol and decimal point; negative numbers are enclosed in parentheses.

The **Percent style** formats numbers as percentages with the % symbol after the number and no decimal places. You can change the number of decimal places that are displayed, as shown here.

Big Flavor, Small Price

## Sales Statistics

| Category | 2015 | 2014 | Net Change | % Change |
|---|---|---|---|---|
| Gross Sales | $ 7,000,000 | $ 8,424,000 | $ (1,424,000) | -16.90% |
| Cost of Sales | 3,374,000 | 2,784,000 | 590,000 | 21.19% |
| Operating Expenses | 5,032,000 | 4,376,000 | 656,000 | 14.99% |
| Net Profit/Loss | $ (1,406,000) | $ 1,264,000 | $ (2,670,000) | -211.23% |

## 2015 Monthly Gross Sales

| State | Jan | Feb | Mar | Apr | May | Jun |
|---|---|---|---|---|---|---|
| Iowa | 26,000 | 24,000 | 27,000 | 28,000 | 29,000 | 32,000 |
|  |  |  |  | 51,000 | 53,000 | 54,0 |
|  |  |  |  | 47,000 | 47,000 | 51,00 |
|  |  |  |  | 27,000 | 28,000 | 29,0 |
| Kansas | 44,000 | 43,000 | 48,000 | 50,000 | 51,000 | 54,00 |
|  | 29,000 | 26,000 | 30,000 | 31,000 | 35,000 | 34,0 |
|  | 20,000 | 21,000 | 24,000 | 25,000 | 28,000 | 27,00 |
|  | 46,000 | 43,000 | 52,000 | 51,000 | 54,000 | 54,0 |
| Colorado | 38,000 | 35,000 | 43,000 | 42,000 | 44,000 | 44,00 |
| Nebr | 27,000 | 28,0 |  |  |  | 37,0 |
|  | 38,000 | 39,000 | 45,000 | 47,000 | 46,000 | 49,00 |

Documentation   **Sales Report**

READY

# Worksheet with Formatting

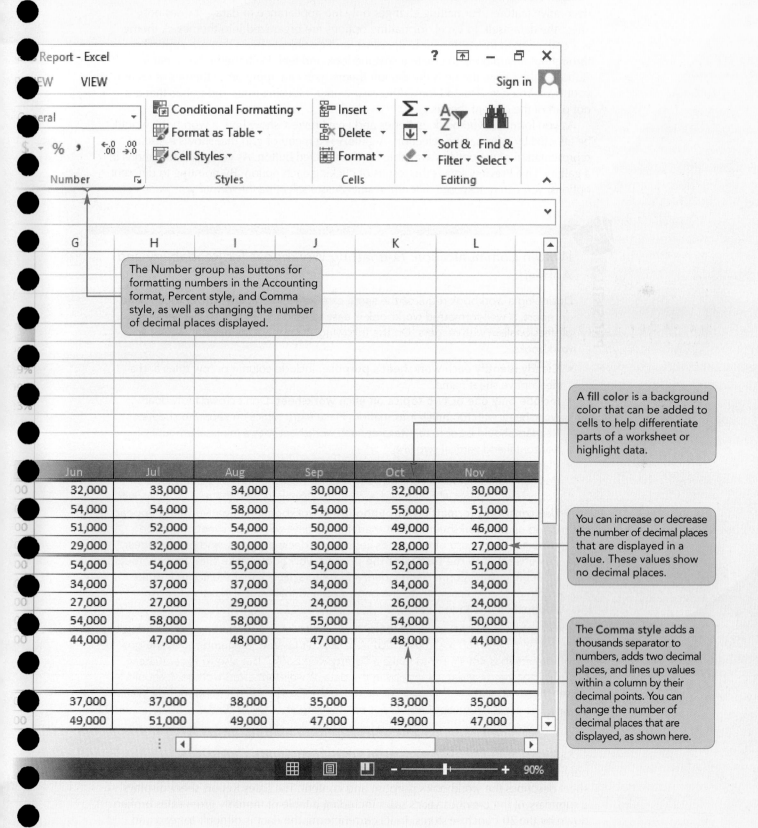

The Number group has buttons for formatting numbers in the Accounting format, Percent style, and Comma style, as well as changing the number of decimal places displayed.

A fill color is a background color that can be added to cells to help differentiate parts of a worksheet or highlight data.

You can increase or decrease the number of decimal places that are displayed in a value. These values show no decimal places.

The Comma style adds a thousands separator to numbers, adds two decimal places, and lines up values within a column by their decimal points. You can change the number of decimal places that are displayed, as shown here.

| Jun | Jul | Aug | Sep | Oct | Nov |
|---|---|---|---|---|---|
| 32,000 | 33,000 | 34,000 | 30,000 | 32,000 | 30,000 |
| 54,000 | 54,000 | 58,000 | 54,000 | 55,000 | 51,000 |
| 51,000 | 52,000 | 54,000 | 50,000 | 49,000 | 46,000 |
| 29,000 | 32,000 | 30,000 | 30,000 | 28,000 | 27,000 |
| 54,000 | 54,000 | 55,000 | 54,000 | 52,000 | 51,000 |
| 34,000 | 37,000 | 37,000 | 34,000 | 34,000 | 34,000 |
| 27,000 | 27,000 | 29,000 | 24,000 | 26,000 | 24,000 |
| 54,000 | 58,000 | 58,000 | 55,000 | 54,000 | 50,000 |
| 44,000 | 47,000 | 48,000 | 47,000 | 48,000 | 44,000 |
| | | | | | |
| 37,000 | 37,000 | 38,000 | 35,000 | 33,000 | 35,000 |
| 49,000 | 51,000 | 49,000 | 47,000 | 49,000 | 47,000 |

# Formatting Cell Text

You can add formatting to a workbook by choosing its fonts, styles, colors, and decorative features. Formatting changes only the appearance of data—it does not affect the data itself. In Excel, formatting options are organized into themes. A **theme** is a collection of formatting for text, colors, and graphical effects that are applied throughout a workbook to create a specific look and feel. Each theme has a name. Although the Office theme is the default theme, you can apply other themes or create your own. You can also add formatting to a workbook using fonts and colors that are not part of the current theme.

As you format a workbook, galleries and Live Preview show how a workbook would be affected by a formatting selection. A **gallery** is a menu or grid that shows a visual representation of the options available for the selected button. As you point to options in a gallery, **Live Preview** shows the results of clicking each option. By pointing to different options, you can quickly see different results before selecting the format you want.

**PROSKILLS**

*Written Communication: Formatting Workbooks for Readability and Appeal*

Designing a workbook requires the same care as designing any written document or report. A well-formatted workbook is easy to read and establishes a sense of professionalism with readers. Do the following to improve the appearance of your workbooks:

- **Clearly identify each worksheet's purpose.** Include column or row titles and a descriptive sheet name.
- **Include only one or two topics on each worksheet.** Don't crowd individual worksheets with too much information. Place extra topics on separate sheets. Readers should be able to interpret each worksheet with a minimal amount of horizontal and vertical scrolling.
- **Place worksheets with the most important information first in the workbook.** Position worksheets summarizing your findings near the front of the workbook. Position worksheets with detailed and involved analysis near the end as an appendix.
- **Use consistent formatting throughout the workbook.** If negative values appear in red on one worksheet, format them in the same way on all sheets. Also, be consistent in the use of thousands separators, decimal places, and percentages.
- **Pay attention to the format of the printed workbook.** Make sure your printouts are legible with informative headers and footers. Check that the content of the printout is scaled correctly to the page size, and that page breaks divide the information into logical sections.

Excel provides many formatting tools. However, too much formatting can be intrusive, overwhelm data, and make the document difficult to read. Remember that the goal of formatting is not simply to make a "pretty workbook," but also to accentuate important trends and relationships in the data. A well-formatted workbook should seamlessly convey your data to the reader. If the reader is thinking about how your workbook looks, it means he or she is not thinking about your data.

Sanjit has already entered the data and some formulas in a workbook, which is only a rough draft of what he wants to submit to the company. The Documentation sheet describes the workbook's purpose and content. The Sales Report sheet displays a summary of the previous year's sales including a table of monthly gross sales broken down by the 20 franchise stores. In its current form, the data is difficult to read and interpret. Sanjit wants you to format the contents of the workbook to improve its readability and visual appeal.

**To open the workbook:**

1. Open the **Sales** workbook located in the Excel2 ▸ Tutorial folder included with your Data Files, and then save the workbook as **Sales Report** in the location specified by your instructor.

2. In the Documentation sheet, enter your name in cell B4 and the date in cell B5.

## Applying Fonts and Font Styles

Excel organizes fonts into theme and non-theme fonts. A **theme font** is associated with a particular theme and used for headings and body text in the workbook. These fonts change automatically when you change the theme applied to the workbook. Text formatted with a **non-theme font** retains its appearance no matter what theme is used with the workbook.

Fonts appear in different character styles. **Serif fonts**, such as Times New Roman, have extra strokes at the end of each character that aid in reading passages of text. **Sans serif fonts**, such as Arial, do not include these extra strokes. Other fonts are purely decorative, such as a font used for specialized logos. Every font can be further formatted with a font style such as *italic*, **bold**, or ***bold italic***; with underline; and with special effects such as ~~strikethrough~~ and color. You can also increase or decrease the font size.

**REFERENCE**

### Formatting Cell Content

- To change the font, select the cell or range. On the HOME tab, in the Font group, click the Font arrow, and then click a font.
- To change the font size, select the cell or range. On the HOME tab, in the Font group, click the Font Size arrow, and then click a font size.
- To change a font style, select the cell or range. On the HOME tab, in the Font group, click the Bold, Italic, or Underline button.
- To change a font color, select the cell or range. On the HOME tab, in the Font group, click the Font Color button arrow, and then click a color.
- To format a text selection, double-click the cell to enter Edit mode, and then select the text to format. Change the font, size, style, or color, and then press the Enter key.

Sanjit wants the company name at the top of each worksheet to appear in large, bold letters using the default heading font from the Office theme. He wants the slogan "Big Flavor, Small Price" displayed below the company name to appear in the heading font, but in smaller, italicized letters.

**To format the company name and slogan in the Documentation sheet:**

1. In the Documentation sheet, select cell **A1** to make it the active cell. The cell with the company name is selected.

2. On the HOME tab, in the Font group, click the **Font button arrow** to display a gallery of fonts available on your computer. Each name is displayed in its corresponding font. When you point to a font in the gallery, Live Preview shows how the text in the selected cell will look with that font. The first two fonts are the theme fonts for headings and body text—Calibri Light and Calibri.

▶ **3.** Point to **Algerian** (or another font) in the All Fonts list. Live Preview shows the effect of the Algerian font on the text in cell A1. See Figure 2-1.

**Figure 2-1** ▶ **Font gallery**

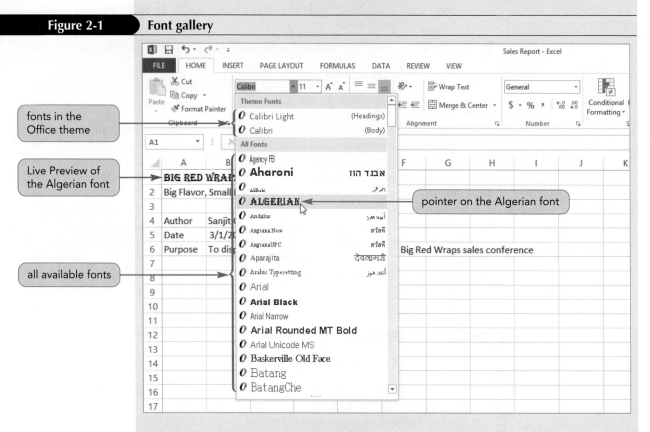

fonts in the Office theme

Live Preview of the Algerian font

all available fonts

pointer on the Algerian font

Big Red Wraps sales conference

▶ **4.** Point to three other fonts in the Font gallery to see the Live Preview showing how cell A1 could look with those fonts.

▶ **5.** Click **Calibri Light** in the Theme Fonts list. The company name in cell A1 changes to the Calibri Light font, the default headings font in the current theme.

▶ **6.** In the Font group, click the **Font Size button arrow** to display a list of font sizes, and then click **26**. The company name changes to 26 points.

▶ **7.** In the Font group, click the **Bold** button **B** (or press the **Ctrl+B** keys). The company name is set in bold.

▶ **8.** Select cell **A2** to make it active. The cell with the slogan text is selected.

▶ **9.** In the Font group, click the **Font Size button arrow**, and then click **10**. The slogan text changes to 10 points.

▶ **10.** In the Font group, click the **Italic** button **I** (or press the **Ctrl+I** keys). The slogan in cell A2 is italicized.

▶ **11.** Select the range **A4:A6**, and then press the **Ctrl+B** keys to change the font to bold.

▶ **12.** Select cell **A7** to deselect the range. The column labels are set in bold. See Figure 2-2.

**Figure 2-2** Formatted cell text

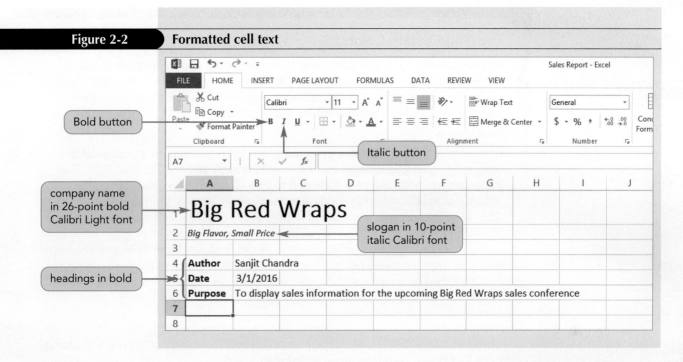

## Applying a Font Color

Color can transform a plain workbook filled with numbers and text into a powerful presentation that captures the user's attention and adds visual emphasis to the points you want to make. By default, Excel displays text in a black font color.

Like fonts, colors are organized into theme and non-theme colors. **Theme colors** are the 12 colors that belong to the workbook's theme. Four colors are designated for text and backgrounds, six colors are used for accents and highlights, and two colors are used for hyperlinks (followed and not followed links). These 12 colors are designed to work well together and to remain readable in all combinations. Each theme color has five variations, or accents, in which a different tint or shading is applied to the theme color.

Ten **standard colors**—dark red, red, orange, yellow, light green, green, light blue, blue, dark blue, and purple—are always available regardless of the workbook's theme. You can open an extended palette of 134 standard colors. You can also create a custom color by specifying a mixture of red, blue, and green color values, making available 16.7 million custom colors—more colors than the human eye can distinguish. Some dialog boxes have an automatic color option that uses your Windows default text and background colors, usually black text on a white background.

**INSIGHT**

### Creating Custom Colors

Custom colors let you add subtle and striking colors to a formatted workbook. To create custom colors, you use the **RGB Color model** in which each color is expressed with varying intensities of red, green, and blue. RGB color values are often represented as a set of numbers in the format

(*red*, *green*, *blue*)

where *red* is an intensity value assigned to red light, *green* is an intensity value assigned to green light, and *blue* is an intensity value assigned to blue light. The intensities are measured on a scale of 0 to 255—0 indicates no intensity (or the absence of the color) and 255 indicates the highest intensity. So, the RGB color value (255, 255, 0) represents a mixture of high-intensity red (255) and high-intensity green (255) with the absence of blue (0), which creates the color yellow.

To create colors in Excel using the RGB model, click the More Colors option located in a color menu or dialog box to open the Colors dialog box. In the Colors dialog box, click the Custom tab, and then enter the red, green, and blue intensity values. A preview box shows the resulting RGB color.

Sanjit wants the labels in the Documentation sheet to stand out, so you will change the Big Red Wraps company name and slogan to red.

### To change the company name and slogan font color:

1. Select the range **A1:A2**. The company name and slogan are selected.

2. On the HOME tab, in the Font group, click the **Font Color button arrow** to display the gallery of theme and standard colors. (The two colors for hyperlinked text are not shown.)

3. Point to the **Red** color (the second color) in the Standard Colors section. The color name appears in a ScreenTip and you see a Live Preview of the text with the red font color. See Figure 2-3.

| Figure 2-3 | Font color gallery |
| --- | --- |

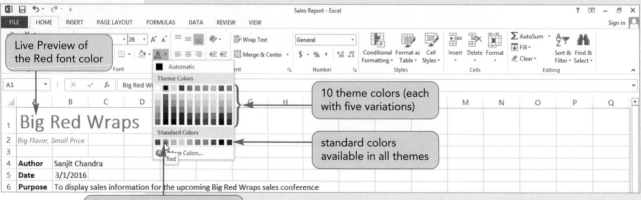

4. Click the **Red** color. The company name and slogan change to red.

## Formatting Text Selections

In Edit mode, you can select and format selections of text within a cell. When the Big Red Wraps slogan is used in marketing materials, "Big Flavor" is set slightly larger than "Small Price." Sanjit wants you to recreate this effect in the workbook by increasing the font size of "Big Flavor" while leaving the rest of the text unchanged. You will use Edit mode to apply a different format to part of the cell text.

### To format part of the company slogan:

1. Double-click cell **A2** to select the cell and enter Edit mode (or click cell **A2** and press the **F2** key). The status bar shows EDIT to indicate that you are working with the cell in Edit mode. The pointer changes to the I-beam pointer.

2. Drag the pointer over the phrase **Big Flavor** to select it. The Mini toolbar appears above the selected text with buttons to change the font, size, style, and color of the selected text in the cell. See Figure 2-4.

**Figure 2-4**     **Mini toolbar in Edit mode**

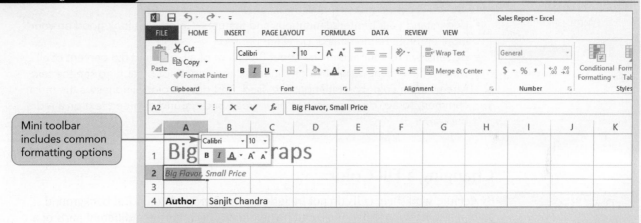

Mini toolbar includes common formatting options

3. On the Mini toolbar, click the **Font Size button arrow**, and then click **14**. The font size of the selected text increases to 14 points.

4. Select cell **A7** to deselect cell A2. See Figure 2-5.

**Figure 2-5**     **Formatted text selection**

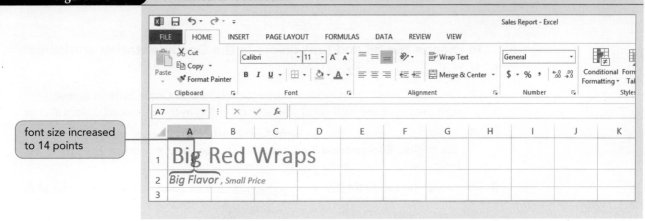

font size increased to 14 points

# Working with Fill Colors and Backgrounds

Another way to distinguish sections of a worksheet is by formatting the cell background. You can fill the cell background with color or an image. Sanjit wants you to add fill colors and background images to the Documentation worksheet.

---

**INSIGHT**

## Using Color to Enhance a Workbook

When used wisely, color can enhance any workbook. However, when used improperly, color can distract the user, making the workbook more difficult to read. As you format a workbook, keep in mind the following tips:

- Use colors from the same theme to maintain a consistent look and feel across the worksheets. If the built-in themes do not fit your needs, you can create a custom theme.
- Use colors to differentiate types of cell content and to direct users where to enter data. For example, format a worksheet so that formula results appear in cells without a fill color and users enter data in cells with a light gray fill color.
- Avoid color combinations that are difficult to read.
- Print the workbook on both color and black-and-white printers to ensure that the printed copy is readable in both versions.
- Understand your printer's limitations and features. Colors that look good on your monitor might not look as good when printed.
- Be sensitive to your audience. About 8 percent of all men and 0.5 percent of all women have some type of color blindness and might not be able to see the text when certain color combinations are used. Red-green color blindness is the most common, so avoid using red text on a green background or green text on a red background.

---

## Changing a Fill Color

**TIP**

You can also change a sheet tab's color. Right-click a sheet tab, point to Tab Color on the shortcut menu, and then click a color.

By default, worksheet cells do not include any background color. But background colors, also known as fill colors, can be helpful for distinguishing different parts of a worksheet or adding visual interest. You add fill colors to selected cells in the worksheet from the Fill Color gallery, which has the same options as the Font Color gallery.

Sanjit wants the labels and text in the Documentation sheet to stand out. You will format the labels in a white font on a red background, and then you'll format the author's name, current date, and purpose of the worksheet in a red font on a white background.

### To change the fill and font colors in the Documentation worksheet:

1. Select the range **A4:A6**.

2. On the HOME tab, in the Font group, click the **Fill Color button arrow** [icon], and then click the **Red** color (the second color) in the Standard Colors section.

3. In the Font group, click the **Font Color button arrow** [icon], and then click the **White, Background 1** color in the Theme Colors section. The labels are formatted in white text on a red background.

4. Select the range **B4:B6**, and then format the cells with a red font and a white background.

5. Increase the width of column B to **30** characters, and then wrap the text in the selected range.

**6.** Select the range **A4:B6**, and then add all borders around each of the selected cells.

**7.** Click cell **A7** to deselect the range. See Figure 2-6.

Figure 2-6 **Font and fill colors in the Documentation sheet**

width of column B is 30 characters

labels are white text on a red background

red text on a white background

text wrapped in the cell

## Adding a Background Image

A background image can provide a textured appearance, like that of granite, wood, or fibered paper, to a worksheet. The image is repeated until it fills the entire sheet. The background image does not affect any cell's format or content. Fill colors added to cells appear on top of the image, covering that portion of the image. Background images are visible only on the screen; they do not print.

Sanjit has provided an image that he wants you to use as the background of the Documentation sheet.

### To add a background image to the Documentation sheet:

**1.** On the ribbon, click the **PAGE LAYOUT** tab to display the page layout options.

**2.** In the Page Setup group, click the **Background** button. The Insert Pictures dialog box opens with options to select a picture from a file, select Office.com Clip Art, or perform a Bing Image Search.

**3.** Click the **Browse** button next to the From a file label. The Sheet Background dialog box opens.

**4.** Navigate to the **Excel2 ▸ Tutorial** folder included with your Data Files, click the **Background** JPEG image file, and then click the **Insert** button. The image is added to the background of the Documentation sheet, and the Background button changes to the Delete Background button, which you can use to remove the background image. See Figure 2-7.

Figure 2-7    **Background image in the Documentation sheet**

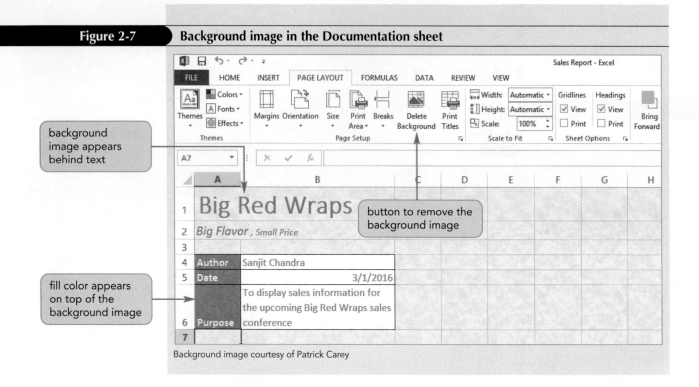

**background image appears behind text**

**button to remove the background image**

**fill color appears on top of the background image**

Background image courtesy of Patrick Carey

# Using Functions and Formulas to Calculate Sales Data

In the Sales Report worksheet, you will format the gross sales from each of the store's 20 restaurants and the summary statistics for those stores. The Sales Report worksheet is divided into two areas. The table at the bottom of the worksheet displays gross sales for the past year for each month by restaurant. The section at the top of the worksheet summarizes the sales data for the past two years. Sanjit collected the following sales data:

- **Gross Sales**—the total amount of sales at all of the restaurants
- **Cost of Sales**—the cost of producing the store's menu items
- **Operating Expenses**—the cost of running the stores including the employment and insurance costs
- **Net Profit/Loss**—the difference between the income from the gross sales and the total cost of sales and operating expenses
- **Units Sold**—the total number of menu items sold by the company during the year
- **Customers Served**—the total number of customers served by the company during the year

Sanjit wants you to calculate these sales statistics for the entire company and per store so he can track how well the stores are performing. First, you will calculate the total gross sales for Big Red Wraps and the company's overall net profit and loss.

**To calculate the company's sales and profit/loss:**

▶ **1.** Click the **Sales Report** sheet tab to make the Sales Report worksheet active.

**2.** Click cell **C6**, type the formula **=SUM(C27:N46)** to calculate the total gross sales from all stores in the previous year, and then press the **Enter** key. Cell C6 displays 9514000, which means that Big Red Wraps' total gross sales for the previous year were more than $9.5 million.

**TIP**

To enter content in a cell, you select the cell, type the specified content, and then press the Enter key.

**3.** In cell **C9**, enter the formula **=C6–(C7+C8)** to calculate the current year's net profit/loss, which is equal to the difference between the gross sales and the sum of the cost of sales and operating expenses. Cell C9 displays 1108000, which means that the company's net profit for 2015 was more than $1.1 million.

**4.** Copy the formula in cell **C9**, and then paste it into cell **D9** to calculate the net profit/loss for 2014. Cell D9 displays 1264000, which means that the company's net profit for that year was more than $1.26 million.

Next, Sanjit asks you to summarize the sales statistics for each store. Sanjit wants the same per-store statistics calculated for the 2015 and 2014 sales data. Per-store sales statistics are calculated by dividing the overall statistics by the number of stores. In this case, you will divide the overall statistics by the value in cell C23, which contains the total number of stores in the Big Red Wraps chain. After you enter the 2015 formulas, you can copy and paste them to calculate the 2014 results.

**To calculate the per-store statistics:**

**1.** In cell **C16**, enter the formula **=C6/C23** to calculate the gross sales per store in 2015. The formula returns 475700, which means that the annual gross sales amount for a Big Red Wraps store in 2015 was more than $475,000.

**2.** In cell **C17**, enter the formula **=C7/C23** to calculate the cost of sales per store in 2015. The formula returns the value 168700, which means that the cost of sales for a Big Red Wraps store in 2015 was typically $168,700.

**3.** In cell **C18**, enter the formula **=C8/C23** to calculate the operating expenses per store in 2015. The formula returns the value 251600, which means that operating expenses of a typical store in 2015 were $251,600.

**4.** In cell **C19**, enter the formula **=C9/C23** to calculate the net profit/loss per store in 2015. The formula returns the value 55400, indicating that the net profit/loss of a typical store in 2015 was $55,400.

**5.** In cell **C21**, enter the formula **=C11/C23** to calculate the units sold per store in 2015. The formula returns the value 67200, indicating that a typical store sold 67,200 units during 2015.

**6.** In cell **C22**, enter the formula **=C12/C23** to calculate the customers served per store in 2015. The formula returns the value 7770, indicating that a typical store served 7,770 customers during that year.

**7.** Copy the formulas in the range **C16:C22** and paste them into the range **D16:D22**. The cell references in the formulas change to calculate the sales data for the year 2014.

**8.** Select cell **B24** to deselect the range. See Figure 2-8.

| Figure 2-8 | Sales statistics for the entire company and per store |
|---|---|

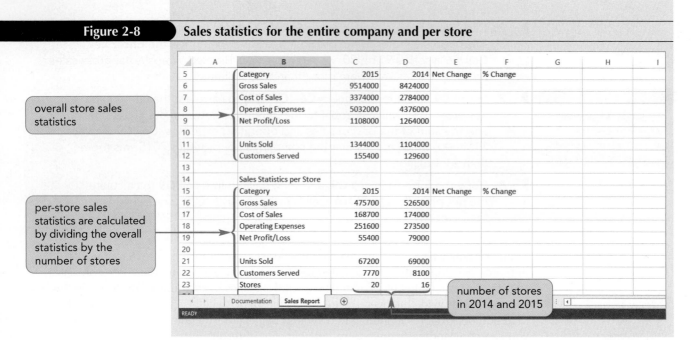

overall store sales statistics

per-store sales statistics are calculated by dividing the overall statistics by the number of stores

number of stores in 2014 and 2015

| | A | B | C | D | E | F | G | H | I |
|---|---|---|---|---|---|---|---|---|---|
| 5 | | Category | 2015 | 2014 | Net Change | % Change | | | |
| 6 | | Gross Sales | 9514000 | 8424000 | | | | | |
| 7 | | Cost of Sales | 3374000 | 2784000 | | | | | |
| 8 | | Operating Expenses | 5032000 | 4376000 | | | | | |
| 9 | | Net Profit/Loss | 1108000 | 1264000 | | | | | |
| 10 | | | | | | | | | |
| 11 | | Units Sold | 1344000 | 1104000 | | | | | |
| 12 | | Customers Served | 155400 | 129600 | | | | | |
| 13 | | | | | | | | | |
| 14 | | Sales Statistics per Store | | | | | | | |
| 15 | | Category | 2015 | 2014 | Net Change | % Change | | | |
| 16 | | Gross Sales | 475700 | 526500 | | | | | |
| 17 | | Cost of Sales | 168700 | 174000 | | | | | |
| 18 | | Operating Expenses | 251600 | 273500 | | | | | |
| 19 | | Net Profit/Loss | 55400 | 79000 | | | | | |
| 20 | | | | | | | | | |
| 21 | | Units Sold | 67200 | 69000 | | | | | |
| 22 | | Customers Served | 7770 | 8100 | | | | | |
| 23 | | Stores | 20 | 16 | | | | | |

Documentation    Sales Report

READY

Sanjit also wants to explore how the company's sales and expenses have changed from 2014 to 2015. To do this, you will calculate the net change in sales from 2014 to 2015 as well as the percent change. The percent change is calculated using the following formula:

$$percent\ change = \frac{2015\ value - 2014\ value}{2014\ value}$$

You will calculate the net and percent changes for all of the sales statistics.

### To calculate the net and percent changes for 2015 and 2014:

1. In cell **E6**, enter the formula **=C6–D6** to calculate the difference between the 2015 and 2014 gross sales. The formula returns 1090000, indicating that gross sales increased by $1.09 million between 2014 and 2015.

Be sure to include the parentheses as shown to calculate the percent change correctly.

2. In cell **F6**, enter the formula **=(C6–D6)/D6** to calculate the percent change in gross sales from 2014 to 2015. The formula returns 0.129392213, indicating a nearly 13% increase in gross sales from 2014 to 2015.

   Next, you'll copy and paste the formulas in cells E6 and F6 to the rest of the sales data to calculate the net change and percent change from 2014 to 2015.

3. Select the range **E6:F6**, and then copy the selected range. The two formulas are copied to the Clipboard.

4. Select the nonadjacent range **E7:F9;E11:F12;E16:F19;E21:F23**, and then paste the formulas from the Clipboard into the selected range. The net and percent changes are calculated for the remaining sales data.

5. Click cell **B24** to deselect the range, and then scroll the worksheet up to display row 5. See Figure 2-9.

**Figure 2-9**    Net and percent changes calculated

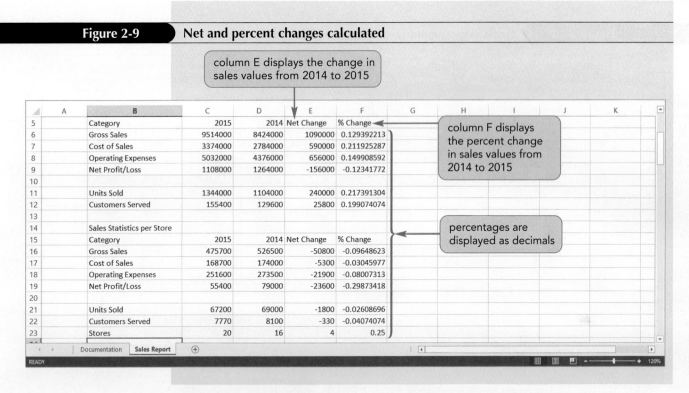

column E displays the change in sales values from 2014 to 2015

column F displays the percent change in sales values from 2014 to 2015

percentages are displayed as decimals

The bottom part of the worksheet contains the sales for each restaurant from 2015. You will use the SUM function to calculate the total gross sales for each restaurant during the entire year, the total monthly sales of all 20 restaurants, and the total gross sales of all restaurants and months.

**To calculate different subtotals of the gross sales:**

1. Select cell **O26**, type **TOTAL** as the label, and then press the **Enter** key. Cell O27 is now the active cell.

2. On the HOME tab, in the Editing group, click the **AutoSum** button, and then press the **Enter** key to accept the suggested range reference and enter the formula =SUM(C27:N27) in cell O27. The cell displays 355000, indicating gross sales in 2015 for the 411 Elm Drive restaurant were $355,000.

3. Copy the formula in cell **O27**, and then paste that formula into the range **O28:O46** to calculate the total sales for each of the remaining 19 restaurants in the Big Red Wraps chain.

4. Select cell **B47**, type **TOTAL** as the label, and then press the **Tab** key. Cell C47 is now the active cell.

5. Select the range **C47:O47** so that you can calculate the total monthly sales for all of the stores.

6. On the HOME tab, in the Editing group, click the **AutoSum** button, and then press the **Enter** key to calculate the total sales for each month as well as the total sales for all months. For example, cell C47 displays 680000, indicating that monthly sales for January 2015 for all stores were $680,000.

7. Select cell **O48** to deselect the range. See Figure 2-10.

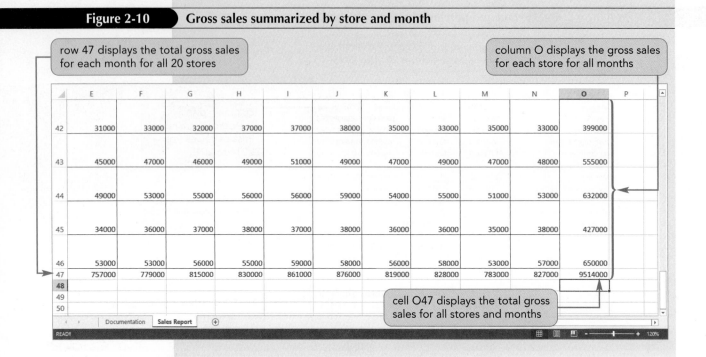

**Figure 2-10**    **Gross sales summarized by store and month**

row 47 displays the total gross sales for each month for all 20 stores

column O displays the gross sales for each store for all months

| | E | F | G | H | I | J | K | L | M | N | O | P |
|---|---|---|---|---|---|---|---|---|---|---|---|---|
| 42 | 31000 | 33000 | 32000 | 37000 | 37000 | 38000 | 35000 | 33000 | 35000 | 33000 | 399000 | |
| 43 | 45000 | 47000 | 46000 | 49000 | 51000 | 49000 | 47000 | 49000 | 47000 | 48000 | 555000 | |
| 44 | 49000 | 53000 | 55000 | 56000 | 56000 | 59000 | 54000 | 55000 | 51000 | 53000 | 632000 | |
| 45 | 34000 | 36000 | 37000 | 38000 | 37000 | 38000 | 36000 | 36000 | 35000 | 38000 | 427000 | |
| 46 | 53000 | 53000 | 56000 | 55000 | 59000 | 58000 | 56000 | 58000 | 53000 | 57000 | 650000 | |
| 47 | 757000 | 779000 | 815000 | 830000 | 861000 | 876000 | 819000 | 828000 | 783000 | 827000 | 9514000 | |
| 48 | | | | | | | | | | | | |
| 49 | | | | | | | | | | | | |
| 50 | | | | | | | | | | | | |

cell O47 displays the total gross sales for all stores and months

Documentation    **Sales Report**    ⊕

READY    120%

# Formatting Numbers

The goal in formatting any workbook is to make the content easier to interpret. For numbers, this can mean adding a comma to separate thousands, setting the number of decimal places, and using percentage and currency symbols to make numbers easier to read and understand. Sanjit asks you to format the numbers in the Sales Report worksheet to improve their readability.

## Applying Number Formats

You can use a number format to display values in a way that makes them easier to read and understand. Changing the number format of the displayed value does not affect the stored value. Numbers are originally formatted in the **General format**, which, for the most part, displays numbers exactly as they are typed. If the number is calculated from a formula or function, the cell displays as many digits after the decimal point as will fit in the cell with the last digit rounded. Calculated values too large to fit into the cell are displayed in scientific notation.

The General format is fine for small numbers, but some values require additional formatting to make the numbers easier to interpret. For example, you might want to:

- Change the number of digits displayed to the right of the decimal point
- Add commas to separate thousands in large numbers
- Apply currency symbols to numbers to identify the monetary unit being used
- Display percentages using the % symbol

**TIP**

To apply the Currency format, click the Number Format button arrow and click Currency, or press the Ctrl+Shift+$ keys.

Excel supports two monetary formats: currency and accounting. Both formats add a thousands separator to the currency values and display two digits to the right of the decimal point. However, the **Currency format** places a currency symbol directly to the left of the first digit of the currency value and displays negative numbers with a negative sign. The **Accounting format** fixes a currency symbol at the left edge of the column, and displays negative numbers within parentheses and zero values with a dash. It also slightly indents the values from the right edge of the cell to allow room for parentheses around negative values. Figure 2-11 compares the two formats.

| Figure 2-11 | Currency and Accounting number formats |
| --- | --- |

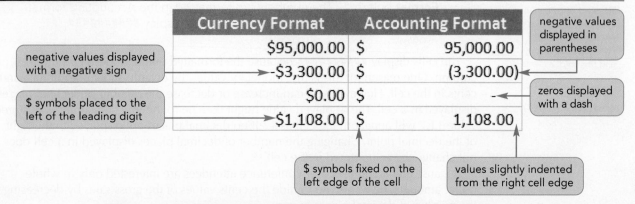

negative values displayed with a negative sign

$ symbols placed to the left of the leading digit

negative values displayed in parentheses

zeros displayed with a dash

$ symbols fixed on the left edge of the cell

values slightly indented from the right cell edge

**PROSKILLS**

### Written Communication: Formatting Monetary Values

Spreadsheets commonly include monetary values. To make these values simpler to read and comprehend, keep in mind the following guidelines when formatting the currency data in a worksheet:

- **Format for your audience.** For general financial reports, round values to the nearest hundred, thousand, or million. Investors are generally more interested in the big picture than in exact values. However, for accounting reports, accuracy is important and often legally required. So, for those reports, be sure to display the exact monetary value.
- **Use thousands separators.** Large strings of numbers can be challenging to read. For monetary values, use a thousands separator to make the amounts easier to comprehend.
- **Apply the Accounting format to columns of monetary values.** The Accounting format makes columns of numbers easier to read than the Currency format. Use the Currency format for individual cells that are not part of long columns of numbers.
- **Use only two currency symbols in a column of monetary values.** Standard accounting format displays one currency symbol with the first monetary value in the column, and optionally displays a second currency symbol with the last value in that column. Use the Accounting format to fix the currency symbols, lining them up within the column.

Following these standard accounting principles will make your financial data easier to read both on the screen and in printouts.

Sanjit wants you to format the gross sales amounts in the Accounting format so that they are easier to read.

## To format the gross sales in the Accounting format:

1. Select the range **C6:E6** with the gross sales.

2. On the HOME tab, in the Number group, click the **Accounting Number Format** button $. The numbers are formatted in the Accounting format. You cannot see the format because the cells display ##########.

**TIP**

To select other currency symbols, click the Accounting Number Format button arrow, and then click a currency symbol.

The cells display ########## because the formatted number doesn't fit into the column. One reason for this is that monetary values, by default, show both dollars and cents in the cell. However, you can increase or decrease the number of decimal places displayed in a cell. The displayed value might then be rounded. For example, the stored value 11.7 will appear in the cell as 12 if no decimal places are displayed to the right of the decimal point. Changing the number of decimal places displayed in a cell does not change the value stored in the cell.

Because Sanjit and the other conference attendees are interested only in whole dollar amounts, he wants you to hide the cents values of the gross sales by decreasing the number of decimal places to zero.

## To decrease the number of decimal places displayed in the gross sales:

1. Make sure the range **C6:E6** is selected.

2. On the HOME tab, in the Number group, click the **Decrease Decimal** button twice. The cents are hidden for gross sales.

3. Select cell **C4** to deselect the range. See Figure 2-12.

**Figure 2-12**    **Formatted gross sales values**

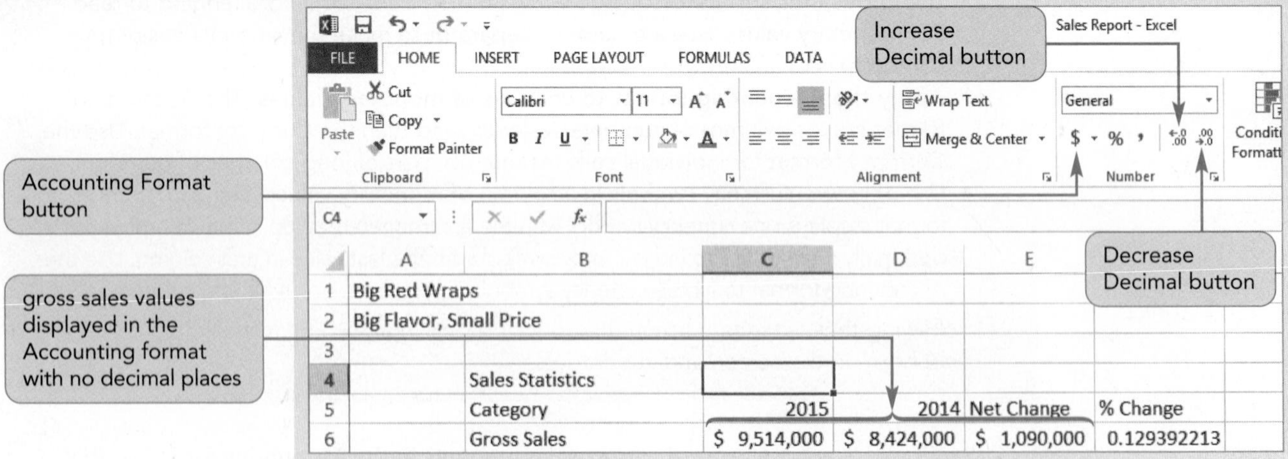

The Comma style is identical to the Accounting format except that it does not fix a currency symbol to the left of the number. The advantage of using the Comma style and the Accounting format together is that the numbers will be aligned in the column.

Sanjit asks you to apply the Comma style to the remaining sales statistics.

## To apply the Comma style to the sales statistics:

1. Select the nonadjacent range **C7:E9;C11:E12** containing the sales figures for all stores in 2014 and 2015.

2. On the HOME tab, in the Number group, click the **Comma Style** button ⁹. In some instances, the number is now too large to be displayed in the cell.

3. In the Number group, click the **Decrease Decimal** button ⁰⁰→.0 twice to remove two decimal places. Digits to the right of the decimal point are hidden for all of the selected cells.

4. Select cell **C13** to deselect the range. See Figure 2-13.

| Figure 2-13 | Formatted sales values |
| --- | --- |

numbers with the Accounting format and no decimal places

numbers with the Comma style and no decimal places

| 4 | Sales Statistics | | | | |
| --- | --- | --- | --- | --- | --- |
| 5 | Category | 2015 | 2014 | Net Change | % Change |
| 6 | Gross Sales | $ 9,514,000 | $ 8,424,000 | $ 1,090,000 | 0.129392213 |
| 7 | Cost of Sales | 3,374,000 | 2,784,000 | 590,000 | 0.211925287 |
| 8 | Operating Expenses | 5,032,000 | 4,376,000 | 656,000 | 0.149908592 |
| 9 | Net Profit/Loss | 1,108,000 | 1,264,000 | (156,000) | -0.12341772 |
| 10 | | | | | |
| 11 | Units Sold | 1,344,000 | 1,104,000 | 240,000 | 0.217391304 |
| 12 | Customers Served | 155,400 | 129,600 | 25,800 | 0.199074074 |
| 13 | | | | | |
| 14 | Sales Statistics per Store | | | | |
| 15 | Category | 2015 | 2014 | Net Change | % Change |
| 16 | Gross Sales | 475700 | 526500 | -50800 | -0.09648623 |
| 17 | Cost of Sales | 168700 | 174000 | -5300 | -0.03045977 |
| 18 | Operating Expenses | 251600 | 273500 | -21900 | -0.08007313 |
| 19 | Net Profit/Loss | 55400 | 79000 | -23600 | -0.29873418 |

numbers aligned within each column

| ◄ ► | Documentation | **Sales Report** | ⊕ | |

READY

The Percent style formats numbers as percentages. When you format values as percentages, the % symbol appears after the number and no digits appear to the right of the decimal point. You can always change how many decimal places are displayed in the cell if that is important to show with your data.

Sanjit wants you to format the percent change from the 2014 to 2015 sales statistics with a percent symbol to make the percent values easier to read.

## To format percentages:

1. Select the nonadjacent range **F6:F9;F11:F12** containing the percent change values.

2. On the HOME tab, in the Number group, click the **Percent Style** button % (or press the **Ctrl+Shift+%** keys). The values are displayed as percentages.

3. In the Number group, click the **Increase Decimal** button ←.0⁰.0 twice. The displayed number includes two decimal places.

4. Select cell **F13** to deselect the range. See Figure 2-14.

**Figure 2-14**     **Formatted percent changes**

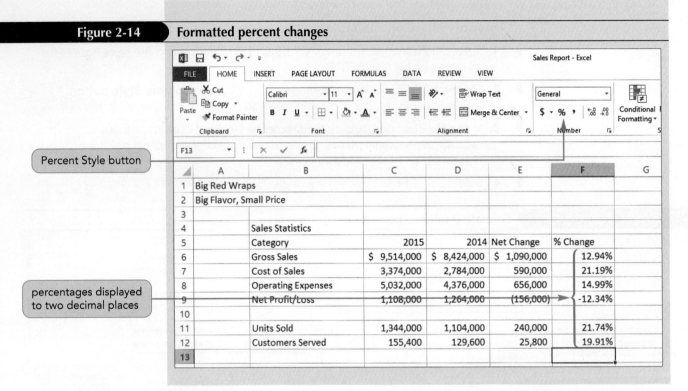

*Percent Style button*

*percentages displayed to two decimal places*

|    | A | B | C | D | E | F | G |
|----|---|---|---|---|---|---|---|
| 1  | Big Red Wraps | | | | | | |
| 2  | Big Flavor, Small Price | | | | | | |
| 3  | | | | | | | |
| 4  | | Sales Statistics | | | | | |
| 5  | | Category | 2015 | 2014 | Net Change | % Change | |
| 6  | | Gross Sales | $ 9,514,000 | $ 8,424,000 | $ 1,090,000 | 12.94% | |
| 7  | | Cost of Sales | 3,374,000 | 2,784,000 | 590,000 | 21.19% | |
| 8  | | Operating Expenses | 5,032,000 | 4,376,000 | 656,000 | 14.99% | |
| 9  | | Net Profit/Loss | 1,108,000 | 1,264,000 | (156,000) | -12.34% | |
| 10 | | | | | | | |
| 11 | | Units Sold | 1,344,000 | 1,104,000 | 240,000 | 21.74% | |
| 12 | | Customers Served | 155,400 | 129,600 | 25,800 | 19.91% | |
| 13 | | | | | | | |

With the data reformatted, the worksheet clearly shows that Big Red Wraps' gross sales increased from 2014 to 2015 by almost 13 percent. However, both the cost of sales and the operating expenses increased by about 21.2 percent and 15 percent, respectively, probably due to the cost of building four new stores. As a result, the company's net profit decreased by $156,000 or about 12.3 percent.

## Formatting Dates and Times

**TIP**

To view the underlying date and time value, apply the General format to the cell or display the formulas instead of the formula results.

Because Excel stores dates and times as numbers and not as text, you can apply different formats without affecting the date and time value. The abbreviated format, *mm/dd/yyyy*, entered in the Documentation sheet is referred to as the **Short Date format**. You can also apply a **Long Date format** that displays the day of the week and the full month name in addition to the day of the month and the year. Other built-in formats include formats for displaying time values in 12- or 24-hour time format.

You will change the date in the Documentation sheet to the Long Date format.

**To format the date in the Long Date format:**

1. Go to the **Documentation** sheet, and then select cell **B5**.

2. On the ribbon, make sure the HOME tab is displayed.

3. In the Number group, click the **Number Format button arrow** to display a list of number formats, and then click **Long Date**. The date is displayed with the weekday name, month name, day, and year. Notice that the date in the formula bar did not change because you changed only the display format, not the date value.

# Formatting Worksheet Cells

You can format the appearance of individual cells by modifying the alignment of text within the cell, indenting cell text, or adding borders of different styles and colors.

## Aligning Cell Content

By default, text is aligned with the left and bottom borders of a cell, and numbers are aligned with the right and bottom borders. You might want to change the alignment to make the text and numbers more readable or visually appealing. In general, you should center column titles, left-align other text, and right-align numbers to keep their decimal places lined up within a column. Figure 2-15 describes the buttons you use to set these alignment options, which are located in the Alignment group on the HOME tab.

| Figure 2-15 | Alignment buttons |
|---|---|

| Button | Name | Description |
|---|---|---|
| | Top Align | Aligns the cell content with the cell's top edge |
| | Middle Align | Vertically centers the cell content within the cell |
| | Bottom Align | Aligns the cell content with the cell's bottom edge |
| | Align Left | Aligns the cell content with the cell's left edge |
| | Center | Horizontally centers the cell content within the cell |
| | Align Right | Aligns the cell content with the cell's right edge |
| | Decrease Indent | Decreases the size of the indentation used in the cell |
| | Increase Indent | Increases the size of the indentation used in the cell |
| | Orientation | Rotates the cell content to any angle within the cell |
| | Wrap Text | Forces the cell text to wrap within the cell borders |
| | Merge & Center | Merges the selected cells into a single cell |

© 2014 Cengage Learning

The date in the Documentation sheet is right-aligned in the cell because Excel treats dates and times as numbers. Sanjit wants you to left-align the date and center the column titles in the Sales Report worksheet.

### To left-align the date and center the column titles:

1. In the Documentation sheet, make sure cell **B5** is still selected.
2. On the HOME tab, in the Alignment group, click the **Align Left** button ⧉. The date shifts to the left edge of the cell.
3. Make the **Sales Report** worksheet the active worksheet.
4. Select the range **C5:F5**. The column titles are selected.
5. In the Alignment group, click the **Center** button ⧉. The column titles are centered in the cells.

## Indenting Cell Content

Sometimes you want a cell's content moved a few spaces from the cell's left edge. This is particularly useful to create subsections in a worksheet or to set off some entries from others. You can increase the indent to shift the contents of a cell away from the left edge of the cell, or you can decrease the indent to shift a cell's contents closer to the left edge of the cell.

Sanjit wants the Cost of Sales and Operating Expenses labels in the sales statistics table offset from the other labels because they represent expenses to the company. You will increase the indent for the expense categories.

**To indent the expense categories:**

1. Select the range **B7:B8** containing the expense categories.

2. On the HOME tab, in the Alignment group, click the **Increase Indent** button twice to indent each label two spaces in its cell.

## Adding Cell Borders

Common accounting practices provide guidelines on when to add borders to cells. In general, a single black border appears above a subtotal, a single bottom border is added below a calculated number, and a double black bottom border appears below the total.

Sanjit wants you to follow these common accounting practices in the Sales Report worksheet. You will add borders below the column titles and below the gross sales values. You will add a top border to the net profit/loss values. Finally, you will add a top and bottom border to the Units Sold and Customers Served rows.

**To add borders to the sales statistics data:**

1. Select the range **B5:F5** containing the table headings.

2. On the HOME tab, in the Font group, click the **All Borders button arrow**, and then click **Bottom Border**. A border is added below the column titles.

3. Select the range **B6:F6** containing the gross sales amounts.

4. In the Font group, click the **Bottom Border** button to add a border below the selected gross sales amounts.

5. Select the range **B9:F9**, click the **Bottom Border button arrow**, and then click **Top Border** to add a border above the net profit/loss amounts.

   The Units Sold and Customers Served rows do not contain monetary values as the other rows do. You will distinguish these rows by adding a top and bottom border.

6. Select the range **B11:F12**, click the **Top Border button arrow**, and then click **Top and Bottom** to add a border above the number of units sold and below the number of customers served.

7. Select cell **B3** to deselect the range. See Figure 2-16.

**Figure 2-16**          **Worksheet with formatted cells**

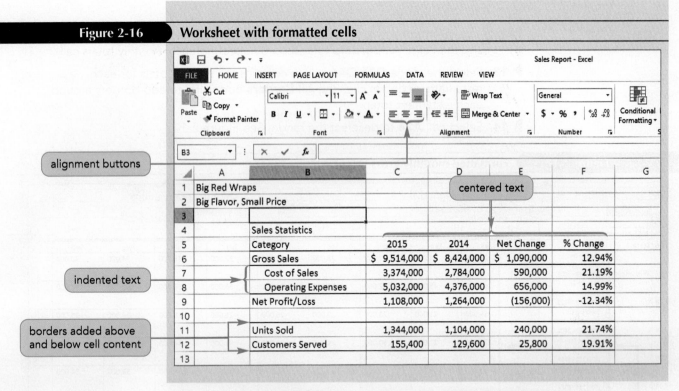

You can apply multiple formats to the same cell to create the look that best fits the data. For example, one cell might be formatted with a number format, alignments, borders, indents, fonts, font sizes, and so on. The monthly sales data needs to be formatted with number styles, alignment, indents, and borders. You'll add these formats now.

## To format the monthly sales table:

1. Click the **Name** box to select the cell reference, type **C27:O47**, and then press the **Enter** key to quickly select the range C27:O47 containing the monthly gross sales for each restaurant.

2. On the HOME tab, in the Number group, click the **Comma Style** button 💬 to add a thousands separator to the values.

3. In the Number group, click the **Decrease Decimal** button to hide the cents from the sales results.

4. In the Alignment group, click the **Top Align** button ≡ to align the sales numbers with the top of each cell.

5. Select the range **C26:O26** containing the labels for the month abbreviations and the TOTAL column.

6. In the Alignment group, click the **Center** button ≡ to center the column labels.

7. Select the range **B27:B46** containing the store addresses.

8. Reduce the font size of the store addresses to **9** points.

9. In the Alignment group, click the **Increase Indent** button to indent the store addresses.

10. In the Alignment group, click the **Top Align** button ≡ to align the addresses at the top of each cell.

11. Select the range **B47:O47** containing the monthly totals.

12. In the Font group, click the **Top and Bottom Borders button arrow** ⊞ ▾, and then click **All Borders** to add borders around each monthly totals cell.

13. Select the range **O26:O46**, which contains the annual totals for each restaurant, and then click the **All Borders** button ⊞ to add borders around each restaurant total.

14. Select cell **A24** to deselect the range. See Figure 2-17.

| Figure 2-17 | Formatted monthly gross sales figures |

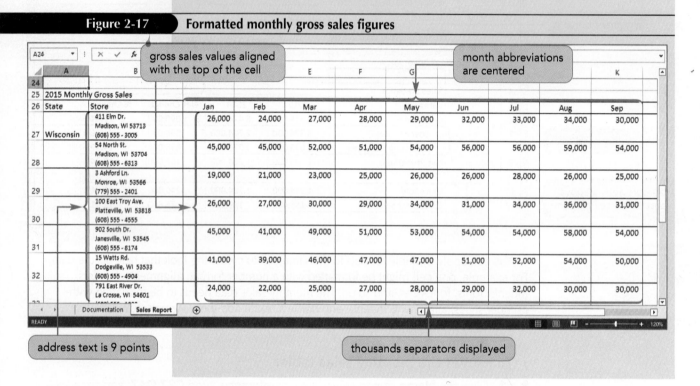

The following annotations appear on the figure: "gross sales values aligned with the top of the cell", "month abbreviations are centered", "address text is 9 points", "thousands separators displayed".

| | State | Store | | Jan | Feb | Mar | Apr | May | Jun | Jul | Aug | Sep |
|---|---|---|---|---|---|---|---|---|---|---|---|---|
| 25 | 2015 Monthly Gross Sales | | | | | | | | | | | |
| 26 | State | Store | | Jan | Feb | Mar | Apr | May | Jun | Jul | Aug | Sep |
| 27 | Wisconsin | 411 Elm Dr. Madison, WI 53713 (608) 555 - 3005 | | 26,000 | 24,000 | 27,000 | 28,000 | 29,000 | 32,000 | 33,000 | 34,000 | 30,000 |
| 28 | | 54 North St. Madison, WI 53704 (608) 555 - 6813 | | 45,000 | 45,000 | 52,000 | 51,000 | 54,000 | 56,000 | 56,000 | 59,000 | 54,000 |
| 29 | | 3 Ashford Ln. Monroe, WI 53566 (779) 555 - 2401 | | 19,000 | 21,000 | 23,000 | 25,000 | 26,000 | 26,000 | 28,000 | 26,000 | 25,000 |
| 30 | | 100 East Troy Ave. Platteville, WI 53818 (608) 555 - 4555 | | 26,000 | 27,000 | 30,000 | 29,000 | 34,000 | 31,000 | 34,000 | 36,000 | 31,000 |
| 31 | | 902 South Dr. Janesville, WI 53545 (608) 555 - 8174 | | 45,000 | 41,000 | 49,000 | 51,000 | 53,000 | 54,000 | 54,000 | 58,000 | 54,000 |
| 32 | | 15 Watts Rd. Dodgeville, WI 53533 (608) 555 - 4904 | | 41,000 | 39,000 | 46,000 | 47,000 | 47,000 | 51,000 | 52,000 | 54,000 | 50,000 |
| | | 791 East River Dr. La Crosse, WI 54601 | | 24,000 | 22,000 | 25,000 | 27,000 | 28,000 | 29,000 | 32,000 | 30,000 | 30,000 |

Documentation    **Sales Report**

## Merging Cells

You can merge, or combine, several cells into one cell. A merged cell contains two or more cells with a single cell reference. When you merge cells, only the content from the upper-left cell in the range is retained. The cell reference for the merged cell is the upper-left cell reference. So, if you merge cells A1 and A2, the merged cell reference is cell A1. After you merge cells, you can align the content within the merged cell. The Merge & Center button in the Alignment group on the HOME tab includes the following options:

- **Merge & Center**—merges the range into one cell and horizontally centers the content
- **Merge Across**—merges each row in the selected range across the columns in the range
- **Merge Cells**—merges the range into a single cell, but does not horizontally center the cell content
- **Unmerge Cells**—reverses a merge, returning the merged cell to a range of individual cells

The first column of the monthly sales data lists the states in which Big Red Wraps has stores. You will merge the cells for each state name.

### To merge the state name cells:

1. Select the range **A27:A33** containing the cells for the Wisconsin stores. You will merge these seven cells into a single cell.

2. On the HOME tab, in the Alignment group, click the **Merge & Center** button. The range A27:A33 merges into one cell with the cell reference A27, and the text is centered and bottom-aligned within the cell.

3. Select the range **A34:A36**, and then click the **Merge & Center** button in the Alignment group to merge and center the Minnesota cells.

4. Select the range **A37:A40**, and then click the **Merge & Center** button to merge and center the Iowa cells.

5. Select cell **A41**, and then center it horizontally to align the Colorado text with the text in the other state cells.

6. Merge and center the range **A42:A43** containing the Nebraska cells.

7. Merge and center the range **A44:A46** containing the Kansas cells. See Figure 2-18. The merged cells make it easier to distinguish restaurants in each state.

**Figure 2-18**    **Merged cells**

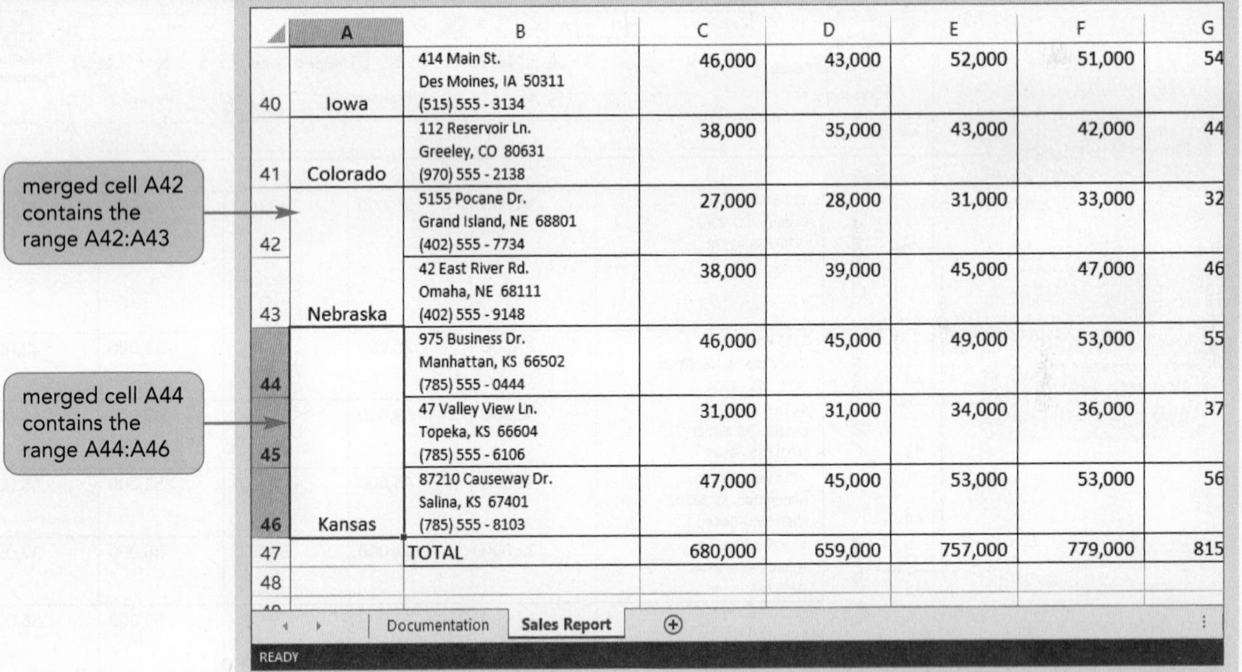

merged cell A42 contains the range A42:A43

merged cell A44 contains the range A44:A46

| | A | B | C | D | E | F | G |
|---|---|---|---|---|---|---|---|
| 40 | Iowa | 414 Main St. Des Moines, IA 50311 (515) 555-3134 | 46,000 | 43,000 | 52,000 | 51,000 | 54 |
| 41 | Colorado | 112 Reservoir Ln. Greeley, CO 80631 (970) 555-2138 | 38,000 | 35,000 | 43,000 | 42,000 | 44 |
| 42 | | 5155 Pocane Dr. Grand Island, NE 68801 (402) 555-7734 | 27,000 | 28,000 | 31,000 | 33,000 | 32 |
| 43 | Nebraska | 42 East River Rd. Omaha, NE 68111 (402) 555-9148 | 38,000 | 39,000 | 45,000 | 47,000 | 46 |
| 44 | | 975 Business Dr. Manhattan, KS 66502 (785) 555-0444 | 46,000 | 45,000 | 49,000 | 53,000 | 55 |
| 45 | | 47 Valley View Ln. Topeka, KS 66604 (785) 555-6106 | 31,000 | 31,000 | 34,000 | 36,000 | 37 |
| 46 | Kansas | 87210 Causeway Dr. Salina, KS 67401 (785) 555-8103 | 47,000 | 45,000 | 53,000 | 53,000 | 56 |
| 47 | | TOTAL | 680,000 | 659,000 | 757,000 | 779,000 | 815 |
| 48 | | | | | | | |

Documentation  **Sales Report**

READY

## Rotating Cell Contents

Text and numbers are displayed horizontally within cells. However, you can rotate cell text to any angle to save space or to provide visual interest to a worksheet. The state names at the bottom of the merged cells would look better and take up less room if they were rotated vertically within their cells. Sanjit asks you to rotate the state names.

**To rotate the state names:**

1. Select the merged cell **A27**.

2. On the HOME tab, in the Alignment group, click the **Orientation** button to display a list of rotation options, and then click **Rotate Text Up**. The state name rotates 90 degrees counterclockwise.

3. In the Alignment group, click the **Middle Align** button ≡ to vertically center the rotated text in the merged cell.

4. Select the merged cell range **A34:A44**, and then repeat Steps 2 and 3 to rotate and vertically center the rest of the state names in their cells.

5. Select cell **A41** to deselect the range, and then increase the height of row 41 (the Colorado row) to **75** points (**100** pixels) so that the entire state name appears in the cell.

6. Reduce the width of column A to **7** characters because the rotated state names take up less space.

7. Select cell **A47**. See Figure 2-19.

| Figure 2-19 | Rotated cell content |

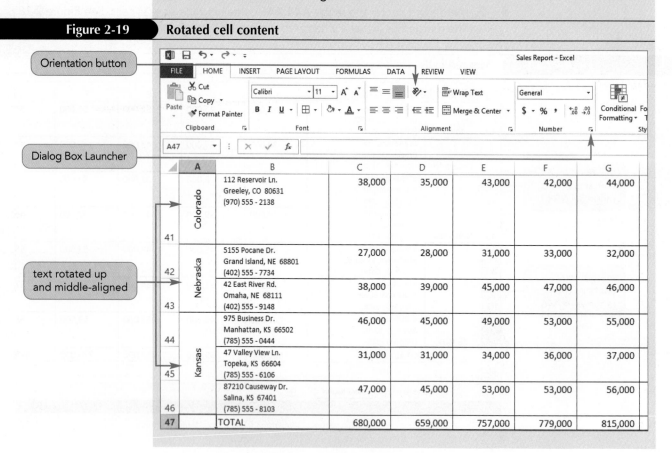

## Exploring the Format Cells Dialog Box

The buttons on the HOME tab provide quick access to the most commonly used formatting choices. For more options, you can use the Format Cells dialog box. You can apply the formats in this dialog box to the selected worksheet cells. The Format Cells dialog box has six tabs, each focusing on a different set of formatting options, as described below:

- **Number**—provides options for formatting the appearance of numbers, including dates and numbers treated as text such as telephone or Social Security numbers
- **Alignment**—provides options for how data is aligned within a cell
- **Font**—provides options for selecting font types, sizes, styles, and other formatting attributes such as underlining and font colors

- **Border**—provides options for adding and removing cell borders as well as selecting a line style and color
- **Fill**—provides options for creating and applying background colors and patterns to cells
- **Protection**—provides options for locking or hiding cells to prevent other users from modifying their contents

Although you have applied many of these formats from the HOME tab, the Format Cells dialog box presents them in a different way and provides more choices. You will use the Font and Fill tabs to format the column titles with a white font on a red background.

### To use the Format Cells dialog box to format the column labels:

**TIP**

You can also open the Format Cells dialog box by right-clicking the selected range, and then clicking Format Cells on the shortcut menu.

1. Select the range **A26:O26** containing the column labels for the table.

2. On the HOME tab, in the Number group, click the **Dialog Box Launcher** located to the right of the group name (refer to Figure 2-19). The Format Cells dialog box opens with the Number tab displayed.

3. Click the **Font** tab to display the font formatting options.

4. Click the **Color** box to display the color palette, and then click the **White, Background 1** theme color. The font is set to white. See Figure 2-20.

**Figure 2-20**    **Font tab in the Format Cells dialog box**

list of available fonts

list of font effects

box shows the selected font color

preview of the selected options

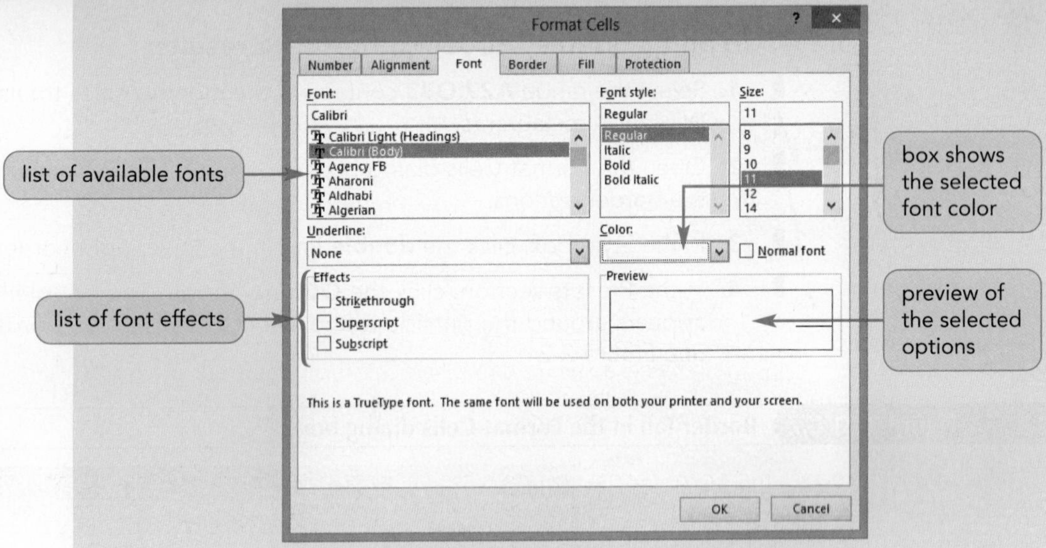

5. Click the **Fill** tab to display background options.

6. In the Background Color palette, click the **red** standard color (the second color in the last row). The background is set to red, as you can see in the Sample box.

7. Click the **OK** button. The dialog box closes, and the font and fill options you selected are applied to the column titles.

You will also use the Format Cells dialog box to change the appearance of the row titles. You'll format them to be displayed in a larger white font on a gray background.

## To format the row labels:

1. Select the range **A27:A46** containing the rotated state names.

2. Right-click the selected range, and then click **Format Cells** on the shortcut menu. The Format Cells dialog box opens with the last tab used displayed—in this case, the Fill tab.

3. In the Background Color palette, click the **gray** theme color (the first color in the seventh column). Its preview is shown in the Sample box.

4. Click the **Font** tab to display the font formatting options.

5. Click the **Color** box, and then click the **White, Background 1** theme color to set the font color to white.

6. Scroll down the **Size** box, and then click **16** to set the font size to 16 points.

7. Click the **OK** button. The dialog box closes, and the font and fill formats are applied to the state names.

The Border tab in the Format Cells dialog box provides options for changing the border style and color as well as placing the border anywhere around a cell or cells in a selected range. Sanjit wants you to format the borders in the monthly sales data so that the sales result from each state is surrounded by a double border.

## To add a double border to the state results:

1. Select the range **A27:O33** containing the monthly sales totals for the Wisconsin restaurants.

2. Open the Format Cells dialog box, and then click the **Border** tab to display the border options.

3. In the Style box, click the **double line** in the lower-right corner of the box.

4. In the Presets section, click the **Outline** option. The double border appears around the outside of the selected cells in the Border preview. See Figure 2-21.

---

**Figure 2-21**     **Border tab in the Format Cells dialog box**

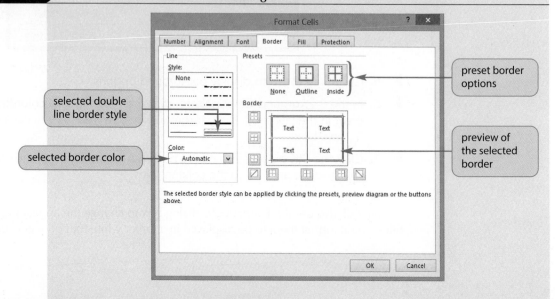

**5.** Click the **OK** button. The selected border is applied to the Wisconsin monthly sales.

**6.** Repeat Steps 2 through 5 to apply double borders to the ranges **A34:O36**, **A37:O40**, **A41:O41**, **A42:O43**, and **A44:O46**.

**7.** Select cell **A48** to deselect the range. See Figure 2-22.

**Figure 2-22**     **Worksheet with font, fill, and border formatting**

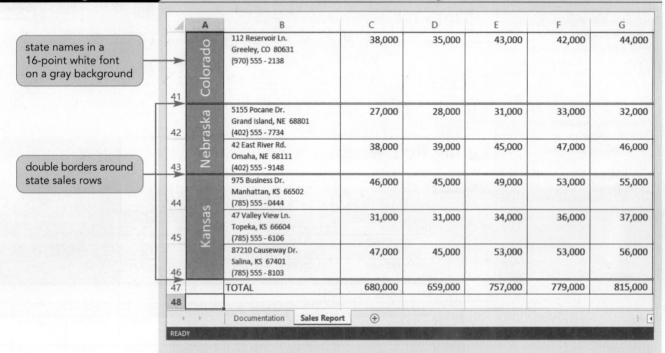

state names in a 16-point white font on a gray background

double borders around state sales rows

| | A | B | C | D | E | F | G |
|---|---|---|---|---|---|---|---|
| | Colorado | 112 Reservoir Ln.<br>Greeley, CO 80631<br>(970) 555 - 2138 | 38,000 | 35,000 | 43,000 | 42,000 | 44,000 |
| 41 | | | | | | | |
| 42 | Nebraska | 5155 Pocane Dr.<br>Grand Island, NE 68801<br>(402) 555 - 7734 | 27,000 | 28,000 | 31,000 | 33,000 | 32,000 |
| 43 | | 42 East River Rd.<br>Omaha, NE 68111<br>(402) 555 - 9148 | 38,000 | 39,000 | 45,000 | 47,000 | 46,000 |
| 44 | Kansas | 975 Business Dr.<br>Manhattan, KS 66502<br>(785) 555 - 0444 | 46,000 | 45,000 | 49,000 | 53,000 | 55,000 |
| 45 | | 47 Valley View Ln.<br>Topeka, KS 66604<br>(785) 555 - 6106 | 31,000 | 31,000 | 34,000 | 36,000 | 37,000 |
| 46 | | 87210 Causeway Dr.<br>Salina, KS 67401<br>(785) 555 - 8103 | 47,000 | 45,000 | 53,000 | 53,000 | 56,000 |
| 47 | | TOTAL | 680,000 | 659,000 | 757,000 | 779,000 | 815,000 |
| 48 | | | | | | | |

Documentation   **Sales Report**   ⊕

READY

**8.** Save the Sales Report worksheet.

You have completed much of the formatting that Sanjit wants in the Sales Report worksheet for the Big Red Wraps sales conference. In the next session, you will explore other formatting options.

## Session 2.1 Quick Check

REVIEW

**1.** What is the difference between a serif font and a sans serif font?

**2.** What is the difference between a theme color and a standard color?

**3.** A cell containing a number displays #######. Why does this occur and what can you do to fix it?

**4.** What is the General format?

**5.** Describe the differences between Currency format and Accounting format.

**6.** The range A1:C5 is merged into a single cell. What is its cell reference?

**7.** How do you format text so that it is set vertically within the cell?

**8.** Where can you access all the formatting options for worksheet cells?

# Session 2.2 Visual Overview:

The PAGE LAYOUT tab has options for setting how the worksheet will print.

The **Format Painter** copies and pastes formatting from one cell or range to another without duplicating any data.

**Print titles** are rows and columns that are included on every page of the printout. In this case, the text in rows 1 and 2 will print on every page.

A **manual page break** is one you set to indicate where a new page of the printout should start and is identified by a solid blue line.

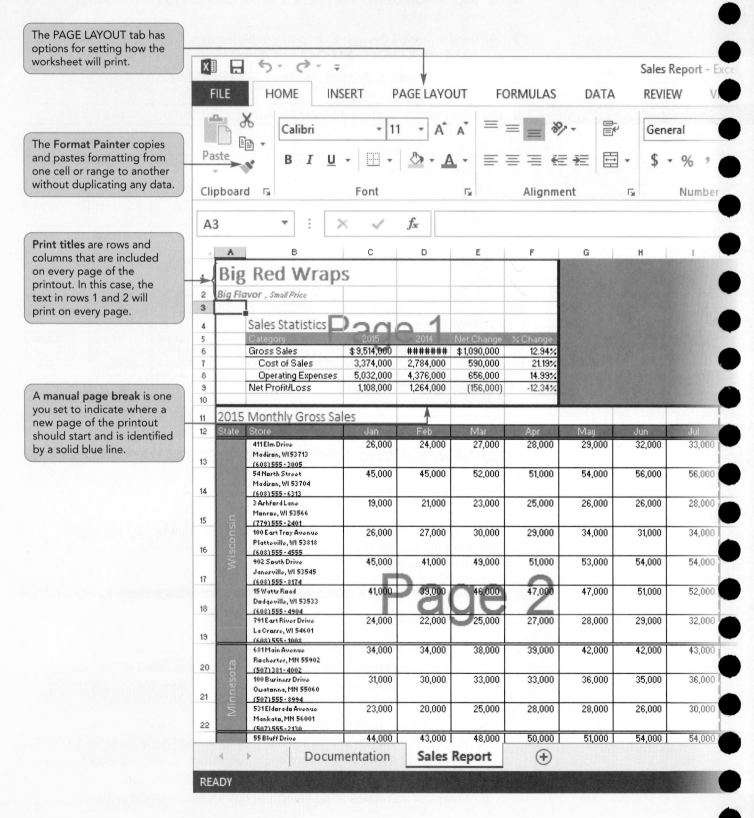

# Worksheet Formatted for Printing

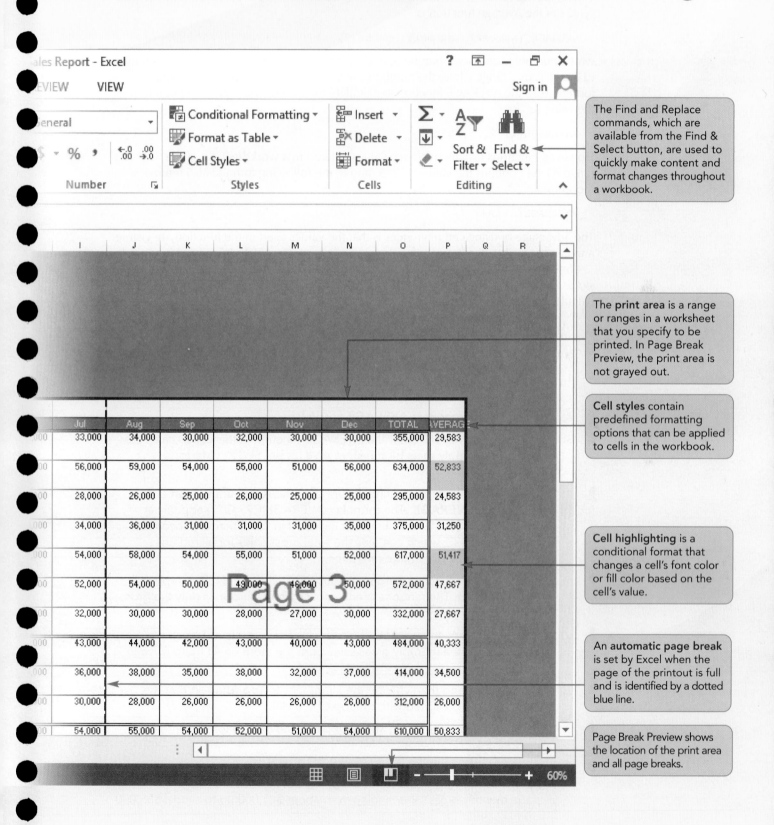

The **Find and Replace** commands, which are available from the Find & Select button, are used to quickly make content and format changes throughout a workbook.

The **print area** is a range or ranges in a worksheet that you specify to be printed. In Page Break Preview, the print area is not grayed out.

**Cell styles** contain predefined formatting options that can be applied to cells in the workbook.

**Cell highlighting** is a conditional format that changes a cell's font color or fill color based on the cell's value.

An **automatic page break** is set by Excel when the page of the printout is full and is identified by a dotted blue line.

Page Break Preview shows the location of the print area and all page breaks.

# Using the Average Function

The **AVERAGE function** calculates the average value from a collection of numbers. The syntax of the Average function is

    AVERAGE (number1, number2, number3, …)

where *number1, number2, number3,* and so forth are either numbers or cell references to the cells or a range where the numbers are stored. For example, the following formula uses the AVERAGE function to calculate the average of 1, 2, 5, and 8, returning the value 4:

    =AVERAGE(1, 2, 5, 8)

However, functions usually reference values entered in a worksheet. So, if the range A1:A4 contains the values 1, 2, 5, and 8, the following formula also returns the value 4:

    =AVERAGE(A1:A4)

The advantage of using cell references is that the values used in the function are visible and can be easily edited.

Sanjit wants to show the average monthly sales for each of the 20 Big Red Wraps stores in addition to the total sales for each store. You will use the AVERAGE function to calculate these values.

### To calculate the average monthly sales for each store:

1. If you took a break after the previous session, make sure the Sales Report workbook is open and the Sales Report worksheet is active.

2. In cell **P26**, enter the text **AVERAGE** as the label.

3. Select cell **P27**. You will enter the AVERAGE function in this cell to calculate the average monthly sales for the store on 411 Elm Drive in Madison, Wisconsin.

4. On the HOME tab, in the Editing group, click the **AutoSum button arrow**, and then click **AVERAGE**. The formula =AVERAGE(C27:O27) appears in the cell. The range reference that was included in the function is incorrect. It includes cell O27, which contains the total gross sales for all months. You need to correct the range reference.

5. Select **O27** in the function's argument, and then click cell **N27** to replace the cell reference. The range reference now correctly includes only the gross sales for each month.

6. Press the **Enter** key to complete the formula. The formula results show 29,583, which is the monthly gross sales from the store on 411 Elm Drive in Madison, Wisconsin.

7. Select cell **P27**, and then change the alignment to **Top Align** so that the calculated value is aligned with the top of the cell.

8. Copy the formula in cell **P27**, and then paste the copied formula into the range **P28:P47**.

9. Select cell **P48** to deselect the range. As shown in Figure 2-23, the average monthly sales from all of the stores are $792,833. Individual stores have average monthly gross sales ranging from about $25,000 up to almost $55,000.

| Figure 2-23 | AVERAGE function results |
|---|---|

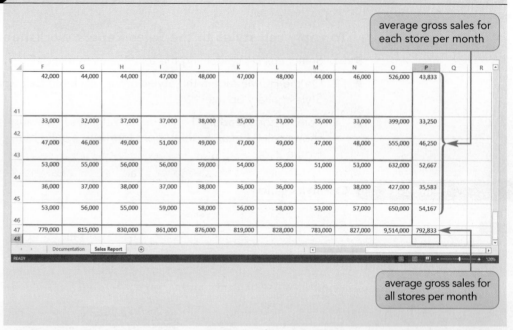

average gross sales for each store per month

average gross sales for all stores per month

With the last formulas added to the worksheet, Sanjit wants you to continue formatting the workbook.

# Applying Cell Styles

A workbook often contains several cells that store the same type of data. For example, each worksheet might have a cell displaying the sheet title, or a range of financial data might have several cells containing totals and averages. It is good design practice to apply the same format to worksheet cells that contain the same type of data.

One way to ensure that similar data is displayed consistently is with styles. A **style** is a collection of formatting options that include a specified font, font size, font styles, font color, fill color, and borders. The Cell Styles gallery includes a variety of built-in styles that you can use to format titles and headings, different types of data such as totals or calculations, and cells that you want to emphasize. For example, you can use the Heading 1 style to display sheet titles in a bold, blue-gray, 15-point Calibri font with no fill color and a blue bottom border. You can then apply the Heading 1 style to all titles in the workbook. If you later revise the style, the appearance of any cell formatted with that style is updated automatically. This saves you the time and effort of reformatting each cell individually.

You already used built-in styles when you formatted data in the Sales Report worksheet with the Accounting, Comma, and Percent styles. You can also create your own cell styles by clicking New Cell Style at the bottom of the Cell Styles gallery.

Sanjit wants you to add more color and visual interest to the Sales Report worksheet. You'll use some of the styles in the Cell Styles gallery to do this.

**To apply cell styles to the Sales Report worksheet:**

▶ **1.** Select cell **B4** containing the text "Sales Statistics."

▶ **2.** On the HOME tab, in the Styles group, click the **Cell Styles** button. The Cell Styles gallery opens.

▶ **3.** Point to the **Heading 1** style in the Titles and Headings section. Live Preview shows cell B4 in a 15-point, bold font with a solid blue bottom border. See Figure 2-24.

**Figure 2-24** Cell Styles gallery

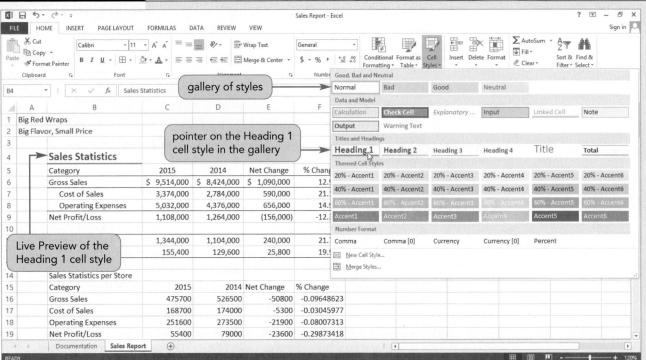

▶ **4.** Move the pointer over different styles in the Cell Styles gallery to see cell B4 with a Live Preview of each style.

▶ **5.** Click the **Title** style. The Title style is applied to cell B4.

▶ **6.** Select the range **B5:F5** containing the column labels for the Sales Statistics data.

▶ **7.** In the Styles group, click the **Cell Styles** button, and then click the **Accent3** style in the Themed Cell Styles section of the Cell Styles gallery.

▶ **8.** Select cell **A25** containing the text "2015 Monthly Gross Sales," and then apply the **Title** cell style to the cell.

▶ **9.** Select cell **A3**. See Figure 2-25.

Figure 2-25    **Cell styles applied to the worksheet**

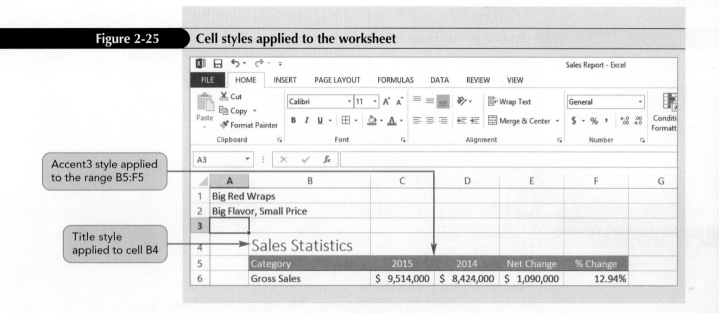

Accent3 style applied to the range B5:F5

Title style applied to cell B4

# Copying and Pasting Formats

Large workbooks often use the same formatting on similar data throughout the workbook, sometimes in widely scattered cells. Rather than repeating the same steps to format these cells, you can copy the format of one cell or range and paste it to another.

## Copying Formats with the Format Painter

The Format Painter provides a fast and efficient way of copying and pasting formats, ensuring that a workbook has a consistent look and feel. The Format Painter does not copy formatting applied to selected text within a cell, and it does not copy data.

Sanjit wants the Sales Report worksheet to use the same formats you applied to the Big Red Wraps company name and slogan in the Documentation sheet. You will use the Format Painter to copy and paste the formats.

**TIP**

To paste the same format multiple times, double-click the Format Painter button to leave the Format Painter on until you click the button again or press the Esc key.

### To use the Format Painter to copy and paste a format:

1. Go to the **Documentation** worksheet, and then select the range **A1:A2**.

2. On the HOME tab, in the Clipboard group, click the **Format Painter** button. The formats from the selected cells are copied to the Clipboard, and a flashing border appears around the selected range and the pointer changes to ⊕🖌.

3. Return to the **Sales Report** worksheet, and then click cell **A1**. The formatting from the Documentation worksheet is removed from the Clipboard and applied to the range A1:A2. Notice that the larger font size you applied to the text "Big Flavor" was not included in the pasted formats.

4. Double-click cell **A2** to enter Edit mode, select **Big Flavor**, and then increase the font size to **14** points. The format for the slogan now matches the slogan on the Documentation sheet.

5. Select cell **A3** to exit Edit mode. See Figure 2-26.

**Figure 2-26** **Formats pasted in the Sales Report worksheet**

Format Painter button

format copied from
Documentation sheet

You can use the Format Painter to copy all of the formats within a selected range and
then apply those formats to another range that has the same size and shape by clicking
the upper-left cell of the range. Sanjit wants you to copy all of the formats you applied
to the Sales Statistics data to the sales statistics per store.

**To copy and paste multiple formats:**

1. Select the range **B4:F12** in the Sales Report worksheet.

2. On the HOME tab, in the Clipboard group, click the **Format Painter** button.

3. Click cell **B14**. All of the number formats, cell borders, fonts, and fill colors
   are pasted into the range B14:F22.

4. Select the range **C23:E23**.

5. On the HOME tab, in the Number group, click the **Comma Style** button ,
   and then click the **Decrease Decimal** button twice to remove the decimal
   places to the right of the decimal point. The numbers are vertically aligned in
   their columns.

6. Select cell **F23**.

7. In the Number group, click the **Percent Style** button % to change the
   number to a percentage, and then click the **Increase Decimal** button
   twice to display two decimal places in the percentage.

8. Click cell **B24**. See Figure 2-27.

**TIP**

If the range in which
you paste the formats is
bigger than the range
you copied, Format
Painter will repeat the
copied formats to fill the
pasted range.

**Figure 2-27**    **Formats pasted from a range**

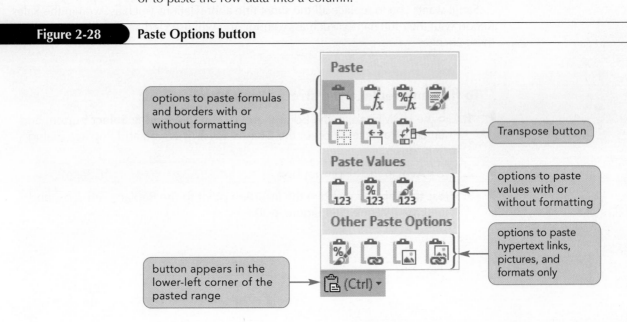

|   | A | B | C | D | E | F | G | H |
|---|---|---|---|---|---|---|---|---|
| 6 | | Gross Sales | $ 9,514,000 | $ 8,424,000 | $ 1,090,000 | 12.94% | | |
| 7 | | Cost of Sales | 3,374,000 | 2,784,000 | 590,000 | 21.19% | | |
| 8 | | Operating Expenses | 5,032,000 | 4,376,000 | 656,000 | 14.99% | | |
| 9 | | Net Profit/Loss | 1,108,000 | 1,264,000 | (156,000) | -12.34% | | |
| 10 | | | | | | | | |
| 11 | | Units Sold | 1,344,000 | 1,104,000 | 240,000 | 21.74% | | |
| 12 | | Customers Served | 155,400 | 129,600 | 25,800 | 19.91% | | |
| 13 | | | | | | | | |
| 14 | | Sales Statistics per Store | | | | | | |
| 15 | | Category | 2015 | 2014 | Net Change | % Change | | |
| 16 | | Gross Sales | $ 475,700 | $ 526,500 | $ (50,800) | -9.65% | | |
| 17 | | Cost of Sales | 168,700 | 174,000 | (5,300) | -3.05% | | |
| 18 | | Operating Expenses | 251,600 | 273,500 | (21,900) | -8.01% | | |
| 19 | | Net Profit/Loss | 55,400 | 79,000 | (23,600) | -29.87% | | |
| 20 | | | | | | | | |
| 21 | | Units Sold | 67,200 | 69,000 | (1,800) | -2.61% | | |
| 22 | | Customers Served | 7,770 | 8,100 | (330) | -4.07% | | |
| 23 | | Stores | 20 | 16 | 4 | 25.00% | | |
| 24 | | | | | | | | |

copied formats — (points to row 9)

pasted formats — (points to rows 16–19)

Documentation    **Sales Report**    ⊕

READY

## Copying Formats with the Paste Options Button

Another way to copy and paste formats is with the Paste Options button 📋 (Ctrl) ▾, which provides options for pasting only values, only formats, or some combination of values and formats. Each time you paste, the Paste Options button appears in the lower-right corner of the pasted cell or range. You click the Paste Options button to open a list of pasting options, shown in Figure 2-28, such as pasting only the values or only the formatting. You can also click the Transpose button to paste the column data into a row, or to paste the row data into a column.

**Figure 2-28**    **Paste Options button**

**Paste**

options to paste formulas and borders with or without formatting

Transpose button

**Paste Values**

options to paste values with or without formatting

**Other Paste Options**

options to paste hypertext links, pictures, and formats only

button appears in the lower-left corner of the pasted range

📋 (Ctrl) ▾

## Copying Formats with Paste Special

The Paste Special command provides another way to control what you paste from the Clipboard. To use Paste Special, select and copy a range, select the range where you want to paste the Clipboard contents, click the Paste button arrow in the Clipboard group on the HOME tab, and then click Paste Special to open the dialog box shown in Figure 2-29.

**Figure 2-29**    **Paste Special dialog box**

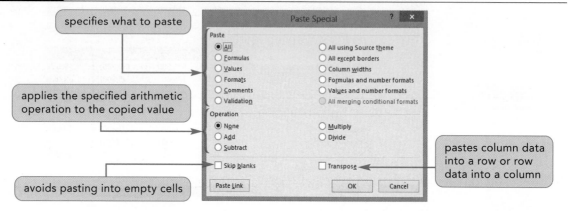

From the Paste Special dialog box, you can control exactly how to paste the copied range.

# Finding and Replacing Text and Formats

The Find and Replace commands let you make content and design changes to a worksheet or the entire workbook quickly. The Find command searches through the current worksheet or workbook for the content or formatting you want to locate, and the Replace command then substitutes it with the new content or formatting you specify.

Sanjit wants you to replace all the street title abbreviations (such as Ave.) in the Sales Report with their full names (such as Avenue). You will use Find and Replace to make these changes.

**To find and replace the street title abbreviations:**

▶ **1.** On the HOME tab, in the Editing group, click the **Find & Select** button, and then click **Replace** (or press the **Ctrl+H** keys). The Find and Replace dialog box opens.

▶ **2.** Type **Ave.** in the Find what box.

▶ **3.** Press the **Tab** key to move the insertion point to the Replace with box, and then type **Avenue**. See Figure 2-30.

**Figure 2-30**    Find and Replace dialog box

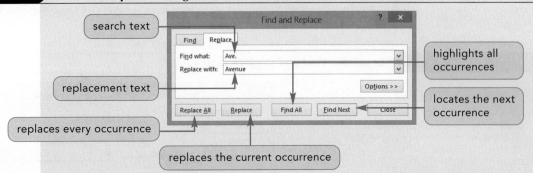

You can choose to find each occurrence of the search text one at a time and decide whether to replace it. You can choose to highlight all occurrences of the search text in the worksheet. Or, you can choose to replace all occurrences at once without reviewing them. In this case, you want to replace every occurrence of the search text with the replacement text.

4. Click the **Replace All** button to replace all occurrences of the search text without reviewing them. A dialog box opens, reporting that three replacements were made in the worksheet.

5. Click the **OK** button to return to the Find and Replace dialog box.

   Next, you will replace the other street title abbreviations.

6. Repeat Steps 2 through 5 to replace all occurrences of each of the following: **St.** with **Street**, **Ln.** with **Lane**, **Dr.** with **Drive**, and **Rd.** with **Road**.

7. Click the **Close** button to close the Find and Replace dialog box.

8. Scroll through the Sales Report worksheet to verify that all street title abbreviations were replaced with their full names.

The Find and Replace dialog box can also be used to replace one format with another or to replace both text and a format simultaneously. Sanjit wants you to replace all occurrences of the white text in the Sales Report worksheet with light yellow text. You'll use the Find and Replace dialog box to make this formatting change.

**To replace white text with yellow text:**

1. On the HOME tab, in the Editing group, click the **Find & Select** button, and then click **Replace** (or press the **Ctrl+H** keys). The Find and Replace dialog box opens.

2. Click the **Options** button to expand the dialog box.

3. Click the **Format** button in the Find what row to open the Find Format dialog box, which is similar to the Format Cells dialog box you used earlier to format a range.

4. Click the **Font** tab to make it active, click the **Color** box, and then click the **White, Background 1** theme color.

5. Click the **OK** button to close the dialog box and return to the Find and Replace dialog box.

6. Click the **Format** button in the Replace with row to open the Replace Format dialog box.

▶ **7.** Click the **Color** box, and then click the **Yellow** standard color.

▶ **8.** Click the **OK** button to close the dialog box and return to the Find and Replace dialog box. See Figure 2-31.

**Figure 2-31**    **Expanded Find and Replace dialog box**

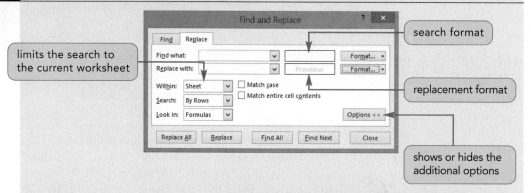

▶ **9.** Verify that the Within box lists **Sheet** to limit the search to the current worksheet.

▶ **10.** Click the **Replace All** button to replace all occurrences of white text in the Sales Report worksheet with yellow text. A dialog box appears, reporting that 32 replacements were made.

▶ **11.** Click the **OK** button to return to the Find and Replace dialog box.

It is a good idea to clear the find and replace formats after you are done so that they won't affect any future searches and replacements. You'll remove the formats from the Find and Replace dialog box.

▶ **12.** Click the **Format button arrow** in the Find what row, and then click **Clear Find Format**. The search format is removed.

▶ **13.** Click the **Format button arrow** in the Replace with row, and then click **Clear Replace Format**. The replacement format is removed.

▶ **14.** Click the **Close** button to return to the worksheet. Notice that every cell in the worksheet that had white text now has yellow text.

# Working with Themes

Recall that a theme is a coordinated selection of fonts, colors, and graphical effects that are applied throughout a workbook to create a specific look and feel. When you switch to a different theme, the theme-related fonts, colors, and effects change throughout the workbook to reflect the new theme. The appearance of non-theme fonts, colors, and effects remains unchanged no matter which theme is applied to the workbook.

Most of the formatting you have applied to the Sales Report workbook is based on the Office theme. Sanjit wants you to change the theme to see how it affects the workbook's appearance.

**To change the workbook's theme:**

▶ 1. Click the **PAGE LAYOUT** tab on the ribbon.

▶ 2. In the Themes group, click the **Themes** button. The Themes gallery opens. Office—the current theme—is the default.

▶ 3. Point to the **Organic** theme in the Themes gallery. Live Preview shows how the appearance of the Sales Report worksheet will change if you select the Organic theme. See Figure 2-32.

| Figure 2-32 | Live Preview of the Organic theme |
|---|---|

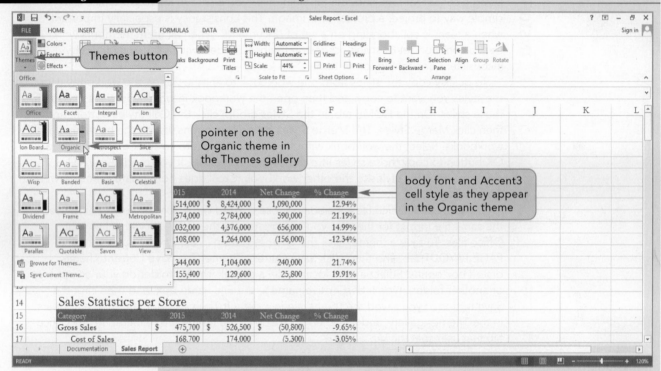

▶ 4. Point to several other themes in the Themes gallery to see how the worksheet appearance would change.

▶ 5. Click the **Wisp** theme to apply that theme to the workbook.

Changing the theme made a significant difference in the worksheet's appearance. The most obvious changes to the worksheet are the fill colors and the fonts. Only formatting options directly tied to a theme change when you select a different theme. Any formatting options you selected that were not theme-based remain unaffected by the change. For example, the yellow standard color you just applied to the different column labels is still yellow, even with the Wisp theme applied, because yellow is not a theme color. For the same reason, the red fill color used in the column labels of the monthly sales table remains unchanged under the new theme.

Sanjit informs you that Big Red Wraps requires all documents to be formatted with the Office theme. You will reapply the Office theme to the workbook.

**To reapply the Office theme to the workbook:**

▶ **1.** On the PAGE LAYOUT tab, in the Themes group, click the **Themes** button, and then click the **Office** theme from the gallery of themes.

The workbook now complies with the company's standard formatting.

**INSIGHT**

*Sharing Styles and Themes*

Using a consistent look and feel for all the files you create in Microsoft Office is a simple way to project a professional image. This consistency is especially important when a team is collaborating on a set of documents. When all team members work from a common set of style and design themes, readers will not be distracted by inconsistent or clashing formatting.

To quickly copy the styles from one workbook to another, open the workbook with the styles you want to copy, and then open the workbook in which you want to copy those styles. On the HOME tab, in the Styles group, click the Cell Styles button, and then click Merge Styles. The Merge Styles dialog box opens, listing the currently open workbooks. Select the workbook with the styles you want to copy, and then click the OK button to copy those styles into the current workbook. If you modify any styles, you must copy the styles to the other workbook; Excel does not update styles between workbooks.

Because other Office files, including those created with Word or PowerPoint, use the same file format for themes, you can create one theme to use with all of your Office files. To save a theme, click the Themes button in the Themes group on the PAGE LAYOUT tab, and then click Save Current Theme. The Save Current Theme dialog box opens. Select a save location (in a default Theme folder on your computer or another folder), type a descriptive name in the File name box, and then click the Save button. If you saved the theme file in a default Theme folder, the theme appears in the Themes gallery, and any changes made to the theme are reflected in any Office file that uses that theme.

# Highlighting Cells with Conditional Formats

Conditional formats are often used to help analyze data. A **conditional format** applies formatting to a cell when its value meets a specified condition. For example, a conditional format can be used to format negative numbers in red and positive numbers in black. Conditional formats are dynamic, which means that the formatting can change when the cell's value changes. Each conditional format has a set of rules that define how the formatting should be applied and under what conditions the format will be changed.

**REFERENCE**

*Highlighting Cells with a Conditional Format*

• Select the range in which you want to highlight cells.
• On the HOME tab, in the Styles group, click the Conditional Formatting button, point to Highlight Cells Rules or Top/Bottom Rules, and then click the appropriate rule.
• Select the appropriate options in the dialog box.
• Click the OK button.

Excel has four conditional formats—data bars, highlighting, color scales, and icon sets. In this tutorial, you will apply cell highlighting, which changes the cell's font color or fill color based on the cell's value, as described in Figure 2-33. You can enter a value or a cell reference if you want to compare other cells with the value in a certain cell.

**Figure 2-33**    **Highlight Cells rules**

| Rule | Highlights Cell Values |
|------|------------------------|
| Greater Than | Greater than a specified number |
| Less Than | Less than a specified number |
| Between | Between two specified numbers |
| Equal To | Equal to a specified number |
| Text that Contains | That contain specified text |
| A Date Occurring | That contain a specified date |
| Duplicate Values | That contain duplicate or unique values |

© 2014 Cengage Learning

## Highlighting Cells Based on Their Values

Sanjit wants to highlight important trends and sales values in the Sales Report worksheet. He wants you to use a conditional format to display sales statistics that showed a negative net or percent change in a red font so that they stand out. You will do this by creating a rule to format the cells in ranges E6:F12 and E16:F22 with numbers that are less than 0.

**To highlight negative numbers in red:**

1. Select the nonadjacent range **E6:F12;E16:F22** in the Sales Report worksheet.
2. On the ribbon, click the **HOME** tab.
3. In the Styles group, click the **Conditional Formatting** button, and then point to **Highlight Cells Rules** to display a menu of the available rules.
4. Click **Less Than**. The Less Than dialog box opens so you can select the value and formatting to highlight negative values.
5. Type **0** (a zero) in the Format cells that are LESS THAN box, click the **with** arrow, and then click **Red Text**. Live Preview shows that the rule formats any cells in the selected range that have a negative value in a red font. See Figure 2-34.

**Figure 2-34**    **Live Preview of the Less Than conditional format**

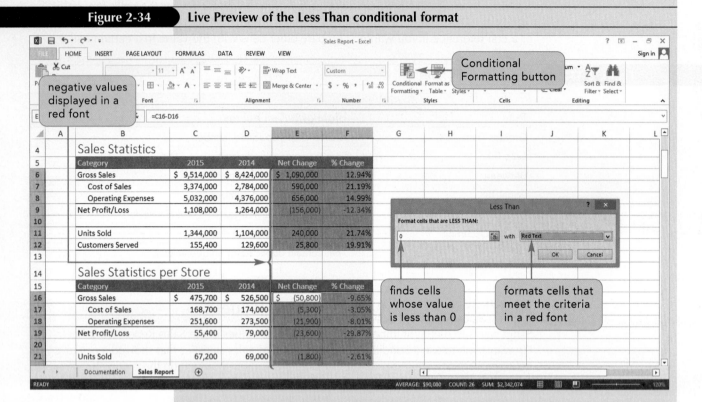

> 6. Click the **OK** button to apply the highlighting rule. You will verify that this format is conditional.

> 7. In cell D8, enter **4,576,000** to change the Operating Expenses value. The now positive values in cells E9 and F9 are formatted in a black font.

> 8. Press the **Ctrl+Z** keys to return the value in cell D8 to 4,376,000. The values in cells E9 and F9 are again negative and in a red font.

The highlighted values show at a glance that Big Red Wraps' gross sales, units sold, and customers served increased from 2014 to 2015, while the company's net profit declined during the same period. The average gross sales per store also declined in 2015. Big Red Wraps opened four new stores in 2015, and Sanjit will argue that the cost of this expansion and low sales from the new stores caused this apparent decline.

## Highlighting Cells with a Top/Bottom Rule

Another way of applying conditional formats is with the Quick Analysis tool. The **Quick Analysis tool**, which appears whenever you select a range of cells, provides access to the most common tools for data analysis and formatting. The FORMATTING category includes buttons for the Greater Than and Top 10% conditional formatting rules. You can highlight cells based on their values in comparison to other cells. For example, you can highlight cells with the 10 highest or lowest values in a selected range, or you can highlight the cells with above-average values in a range.

Sanjit wants you to highlight the five stores in the Big Red Wraps chain that had the highest gross sales in the last fiscal year. You will use a Top/Bottom rule to do this.

### To use a Top/Bottom Rule to highlight the stores with the highest gross sales:

1. Select the range **P27:P46** containing the average monthly gross sales for each of the 20 Big Red Wraps stores. The Quick Analysis button appears in the lower-right corner of the selected range.

2. Click the **Quick Analysis** button 📊, and then point to **Top 10%**. Live Preview colors the cells in the top 10 percent with red font and a red fill. See Figure 2-35.

| Figure 2-35 | Quick Analysis tool |

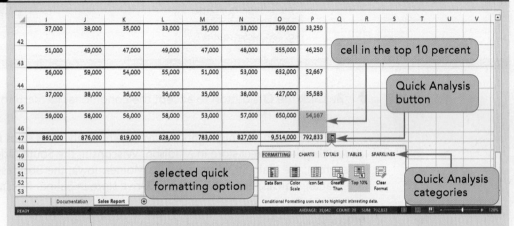

Sanjit wants to see the top five items rather than the cells with values in the top 10 percent, so you won't apply this conditional formatting.

3. Press the **Esc** key to close the Quick Analysis tool. The range P27:P46 remains selected.

4. On the HOME tab, in the Styles group, click the **Conditional Formatting** button, and then point to **Top/Bottom Rules** to display a menu of available rules.

5. Click **Top 10 Items** to open the Top 10 Items dialog box.

6. Click the down arrow on the spin box five times to change the value from 10 to 5. This specifies that the top five values in the selected range will be formatted.

7. Click the **with** arrow, and then click **Green Fill with Dark Green Text** to specify the formatting to apply to the five cells with the top values. Live Preview highlights the top five stores in terms of gross sales. See Figure 2-36.

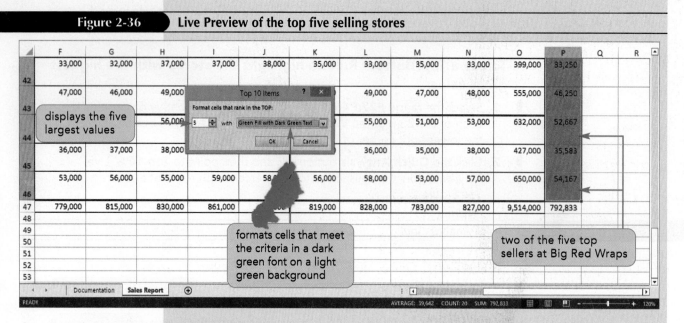

**Figure 2-36**    **Live Preview of the top five selling stores**

▶ **8.** Click the **OK** button to accept the conditional formatting.

The Top/Bottom rule highlights the average monthly gross sales for the five top-selling stores: the North Street store in Madison, Wisconsin; the South Drive store in Janesville, Wisconsin; the Main Street store in Des Moines, Iowa; the Business Drive store in Manhattan, Kansas; and the Causeway Drive store in Salina, Kansas.

## Clearing a Conditional Format

You can remove a conditional format at any time without affecting the underlying data by selecting the range containing the conditional format, clicking the Conditional Formatting button, and then clicking the Clear Rules button. A menu opens, providing options to clear the conditional formatting rules from the selected cells or the entire worksheet. You can also click the Quick Analysis button that appears in the lower-right corner of the selected range, and then click the Clear Format button in the FORMATTING category.

## Creating a Conditional Formatting Legend

When you use conditional formatting to highlight cells in a worksheet, the purpose of the formatting is not always immediately apparent. To ensure that everyone knows why certain cells are highlighted, you should include a **legend**, which is a key that identifies each color and its meaning.

You will add a legend to the Sales Report worksheet to document the Top 5 highlighting rule you just created.

**To create a conditional formatting legend:**

▶ **1.** Select cell **P49**, type **light green**, and then press the **Enter** key. You will use a highlight rule to fill this cell with a dark green font on a light green fill.

▶ **2.** Select cell **P49** to make it the active cell.

▶ **3.** On the HOME tab, in the Styles group, click the **Conditional Formatting** button, point to **Highlight Cells Rules**, and then click **Text that Contains**. The Text That Contains dialog box opens.

4. Verify that **light green** appears in the Format cells that contain the text box. The box shows the text entered in the selected cell.

5. Click the **with** arrow, and then click **Green Fill with Dark Green Text** to format cell P49 with the same format used for the top five gross sales.

6. Click the **OK** button. Cell P49 remains selected.

7. In the Alignment group, click the **Center** button  to center the text in the cell.

8. In cell **O49**, enter **Top 5 Stores** to identify the format's purpose, and then select cell **O49**.

9. In the Styles group, click the **Cell Styles** button, and then click the **Explanatory Text** style (the third style in the first row of the Data and Model section). The cell style is applied to the selected cell.

10. Click cell **O51**. The legend is complete, as shown in Figure 2-37.

| Figure 2-37 | Conditional formatting legend |

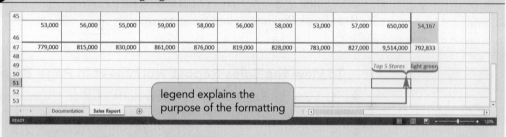

The conditional formatting makes the top-selling stores stand out.

## Written Communication: Using Conditional Formatting Effectively

**PROSKILLS**

Conditional formatting is an excellent way to highlight important trends and data values to clients and colleagues. However, be sure to use it judiciously. Overusing conditional formatting might obscure the very data you want to emphasize. Keep in mind the following tips as you make decisions about what to highlight and how it should be highlighted:

- **Document the conditional formats you use.** If a bold, green font means that a sales number is in the top 10 percent of all sales, include that information in a legend in the worksheet.
- **Don't clutter data with too much highlighting.** Limit highlighting rules to one or two per data set. Highlights are designed to draw attention to points of interest. If you use too many, you will end up highlighting everything—and, therefore, nothing.
- **Use color sparingly in worksheets with highlights.** It is difficult to tell a highlight color from a regular fill color, especially when fill colors are used in every cell.
- **Consider alternatives to conditional formats.** If you want to highlight the top 10 sales regions, it might be more effective to simply sort the data with the best-selling regions at the top of the list.

Remember that the goal of highlighting is to provide a strong visual clue to important data or results. Careful use of conditional formatting helps readers to focus on the important points you want to make rather than distracting them with secondary issues and facts.

# Formatting a Worksheet for Printing

You should format any worksheets you plan to print so that they are easy to read and understand. You can do this using the print settings, which enable you to set the page orientation, the print area, page breaks, print titles, and headers and footers. Print settings can be applied to an entire workbook or to individual sheets. Because other people will likely see your printed worksheets, you should format the printed output as carefully as you format the electronic version. Sanjit wants you to format the Sales Report worksheet so he can distribute the printed version at the upcoming sales conference.

## Using Page Break Preview

Page Break Preview shows only those parts of the active sheet that will print and how the content will be split across pages. A dotted blue border indicates a page break, which separates one page from another. As you format the worksheet for printing, you can use this view to control what content appears on each page.

Sanjit wants to know how the Sales Report worksheet would print in portrait orientation and how many pages would be required. You will look at the worksheet in Page Break Preview to find these answers.

**To view the Sales Report worksheet in Page Break Preview:**

▶ **1.** Click the **Page Break Preview** button 🔲 on the status bar. The worksheet switches to Page Break Preview.

▶ **2.** Change the zoom level of the worksheet to **30%** so you can view the entire contents of this large worksheet. See Figure 2-38.

**Figure 2-38**     **Sales Report worksheet in Page Break Preview**

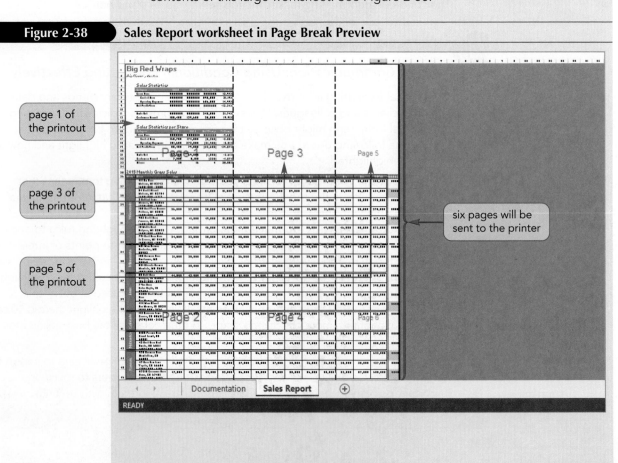

page 1 of the printout

page 3 of the printout

page 5 of the printout

six pages will be sent to the printer

**Trouble?** If you see a different page layout or the worksheet is split onto a different number of pages, don't worry. Each printer is different, so the layout and pages might differ from what is shown in Figure 2-38.

Page Break Preview shows that a printout of the Sales Report worksheet requires six pages in portrait orientation, and that pages 3 and 5 would be mostly blank. Note that each printer is different, so your Page Break Preview might show a different number of pages. With this layout, each page would be difficult to interpret because the data is separated from the descriptive labels. Sanjit wants you to fix the layout so that the contents are easier to read and understand.

## Defining the Print Area

By default, all cells in a worksheet containing text, formulas, or values are printed. If you want to print only part of a worksheet, you can set a print area, which is the region of the worksheet that is sent to the printer. Each worksheet has its own print area. Although you can set the print area in any view, Page Break Preview shades the areas of the worksheet that are not included in the print area, making it simple to confirm what will print.

Sanjit doesn't want the empty cells in the range G1:O24 to print, so you will set the print area to eliminate those cells.

**To set the print area of the Sales Report worksheet:**

1. Change the zoom level of the worksheet to **80%** to make it easier to select cells and ranges.

2. Select the nonadjacent range **A1:F24;A25:P49** containing the cells with content.

3. On the ribbon, click the **PAGE LAYOUT** tab.

4. In the Page Setup group, click the **Print Area** button, and then click **Set Print Area**. The print area changes to cover only the nonadjacent range A1:F24;A25:P49. The rest of the worksheet content is shaded to indicate that it will not be part of the printout.

5. Select cell **A1** to deselect the range.

6. Change the zoom level to **50%** so you can view more of the worksheet. See Figure 2-39.

Figure 2-39    **Print area set for the Sales Report worksheet**

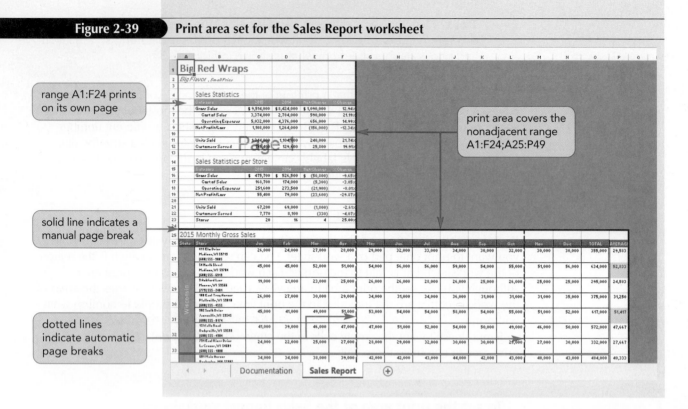

range A1:F24 prints on its own page

print area covers the nonadjacent range A1:F24;A25:P49

solid line indicates a manual page break

dotted lines indicate automatic page breaks

## Inserting Page Breaks

Often, the contents of a worksheet will not fit onto a single printed page. When this happens, Excel prints as much of the content that fits on a single page without resizing, and then inserts automatic page breaks to continue printing the remaining worksheet content on successive pages. The resulting printouts might split worksheet content in awkward places, such as within a table of data.

**TIP**

When you remove a page break, Excel will automatically rescale the printout to fit into the allotted pages.

To split the printout into logical segments, you can insert manual page breaks. Page Break Preview identifies manual page breaks with a solid blue line and automatic page breaks with a dotted blue line. When you specify a print area for a nonadjacent range, as you did for the Sales Report worksheet, you also insert manual page breaks around the adjacent ranges. So a manual page break already appears in the print area you defined (see Figure 2-39). You can remove a page break in Page Break Preview by dragging it out of the print area.

**REFERENCE**

### Inserting and Removing Page Breaks

**To insert a page break:**
- Click the first cell below the row where you want to insert a page break, click a column heading, or click a row heading.
- On the PAGE LAYOUT tab, in the Page Setup group, click the Breaks button, and then click Insert Page Break.

**To remove a page break:**
- Select any cell below or to the right of the page break you want to remove.
- On the PAGE LAYOUT tab, in the Page Setup group, click the Breaks button, and then click Remove Page Break.

*or*
- In Page Break Preview, drag the page break line out of the print area.

The Sales Report worksheet has automatic page breaks along columns F and L. You will remove these automatic page breaks from the Sales Report worksheet.

**To remove the automatic page breaks and insert manual page breaks:**

▶ 1. Point to the dotted blue page break directly to the right of column L until the pointer changes to ↔.

▶ 2. Drag the page break to the right and out of the print area. The page break is removed from the worksheet.

▶ 3. Point to the page break located in cell F31 until the pointer changes to ↔, and then drag the page break to the right and out of the print area.

On the PAGE LAYOUT tab, in the Scale to Fit section, notice that the Scale box shows 43%. After removing the two page breaks from the Sales Report printout, Excel scaled the printout from 100% of its actual size to 43% to fit the printout onto two pages.

▶ 4. Click the **column I** heading to select the entire column. You will add a manual page break between columns H and I to split the monthly gross sales data onto two pages so the printout will be larger and easier to read.

▶ 5. On the PAGE LAYOUT tab, in the Page Setup group, click the **Breaks** button, and then click **Insert Page Break**. A manual page break is added between columns H and I, forcing the monthly gross sales onto a new page after the June data.

▶ 6. Select cell **A1** to deselect the column. The printout of the Sales Report worksheet is now limited to three pages. However, the gross sales data in the range A25:O49 is split across pages. See Figure 2-40.

| Figure 2-40 | Manual page break added to the print area |

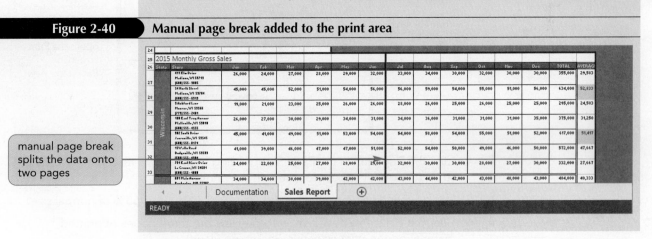

manual page break splits the data onto two pages

## Adding Print Titles

It is a good practice to include descriptive information such as the company name, logo, and worksheet title on each page of a printout in case a page becomes separated from the other pages. You can repeat information, such as the company name, by specifying which rows or columns in the worksheet act as print titles. If a worksheet contains a large table, you can print the table's column headings and row headings on every page of the printout by designating those columns and rows as print titles.

In the Sales Report worksheet, the company name and slogan currently appear on the first page of the printout, but do not appear on subsequent pages. Also, the descriptive row labels for the monthly sales table in column A do not appear on the third page of the printout. You will add print titles to fix these issues.

**To set the print titles:**

**TIP**

You can also open the Page Setup dialog box by clicking the Dialog Box Launcher in the Page Setup group on the PAGE LAYOUT tab.

1. On the PAGE LAYOUT tab, in the Page Setup group, click the **Print Titles** button. The Page Setup dialog box opens with the Sheet tab displayed.

2. In the Print titles section, click the **Rows to repeat at top** box, move the pointer over the worksheet, and then select the range **A1:A2**. A flashing border appears around the first two rows of the worksheet to indicate that the contents of the first two rows will be repeated on each page of the printout. The row reference $1:$2 appears in the Rows to repeat at top box.

3. Click the **Columns to repeat at left** box, and then select columns A and B from the worksheet. The column reference $A:$B appears in the Columns to repeat at left box. See Figure 2-41.

**Figure 2-41**  **Sheet tab in the Page Setup dialog box**

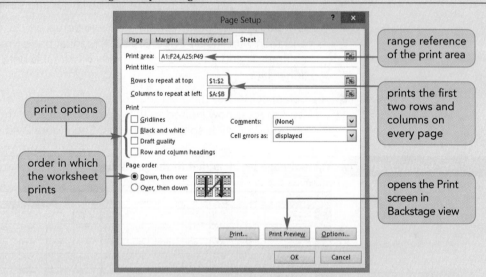

4. Click the **Page** tab in the Page Setup dialog box. You will rescale the worksheet so that it doesn't appear too small in the printout.

5. In the Scaling section, change the Adjust to amount to **65%** of normal size.

6. Click the **Print Preview** button to preview the three pages of printed material on the Print screen in Backstage view.

7. Verify that each of the three pages has the Big Red Wraps title and slogan at the top of the page, and that the state and store names appear in the leftmost columns of pages 2 and 3. See Figure 2-42.

| Figure 2-42 | Print titles on page 3 of the Sales Report worksheet |

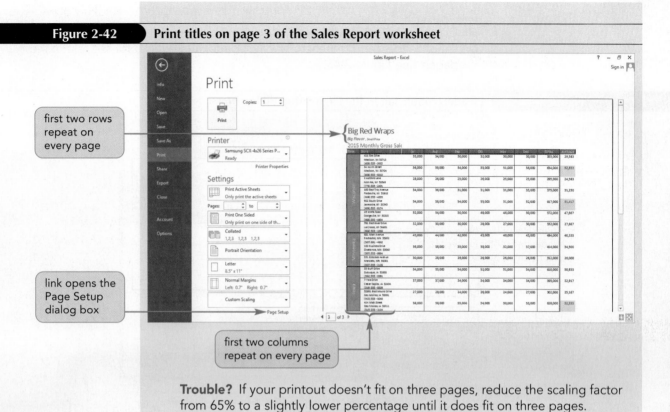

first two rows repeat on every page

link opens the Page Setup dialog box

first two columns repeat on every page

**Trouble?** If your printout doesn't fit on three pages, reduce the scaling factor from 65% to a slightly lower percentage until it does fit on three pages.

## Creating Headers and Footers

You can also use headers and footers to repeat information on each printed page. A **header** appears at the top of each printed page; a **footer** appears at the bottom of each printed page. Headers and footers contain helpful and descriptive text that is usually not found within the worksheet, such as the workbook's author, the current date, or the workbook's filename. If the printout spans multiple pages, you can display the page number and the total number of pages in the printout to help ensure you and others have all the pages.

Each header and footer has three sections—a left section, a center section, and a right section. Within each section, you type the text you want to appear, or you insert elements such as the worksheet name or the current date and time. These header and footer elements are dynamic; if you rename the worksheet, for example, the name is automatically updated in the header or footer. Also, you can create one set of headers and footers for even and odd pages, and you can create another set for the first page in the printout.

Sanjit wants the printout to display the workbook's filename in the header's left section, and the current date in the header's right section. He wants the center footer to display the page number and the total number of pages in the printout, and the right footer to display your name as the workbook's author.

### To create the header and footer:

1. Click the **Page Setup** link near the bottom of the Print screen to open the Page Setup dialog box.

2. Click the **Header/Footer** tab to display the header and footer options.

> **3.** Click the **Different first page** check box to select it. This lets you create one set of headers and footers for the first page, and one set for the rest of the pages. See Figure 2-43.

**Figure 2-43**    **Header/Footer tab in the Page Setup dialog box**

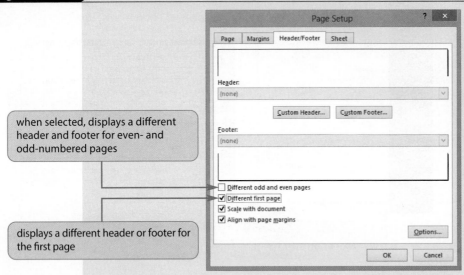

when selected, displays a different header and footer for even- and odd-numbered pages

displays a different header or footer for the first page

> **4.** Click the **Custom Header** button to open the Header dialog box. The dialog box contains two tabs—Header and First Page Header—because you selected the Different first page option.

**TIP**

You can create or edit headers and footers in Page Layout view by clicking in the header/footer section and using the tools on the DESIGN tab.

> **5.** On the Header tab, type **Filename:** in the Left section box, press the **spacebar**, and then click the **Insert File Name** button 📄. The code &[File], which displays the filename of the current workbook, is added to the left section of the header.

> **6.** Press the **Tab** key twice to move to the right section of the header, and then click the **Insert Current Date** button 📅. The code &[Date] is added to the right section of the header. See Figure 2-44.

**Figure 2-44**    **Header dialog box**

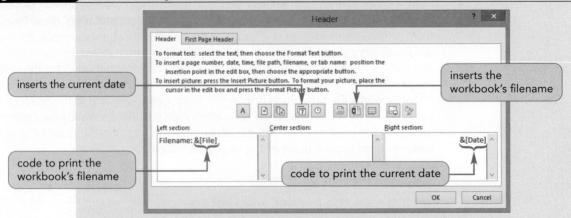

inserts the current date

inserts the workbook's filename

code to print the workbook's filename

code to print the current date

> **7.** Click the **OK** button to return to the Header/Footer tab in the Page Setup dialog box. You did not define a header for the first page of the printout, so no header information will be added to that page.

Now you will format the page footer for all pages of the printout.

**8.** Click the **Custom Footer** button to open the Footer dialog box, which is similar to the Header dialog box.

**9.** Click the **Center section** box, type **Page**, press the **spacebar**, and then click the **Insert Page Number** button. The code &[Page], which inserts the current page number, appears after the label "Page."

**10.** Press the **spacebar**, type **of**, press the **spacebar**, and then click the **Insert Number of Pages** button. The code &[Pages], which inserts the total number of pages in the printout, is added to the Center section box. See Figure 2-45.

**Figure 2-45** Footer dialog box

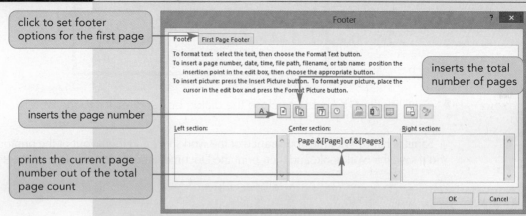

**11.** Click the **First Page Footer** tab so you can create the footer for the first page of the printout.

**12.** Click the **Right section** box, type **Prepared by:**, press the **spacebar**, and then type your name.

**13.** Click the **OK** button to return to the Page Setup dialog box.

## Setting the Page Margins

A **margin** is the space between the page content and the edges of the page. By default, Excel sets the page margins to 0.7 inch on the left and right sides, and 0.75 inch on the top and bottom; and it allows for 0.3-inch margins around the header and footer. You can reduce or increase these margins as needed by selecting predefined margin sizes or setting your own.

Sanjit's reports need a wider margin along the left side of the page to accommodate the binding. He asks you to increase the left margin for the printout from 0.7 inch to 1 inch.

**To set the left margin:**

**1.** Click the **Margins** tab in the Page Setup dialog box to display options for changing the page margins.

**2.** Double-click the **Left** box to select the setting, and then type **1** to increase the size of the left margin. See Figure 2-46.

**TIP**
To select preset margins, click the Margins button in the Page Setup group on the PAGE LAYOUT tab.

**Figure 2-46**   Margins tab in the Page Setup dialog box

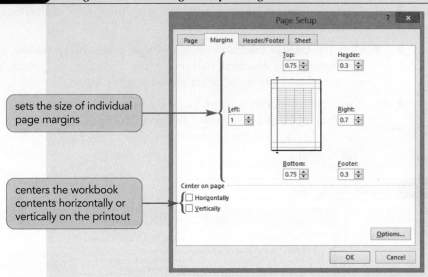

sets the size of individual page margins

centers the workbook contents horizontally or vertically on the printout

▶ **3.** Click the **OK** button to close the dialog box and return to the worksheet.

Sanjit is happy with the appearance of the worksheet and the layout of the printout. You'll save the workbook, and then print the Documentation and Sales Report sheets.

**To save and print the workbook:**

▶ **1.** Return the Sales Report worksheet to **Normal** view, and then save the workbook.

▶ **2.** Display the Print screen in Backstage view, and then change the first Settings box to **Print Entire Workbook**. Both the Sales Report worksheet and the Documentation sheet appear in the preview. As you can see, the printout will include a header with the filename and date on every page except the first page, and a footer with your name on the first page and the page number along with the total number of pages on subsequent pages.

▶ **3.** If you are instructed to print, print the entire workbook, and then close it.

## Session 2.2 Quick Check

REVIEW

1. Describe two methods of applying the same format to different ranges.
2. Red is a standard color. What happens to red text when you change the workbook's theme?
3. What is a conditional format?
4. How would you highlight the top five values in the range A1:C20?
5. How do you insert a manual page break in a worksheet?
6. What is a print area?
7. What are print titles?
8. Describe how to add the workbook filename to the center section of the footer on every page of the printout.

### SAM Projects

Put your skills into practice with SAM Projects! SAM Projects for this tutorial can be found online. If you have a SAM account, go to www.cengage.com/sam2013 to download the most recent Project Instructions and Start Files.

## Review Assignments

**Data Files needed for the Review Assignments: Menu.xlsx, Background2.png**

Sanjit has a worksheet that details the sales of individual items from the Big Red Wraps menu. He asks you to format the sales figures and design a layout for the printed sheet as you did for the Sales Report workbook. Complete the following:

1. Open the **Menu** workbook located in the Excel2 ▸ Review folder included with your Data Files, and then save the workbook as **Menu Sales** in the location specified by your instructor.

2. In the Documentation sheet, enter your name in cell B4 and the date in cell B5.

3. Make the following formatting changes to the Documentation sheet:
   a. Set the background image to the **Background2.png** file located in the Excel2 ▸ Review folder.
   b. Format the text in cell A1 in red 26-point bold Calibri Light.
   c. Format the text in cell A2 to red 10-point italic Calibri Light. Change the text string "Big Flavor" to 14 points.
   d. Apply the Accent2 cell style to the range A4:A6.
   e. Change the font color of range B4:B6 to red and change its fill color to white.
   f. Format the date in the Long Date format and left-align the cell contents.

4. Use the Format Painter to copy the formatting in the range A1:A2 in the Documentation sheet and paste it to the same range in the Menu Sales worksheet. (*Hint*: You must increase the size of the text "Big Flavor" manually.)

5. Apply the Title cell style to the titles in cells B4, B12, and A20.

6. Make the following changes to the Units Sold table in the range B5:F10:
   a. In cell C6, calculate the total number of wraps sold by the company (found in the range C22:N31). In cell C7, calculate the total number of soups. In cell C8, calculate the total number of sides. In cell C9, calculate the total number of salads.
   b. In cell C10, calculate the sum of the range C6:C9. Copy the formula to cell D10.
   c. In the range E6:E10, calculate the difference between the 2015 and 2014 values. In the range F6:F10, calculate the percent change from 2014 to 2015.
   d. Apply the Accent2 cell style to the headings in the range B5:F5. Center the headings in the range C5:F5.
   e. Apply the Comma style to the values in the range C6:E10. Do not display any numbers to the right of the decimal point.
   f. Apply the Percent style to the values in the range F6:F10 and show two decimal places.
   g. Add a top border to the values in the range B10:F10.

7. Make the following changes to the range B13:F18:
   a. In cells C18 and D18, calculate the totals of the 2014 and 2015 sales. In the range E14:F18, calculate the change in sales and the percent change.
   b. Copy the format from the range B5:F10 and paste it into the range B13:F18.
   c. Change the format for the values in the ranges C14:E14 and C18:E18 to Accounting format with no decimal places.

8. Make the following changes to the Units Sold per Month table in the range A21:O46:

   a. In the range O22:O45, calculate the total units sold for each menu item. In the range C46:O46, calculate the total items sold per month and overall.

   b. Format the headings in the range A21:O21 with the Accent2 cell style. Center the headings in the range C21:O21.

   c. Format the units sold values in the range C22:O46 with the Comma style and no decimal places.

   d. Change the fill color of the subtotals in the range O22:O45 and C46:N46 to White, Background 1, Darker 15% (the first color in the third row of the theme colors).

   e. Merge each of the menu categories in the range A22:A45 into single cells. Rotate the text of the cells up. Increase the font size to 18 points and middle-align the cell contents.

   f. Format cell A22 with the "Wraps" label in a white font on a Gray-25%, Background 2, Darker 50% fill. Format cell A32 with the "Soups" label in a white font on Blue, Accent 1, Darker 25% fill. Format of cell A37 with the "Sides" label in a white font on a Gold, Accent 4, Darker 25% fill. Format cell A42 with the "Salads" label in a white font on a Green, Accent 6, Darker 25% fill.

   g. Add a thick box border around each category of menu item in the ranges A22:O31, A32:O36, A37:O41, and A42:O45.

9. Create a conditional format for the subtotals in the range O22:O45 highlighting the top five selling items with a yellow fill and dark yellow text.

10. Create a legend for the conditional format. Enter the text **Top 5 Sellers** in cell O48. Add a thick box border around the cell, and then use a conditional format that displays this text in dark yellow text on a yellow fill.

11. Set the following print formats for the Menu Sales worksheet:

    a. Set the print area to the nonadjacent range A1:F19;A20:O48.

    b. Remove any automatic page breaks in the large Units Sold table. Insert a manual page break to separate the June and July sales figures. The printout of the Menu Sales worksheet should fit on three pages.

    c. Scale the printout to 70 percent of normal size.

    d. Define the print titles to repeat the first three rows at the top of the sheet, and the first two columns at the left of the sheet.

    e. Increase the left margin of the printout from 0.7 inch to 1 inch.

    f. Create headers and footers for the printout with a different header for the first page.

    g. For the first page header, print **Prepared by** *your name* in the right section. For every other page, print **Filename:** *file* in the left section and *date* in the right section, where *file* is the name of the workbook file and *date* is the current date. (*Hint*: Use the buttons in the Header dialog box to insert the filename and date.)

    h. For every footer, print **Page** *page* **of** *pages* in the center section, where *page* is the page number and *pages* is the total number of pages in the printout.

12. If you are instructed to print, print the entire workbook in portrait orientation. Verify that the company name and slogan appear on every page of the Menu Sales worksheet printout, and that the menu category and menu item name appear on both pages with the Units Sold table.

13. Save and close the workbook.

## Case Problem 1

**Data File needed for this Case Problem: Salon.xlsx**

*Special Highlights Hair Salon*    Sarah Jones is developing a business plan for a new hair salon, Special Highlights Hair Salon, located in Hatton, North Dakota. As part of the business plan, she needs a projected income statement for the company. You will help her develop and format the income statement. Complete the following:

1. Open the **Salon** workbook located in the Excel2 ▸ Case1 folder included with your Data Files, and then save the workbook as **Salon Income Statement** in the location specified by your instructor.

2. In the Documentation sheet, enter your name in cell B3 and the date in cell B4.

3. Apply the following formatting to the Documentation sheet:
   a. Format cell A1 using the Title cell style.
   b. Format the range A3:A5 using the Accent6 cell style.
   c. In cell B4, format the date value using the long date format, and left-align the cell contents.
   d. In cell B5, format the text string "Special Highlights Hair Salon" in italic.

4. In the Income Statement worksheet, format cell A1 using the Title cell style.

5. Calculate the following items in the Income Statement worksheet:
   a. In cell C7, calculate the Gross Profit, which is equal to the Gross Sales minus the Cost of Sales.
   b. In cell C21, calculate the Total Operating Expenses, which is equal to the sum of the operating expenses.
   c. In cell C22, calculate the Total Operating Profit/Loss, which is equal to the Gross Profit minus the Total Operating Expenses.
   d. In cell C23, calculate the projected Income Taxes, which is equal to 35 percent of the Total Operating Profit/Loss.
   e. In cell C24, calculate the Net Profit/Loss, which is equal to the Total Operating Profit/Loss minus the projected Income Taxes.

6. Set the following formats to the Income Statement worksheet:
   a. Format cells A3 and A26 using the Heading 2 cell style.
   b. Format cells A4 and A9 and the range A27:A38 in bold.
   c. Format cells B5, C7, B10, C21, and C24 using the Accounting format with no decimal places.
   d. Format cells B6, B11:B19, C22, and C23 using the Comma style with no decimal places.
   e. Indent the text in the ranges A5:A6 and A10:A19 two spaces. Indent the text in cell A7 and the range A21:A24 four spaces.
   f. Add a bottom border to cells B6, C7, C21, C22, and C23. Add a double bottom border to cell C24.

7. Merge cells A26:E26 and then left-align the merged cell's contents.

8. Merge the contents of the range B27:E27. Left-align the merged cell's contents and wrap the text within the cell. Increase the height of row 27 to display the entire contents of the cell.

9. Top-align and left-align the range A27:B38.

10. Copy the format from the range A27:B27 to the range A28:B38. Merge columns B through E in each row, left-align the text, and resize the row heights to display the complete contents of the cells.

11. Italicize the text string "National Salon News" in cells B27 and B28.

12. Set the following printing formats to the Income Statement worksheet:

   a. Insert a manual page break directly above row 26 so that the Income Statement prints on two pages.

   b. Set rows 1 and 2 as a print title to print on both pages.

   c. Change the page margins to 1 inch on every side.

   d. On the first page of the printout, print **Prepared by *your name*** in the left section of the header, where *your name* is your name. Print the ***current date*** in the right section of the header. Do not display header text on any other page.

   e. For every page, add a footer that prints the workbook ***filename*** in the left section, **Page *page*** in the center section, and the ***worksheet name*** in the right section.

13. If you are instructed to print, print the entire contents of the workbook in portrait orientation.

14. Save and close the workbook.

## Case Problem 2

**APPLY**

**Data File needed for this Case Problem: Waist.xlsx**

*Waist Trainers*   Alexandra Roulez is a dietician at Waist Trainers, a company in Fort Smith, Arkansas, that specializes in personal improvement, particularly in areas of health and fitness. Alexandra wants to create a meal-planning workbook for her clients who want to lose weight and improve their health. One goal of meal planning is to decrease the percentage of fat in the diet. Alexandra thinks it would be helpful to highlight foods that have a high percentage of fat as well as list their total fat calories. She already created a workbook that contains a few sample food items and lists the number of calories and grams of fat in each item. She wants you to format this workbook. Complete the following:

1. Open the **Waist** workbook located in the Excel2 ▸ Case2 folder included with your Data Files, and then save the workbook as **Waist Trainers Nutrition Table** in the location specified by your instructor.

2. In the Documentation sheet, enter your name in cell B3 and the date in cell B4.

3. Set the following formatting to the Documentation sheet:

   a. In cell A1, apply the Title cell style, increase the font size to 24 points, and then change the font color to a medium orange.

   b. Apply the Accent2 cell style to the range A3:A5.

   c. Wrap the text within the range B3:B5, and then left- and top-align the text in the cells.

   d. Change the format of the date in cell B4 to the long date format.

   e. Add borders around all of the cells in the range A3:B5.

4. Copy the cell format for cell A1 in the Documentation sheet to cell A1 in the Meal Planner worksheet.

5. In cell F4, enter the text **Calories from Fat**. In cell G4, enter the text **Fat Percentage**.

6. In the range F5:F54, calculate the calories from fat for each food item, which is equal to the Grams of Fat multiplied by 9. In the range G5:G54, calculate the fat percentage of each food item, which is equal to the Calories from Fat divided by the Calories.

7. Format cell A3 using the Heading 4 cell style.

8. Format the range A4:G4 using the Accent2 cell style.

9. Format the range D5:F54 with the Comma style and display one decimal place.

10. Format the range G5:G54 with the Percent style and display two decimal places.

11. Merge the cells in the range A5:A8, rotate the text up, and then center-align the cell content both horizontally and vertically. Change the fill color to medium gold, increase the font size to 14 points, and then change the font color to white.

12. Place a thick box border around the beef food items in the range A5:G8.

13. Repeat Steps 11 and 12 for the other six food categories.

14. For good health, the FDA recommends that the fat percentage in a person's diet should not exceed 30 percent of the total calories per day. Create a Conditional Formatting rule for the fat percentages to highlight those food items that exceed the FDA recommendation in dark red text on a light red fill.

15. In cell G2, enter the text **High Fat Food**. Center the text in the cell. Change the format of the cell to dark red text on a light red fill. Add a thick black border around the cell.

16. Set the following print formats for the Meal Planner worksheet:

   a. Change the page orientation to landscape.

   b. Scale the printout so that the width of the worksheet fits on a single page.

   c. If necessary, create manual page breaks directly above row 25 and above row 44. The worksheet should print on three separate pages.

   d. Repeat the first four rows of the worksheet on every printed page.

   e. For every page, add a footer that prints **Prepared by** *your name* in the left section, **Page** *page* in the center section, and the *worksheet name* in the right section.

17. If you are instructed to print, print the entire contents of the workbook.

18. Save and close the workbook.

## Case Problem 3

**CHALLENGE**

Data File needed for this Case Problem: Wind.xlsx

***Winds of Change***   Odette Ferris is a researcher at Winds of Change, a privately run wind farm providing supplemental power for communities near Topeka, Kansas. One of Odette's jobs is to record wind speeds from different sectors of the wind farm. She has entered the wind speed data into a workbook as a table with wind speed measures laid out in a grid. Because the numbers are difficult to read and interpret, she wants you to color code the wind speed values using conditional formatting. Complete the following:

1. Open the **Wind** workbook located in the Excel2 ► Case3 folder included with your Data Files, and then save the workbook as **Wind Speed Grid** in the location specified by your instructor.

2. In the Documentation sheet, enter your name in cell B3 and the date in cell B4.

3. In the Wind Speed Grid worksheet, merge the range A1:V1, and then apply the Heading 1 cell style to the merged cell and set the font size to 20 points.

4. Format the range B3:V3 as white text on a black background. Copy this formatting to the grid coordinates in the range A4:A64.

⊕ **Explore**  5. Create a conditional format that highlights cells in the range B4:V64 whose value equals 18 with fill color equal to (99, 37, 35). (*Hint*: In the Equal To dialog box, select Custom Format in the with box to open the Format Cells dialog box. On the Fill tab, in the Background Color section, click the More Colors button, and then click the Custom tab to enter the RGB color value.)

⊕ **Explore**  6. Repeat Step 5 to continue creating conditional formats that set highlight colors for the wind speed values in the range B4:V64 using the wind speeds and color values shown in Figure 2-47.

**Figure 2-47**    **Wind speed color values**

| Wind Speed | RGB Color Value |
|---|---|
| 16 m/s | (150, 54, 52) |
| 14 m/s | (218, 150, 148) |
| 12 m/s | (230, 184, 183) |
| 10 m/s | (242, 220, 219) |
| 8 m/s | (242, 242, 242) |
| 6 m/s | (255, 255, 255) |
| 4 m/s | (197, 217, 241) |
| 2 m/s | (141, 180, 226) |
| 0 m/s | (83, 141, 213) |

© 2014 Cengage Learning

7. Reduce the font size of the values in the range B4:V64 to 1 point.

**Explore** 8. Enclose each cell in the range B4:V64 in a light gray border. (*Hint*: Use the Border tab in the Format Cells dialog box.)

9. Use the Format Painter to copy the formats from the range B4:V64 and apply them to the range X3:X12. Increase the font size of the cells in that range to 11 points.

10. Merge the range Y3:Y12, center the contents of the merged cell horizontally and vertically, and then rotate the text down. Format the text in a bold 18-point font.

11. Set the following print formats to the Wind Speed Grid worksheet:
   a  Change the page orientation to landscape.
   b. Set the print area to the range A1:Y64.
   c. Scale the worksheet so that the width and the height of the sheet fit on a single page.
   d. Add a header to the printed page with your name in the left section of the header and the worksheet name in the right section of the header.

12. Save and close the workbook.

## Case Problem 4

**CREATE**

**Data File needed for this Case Problem: Office.xlsx**

*Office Cart*  Robert Trenton is a shipping manager at Office Cart, an online office supply store located in Muncie, Indiana. He wants to use an Excel workbook to track shipping orders. Robert asks you to create and format a worksheet that he can use to enter information for packing slips. Complete the following:

1. Open the **Office** workbook located in the Excel2 ▸ Case4 folder included with your Data Files, and then save the workbook as **Office Cart Packing Slip** in the location specified by your instructor.

2. In the Documentation sheet, enter your name in cell B3 and the date in cell B4.

3. Set the following formats in the Documentation sheet:
   a. Merge cells A1 and B1, and then left-align the contents of the merged cell. Change the font to 28-point white Calibri Light on a dark green background.
   b. Change the font of the range A3:A5 to 14-point white Calibri Light on a dark green background.
   c. Change the format of the date value in cell B4 to the Long Date style, and then left-align the date in the cell.
   d. Italicize the text "Office Cart" in cell B5.
   e. Add a border around each cell in the range A3:B5.

4. Insert a new worksheet at the end of the workbook and name it **Packing Slip**.

5. In the Packing Slip worksheet, select all of the cells in the worksheet. (*Hint*: Click the Select All button at the intersection of the row and column headings, or press the Ctrl+A keys.) Change the font to 10-point dark green Calibri.

6. Add a thick box border around the range A1:D40.

7. For the range A1:D3, change the format to a white Calibri Light font on a dark green background.

8. Set the width of column A to 15 characters. Set the width of column B to 20 characters. Set the width of column C to 30 characters. Set the width of column D to 20 characters.

9. Merge the range A1:B3. Merge the range C1:D3, and then right- and top-align the merged cell. Set the row height of row 1 to 36 points and the heights of rows 2 and 3 to 15 points.

10. In cell A1, enter the following three lines of text, pressing the Alt+Enter keys to start a new line within the cell:
**Office Cart**
**14 Trenke Lane**
**Muncie, IN 47303**
Format the first line in a 26-point bold font.

11. In cell C1, enter **Packing Slip**, and then format the text in a 26-point bold font using the Headings font of the current theme.

12. In the range A5:A7, enter the following three lines of text in a bold font, and then right-align the text and indent the text one character:
**Order Date**
**Order Number**
**Purchase Order**

13. Format cell B5 in the Long Date format and left-align the cell contents. Insert border lines around each of the cells in the range B5:B7.

14. In the range C5:C7, enter the following three lines of text, and then use the Format Painter to copy the formats from the range A5:B7 to the range C5:D7:
**Date**
**Sales Rep**
**Account Num**

15. In cell B9, enter **Ship To**. In cell D9, enter **Bill To**. Format the text in both cells in bold.

16. In cell A10, enter **Address**, format the text in bold, right-align the text, and then indent it one character.

17. Merge the cells in the range B10:B15, left- and top-align the cell contents, insert a border around the merged cell, and then wrap the text within this cell.

18. In cell C10, enter **Address**. Copy the format from the range A10:B15 to the range C10:D15.

19. Enter the following data in the indicated cells in the worksheet:
cell A17: **Item**
cell B17: **Product No.**
cell C17: **Description**
cell D17: **Order Quantity**

20. Format the range A17:D17 in bold white Calibri on a dark green background.

21. Format the range A18:D18 with a bottom border and a light green background. Format the range A19:D19 with a bottom border and a white background. Copy the format in the range A18:D19 to the range A20:D27.

22. Apply a Top and Double Bottom Border to the range A28:D28. Merge the contents of the range A28:C28. Enter **Total** in cell A28, bold the text, and right-align the cell contents.

23. In cell D28, enter a formula to calculate the sum of the values in the range D18:D27. Bold the text.

24. In cell A30, enter **Comments** and then bold the text.

25. Merge the range A31:D39, left- and top-align the cell contents, and then add a thick box border around the merged cell.

26. In cell D40, enter **Thank you for your business!** in italic 16-point Calibri, and then right-align the cell contents.

27. Make sure the worksheet is set to portrait orientation, and then add a footer that displays your name in the left section, the filename in the center section, and the current date in the right section. Scale the printout so that it fits onto a single page.

28. Enter the packing slip data shown in Figure 2-48. Save and close the workbook.

**Figure 2-48**    **Office Cart packing slip form**

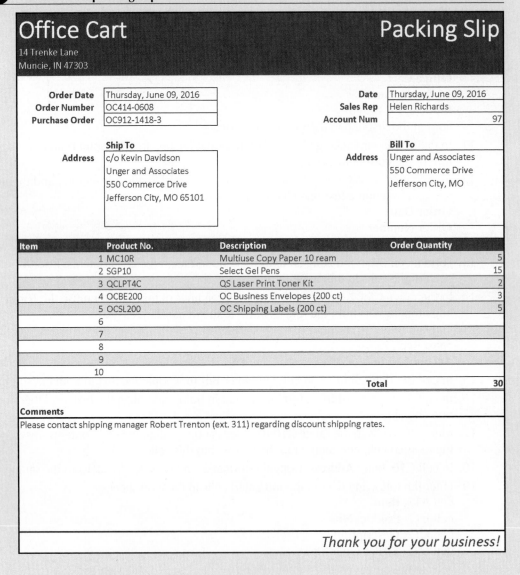

Office Cart packing slip form:

# Office Cart                                 Packing Slip

14 Trenke Lane
Muncie, IN 47303

| | | | | |
|---|---|---|---|---|
| **Order Date** | Thursday, June 09, 2016 | **Date** | Thursday, June 09, 2016 |
| **Order Number** | OC414-0608 | **Sales Rep** | Helen Richards |
| **Purchase Order** | OC912-1418-3 | **Account Num** | 97 |

**Ship To**                                   **Bill To**

**Address**   c/o Kevin Davidson              **Address**   Unger and Associates
              Unger and Associates                          550 Commerce Drive
              550 Commerce Drive                            Jefferson City, MO
              Jefferson City, MO 65101

| Item | Product No. | Description | Order Quantity |
|---|---|---|---|
| 1 | MC10R | Multiuse Copy Paper 10 ream | 5 |
| 2 | SGP10 | Select Gel Pens | 15 |
| 3 | QCLPT4C | QS Laser Print Toner Kit | 2 |
| 4 | OCBE200 | OC Business Envelopes (200 ct) | 3 |
| 5 | OCSL200 | OC Shipping Labels (200 ct) | 5 |
| 6 | | | |
| 7 | | | |
| 8 | | | |
| 9 | | | |
| 10 | | | |
| | | **Total** | 30 |

**Comments**

Please contact shipping manager Robert Trenton (ext. 311) regarding discount shipping rates.

*Thank you for your business!*

TUTORIAL **3**

EXCEL

## OBJECTIVES

**Session 3.1**
- Make a workbook user-friendly
- Translate an equation into an Excel formula
- Understand function syntax
- Enter formulas and functions with the Quick Analysis tool
- Enter functions with the Insert Function dialog box
- Interpret error values
- Change cell references between relative and absolute

**Session 3.2**
- Use the AutoFill tool to enter formulas and data and complete a series
- Display the current date with the TODAY function
- Find the next weekday with the WORKDAY function
- Use the COUNT and COUNTA functions to tally cells
- Use an IF function to return a value based on a condition
- Perform an exact match lookup with the VLOOKUP function
- Perform what-if analysis using trial and error and Goal Seek

# Calculating Data with Formulas and Functions

*Creating a Fitness Tracker*

## Case | Fit Fathers Inc.

Ken Dorsett is a certified fitness professional and founder of Fit Fathers Inc., which is a fitness program he developed to help fathers stay fit and active. From its beginnings in Blue Springs, Missouri, where Ken led daily workouts with three other dads, his program has grown to an enrollment of 318 fathers in five different cities in the northwest corner of the state.

Ken wants to help his members evaluate their fitness goals and track their workouts. He has been working on an Excel workbook that can assess each participant's fitness level and track his workout progress. Ken has developed the basic structure of the workbook, but still needs to enter the formulas to calculate the different statistics and data that are important for his clients. He asks you to enter the appropriate formulas to complete the workbook. To do this, you will use a variety of formulas and functions.

## STARTING DATA FILES

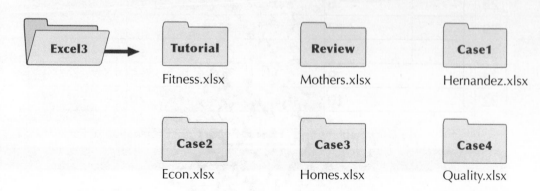

Excel3 → Tutorial
Fitness.xlsx

Review
Mothers.xlsx

Case1
Hernandez.xlsx

Case2
Econ.xlsx

Case3
Homes.xlsx

Case4
Quality.xlsx

Microsoft product screenshots used with permission from Microsoft Corporation.

# Session 3.1 Visual Overview:

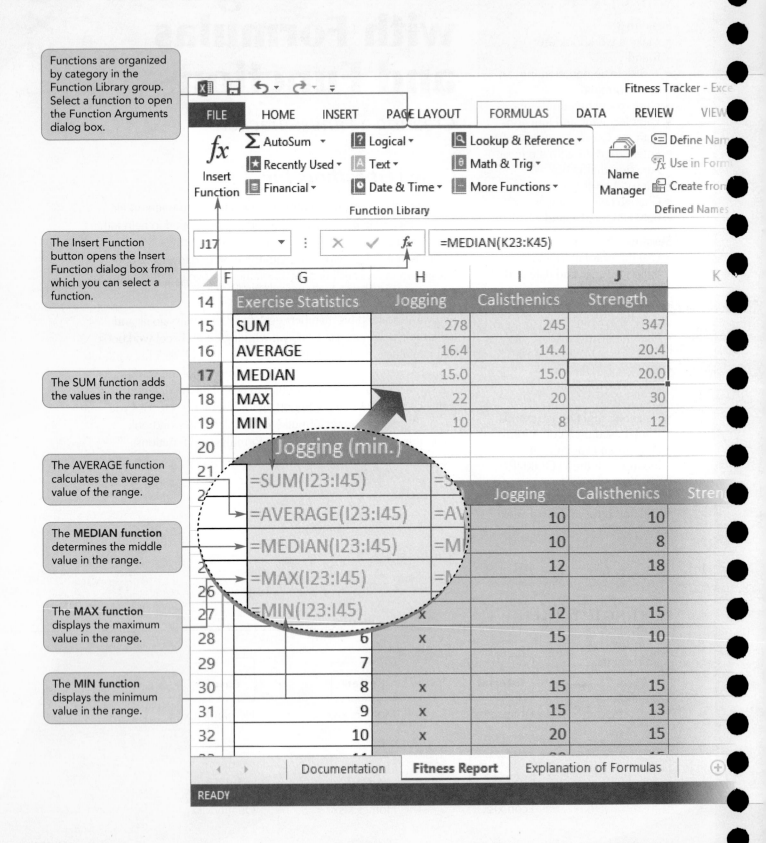

Functions are organized by category in the Function Library group. Select a function to open the Function Arguments dialog box.

The Insert Function button opens the Insert Function dialog box from which you can select a function.

The SUM function adds the values in the range.

The AVERAGE function calculates the average value of the range.

The **MEDIAN function** determines the middle value in the range.

The **MAX function** displays the maximum value in the range.

The **MIN function** displays the minimum value in the range.

FILE    HOME    INSERT    PAGE LAYOUT    FORMULAS    DATA    REVIEW    VIEW

Fitness Tracker - Exce

Insert Function

Σ AutoSum ▾
★ Recently Used ▾
Financial ▾

? Logical ▾
A Text ▾
Date & Time ▾

Lookup & Reference ▾
Math & Trig ▾
More Functions ▾

Name Manager

Define Nam
Use in Form
Create from

Function Library

Defined Names

J17          fx     =MEDIAN(K23:K45)

| | Exercise Statistics | Jogging | Calisthenics | Strength | |
|---|---|---|---|---|---|
| 14 | Exercise Statistics | Jogging | Calisthenics | Strength | |
| 15 | SUM | 278 | 245 | 347 | |
| 16 | AVERAGE | 16.4 | 14.4 | 20.4 | |
| 17 | MEDIAN | 15.0 | 15.0 | 20.0 | |
| 18 | MAX | 22 | 20 | 30 | |
| 19 | MIN | 10 | 8 | 12 | |

Jogging (min.)

=SUM(I23:I45)
=AVERAGE(I23:I45)
=MEDIAN(I23:I45)
=MAX(I23:I45)
=MIN(I23:I45)

| | | Jogging | Calisthenics | Stren |
|---|---|---|---|---|
| 21 | | 10 | 10 | |
| | | 10 | 8 | |
| | | 12 | 18 | |
| 27 | | 12 | 15 | |
| 28 | 6 | 15 | 10 | |
| 29 | 7 | | | |
| 30 | 8 | 15 | 15 | |
| 31 | 9 | 15 | 13 | |
| 32 | 10 | 20 | 15 | |

Documentation     **Fitness Report**     Explanation of Formulas

READY

# Functions and Cell References

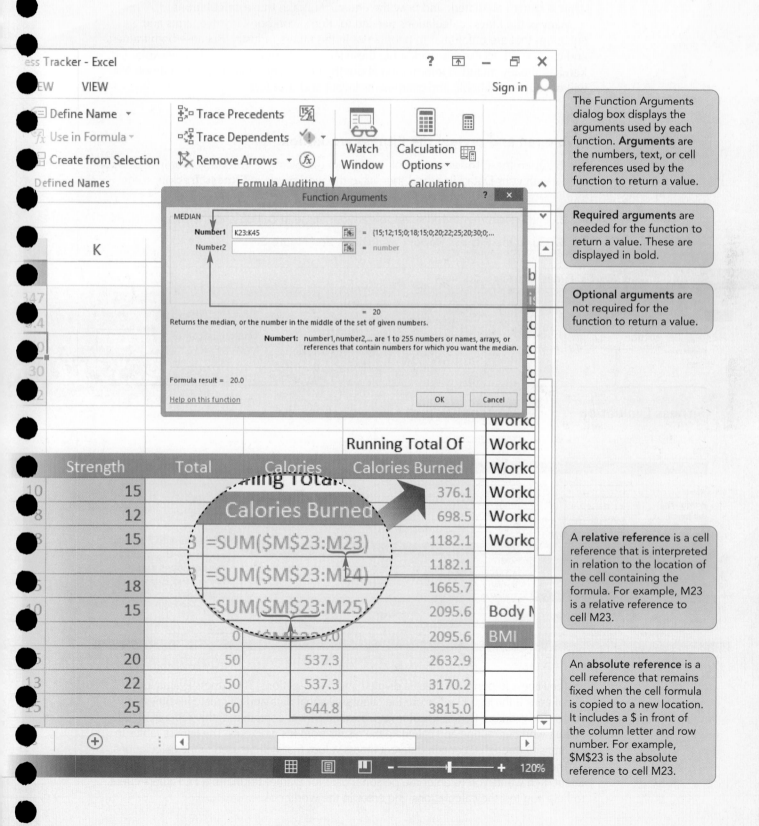

The Function Arguments dialog box displays the arguments used by each function. **Arguments** are the numbers, text, or cell references used by the function to return a value.

**Required arguments** are needed for the function to return a value. These are displayed in bold.

**Optional arguments** are not required for the function to return a value.

A **relative reference** is a cell reference that is interpreted in relation to the location of the cell containing the formula. For example, M23 is a relative reference to cell M23.

An **absolute reference** is a cell reference that remains fixed when the cell formula is copied to a new location. It includes a $ in front of the column letter and row number. For example, $M$23 is the absolute reference to cell M23.

# Making Workbooks User-Friendly

Every workbook should be accessible to its intended users. When a workbook is user-friendly, anyone who needs to enter data in the workbook or interpret its results can understand the workbook's contents, including any jargon or unusual terms, what is being calculated, and how the equations make those calculations.

Many of the fitness calculations needed for Ken's workbook involve terms and equations that are unfamiliar to people not in the fitness industry. Because both trainers and clients will access this workbook, these terms and equations need to be explained. Ken has already included information about the fitness equations in the workbook. You will open the workbook, and examine its layout and structure.

### To open and review the Fitness workbook:

1. Open the **Fitness** workbook located in the Excel3 ▶ Tutorial folder included with your Data Files, and then save the workbook as **Fitness Tracker** in the location specified by your instructor.

2. In the Documentation sheet, enter your name in cell B3 and the date in cell B4.

3. Go to the **Fitness Report** worksheet. See Figure 3-1.

**Figure 3-1** Fitness Tracker workbook

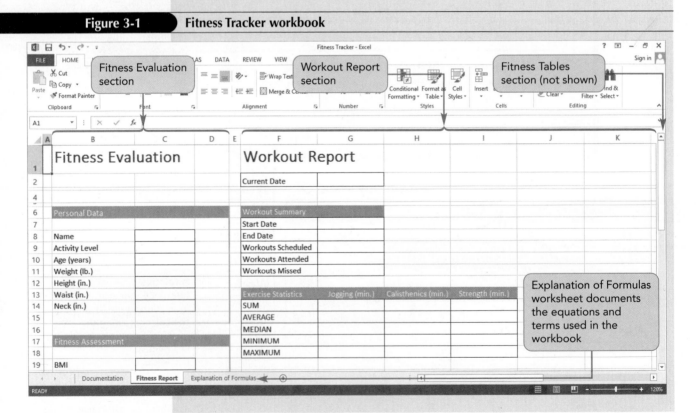

The Fitness Report worksheet is divided into three sections. The Fitness Evaluation in columns B through D will store the client's personal data and calculate his fitness status. The Workout Report in columns F through M will contain monthly reports on the client's workout routine and calculate the results from his workouts. The Fitness Tables in columns O through P contain different fitness values that will be used in the calculations.

The Fitness Evaluation contains a section for personal information on a Fit Fathers client. Ken wants you to enter the personal data for Daniel Pridham, a Fit Fathers client, to help you test the calculations you enter in the workbook.

**To enter Daniel's personal data:**

▶ **1.** In cell **C8**, enter **Daniel Pridham** as the client's name.

▶ **2.** In cell **C9**, enter **Sedentary** to describe Daniel's activity level.

▶ **3.** In the range **C10:C14**, enter **45** for his age, **193** for his weight in pounds, **70** for his height in inches, **37** for his waist size in inches, and **15.5** for his neck size in inches.

## Documenting Formulas

Documenting the contents of a workbook helps to avoid errors and confusion. This type of information can make a workbook easier for other people to understand. For workbooks that include many calculations, as the Fitness Tracker workbook does, it is helpful to explain the formulas and terms used in the calculations. Such documentation also can serve as a check that the equations are accurate. Another way to document formulas and terms is to include notes of explanation within the worksheet where the equations are used.

Ken has included explanations of different fitness terms and equations in the Explanation of Formulas worksheet, and explanatory notes in cells B26 and F46 of the Fitness Report worksheet. Before proceeding, he wants you to review the documentation in these worksheets.

**To review the documentation in the Fitness Tracker workbook:**

▶ **1.** Click the **Explanation of Formulas** sheet tab to make it the active sheet.

▶ **2.** Read the sheet contents, reviewing the descriptions of common fitness terms and formulas. As you continue developing the Fitness Tracker workbook, you'll learn about these terms and formulas in more detail.

▶ **3.** Click the **Fitness Report** sheet tab to return to the Fitness Report worksheet.

▶ **4.** Read the explanatory notes in cells B26 and F46.

## Using Constants in Formulas

The first fitness equation Ken wants you to enter is BMI, or body mass index, which estimates the amount of human body fat. The BMI equation is based on the individual's body weight divided by the square of his or her height. The specific formula is

$$BMI = \frac{703w}{h^2}$$

where $w$ is the body weight in pounds and $h$ is the height in inches. BMI values from 18.5 to 24.9 are considered normal; anything higher is considered overweight.

One common skill you need when creating a workbook is to translate an equation like the BMI equation into an Excel formula. Some equations use constants. A **constant** is a value in a formula that doesn't change. In the BMI equation, 703 is a constant because that value never changes when calculating the body mass index.

**INSIGHT**

### Deciding Where to Place a Constant

Should a constant be entered directly into the formula or placed in a separate worksheet cell and referenced in the formula? The answer depends on the constant being used, the purpose of the workbook, and the intended audience. Placing constants in separate cells that you reference in the formulas can help users better understand the worksheet because no values are hidden within the formulas. Also, when a constant is entered in a cell, you can add explanatory text next to each constant to document how it is being used in the formula. On the other hand, you don't want a user to inadvertently change the value of a constant and throw off all the formula results. You will need to evaluate how important it is for other people to immediately see the constant, and whether the constant requires any explanation for other people to understand the formula. For example, Ken wants you to include the 703 constant in the BMI formula rather than in a separate cell because he doesn't feel that clients need to see this constant to understand BMI.

To convert the BMI equation into a formula, you need to replace $w$ and $h$ in the equation with Daniel's actual weight and height. Because Daniel's weight is stored in cell C11 and his height is stored in cell C12, you replace the $w$ in the formula with the C11 cell reference, and replace the $h$ in the formula with the C12 cell reference. The resulting Excel formula is:

```
=703*C11/C12^2
```

Note that the exponent operator ^ is used to square the height value in the denominator of the fraction. Recall that exponentiation raises a value to a power; in this case, the value in cell C12 is raised to the second power, or squared. Following the order of operations, Excel will first square the height value, then multiply the weight value by 703, and finally divide that product by the squared height. You will enter the BMI formula in the Fitness Report worksheet now.

### To enter the BMI formula in the Fitness Report worksheet:

1. In cell **C19**, enter the formula **=703*C11/C12^2**. The formula multiplies the weight in cell C11 by the constant 703, and then divides the resulting value by the square of the height in cell C12. The calculated BMI value that is displayed in cell C19 is 27.68959184.

   **Trouble?** If your BMI formula results differ from 27.68959184, you probably entered the formula incorrectly. Edit your formula as needed so that the numbers and cell references match those shown in the formula in Step 1.

2. Select cell **C19**, and then reduce the number of displayed decimals to one. Cell C19 displays 27.7 as the formula results.

The next fitness equation, which calculates the individual's resting basal metabolic rate (BMR), includes four constants. The resting BMR estimates the number of calories a person expends daily (not counting any actual activity). For men, the BMR is calculated with the equation

$$BMR = 6.23w + 12.7h - 6.76a + 66$$

where *w* is the weight in pounds, *h* is the height in inches, and *a* is the age in years. BMR is calculated by multiplying the weight, height, and age by different constants, and then adding the results to another constant. Heavier and taller people require more daily calories to sustain them. As people age, their metabolism slows, resulting in a lower BMR. Daniel's weight, height, and age are stored in cells C11, C12, and C10, respectively, so the BMR equation translates to the following Excel formula:

```
=6.23*C11+12.7*C12–6.76*C10+66
```

You will enter this formula in the Fitness Report worksheet to calculate Daniel's BMR.

### To enter the BMR formula in the Fitness Report worksheet:

▶ **1.** In cell **C21**, enter the formula **=6.23*C11+12.7*C12–6.76*C10+66**. Cell C21 displays 1853.19, indicating that Daniel burns about 1853 calories per day before performing any activity.

   **Trouble?** If your BMR formula results differ from 1853.19, you might have entered the formula incorrectly. Edit the formula as needed so that the numbers and cell references match those shown in the formula in Step 1.

▶ **2.** Select cell **C21**, and then reduce the number of decimals displayed in the cell to zero. The number of calories per day displayed in cell C21 is 1853.

The 1853 calories per day amount assumes no physical activity. However, even the most sedentary person moves a little bit during the day, which increases the BMR value. The table in the range O7:P12 in the Fitness Report worksheet lists the constant multipliers for different activity levels. For example, the BMR of a sedentary man like Daniel is multiplied by 1.2 (shown in cell P8) to account for daily movements. If Daniel were to increase his activities to a moderate level, the multiplier would increase to 1.55 (as shown in cell P10).

You will enter the formula to calculate Daniel's active BMR based on his sedentary lifestyle. Ken wants you to use the constant value stored in the table rather entering it into the formula because he anticipates that Daniel will increase his activity level under the direction of Fit Fathers, and it is easier to update the amount in a cell rather than editing a formula.

### To calculate Daniel's active BMR:

▶ **1.** In cell **C22**, enter the formula **=C21*P8** to multiply Daniel's resting BMR by the sedentary activity level. Based on this calculation, Daniel's active BMR is 2223.828 calories per day.

▶ **2.** Select cell **C22**, and then decrease the number of decimal places displayed in the cell to zero. The displayed value changes to 2224. See Figure 3-2.

Figure 3-2    **BMI and BMR calculated values**

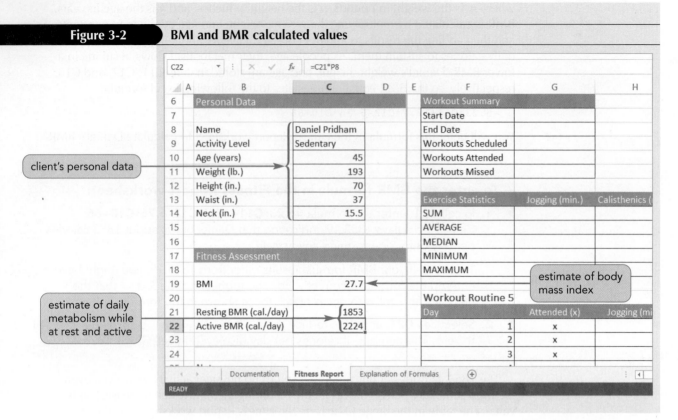

The active BMR shows that Daniel needs about 2224 calories per day to maintain his current weight.

## Identifying Notes, Input Values, and Calculated Values

When worksheets involve notes and many calculations, it is useful to distinguish input values that are used in formulas from calculated values that are returned by formulas. Formatting that clearly differentiates input values from calculated values helps others more easily understand the worksheet. Such formatting also helps prevent anyone from entering a value in a cell that contains a formula.

You can use cell styles to identify cells as containing explanatory text, input values, and calculated values. When you use cell styles or other formatting to identify a cell's purpose, you should include a legend in the worksheet describing the purpose of the formatting.

Ken wants to be sure that whenever he and his staff members update a client's workbook, they can easily see where to enter numbers. You will apply cell styles to distinguish between notes, input cells, and formula cells.

**To apply cell styles to differentiate cells with notes, input values, and calculated values:**

1. Select the merged cell **B26**.

2. On the HOME tab, in the Styles group, click the **Cell Styles** button to open the Cell Styles gallery.

3. Click the **Explanatory Text** cell style located in the Data and Model group. Cell B26 is formatted with the Explanatory Text cell style.

4. Format cell **F46** with the **Explanatory Text** cell style.

5. Format the range **C8:C14** with the **Input** cell style. These cells contain the personal information about Daniel that you entered earlier.

6. Format the nonadjacent range **C19;C21:C22** containing the calculated BMI and BMR values with the **Calculation** cell style.

7. Format the range **G22:J44** with the **Input** cell style. These cells store information about Daniel's workout routine, which Ken enters after each workout.

Next, you'll create a legend to identify which cells are input cells and which cells are calculated cells.

8. In cell **C2**, enter **Input Values** as the label, format the cell with the **Explanatory Text** cell style, and then right-align the text in the cell.

9. In cell **C4**, enter **Calculated Values** as the label, and then use the Format Painter to copy the formatting in cell C2 and paste it to cell C4.

10. Format cell **D2** with the **Input** cell style, and then format cell **D4** with the **Calculation** cell style.

11. Select cell **C19**. See Figure 3-3.

| Figure 3-3 | Input and calculated values formatted with cell styles |
|---|---|

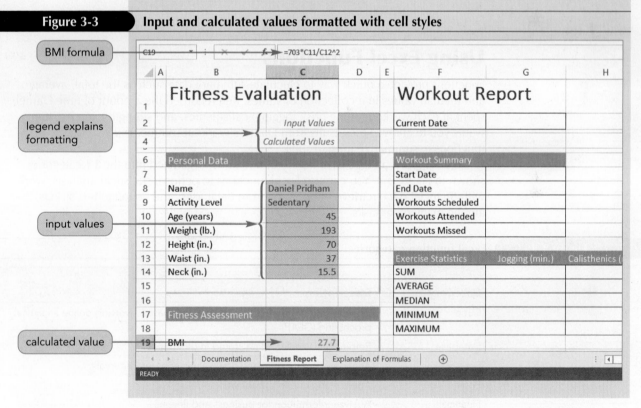

The built-in cell styles are a quick way of marking different types of values in your worksheet. If the formats do not match what you want for your workbook, you can create your own cell styles. However you design your worksheet, your purpose is to make the values easy to interpret.

**PROSKILLS**

*Written Communication: Displaying Significant Digits*

Excel stores numbers with up to 15 digits and displays as many digits as will fit into the cell. So even the result of a simple formula such as =10/3 will display 3.33333333333333 if the cell is wide enough.

A number with 15 digits is difficult to read, and calculations rarely need that level of accuracy. Many scientific disciplines, such as chemistry or physics, have rules for specifying exactly how many digits should be displayed with any calculation. These digits are called **significant digits** because they indicate the accuracy of the measured and calculated values. For example, an input value of 19.32 has four significant digits.

The rules are based on several factors and vary from one discipline to another. Generally, a calculated value should display no more digits than are found in any of the input values. For example, because the input value 19.32 has four significant digits, any calculated value based on that input should have no more than four significant digits. Showing more digits would be misleading because it implies a level of accuracy beyond that which was actually measured.

Because Excel displays calculated values with as many digits as can fit into a cell, you need to know the standards for your profession and change the display of your calculated values accordingly.

# Using Excel Functions

Functions provide a quick way to calculate summary data such as the total, average, and median values in a collection of values. Ken recorded the amount of time Daniel spent at each workout doing brisk jogging, calisthenics, and strength exercise. Ken wants you to analyze the results from Daniel's workout routine. You will use Excel functions to summarize these results.

Excel supports an extensive library of functions, organized into the 12 categories shown in Figure 3-4. You can use Excel functions to perform statistical analysis, work with financial data, retrieve information from databases, and generate text strings, among many other tasks.

| Figure 3-4 | Excel function categories |
| --- | --- |

| Category | Description |
| --- | --- |
| Cube | Retrieve data from multidimensional databases involving online analytical processing (OLAP) |
| Database | Retrieve and analyze data stored in databases |
| Date & Time | Analyze or create date and time values and time intervals |
| Engineering | Analyze engineering problems |
| Financial | Analyze information for business and finance |
| Information | Return information about the format, location, or contents of worksheet cells |
| Logical | Return logical (true-false) values |
| Lookup & Reference | Look up and return data matching a set of specified conditions from a range |
| Math & Trig | Perform math and trigonometry calculations |
| Statistical | Provide statistical analyses of data sets |
| Text | Return text values or evaluate text |
| Web | Provide information on web-based connections |

© 2014 Cengage Learning

The Excel Help system provides information on all of the Excel functions.

## Exploring Function Syntax

Before you use functions, you should understand the function syntax. Recall that the syntax of an Excel function follows the general pattern

FUNCTION(*argument1*,*argument2*,...)

where FUNCTION is the name of the function, and *argument1*, *argument2*, and so forth are arguments used by the function. An argument can be any type of value including text, numbers, cell references, or even other formulas or functions. Not all functions require arguments.

**TIP**

Optional arguments are always placed last in the argument list.

Some arguments are optional. You can include an optional argument in the function or omit it from the function. Some optional arguments have default values associated with them, so that if you omit the optional argument, Excel will use the default value. These tutorials show optional arguments within square brackets along with the argument's default value (if any), as

FUNCTION(*argument1*[, *argument2*=*value2*,...])

where *argument1* is a required argument, *argument2* is optional, and *value2* is the default value for *argument2*. As you work with specific functions, you will learn which arguments are required and which are optional as well as any default values associated with optional arguments.

Figure 3-5 describes some of the more common Math, Trig, and Statistical functions and provides the syntax of those functions.

| Figure 3-5 | Common Math, Trig, and Statistical functions |

| Function | Category | Description |
|---|---|---|
| AVERAGE(*number1*[, *number2*, *number3*, ...]) | Statistical | Calculates the average of a collection of numbers, where *number1*, *number2*, and so forth are numbers or cell references; only *number1* is required |
| COUNT(*value1*[, *value2*, *value3*, ...]) | Statistical | Counts how many cells in a range contain numbers, where *value1*, *value2*, and so forth are text, numbers, or cell references; only *value1* is required |
| COUNTA(*value1*[, *value2*, *value3*, ...]) | Statistical | Counts how many cells are not empty in ranges *value1*, *value2*, and so forth, or how many numbers are listed within *value1*, *value2*, etc. |
| INT(*number*) | Math & Trig | Displays the integer portion of *number* |
| MAX(*number1*[, *number2*, *number3*, ...]) | Statistical | Calculates the maximum value of a collection of numbers, where *number1*, *number2*, and so forth are either numbers or cell references |
| MEDIAN(*number1*[, *number2*, *number3*, ...]) | Statistical | Calculates the median, or middle, value of a collection of numbers, where *number1*, *number2*, and so forth are either numbers or cell references |
| MIN(*number1*[, *number2*, *number3*, ...]) | Statistical | Calculates the minimum value of a collection of numbers, where *number1*, *number2*, and so forth are either numbers or cell references |
| RAND() | Math & Trig | Returns a random number between 0 and 1 |
| ROUND(*number*, *num_digits*) | Math & Trig | Rounds *number* to the number of digits specified by *num_digits* |
| SUM(*number1*[, *number2*, *number3*, ...]) | Math & Trig | Adds a collection of numbers, where *number1*, *number2*, and so forth are either numbers or cell references |

For example, the ROUND function rounds a number to a specified number of decimal places and has the syntax

```
ROUND(number, num_digits)
```

where *number* is the number to be rounded and *num_digits* is the number of decimal places to which you want to round the *number* argument. The following function rounds 2.718282 to two decimal places, resulting in 2.72:

```
ROUND(2.718282, 2)
```

However, you usually reference data values stored in worksheet cells rather than entering the numbers directly in the function. For example, the following function rounds the number in cell A10 to three decimal places:

```
ROUND(A10, 3)
```

Both arguments in the ROUND function are required. An example of a function that uses optional arguments is the AVERAGE function, which can calculate averages from several ranges or entered values. For example, the function

```
AVERAGE(A1:A10)
```

averages the values in the range A1:A10, while the function

```
AVERAGE(A1:A10, C5:C10, E10)
```

includes two optional arguments and averages the values from the cells in range A1:A10, range C5:C10, and cell E10.

Functions can be included as part of larger formulas. The following formula calculates the average of the values in the range A1:A100, and then squares that result using the $\wedge$ operator:

```
=AVERAGE(A1:A100)^2
```

Functions can also be placed inside another function, or **nested**. If a formula contains several functions, Excel starts with the innermost function and then moves outward. For example, the following formula first calculates the average of the values in the range A1:A100 using the AVERAGE function, and then rounds that value to two decimal places:

```
=ROUND(AVERAGE(A1:A100),2)
```

One challenge of nesting functions is to make sure that you include all of the parentheses. You can check this by counting the number of opening parentheses and making sure that number matches the number of closing parentheses. Excel also displays each level of nested parentheses in different colors to make it easier for you to match the opening and closing parentheses in the formula. If the number of parentheses doesn't match, Excel will not accept the formula and will provide a suggestion for how to rewrite the formula so the number of opening and closing parentheses does match.

There are several ways to enter a function. You have already entered a function by typing directly in a cell and using the AutoSum button. Another way to enter a function is with the Quick Analysis tool.

## Entering Functions with the Quick Analysis Tool

The Quick Analysis tool, which you have already used to apply conditional formats that highlight specific data values, can also be used to generate columns and rows of summary statistics that can be used for analyzing data.

Columns F through M in the Fitness Report worksheet will contain the workout report. The range H22:J44 records the number of minutes Daniel spent at each workout jogging, doing calisthenics, and doing strength training. Ken needs to know the total minutes Daniel spent at each exercise to evaluate Daniel's workout effort during the past month. The most efficient way to calculate these totals is with the SUM function. You will use the Quick Analysis tool to enter the SUM function to calculate the total minutes spent at each exercise.

### To calculate the total minutes spent on each exercise:

▶ 1. Select the range **H22:J44** containing the minutes spent on each exercise during each workout. The Quick Analysis button 📧 appears in the lower-right corner of the selected range.

▶ 2. Click the **Quick Analysis** button 📧 (or press the **Ctrl+Q** keys) to display the Quick Analysis tool.

▶ 3. Click the **TOTALS** category to display Quick Analysis tools for calculating totals.

▶ 4. Point to the **Sum** button. Live Preview shows the results of Sum. See Figure 3-6.

| Figure 3-6 | Quick Analysis tool to calculate totals |

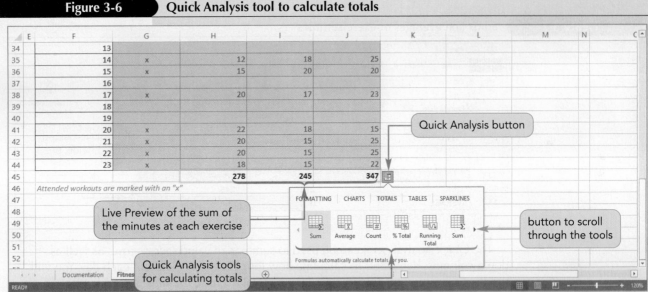

▶ 5. Click **Sum** to enter the SUM function for each cell in the selected range. The results show that Daniel spent 278 minutes jogging, 245 minutes doing calisthenics, and 347 minutes doing strength exercises during the previous month's workouts.

The Quick Analysis tool automatically inserts the formulas containing the SUM function at the bottom of the table. Ken wants you to move this information near the top of the worksheet where it can be viewed first.

▶ 6. Select the range **H45:J45**, and then cut the selected range.

▶ 7. Select cell **G14**, and then paste the formulas with the SUM functions. The totals now appear in the range G14:I14.

The Quick Analysis tool can also be used to quickly calculate averages. An average provides an estimate of the most typical value from a data sample. Ken wants to know the average number of minutes that Daniel spent on each exercise during his sessions.

### To calculate the average minutes spent per exercise:

▶ 1. Select the range **H22:J44**, and then click the **Quick Analysis** button 🔳 that appears in the lower-right corner of the selected range (or press the **Ctrl+Q** keys).

▶ 2. Click the **TOTALS** category, and then click **Average** to enter the AVERAGE function in the range H45:J45 and calculate the average minutes per exercise type.

▶ 3. Cut the formulas from the range **H45:J45**, and then paste them into the range **G15:I15**.

Excel displays the averages to eight decimal places, which implies a far greater accuracy in measuring the exercise time than could be recorded.

▶ 4. In the range **G15:I15**, decrease the number of decimal places displayed to one. On average, Daniel spent about 16.4 minutes per session jogging, 14.4 minutes on calisthenics, and 20.4 minutes on strength exercises. See Figure 3-7.

**Figure 3-7**    Sums and averages of exercise times

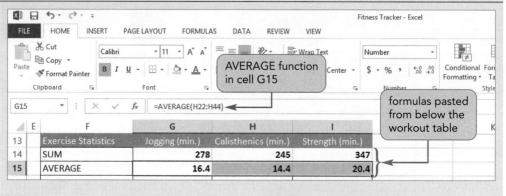

The Quick Analysis tool can be used to summarize values across rows as well as down columns. Ken wants to calculate how long Daniel worked out each day. You will use the Quick Analysis tool to calculate the total exercise minutes per workout.

### To calculate the total workout times per session:

▶ 1. In cell **K21**, enter **Total Minutes** as the heading.

▶ 2. Select the range **H22:J44**, and then open the Quick Analysis tool.

▶ 3. Click the **TOTALS** category, and then click the right scroll button to scroll to the right through the list of calculations.

▶ 4. Click the **Sum** button for the column of summary statistics. SUM functions are entered in the range K22:K44, calculating the sum of the workout minutes per session.

The Quick Analysis tool applies its own style to the formulas it generates. Instead of the bold text, you want the formulas to be formatted with the Calculation style.

▶ 5. Format the range **K22:K44** with the **Calculation** cell style.

6. In cell **J13**, enter **Total Minutes** as the heading.

7. Copy the formulas in the range **I14:I15**, and then paste them into the range **J14:J15** to calculate the sum and average of the total exercise minutes from all of the workouts. As shown in Figure 3-8, Daniel worked out for 870 minutes during the month with an average of 37.8 minutes per workout.

**Figure 3-8** | **Total exercise time per workout**

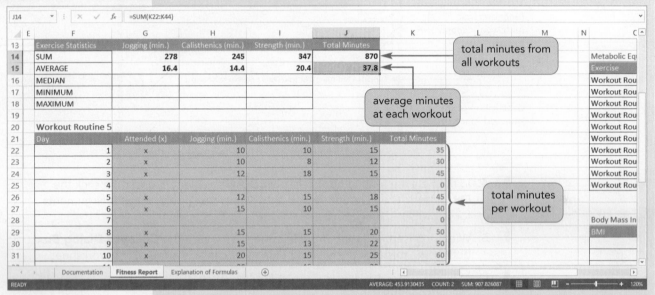

## Entering Functions with the Insert Function Dialog Box

Functions are organized in the Function Library group on the FORMULAS tab. In the Function Library, you can select a function from a function category. You can also open the Insert Function dialog box to search for a particular function based on a description you enter. When you select a function, the Function Arguments dialog box opens, listing all of the arguments associated with that function. Required arguments are in bold type; optional arguments are in normal type.

Ken wants his report to include the median exercise times for the three exercise categories. The **median** provides the middle value from a data sample. You can use the MEDIAN function to determine the middle value in a range of numbers. The Quick Analysis tool doesn't include median, so you will use the Insert Function and Function Arguments dialog boxes to help you correctly insert the MEDIAN function.

### To calculate the median exercise time:

1. Select cell **G16**. This is the cell in which you will enter the MEDIAN function.

2. Click the **Insert Function** button $f_x$ to the left of the formula bar to open the Insert Function dialog box. From the Insert Function dialog box, you can describe the function you want to search for.

3. In the Search for a function box, type **middle value**, and then click the **Go** button. Functions for finding a middle value appear in the Select a function box. The second entry in the list, MEDIAN, is the one you want to use. See Figure 3-9.

**Figure 3-9** **Insert Function dialog box**

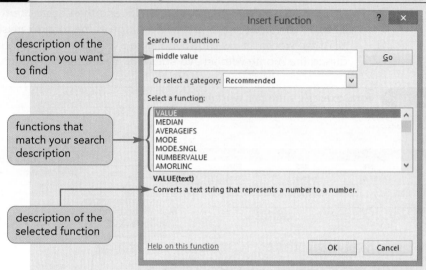

description of the function you want to find

functions that match your search description

description of the selected function

▶ **4.** In the Select a function box, click **MEDIAN** to select it, and then click the **OK** button. The Function Arguments dialog box opens with the arguments for the MEDIAN function.

▶ **5.** With the insertion point in the Number1 box, click the **Collapse Dialog Box** button 🔳 to shrink the dialog box so you can see more of the worksheet.

▶ **6.** In the worksheet, select the range **H22:H44**. These cells contain the times Daniel spent jogging.

▶ **7.** In the Function Arguments dialog box, click the **Expand Dialog Box** button 🔳 to redisplay the entire dialog box. The dialog box now shows a preview of the MEDIAN function and the value it will return to the formula. See Figure 3-10.

**Figure 3-10** **Function Arguments dialog box**

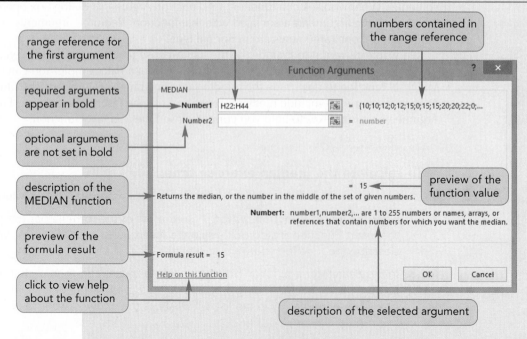

numbers contained in the range reference

range reference for the first argument

required arguments appear in bold

optional arguments are not set in bold

description of the MEDIAN function

preview of the function value

preview of the formula result

click to view help about the function

description of the selected argument

**8.** Click the **OK** button. The formula =MEDIAN(H22:H44) is entered in cell G16, which displays 15 (the median exercise time for jogging).

**9.** Copy cell **G16**, and then paste the copied formula into the range **H16:J16** to calculate the median exercise times for calisthenics, strength training, and all exercises. See Figure 3-11.

| Figure 3-11 | Median exercise times |
| --- | --- |

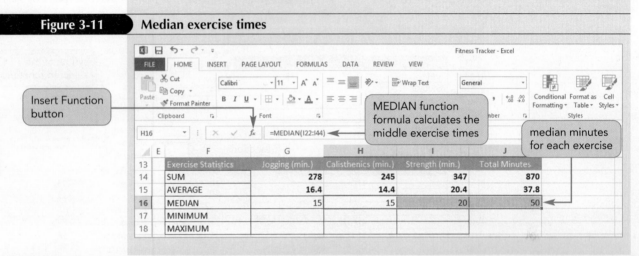

Daniel spent a median time of 15 minutes on calisthenics and 20 minutes on strength training. The median total exercise time was 50 minutes, which is quite a bit higher than the average total exercise time of 37.8 minutes. Why this difference? One reason is that averages are greatly influenced by extremely low or high values. Because Daniel missed several workouts, his exercise time for those days was 0, bringing down the overall average. A median, or middle value, is not as affected by these extreme values, which is why some statisticians advocate medians over averages for analyzing data with widely spaced values.

Ken also wants to know the minimum and maximum minutes Daniel spent exercising during the month. You can access functions by scrolling through the Function Library. You will use this method to enter the functions to calculate the minimum and maximum exercise times.

### To calculate the minimum and maximum minutes of exercise:

**1.** Select cell **G17**, which is where you will calculate the minimum exercise time.

**2.** On the ribbon, click the **FORMULAS** tab to display the function categories in the Function Library.

**3.** Click the **More Functions** button to display the rest of the function categories. Calculations involving maximums and minimums are included with the Statistical functions.

**4.** Click **Statistical** to display the statistical functions, and then scroll down and point to **MIN**. A ScreenTip appears, displaying the MIN function syntax and a description of the function. See Figure 3-12.

**Figure 3-12** MIN function in the Function Library

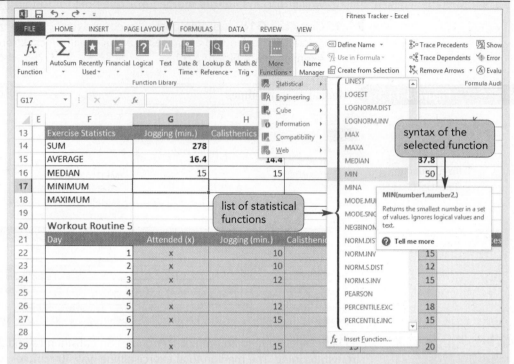

functions organized into categories

list of statistical functions

syntax of the selected function

▶ **5.** Click **MIN** to open the Function Arguments dialog box.

▶ **6.** With the insertion point in the Number1 box, select the range **H22:H44** in the worksheet. These cells store the amount of time Daniel spent jogging.

▶ **7.** Click the **OK** button. The dialog box closes, and the formula =MIN(H22:H44) is entered in cell G17, which displays 10, the minimum minutes that Daniel spent jogging during the month.

▶ **8.** Select cell **G18**, click the **More Functions** button in the Function Library group, click **Statistical**, and then scroll down and click **MAX**. The Function Arguments dialog box opens.

▶ **9.** With the insertion point in the Number1 box, select the range **H22:H44** in the worksheet, and then click the **OK** button. The formula =MAX(H22:H44) is entered in cell G18, which displays 22, the maximum minutes that Daniel spent jogging.

▶ **10.** Copy the range **G17:G18**, and then paste the formulas in the range **H17:J18** to calculate the minimum and maximum times for the other exercises and overall.

▶ **11.** Format the range **G14:J18** with the **Calculation** cell style, and then select cell **F19**. See Figure 3-13.

**Figure 3-13**     Summary statistics of the exercise times

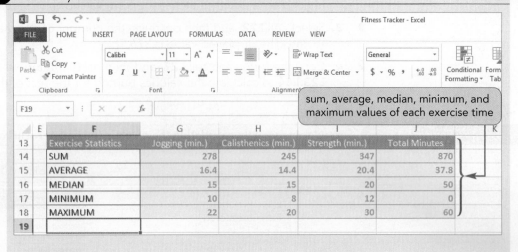

# Referencing Function Results in a Formula

The amount of calories burned during exercise is a function of intensity and time. The more intense the exercise or the longer it lasts, the more calories burned. Ken uses the fitness equation

$$\text{Calories} = \frac{METS \times w \times t}{125.7143}$$

to calculate how many calories will be used during exercise, where *METS* is a metabolic factor that measures the intensity of the exercise, *w* is the individual's weight in pounds, *t* is the exercise time in minutes, and 125.7143 is a constant that converts the quantity into calories. Ken listed the METS values for the different workout routines he created in the range O15:P25 of the Fitness Report worksheet. For example, the METS for Workout Routine 5 is 7.0 and the METS for Workout Routine 10 is 16.0. Using the METS information and the weight and exercise times, you can calculate the total calories burned during each workout.

The fitness equation that calculates calories burned during the first workout translates into the formula

```
=P20*C11*K22/125.7143
```

where P20 references the cell with the METS for Workout Routine 5, C11 references the cell that stores Daniel's weight, and K22 references the cell that calculates the total exercise time of the first workout.

You will enter this formula in cell L22, and then copy it to the remaining cells in the column to calculate the calories burned during each workout.

## To calculate the calories burned during Daniel's first workout:

1. In cell **L21**, enter **Calories Burned** as the label.

2. In cell **L22**, enter the formula **=P20*C11*K22/125.7143** to calculate the calories Daniel burned at his first workout. Cell P20 stores the METS value, cell C11 contains Daniel's weight, and cell K22 is the total exercise time for Workout Routine 5 on the first day of the month. Cell L22 displays 376.1306391, which is the number of calories burned at the first workout.

**Trouble?** If your value differs from 376.1306391, edit your formula as needed so it exactly matches the formula shown in Step 2.

▶ **3.** Select cell **L22**, and then decrease the number of decimal places shown to one. The displayed value is 376.1.

▶ **4.** Copy the formula in cell **L22**, and then paste the formula to the range **L23:L44** to calculate the calories burned for the rest of the workouts. See Figure 3-14.

**Figure 3-14**    **Formulas incorrectly calculating the calories burned per workout**

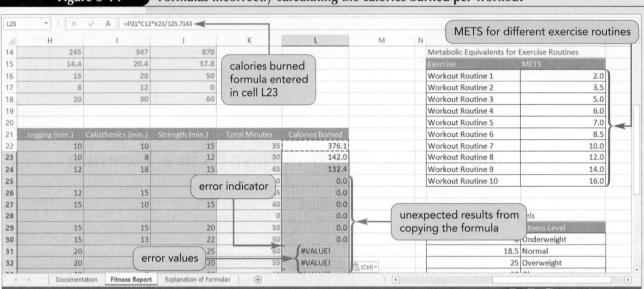

The first few values seem somewhat reasonable, but then several workouts show no calories burned. These are followed by cells displaying #VALUE! rather than a number. Obviously something went wrong when you copied and pasted the formula.

# Interpreting Error Values

The #VALUE! that appears in some of the cells in the Fitness Report worksheet is an error value. An **error value** indicates that some part of a formula is preventing Excel from returning a calculated value. An error value begins with a pound sign (#) followed by an error name that indicates the type of error. Figure 3-15 describes common error values that you might see instead of the results from formulas and functions. For example, the error value #VALUE! indicates that the wrong type of value is used in a function or formula. You will need to examine the formulas in the cells with error values to determine exactly what went wrong.

| Figure 3-15 | Excel error values |
| --- | --- |

| Error Value | Description |
| --- | --- |
| #DIV/0! | The formula or function contains a number divided by 0. |
| #NAME? | Excel doesn't recognize text in the formula or function, such as when the function name is misspelled. |
| #N/A | A value is not available to a function or formula, which can occur when a workbook is initially set up prior to entering actual data values. |
| #NULL! | A formula or function requires two cell ranges to intersect, but they don't. |
| #NUM! | Invalid numbers are used in a formula or function, such as text entered in a function that requires a number. |
| #REF! | A cell reference used in a formula or function is no longer valid, which can occur when the cell used by the function was deleted from the worksheet. |
| #VALUE! | The wrong type of argument is used in a function or formula. This can occur when you reference a text value for an argument that should be strictly numeric. |

© 2014 Cengage Learning

The error value messages are not particularly descriptive or helpful. To help you locate the error, an error indicator appears in the upper-left corner of the cell with the error value. When you point to the error indicator, a ScreenTip appears with more information about the source of the error.

**INSIGHT**

### Deciding When to Correct an Error Value

An error value does not mean that you must correct the cell's formula or function. Some error values appear simply because you have not yet entered any data into the workbook. For example, if you use the AVERAGE function to find the average value of an empty column, the #DIV/0! error value appears because the formula cannot calculate the average of a collection of empty cells. However, as soon as you begin entering data, the #DIV/0! message will disappear.

Ken wants you to figure out why the #VALUE error value appears in some of the cells where you copied the calories burned formula. To figure this out, you will examine the formula in cell L31, which is the first cell that displays the error value instead of the expected number results.

### To view the formula in cell L31 that results in an error value:

1. Double-click cell **L31**, which displays the #VALUE! error value. In Edit mode, the cell references used in the formula are color coded to match the corresponding cells, making it easier to see which cells are used in the formula.

2. Observe that cell L31 contains the formula =P29*C20*K31/125.7143.

**3.** Look at the first cell reference in the formula. The first cell reference is to cell P29 containing the text "Fitness Level" instead of cell P20 containing the METS value for Workout Routine 5. The formula is attempting to multiply the text in cell P29, but multiplication can be done only with numbers. This is the problem causing the #VALUE! error value.

**4.** Look at the second cell reference in the formula. The second cell reference is to cell C20, an empty cell, rather than to cell C11 containing Daniel's weight.

**5.** Look at the third cell reference in the formula. The third cell reference is to cell K31, which contains the total exercise times for the tenth workout—the correct cell reference.

# Exploring Cell References

Most workbooks include data entered in cells that are then referenced in formulas to perform calculations on that data. The formulas can be simple, such as the formulas you entered to add the total minutes of each workout, or they can be more complex, such as the formulas you entered to calculate the calories burned during each workout. Each of these formulas includes one or more cell references.

## Understanding Relative References

When a formula includes a cell reference, Excel interprets that cell reference as being located relative to the position of the current cell. For example, Excel interprets the following formula entered in cell A1 to mean "add the value of the cell one column to the right of this cell to the value of the cell one column to the right and one row below this cell":

```
=B1+B2
```

This relative interpretation is retained when the formula is copied to a new location. So, if the formula in cell A1 is copied to cell A3 (two rows down in the worksheet), the relative references in the formula also shift two rows down, resulting in the following formula:

```
=B3+B4
```

Figure 3-16 shows another example of how relative references change when a formula is copied to new cell locations. In this figure, the formula =A4 entered in cell D7 displays 10, which is the number entered in cell A4. When pasted to a new location, each of the pasted formulas contains a reference to a cell that is three rows up and three rows to the left of the current cell's location.

Figure 3-16    Formulas using relative references

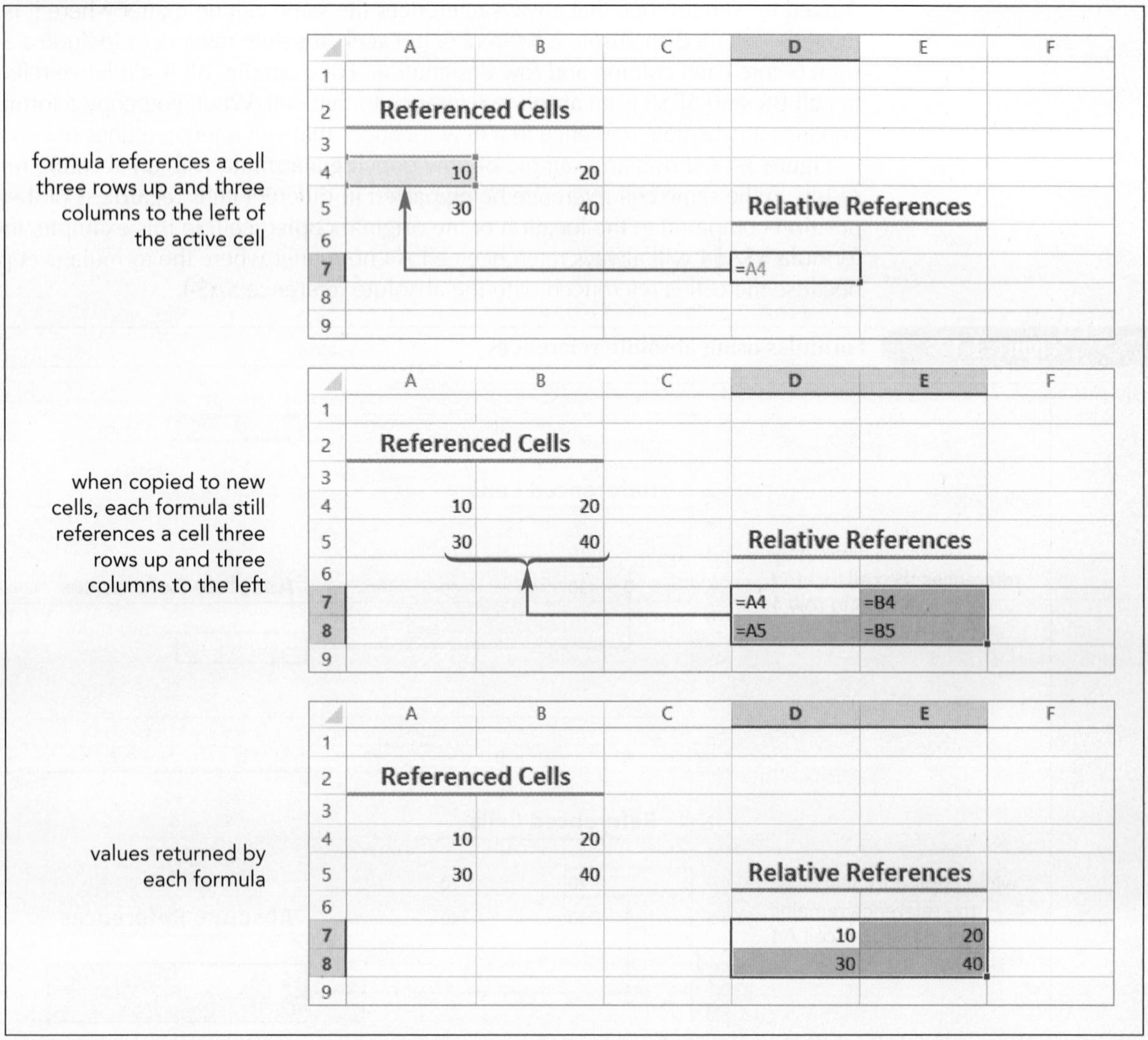

formula references a cell three rows up and three columns to the left of the active cell

when copied to new cells, each formula still references a cell three rows up and three columns to the left

values returned by each formula

This explains what happened with the relative references you used to calculate calories burned for each workout. When you entered the following formula in cell L22, cell C11 correctly references the client's weight and the other cells correctly reference the METS for Workout Routine 5 and the total exercise time:

```
=P20*C11*K22/125.7143
```

When you copied the formula down to cell L31, all of the cell references contained in that formula also shifted down nine rows, resulting in the following formula, which accurately references the total exercise time for the corresponding workout but no longer references Daniel's weight or the METS for Workout Routine 5—both of which are necessary for the calculation:

```
=P29*C20*K31/125.7143
```

What you need is a cell reference that remains fixed when the formula is copied to a new location.

## Understanding Absolute References

A fixed reference—one that always references the same cell no matter where it is moved—is called an **absolute reference**. In Excel, absolute references include a $ (dollar sign) before each column and row designation. For example, B8 is a relative reference to cell B8, and $B$8 is an absolute reference to that cell. When you copy a formula that contains an absolute reference to a new location, that cell reference does not change.

Figure 3-17 shows an example of how copying a formula with an absolute reference results in the same cell reference being pasted in different cells regardless of their position compared to the location of the original copied cell. In this example, the formula =$A$4 will always reference cell A4 no matter where the formula is copied to, because the cell is referenced with the absolute reference $A$4.

**Figure 3-17**     **Formulas using absolute references**

formula absolutely references the cell located in column A and row 4

when copied to new cells, the reference remains fixed on cell A4

values returned by each formula

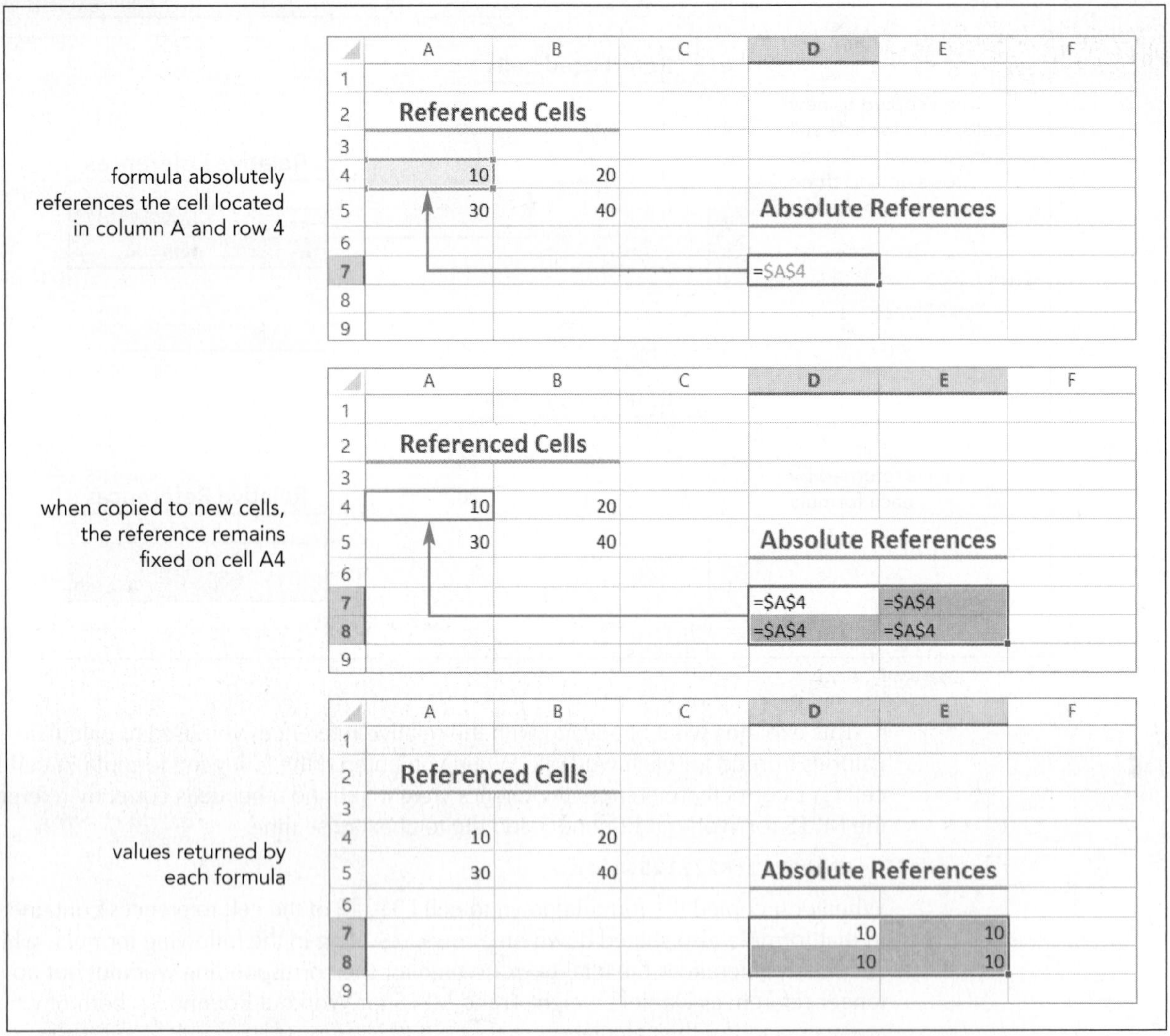

© 2014 Cengage Learning

## Understanding Mixed References

A formula can also include cell references that are mixed. A **mixed reference** contains both relative and absolute references. For example, a mixed reference for cell A2 can be either $A2 or A$2. In the mixed reference $A2, the reference to column A is absolute and the reference to row 2 is relative. In the mixed reference A$2, the column reference is relative and the row reference is absolute. A mixed reference "locks" one part of the cell reference while the other part can change. When you copy and paste a cell with a mixed reference to a new location, the absolute portion of the cell reference remains fixed and the relative portion shifts along with the new location of the pasted cell.

Figure 3-18 shows an example of using mixed references to complete a multiplication table. The first cell in the table, cell B3, contains the formula =$A3*B$2, which multiplies the first column entry (A3) by the first row entry (B2), returning 1. When this formula is copied to another cell, the absolute portions of the cell references remain unchanged and the relative portions of the references change. For example, if the formula is copied to cell E6, the first mixed cell reference changes to $A6 because the column reference is absolute and the row reference is relative, and the second cell reference changes to E$2 because the row reference is absolute and the column reference is relative. The result is that cell E6 contains the formula =$A6*E$2 and returns 16. Other cells in the multiplication table are similarly modified so that each entry returns the multiplication of the intersection of the row and column headings.

**Figure 3-18**    **Formulas using mixed references**

mixed cell reference that fixes the column reference for the first term and the row reference for the second term

| | A | B | C | D | E | F | G |
|---|---|---|---|---|---|---|---|
| 1 | | | Multiplication Table | | | | |
| 2 | | 1 | 2 | 3 | 4 | 5 | |
| 3 | 1 | =$A3*B$2 | | | | | |
| 4 | 2 | | | | | | |
| 5 | 3 | | | | | | |
| 6 | 4 | | | | | | |
| 7 | 5 | | | | | | |
| 8 | | | | | | | |

when copied to the B3:B7 range, the fixed references remain unchanged and the relative references are shifted

| | A | B | C | D | E | F | G |
|---|---|---|---|---|---|---|---|
| 1 | | | Multiplication Table | | | | |
| 2 | | 1 | 2 | 3 | 4 | 5 | |
| 3 | 1 | =$A3*B$2 | =$A3*C$2 | =$A3*D$2 | =$A3*E$2 | =$A3*F$2 | |
| 4 | 2 | =$A4*B$2 | =$A4*C$2 | =$A4*D$2 | =$A4*E$2 | =$A4*F$2 | |
| 5 | 3 | =$A5*B$2 | =$A5*C$2 | =$A5*D$2 | =$A5*E$2 | =$A5*F$2 | |
| 6 | 4 | =$A6*B$2 | =$A6*C$2 | =$A6*D$2 | =$A6*E$2 | =$A6*F$2 | |
| 7 | 5 | =$A7*B$2 | =$A7*C$2 | =$A7*D$2 | =$A7*E$2 | =$A7*F$2 | |
| 8 | | | | | | | |

values returned by each formula

| | A | B | C | D | E | F | G |
|---|---|---|---|---|---|---|---|
| 1 | | | Multiplication Table | | | | |
| 2 | | 1 | 2 | 3 | 4 | 5 | |
| 3 | 1 | 1 | 2 | 3 | 4 | 5 | |
| 4 | 2 | 2 | 4 | 6 | 8 | 10 | |
| 5 | 3 | 3 | 6 | 9 | 12 | 15 | |
| 6 | 4 | 4 | 8 | 12 | 16 | 20 | |
| 7 | 5 | 5 | 10 | 15 | 20 | 25 | |
| 8 | | | | | | | |

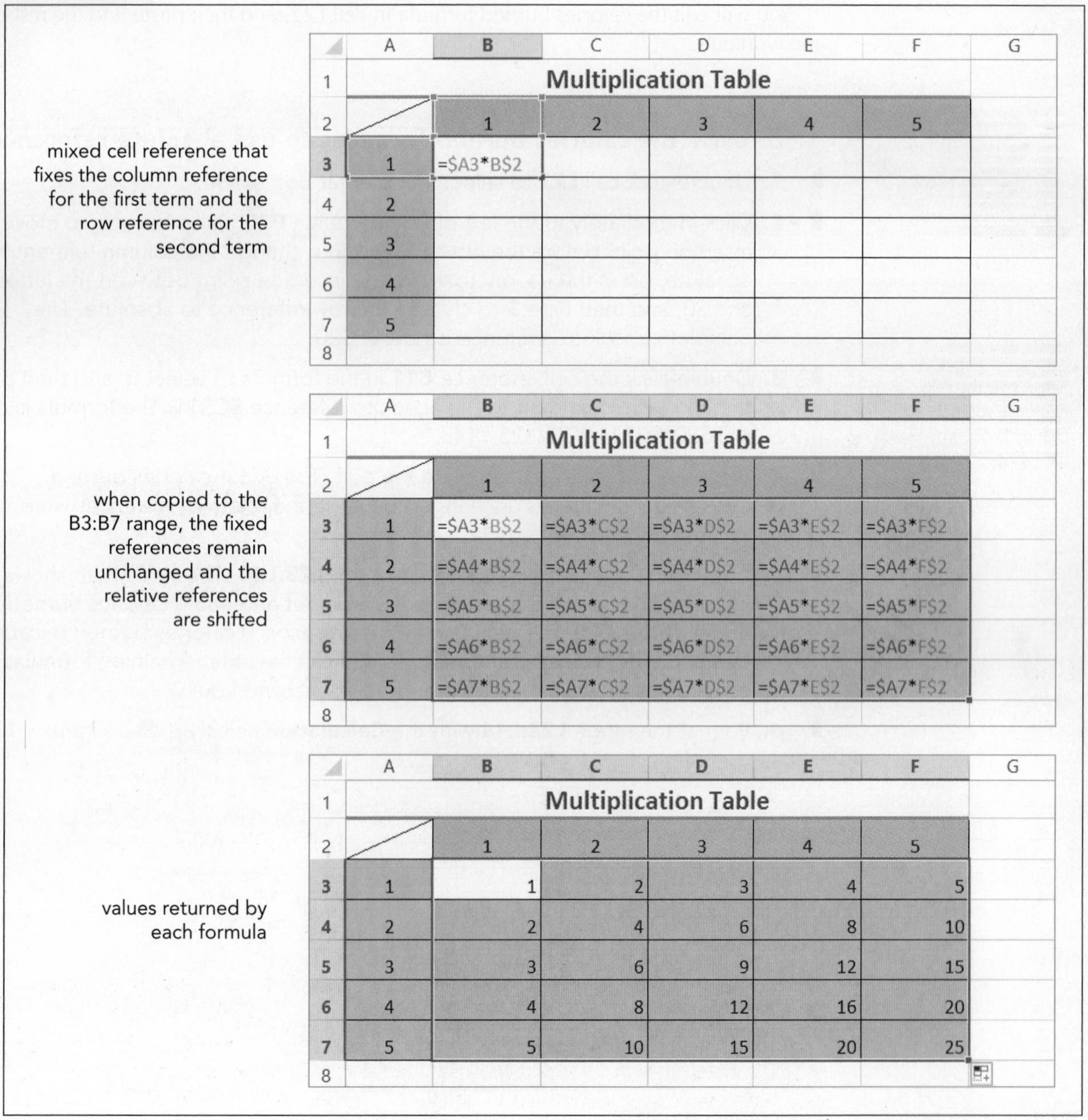

## Changing Cell References in a Formula

You can quickly switch a cell reference from relative to absolute or mixed. Rather than retyping the formula, you can select the cell reference in Edit mode and then press the F4 key. As you press the F4 key, Excel cycles through the different reference types—starting with the relative reference, followed by the absolute reference, then to a mixed reference with the row absolute, and finally to a mixed reference with the column absolute.

Ken wants you to fix the problem with the cell references in the calories burned formulas. You need to revise the formula to use absolute references to Daniel's weight and the METS value that will not change when the formula is copied to new locations. You will leave the relative reference to the total exercise time so that the copied formulas will retrieve the exercise times from the corresponding workouts. The revised formula in cell L22 uses an absolute reference to the METS values in $P$20 and an absolute reference to Daniel's weight in $C$11, as follows:

```
=$P$20*$C$11*K22/125.7143
```

You will edit the calories burned formula in cell L22, and then paste it to the rest of the workouts.

### To revise the calories burned formulas to use absolute references:

1. Double-click cell **L22** to select it and enter Edit mode.

2. Click immediately to the left of cell reference **P20** in the formula to move the insertion point before the letter P, type **$** to change the column reference to absolute, press the → key to move the insertion point between the letter P and 20, and then type **$** to change the row reference to absolute. The complete absolute reference is now $P$20.

3. Double-click the cell reference **C11** in the formula to select it, and then press the **F4** key to change it to the absolute reference $C$11. The formula is now =$P$20*$C$11*K22/125.7143.

Select only the cell reference you want to change before you press the F4 key.

4. Press the **Enter** key to complete the edit. The 376.1 calories burned displayed in the cell is unchanged because the relative references were accurate in this first formula.

5. Copy cell **L22** and paste it into the range **L23:L44**. The worksheet shows 322.4 calories burned for the second workout and 483.6 calories burned for the third workout. The next row in the list shows 0 calories burned because Daniel did not work out that day. As you can see, the remaining formulas now correctly calculate the calories burned at each workout.

6. Format the range **L22:L44** with the **Calculation** cell style. See Figure 3-19.

**Figure 3-19**    **Formulas with absolute and relative references**

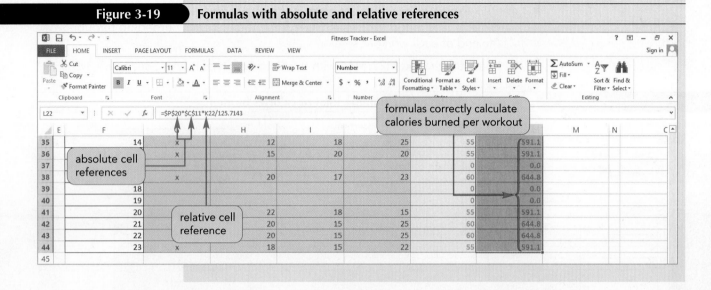

## Planning Which Cell Reference to Use in a Formula

You can include the correct type of cell reference in a formula as you create the formula. This requires a little more thought up front, as you consider how each cell in a formula needs to be referenced before you create the formula. Ken wants you to create a running total of the calories burned during each workout. You can use the SUM function with a combination of absolute and relative cell references to add the values in a range. The formula to calculate the total in the first cell is:

    =SUM($L$22:L22)

In this formula, the starting cell of the range is fixed at cell L22, but the ending cell of the range is relative. When you copy this formula down the column, the starting cell remains absolutely referenced to cell L22, but the ending cell changes to include the current row. For example, when the formula is pasted three rows down, the formula changes to add the numbers in cells L22, L23, L24, and L25, as follows:

    =SUM($L$22:L25)

Continuing in this way, the last cell will contain the sum of all of the calories burned totals using the following formula:

    =SUM($L$22:L44)

Instead of entering the formulas yourself, you can use the Quick Analysis tool to calculate the total calories burned up through the end of each workout session.

### To calculate the running total of calories burned:

▶ 1. In cell **M21**, enter **Calories Subtotal** as the label.

▶ 2. Select the range **L22:L44** containing the calories burned during each workout, and then click the **Quick Analysis** button 📲 (or press the **Ctrl+Q** keys).

▶ 3. Click the **TOTALS** category, and then scroll right to the end of the TOTALS tools.

4. Click **Running Total** (the last entry in the list, which is the Running Total of a column). The range M22:M44 displays the total calories burned up through the end of each workout session.

5. Format the range **M22:M44** with the **Calculation** cell style. See Figure 3-20.

**Figure 3-20**    Formulas calculating the running total of calories burned

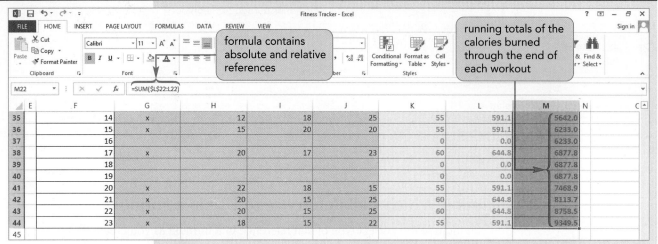

Daniel burned 698.5 calories during the first two workouts and more than 1180 calories after the first three workouts. The formula used to calculate the running totals for the column includes both absolute and relative references. You will review the formulas in column M to see the formulas calculating the running totals.

## To view the formulas for the running totals:

1. Select cell **M22**, and then review the formula, which is =SUM($L$22:L22). Notice the absolute and relative references to cell L22.

2. Select cell **M23**, and then review the formula, which is =SUM($L$22:L23). Notice that the absolute reference to cell L22 remains unchanged, but the relative reference is now cell L23, expanding the range being added with the SUM function.

3. Select each cell in column M and review its formula, noticing that the absolute reference $L$22 always appears as the top cell of the range but the relative reference for the last cell of the range changes.

4. Save the workbook.

You can see that the running total is calculated with the SUM function using a combination of absolute and relative cell references. The top of the range used in the SUM function is locked at cell L22, but the bottom of the range is relative, expanding in size as the formula was copied down column M. Entered this way, with absolute and relative cell references, the SUM function calculates partial sums, providing the total calories burned up through the end of each workout session.

INSIGHT

## Understanding When to Use Relative, Absolute, and Mixed References

Part of effective workbook design is knowing when to use relative, absolute, and mixed references. Use relative references when you want to apply the same formula with input cells that share a common layout or pattern. Relative references are commonly used when copying a formula that calculates summary statistics across columns or rows of data values. Use absolute references when you want your copied formulas to always refer to the same cell. This usually occurs when a cell contains a constant value, such as a tax rate, that will be referenced in formulas throughout the worksheet. Mixed references are seldom used other than when creating tables of calculated values such as a multiplication table in which the values of the formula or function can be found at the intersection of the rows and columns of the table.

So far, you have entered the fitness formulas and summary statistics in the Fitness Tracker workbook. In the next session, you will explore date and time functions, and then look up values to use in formulas and functions.

REVIEW

## Session 3.1 Quick Check

1. What is an optional argument? What does Excel do if you do not include an optional argument?
2. Write the function to return the middle value from the values in the range X1:X10.
3. Write the function to round the value in cell A5 to the fourth decimal place.
4. The range of a set of values is defined as the maximum value minus the minimum value. Write the formula to calculate the range of values in the range Y1:Y10.
5. If cell A11 contains the formula =SUME(A1:A10), what error value will appear in the cell?
6. You need to reference cell Q57 in a formula. What is its relative reference? What is its absolute reference? What are the two mixed references?
7. If cell R10 contains the formula =R1+R2, which is then copied to cell S20, what formula is entered in cell S20?
8. If cell V10 contains the formula = AVERAGE($U1:$U5), which is then copied to cell W20, what formula is entered in cell W20?

# Session 3.2 Visual Overview:

A **lookup table** stores the data you want to retrieve in categories. This is a vertical lookup table that organizes the categories in the first column of the table.

**Compare values** are the categories located in the first column of the lookup table and are used for matching to a lookup value specified by the user.

**Return values** are the data values you want to retrieve from the lookup table and are located in the second and subsequent columns.

A **lookup value** is the category you want to find in a lookup table.

The **VLOOKUP function** returns values from a vertical lookup table by specifying the lookup value to match to a compare value, the location of the lookup table, and the column in the table that contains the return values.

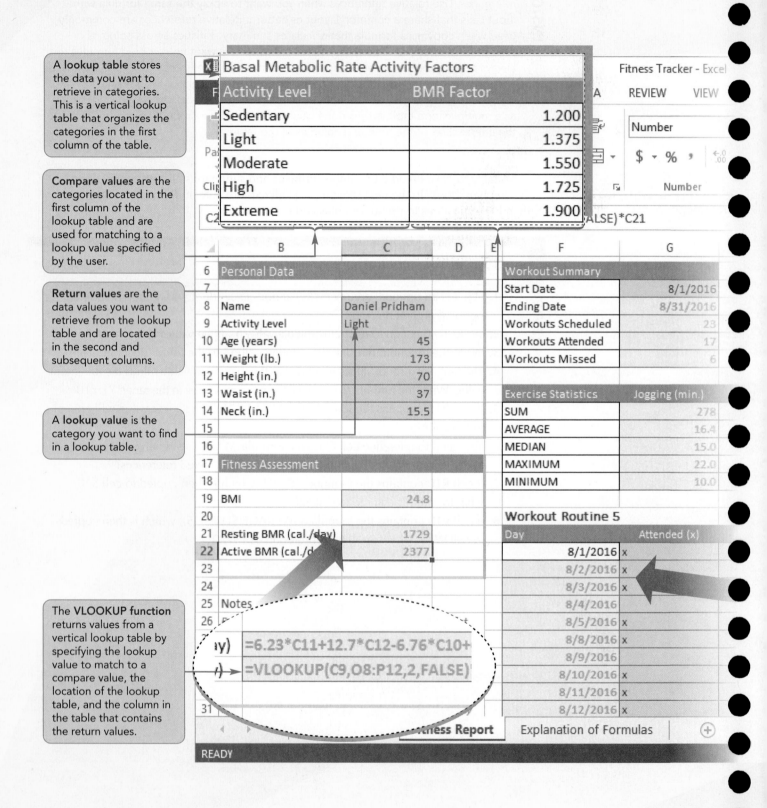

**Basal Metabolic Rate Activity Factors**

| Activity Level | BMR Factor |
|---|---|
| Sedentary | 1.200 |
| Light | 1.375 |
| Moderate | 1.550 |
| High | 1.725 |
| Extreme | 1.900 |

Fitness Tracker - Excel

REVIEW    VIEW

Number

$ ▾ % ,    ₀₀

Number

C2... ...LSE)*C21

| | B | C | D | E | F | G |
|---|---|---|---|---|---|---|
| 6 | Personal Data | | | | Workout Summary | |
| 7 | | | | | Start Date | 8/1/2016 |
| 8 | Name | Daniel Pridham | | | Ending Date | 8/31/2016 |
| 9 | Activity Level | Light | | | Workouts Scheduled | 23 |
| 10 | Age (years) | 45 | | | Workouts Attended | 17 |
| 11 | Weight (lb.) | 173 | | | Workouts Missed | 6 |
| 12 | Height (in.) | 70 | | | | |
| 13 | Waist (in.) | 37 | | | Exercise Statistics | Jogging (min.) |
| 14 | Neck (in.) | 15.5 | | | SUM | 278 |
| 15 | | | | | AVERAGE | 16.4 |
| 16 | | | | | MEDIAN | 15.0 |
| 17 | Fitness Assessment | | | | MAXIMUM | 22.0 |
| 18 | | | | | MINIMUM | 10.0 |
| 19 | BMI | 24.8 | | | | |
| 20 | | | | | Workout Routine 5 | |
| 21 | Resting BMR (cal./day) | 1729 | | | Day | Attended (x) |
| 22 | Active BMR (cal./d... | 2377 | | | 8/1/2016 | x |
| 23 | | | | | 8/2/2016 | x |
| 24 | | | | | 8/3/2016 | x |
| 25 | Notes | | | | 8/4/2016 | |
| 26 | | | | | 8/5/2016 | x |
| 2... | | | | | 8/8/2016 | x |
| | | | | | 8/9/2016 | |
| | | | | | 8/10/2016 | x |
| | | | | | 8/11/2016 | x |
| 31 | | | | | 8/12/2016 | x |

$=6.23*C11+12.7*C12-6.76*C10+$

$=VLOOKUP(C9,O8:P12,2,FALSE)$

...ness Report    Explanation of Formulas    ⊕

READY

# Logical and Lookup Functions

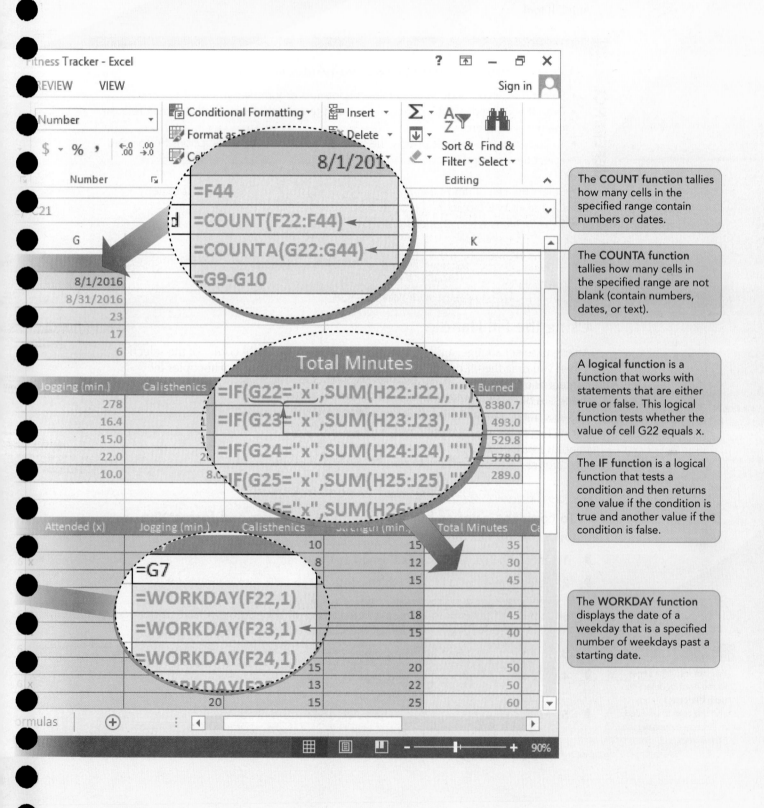

The **COUNT function** tallies how many cells in the specified range contain numbers or dates.

The **COUNTA function** tallies how many cells in the specified range are not blank (contain numbers, dates, or text).

A **logical function** is a function that works with statements that are either true or false. This logical function tests whether the value of cell G22 equals x.

The **IF function** is a logical function that tests a condition and then returns one value if the condition is true and another value if the condition is false.

The **WORKDAY function** displays the date of a weekday that is a specified number of weekdays past a starting date.

# AutoFilling Formulas and Data

**AutoFill** provides a quick way to enter content and formatting in cells based on existing entries in adjacent cells. Ken wants you to include summary statistics for calories burned across all of the scheduled workouts. To add these statistics, you'll use the AutoFill tool.

---

**REFERENCE**

## Copying Formulas and Formats with AutoFill

- Select the cell or range that contains the formula or formulas you want to copy.
- Drag the fill handle in the direction you want to copy the formula(s), and then release the mouse button.
- To copy only the formats or only the formulas, click the Auto Fill Options button and select the appropriate option.

*or*

- Select the cell or range that contains the formula or formulas you want to copy.
- On the HOME tab, in the Editing group, click the Fill button.
- Select a fill direction and fill type.

*or*

- On the HOME tab, in the Editing group, click Series.
- Enter the desired fill series options, and then click the OK button.

---

## Using the Fill Handle

After you select a range, a **fill handle** appears in the lower-right corner of the selection. When you drag the fill handle over an adjacent cell or range, AutoFill copies the content and formats from the original cell or range into the adjacent cell or range. This process is often more efficient than the two-step process of copying and pasting.

Ken wants you to calculate the same summary statistics for the calories burned during the workouts as you did for the total minutes of each workout. Because the total minutes formulas use relative references, you can use the fill handle to copy these for the calories burned statistics.

---

### To copy the calories burned summary statistics and formatting with the fill handle:

▶ 1. In cell **K13**, enter **Calories Burned** as the label.

▶ 2. Select the range **J14:J18**, which contains the cells with formulas for calculating the sum, average, median, minimum, and maximum total minutes. A fill handle appears in the lower-right corner of the selected range, directly above and to the left of the Quick Analysis button.

▶ 3. Point to the **fill handle**. The pointer changes to ✚.

▶ 4. Click and drag the fill handle over the range **K14:K18**. A solid outline appears around the selected range as you move the pointer.

▶ 5. Release the mouse button. The selected range is filled in with the formulas and formatting from the range J14:J18, and the Auto Fill Options button appears in the lower-right corner of the selected cells. See Figure 3-21.

**TIP**

You can also fill a series to the right by selecting both the cells to copy and the cells to be filled in, and then pressing the Ctrl+R keys.

**Figure 3-21**    Formulas and formatting copied with AutoFill

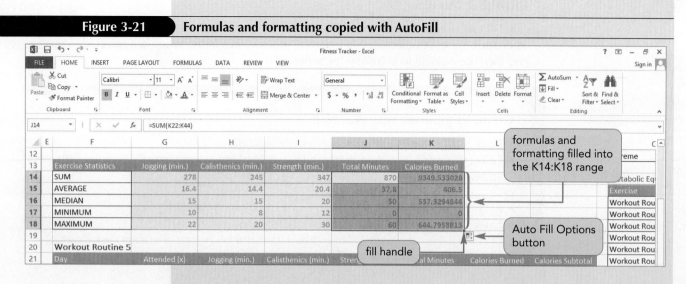

**6.** Format the range **K14:K18** to display one decimal place.

Based on the summary statistics, Ken can see that Daniel burned 9349.5 calories during the month, burned an average of 406.5 calories per session, burned a median of 537.3 calories per session, and burned a minimum of 0.0 calories and a maximum of 644.8 calories per session during the month.

## Using the Auto Fill Options Button

By default, AutoFill copies both the content and the formatting of the original range to the selected range. However, sometimes you might want to copy only the content or only the formatting. The Auto Fill Options button that appears after you release the mouse button lets you specify what is copied. As shown in Figure 3-22, clicking this button provides a menu of AutoFill options. The Copy Cells option, which is the default, copies both the content and the formatting. The Fill Formatting Only option copies the formatting into the selected cells but not any content. The Fill Without Formatting option copies the content but not the formatting.

**Figure 3-22**    Auto Fill Options button

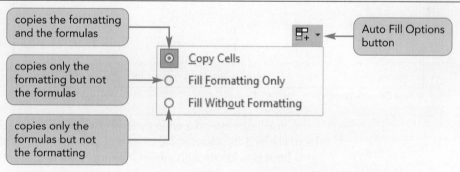

Because you want to copy the content and the formatting of the summary statistics, you don't need to use the Auto Fill Options button.

## Filling a Series

AutoFill can also be used to create a series of numbers, dates, or text based on a pattern. To create a series of numbers, you enter the initial values in the series in a selected range and then use AutoFill to complete the series.

Figure 3-23 shows how AutoFill can be used to insert the numbers from 1 to 10 in a selected range. You enter the first few numbers in the range A2:A4 to establish the pattern you want AutoFill to use—consecutive positive numbers in this example. Then, you select the range and drag its fill handle over the cells where you want the pattern continued—in this case, the range A5:A11—and Excel fills in the rest of the series.

| **Figure 3-23** | **AutoFill extends a numeric sequence** |

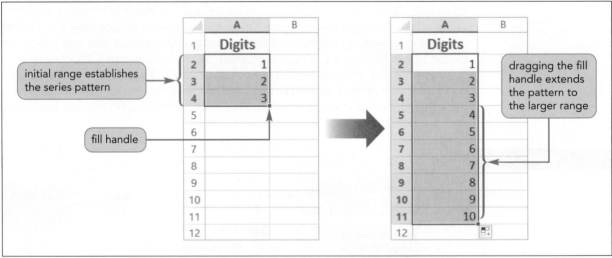

© 2014 Cengage Learning

AutoFill can extend a wide variety of series, including dates and times and patterned text. Figure 3-24 shows some examples of series that AutoFill can generate. In each case, you must provide enough information for AutoFill to identify the pattern. AutoFill can recognize some patterns from only a single entry—such as Jan or January, to create a series of month abbreviations or names, or Mon or Monday, to create a series of the days of the week. A text pattern that includes text and a number such as Region 1, Region 2, and so on can also be automatically extended using AutoFill. You can start the series at any point, such as Weds, June, or Region 10, and AutoFill will complete the next days, months, or text.

| Figure 3-24 | AutoFill extends numbers, dates and times, and patterned text |

| Type | Initial Pattern | Extended Series |
|------|-----------------|-----------------|
| Numbers | 1, 2, 3 | 4, 5, 6, .. |
| | 2, 4, 6 | 8, 10, 12, ... |
| Dates and Times | Jan | Feb, Mar, Apr, ... |
| | January | February, March, April, ... |
| | 15-Jan, 15-Feb | 15-Mar, 15-Apr, 15-May, ... |
| | 12/30/2016 | 12/31/2016, 1/1/2017, 1/2/2017, ... |
| | 12/31/2016, 1/31/2017 | 2/29/2017, 3/31/2017, 4/30/2017, ... |
| | Mon | Tue, Wed, Thu, ... |
| | Monday | Tuesday, Wednesday, Thursday, ... |
| | 11:00AM | 12:00PM, 1:00PM, 2:00PM, ... |
| Patterned Text | 1st period | 2nd period, 3rd period, 4th period, ... |
| | Region 1 | Region 2, Region 3, Region 4, ... |
| | Quarter 3 | Quarter 4, Quarter 1, Quarter 2, ... |
| | Qtr3 | Qtr4, Qtr1, Qtr2, ... |

© 2014 Cengage Learning

Ken wants you to fill in the dates of the workouts, replacing the numbers in the range F22:F44. You will use AutoFill to insert the calendar dates starting with 8/1/2016.

### To use AutoFill to enter the calendar dates:

1. In cell **F22**, enter **8/1/2016**. This is the first date you want to use for the series.

2. Select cell **F22** to select the cell with the first date in the series.

3. Drag the fill handle over the range **F23:F44**.

4. Release the mouse button. AutoFill enters the calendar dates ending with 8/23/2016 in cell F44.

**TIP**

You can also fill a series down by selecting both the cells to copy and the cells to be filled in, and then pressing the Ctrl+D keys.

For more complex AutoFill patterns, you can use the Series dialog box to specify a linear or growth series for numbers; a date series for dates that increase by day, weekday, month, or year; or an AutoFill series for patterned text. With numbers, you can also specify the step value (how much each number increases over the previous entry) and a stop value (the endpoint for the entire series).

Ken notices that the workout dates are wrong in the Fitness Report worksheet. Fit Fathers meets only Monday through Friday. He asks you to change the fill pattern to include only weekdays. You will use the Series dialog box to set the fill pattern for the rest of the weekdays in the month.

### To fill the dates of weekdays in August:

1. Make sure the range **F22:F44** is selected. Cell F22 contains the first value for the series that will be entered in the range F23:F44.

2. On the HOME tab, in the Editing group, click the **Fill** button, and then click **Series**. The Series dialog box opens.

3. In the Type section, make sure that the **Date** option button is selected.

> **4.** In the Date unit section, click the **Weekday** option button so that the series includes only dates for Mondays through Fridays. See Figure 3-25.

**Figure 3-25** | **Series dialog box**

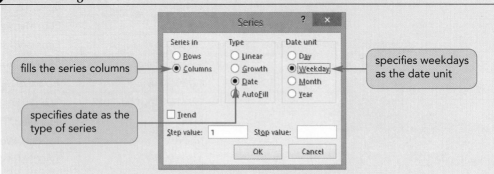

fills the series columns

specifies date as the type of series

specifies weekdays as the date unit

> **5.** Click the **OK** button. The dates of weekdays in August are filled into the selected range ending with 8/31/2016. See Figure 3-26.

**Figure 3-26** | **Weekday values filled in**

only weekdays are entered in the selected range

| | E | F | G | H | I | J | |
|---|---|---|---|---|---|---|---|
| 20 | | Workout Routine 5 | | | | | |
| 21 | | Day | Attended (x) | Jogging (min.) | Calisthenics (min.) | Strength (min.) | Tot |
| 22 | | 8/1/2016 | x | 10 | 10 | 15 | |
| 23 | | 8/2/2016 | x | 10 | 8 | 12 | |
| 24 | | 8/3/2016 | x | 12 | 18 | 15 | |
| 25 | | 8/4/2016 | | | | | |
| 26 | | 8/5/2016 | x | 12 | 15 | 18 | |
| 27 | | 8/8/2016 | x | 15 | 10 | 15 | |
| 28 | | 8/9/2016 | | | | | |
| 29 | | 8/10/2016 | x | 15 | 15 | 20 | |
| 30 | | 8/11/2016 | x | 15 | 13 | 22 | |
| 31 | | 8/12/2016 | x | 20 | 15 | 25 | |
| 32 | | 8/15/2016 | x | 20 | 15 | 20 | |
| 33 | | 8/16/2016 | x | 22 | 8 | 30 | |
| 34 | | 8/17/2016 | | | | | |
| 35 | | 8/18/2016 | x | 12 | 18 | 25 | |
| 36 | | 8/19/2016 | x | 15 | 20 | 20 | |
| 37 | | 8/22/2016 | | | | | |
| 38 | | 8/23/2016 | x | 20 | 17 | 23 | |

Documentation    **Fitness Report**    Explanation of Formulas    ⊕

READY                                                                    AVERAGE: 8

# Working with Date Functions

Excel has several functions that work with dates and times. **Date functions** insert or calculate dates and times. They are particularly useful in business workbooks that involve production schedules and calendar applications. Figure 3-27 describes some of the commonly used Date functions.

| Figure 3-27 | Date functions |
| --- | --- |

| Function | Description |
| --- | --- |
| DATE(*year*, *month*, *day*) | Creates a date value for the date represented by the *year*, *month*, and *day* arguments |
| DAY(*date*) | Extracts the day of the month from *date* |
| MONTH(*date*) | Extracts the month number from *date* where 1=January, 2=February, and so forth |
| YEAR(*date*) | Extracts the year number from *date* |
| NETWORKDAYS(*start*, *end*[, *holidays*]) | Calculates the number of whole working days between *start* and *end*; to exclude holidays, add the optional *holidays* argument containing a list of holiday dates to skip |
| WEEKDAY(*date*[, *return_type*]) | Calculates the weekday from *date*, where 1=Sunday, 2=Monday, and so forth; to choose a different numbering scheme, set *return_type* to 1 (1=Sunday, 2=Monday, ...), 2 (1=Monday, 2=Tuesday, ...), or 3 (0=Monday, 1=Tuesday, ...) |
| WORKDAY(*start*, *days*[, *holidays*]) | Returns the workday after *days* workdays have passed since the *start* date; to exclude holidays, add the optional *holidays* argument containing a list of holiday dates to skip |
| NOW( ) | Returns the current date and time |
| TODAY( ) | Returns the current date |

© 2014 Cengage Learning

## Displaying the Current Date with the TODAY function

Many workbooks include the current date. You can use the **TODAY function** to display the current date in a worksheet. The TODAY function has the following syntax:

    =TODAY( )

Note that although the TODAY function doesn't have any arguments, you still must include the parentheses for the function to work. The date displayed by the TODAY function is updated automatically whenever you reopen the workbook or enter a new calculation.

Ken wants the Fitness Report worksheet to show the current date each time it is used or printed. You will use the TODAY function to display the current date in cell G2.

### To display the current date with the TODAY function:

1. Select cell **G2**.

2. On the FORMULAS tab, in the Function Library group, click the **Date & Time** button to display the date and time functions.

3. Click **TODAY**. The Function Arguments dialog box opens and indicates that the TODAY function requires no arguments.

4. Click the **OK** button. The formula =TODAY() is entered in cell G2.

5. Verify that the current date is displayed in the cell.

6. Format the cell using the **Calculation** style.

## Finding the Next Weekday with the WORKDAY function

Instead of using AutoFill to enter a series of dates in a range, you can use the WORKDAY function to fill in the remaining weekdays based on the start date you specify. The WORKDAY function displays the date of the weekday a specific number of weekdays past a starting date. The syntax of the WORKDAY function is

=WORKDAY(*start*, *days*[, *holiday*])

**TIP**

You can enter the dates to skip into worksheet cells, and then reference that range in the *holiday* argument of the WORKDAY function.

where *start* is a start date, *days* is the number of weekdays after *start*, and *holiday* is an optional list of dates to skip. If you do not include anything for the optional *holiday* argument, the WORKDAY function does not skip any days. For example, if cell A1 contains the date 11/4/2016, a Friday, the following formula displays the date 11/9/2016, a Wednesday that is three working days after 11/4/2016:

=WORKDAY(A1, 3)

Ken wants to automate the process of inserting the exercise dates. You will use the WORKDAY function to do this.

### To insert the exercise dates using the WORKDAY function:

1. In cell **G7**, enter **8/1/2016** to specify the date the workouts will begin, and then format the cell using the **Input** cell style.

2. In cell **G8**, enter the formula **=F44** to display the date of the last scheduled workout, which is 8/31/2016 in this instance, and then format the cell using the **Calculation** cell style.

3. In cell **F22**, enter the formula **=G7** to replace the date with a reference to the start date you specified in cell G7. The cell still displays 8/1/2016.

4. Select cell **F23**, if necessary, and then click the **Insert Function** button $f_x$ next to the formula bar. The Insert Function dialog box opens.

5. Type **working days** in the Search for a function box, and then click the **Go** button to find all of the functions related to working days.

6. In the Select a function box, click **WORKDAY** to select the function, and then click the **OK** button. The WORKDAY Function Arguments dialog box opens.

7. In the Start_date box, type the cell reference **F22** to specify that cell F22 contains the start date you want to use.

8. In the Days box, type **1** to specify the number of workdays after the date in cell F22 that you want the formula results to show. See Figure 3-28.

---

**Figure 3-28**    **Function Arguments dialog box for the WORKDAY function**

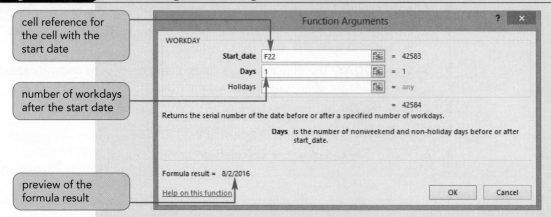

cell reference for the cell with the start date

number of workdays after the start date

preview of the formula result

**TIP**

To select a working day prior to the start date, enter a negative number rather than a positive number.

**9.** Click the **OK** button. Cell F23 contains the formula =WORKDAY(F22, 1) and displays the date 8/2/2016, which is the next workday after 8/1/2016.

You want to use the same formula to calculate the rest of the workout dates. You can use AutoFill to quickly repeat the formula.

**10.** Select cell **F23**, and then drag the fill handle down over the range **F23:F44** to copy the formula and enter the rest of the workdays in the month.

Because the copied formulas use relative references, each cell displays a date that is one workday after the date in the previous cell. The dates should not be different from the dates you entered previously using AutoFill.

**11.** Format the range **F22:F44** with the **Calculation** cell style to show that these dates are calculated by a formula rather than entered manually.

You will test that the formulas in the range F22:F44 are working correctly by entering a different start date.

**12.** In cell **G7**, enter **9/1/2016** as the new start date.

**13.** Review the dates in the range F22:F44, verifying that the workout dates start with 9/2/2016 in cell F23, continue with 9/5/2016 in cell F24, and end with 10/3/2016 in cell F44.

**Trouble?** If the workout dates do not end with 10/3/2016, compare the formula in cell F23 to the formula shown in Step 9, make any edits needed, and then repeat Step 10.

**14.** In cell **G7**, enter **8/1/2016** to return to the original start date.

## INSIGHT

### Selecting the Days in the Work Week

Different countries, regions, and even businesses might have different rules for what constitutes a workday. If you need to create a schedule that doesn't follow the standard U.S. business days (Monday through Friday), you can use the WORKDAY.INTL function to specify the days to use as the work week. The syntax of the WORKDAY.INTL function is:

```
=WORKDAY.INTL(start, days[, weekend=1, holidays])
```

The only difference between the syntax of the WORKDAY.INTL function and the syntax of the WORKDAY function is the optional *weekend* argument, which specifies the days of the week considered to be weekend or nonworking days. If you omit the *weekend* argument, weekends are considered to occur only on Saturday and Sunday. If you include the *weekend* argument, you enter one of the following numbers to specify the two days or the one day to consider as the weekend:

| Weekend | Two-Day Weekend | Weekend | One-Day Weekend |
|---|---|---|---|
| 1 | Saturday, Sunday | 11 | Sunday |
| 2 | Sunday, Monday | 12 | Monday |
| 3 | Monday, Tuesday | 13 | Tuesday |
| … | | … | |
| 7 | Friday, Saturday | 17 | Saturday |

For example, a business that is open every day except Sunday would use a *weekend* value of 11 to indicate that only Sunday is considered a nonworking day, and a business that is closed on Monday and Tuesday would use a *weekend* value of 3 to specify a work week of Wednesday through Sunday. For other working week schedules, you can enter text to specify which days are workdays. See Excel Help for more information.

# Counting Cells

Excel has two functions for counting cells—the COUNT function and the COUNTA function. The COUNT function tallies how many cells in a range contain numbers or dates (because they are stored as numeric values). The COUNT function does not count blank cells or cells that contain text. Its syntax is

    COUNT(value1[, value2, value3, ...])

where *value1* is the first item or cell reference containing the numbers you want to count. The remaining *value* arguments are used primarily when you want to count numbers and dates in nonadjacent ranges. For example, the following function counts how many cells in the range A1:A10, the range C1:C5, and cell E5 contain numbers or dates:

    COUNT(A1:A10, C1:C5, E5)

If you want to know how many cells contain entries—whether those entries are numbers, dates, or text—you use the COUNTA function, which tallies the nonblank cells in a range. The following is the syntax of the COUNTA function, which has the same arguments as the COUNT function:

    COUNTA(value1[, value2, value3, ...])

Ken wants the Workout Summary to show the total number of scheduled workouts for the month, the number of attended workouts, and the number of missed workouts. You will use the COUNT function to count the total number of workout dates in the Workout Routine 5 table. Then, you will use the COUNTA function to count the number of workouts actually attended. Each attended workout is marked by an "x" in column G of the Workout Routine 5 table; missing workouts are left blank. Finally, you will enter a formula to calculate the missed workouts.

### To count the scheduled, attended, and missed workouts:

1. In cell **G9**, enter the formula **=COUNT(F22:F44)**. Cell G9 displays 23, indicating that Ken scheduled 23 workouts for the month.

2. In cell **G10**, enter the formula **=COUNTA(G22:G44)**. Cell G10 displays 17, indicating that Daniel attended 17 of the 23 scheduled workouts.

3. In cell **G11**, enter the formula **=G9–G10** to calculate the difference between the number of scheduled workouts and the number of attended workouts. Cell G11 displays 6, which is the number of missed workouts.

4. Format the range **G9:G11** with the **Calculation** cell style.

5. Select cell **G10**. See Figure 3-29.

**Figure 3-29** **Completed Workout Summary**

COUNTA function counts the number of nonblank cells in the specified range

difference between the scheduled and attended workouts

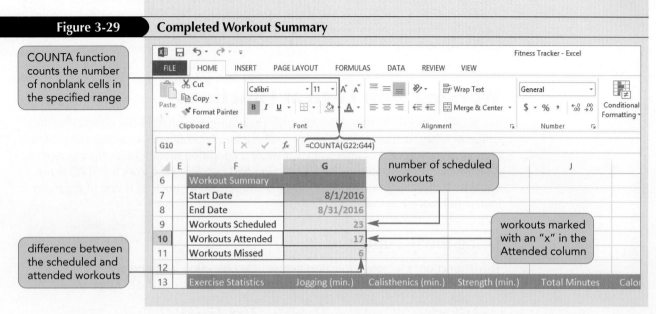

number of scheduled workouts

workouts marked with an "x" in the Attended column

It is important to understand the difference between the COUNT and COUNTA functions. For example, if you had used the COUNT function in cell G10 to tally the number of attended workouts, the result would have been 0 because the range G22:G44 contains no entries with numbers.

Like the COUNT function, many of Excel's statistical functions ignore cells that are blank or contain text. This can create unexpected results with calculated values if you are not careful. Figure 3-30 shows how some of the common summary statistics change when blank cells are used in place of zeroes.

**Figure 3-30** **Calculations involving blank cells and zeroes**

cells with zeroes

cells left blank

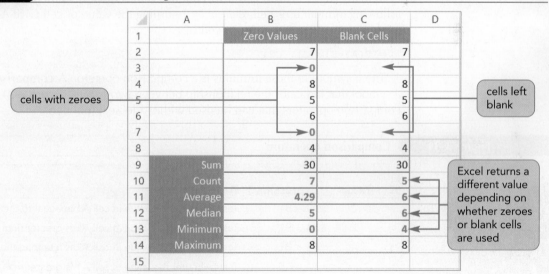

Excel returns a different value depending on whether zeroes or blank cells are used

Some of the fitness statistics for total exercise minutes and calories burned include the six workouts that Daniel missed. For example, the minimum exercise minutes and calories burned are both listed as 0 because the calculated values show up as 0 in the worksheet when the workout session was missed. Ken wants the summary statistics based on only the workouts actually attended. One way to exclude missed workouts is to delete the zeroes, leaving blank cells. However, Ken wants the worksheet to be user-friendly and not require anyone to double-check and edit entries for missed workouts. Instead of editing the worksheet, you can use a logical function to automatically replace zeroes with blanks for missed workouts.

# Working with Logical Functions

A logical function returns a different value depending on whether the given condition is true or false, such as whether or not a scheduled workout was attended. In Excel, the condition is expressed as a formula. Consider a condition that includes the expression A5=3. If cell A5 is equal to 3, this expression and condition are true; if cell A5 is not equal to 3, this expression and condition are false. The IF function is one of the many logical functions you can use in Excel.

## Using the IF Function

The IF function is a logical function that returns one value if a condition is true, and returns a different value if that condition is false. The syntax of the IF function is

    IF(*logical_test*, *value_if_true*, *value_if_false*)

where *logical_test* is a condition that is either true or false, *value_if_true* is the value returned by the function if the condition is true, and *value_if_false* is the value returned if the condition is false. The value can be a number, text, a date, or a cell reference. For example, the following formula tests whether the value in cell A1 is equal to the value in cell B1:

    =IF(A1=B1, 100, 50)

If the value in cell A1 equals the value in cell B1, the formula result is 100; otherwise, the formula result is 50.

In many cases, however, you will not use values directly in the IF function. The following formula uses cell references, returning the value of cell C1 if A1 equals B1; otherwise, it returns the value of cell C2:

    =IF(A1=B1, C1, C2)

The = symbol in these formulas is a comparison operator. A **comparison operator** is a symbol that indicates the relationship between two values. Figure 3-31 describes the comparison operators that can be used within a logical function.

**Figure 3-31**     Comparison operators

| Operator | Expression | Description |
|---|---|---|
| = | A1 = B1 | Tests whether the value in cell A1 is equal to the value in cell B1 |
| > | A1 > B1 | Tests whether the value in cell A1 is greater than the value in cell B1 |
| < | A1 < B1 | Tests whether the value in cell A1 is less than the value in cell B1 |
| >= | A1 >= B1 | Tests whether the value in cell A1 is greater than or equal to the value in cell B1 |
| <= | A1 <= B1 | Tests whether the value in cell A1 is less than or equal to the value in cell B1 |
| <> | A1 <> B1 | Tests whether the value in cell A1 is not equal to the value in cell B1 |

© 2014 Cengage Learning

The IF function also works with text. For example, the following formula tests whether the value of cell A1 is equal to "yes":

```
=IF(A1="yes", "done", "restart")
```

If true (the value of cell A1 is equal to "yes"), the formula returns the text "done"; otherwise, it returns the text "restart". Notice that the text in the function is enclosed in quotation marks.

In addition, you can nest other functions inside an IF statement. The following formula first tests whether cell A5 is equal to the maximum of values within the range A1:A100:

```
=IF(A5=MAX(A1:A100), "Maximum", "")
```

If it is, the formula returns the text "Maximum"; otherwise, it returns no text.

In the Fitness Report worksheet, you need to rewrite the formulas that calculate the total minutes and total calories from each workout as IF functions that test whether Daniel actually attended the workout. Because every attended workout is marked with an "x" in column G, you can test whether the cell entry in column G is an "x". For example, the following formula in cell K22 is currently being used to calculate the total minutes from the first workout:

```
=SUM(H22:J22)
```

This formula can be revised to the following IF function, which first determines if cell G22 contains an "x" (indicating that the workout was attended), and then uses the SUM function to calculate the total minutes if there is an "x":

```
=IF(G22="x", SUM(H22:J22), "")
```

Otherwise, the formula displays nothing, leaving the cell blank.

You will use relative references in the revised formula so that you can copy it for the other workouts and total columns. You will create the formula with the IF function for the total minutes column now.

> **TIP**
>
> For the formula result to show no text, include opening and closing quotation marks with nothing between them.

## To use an IF function to calculate total minutes for attended workouts:

1. Select cell **K22**, and then press the **Delete** key to clear the original formula from the cell.

2. Click the **Insert Function** button $f_x$ next to the formula bar to open the Insert Function dialog box.

3. Type **if function** in the Search for a function box, and then press the **Enter** key. Functions that match your description appear in the Select a function box.

4. Click **IF** in the Select a function box, and then click the **OK** button to open the Function Arguments dialog box.

5. In the Logical_test box, type **G22="x"** as the expression that tests whether cell G22 is equal to x.

6. Press the **Tab** key to move the insertion point to the Value_if_true box, and then type **SUM(H22:J22)**. If cell G22 does contain an x (the logical test is true), the sum of the values in the range H22:J22 will be displayed in cell K22.

7. Press the **Tab** key to move the insertion point to the Value_if_false box, and then type **""** (opening and closing quotation marks). If cell G22 does not contain an x (the logical test is false), the cell will be left blank. See Figure 3-32.

**Figure 3-32**    **Function Arguments dialog box for the IF function**

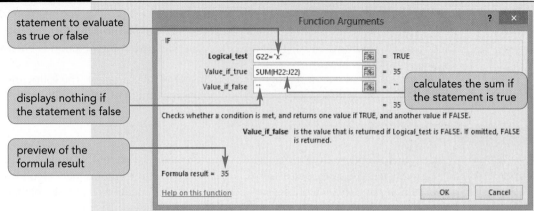

statement to evaluate as true or false

displays nothing if the statement is false

preview of the formula result

calculates the sum if the statement is true

8. Click the **OK** button. The formula =IF(G22="x", SUM(H22:J22), "") is entered into cell K22. The cell displays 35, which is the number of minutes Daniel spent exercising at that workout session.

   You will copy the formula with the IF function to calculate the total minutes for the rest of the workouts.

9. Select cell **K22**, and then drag the fill handle down over the range **K22:K44** to copy the IF formula to the remaining cells in the column. The total number of minutes for each workout is recalculated so that the missed workouts in cells K25, K28, K34, K37, K39, and K40 are now left blank.

10. Select cell **K22**. The #VALUE! error value appears in columns L and M for each of the missed workouts because the current formulas cannot calculate calories burned when no total minutes are provided. See Figure 3-33.

**Figure 3-33**    **IF function excludes the total minutes for missed workouts**

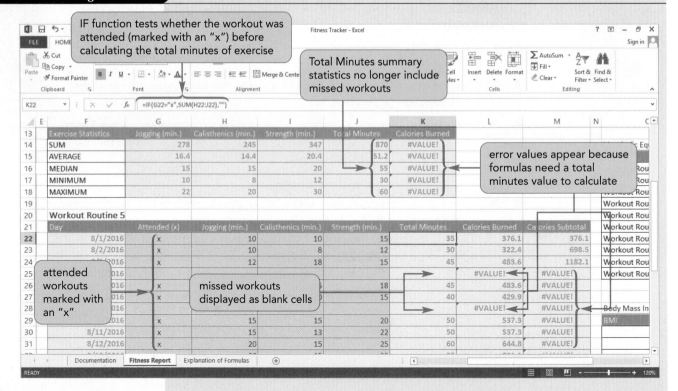

Next, you will update the calories burned formulas so that they don't display the #VALUE! error value when a workout is missed. This requires another IF statement similar to the one you used to calculate total minutes. As with the total minutes calculation, any missed workout will display a blank cell for the calories burned in place of a 0. Rather than reentering the complete formula for calories burned, you can edit the existing formula, inserting the IF function.

## To change the calories burned formulas to IF functions:

1. Double-click cell **L22** to enter Edit mode.

2. Press the **Home** key to move the insertion point to the beginning of the formula, and then press the → key to move the insertion point one space to the right, directly after = (the equal sign). You will begin the IF function after the equal sign.

3. Type **IF(G22="x",** to insert the function name and the expression for the logical test.

4. Press the **Ctrl+End** keys to move the insertion point to the end of the formula.

> Make sure your formula matches the one shown here.

5. Type **, "")** to enter the value if false and complete the IF function. The complete formula is now =IF(G22="x", $P$20*$C$11*K22/125.7143, "").

6. Press the **Enter** key to exit Edit mode and make cell L23 active. Cell L22 still displays 376.1 because Ken did not miss the first workout.

   You will use AutoFill to copy the IF function to the rest of the cells in the Calories Burned column.

7. Select cell **L22**, and then drag the fill handle down over the range **L22:L44**. As shown in Figure 3-34, the missed workouts now display blank cells instead of zeroes, and the attended workouts show the same calculated values as earlier.

**Figure 3-34**    **IF function excludes the calories burned for missed workouts**

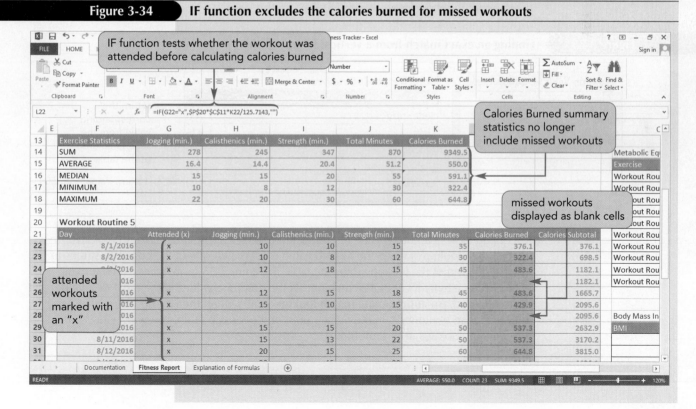

By excluding the missed workouts, Daniel's average exercise time increased from 37.8 minutes to 51.2 minutes, and the average calories burned increased to 550 calories. These averages more closely match the median values because zeroes were removed from the calculations. The minimum values for Total Minutes and Calories Burned now also reflect only attended workouts, changing from 0 (when they were based on a missed workout) to 30 minutes and 322.4 calories, respectively. These measures reflect the true results of the workouts Daniel attended.

# Using a Lookup Function

**Lookup functions** find values in tables of data and insert them in another location in the worksheet such as cells or in formulas. For example, consider the active BMR calculated in cell C22, which adjusts the calculation of Daniel's metabolic rate to account for his activity level. The more active Daniel is, the more calories he can consume without gaining weight. The multiplying factors for each activity level (Sedentary, Light, Moderate, High, or Extreme) are stored in a table in the range O8:P12; you used the value in cell P8 to adjust Daniel's BMR value for his sedentary lifestyle. Instead of including a direct reference to one of the multiplying factors in the table, you can use a function to have Excel choose the multiplying factor that corresponds to the specified activity level.

The table that stores the data you want to retrieve is called a lookup table. A lookup table organizes numbers or text into categories. This particular lookup table organizes the BMR factors by activity levels, as shown in Figure 3-35. Every activity level category in the first column of the lookup table has a corresponding BMR factor in the second column of the table. This table is a vertical lookup table because the categories are arranged vertically. The entries in the first column of a vertical lookup table are referred to as the compare values because they are compared to the category you want to find (called the lookup value). When a match is found, the corresponding value in one of the subsequent columns is returned. For example, to find the return value for the Moderate lookup value, you look down the first column of the lookup table until you find the Moderate entry. Then, you move to the second column to locate the corresponding return value, which is 1.550, in this case.

**Figure 3-35**   **Finding an exact match from a vertical lookup table**

© 2014 Cengage Learning

Lookup tables can be constructed for exact match or approximate match lookups. An **exact match lookup** is when the lookup value must match one of the compare values in the first column of the lookup table. The table in Figure 3-35 is an exact match lookup because the activity level must match one of the compare values in the table or a value is not returned. An **approximate match lookup** occurs when the lookup value falls within a range of numbers in the first column of the lookup table. You will work with exact match lookups in this tutorial.

# Finding an Exact Match with the VLOOKUP Function

To retrieve the return value from a vertical lookup table, you use the VLOOKUP function. The syntax of the VLOOKUP function is

```
VLOOKUP(lookup_value, table_array, col_index_num[, range_lookup=TRUE])
```

where *lookup_value* is the compare value to find in the first column of the lookup table, *table_array* is the range reference to the lookup table, and *col_index_num* is the number of the column in the lookup table that contains the return value. Keep in mind that *col_index_num* refers to the number of the column within the lookup table, not the worksheet column. For example, *col_index_num* 2 refers to the second column of the table, *col_index_num* 3 refers to the third column of the table, and so forth. Finally, *range_lookup* is an optional argument that specifies whether the compare values are an exact match or a range of values (for an approximate match). For an exact match, you set the *range_lookup* value to FALSE. For approximate match lookups, you set the *range_lookup* value to TRUE or you can omit it because its default value is TRUE.

For example, the following formula performs an exact match lookup to find the BMR factor for an Extreme activity level based on the values from the lookup table in the range O8:P12 (shown earlier in Figure 3-35):

```
=VLOOKUP("Extreme", O8:P12, 2, FALSE)
```

**TIP**

If the VLOOKUP function cannot find the lookup value, the #N/A error value is displayed in the cell.

The *col_index_num* is 2 because the BMR factors are in the second column of the table. The *range_lookup* is FALSE because this is an exact match. The function looks through the compare values in the first column of the table to locate the "Extreme" entry. When the exact entry is found, the function returns the corresponding value in the second column of the table, which in this case is 1.900.

Daniel's activity level in cell C9 is entered as Sedentary, which has a BMR factor of 1.2. The following active BMR formula you entered earlier calculated that Daniel can consume about 2224 calories per day and maintain his current weight:

```
=P8*C21
```

In this formula, P8 references the Sedentary BMR value in cell P8 and C21 references Daniel's base or resting metabolic rate. To have Excel look up the BMR value, you need to replace the P8 cell reference with a VLOOKUP function, as follows:

```
=VLOOKUP(C9, O8:P12, 2, FALSE)*C21
```

In this formula, C9 contains Daniel's activity level (Sedentary), O8:P12 references the lookup table, 2 specifies the table column to find the BMR factors, and FALSE indicates that this is an exact match lookup. You will enter this formula into the worksheet now.

**To use the VLOOKUP function to calculate Daniel's active BMR:**

1. Select cell **C22**, and then press the **Delete** key to clear the formula currently in the cell.

2. On the ribbon, click the **FORMULAS** tab. Because VLOOKUP has several arguments to manage, you will enter the function using the Function Arguments dialog box.

3. In the Function Library group, click **Lookup & Reference** to display a list of functions, and then click **VLOOKUP**. The Function Arguments dialog box opens.

4. With the insertion point in the Lookup_value box, click cell **C9** in the worksheet to enter that cell reference as the location containing the value to look up in the first column of the lookup table.

5. Press the **Tab** key to move the insertion point into the Table_array box, and then select the range **O8:P12**, which contains the vertical lookup table in the worksheet.

6. Press the **Tab** key to move the insertion point to the Col_index_num box, and then type **2** to return a value from the second column of the lookup table.

7. Press the **Tab** key to move the insertion point to the Range_lookup box, and then type **FALSE** to specify an exact match lookup. The dialog box shows the resulting value of the function with these arguments, which in this case is 1.2. See Figure 3-36.

| Figure 3-36 | Function Arguments dialog box for the VLOOKUP function |
| --- | --- |

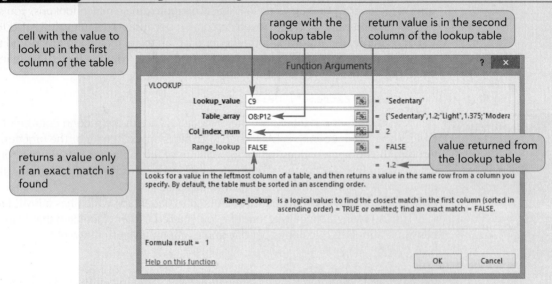

cell with the value to look up in the first column of the table

range with the lookup table

return value is in the second column of the lookup table

returns a value only if an exact match is found

value returned from the lookup table

8. Click the **OK** button to close the dialog box.

9. Double-click cell **C22** to enter Edit mode, press the **Ctrl+End** keys to move the insertion point to the end of the formula, type **\*C21** to complete the formula, and then press the **Enter** key. The completed formula in cell C22 is =VLOOKUP(C9,O8:P12,2,FALSE)\*C21, resulting in an active BMR of 2224 calories per day for a Sedentary activity level.

   You will change the activity level to ensure that the formula works correctly.

10. In cell **C9**, enter **Moderate** to change the activity level from Sedentary. The active BMR value changes to 2872 because the VLOOKUP function returns a 1.55 BMR factor from the lookup table.

    Ken decides that Light is a more accurate description of Daniel's activity level.

11. In cell **C9**, enter **Light** as the activity level. At that activity level, the active BMR changes to 2548. With a Light activity level, Daniel can consume about 2548 calories per day and maintain his current weight.

12. Select cell **C22** to view the formula. See Figure 3-37.

**TIP**

Exact matches are not case sensitive, so the lookup values Light, light, and LIGHT are considered to be the same.

**Figure 3-37**     **VLOOKUP function calculates the active BMR**

VLOOKUP function looks up the BMR factor from the table in the range O8:P12

updated activity level

formula results show the daily calories for light activity

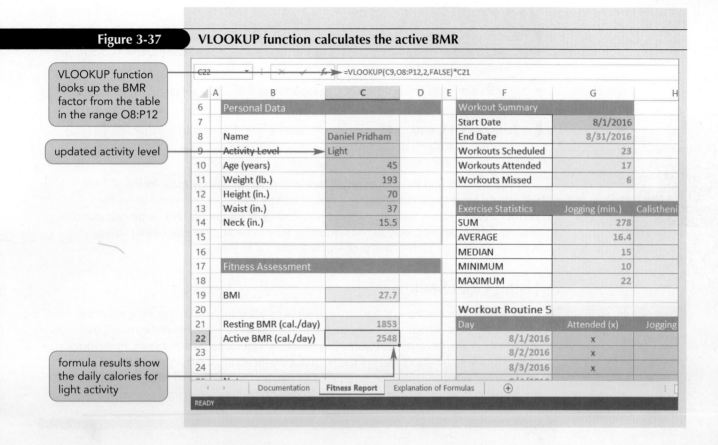

# Performing What-If Analysis

A **what-if analysis** lets you explore the impact that changing input values has on the calculated values in the workbook. For example, Ken could perform a what-if analysis to determine how many pounds Daniel needs to lose to reach a more healthy weight. Current fitness standards suggest that a body mass index between 18.5 and 24.9 is considered to be within the "normal" classification. Daniel's body mass index is 27.7, which is rated as overweight. So Ken wants to know how many pounds Daniel needs to lose to reduce his body mass index to 24.9.

## Using Trial and Error

One way to perform a what-if analysis is by changing one or more of the input values to see how they affect the calculated results. This **trial-and-error method** requires some guesswork as you estimate which values to change and by how much. In this case, Ken wants you to find out the weight at which Daniel would reach a BMI of 24.9. You'll start by checking the resulting body mass index if Daniel were to lose 10 pounds, reducing his weight to 183 pounds.

### To perform a what-if analysis by trial and error:

1. In cell **C11**, change the weight from 193 pounds to **183** pounds. Daniel's body mass index decreases from 27.7 to 26.3, as shown in cell C19. At this weight, he is still considered overweight.

**2.** In cell **C11**, enter **163** pounds. At this weight, Daniel's BMI shown in cell C19 is 23.4. So losing 30 pounds is more than enough to classify Daniel's body weight as normal.

Ken wants to know if Daniel can lose fewer than 30 pounds to reach that classification.

**3.** In cell **C11**, enter **168** pounds. At this weight, Daniel's BMI value is 24.1, which is still within the normal classification, but not exactly equal to 24.9.

If you want to find the exact weight that will result in a body mass index of 24.9, you would have to continue trying different weight values as you close in on the correct weight. This is why the method is called "trial and error." For some calculations, trial and error can be a very time-consuming way to locate the exact input value. A more direct approach to this problem is to use Goal Seek.

## Using Goal Seek

**Goal Seek** automates the trial-and-error process by allowing you to specify a value for a calculated item, which Excel uses to determine the input value needed to reach that goal. In this case, because Ken wants to know how Daniel can reach a body mass index of exactly 24.9 (the upper level of the normal classification), the question that Goal Seek answers is: "What weight value is required to reach that goal?" Goal Seek starts by setting the calculated value and works backward to determine the correct input value.

**REFERENCE**

### Performing What-If Analysis and Goal Seek

**To perform a what-if analysis by trial and error:**
- Change the value of a worksheet cell (the input cell).
- Observe its impact on one or more calculated cells (the result cells).
- Repeat until the desired results are achieved.

**To perform a what-if analysis using Goal Seek:**
- On the DATA tab, in the Data Tools group, click the What-If Analysis button, and then click Goal Seek.
- Select the result cell in the Set cell box, and then specify its value (goal) in the To value box.
- In the By changing cell box, specify the input cell.
- Click the OK button. The value of the input cell changes to set the value of the result cell.

You will use Goal Seek to find the weight that will result in Daniel's BMI reaching exactly 24.9.

### To use Goal Seek to find a weight resulting in a 24.9 BMI:

**1.** On the ribbon, click the **DATA** tab.

**2.** In the Data Tools group, click the **What-If Analysis** button, and then click **Goal Seek**. The Goal Seek dialog box opens.

**3.** Make sure the value in the Set cell box is selected, and then click cell **C19** in the Fitness Report worksheet. The absolute cell reference $C$19 appears in the Set cell box. The set cell is the calculated value you want Goal Seek to change to meet your goal.

4. Press the **Tab** key to move the insertion point to the To value box, and then type **24.9**. This indicates that you want Goal Seek to set this value to 24.9 (the highest body mass index in the normal classification).

5. Press the **Tab** key to move the insertion point to the By changing cell box. There are often various input values you can change to meet a goal. In this case, you want to change the weight value in cell C11.

6. Click cell **C11**. The absolute reference $C$11 appears in the By changing cell box. See Figure 3-38.

| Figure 3-38 | Goal Seek dialog box |
| --- | --- |

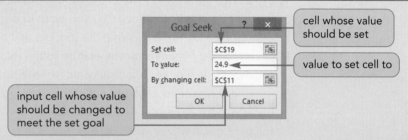

7. Click the **OK** button. The Goal Seek dialog box closes, and the Goal Seek Status dialog box opens, indicating that Goal Seek found a solution.

8. Click the **OK** button. A weight value of about 173 pounds is displayed in cell C11. Daniel would need to lose roughly 20 pounds, reducing his weight to 173 pounds to reach a weight within the normal classification for BMI. See Figure 3-39.

| Figure 3-39 | Target weight determined by Goal Seek |
| --- | --- |

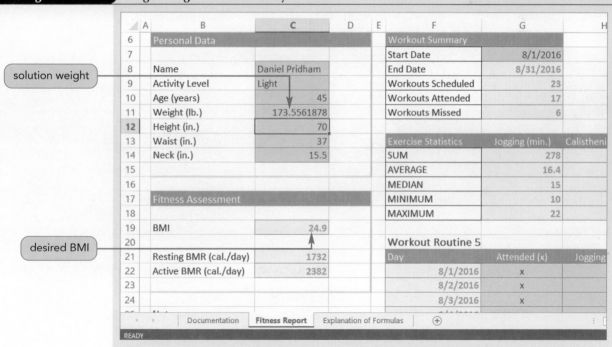

9. Save and close the workbook.

Ken appreciates all of the work you have done in developing the Fitness Tracker workbook. He will use this workbook as a model for all of his other clients at Fit Fathers.

**REVIEW**

## Session 3.2 Quick Check

1. The first three values in a selected series are 3, 6, and 9. What are the next three values that will be inserted by AutoFill?
2. Write a formula to display the current date.
3. Write a formula to find the date four workdays after the date value stored in cell B10. There are no holidays.
4. Explain the difference between the COUNT function and the COUNTA function.
5. If cell Q3 is greater than cell Q4, you want to display the text "OK"; otherwise, display the text "RETRY". Write the formula that accomplishes this.
6. Jan is entering hundreds of temperature values into an Excel worksheet for a climate research project, and she wants to save time on data entry by leaving freezing point values as blanks rather than typing zeroes. Will this cause complications if she later tries to calculate an average temperature from her data values? Explain why or why not.
7. Provide the formula to perform an exact match lookup with the lookup value from cell G5 using a lookup table located in the range A1:F50. Return the value from the third column of the table.
8. What is the difference between a what-if analysis by trial and error and by Goal Seek?

ASSESS

PRACTICE

## Review Assignments

**Data File needed for the Review Assignments: Mothers.xlsx**

Ken and his wife, Sally, are expanding the business, changing its name to Fit Fathers and Mothers Inc., and adding fitness classes for mothers with a special emphasis on pregnant women. The fitness equations for women are different from those for men. Ken and Sally want you to create a workbook similar to the one you created for fathers, but focused on the fitness needs of women. Sally also wants you to calculate the total fat burned in the course of completing the workout schedule. She has already designed much of the workbook's contents, but she needs you to add the formulas and functions. Complete the following:

1. Open the **Mothers** workbook located in the Excel3 ▶ Review folder included with your Data Files, and then save the workbook as **Mothers Fitness** in the location specified by your instructor.

2. In the Documentation sheet, enter your name and the date.

3. Go to the Fitness Analysis worksheet. In the range C8:C15, enter the personal data for **Dorothy Young**. Her activity level is **Moderate**, she is **38** years old, **152** pounds, **64** inches tall, with a **33**-inch waist, **35**-inch hips, and a **14**-inch neck.

4. In cell C20, enter a formula to calculate Dorothy's body mass index based on the equation
   $$BMI = 703w/h^2$$
   where $w$ is the weight in pounds and $h$ is the height in inches. Display the formula results with one decimal place.

5. In cell C22, enter a formula to calculate the resting metabolism rate for women based on the equation
   $$BMR = 4.338w + 4.698h - 4.68a + 655$$
   where $w$ is the weight in pounds, $h$ is the height in inches, and $a$ is the age in years. Display the formula results with no decimal places.

6. In cell C23, enter a formula using the VLOOKUP function to calculate the active BMR based on the equation
   Active BMR = *Activity Factor* × *BMR*
   where *Activity Factor* is an exact match lookup for the value in the range O8:Q12 that corresponds to the activity level entered in cell C9, and *BMR* is the value in cell C22. Display the formula results with no decimal places.

7. In cell K22, enter a formula using an IF function to calculate the total minutes for the first workout that displays a blank cell if Dorothy did not attend a workout that day.

8. Use AuotFill to copy the formula you entered in cell K22 to the range K23:K44 to calculate the total minutes for each workout.

9. In cell L22, enter a formula to calculate the calories burned at the first workout based on the equation
   $$Calories = \frac{METS \times w \times t}{125.7143}$$
   where *METS* is the metabolic factor for the exercise, $w$ is the client's weight, and $t$ is the exercise time. Use the METS value located in cell P19, the weight value located in cell C11, and the time value located in the corresponding cell in column K. Be sure to use an absolute reference for both weight and METS.

10. Edit the formula you entered in cell L22 to be included as part of an IF function that returns a blank cell if Dorothy did not attend the workout that day. Display the formula results with one decimal place.

11. Use AutoFill to copy the formula you entered in cell L22 to the range L23:L44 to calculate the calories burned at each workout.

12. In the range M22:M44, use the Quick Analysis tool to calculate a column running total of the calories burned in the range L22:L44. Display the formula results with two decimal places.

13. Complete the exercise statistics in the range G14:K18 by entering formulas calculating the sum, average, median, maximum, and minimum values of the exercise times, and calories burned values from the workout log. Display the averages and the calories burned statistics with one decimal place.

14. In cell G2, use a function to display the current date whenever the workbook is opened.

15. In cell F22, enter a formula to reference the start date entered in cell G7.

16. In the range F23:F44, use a function to increase the value of the date in the previous row by 1 workday. Format the formula results with the Short Date format.

17. In cell G8, enter a formula to display the ending date entered in cell F44.

18. In cell G9, enter a formula to count the number of days included in the range F22:F44.

19. In cell G10, enter a formula to count the number of attended workouts as indicated in the range G22:G44.

20. In cell G11, enter a formula to calculate the difference between the number of scheduled workouts and the number of attended workouts. Save the workbook.

21. Use Goal Seek to determine the weight Dorothy must attain to reach a body mass index of 22.

22. Save the revised workbook as **Mothers Fitness Goal**, and then close the workbook.

## Case Problem 1

APPLY

**Data File needed for this Case Problem: Hernandez.xlsx**

**Hernandez Family**   Juan and Olivia Hernandez are a recently married couple in Fort Wayne, Indiana. Juan is currently in graduate school and Olivia is the manager at a local bakery. They want to use Excel to help manage their family budget, but they need help setting up the formulas and functions to project their monthly expenses and help them meet their financial goals. Complete the following:

1. Open the **Hernandez** workbook located in the Excel3 ▶ Case1 folder included with your Data Files, and then save the workbook as **Hernandez Budget** in the location specified by your instructor.

2. In the Documentation sheet, enter your name and the date.

3. Go to the Budget worksheet. In cell B7, calculate the couple's total monthly income.

4. In row 23, use AutoFill to replace the numbers 1 through 12 with the month abbreviations **Jan** through **Dec**.

5. In rows 24 and 25, enter the couple's monthly income by referencing the monthly income estimates in cells B5 and B6. Use an absolute cell reference.

6. In row 26, calculate the couple's monthly income.

7. In row 37, enter formulas to calculate the total estimated expenses for each month.

8. In row 38, calculate each month's net cash flow, which is equal to the total income minus the total expenses.

9. In row 39, calculate the running total of the net cash flow so that Olivia and Juan can see how their net cash flow changes as the year progresses.

10. In the range B10:B19, calculate the average monthly expenses by category based on the values previously entered in rows 27 through 36.

11. In cell B20, calculate the total average monthly expenses.

12. The couple currently has $7,350 in their savings account. Each month the couple will either take money out of their savings account or deposit money. In row 41, calculate the end-of-month balance in their savings account by adding the value in cell E5 to the running total values of the net cash flow in row 39. Use an absolute cell reference for cell E5.

13. In cell E6, enter a formula to display the value of the savings balance at the end of December.

14. Juan and Olivia would like to have $15,000 in their savings account by the end of the year. Olivia is planning to ask for a raise at her job. Use Goal Seek to determine the value of cell B6 that will achieve a final savings balance of $15,000.

15. Save and close the workbook.

## Case Problem 2

**CHALLENGE**

Data File needed for this Case Problem: Econ.xlsx

***Introduction to Economics 102***   Alice Keyes teaches Introduction to Economics 102 at Mountain View Business School in Huntington, West Virginia. She wants to use Excel to track the grades from her class. Alice has already entered the homework, quiz, and final exam scores for all of her students in a workbook, and she has asked you to set up the formulas and functions for her.

You will calculate each student's final average based on his or her homework score, quiz scores, and final exam. Homework counts for 20 percent of the student's final grade. The first two quizzes count for 10 percent each. The second two quizzes count for 15 percent each. The final exam counts for 30 percent of the final grade.

You will also calculate each student's rank in the class. The rank will display which student placed first in terms of his or her overall score, which student placed second, and so forth. Ranks are calculated using the function

    RANK(*number*, *ref*, [*order*=0])

where *number* is the value to be ranked, *ref* is a reference to the cell range containing the values against which the ranking is done, and *order* is an optional argument that specifies whether to rank in descending order or ascending order. The default *order* value is 0 to rank the values in descending order.

Finally, you will create formulas that will look up information on a particular student based on that student's ID so Alice doesn't have to scroll through the complete class roster to find a particular student. Complete the following:

1. Open the **Econ** workbook located in the Excel3 ► Case2 folder included with your Data Files, and then save the workbook as **Econ Grades** in the location specified by your instructor.

2. In the Documentation sheet, enter your name and the date.

3. Go to the Grade Book worksheet. In cell B5, count the number of student IDs in the range A22:A57.

✚ **Explore**  4. Cells C15 through H15 contain the weights assigned to each assignment, quiz, or exam. In cell J22, calculate the weighted average of the first student's scores by entering a formula that multiplies each score by its corresponding weight and adds the resulting products.

5. Edit the formula in cell J22, changing the references to the weights in cells C15 through H15 from relative references to absolute references.

6. Use AutoFill to copy the formula from cell J22 into the range J23:J57.

✚ **Explore**  7. In cell K22, use the RANK function to calculate how the first student compares to the other students in the class. Use the weighted average from cell J22 for the *number* argument and the range of weighted averages in the cell range $J$22:$J$57 for the *ref* argument. You do not need to specify a value for the *order* argument.

8. Use AutoFill to copy the formula you entered in cell K22 into the range K23:K57.

9. In the range C16:H18, calculate the class average, minimum, and maximum for each of the six grading components (homework, quizzes, and final exam).

10. In cell B8, enter the student ID **14858**.

✦ **Explore** 11. Using the VLOOKUP function with an exact match and the student data table in the range A22:K57, retrieve the first name, last name, weighted average, and class rank for student 14858 in the range B9:B12. Use an absolute reference to the lookup table. Note that the first name is found in the third column of the student data table, the last name is found in the second column, the weighted average is found in the tenth column, and the class rank is found in the eleventh column.

12. Brenda Dunford missed the final exam and will be taking a make-up exam. She wants to know what score she would need on the final exam to achieve an overall weighted average of 90. Use Goal Seek to calculate what final exam score Brenda needs to result in a weighted average of 90.

13. Save and close the workbook.

## Case Problem 3

**CHALLENGE**

Data File needed for this Case Problem: Homes.xlsx

*Homes of Dreams* Larry Helt is a carpenter and a woodcrafter in Coventry, Rhode Island, who loves to design and build custom dollhouses. He started his business, Homes of Dreams, a few years ago and it has expanded into a very profitable sideline to his ongoing carpentry work. Larry wants to create a shipping form that will calculate the cost for the purchased items, including taxes, shipping, and handling. Larry already designed the worksheet, which includes a table of shipping rates, shipping surcharges, and items sold by Homes of Dreams. He asks you to complete the worksheet. Complete the following:

1. Open the **Homes** workbook located in the Excel3 ▸ Case3 folder included with your Data Files, and then save the workbook as **Homes of Dreams** in the location specified by your instructor.

2. In the Documentation sheet, enter your name and the date.

3. Go to the Order Form worksheet.

4. In cell B21, enter the Item ID **DH007**.

5. In cell C21, enter the VLOOKUP function with an exact match to return the name of the item referenced in cell B21. Reference the lookup table in the range M4:O50 using an absolute cell reference. Return the value from the second column of the table.

6. In cell E21, enter the VLOOKUP function with an exact match to return the price of the item referenced in cell B21. Use an absolute reference to the lookup table in the range M4:O50. Return the value from the third column of the table.

7. In cell F21, enter **1** as the quantity of the item ordered.

8. In cell G21, calculate the price of the item multiplied by the quantity ordered.

✦ **Explore** 9. Revise your formulas in cells C21, E21, and G21, nesting them within an IF formula. For each cell, test whether the value of cell B21 is not equal to "" (a blank). If it is not, return the value of the VLOOKUP function in cells C21 and E21 and the calculated value in cell G21. Otherwise, those cells should return a blank ("") value.

10. Use AutoFill to copy the formulas in cells C21, E21, and G21 through row 30 in the order items table.

11. In row 22, enter **BD002** as the Item ID and **3** as the quantity of items ordered. Verify that the formulas you created automatically enter the name, price, and charge for the item.

12. In rows 23 through 25, enter **1** order for item **BH003**, **1** order for item **DR002**, and **1** order for item **KR009**.

13. In cell G32, calculate the sum of the item charges from all possible orders.

14. In cell G33, calculate the sales tax on the order, which is equal to the subtotal multiplied by the tax rate (entered in cell J9).

15. In cell C15, enter a function to insert the current date whenever the workbook is opened.

16. In cell C16, enter **3 Day** as the type of delivery for this order.

17. In cell C17, calculate the number of working days it will take to ship the order by inserting a VLOOKUP function using an exact match lookup. Use the delivery type in cell C16 as the lookup value, and use the shipping data in the range I4:K7 as the lookup table. Return the value from the third column of the table.

⊕ **Explore** 18. In cell C18, estimate the date of delivery. Use cell C15 as the start date and cell C17 as the number of working days after the start date.

⊕ **Explore** 19. The shipping and handling fee is based on the delivery method (Standard, 3 Day, 2 Day, or Overnight). In cell G34, calculate the shipping and handling fee for the order using an exact match lookup with the data in the range I4:J7. Use the delivery method specified in cell C16 to find the corresponding shipping and handling fee in the Delivery table.

20. In cell G36, calculate the sum of the merchandise subtotal, sales tax, and shipping and handling fee.

21. Save the workbook, and then delete the item IDs and quantities from the order table.

22. Save the workbook as **Homes of Dreams 2**, calculate the cost of ordering 1 of item BD001 using overnight delivery, and then save the workbook.

23. Save the workbook as **Homes of Dreams 3**, and then delete the item IDs and quantities from the order table. Calculate the cost of ordering 1 of item KR001, 2 of item BH004, and 1 of item DR001 using standard delivery. Save and close the workbook.

## Case Problem 4

**TROUBLESHOOT**

**Data File needed for this Case Problem: Quality.xlsx**

*Karleton Manufacturing*   Carmen Garza is a quality control manager at Karleton Manufacturing, a manufacturing plant located in Trotwood, Ohio. One project that Carmen oversees is the manufacture of tin cans for a major food company. The can widths must be consistent. To compensate for the fact that metal working tools tend to wear down during the day, the pressure behind the tools is increased as the blades become worn. Quality control technicians monitor the process to check that it remains "in control" creating cans whose widths are neither too narrow nor too wide. Carmen has recorded the widths of four cans from 39 batches in an Excel workbook that she wants to use to determine whether the process is "in control." One standard for determining whether a process is "in control" is whether the average value from a process batch falls within the lower and upper control limits. The workbook itself is in need of quality control as some of the formulas are not calculating correctly. You will fix these and then enter the remainder of the formulas needed in the worksheet. Complete the following:

1. Open the **Quality** workbook located in the Excel3 ▶ Case4 folder included with your Data Files, and then save the workbook as **Quality Control Analysis** in the location specified by your instructor.

2. In the Documentation sheet, enter your name and the date.

3. In the Quality Control worksheet, use AutoFill with the value in cell A7 and fill the series of batch numbers from B-1 to B-39 into the range A7:A45.

⚙ **Troubleshoot** 4. In the Quality Control worksheet, cells M3 and M4 display the #NAME? error value instead of the averages. Make the necessary changes to correct the formulas.

⚙ **Troubleshoot** 5. The formulas in the range H7:H45 are supposed to calculate the range of values (maximum minus minimum) within each batch. However, the formula results display 6.2 for every batch. Make the necessary changes in the formulas to fix the problem.

⚙ **Troubleshoot** 6. The formulas in the range I7:I45 are supposed to calculate the average width of the four cans tested in each batch. Unfortunately, the formulas' results don't equal the average widths. Make the necessary changes in the formulas to fix the problem.

7. In cell J7, calculate the lower control limit for the first batch based on the equation

$LCL=XBAR-A2\times RBAR$

where $LCL$ is the lower and upper control limits, $XBAR$ is the average value from all batches, $RBAR$ is the average range from all batches, and $A2$ is a correction factor that depends on the sample size of the batch. In this case, use the $XBAR$ value from cell M3 and the $RBAR$ value from cell M4. Determine the $A2$ value using an exact match lookup with the sample size in cell G7 as the reference value, and the second column from the table in the range O7:P30 as the return value.

8. AutoFill the lower control limit formula from cell J7 into the rest of the LCL column in the Control Limits table. Check to make sure your formulas were properly copied and that they still reference the correct cells.

9. In cell K7, calculate the upper control limit for the first batch based on the equation

$$UCL = XBAR + A2 \times RBAR$$

where $UCL$ is the upper control limit. Copy your formula into the rest of the UCL column in the Control Limits table.

10. In cell L7, indicate whether the B-1 batch process is "in control low" by testing whether the batch's average is less than its LCL value. If it is, display "NO"; otherwise, display a blank cell.

11. In cell M7, indicate whether the B-1 batch process is "in control high" by testing whether the batch's average is greater than its UCL value. If it is, display "NO"; otherwise, display a blank cell.

12. Fill the in control low and in control high formulas for the rest of the batches.

13. Add conditional formatting to the range L7:M45 so that cells displaying "NO" are formatted in dark red text on a light red background.

⚙ **Troubleshoot** 14. The computer program that recorded the width values entered a missing width value as a 0 instead of leaving the cells blank. This affects the calculations about sample size and which batches are in control. Fix this in the data set and any formulas so that the worksheet accurately indicates which batches are not in control on the low side or not in control on the high side.

15. Save and close the workbook.

# Creating a Presentation

*Presenting Information About Community Supported Agriculture*

## OBJECTIVES

**Session 1.1**
- Plan and create a new presentation
- Create a title slide and slides with lists
- Edit and format text
- Move and copy text
- Convert a list to a SmartArt diagram
- Duplicate, rearrange, and delete slides
- Close a presentation

**Session 1.2**
- Open an existing presentation
- Change the theme and theme variant
- Insert and crop photos
- Modify photo compression options
- Resize and move objects
- Create speaker notes
- Check the spelling
- Run a slide show
- Print slides, handouts, speaker notes, and the outline

## Case | *Valley Falls CSA*

Isaac DeSoto graduated from Claflin University in Orangeburg, South Carolina, with a degree in Agriculture Production Technology. He began his career working for the South Carolina Department of Agriculture. Recently, he bought a large farm near Spartanburg, South Carolina, and started a community-supported agriculture program, or CSA. In a CSA, people buy shares each season and, in return, receive weekly portions of produce from the farm. Isaac also created a partnership with other local farmers and founded Valley Falls CSA. Isaac wants to use a PowerPoint presentation to attract new co-op members.

**Microsoft PowerPoint 2013** (or simply **PowerPoint**) is a computer program you use to create a collection of slides that can contain text, charts, pictures, sounds, movies, multimedia, and so on. In this tutorial, you'll use PowerPoint to create a presentation that Isaac can use to explain what Valley Falls CSA is and what it has to offer to potential members and the community. After Isaac reviews it, you'll add graphics and speaker notes to the presentation. Finally, you'll check the spelling, run the slide show to evaluate it, and print the file.

## STARTING DATA FILES

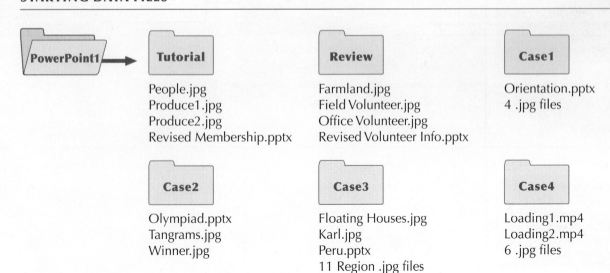

**PowerPoint1** →

**Tutorial**
People.jpg
Produce1.jpg
Produce2.jpg
Revised Membership.pptx

**Review**
Farmland.jpg
Field Volunteer.jpg
Office Volunteer.jpg
Revised Volunteer Info.pptx

**Case1**
Orientation.pptx
4 .jpg files

**Case2**
Olympiad.pptx
Tangrams.jpg
Winner.jpg

**Case3**
Floating Houses.jpg
Karl.jpg
Peru.pptx
11 Region .jpg files

**Case4**
Loading1.mp4
Loading2.mp4
6 .jpg files

# Session 1.1 Visual Overview:

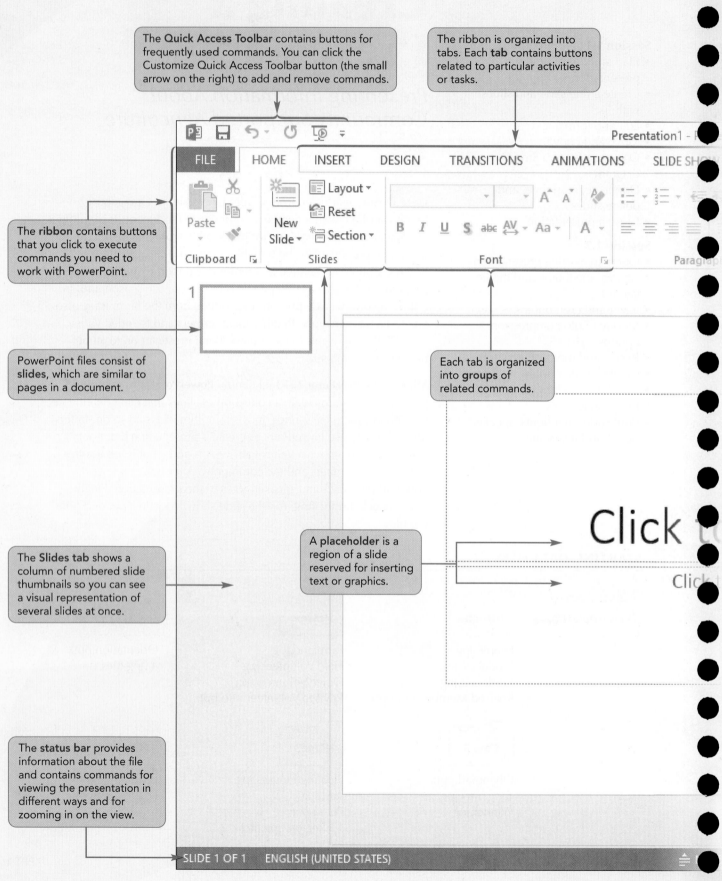

The **Quick Access Toolbar** contains buttons for frequently used commands. You can click the Customize Quick Access Toolbar button (the small arrow on the right) to add and remove commands.

The ribbon is organized into tabs. Each **tab** contains buttons related to particular activities or tasks.

The **ribbon** contains buttons that you click to execute commands you need to work with PowerPoint.

PowerPoint files consist of **slides**, which are similar to pages in a document.

Each tab is organized into **groups** of related commands.

The **Slides tab** shows a column of numbered slide thumbnails so you can see a visual representation of several slides at once.

A **placeholder** is a region of a slide reserved for inserting text or graphics.

The **status bar** provides information about the file and contains commands for viewing the presentation in different ways and for zooming in on the view.

# The PowerPoint Window

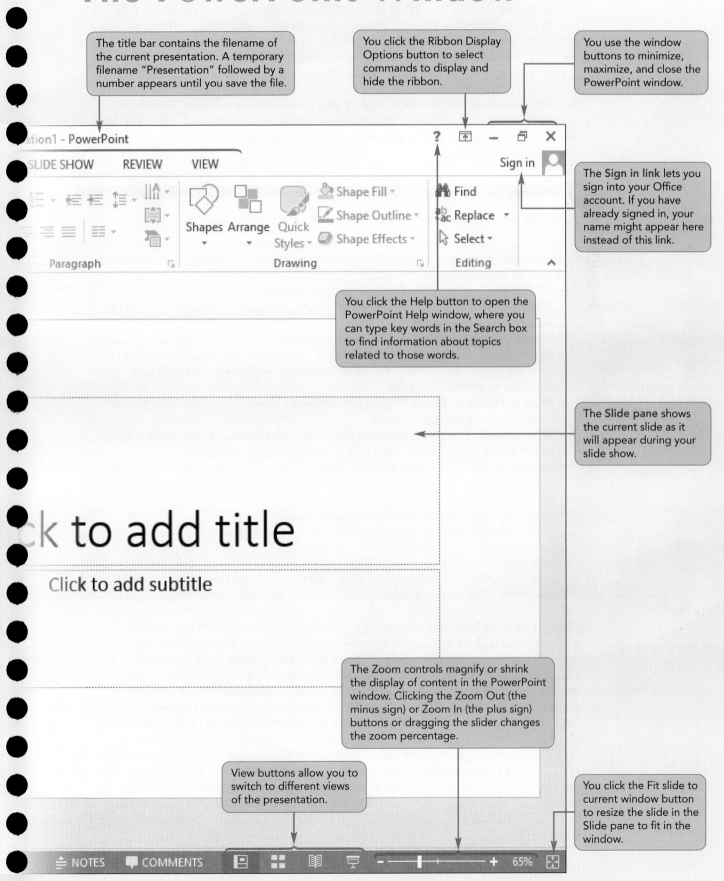

The title bar contains the filename of the current presentation. A temporary filename "Presentation" followed by a number appears until you save the file.

You click the Ribbon Display Options button to select commands to display and hide the ribbon.

You use the window buttons to minimize, maximize, and close the PowerPoint window.

The **Sign in link** lets you sign into your Office account. If you have already signed in, your name might appear here instead of this link.

You click the Help button to open the PowerPoint Help window, where you can type key words in the Search box to find information about topics related to those words.

The **Slide pane** shows the current slide as it will appear during your slide show.

The Zoom controls magnify or shrink the display of content in the PowerPoint window. Clicking the Zoom Out (the minus sign) or Zoom In (the plus sign) buttons or dragging the slider changes the zoom percentage.

View buttons allow you to switch to different views of the presentation.

You click the Fit slide to current window button to resize the slide in the Slide pane to fit in the window.

# Planning a Presentation

A **presentation** is a talk (lecture) or prepared file in which the person speaking or the person who prepared the file—the presenter—wants to communicate with an audience to explain new concepts or ideas, sell a product or service, entertain, train the audience in a new skill or technique, or any of a wide variety of other topics.

Most people find it helpful to use **presentation media**—visual and audio aids to support key points and engage the audience's attention. Microsoft PowerPoint is one of the most commonly used tools for creating effective presentation media. The features of PowerPoint make it easy to incorporate photos, diagrams, music, and video with key points of a presentation. Before you create a presentation, you should spend some time planning its content.

**PROSKILLS**

### Verbal Communication: Planning a Presentation

Answering a few key questions will help you create a presentation using appropriate presentation media that successfully delivers its message or motivates the audience to take an action.

- **What is the purpose of your presentation?** In other words, what action or response do you want your audience to have? For example, do you want them to buy something, follow instructions, or make a decision?
- **Who is your audience?** Think about the needs and interests of your audience as well as any decisions they'll make as a result of what you have to say. What you choose to say to your audience must be relevant to their needs, interests, and decisions or it will be forgotten.
- **What are the main points of your presentation?** Identify the information that is directly relevant to your audience.
- **What presentation media will help your audience absorb the information and remember it later?** Do you need lists, photos, charts, or tables?
- **What is the format for your presentation?** Will you deliver the presentation orally or will you create a presentation file that your audience members will view on their own, without you present?
- **How much time do you have for the presentation?** Keep that in mind as you prepare the presentation content so that you have enough time to present all of your key points.
- **Will your audience benefit from handouts?** **Handouts** are printed documents you give to your audience before, during, or after your presentation.

The purpose of Isaac's presentation is to sell shares in the new CSA. His audience will be members of the local community who are interested in the benefits of belonging to a CSA and want to learn more about it. His key points are that being a member of a CSA is good for consumers because they will be eating fresher, more nutritious food, and good for the community because local farms are supported and there is less of an impact on the environment. He also plans to explain pricing and how members get their produce so that audience members have enough information to make a decision about becoming a member. Isaac will use PowerPoint to display lists and graphics to help make his message clear. He plans to deliver his presentation orally to small groups of people in a classroom-sized room, and his presentation will be 15 to 20 minutes long. For handouts, he plans to have membership applications available to distribute to anyone who is interested, but he will not distribute anything before his presentation because he wants the audience's full attention to be on him and the details are not complex enough that the audience will need a sheet to refer to as he is speaking.

Once you know what you want to say or communicate, you can prepare the presentation media to help communicate your ideas.

# Starting PowerPoint and Creating a New Presentation

Microsoft PowerPoint 2013 is a tool you can use to create and display visual and audio aids on slides to help clarify the points you want to make in your presentation or to create a presentation that people view on their own without you being present.

When PowerPoint starts, the Recent screen in Backstage view is displayed. **Backstage view** contains commands that allow you to manage your presentation files and PowerPoint options. When you first start PowerPoint, the only actions available to you in Backstage view are to open an existing PowerPoint file or create a new file. You'll start PowerPoint now.

## To start PowerPoint:

▶ **1.** Display the Windows Start screen, if necessary.

**Using Windows 7?** To complete Step 1, click the Start button on the taskbar.

▶ **2.** Click the **PowerPoint 2013** tile. PowerPoint starts and displays the Recent screen in Backstage view. See Figure 1-1. In the orange bar on the left is a list of recently opened presentations, and on the right are options for creating new presentations.

**Figure 1-1**    Recent screen in Backstage view

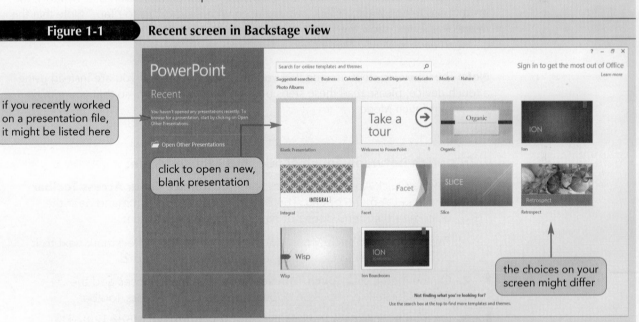

if you recently worked on a presentation file, it might be listed here

click to open a new, blank presentation

the choices on your screen might differ

**Trouble?** If you don't see the PowerPoint 2013 tile, type PowerPoint to display the Apps screen with the PowerPoint 2013 tile highlighted, and then click the tile.

**Using Windows 7?** To complete Step 2, point to All Programs on the Start menu, click Microsoft Office 2013, and then click PowerPoint 2013.

▶ **3.** Click **Blank Presentation**. Backstage view closes and a new presentation window appears. The temporary filename "Presentation1" appears in the title bar. There is only one slide in the new presentation—Slide 1.

**Trouble?** If you do not see the area on the ribbon that contains buttons and you see only the ribbon tab names, click the HOME tab to expand the ribbon and display the commands, and then in the bottom-right corner of the ribbon, click the Pin the ribbon button ⊞ that appears.

**Trouble?** If the window is not maximized, click the Maximize button ▢ in the upper-right corner.

When you create a new presentation, it is displayed in Normal view. **Normal view** displays slides one at a time in the Slide pane, allowing you to see how the text and graphics look on each slide, and displays **thumbnails**—miniature images—of all the slides in the presentation in the Slides tab on the left. The HOME tab on the ribbon is orange to indicate that it is selected when you first open or create a presentation. The Session 1.1 Visual Overview identifies elements of the PowerPoint window.

## Working in Touch Mode

In Office 2013, you can work with a mouse or, if you have a touch screen, you can work in Touch Mode. In **Touch Mode** the ribbon increases in height so that there is more space around each button on the ribbon, making it easier to use your finger to tap the specific button you need. Also, in the main part of the PowerPoint window, the instructions telling you to "Click" are replaced with instructions to "Tap." Note that the figures in this text show the screen with Mouse Mode on. You'll switch to Touch Mode and then back to Mouse Mode now.

**Note:** The following steps assume that you are using a mouse. If you are instead using a touch device, please read these steps but don't complete them, so that you remain working in Touch Mode.

**To switch between Touch Mode and Mouse Mode:**

1. On the Quick Access Toolbar, click the **Customize Quick Access Toolbar** button ▾. A menu opens. The Touch/Mouse Mode command near the bottom of the menu does not have a checkmark next to it.

   **Trouble?** If the Touch/Mouse Mode command has a checkmark next to it, press the Esc key to close the menu, and then skip Step 2.

2. On the menu, click **Touch/Mouse Mode**. The menu closes and the Touch/Mouse Mode button appears on the Quick Access Toolbar.

3. On the Quick Access Toolbar, click the **Touch/Mouse Mode** button ▣. A menu opens listing Mouse and Touch, and the icon next to Mouse is shaded orange to indicate it is selected.

   **Trouble?** If the icon next to Touch is shaded orange, press the Esc key to close the menu and skip Step 4.

4. On the menu, click **Touch**. The menu closes and the ribbon increases in height so that there is more space around each button on the ribbon. Notice that the instructions in the main part of the PowerPoint window changed by replacing the instruction to "Click" with the instruction to "Tap." See Figure 1-2. Now you'll change back to Mouse Mode.

**Figure 1-2**    **PowerPoint window with Touch mode active**

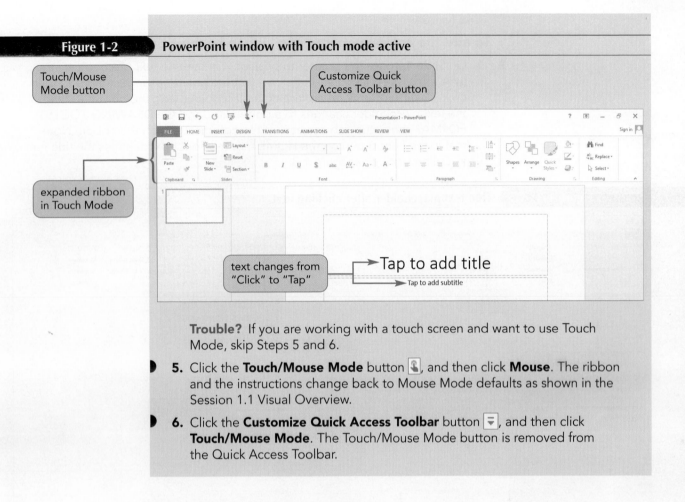

Touch/Mouse Mode button

Customize Quick Access Toolbar button

expanded ribbon in Touch Mode

text changes from "Click" to "Tap"

Tap to add title

Tap to add subtitle

**Trouble?** If you are working with a touch screen and want to use Touch Mode, skip Steps 5 and 6.

5. Click the **Touch/Mouse Mode** button, and then click **Mouse**. The ribbon and the instructions change back to Mouse Mode defaults as shown in the Session 1.1 Visual Overview.

6. Click the **Customize Quick Access Toolbar** button, and then click **Touch/Mouse Mode**. The Touch/Mouse Mode button is removed from the Quick Access Toolbar.

# Creating a Title Slide

The **title slide** is the first slide in a presentation. It generally contains the title of the presentation plus any other identifying information you want to include, such as a company's slogan, the presenter's name, or a company name. The **font**—a set of characters with the same design—used in the title and subtitle may be the same or may be different fonts that complement each other.

The title slide contains two objects called text placeholders. A placeholder is a region of a slide reserved for inserting text or graphics. A **text placeholder** is a placeholder designed to contain text. Text placeholders usually display text that describes the purpose of the placeholder and instructs you to click so that you can start typing in the placeholder. The larger text placeholder on the title slide is designed to hold the presentation title, and the smaller text placeholder is designed to contain a subtitle. Once you enter text into a text placeholder, it is no longer a placeholder and becomes an object called a **text box**.

When you click in the placeholder, the **insertion point**, which indicates where text will appear when you start typing, appears as a blinking line in the center of the placeholder. In addition, a contextual tab, the DRAWING TOOLS FORMAT tab, appears on the ribbon. A **contextual tab** appears only in context—that is, when a particular type of object is selected or active—and contains commands for modifying that object.

You'll add a title and subtitle for Isaac's presentation now. Isaac wants the title slide to contain the company name and slogan.

### To add the company name and slogan to the title slide:

1. On **Slide 1**, move the pointer to position it in the title text placeholder (where it says "Click to add title") so that the pointer changes to ⊺, and then click. The insertion point replaces the placeholder text; the border around the text placeholder changes to a dotted line, and the DRAWING TOOLS FORMAT contextual tab appears as the rightmost tab on the ribbon. Note that in the Font group on the HOME tab, the Font box identifies the title font as Calibri Light. See Figure 1-3.

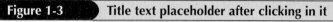

**Figure 1-3**   Title text placeholder after clicking in it

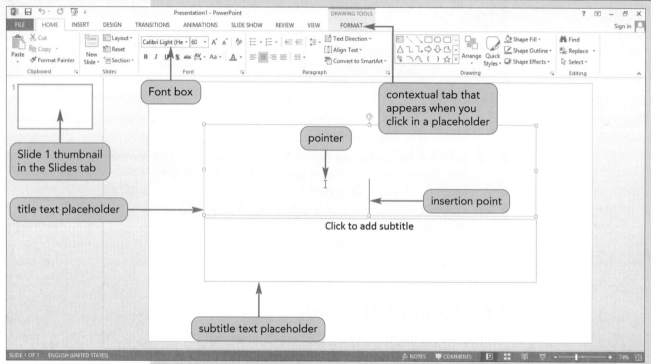

**Trouble?** The insertion point might appear as a thin, blue rectangle with the Mini toolbar above and to the right of it. Ignore this and continue with Step 2.

2. Type **Valley Farms CSA**. The placeholder is now a text box.

3. Click a blank area of the slide. The border of the text box disappears, and the DRAWING TOOLS FORMAT tab no longer appears on the ribbon.

4. Click in the **subtitle text placeholder** (where it says "Click to add subtitle"), and then type **Freshest, most delicious food!**. Notice in the Font group that the subtitle font is Calibri, a font which works well with the Calibri Light font used in the title text.

5. Click a blank area of the slide.

## Saving and Editing a Presentation

Once you have created a presentation, you should name and save the presentation file. You can save the file on a hard drive or a network drive, on an external drive such as a USB drive, or to your account on SkyDrive, Microsoft's free online storage area.

## To save the presentation for the first time:

▶ **1.** On the Quick Access Toolbar, point to the **Save** button 🖫. The button becomes shaded and its ScreenTip appears. A **ScreenTip** identifies the names of buttons; sometimes they also display a key combination you can press instead of clicking the button and information about how to use the button. In this case, the ScreenTip displays the word "Save" and the key combination for the Save command, Ctrl+S.

▶ **2.** Click the **Save** button 🖫. The Save As screen in Backstage view appears. See Figure 1-4. Because a presentation is open, more commands are available in Backstage view than when you started PowerPoint. The **navigation bar** on the left contains commands for working with the file and program options.

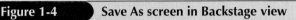

**Figure 1-4** ▶ Save As screen in Backstage view

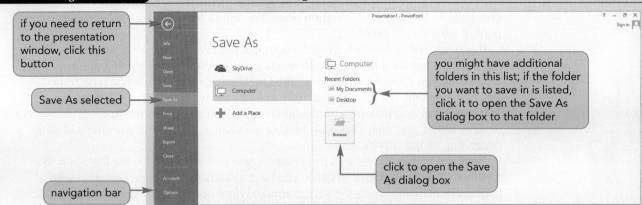

if you need to return to the presentation window, click this button

Save As selected

navigation bar

you might have additional folders in this list; if the folder you want to save in is listed, click it to open the Save As dialog box to that folder

click to open the Save As dialog box

▶ **3.** Click **Computer**, if necessary, and then click the **Browse** button. The Save As dialog box opens, similar to the one shown in Figure 1-5.

**Figure 1-5** ▶ Save As dialog box

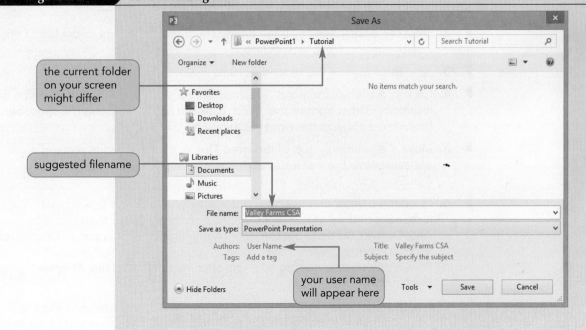

the current folder on your screen might differ

suggested filename

your user name will appear here

**Trouble?** If you are saving your files to your SkyDrive account, click SkyDrive on the Save As screen, log in to your account if necessary, and then click the Browse button.

4. Navigate to the drive and folder where you are storing your Data Files, and then click in the **File name** box. The suggested filename, Valley Falls CSA, is selected.

5. Type **Membership Info**. The text you type replaces the selected text in the File name box.

6. Click the **Save** button. The file is saved, the dialog box and Backstage view close, and the presentation window appears again with the new filename in the title bar.

Once you have created a presentation, you can make changes to it. For example, if you need to change text in a text box, you can easily edit it. The Backspace key deletes characters to the left of the insertion point, and the Delete key deletes characters to the right of the insertion point.

If you mistype or misspell a word, you might not need to correct it because the **AutoCorrect** feature automatically corrects many commonly mistyped and misspelled words after you press the spacebar or the Enter key. For instance, if you type "cna" and then press the spacebar, PowerPoint corrects the word to "can." If you want AutoCorrect to stop making a particular change, you can display the AutoCorrect Options menu, and then click Stop making the change. (The exact wording will differ depending on the change made.)

After you make changes to a presentation, you will need to save the file again so that the changes are stored. Because you have already saved the presentation with a permanent filename, using the Save command does not open the Save As dialog box; it simply saves the changes you made to the file.

**To edit the text on Slide 1 and save your changes:**

1. On Slide 1, click the **title**, and then use the ← and → keys as needed to position the insertion point to the right of the word "Farms."

2. Press the **Backspace** key three times. The three characters to the left of the insertion point, "rms," are deleted.

3. Type **lls** to change the second word to "Falls."

4. Click to the left of the word "Freshest" in the subtitle text box to position the insertion point in front of that word, type **Teh**, and then press the **spacebar**. PowerPoint corrects the word you typed to "The."

5. Move the pointer on top of the word **The**. A small, very faint rectangle appears below the first letter of the word. This indicates that an AutoCorrection has been made.

6. Move the pointer on top of the AutoCorrection indicator box so that it changes to the AutoCorrect Options button ⚡ ▾, and then click the **AutoCorrect Options button** ⚡ ▾. A menu opens, as shown in Figure 1-6. You can change the word back to what you originally typed, instruct PowerPoint to stop making this type of correction in this file, or open the AutoCorrect dialog box.

**Trouble?** If you can't see the AutoCorrection indicator box, point to the letter T, and then slowly move the pointer down until it is on top of the box and changes it to the AutoCorrect Options button.

**Figure 1-6**    AutoCorrect Options button menu

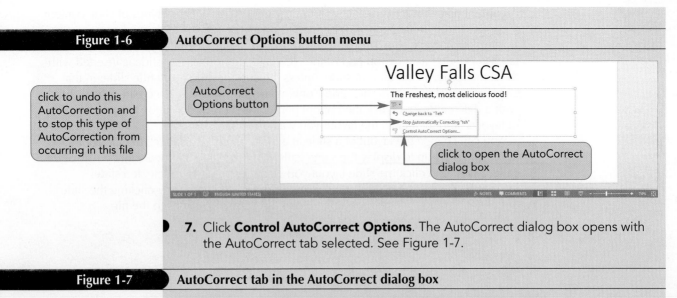

click to undo this AutoCorrection and to stop this type of AutoCorrection from occurring in this file

AutoCorrect Options button

click to open the AutoCorrect dialog box

**7.** Click **Control AutoCorrect Options**. The AutoCorrect dialog box opens with the AutoCorrect tab selected. See Figure 1-7.

**Figure 1-7**    AutoCorrect tab in the AutoCorrect dialog box

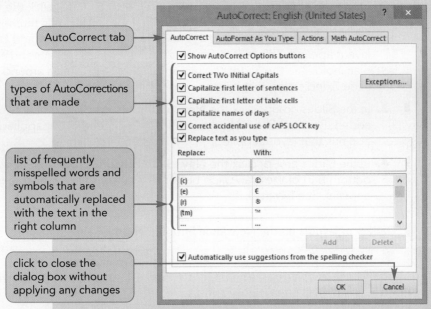

AutoCorrect tab

types of AutoCorrections that are made

list of frequently misspelled words and symbols that are automatically replaced with the text in the right column

click to close the dialog box without applying any changes

**8.** Examine the types of changes the AutoCorrect feature makes, and then click the **Cancel** button.

**9.** Click to the left of the "F" in "Freshest, if necessary, press the **Delete** key, and then type **f**. The subtitle now is "The freshest, most delicious food!" Now that you have modified the presentation, you need to save your changes.

**10.** On the Quick Access Toolbar, click the **Save** button. The changes you made are saved to the file you named Membership Info.

## Adding New Slides

Now that you've created the title slide, you need to add more slides. Every slide has a **layout**, which is the arrangement of placeholders on the slide. The title slide uses the Title Slide layout. A commonly used layout is the Title and Content layout, which contains a title text placeholder for the slide title and a content placeholder.

A **content placeholder** is a placeholder designed to hold several types of slide content including text, a table, a chart, a picture, or a video.

To add a new slide, you use the New Slide button in the Slides group on the HOME tab. When you click the top part of the New Slide button, a new slide is inserted with the same layout as the current slide, unless the current slide is the title slide; in that case the new slide has the Title and Content layout. If you want to create a new slide with a different layout, click the bottom part of the New Slide button to open a gallery of layouts, and then click the layout you want to use.

You can change the layout of a slide at any time. To do this, click the Layout button in the Slides group to display the same gallery of layouts that appears in the Add Slide gallery, and then click the slide layout you want to apply to the selected slide.

As you add slides, you can switch from one slide to another by clicking the slide thumbnails in the Slides tab. You need to add several new slides to the file.

### To add new slides and apply different layouts:

1. Make sure the HOME tab is displayed on the ribbon.

2. In the Slides group, click the **New Slide** button (that is, click the top part of the button). A new slide appears in the Slide pane and its thumbnail appears in the Slides tab below Slide 1. The new slide has the Title and Content layout applied. This layout contains a title text placeholder and a content placeholder. In the Slides tab, an orange border appears around the new Slide 2, indicating that it is the current slide.

3. In the Slides group, click the **New Slide** button again. A new Slide 3 is added. Because Slide 2 had the Title and Content layout applied, Slide 3 also has that layout applied.

4. In the Slides group, click the **New Slide button arrow** (that is, click the bottom part of the New Slide button). A gallery of the available layouts appears. See Figure 1-8.

| Figure 1-8 | Gallery of layouts on the New Slide button menu |
| --- | --- |

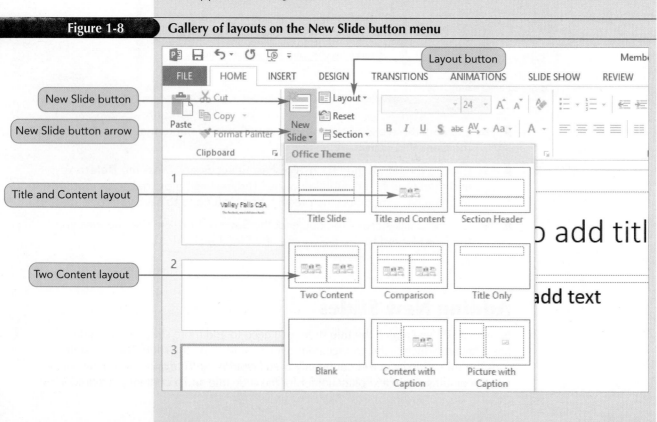

5.  In the gallery, click the **Two Content** layout. The gallery closes and a new Slide 4 is inserted with the Two Content layout applied. This layout includes three objects: a title text placeholder and two content placeholders.

6.  In the Slides group, click the **New Slide** button. A new Slide 5 is added to the presentation. Because Slide 4 had the Two Content layout applied, that layout is also applied to the new slide. You need to change the layout of Slide 5.

7.  In the Slides group, click the **Layout** button. The same gallery of layouts that appeared when you clicked the New Slide button arrow appears. The Two Content layout is selected, as indicated by the orange shading behind it, showing you that this is the layout applied to the current slide, Slide 5.

8.  Click the **Title and Content** layout. The layout of Slide 5 is changed to Title and Content.

9.  In the Slides group, click the **New Slide** button three more times to add three more slides with the Title and Content layout. There are now eight slides in the presentation. In the Slides tab, Slides 1 through 3 have scrolled up out of view, and vertical scroll bars are now visible in both the Slides tab and in the Slide pane.

10. In the Slides tab, drag the **scroll box** to the top of the vertical scroll bar, and then click the **Slide 2** thumbnail. Slide 2 becomes the current slide—it appears in the Slide pane and is selected in the Slides tab. See Figure 1-9.

| Figure 1-9 | Slide 2 with the Title and Content layout |
| --- | --- |

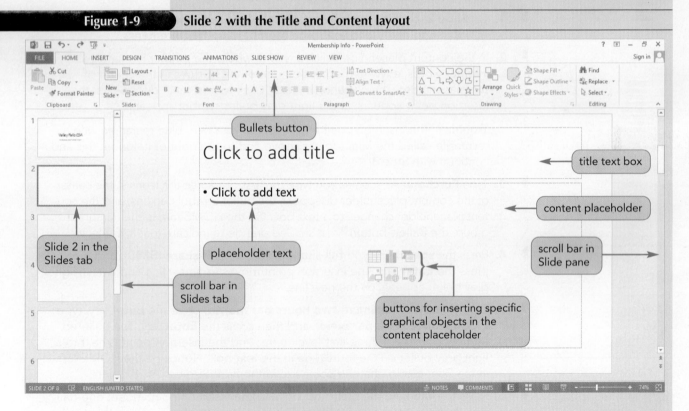

11. On the Quick Access Toolbar, click the **Save** button 🖫. The changes you made are saved in the file.

If you accidentally close a presentation without saving changes and need to recover it, you can do so by clicking the FILE tab, clicking Open in the navigation bar, and then clicking the Recover Unsaved Presentations button.

# Creating Lists

One way to help explain the topic or concept you are describing in your presentation is to use lists. For oral presentations, the intent of lists is to enhance the oral presentation, not replace it. In self-running presentations, items in lists might need to be longer and more descriptive. However, keep in mind that PowerPoint is a presentation graphics program intended to help you present information in a visual, graphical manner, not create a written document in an alternate form.

Items in a list can appear at different levels. A **first-level item** is a main item in a list; a **second-level item**—sometimes called a **subitem**—is an item beneath and indented from a first-level item. Usually, the font size—the size of the text—in subitems is smaller than the size used for text in the level above. Text is measured in **points**, which is a unit of measurement. Text in a book is typically printed in 10- or 12-point type; text on a slide needs to be much larger so the audience can easily read it.

## Creating a Bulleted List

A **bulleted list** is a list of items with some type of bullet symbol in front of each item or paragraph. When you create a subitem in the list, a different or smaller symbol is often used. You need to create a bulleted list that describes the requirements of a membership in Valley Farms CSA.

**To create bulleted lists on Slides 2 and 3:**

1. On **Slide 2**, click in the **title text placeholder** (with the placeholder text "Click to add title"), and then type **Membership Requirements**.

2. In the content placeholder, click any area where the pointer is shaped as $\text{I}$; in other words, anywhere except on one of the buttons in the center of the placeholder. The placeholder text "Click to add text" disappears, the insertion point appears, and a light gray bullet symbol appears.

   **Trouble?** The insertion point might appear as a thin, blue rectangle with a rectangle called the Mini toolbar above and to the right of it. Ignore this and continue with Step 3.

3. Type **Purchase**. As soon as you type the first character, the icons in the center of the content placeholder disappear, the bullet symbol darkens, and the content placeholder changes to a text box. On the HOME tab, in the Paragraph group, the Bullets button is shaded orange to indicate that it is selected.

4. Press the **spacebar**, type **full-share ($425) or half-share ($250)**, and then press the **Enter** key. The insertion point moves to a new line and a new, light gray bullet appears on the new line.

5. Type **Volunteer minimum two hours per month**, press the **Enter** key, type **Pick up share once per week**, and then press the **Enter** key. The bulleted list now consists of three first-level items, and the insertion point is next to a light gray bullet on the fourth line in the text box. Notice on the HOME tab, in the Font group, that the point size in the Font Size box is 28 points.

6. Press the **Tab** key. The bullet symbol and the insertion point indent one-half inch to the right, the bullet symbol changes to a smaller size, and the number in the Font Size box changes to 24. See Figure 1-10.

**Figure 1-10** **Subitem created on Slide 2**

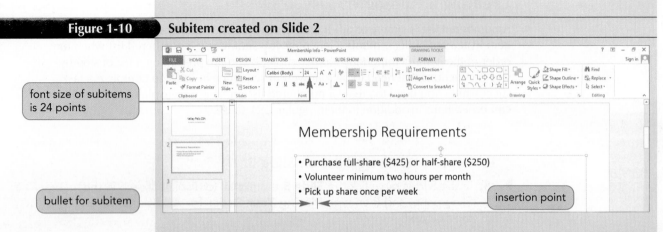

font size of subitems is 24 points

bullet for subitem

insertion point

7. Type **Fridays, 3 p.m. - 5 p.m.** and then press the **Enter** key. When you pressed the spacebar key after typing 5, AutoCorrect changed the dash to an en-dash, a typographical character slightly longer than a hyphen.

8. Type **Saturdays, 7 a.m. - noon**, and then press the **Enter** key. A third subitem is created. You will change it to a first-level item using a key combination. In this book, when you need to press two keys together, the keys will be listed separated by a plus sign. You don't need to press the keys at exactly the same time—press and hold the first key, press and release the second key, and then release the first key.

9. Press the **Shift+Tab** keys. The bullet symbol and the insertion point shift back to the left margin of the text box, the bullet symbol changes back to the larger size, and 28 again appears in the Font Size box because this line is now a first-level bulleted item.

**TIP**

Avoid putting information on the bottom quarter of the slide because people in the back of a large room will not be able to see it.

10. Type **Or have it delivered (additional fee)**, press the **Enter** key, and then type **October community celebration**.

11. In the Slides tab, click the **Slide 3** thumbnail to display Slide 3 in the Slide pane, click in the **title text placeholder**, and then type **Members Receive**.

12. In the content placeholder, click the **placeholder text**, type **Share of pre-selected produce**, press the **Enter** key, and then type **Self-selected items**.

If you add more text than will fit in the text box with the default font sizes and line spacing, **AutoFit** adjusts these features to make the text fit. When AutoFit is activated, the AutoFit Options button appears below the text box. You can click this button and then select from among several options, including turning off AutoFit for this text box and splitting the text between two slides. Although AutoFit can be helpful, be aware that it also allows you to crowd text on a slide, making the slide less effective.

**PROSKILLS**

*Written Communication: How Much Text Should I Include?*

Text can help audiences retain the information you are presenting by allowing them to read the main points while hearing you discuss them. But be wary of adding so much text to your slides that your audience can ignore you and just read the slides. Try to follow the 7x7 rule—no more than seven items per slide, with no more than seven words per item. A variation of this rule is 6x6, and some presenters even prefer 4x4. If you create a self-running presentation (a presentation file others will view on their own) you will usually need to add more text than you would if you were presenting the material in person.

## Creating a Numbered List

A **numbered list** is similar to a bulleted list except that numbers appear in front of each item instead of bullet symbols. Generally you should use a numbered list when the order of the items is important—for example, if you are presenting a list of step-by-step instructions that need to be followed in sequence in order to complete a task successfully. You need to create a numbered list on Slide 5 to explain how members can order items in addition to their regular CSA share.

### To create a numbered list on Slide 5:

1. In the Slides tab, click the **Slide 5** thumbnail to display Slide 5 in the Slide pane, and then type **Placing Your Order for Additional Items** as the title text.

2. In the content placeholder, click the **placeholder text**.

3. On the HOME tab, in the Paragraph group, click the **Numbering** button ⊟. The Numbering button is selected, the Bullets button is deselected, and in the content placeholder, the bullet symbol is replaced with the number 1 followed by a period.

   **Trouble?** If a menu containing a gallery of numbering styles appears, you clicked the Numbering button arrow on the right side of the button. Click the Numbering button arrow again to close the menu, and then click the left part of the Numbering button.

4. Type **Place online by Wednesday**, and then press the **Enter** key. As soon as you start typing, the number 1 darkens to black. After you press the Enter key, the insertion point moves to the next line, next to the light gray number 2.

5. Type **Verify payment information**, and then press the **Enter** key. The number 3 appears on the next line.

6. In the Paragraph group, click the **Increase List Level** button ⊒. The third line is indented to be a subitem under the second item, and the number 3 that had appeared changes to a number 1 in a smaller size than the first-level items. Clicking the Increase List Level button is an alternative to pressing the Tab key to create a subitem.

7. Type **Credit card**, press the **Enter** key, type **Debit from checking account**, press the **Enter** key.

8. In the Paragraph group, click the **Decrease List Level** button ⊟. The fifth line is now a first-level item and the number 3 appears next to it. Clicking the Decrease List Level button is an alternative to pressing the Shift+Tab keys to promote a subitem.

9. Type **Submit**. The list now consists of three first-level numbered items and two subitems under number 2.

10. In the second item, click before the word "Verify," and then press the **Enter** key. A blank line is inserted above the second item.

11. Press the ↑ key. A light-gray number 2 appears in the blank line. The item on the third line in the list is still numbered 2.

12. Type **Specify pickup or delivery**. As soon as you start typing, the new number 2 darkens in the second line and the third item in the list is numbered 3. Compare your screen to Figure 1-11.

**Figure 1-11**    **Numbered list on Slide 5**

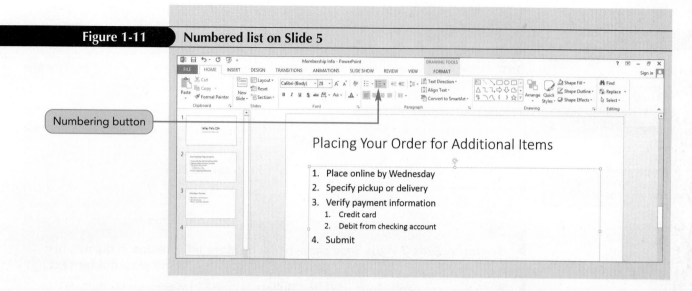

Numbering button

## Creating an Unnumbered List

An **unnumbered list** is a list that does not have bullets or numbers preceding each item. Unnumbered lists are useful in slides when you want to present information on multiple lines without actually itemizing the information. For example, contact information for the presenter, including his or her email address, street address, city, and so on would be clearer if it were in an unnumbered list.

As you have seen, items in a list have a little extra space between each item to visually separate bulleted items. Sometimes, you don't want the extra space between lines. If you press the Shift+Enter keys instead of just the Enter key, a new line is created, but it is still considered to be part of the item above it. Therefore, there is no extra space between the lines. Note that this also means that if you do this in a bulleted or numbered list, the new line will not have a bullet or number next to it because it is not a new item.

You need to create a slide that defines CSA. Also, Isaac asks you to create a slide containing contact information.

**To create unnumbered lists on Slides 4 and 7:**

1. In the Slides tab, click the **Slide 4** thumbnail to display Slide 4 in the Slide pane. Slide 4 has the Two Content layout applied.

2. Type **What Is a CSA?** as the title text, and then in the left content placeholder, click the **placeholder text**.

3. On the HOME tab, in the Paragraph group, click the **Bullets** button. The button is no longer selected, and the bullet symbol disappears from the content placeholder.

4. Type **Community**, press the **Enter** key, type **Supported**, press the **Enter** key, and then type **Agriculture**. Compare your screen to Figure 1-12.

**Figure 1-12**  **Unnumbered list on Slide 4**

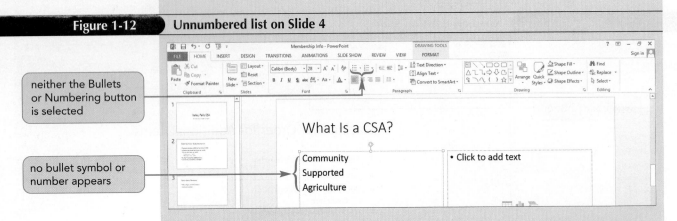

neither the Bullets or Numbering button is selected

no bullet symbol or number appears

5. Display **Slide 7** in the Slide pane, type **For More Information** in the title text placeholder, and then in the content placeholder, click the **placeholder text**.

6. In the Paragraph group, click the **Bullets** button to remove the bullets, type **Valley Falls CSA**, and then press the **Enter** key. A new line is created, but there is extra space above the insertion point. This is not how addresses usually appear.

7. Press the **Backspace** key to delete the new line and move the insertion point back to the end of the first line, and then press the **Shift+Enter** keys. The insertion point moves to the next line and, this time, there is no extra space above it.

8. Type **300 County Fair Road**, press the **Shift+Enter** keys, and then type **Spartanburg, SC 29301**. You need to insert the phone number on the next line, the general email address for the group on the line after that, and the website address on the last line. The extra space above these lines will set this information apart from the address and make it easier to read.

9. Press the **Enter** key to create a new line with extra space above it, type **(864) 555-FOOD**, press the **Enter** key, type **csainfo@valleyfallscsa.example.org**, and then press the **Enter** key. The insertion point moves to a new line with extra space above it, and the email address you typed changes color to blue and is underlined.

   When you type text that PowerPoint recognizes as an email or website address and then press the spacebar or Enter key, it automatically formats it as a link that can be clicked during a slide show, and changes its color and adds the underline to indicate this. You can only click links during a slide show.

10. Type **www.valleyfallscsa.example.org**, and then press the **spacebar**. The text is formatted as a link. Isaac plans to click the link during his presentation to show the audience the website, so he wants it to stay formatted as a link. However, there is no need to have the email address formatted as a link because no one will click it during the presentation.

11. Right-click **csainfo@valleyfallscsa.example.org**. A shortcut menu opens.

12. On the shortcut menu, click **Remove Hyperlink**. The email address is no longer formatted as a hyperlink. Compare your screen to Figure 1-13.

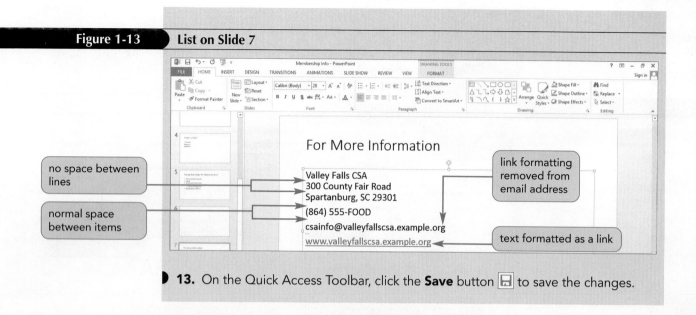

**Figure 1-13**   **List on Slide 7**

no space between lines

normal space between items

link formatting removed from email address

text formatted as a link

13. On the Quick Access Toolbar, click the **Save** button 🔲 to save the changes.

# Formatting Text

Slides in a presentation should have a cohesive look and feel. For example, the slide titles and the text in content placeholders should be in complementary fonts. However, there are times when you need to change the format of text. For instance, you might want to make specific words bold to make them stand out more.

To apply a format to text, either the text or the text box must be selected. If you want to apply the same formatting to all the text in a text box, you can click the border of the text box. When you do this, the dotted line border changes to a solid line to indicate that the contents of the entire text box are selected.

The commands in the Font group on the HOME tab are used to apply formatting to text. Some of these commands are also available on the Mini toolbar, which appears when you select text with the mouse. The **Mini toolbar** contains commonly used buttons for formatting text. If the Mini toolbar appears, you can use the buttons on it instead of those in the Font group.

Some of the commands in the Font group use the Microsoft Office **Live Preview** feature, which previews the change on the slide so you can instantly see what the text will look like if you apply that format.

Isaac wants the contact information on Slide 7 to be larger. He also wants the first letter of each item in the unnumbered list on Slide 4 ("What Is a CSA?") formatted so they are more prominent.

**TIP**

To remove all formatting from selected text, click the Clear All Formatting button in the Font group.

## To format the text on Slides 4 and 7:

1. On **Slide 7** ("For More Information"), position the pointer on the text box border so that it changes to ⬆, and then click the border of the text box containing the contact information. The border changes to a solid line to indicate that the entire text box is selected.

2. On the HOME tab, in the Font group, click the **Increase Font Size** button A̋ twice. All the text in the text box increases in size with each click.

3. Display **Slide 4** ("What Is a CSA?") in the Slide pane.

**4.** In the unnumbered list, click to the left of "Community," press and hold the **Shift** key, press the → key, and then release the **Shift** key. The letter "C" is selected. See Figure 1-14.

| Figure 1-14 | Text selected to be formatted |

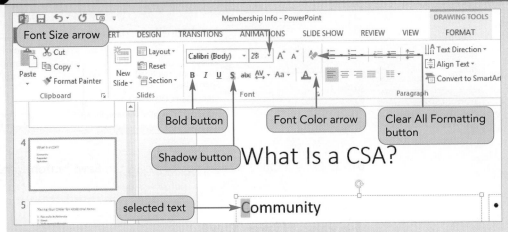

**5.** In the Font group, click the **Bold** button B. The Bold button becomes selected and the selected text is formatted as bold.

**6.** Make sure the letter "C" is still selected, and then in the Font group, click the **Shadow** button S. The selected text is now bold with a slight drop shadow.

**7.** In the Font group, click the **Font Size arrow** to open the Font Size menu, and then click **48**. The selected text is now 48 points.

**8.** In the Font group, click the **Font Color arrow**. A menu containing colors opens.

**9.** Under Theme Colors, move the pointer over each color, noting the ScreenTips that appear and watching as Live Preview changes the color of the selected text as you point to each color. Figure 1-15 shows the pointer pointing to the Orange, Accent 2, Darker 25% color.

| Figure 1-15 | Font Color button menu |

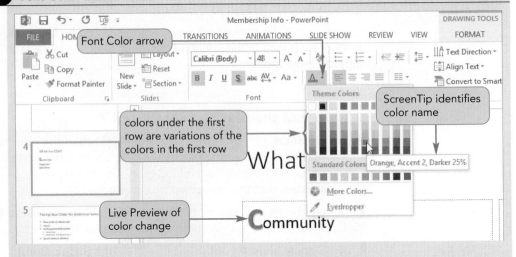

**10.** Using the ScreenTips, locate the **Orange, Accent 2, Darker 25%** color and then click it. The selected text changes to the orange color you clicked.

Now you need to format the first letters in the other words in the list to match the letter "C." You can repeat the steps you did when you formatted the letter "C," or you use the Format Painter to copy all the formatting of the letter "C" to the other letters you need to format.

Also, Isaac wants the text in the unnumbered list to be as large as possible. Because the first letters of each word are larger than the rest of the letters, the easiest way to do this is to select all of the text, and then use the Increase Font Size button. All of the letters will increase in size by four points with each click.

**To use the Format Painter to copy and apply formatting on Slide 4:**

1. Make sure the letter "C" is still selected.

2. On the HOME tab, in the Clipboard group, click the **Format Painter** button, and then move the pointer back to the Slide pane. The button is selected, and the pointer changes to 🖌.

3. Position the pointer before the letter "S" in "Supported," press and hold the mouse button, drag over the letter **S**, and then release the mouse button. The formatting you applied to the letter "C" is copied to the letter "S" and the Mini toolbar appears. See Figure 1-16. The Mini toolbar appears whenever you drag over text to select it.

**Figure 1-16**  ▶  **The Mini toolbar**

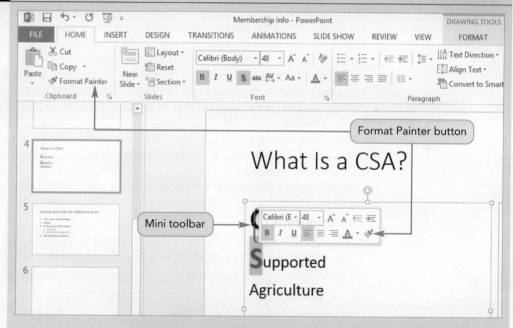

**TIP**

If you need to copy formatting to more than one location, double-click the Format Painter button to keep it selected until you deselect it.

4. On the Mini toolbar, click the **Format Painter** button 🖌, and then drag across the letter **A** in Agriculture.

5. Click the border of the text box to select the entire text box, and then in the Font group, click the **Increase Font Size** button A˄ five times. In the Font group, the Font Size button indicates that the text is 48+ points. This means that in the selected text box, the text that is the smallest is 48 points and there is some text that is a larger point size.

6. On the Quick Access Toolbar, click the **Save** button 💾 to save the changes.

### Undoing and Redoing Actions

If you make a mistake or change your mind about an action as you are working, you can reverse the action by clicking the Undo button on the Quick Access Toolbar. You can undo up to the most recent 20 actions by continuing to click the Undo button, or by clicking the Undo button arrow and then selecting as many actions in the list as you want. You can also Redo an action that you undid by clicking the Redo button on the Quick Access Toolbar.

When there are no actions that can be redone, the Redo button changes to the Repeat button. You can use the Repeat button to repeat an action, such as formatting text as bold. If the Repeat button is light gray, this means it is unavailable because there is no action to repeat (or to redo).

# Moving and Copying Text

You can move or copy text and objects in a presentation using the Clipboard. The **Clipboard** is a temporary storage area available to all Windows programs on which text or objects are stored when you cut or copy them. To **cut** text or objects—that is, remove the selected text or objects from one location so that you can place it somewhere else—you select the text or object, and then use the Cut button in the Clipboard group on the HOME tab to remove the selected text or object and place it on the Clipboard. To **copy** selected text or objects, you use the Copy button in the Clipboard group on the HOME tab, which leaves the original text or object on the slide and places a copy of it on the Clipboard. You can then **paste** the text or object stored on the Clipboard anywhere in the presentation, or, in fact, in any file in any Windows program.

You can paste an item on the Clipboard as many times and in as many locations as you like. However, the Clipboard can hold only the most recently cut or copied item. As soon as you cut or copy another item, it replaces the previously cut or copied item on the Clipboard.

Note that cutting text or an object is different from using the Delete or Backspace key to delete it. Deleted text and objects are not placed on the Clipboard; this means they cannot be pasted.

Isaac wants a few changes made to Slides 5 and 3. You'll use the Clipboard as you make these edits.

### To copy and paste text using the Clipboard:

▶ 1. Display **Slide 5** ("Placing Your Order for Additional Items") in the Slide pane, and then double-click the word **Order** in the title text. The word "Order" is selected.

▶ 2. On the HOME tab, in the Clipboard group, click the **Copy** button. The selected word is copied to the Clipboard.

▶ 3. In the last item in the numbered list, click after the word "Submit," and then press the **spacebar**.

▶ 4. In the Clipboard group, click the **Paste** button. The text is pasted and picks up the formatting of its destination; that is, the pasted text is the 28-point Calibri font, the same font and size as the rest of the first-level items in the list, instead of 44-point Calibri Light as in the title. The Paste Options button ▾ appears below the pasted text.

▶ 5. Click the **Paste Options** button ▾. A menu opens with four buttons on it. See Figure 1-17.

| Figure 1-17 | Buttons on the Paste Options button menu when text is on the Clipboard |

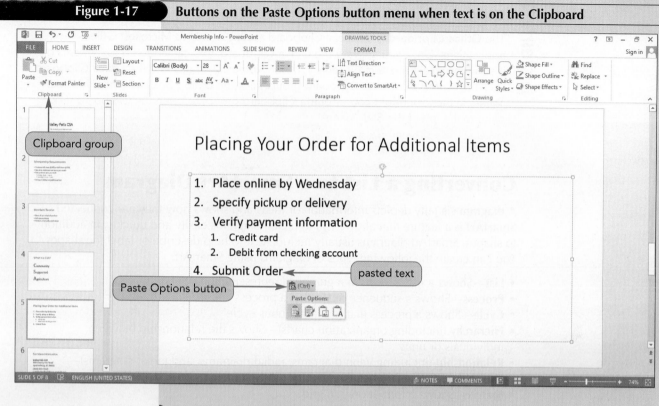

6. Point to each button on the menu, reading the ScreenTips and watching to see how the pasted text changes in appearance. The first button is the Use Destination Theme button, and this is the default choice when you paste text.

7. Click a blank area of the slide to close the menu without making a selection, click to the left of "Order" in the last item in the numbered list, press the **Delete** key, and then type **o**. The word "order" in in the numbered list is now all lowercase.

8. Display **Slide 2** ("Membership Requirements") in the Slide pane. The last bulleted item ("October community celebration") belongs on Slide 3.

9. In the last bulleted item, position the pointer on top of the bullet symbol so that the pointer changes to ⊕, and then click. The entire bulleted item is selected.

10. In the Clipboard group, click the **Cut** button. The last bulleted item is removed from the slide and placed on the Clipboard.

11. Display **Slide 3** ("Members Receive") in the Slide pane, click after the second bulleted item, and then press the **Enter** key to create a third line.

12. In the Clipboard group, click the **Paste** button. The bulleted item you cut is pasted as the third bulleted item on Slide 3 using the default Paste option of Use Destination Theme. The insertion point appears next to a fourth bulleted item.

13. Press the **Backspace** key twice. The extra line is deleted.

### Using the Office Clipboard

The **Office Clipboard** is a special Clipboard available only to Microsoft Office applications. Once you activate the Office Clipboard, you can store up to 24 items on it and then select the item or items you want to paste. To activate the Office Clipboard, click the HOME tab. In the Clipboard group, click the Dialog Box Launcher (the small square in the lower-right corner of the Clipboard group) to open the Clipboard task pane to the left of the Slide pane.

# Converting a List to a SmartArt Diagram

A **diagram** visually depicts information or ideas and shows how they are connected. **SmartArt** is a feature that allows you to create diagrams easily and quickly. In addition to shapes, SmartArt diagrams usually include text to help describe or label the shapes. You can create the following types of diagrams using SmartArt:

- **List**—Shows a list of items in a graphical representation
- **Process**—Shows a sequence of steps in a process
- **Cycle**—Shows a process that is a continuous cycle
- **Hierarchy** (including organization charts)—Shows the relationship between individuals or units
- **Relationship** (including Venn diagrams, radial diagrams, and target diagrams)— Shows the relationship between two or more elements
- **Matrix**—Shows information in a grid
- **Pyramid**—Shows foundation-based relationships
- **Picture**—Provides a location for a picture or pictures that you insert

There is also an Office.com category of SmartArt, which, if you are connected to the Internet, displays additional SmartArt diagrams available in various categories on Office.com, a Microsoft website that contains tools for use with Office programs.

A quick way to create a SmartArt diagram is to convert an existing list. When you select an existing list and then click the Convert to SmartArt Graphic button in the Paragraph group on the HOME tab, a gallery of SmartArt layouts appears. For SmartArt, a **layout** is the arrangement of the shapes in the diagram. Each first-level item in the list is converted to a shape in the SmartArt diagram. If the list contains subitems, you might need to experiment with different layouts to find one that best suits the information in your list.

### Converting a Bulleted List into a SmartArt Diagram

- Click anywhere in the bulleted list.
- In the Paragraph group on the HOME tab, click the Convert to SmartArt Graphic button, and then click More SmartArt Graphics.
- In the Choose a SmartArt Graphic dialog box, select the desired SmartArt type in the list on the left.
- In the center pane, click the SmartArt diagram you want to use.
- Click the OK button.

Isaac wants the numbered list on Slide 5 converted into a SmartArt diagram.

**To convert the list on Slide 5 into a SmartArt diagram:**

1. Display **Slide 5** ("Placing Your Order for Additional Items") in the Slide pane, and then click anywhere on the numbered list to make the text box border appear.

2. On the HOME tab, in the Paragraph group, click the **Convert to SmartArt Graphic** button. A gallery of SmartArt layouts appears.

3. Point to the first layout. The ScreenTip identifies this layout as the Vertical Bullet List layout, and Live Preview shows you what the numbered list will look like with that layout applied. See Figure 1-18. Notice that the subitems are not included in a shape in this diagram.

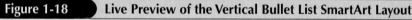

| Figure 1-18 | Live Preview of the Vertical Bullet List SmartArt Layout |

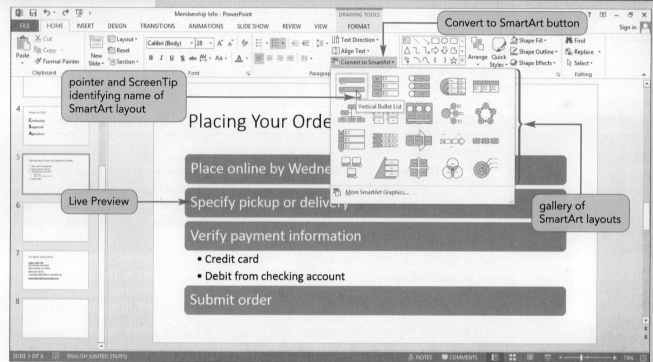

4. Point to several other layouts in the gallery, observing the Live Preview of each one. In some of the layouts, the subitems are included in a shape.

5. At the bottom of the gallery, click **More SmartArt Graphics**. The Choose a SmartArt Graphic dialog box opens. See Figure 1-19. You can click a type in the left pane to filter the middle pane to show only that type of layout.

Figure 1-19 **Choose a SmartArt Graphic dialog box**

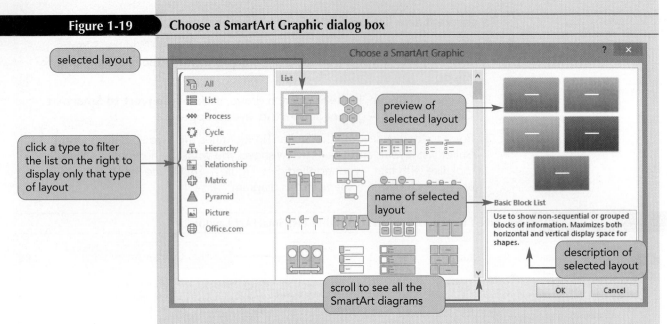

6. In the left pane, click **Process**, and then in the middle pane, click the **Continuous Block Process** layout, using the ScreenTips to identify it (it's the first layout in the third row). The right pane changes to show a description of that layout.

7. Click the **OK** button. The dialog box closes, and each of the first level items in the list appears in the square shapes in the diagram. The items also appear as a bulleted list in the Text pane, which is open to the left of the diagram. The SMARTART TOOLS contextual tabs appear on the ribbon. See Figure 1-20.

In this layout, the subitems below "Verify payment information" are included in the third square; they are not placed in their own shapes in the diagram. Isaac decides the information in the subitems does not need to be on the slide because people will see those options on the website when they log in.

**Trouble?** If you do not see the Text pane, click the Text pane button 🔲 on the left border of the selected SmartArt diagram.

**Figure 1-20**    **SmartArt diagram with the Continuous Block Process layout**

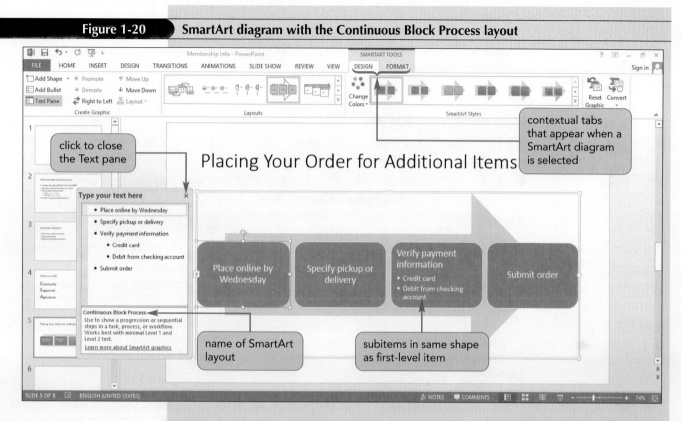

8. In the "Verify payment information shape," select **Debit from checking account**, and then press the **Delete** key. The text is deleted from the shape and from the Text pane.

9. In the Text pane, click after the word "card," press the **Backspace** key as many times as necessary to delete all of the bullet text, and then press the **Backspace** key once more. The bullet changes to a first-level bullet and a new square shape is inserted in the diagram.

10. Press the **Backspace** key one more time. The empty bullet and the blank line are deleted in the Text pane, and the newly added shape is removed from the diagram. The "Verify payment information" square now contains only the first-level item. Notice that AutoFit increased the size of the text in all the boxes so that the text still fills the boxes and is as large as possible.

11. Click a blank area of the slide to deselect the diagram, and then on the Quick Access Toolbar, click the **Save** button 🔲 to save your changes.

## Manipulating Slides

You can manipulate the slides in a presentation to suit your needs. For instance, if you need to create a slide that is similar to another slide, you can duplicate the existing slide and then modify the copy. If you decide that slides need to be rearranged, you can reorder them. And if you no longer want to include a slide in your presentation, you can delete it.

To duplicate, rearrange, or delete slides, you select the slides in the Slides tab in Normal view or switch to Slide Sorter view. In **Slide Sorter view** all the slides in the presentation are displayed as thumbnails in the window; the Slides tab does not appear. You already know that to select a single slide you click its thumbnail. You can also select more than one slide at a time. To select sequential slides, click the first slide, press and hold the Shift key, and then click the last slide you want to select. To select nonsequential slides, click the first slide, press and hold the Ctrl key, and then click any other slides you want to select.

Isaac wants to show the slide that explains what the letters "CSA" stand for at the end of the presentation. You will duplicate that slide instead of recreating it.

**To duplicate Slide 4:**

▶ **1.** In the Slides tab, click the **Slide 4** ("What Is a CSA?") thumbnail to display Slide 4 in the Slide pane.

▶ **2.** On the HOME tab, in the Slides group, click the **New Slide button arrow**, and then click **Duplicate Selected Slides**. Slide 4 is duplicated and the copy is inserted as a new Slide 5 in the Slides tab. Slide 5 is now the current slide. If more than one slide were selected, they would all be duplicated. The duplicate slide doesn't need the title; Isaac just wants to reinforce the term.

▶ **3.** Click in the title "What Is a CSA?", click the text box border to select the text box, and then press the **Delete** key. The title and the title text box are deleted and the title text placeholder reappears.

You could delete the title text placeholder, but it is not necessary. When you display the presentation to an audience as a slide show, any unused placeholders will not appear.

Next you need to rearrange the slides. You need to move the duplicate of the "What Is a CSA?" slide so it is the last slide in the presentation because Isaac wants to leave it displayed after the presentation is over. He hopes this visual will reinforce for the audience that CSAs are good for the entire community. Isaac also wants the "Members Receive" slide moved so it appears before the "Membership Requirements" slide, and he wants the original "What Is a CSA?" slide to be the second slide in the presentation.

**To move slides in the presentation:**

▶ **1.** In the Slides tab, scroll up, if necessary, so that you can see Slides 2 and 3, and then drag the **Slide 3** ("Members Receive") thumbnail above the Slide 2 ("Membership Requirements") thumbnail. As you drag, the Slide 3 thumbnail follows the pointer and Slide 2 moves down. The "Members Receive" slide is now Slide 2 and "Membership Requirements" is now Slide 3. You'll move the other two slides in Slide Sorter view.

**TIP**
You can also use the buttons in the Presentation Views group on the VIEW tab to switch views.

▶ **2.** On the status bar, click the **Slide Sorter** button. The view switches to Slide Sorter view. Slide 2 has an orange border, indicating that it is selected.

▶ **3.** On the status bar, click the **Zoom Out** button as many times as necessary until you can see all nine slides in the presentation. See Figure 1-21.

| Figure 1-21 | Slide Sorter view |

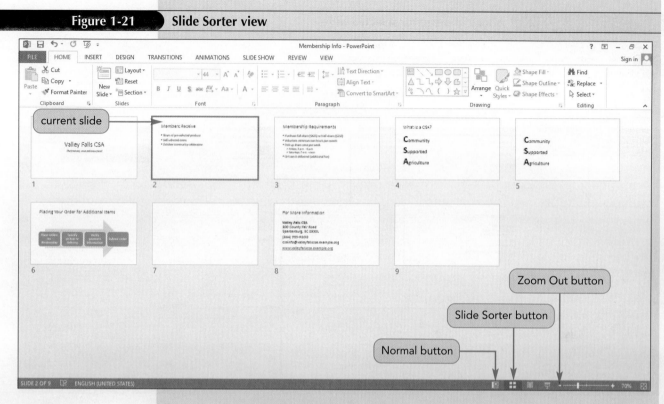

4. Drag the **Slide 4** ("What Is a CSA?") thumbnail between Slides 1 and 2. As you drag, the other slides move out of the way. The slide is repositioned and the slides are renumbered so that the "What Is a CSA?" slide is now Slide 2.

5. Drag the **Slide 5** (the CSA slide without a title) thumbnail so it becomes the last slide in the presentation (Slide 9).

Now you need to delete the two blank slides. To delete a slide, you need to right-click its thumbnail to display a shortcut menu.

## To delete slides:

1. Click **Slide 6** (a blank slide), press and hold the **Shift** key, and then click **Slide 8** (the other blank slide), and then release the **Shift** key. The two slides you clicked are selected, as well as the slide between them. You want to delete only the two blank slides.

2. Click a blank area of the window to deselect the slides, click **Slide 6**, press and hold the **Ctrl** key, click **Slide 8**, and then release the **Ctrl** key. Only the two slides you clicked are selected.

3. Right-click either selected slide. A shortcut menu appears. See Figure 1-22.

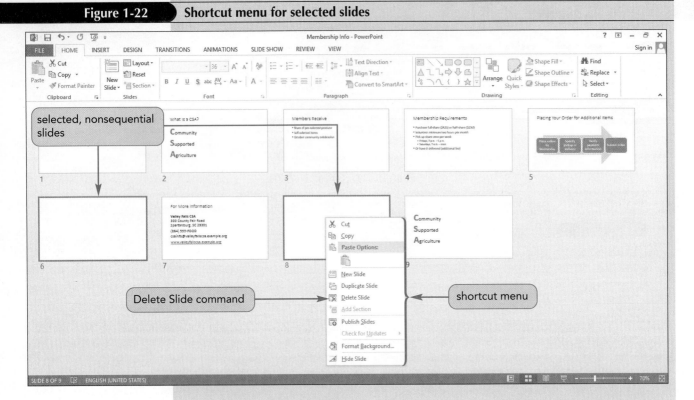

**Figure 1-22**    Shortcut menu for selected slides

> **4.** On the shortcut menu, click **Delete Slide**. The shortcut menu closes and the two selected slides are deleted. The presentation now contains seven slides.

> **5.** On the status bar, click the **Normal** button 🖳. The presentation appears in Normal view.

> **6.** On the Quick Access Toolbar, click the **Save** button 🖫 to save the changes to the presentation.

# Closing a Presentation

When you are finished working with a presentation, you can close it and leave PowerPoint open. To do this, you click the FILE tab to open Backstage view, and then click the Close command. If you click the Close button ✖ in the upper-right corner of the PowerPoint window and only one presentation is open, you will not only close the presentation, you will exit PowerPoint as well.

You're finished working with the Membership Info file for now, so you will close it. First you will add your name to the title slide.

### To close the Membership Info presentation:

> **1.** Display **Slide 1** (the title slide) in the Slide pane, click the **subtitle**, position the insertion point after "food!," press the **Enter** key, and then type your full name.

> **2.** On the ribbon, click the **FILE** tab. Backstage view appears with the Info screen displayed. See Figure 1-23. The Info screen contains information about the current presentation, including the name, drive, and folder of the current presentation.

**Figure 1-23** | **Info screen in Backstage view**

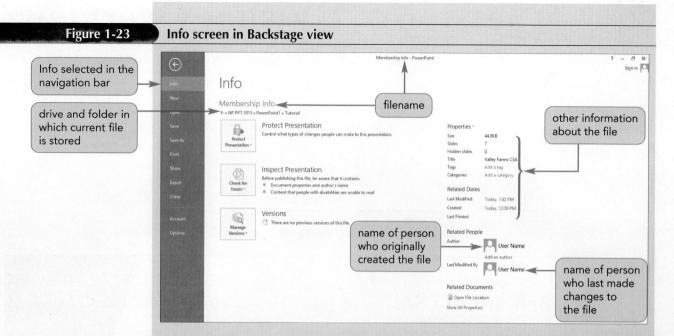

3. In the navigation bar, click **Close**. Backstage view closes and a dialog box opens asking if you want to save your changes.

4. In the dialog box, click the **Save** button. The dialog box and the presentation close, and the empty presentation window appears.

   **Trouble?** If you want to take a break, you can exit PowerPoint by clicking the Close button ☒ in the upper-right corner of the PowerPoint window.

You've created a presentation that includes slides to which you added bulleted, numbered, and unnumbered lists. You also edited and formatted text, converted a list to a SmartArt diagram, and duplicated, rearranged, and deleted slides. You are ready to give the presentation draft to Isaac to review.

## Session 1.1 Quick Check

**REVIEW**

1. Define "presentation."

2. How do you display Backstage view?

3. What is the main area of the PowerPoint window called?

4. What is a layout?

5. In addition to a title text placeholder, what other placeholder do most layouts contain?

6. What is the term for an object that contains text?

7. What is the difference between the Clipboard and the Office Clipboard?

8. How do you convert a list to a SmartArt diagram?

# Session 1.2 Visual Overview:

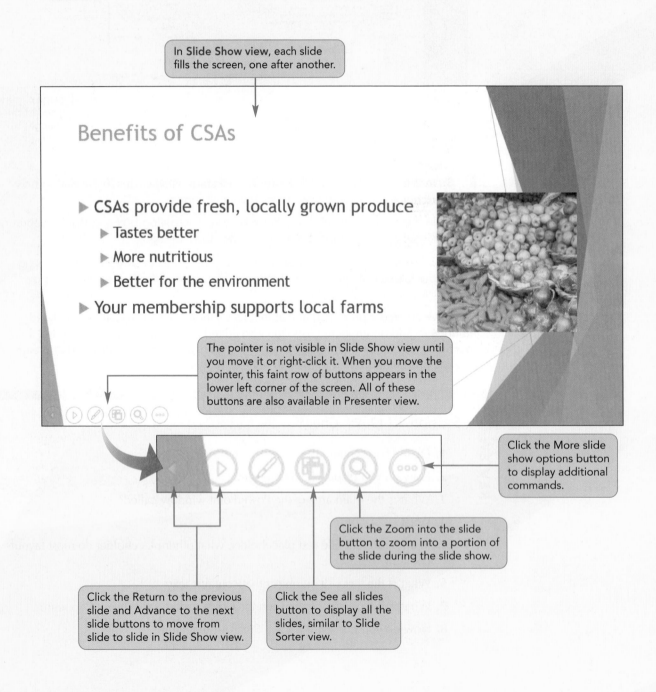

In **Slide Show** view, each slide fills the screen, one after another.

Benefits of CSAs

▶ CSAs provide fresh, locally grown produce
  ▶ Tastes better
  ▶ More nutritious
  ▶ Better for the environment
▶ Your membership supports local farms

The pointer is not visible in Slide Show view until you move it or right-click it. When you move the pointer, this faint row of buttons appears in the lower left corner of the screen. All of these buttons are also available in Presenter view.

Click the More slide show options button to display additional commands.

Click the Zoom into the slide button to zoom into a portion of the slide during the slide show.

Click the Return to the previous slide and Advance to the next slide buttons to move from slide to slide in Slide Show view.

Click the See all slides button to display all the slides, similar to Slide Sorter view.

# Slide Show and Presenter Views

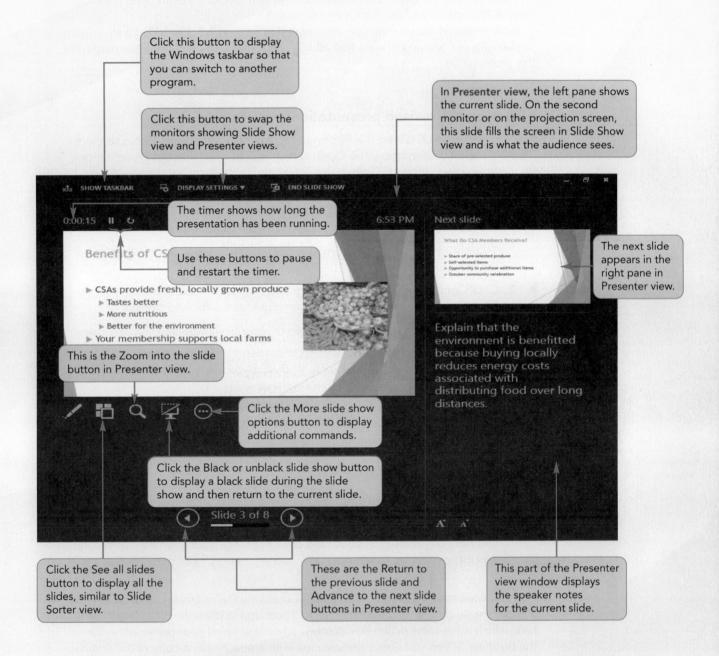

Click this button to display the Windows taskbar so that you can switch to another program.

Click this button to swap the monitors showing Slide Show view and Presenter views.

In **Presenter view**, the left pane shows the current slide. On the second monitor or on the projection screen, this slide fills the screen in Slide Show view and is what the audience sees.

The timer shows how long the presentation has been running.

Use these buttons to pause and restart the timer.

The next slide appears in the right pane in Presenter view.

This is the Zoom into the slide button in Presenter view.

Click the More slide show options button to display additional commands.

Click the Black or unblack slide show button to display a black slide during the slide show and then return to the current slide.

Click the See all slides button to display all the slides, similar to Slide Sorter view.

These are the Return to the previous slide and Advance to the next slide buttons in Presenter view.

This part of the Presenter view window displays the speaker notes for the current slide.

# Opening a Presentation and Saving It with a New Name

If you have closed a presentation, you can always reopen it to modify it. To do this, you can double-click the file in a Windows Explorer window, or you can open Backstage view in PowerPoint and use the Open command.

Isaac reviewed the presentation you created in Session 1.1. He added a slide listing the benefits of CSAs and made a few additional changes. You will continue modifying this presentation.

**To open the revised presentation:**

▶ **1.** Click the **FILE** tab on the ribbon to display Backstage view. Because there is no open presentation, the Open screen is displayed. Recent Presentations is selected, and you might see a list of the 25 most recently opened presentations on the right.

   **Trouble?** If PowerPoint is not running, start PowerPoint, and then in the navigation bar on the Recent screen, click the Open Other Presentations link.

   **Trouble?** If another presentation is open, click Open in the navigation bar in Backstage view.

▶ **2.** Click **Computer**. The list of recently opened files is replaced with a list of recently accessed folders on your computer and a Browse button.

   **Trouble?** If you are storing your files on your SkyDrive, click SkyDrive, and then log in if necessary.

▶ **3.** Click the **Browse** button. The Open dialog box appears. It is similar to the Save As dialog box.

▶ **4.** Navigate to the drive that contains your Data Files, navigate to the **PowerPoint1 ▶ Tutorial** folder, click **Revised Membership** to select it, and then click the **Open** button. The Open dialog box closes and the Revised Membership presentation opens in the PowerPoint window, with Slide 1 displayed in the Slide pane.

   **Trouble?** If you don't have the starting Data Files, you need to get them before you can proceed. Your instructor will either give you the Data Files or ask you to obtain them from a specified location (such as a network drive). If you have any questions about the Data Files, see your instructor or technical support person for assistance.

If you want to edit a presentation without changing the original, you need to create a copy of it. To do this, you use the Save As command to open the Save As dialog box, which is the same dialog box you saw when you saved your presentation for the first time. When you save a presentation with a new name, a copy of the original presentation is created, the original presentation is closed, and the newly named copy remains open in the PowerPoint window.

**To save the Revised Membership presentation with a new name:**

▶ **1.** Click the **FILE** tab, and then in the navigation bar, click **Save As**. The Save As screen in Backstage view appears.

▶ **2.** Click **Computer**, if necessary. On the right under Computer is a list of recently accessed folders with the folder containing the current file at the top.

3. If the folder in which you are saving your Data Files is listed on the right, click it; if the folder in which you are saving your files is not listed, click the **Browse** button. The Save As dialog box opens.

4. If necessary, navigate to the drive and folder where you are storing your Data Files.

5. In the File name box, change the filename to **CSA New Member**, and then click the **Save** button. The Save As dialog box closes, a copy of the file is saved with the new name CSA New Member, and the CSA New Member presentation appears in the PowerPoint window.

# Changing the Theme and the Theme Variant

A **theme** is a coordinated set of colors, fonts, backgrounds, and effects. All presentations have a theme. If you don't choose one, the default Office theme is applied; that is the theme currently applied to the CSA New Member presentation.

You saw the Office theme set of colors when you changed the color of the text on the "What Is a CSA?" slide. You have also seen the Office theme fonts in use on the slides. In the Office theme, the font of the slide titles is Calibri Light and the font of the text in content text boxes is Calibri. In themes, the font used for slide titles is the Headings font, and the font used for the content text boxes is the Body font.

In PowerPoint, each theme has several variants with different coordinating colors and sometimes slightly different backgrounds. A theme and its variants are called a **theme family**. PowerPoint comes with several installed themes, and many more themes are available online at Office.com. In addition, you can use a custom theme stored on your computer or network.

You can select a different installed theme when you create a new presentation by clicking one of the themes on the New or Recent screen in Backstage view instead of clicking Blank Presentation, and then clicking one of the variants. If you want to change the theme of an open presentation, you can choose an installed theme on the DESIGN tab or you can apply a custom theme stored on your computer or network. When you change the theme, the colors, fonts, and slide backgrounds change to those used in the new theme.

Isaac wants the theme of the CSA New Member presentation changed to one that has more color in the background. First you'll display Slide 2 in the Slide pane so you can see the effect a different theme has on the text formatted with a theme color.

**To examine the current theme and then change the theme and theme variant:**

1. Display **Slide 2** ("What Is a CSA?") in the Slide pane, and then, in the unnumbered list select the orange letter **C**.

2. On the HOME tab, in the Font group, click the **Font Color arrow**. Look at the colors under Theme Colors and note the second to last color is selected in the column containing shades of orange. Notice also the row of Standard Colors below the theme colors.

3. In the Font group, click the **Font arrow**. A menu of fonts installed on the computer opens. At the top under Theme Fonts, Calibri (Body) is selected because the letter C that you selected is in a content text box. See Figure 1-24.

**Figure 1-24**    **Theme fonts on the Font box menu**

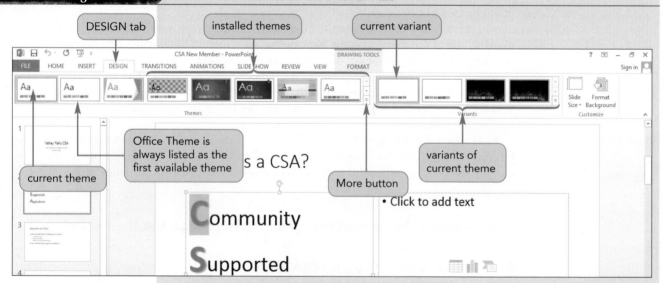

4. On the ribbon, click the **DESIGN** tab. The Font menu closes and the installed themes appear in the Themes gallery on the DESIGN tab. See Figure 1-25. The current theme is the first theme listed in the Themes group on the DESIGN tab. The next theme is the Office theme, which, in this case, is also the current theme.

**Figure 1-25**    **Themes and variants on the DESIGN tab**

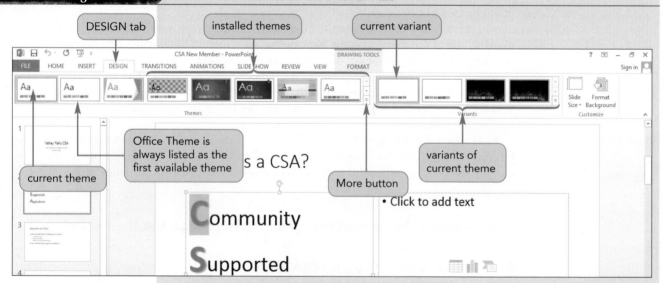

**TIP**

To apply a theme from a presentation stored on your computer or network, click the Themes More button, and then click Browse for Themes.

To see all of the installed themes, you need to scroll through the gallery by clicking the up and down scroll buttons on the right end of the gallery or clicking the More button to expand the gallery to see all of the themes at once. The **More button** appears on all galleries that contain additional items or commands that don't fit in the group on the ribbon.

5. In the Themes group, click the **More** button ⤓. The gallery of themes opens. See Figure 1-26. When the gallery is open, the theme applied to the current presentation appears in the first row. In the next row, the first theme is the Office theme, and then the rest of the installed themes appear. Some of these themes appear on the Recent and New screens in Backstage view.

**Figure 1-26** Theme gallery expanded

current theme is the Office theme

installed themes (your gallery might differ)

6. Point to several of the themes in the gallery to display their ScreenTips and to see a Live Preview of the theme applied to the current slide, and then click the **Facet** theme. The gallery closes and the Facet theme is applied to all the slides with the default variant (the first variant in the Variants group).

   The title text on each slide changes from black to green, the letters that you had colored orange on Slide 2 are dark green, the bullet symbols change from black circles to green triangles, and in the Slides tab, you can see on the Slide 6 thumbnail that the SmartArt shapes are now green as well.

7. In the Variants group, point to the other three variants to see a Live Preview of each of them. Isaac likes the default green variant best, so you will not change it.

8. Click the **HOME** tab, and then in the Font group, click the **Font Color arrow**. The selected color—the color of the selected letter "C"—is now a shade of green in the Theme Colors of the Facet theme. Notice also that the row of Standard Colors is the same as it was when the Office theme was applied.

9. In the Font group, click the **Font arrow**. You can see that the Theme Fonts are now Trebuchet MS for both Headings (slide titles) and the Body (content text boxes).

10. Press the **Esc** key. The Font menu closes.

After you apply a new theme, you should examine your slides to make sure that they look the way you expect them to. The font sizes used in the Facet theme are considerably smaller than those used in the Office theme. You know that Isaac wants the slides to be legible and clearly visible from a distance, so you will increase the font sizes on some of the slides. The title slide and Slide 2 are fine, but you need to examine the rest of the slides.

### To examine the slides with the new theme and adjust font sizes:

1. Display **Slide 3** ("Benefits of CSAs") in the Slide pane, and then in the bulleted list, click the first bulleted item. (This is the new slide that Isaac added.) In the Font group, the font size is 18 points, quite a bit smaller than the font size of first-level bulleted items in the Office theme, which is 28 points. You can see that the font size of the subitems is also fairly small.

▶ **2.** In the bulleted list, click the text box border to select the entire text box. In the Font group, 16+ appears in the Font Size box. The smallest font size used in the selected text box—the font size of the subitems—is 16, and the plus sign indicates that there is text in the selected text box larger than 16 points.

▶ **3.** In the Font group, click the **Increase Font Size** button [A˄] three times. The font size of the first-level bullets changes to 28 points, and the font size of the second-level bullets changes to 24 points. This is the same as the font sizes used in lists in the Office theme.

   **Trouble?** If the DRAWING TOOLS FORMAT tab becomes selected on the ribbon, click the HOME tab.

▶ **4.** Display **Slide 4** ("What Do CSA Members Receive?") in the Slide pane, and then increase the size of the text in the bulleted list to 28 points. There are misspelled words on this slide and on Slide 5; ignore them for now.

▶ **5.** Display **Slide 5** ("Membership Requirements") in the Slide pane, and then increase the font size of the text in the bulleted list so that the font size of the first-level items is 28 points and of the subitems is 24 points.

▶ **6.** Display **Slides 6, 7, 8,** and then **Slide 1** in the Slide pane. These remaining slides look fine.

▶ **7.** On the Quick Access Toolbar, click the **Save** button [💾]. The changes to the presentation are saved.

## INSIGHT

### Understanding the Difference Between Themes and Templates

As explained earlier, a theme is a coordinated set of colors, fonts, backgrounds, and effects. A **template**, like any presentation, has a theme applied, but it also contains text, graphics, and placeholders to help direct you in creating content for a presentation. You can create and save your own custom templates or find everything from calendars to marketing templates among the thousands of templates available on Office.com. To find a template on Office.com, display the Recent or New screen in Backstage view, type key words in the Search box or click one of the category links below the Search box to display templates related to the search terms or category. If you create a new presentation based on a template, you can make any changes you want to the slides.

If a template is stored on your computer, you can apply the theme used in the template to an existing presentation. However, if you want to apply the theme used in a template on Office.com to an existing presentation, you need to download and save the template to your computer first, and then you can apply it to an existing presentation.

## Working with Photos

Most people are exposed to multimedia daily and expect to have information conveyed visually as well as verbally. In many cases, graphics are more effective than words for communicating an important point. For example, if a sales force has reached its sales goals for the year, including a photo in your presentation of a person reaching the top of a mountain can convey a sense of exhilaration to your audience.

## Inserting Photos Stored on Your Computer or Network

Content placeholders contain buttons that you can use to insert things other than a list, including photos stored on your hard drive, a network drive, a USB drive, an SD card from a digital camera, or any other medium to which you have access. You can also use the Picture button in the Images group on the INSERT tab to add photos to slides.

Isaac has photos showing produce from his farm that he wants inserted on two of the slides in the presentation. He also wants a photo of people volunteering on the farm to appear on the last slide in the presentation.

### To insert photos stored on your computer or network on slides:

1. Display **Slide 2** ("What Is a CSA?") in the Slide pane, and then in the content placeholder on the right, click the **Pictures** button ⬚. The Insert Picture dialog box appears. This dialog box is similar to the Open dialog box.

2. Navigate to the **PowerPoint1 ▸ Tutorial** folder included with your Data Files, click **Produce1**, and then click the **Insert** button. The dialog box closes, and a picture of produce in bins appears in the placeholder and is selected. The contextual PICTURE TOOLS FORMAT tab appears on the ribbon to the right of the VIEW tab and is the active tab. See Figure 1-27.

| Figure 1-27 | Picture inserted on Slide 2 |
| --- | --- |

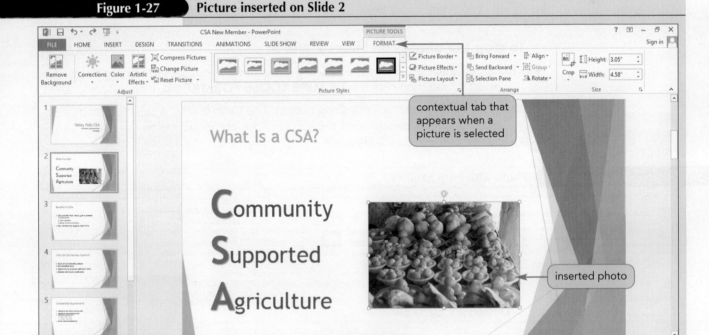

Photo courtesy of S. Scott Zimmerman

3. Display **Slide 3** ("Benefits of CSAs") in the Slide pane. This slide uses the Title and Content layout and does not have a second content placeholder. You can change the layout to include a second content placeholder or you can use a command on the ribbon to insert a photo.

4. Click the **INSERT** tab, and then in the Images group, click the **Pictures** button. The Insert Picture dialog box opens.

> **5.** In the PowerPoint1 ▸ Tutorial folder, click **Produce2**, and then click the **Insert** button. The dialog box closes and the picture is added to the center of the slide, covering much of the bulleted list. You will fix this later.

> **6.** Display **Slide 8** (the copy of the "What Is a CSA?" slide), and then click the **INSERT** tab on the ribbon.

> **7.** In the Images group, click the **Pictures** button, click **People** in the PowerPoint1 ▸ Tutorial folder, and then click the **Insert** button. The picture replaces the content placeholder on the slide.

## Cropping Photos

Sometimes you want to display only part of a photo. For example, if you insert a photo of a party scene that includes a bouquet of colorful balloons, you might want to show only the balloons. To do this, you can **crop** the photo—cut out the parts you don't want to include. In PowerPoint, you can crop it manually to any size you want, crop it to a preset ratio, or crop it to a shape.

On Slide 2, Isaac wants you to crop the photo to a diamond shape to make it more interesting, and to crop the photo on Slide 3 to make the dimensions of the final photo smaller without making the images in the photo smaller.

### To crop the photos on Slides 2 and 3:

> **1.** Display **Slide 3** ("Benefits of CSAs") in the Slide pane, click the photo to select it, and then click the **PICTURE TOOLS FORMAT** tab, if necessary.

> **2.** In the Size group, click the **Crop** button. The Crop button is selected, and crop handles appear around the edges of the photo just inside the sizing handles. See Figure 1-28.

**Figure 1-28**    **Photo with crop handles**

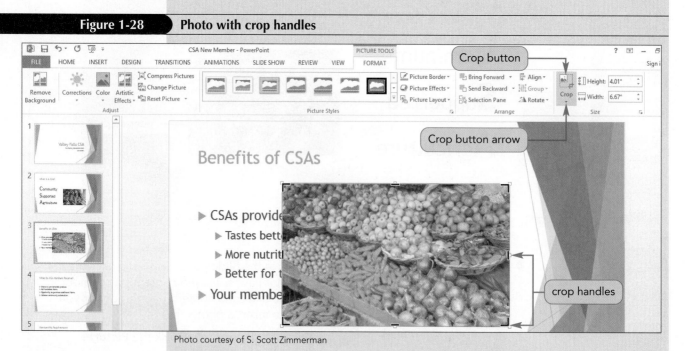

Photo courtesy of S. Scott Zimmerman

3. Position the pointer directly on top of the **left-middle crop handle** so that it changes to ⊣, press and hold the mouse button, and then drag the crop handle to the right approximately two inches.

4. Drag the crop handles on the bottom and right of the photo to match the cropped photo shown in Figure 1-29.

**Figure 1-29**    **Cropped photo**

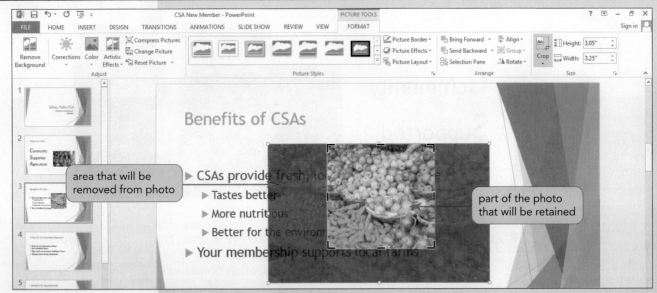

Photo courtesy of S. Scott Zimmerman

5. Click the **Crop** button again. The Crop feature is turned off, but the photo is still selected and the FORMAT tab is still the active tab. The photo is still on top of the bulleted list, but you'll fix this later.

6. Display **Slide 2** ("What Is a CSA?") in the Slide pane, click the photo to select it, and then click the **FORMAT** tab, if necessary.

7. In the Size group, click the **Crop button arrow**. The Crop button menu opens. See Figure 1-30.

Figure 1-30    Crop button menu

Photo courtesy of S. Scott Zimmerman

8.  Point to **Crop to Shape** to open a gallery of shapes, and then under Basic Shapes, click the **Diamond** shape. The photo is cropped to a diamond shape. Notice that the rectangular selection border of the original photo is still showing.

9.  In the Size group, click the **Crop** button. You can now see the cropped portions of the original, rectangle photo that are shaded gray.

10. Click a blank area of the slide. The picture is no longer selected and the HOME tab is the active tab on the ribbon.

## Modifying Photo Compression Options

When you save a presentation that contains photos, PowerPoint automatically compresses the photos to a resolution of 220 pixels per inch (ppi). (For comparison, photos printed in magazines are typically 300 ppi.) Compressing photos reduces the size of the presentation file, but it also reduces the quality of the photos. See Figure 1-31 for a description of the compression options available. If an option in the dialog box is gray, the photo is a lower resolution than that setting. Note that many monitors and projectors are capable of displaying resolutions only a little higher (98 ppi) than the resolution designated for email (96 ppi).

| Figure 1-31 | Photo compression settings |

| Compression Setting | Description |
|---|---|
| 220 ppi | Photos are compressed to 220 pixels per inch; use when you need to maintain the quality of the photograph when the slides are printed. This is the default setting for PowerPoint presentations. (Note that although this setting compresses the photos minimally, they are still compressed, and if photograph quality is the most important concern, do not compress photos at all.) |
| 150 ppi | Photos are compressed to 150 pixels per inch; use when the presentation will be viewed on a monitor or screen projector. |
| 96 ppi | Photos are compressed to 96 pixels per inch; use for presentations that need to be emailed or uploaded to a Web page or when it is important to keep the overall file size small. |
| Document resolution | Photos are compressed to the resolution specified on the Advanced tab in the PowerPoint Options dialog box. The default setting is 220 ppi. |
| No compression | Photos are not compressed at all; used when it is critical that photos remain at their original resolution. |

© 2014 Cengage Learning

You can change the compression setting for each photo that you insert or you can change the settings for all the photos in the presentation. If you cropped photos, you also can discard the cropped areas of the photo to make the presentation file size smaller. (Note that when you crop to a shape, the cropped portions are not discarded.) If you insert additional photos or crop a photo after you apply the new compression settings to all the slides, you will need to apply the new settings to the new photos.

**REFERENCE**

*Modifying Photo Compression Settings and Removing Cropped Areas*

- After all photos have been added to the presentation file, click any photo in the presentation to select it.
- Click the PICTURE TOOLS FORMAT tab. In the Adjust group, click the Compress Pictures button.
- Click the option button next to the resolution you want to use.
- To apply the new compression settings to all the photos in the presentation, click the Apply only to this picture check box to deselect it.
- To keep cropped areas of photos, click the Delete cropped area of pictures check box to deselect it.
- Click the OK button.

You will adjust the compression settings to make the file size of the presentation as small as possible so that Isaac can easily send it or post it for others without worrying about file size limitations on the receiving server.

**To modify photo compression settings and remove cropped areas from photos:**

1. On **Slide 2** ("What Is a CSA?"), click the photo, and then click the **PICTURE TOOLS FORMAT** tab, if necessary.

2. In the Adjust group, click the **Compress Pictures** button. The Compress Pictures dialog box opens. See Figure 1-32. Under Target output, the Use document resolution option button is selected.

**Figure 1-32** Compress Pictures dialog box

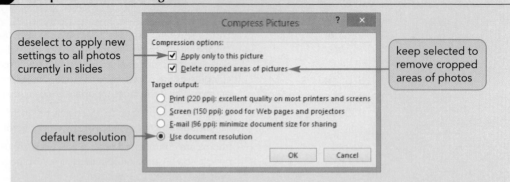

3. Click the **E-mail (96 ppi)** option button. This setting compresses the photos to the smallest possible size. At the top of the dialog box under Compression options, the Delete cropped area of pictures check box is already selected. This option is not applied to cropped photos until you open this dialog box and then click the OK button to apply it. Because you want the presentation file size to be as small as possible, you do want cropped portions of photos to be deleted, so you'll leave this selected. The Apply only to this picture check box is also selected; however, you want the settings applied to all the photos in the file.

4. Click the **Apply only to this picture** check box to deselect it.

5. Click the **OK** button.

   The dialog box closes and the compression settings are applied to all the photos in the presentation. You can confirm that the cropped areas of photos were removed by examining the photo on Slide 3. (The photo on Slide 2 was cropped to a shape, so the cropped areas on it were not removed.)

6. Display **Slide 3** ("Benefits of CSAs") in the Slide pane, click the photo to select it, click the **FORMAT** tab, if necessary, and then in the Size group, click the **Crop** button. The Crop handles appear around the photo, but the portions of the photo that you cropped out no longer appear.

7. Click the **Crop** button again to deselect it, and then save the changes to the presentation.

Be sure you are satisfied with the way you cropped the photo on Slide 3 before you delete the cropped areas.

### INSIGHT

### Keeping Photos Uncompressed

Suppose you are a photographer and want to create a presentation to show your photos. In that case, you would want to display them at their original, uncompressed resolution. To do this, you need to change a setting in the PowerPoint Options dialog box before you add photos to slides. Click the FILE tab to open Backstage view, click Options in the navigation bar to open the PowerPoint Options dialog box, click Advanced in the navigation bar, and then locate the Image Size and Quality section. To keep images at their original resolution, click the Do not compress images in file check box to select it. Note that you can also change the default compression setting for photos in this dialog box; you can increase the compression or choose to automatically discard cropped portions of photos. Note that these changes affect only the current presentation.

# Resizing and Moving Objects

You can resize and move any object to best fit the space available on a slide. One way to resize an object is to drag a sizing handle. **Sizing handles** are the small squares that appear in the corners and in the middle of the sides of the border of a selected object. When you use this method, you can adjust the size of the object so it best fits the space visually. If you need to size an object to exact dimensions, you can modify the measurements in the Size group on the FORMAT tab that appears when you select the object.

You can also drag an object to reposition it anywhere on the slide. If more than one object is on a slide, **smart guides**, dashed red lines, appear as you drag to indicate the center and the top and bottom borders of the objects. Smart guides can help you position objects so they are aligned and spaced evenly.

In addition to using the smart guides, it can be helpful to display rulers and gridlines in the window. The rulers appear along the top and left sides of the Slide pane. Gridlines are one-inch squares made up of dots one-sixth of an inch apart. As you drag an object, it snaps to the grid, even if it is not visible.

## Resizing and Moving Pictures

Pictures and other objects that cause the PICTURE TOOLS FORMAT tab to appear when selected have their aspect ratios locked by default. The **aspect ratio** is the ratio of the object's height to its width. When the aspect ratio is locked, if you resize the photo by dragging a corner sizing handle or if you change one dimension in the Size group on the PICTURE TOOLS FORMAT tab, the other dimension will change by the same percentage. However, if you drag one of the sizing handles in the middle of an object's border, you will override the locked aspect ratio setting and resize the object only in the direction you drag. Generally you do not want to do this with photos because the images will become distorted.

You need to resize and move the cropped photo on Slide 3 so it is not obscuring the text. You also want to resize and move the photos you inserted on Slides 2 and 8 so the slides are more attractive. You'll display the rulers and gridlines to help you as you do this.

### To move and resize the photos:

1. Click the **VIEW** tab, and then in the Show group, click the **Ruler** and the **Gridlines** check boxes. Rulers appear along the top and left sides of the Slide pane, and the gridlines appear in the Slide pane.

2. On **Slide 3** ("Benefits of CSAs"), select the photo, if necessary, and then position the pointer on the photo anywhere except on a sizing handle so that the pointer changes to ⁺⁺⁺.

3. Press and hold the mouse button, drag the photo down and to the right so that the right edge of the photo is approximately one inch from the right side of the slide and a smart guide appears indicating that the top of the photo and the top of the bulleted list text box are aligned, as shown in Figure 1-33.

**TIP**

If you don't want objects you are moving to snap to the grid, press and hold the Alt key while you are dragging.

**Figure 1-33**　**Repositioning photo on Slide 3 using smart guides and gridlines**

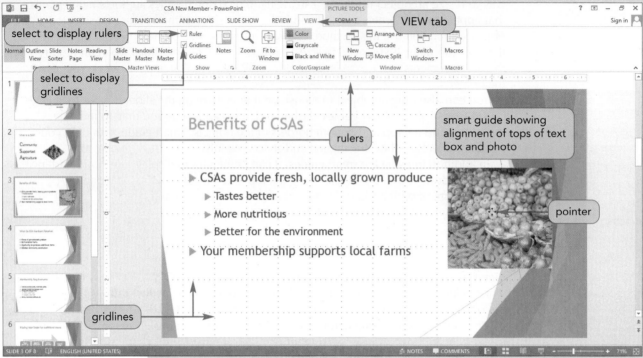

Photo courtesy of S. Scott Zimmerman

4. Release the mouse button. The photo is repositioned to the right of the bulleted list.

5. Display **Slide 2** ("What Is a CSA?") in the Slide pane, click the photo to select it, and then click the **PICTURE TOOLS FORMAT** tab if necessary. Instead of the border and sizing handles being on the diamond border, a rectangular border appears representing the original, uncropped photo's borders. (Remember that cropped portions of photos that are cropped to a shape are not removed.)

6. In the Size group, click in the **Height** box to select the current measurement, type **4**, and then press the **Enter** key. The measurement in the Width box in the Size group changes proportionately, and the new measurements are applied to the photo.

7. Drag the photo up and to the left until a horizontal smart guide appears indicating the alignment of the middle of the text box and the middle of the photo, and a vertical smart guide appears on the left side of the photo indicating the alignment of the left edge of the photo and the right edge of the bulleted list text box, as shown in Figure 1-34.

| Figure 1-34 | Moving resized photo on Slide 2 |

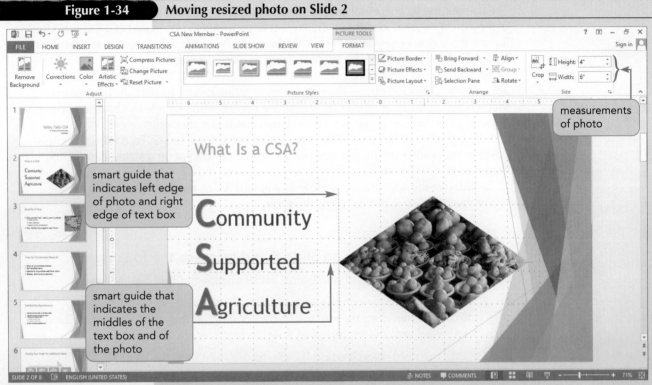

Photo courtesy of S. Scott Zimmerman

**8.** Display **Slide 8** (the last slide in the presentation) in the Slide pane, click the photo to select it, position the pointer on the top-middle sizing handle to that it changes to ↕, press and hold the mouse button, and then drag the sizing handle approximately two inches up. The photo is two inches taller, but the image is distorted.

**9.** On the Quick Access Toolbar, click the **Undo** button ↶. You need to resize the photo by dragging a corner sizing handle to maintain the aspect ratio.

**10.** Click the **FORMAT** tab, and note the measurements in the Size group. The photo is 3.05 inches high and 4.58 inches wide.

**11.** Position the pointer on the bottom-right corner sizing handle so that it changes to ⤡, press and hold the mouse button, and then drag the sizing handle down. Even though you are dragging in only one direction, because you are dragging a corner sizing handle, both the width and height are changing proportionately.

**12.** When the photo is approximately four inches high and six inches wide, release the mouse button. Note that the measurements in the Height and Width boxes changed to reflect the picture's new size.

**13.** Drag the photo up until the top of the photo aligns with the 2-inch mark on the ruler on the left and the right edge of the photo is aligned with the 6-inch mark on the ruler at the top of the Slide pane. You are done using the ruler and gridlines so you can turn these features off.

**14.** Click the **VIEW** tab, and then click the **Ruler** and **Gridlines** check boxes to deselect them.

## Resizing and Moving Text Boxes

The themes and layouts installed with PowerPoint are designed by professionals, so much of the time it's a good idea to use the layouts as provided to be assured of a cohesive look among the slides. However, occasionally there will be a compelling reason to adjust the layout of objects on a slide, by either resizing or repositioning them.

Text boxes and other objects that cause the DRAWING TOOLS FORMAT tab to appear when selected do not have their aspect ratios locked by default. This means that when you resize an object by dragging a corner sizing handle or changing one dimension in the Size group, the other dimension is not affected.

Like any other object on a slide, you can reposition text boxes. To do this, you must position the pointer on the text box border, anywhere except on a sizing handle, to drag it to its new location.

To improve the appearance of Slide 8, you will resize the text box containing the unnumbered list so it vertically fills the slide.

### To resize the text box on Slide 8 and increase the font size:

1. On Slide 8, click the unnumbered list to display the text box border.

2. Position the pointer on the top-middle sizing handle so that it changes to ↕, and then drag the sizing handle up until the top edge of the text box is aligned with the top edge of the title text placeholder.

3. Drag the right-middle sizing handle to the right until the right edge of the text box is touching the left edge of the photo.

4. Click the **HOME** tab, and then in the Font group, click the **Increase Font Size** button A˘ three times. Even though the title text placeholder will not appear during a slide show, you will delete it so that it is easier to see how the final slide will look.

5. Click the title text placeholder border, and then press the **Delete** key. See Figure 1-35 and adjust the position of the photo if necessary.

**Figure 1-35**    Slide 8 with resized text box

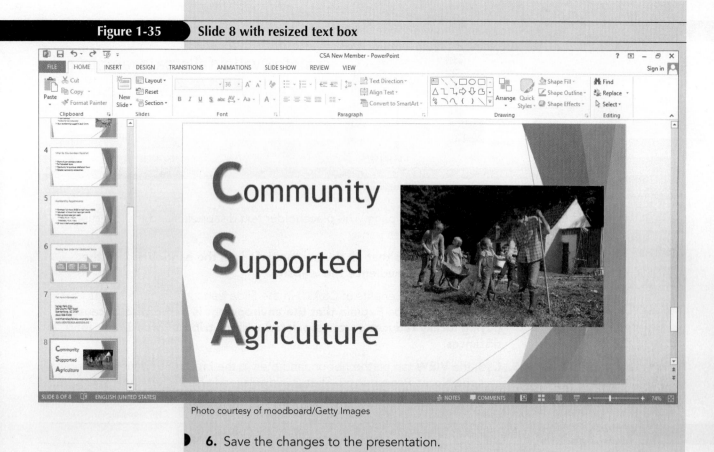

Photo courtesy of moodboard/Getty Images

▶ **6.** Save the changes to the presentation.

# Adding Speaker Notes

**Speaker notes**, or simply **notes**, are information you add about slide content to help you remember to bring up specific points during the presentation. Speaker notes should not contain all the information you plan to say during your presentation, but they can be a useful tool for reminding you about facts and details related to the content on specific slides. You add notes in the **Notes pane**, which you can display below the Slide pane in Normal view, or you can switch to **Notes Page view**, in which an image of the slide appears in the top half of the presentation window and the notes for that slide appear in the bottom half.

### To add notes to Slides 3 and 7:

▶ **1.** Display **Slide 7** ("For More Information") in the Slide pane, and then, on the status bar, click the **NOTES** button. The Notes pane appears below the Slide pane with "Click to add notes" as placeholder text. See Figure 1-36.

**Figure 1-36** Notes pane below the Slide pane

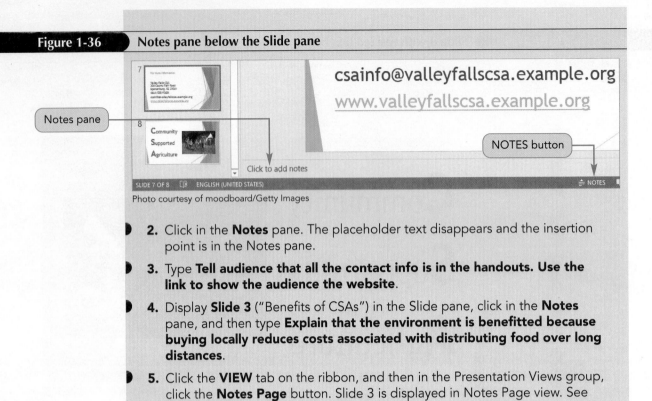

Photo courtesy of moodboard/Getty Images

2. Click in the **Notes** pane. The placeholder text disappears and the insertion point is in the Notes pane.

3. Type **Tell audience that all the contact info is in the handouts. Use the link to show the audience the website**.

4. Display **Slide 3** ("Benefits of CSAs") in the Slide pane, click in the **Notes** pane, and then type **Explain that the environment is benefitted because buying locally reduces costs associated with distributing food over long distances**.

5. Click the **VIEW** tab on the ribbon, and then in the Presentation Views group, click the **Notes Page** button. Slide 3 is displayed in Notes Page view. See Figure 1-37.

**Figure 1-37** Slide 3 in Notes Page view

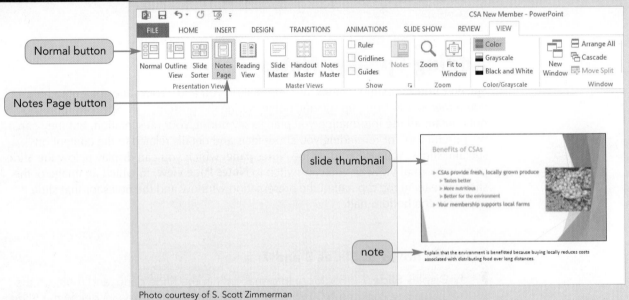

Photo courtesy of S. Scott Zimmerman

**TIP**

Use the Zoom in button on the status bar to magnify the text to make it easier to edit the note.

6. In the note, click after "reduces," press the **spacebar**, and then type **energy**.

7. In the Presentation Views group, click the **Normal** button to return to Normal view. The Notes pane stays displayed until you close it again.

8. On the status bar, click the **NOTES** button to close the Notes pane, and then save the changes to the presentation.

# Checking Spelling

You should always check the spelling and grammar in your presentation before you finalize it. To make this task easier, you can use PowerPoint's spelling checker. You can quickly tell if there are words on slides that are not in the built-in dictionary by looking at the Spelling button at the left end of the status bar. If there are no words flagged as possibly misspelled, the button is 🗐; if there are flagged words, the button changes to 🗐. To indicate that a word might be misspelled, a wavy red line appears under it.

To correct misspelled words, you can right-click a flagged word to see a list of suggested spellings on the shortcut menu, or you can check the spelling of all the words in the presentation. To check the spelling of all the words in the presentation, you click the Spelling button in the Proofing group on the REVIEW tab. This opens the Spelling task pane to the right of the Slide pane and starts the spell check from the current slide. A **task pane** is a pane that opens to the right or left of the Slide pane and contains commands and options related to the task you are doing. When a possible misspelled word is found, suggestions are displayed for the correct spelling. Synonyms for the selected correct spelling are also listed.

**To check the spelling of words in the presentation:**

1. Display **Slide 4** ("What Do CSA Members Receive?") in the Slide pane, and then right-click the misspelled word **Oportunity**. A shortcut menu opens listing spelling options. See Figure 1-38.

| Figure 1-38 | Shortcut menu for a misspelled word |
| --- | --- |

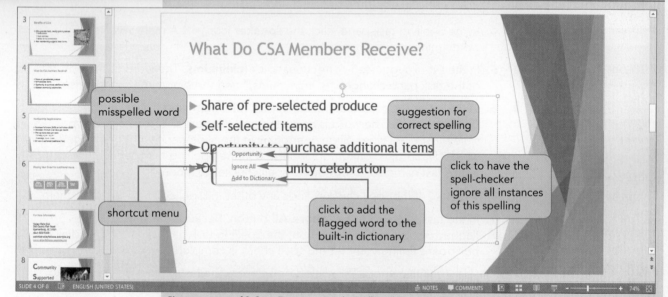

Photos courtesy of S. Scott Zimmerman and moodboard/Getty Images

2. On the shortcut menu, click **Opportunity**. The menu closes and the spelling is corrected.

**TIP**

You can also click the Spelling button on the status bar to start the spell check.

3. Click the **REVIEW** tab, and then in the Proofing group, click the **Spelling** button. The Spelling task pane opens to the right of the Slide pane, and the next slide that contains a possible misspelled word, Slide 5 ("Membership Requirements"), appears in the Slide pane with the flagged word, "minmum," highlighted. See Figure 1-39. In the Spelling task pane, the first suggested correct spelling is selected. The selected correct spelling also appears at the bottom of the task pane with synonyms for the word listed below it and a speaker icon next to it.

| Figure 1-39 | Spelling task pane displaying a misspelled word |

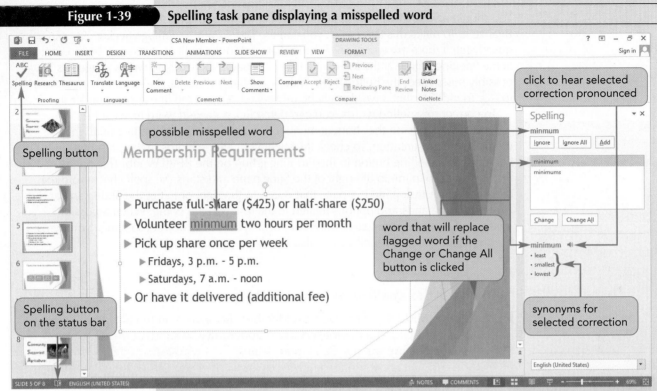

Photos courtesy of S. Scott Zimmerman and moodboard/Getty Images

**4.** In the Spelling task pane, click the **speaker** icon 🔊. A male voice says the word "minimum."

**5.** In the list of suggested corrections, click **minimums**. The word at the bottom of the task pane changes to "minimums," and the synonyms change also.

**6.** In the list of suggested corrections, click **minimum**, and then click the **Change** button. The word is corrected and the next slide containing a possible misspelled word, Slide 1, appears in the Slide pane with the flagged word, "DeSoto," highlighted and listed in the Spelling task pane. This is Isaac's last name so you want the spell checker to ignore this.

**Trouble?** If the spell checker finds any other misspelled words, correct them.

**7.** In the task pane, click the **Ignore All** button. Because that was the last flagged word in the presentation, the Spelling task pane closes and a dialog box opens telling you that the spell check is complete.

**8.** Click the **OK** button. The dialog box closes. The last flagged word, DeSoto, is still selected on Slide 1.

**9.** Click a blank area of the slide to deselect the text, and then save the changes to your presentation.

# Running a Slide Show

After you have created and proofed your presentation, you should view it as a slide show to see how it will appear to your audience. There are several ways to do this—Slide Show view, Presenter view, and Reading view.

## Using Slide Show View and Presenter View

You can use Slide Show view if your computer has only one monitor and you don't have access to a screen projector. If your computer is connected to a second monitor or a screen projector, Slide Show view is the way an audience will see your slides. Refer to the Session 1.2 Visual Overview for more information about Slide Show view.

Isaac asks you to review the slide show in Slide Show view to make sure the slides look good.

**TIP**

To start the slide show from the current slide, click the Slide Show button on the status bar.

**To use Slide Show view:**

1. On the Quick Access Toolbar, click the **Start From Beginning** button. Slide 1 appears on the screen in Slide Show view. Now you need to advance the slide show.

2. Press the **spacebar**. Slide 2 ("What Is a CSA?") appears on the screen.

3. Click the mouse button. The next slide, Slide 3 ("Benefits of CSAs"), appears on the screen.

4. Press the **Backspace** key. The previous slide, Slide 2, appears again.

5. Type **7**, and then press the **Enter** key. Slide 7 ("For More Information") appears on the screen.

6. Move the mouse to display the pointer, and then position the pointer on the website address **www.valleyfoodscsa.example.org**. The pointer changes to 🖑 to indicate that this is a link, and the ScreenTip that appears shows the full website address including "http://". If this were a real website, you could click the link to open your Web browser and display the website to your audience. Because you moved the pointer, a very faint row of buttons appears in the lower-left corner. See Figure 1-40.

**Figure 1-40**     Link and buttons in Slide Show view

(864) 555-FOOD

csainfo@valleyfallscsa.example.org

www.valleyfallscsa.example.org

- pointer on a link in Slide Show view
- row of buttons that appears when you move the pointer
- ScreenTip identifying the link

7. Move the pointer again, if necessary, to display the row of buttons that appears in the lower left corner of the screen, and then click the **Return to the previous slide** button four times to return to Slide 3 ("Benefits of CSAs").

   **Trouble?** If you can't see the buttons on the toolbar, move the pointer to the lower left corner so it is on top of the first button to darken that button, and then move the pointer to the right to see the rest of the buttons.

8. Display the faint row of buttons again, and then click the **Zoom into the slide** button. The pointer changes to ⊕ and three-quarters of the slide is darkened. See Figure 1-41.

**Figure 1-41**     **Zoom feature activated in Slide Show view**

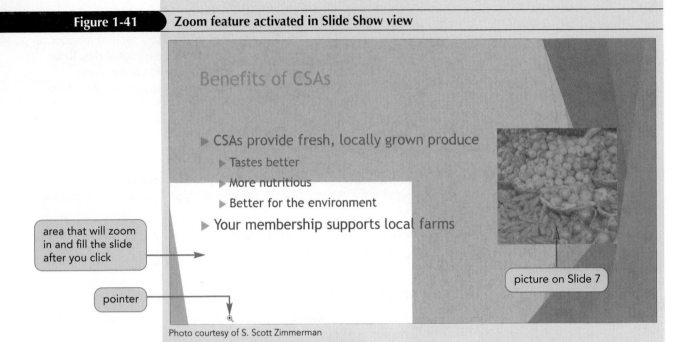

Photo courtesy of S. Scott Zimmerman

▶ **9.** Move the pointer to the picture, watching as the bright rectangle follows it, and then click the picture. The view zooms so that the part of the slide inside the bright rectangle fills the screen, and the pointer changes to ⌠🖐⌡.

▶ **10.** Press and hold the mouse button to change the pointer to ⌠✊⌡, and then drag down and to the right to pull another part of the zoomed in slide into view.

▶ **11.** Press the **Esc** key to zoom back out to see the whole slide.

Presenter view provides additional tools for running a slide show. In addition to seeing the current slide, you can also see the next slide, speaker notes, and a timer showing you how long the slide show has been running. Refer to the Session 1.2 Visual Overview for more information about Presenter view. Because of the additional tools available in Presenter view, you should consider using it if your computer is connected to a second monitor or projector. If, for some reason, you don't want to use Presenter view in that circumstance, you can switch to Slide Show view.

If your computer is connected to a projector or second monitor, and you start a slide show in Slide Show view, Presenter view starts on the computer and Slide Show view appears on the second monitor or projection screen. If you want to practice using Presenter view when your computer is not connected to a second monitor or projector, you can switch to Presenter view from Slide Show view.

Isaac wants you to switch to Presenter view and familiarize yourself with the tools available there.

### To use Presenter view to review the slide show:

▶ **1.** Move the pointer to display the row of buttons in the lower left corner of the screen, click the **More slide show options** button ⊙ to open a menu of commands, and then click **Show Presenter View**. The screen changes to show the presentation in Presenter view.

▶ **2.** Below the current slide, click the **See all slides** button ▦. The screen changes to show thumbnails of all the slides in the presentation, similar to Slide Sorter view.

3. Click the **Slide 4** thumbnail. Presenter view reappears, displaying Slide 4 ("What Do CSA Members Receive?") as the current slide.

4. Click anywhere on the current slide, Slide 4. The slide show advances to display Slide 5.

5. At the bottom of the screen, click the **Advance to the next slide** button ▶. Slide 6 ("Placing Your Order for Additional Items") appears.

6. Press the **spacebar** twice. The slide show advances again to display Slides 7 and then 8.

7. Press the **spacebar** again. A black slide appears. As noted on the slide, the black screen indicates the end of the slide show.

8. Press the **spacebar** once more. Presentation view closes and you return to Normal view.

### Decision Making: Displaying a Blank Slide During a Presentation

Sometimes during a presentation, the audience has questions about the material and you want to pause the slide show to respond to their questions. Or you might want to refocus the audience's attention on you instead of on the visuals on the screen. In these cases, you can display a blank slide (either black or white). When you do this, the audience, with nothing else to look at, will shift all of their attention to you. Some presenters plan to use blank slides and insert them at specific points during their slide shows. Planning to use a blank slide can help you keep your presentation focused and remind you that the purpose of the PowerPoint slides is to provide visual aids to enhance your presentation; the slides themselves are not the presentation.

If you did not create blank slides in your presentation file, but during your presentation you feel you need to display a blank slide, you can easily do this in Slide Show or Presenter view by pressing the B key to display a blank black slide or the W key to display a blank white slide. You can also click the Menu button in the row of buttons or right-click the screen to open a menu, point to Screen on the menu, and then click Black or White. To remove the black or white slide and redisplay the slide that had been on the screen before you displayed the blank slide, press any key on the keyboard or click anywhere on the screen. In Presenter view, you can also use the Black or unblack slide show button 🔲 to toggle a black slide on or off.

An alternative to redisplaying the slide that had been displayed prior to the blank slide is to click the Advance to the next slide button ▶. This can be more effective than redisplaying the slide that was onscreen before the blank slide because, after you have grabbed the audience's attention and prepared them to move on, you won't lose their focus by displaying a slide they have already seen.

## Using Reading View

Reading view displays the slides so that they almost fill the screen, similar to Slide Show view; however, in Reading view, a status bar appears identifying the number of the current slide and providing buttons to advance the slide show. You can also resize the window in Reading view to allow you to work in another window on the desktop.

**To use Reading view to review the presentation:**

▶ 1. Display **Slide 2** ("What Is a CSA?"), in the Slide pane, and then on the status bar, click the **Reading View** button 📖. The presentation changes to Reading view with Slide 2 displayed. See Figure 1-42.

| Figure 1-42 | Slide 2 in Reading view |
|---|---|

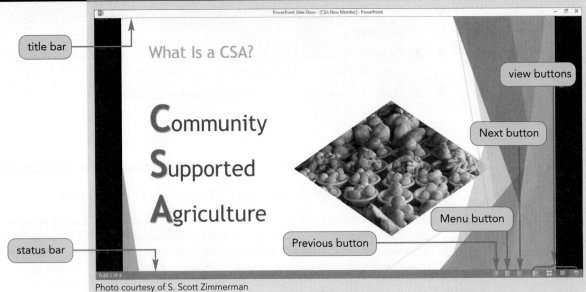

Photo courtesy of S. Scott Zimmerman

▶ 2. On the status bar, click the **Menu** button 📋. A menu appears with commands for working in Reading view, some of which are also available in Slide Show and Presenter views.

▶ 3. Click **Full Screen**. The presentation switches to Slide Show view displaying the current slide, Slide 2.

▶ 4. Press the **Esc** key. Slide Show view closes and you return to Reading view.

▶ 5. On the status bar, click the **Next** button ⏵. The next slide, Slide 3, appears on the screen.

▶ 6. On the status bar, click the **Normal** button 🖥 to return to Normal view with Slide 1 displayed in the Slide pane.

# Printing a Presentation

Before you deliver your presentation, you might want to print it. PowerPoint provides several printing options. For example, you can print the slides in color, grayscale (white and shades of gray), or pure black and white, and you can print one, some, or all of the slides in several formats.

You use the Print screen in Backstage view to set print options such as specifying a printer and color options.

First, you will replace Isaac's name on Slide 1 with your name.

## To choose a printer and color options:

1. Display **Slide 1** in the Slide pane, and then replace Isaac's name in the subtitle with your name.

2. Click the **FILE** tab to display Backstage view, and then click **Print** in the navigation bar. Backstage view changes to display the Print screen. The Print screen contains options for printing your presentation, and a preview of the first slide as it will print with the current options. See Figure 1-43.

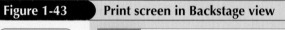

**Figure 1-43**    **Print screen in Backstage view**

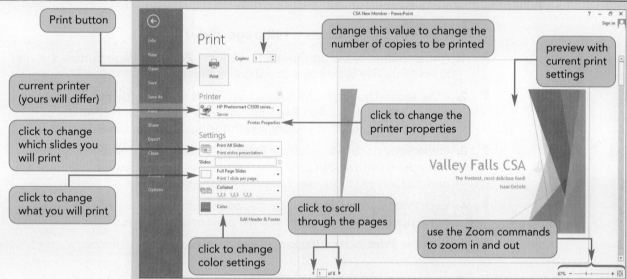

3. If you are connected to a network or to more than one printer, make sure the printer listed in the Printer box is the one you want to use; if it is not, click the **Printer** button, and then click the correct printer in the list.

4. Click the **Printer Properties** link to open the Properties dialog box for your printer. Usually, the default options are correct, but you can change any printer settings, such as print quality or the paper source, in this dialog box.

5. Click the **Cancel** button to close the Properties dialog box. Now you can choose whether to print the presentation in color, black and white, or grayscale. If you plan to print in black and white or grayscale, you should change this setting so you can see what your slides will look like without color and to make sure they are legible.

6. Click the **Color** button, and then click **Grayscale**. The preview changes to grayscale.

7. At the bottom of the preview pane, click the **Next Page** button ▶ twice to display Slide 3 ("Benefits of CSAs"). The slides are legible in grayscale.

8. If you will be printing in color, click the **Grayscale** button, and then click **Color**.

In the Settings section on the Print screen, you can click the Full Page Slides button to choose from among several choices for printing the presentation, as described below:

- **Full Page Slides**—Prints each slide full size on a separate piece of paper.
- **Notes Pages**—Prints each slide as a notes page.
- **Outline**—Prints the text of the presentation as an outline.
- **Handouts**—Prints the presentation with one or more slides on each piece of paper. When printing four, six, or nine slides, you can choose whether to order the slides from left to right in rows (horizontally) or from top to bottom in columns (vertically).

Isaac wants you to print the title slide as a full page slide so that he can use it as a cover page for his handouts.

### To print the title slide as a full page slide:

1. At the bottom of the preview pane, click the **Previous Page** button ◀ three times to display Slide 1 (the title slide) as the preview.

2. If the second button in the Settings section is not labeled "Full Page Slides," click it, and then click **Full Page Slides**. Note that below the preview of Slide 1, it indicates that you are viewing Slide 1 of eight slides to print.

3. In the Settings section, click the **Print All Slides** button. Note on the menu that opens that you can print all the slides, selected slides, the current slide, or a custom range. You want to print just the title slide as a full page slide.

4. Click **Print Current Slide**. Slide 1 appears in the preview pane, and at the bottom, it now indicates that you will print only one slide.

5. Click the **Print** button. Backstage view closes and Slide 1 prints.

Next, Isaac wants you to print the slides as a handout, with all eight slides on a single sheet of paper.

### To print the slides as a handout:

1. Click the **FILE** tab, and then click **Print** in the navigation bar.

2. In the Settings section, click the **Full Page Slides** button. A menu opens listing the various ways you can print the slides. See Figure 1-44.

---

**Figure 1-44**  **Print screen in Backstage view with print options menu open**

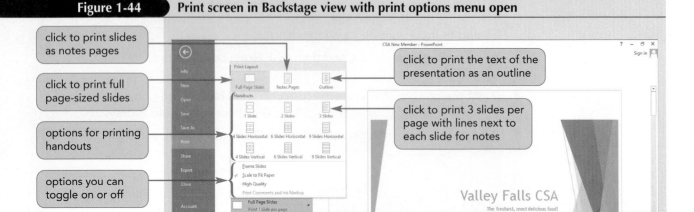

click to print slides as notes pages

click to print full page-sized slides

options for printing handouts

options you can toggle on or off

click to print the text of the presentation as an outline

click to print 3 slides per page with lines next to each slide for notes

Valley Falls CSA
The freshest, most delicious food!

3. In the Handouts section, click **9 Slides Horizontal**. The preview changes to show Slide 1 in the upper-left corner. You need to specify that all eight slides will print.

4. Click the **Print Current Slide** button, and then click **Print All Slides**. All eight slides appear in the preview pane, arranged in order horizontally, that is, in three rows from left to right. Notice that the current date appears in the top-right corner and a page number appears in the bottom-right corner.

5. At the top of the Print section, click the **Print** button. Backstage view closes and the handout prints.

Recall that you created speaker notes on Slides 3 and 7. Isaac would like you to print these slides as notes pages.

**To print the nonsequential slides containing speaker notes:**

1. Open the Print screen in Backstage view again, and then click the **9 Slides Horizontal** button. The menu opens. "9 Slides Horizontal" appeared on the button because that was the last printing option you chose.

2. In the Print Layout section of the menu, click **Notes Pages**. The menu closes and the preview displays Slide 1 as a Notes Page.

3. In the Settings section, click in the **Slides** box, type **3,7** and then click a blank area of the Print screen.

4. Scroll through the preview to confirm that Slides 3 and 7 will print, and then click the **Print** button. Backstage view closes and Slides 3 and 7 print as notes pages.

Finally, Isaac would like you to print the outline of the presentation. Recall that Slide 8 is designed to be a visual Isaac can leave displayed at the end of the presentation, so you don't need to include it in the outline.

**To print Slides 1 through 7 as an outline on a single page:**

1. Open the Print tab in Backstage view, click the **Notes Pages** button, and then in the Print Layout section, click **Outline**. The text on Slides 3 and 7 appears as an outline in the preview pane.

2. Click in the **Slides** box, type **1-7**, and then click a blank area of the Print screen. See Figure 1-45.

**Figure 1-45** | Print screen in Backstage view with Slides 1-7 previewed as an outline

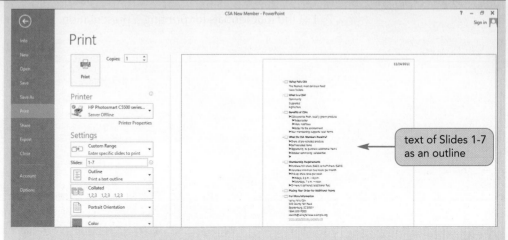

3. At the top of the Print section, click the **Print** button. Backstage view closes and the text of Slides 1-7 prints on one sheet of paper.

# Exiting PowerPoint

When you are finished working with your presentation, you can exit PowerPoint. If there is only one presentation open, you click the Close button ☒ in the upper-right corner of the program window to exit the program. If more than one presentation is open, clicking this button will only close the current presentation; to exit PowerPoint, you would need to click the Close button in each of the open presentation's windows.

**To exit PowerPoint:**

1. In the upper-right corner of the program window, click the **Close** button ☒. A dialog box opens asking if you want to save your changes. This is because you did not save the file after you replaced Isaac's name with your own.

2. In the dialog box, click the **Save** button. The dialog box closes, the changes are saved, and PowerPoint exits.

In this session, you opened an existing presentation and saved it with a new name, changed the theme, added and cropped photos and adjusted the photo compression, and resized and moved objects. You have also added speaker notes and checked the spelling. Finally, you printed the presentation in several forms and exited PowerPoint. Your work will help Isaac give an effective presentation to potential customers of Valley Farms CSA.

## REVIEW

### Session 1.2 Quick Check

1. Explain what a theme is and what changes with each variant.
2. Describe what happens when you crop photos.
3. Describe sizing handles.
4. Describe smart guides.
5. Why is it important to maintain the aspect ratio of photos?
6. What is the difference between Slide Show view and Presenter view?
7. List the four formats for printing a presentation.

ASSESS

## SAM Projects

Put your skills into practice with SAM Projects! SAM Projects for this tutorial can be found online. If you have a SAM account, go to www.cengage.com/sam2013 to download the most recent Project Instructions and Start Files.

PRACTICE

## Review Assignments

**Data Files needed for the Review Assignments: Farmland.jpg, Field Volunteer.jpg, Office Volunteer.jpg, Revised Volunteer Info.pptx**

Chris Kopache is the Volunteer Coordinator for Valley Falls CSA. He needs to create a presentation for CSA members to explain the various ways they can volunteer. He will give the presentation to small groups. He doesn't want to overwhelm people, but he wants them to have enough information about each type of job so that they can choose one that best suits their abilities. He asks you to begin creating the presentation.

1. Start PowerPoint and create a new, blank presentation. On the title slide, type **Information for Volunteers** as the title, and then type your name as the subtitle. Save the presentation as **Volunteer Info** to the drive and folder where you are storing your files.

2. Edit the title by adding **Valley Falls CSA** before the word "Volunteers."

3. Add a new Slide 2 with the Title and Content layout, type **Jobs for Volunteers** as the slide title, and then in the content placeholder type the following:
   - **Field work**
   - **Work in store**
   - **Deliver shares**
   - **Office work**
     - **Must be familiar with Excel and Word**
     - **Only 3 positions available**

4. Create a new Slide 3 with the Title and Content layout. Add **Expectations** as the slide title, and then type the following as a numbered list on the slide:
   1. **Submit job preferences with membership application**
   2. **Volunteer minimum two hours per month**
   3. **Submit shift changes one week in advance**
   4. **Contact Chris Kopache**

5. Create a new Slide 4 using the Two Content layout. Add **Questions?** as the slide title.

6. Use the Cut and Paste commands to move the last bulleted item on Slide 3 ("Contact Chris Kopache") to the left content placeholder on Slide 4.

7. On Slide 4, remove the bullet symbol from the text you pasted, and then add the following as the next two items in the unnumbered list:
   **Email: c_kopache@example.org**
   **Cell: 803-555-8723**

8. Click after "Kopache" in the first item in the list, and then create a new line below it without creating a new item in the list and so that there is no extra space above the new line. On the new line, type **Volunteer Coordinator**.

9. Remove the hyperlink formatting from the email address.

10. Create a new Slide 5 using the Title and Content layout. Delete the title text placeholder. In the content placeholder, type **Thank You!** as a single item in an unnumbered list. Increase the size of the text "Thank You!" to 96 points, and then change the color of this text to Blue, Accent 1.

11. On Slide 3 ("Expectations"), change the numbered list to a SmartArt graphic. Use the Vertical Curved List layout, which is a List type of diagram.

12. Save your changes, and then close the presentation.

13. Open the file **Revised Volunteer Info**, located in the PowerPoint1 ▸ Review folder included with your Data Files, add your name as the subtitle on the title slide, and then save it as **New CSA Volunteers** to the drive and location where you are storing your files.

14. Change the theme to Wisp and keep the default variant. On Slide 2, change the size of the text in the bulleted list so that the size of the text of the first-level items is 28 points.

15. On Slide 1 (the title slide), insert the photo **Farmland**, located in the PowerPoint1 ▸ Review folder included with your Data Files. Resize the photo, maintaining the aspect ratio, so that it is the same width as the slide, and then reposition the photo so that the top of the photo aligns with the top of the slide. Crop the photo from the bottom, up to the base of the trees on the right, leaving approximately one-quarter inch between the bottom of the photo and the slide title.

16. Change the layout of Slide 4 ("Volunteer in the Fields") to Title and Content, and then duplicate Slide 4. In the title of Slide 5 (the duplicate slide), replace "Fields" with **Office**.

17. On Slide 4, insert the photo **Field Volunteer**, located in the PowerPoint1 ▸ Review folder. Resize the photo so it is 4.9 inches high, maintaining the aspect ratio, and reposition it so it is approximately centered in the space below the slide title.

18. On Slide 5, insert the photo **Office Volunteer**. Crop the top portion of the photo so that there is approximately one-half inch of wall above the top of the paintings in the photo. Resize the cropped photo so it is 5.1 inches high, maintaining the aspect ratio, and then reposition the photo as you did for the photo on Slide 4.

19. Move Slide 5 ("Volunteer in the Office") so it becomes Slide 7.

20. On Slide 9 ("Questions?"), crop the photo to the Oval shape. Increase the size of the text in the unnumbered list to 24 points, and then resize the text box to make it wide enough so that the line containing the email address fits on one line.

21. Compress all the photos in the slides to 96 ppi and delete cropped areas of pictures.

22. Display Slide 3 ("Description of Volunteer Jobs") in the Slide pane and review the information on this slide. Chris wants to include this information as notes on Slides 4 through 7 instead of displaying it as a bulleted list. He has already added the notes to Slides 5 and 6. Display Slide 4 ("Volunteer in the Fields") in the Slide pane, display the Notes pane, and then add **Field workers pull weeds and participate in harvesting produce**. in the Notes pane. Then display Slide 7 ("Volunteer in the Office") in the Slide pane, and add **Office workers use Excel to maintain volunteer schedules and use Word to publish the newsletter**. as a note on this slide.

23. Delete Slide 3 ("Description of Volunteer Jobs") and the last slide (the blank slide).

24. Correct the two spelling errors on Slide 2 and the error on Slide 7, and ignore all instances of Chris's last name. If you made any additional spelling errors, correct them as well. Save the changes to the presentation.

25. Review the slide show in Slide Show, Presenter, and Reading views.

26. View the slides in grayscale, and then print the following: the title slide as a full page-sized slide in color or in grayscale depending on your printer; Slides 1–9 as a handout on a single piece of paper with the slides in order horizontally; Slides 3 and 6 as notes pages, and Slides 1–8 as an outline. Close the presentation when you are finished.

**APPLY**

## Case Problem 1

Data Files needed for this Case Problem: Apartment.jpg, Center.jpg, Couple.jpg, Orientation.pptx, Room.jpg

*Wind Lake Assisted Living Center* Sylvia Prater is director of human resources at Wind Lake Assisted Living Center in Muskego, Wisconsin. She is in charge of hiring employees and training them. She decided to create a presentation that she will give to new employees as part of their orientation. She asks you to help her create PowerPoint slides that she will use while she gives her presentation. Complete the following steps:

1. Open the presentation named **Orientation**, located in the PowerPoint1 ▶ Case1 folder included with your Data Files, and then save it as **Employee Orientation** to the drive and folder where you are storing your files.

2. Insert a new slide using the Title Slide layout. Move this new slide so it is Slide 1. Type **Employee Orientation** as the presentation title on the title slide. In the subtitle text placeholder, type your name.

3. Create a new Slide 2 with the Title and Content layout. Type **What Is Assisted Living?** as the slide title, and **Residence for people who need some assistance with daily living activities**. as the only item in the content placeholder. Change this to an unnumbered list.

4. Apply the View theme, and then apply its third variant. (If the View theme is not listed in the Themes gallery, choose any other theme and variant that uses a white or mostly white background, places the slide titles at the top of the slides, uses bullet symbols for first-level bulleted items, and positions the content in the bulleted lists starting at the top of the content text box, not the middle.)

5. On Slide 2 ("What Is Assisted Living?"), increase the size of the text of the in the text box below the slide titles to 28 points. On Slide 3 ("What Do We Provide?") increase the size of the text in the bulleted list so it is 24 points. On Slide 4 ("Our Employees") and Slide 7 ("Our Residents"), increase the size of the text in the bulleted list so that the first-level items are 28 points.

6. On Slide 2, insert the photo **Center**, located in the PowerPoint1 ▶ Case1 folder. Crop the top part of the photo off so that there is about one inch of sky above the building. Position the photo so the bottom of the photo aligns with the bottom of the slide and the left edge of the photo aligns with the right edge of the gray bar on the left. Resize the photo, maintaining the aspect ratio, so that it stretches from the gray bar on the left to the orange bar on the right. (If you used a different theme, center the photo horizontally in the space at the bottom of the slide.)

7. On Slide 3 ("What Do We Provide?"), add the speaker note **Personal care, such as bathing, grooming, and dressing, is provided by certified personal care attendants**.

8. On Slide 6 ("Living Quarters"), change the layout to the Comparison layout, which includes two content placeholders and a small text placeholder above each content placeholder. In the large content placeholder on the left, insert the photo **Room**, and in the large content placeholder on the right, insert the photo **Apartment**. Resize the Room photo so it is approximately the same height as the Apartment photo, maintaining the aspect ratio, and then reposition it, if needed, so that it is center-aligned with the caption placeholder above it and top-aligned with the Room photo on the left.

9. On Slide 5 ("Our Facility"), cut the first bulleted item, and then paste it in on Slide 6 in the small text placeholder on the left. If a blank line is added below the pasted text, delete it. On Slide 5, cut the remaining bulleted item, and then paste it on Slide 6 in the small text placeholder on the right, deleting the blank line if necessary.

10. On Slide 7 ("Our Residents"), add **Age** as the third bulleted item in the list, and then add **Minimum 60 years** and **Average 78 years** as subitems under the "Age" first-level item. Change the layout to Two Content.

11. On Slide 7, in the content placeholder, insert the photo **Couple**, located in the PowerPoint1 ▸ Case1 folder. Crop off the part of the photo to the right of the man, resize the photo so it is 5 inches high, maintaining the aspect ratio, and then reposition it as needed so that the top of the photo and the top of the content text box are aligned.

12. Compress all the photos in the presentation to 96 ppi and delete cropped portions of photos.

13. On Slide 8 ("New Employee To Do List"), change the list to a numbered list, and then add the following as a new item 2:

    **2. Attend certification seminars**
       **1. First aid**
       **2. CPR**

14. On Slide 8, convert the numbered list to a SmartArt diagram using the Vertical Block List layout, which is a List type of diagram. In the Text pane, click before "Confidentiality agreement," and then press the Tab key to make it a subitem under "Fill out paperwork." Change "W-4 and other personnel forms" to a second subitem under "Fill out paperwork."

15. Delete Slide 5 ("Our Facility"). Move Slide 4 ("Our Employees") so it becomes Slide 6.

16. Check the spelling in the presentation, and then read the text in the presentation carefully. On Slide 3 ("What Do We Provide?"), change the incorrect word "sight" to **site**.

17. Save the changes to the presentation, view the slide show in Presenter view, and then print the title slide as a full page slide, print Slides 2–7 as a handout using the 6 Slides Horizontal arrangement, and print Slide 3 as a notes page.

## Case Problem 2

**TROUBLESHOOT**

**Data Files needed for this Case Problem: Olympiad.pptx, Tangrams.jpg, Winner.jpg**

***Chandler, AZ School District*** Manuel Resendez is the Director of Science Curriculum Development for the Chandler, Arizona school district. One of his responsibilities is to organize an annual district-wide Math and Science Olympiad, during which school children in grades 4 through 6 can demonstrate their skills in math and science. To make sure that the teachers, coaches, parents, and volunteers at the Olympiad understand the purpose of the event and the activities the students will be doing, he plans to visit each school and give a presentation to those involved. He created a PowerPoint presentation with text describing the event, and he asks you to finish it by inserting photos from the previous year's event. Complete the following steps:

1. Open the file named **Olympiad**, located in the PowerPoint1 ▸ Case2 folder included with your Data Files, and then save it as **Math-Science Olympiad** to the drive and folder where you are storing your files. Add your name as the subtitle on Slide 1.

2. Apply the Frame theme. Change the variant to the third variant.

⚙ **Troubleshoot** 3. Evaluate the problem that the theme change caused on the title slide and fix it.

4. On Slide 3, in the first item in the bulleted list, move "9:00 a.m. to 8:00 p.m." to a new line below the first line starting with "When" without creating a new bulleted item. Do the same with "180 S. Arizona Ave." in the second item.

5. Move Slide 4 ("Rules") so it becomes Slide 10.

6. On Slide 10 ("Rules"), change the bulleted list to a numbered list. Add as a new item 4 **Only event administrators allowed on the contest floor**. Change the size of the text in the numbered list to 28 points.

7. Change the layout of Slide 9 ("Tangrams") to Two Content, and then insert the photo **Tangrams**, located in the PowerPoint1 ▸ Case2 folder, in the content placeholder. Increase the size of the picture, maintaining the aspect ratio, and reposition it so it better fills the space on the right.

8. Change the layout of Slide 11 ("Awards") to Two Content, and then insert the photo **Winner**, located in the PowerPoint1 ▸ Case2 folder, in the content placeholder.

⚙ **Troubleshoot** 9. One of the slides contains information that should be explained orally rather than presented as a list. Review the presentation to identify this slide and change that information to a speaker note on that slide. Make any other adjustments necessary to make this an effective slide.

⚙ **Troubleshoot** 10. Review the presentation to identify the slide that contains information that is repeated in the presentation and delete that slide.

⚙ **Troubleshoot** 11. Consider how changing the theme in Step 2 affected the readability of the lists on the slides. Make the appropriate changes to the slides.

12. Compress all the photos in the presentation to 96 ppi, check the spelling in the presentation, and then save the changes. (*Hint*: If the E-mail (96 ppi) option in the Compress Pictures dialog box is gray and not available, close the dialog box, select a different picture, and try again.)

13. View the slide show in Presenter view, zooming in on the pictures of the different events.

14. Print the title slide as a full page slide in grayscale. Print Slides 1–3 and Slides 5–10 as an outline by typing **1-3, 5-10** in the Slides box.

## Case Problem 3

CREATE

**Data Files needed for this Case Problem: Floating Houses.jpg, Karl.jpg, Peru.pptx, Region1.jpg – Region8 Right.jpg**

***Karl Benson Photography*** Karl Benson is a photographer who specializes in scenic photos. He also teaches a course for beginner photographers. Karl recently returned from a trip to Peru. On his trip, he was very interested to learn that Peru has eight distinct regions with different geography and climates. Karl asks you to create a presentation that contains some of the photos he took on his trip. He will not be giving an oral presentation using this file. Instead, he wants his students to view the slides on their own, so he prepared a file with text describing the photos and the regions in Peru. Slides 2 through 10 of the final presentation are shown in Figure 1-46. Refer to Figure 1-46 as you complete the following steps:

**Figure 1-46**    **Slides 2-11 of Peruvian Regions presentation**

Maps used with permission of Microsoft Corporation; Photos courtesy of S. Scott Zimmerman

1. Open the file named **Peru**, located in the PowerPoint1 ▶ Case3 folder included with your Data Files, and then save it as **Peruvian Regions** to the drive and folder where you are storing your files.

2. Add a new slide with the Title Slide layout, and move it so it is Slide 1. Type **The Eight Regions of Peru** as the title and your name as the subtitle.

3. Change the variant of the Office theme to the third variant.

4. On Slide 2, drag the map of Peru on top of the map of South America as in Figure 1-46. (Use the left edges of the maps as a guide.) Resize the title text box to 4" x 5", change the font size of the text in the title text box to 32 points, and then position it on the left side of the slide, approximately centered vertically.

5. Change the layout of Slides 3 through 7 to Picture with Caption. On all five slides, change the font size of the captions in the text boxes below the titles from 16 points to 18 points.

6. Use the Region numbers on the slides to reorder Slides 3 through 10 in order by Region, starting with Region 1 on Slide 3 and ending with Region 8 on Slide 10.

7. On Slides 3 through 10, insert the photos provided in the PowerPoint1 ▶ Case3 folder that correspond to the region numbers described on each slide. Refer to Figure 1-46 as needed.

8. On Slide 11 ("Want More?"), insert the **Floating Houses** photo, located in the PowerPoint1 ▶ Case3 folder, in the content placeholder on the left and the **Karl** photo, located in the PowerPoint1 ▶ Case3 folder, in the content placeholder on the right.

9. Karl needs to post this presentation to a website that has file size limitations, so he needs the presentation file size to be as small as possible, even though he realizes that compressing the photos will reduce their quality. Compress all the photos in the presentation to 96 ppi.

10. Save the changes to the presentation, and then view the presentation in Reading view.

## Case Problem 4

Data Files needed for this Case Problem: Cargo.jpg, Corpus Christi.jpg, Freight.jpg, Loading1.mp4, Loading2.mp4, Submit.jpg, URL.jpg, Woman.jpg

**CHALLENGE**

***Corpus Christi Freight Transport, Inc.*** Quentin Hershey is a customer relations representative for Corpus Christi Freight Transport, Inc., a large shipping company headquartered in Corpus Christi, Texas, and with offices in Argentina and Sydney. He wants you to help him create a PowerPoint presentation to explain features of the company and the services it offers. Quentin wants to give the presentation to organizations that require shipping services to U.S. waterways and to foreign ports. Complete the following steps:

**Explore** 1. Create a new presentation using the Striped black border presentation template from Office.com. (*Hint*: Use **striped black border** as the search term. If you get no results, type **white** as the search term, and then choose a template with a simple theme.)

2. Replace the title text on the title slide with **Corpus Christi Freight Transport, Inc**. and replace the subtitle text with your name. Save the presentation as **Freight Transport** to the drive and folder where you are storing your files.

3. Delete all the slides except the title slide.

4. Add a new Slide 2 with the Two Content layout. Type **Who We Are** as the title, and then type the following as a bulleted list in the left content placeholder:
   - **International shipping company**
   - **Licensed by Federal Maritime Commission**
   - **Bonded as international freight transporter**
   - **Registered as cosmetic freight forwarder**

5. On Slide 2, in the right content placeholder, insert the photo **Freight**, located in the PowerPoint1 ▶ Case4 folder included with your Data Files. Resize it, maintaining the aspect ratio, so it is 4.8 inches high, and then reposition it as needed so that the middle of the photo and the middle of the bulleted list text box are aligned.

6. Add a new Slide 3 with the Title and Content layout. Type **Online Scheduling** as the title, and then type the following as a bulleted list in the content placeholder:
   - **Register at www.freight.example.com**
   - **Enter type and amount**
   - **Submit information**
   - **Receive confirmation within 24 hours**

7. On Slide 3, remove the link formatting from the website address in the first bulleted item.

8. On Slide 3, convert the bulleted list to a SmartArt diagram with the Vertical Picture List layout, which is a List type of diagram.

⊕ **Explore** 9. Change the colors of the diagram to Colored Fill – Accent 3 by using the Change Colors button in the SmartArt Styles group on the SMARTART TOOLS DESIGN tab.

⊕ **Explore** 10. Insert the following pictures, located in the PowerPoint1 ▸ Case4 folder, in the picture placeholders in the SmartArt diagram, in order from top to bottom: **URL, Cargo, Submit,** and **Woman**.

11. Add a new Slide 4 with the Two Content layout. Type **U.S. Office** as the title. In the content placeholder on the left, type the following as an unnumbered list without extra space between the lines:

   **Corpus Christi Freight**

   **2405 Shoreline Road**

   **Corpus Christi, TX 78401**

12. On Slide 4, add the phone number **(361) 555-1254** and the website address **www.freight.example.com** as new items in the unnumbered list. Press the spacebar after typing the website address to format it as a link.

13. On Slide 4, add the photo **Corpus Christi**, located in the PowerPoint1 ▸ Case4 folder, to the content placeholder on the right. Resize it so it is 3.9 inches high, maintaining the aspect ratio, and then position it so the top edge aligns with the top edge of the text box on the left and there is approximately one inch of space between the right side of the photo and the right edge of the slide.

14. Compress all the photos in the presentation to 96 ppi, and then save the changes.

15. Add a new Slide 5 with the Comparison layout. Type **How Are Containers Loaded?** as the title, type **First a container is selected** in the small text placeholder on the left, and then type **Then it is transported to the ship and loaded** in the small text placeholder on the right. Move this slide so it becomes Slide 4.

⊕ **Explore** 16. On Slide 4 ("How Are Containers Loaded?"), insert the video **Loading1**, located in the PowerPoint1 ▸ Case4 folder, in the left content placeholder, and insert the video **Loading2**, located in the same folder, in the right content placeholder. (The video objects might be filled with black when they are inserted.)

⊕ **Explore** 17. Open the Info tab in Backstage view. Use the Compress Media command to compress the videos to the lowest quality possible. Use the Back button at the top of the navigation bar in Backstage view to return to Normal view.

18. Run the slide show in Slide Show view. When Slide 4 ("How Are Containers Loaded?") appears, point to each video to make a Play button appear, and then click the Play button to play each video. Note that there is no sound in the videos. (*Hint*: Point to the video as it plays to display the play bar again.)

# Adding Media and Special Effects

*Using Media in a Presentation for a Norwegian Tourism Company*

## OBJECTIVES

**Session 2.1**
- Apply a theme used in another presentation
- Insert online pictures
- Insert shapes
- Format shapes and pictures
- Rotate and flip objects
- Create a table
- Modify and format a table
- Insert symbols
- Change the proofing language

**Session 2.2**
- Apply and modify transitions
- Animate objects and bulleted lists
- Change how an animation starts
- Add video and modify playback options
- Understand animation effects applied to videos
- Trim video and set a poster frame
- Compress media
- Add footers and headers

## Case | *Essential Norway Tours*

Inger Halvorsen was born and raised in Myrdal, Norway, not far from the Flåm Railway that travels through the beautiful mountains of central Norway. She attended college in the United States and graduated with a degree in geography. She then returned to her home country and started a travel agency, Essential Norway Tours, in Oslo. She hired a photographer to take photos and video of scenes from one of her tours from Hønefoss to Myrdal on the Bergen Train, from Myrdal to Flåm on the Flåm Train, and by boat through Aurlandsfjord and Nærøfjords, two of the most beautiful fjords in Norway. She wants to include the photos and video in a presentation that she wants you to give to U.S. travel agents and others who might be interested in booking trips through her agency.

In this tutorial, you will modify a presentation to highlight the beautiful scenery visitors will enjoy when they go on an Essential Norway tour. You will add formatting and special effects to photos and shapes, add transitions and animations to slides, and add and modify video.

## STARTING DATA FILES

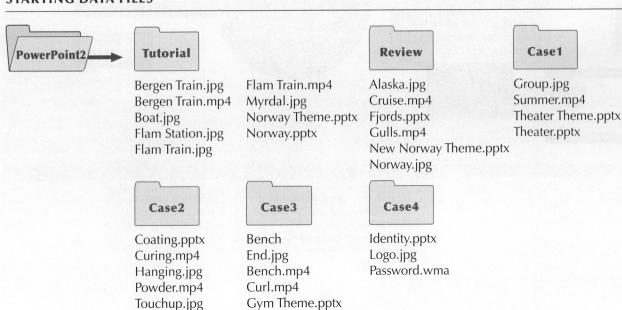

**PowerPoint2** →

**Tutorial**
Bergen Train.jpg
Bergen Train.mp4
Boat.jpg
Flam Station.jpg
Flam Train.jpg
Flam Train.mp4
Myrdal.jpg
Norway Theme.pptx
Norway.pptx

**Review**
Alaska.jpg
Cruise.mp4
Fjords.pptx
Gulls.mp4
New Norway Theme.pptx
Norway.jpg

**Case1**
Group.jpg
Summer.mp4
Theater Theme.pptx
Theater.pptx

**Case2**
Coating.pptx
Curing.mp4
Hanging.jpg
Powder.mp4
Touchup.jpg
Wash.mp4
Welding.jpg

**Case3**
Bench
End.jpg
Bench.mp4
Curl.mp4
Gym Theme.pptx
Gym.pptx
Military.mp4

**Case4**
Identity.pptx
Logo.jpg
Password.wma

# Session 2.1 Visual Overview:

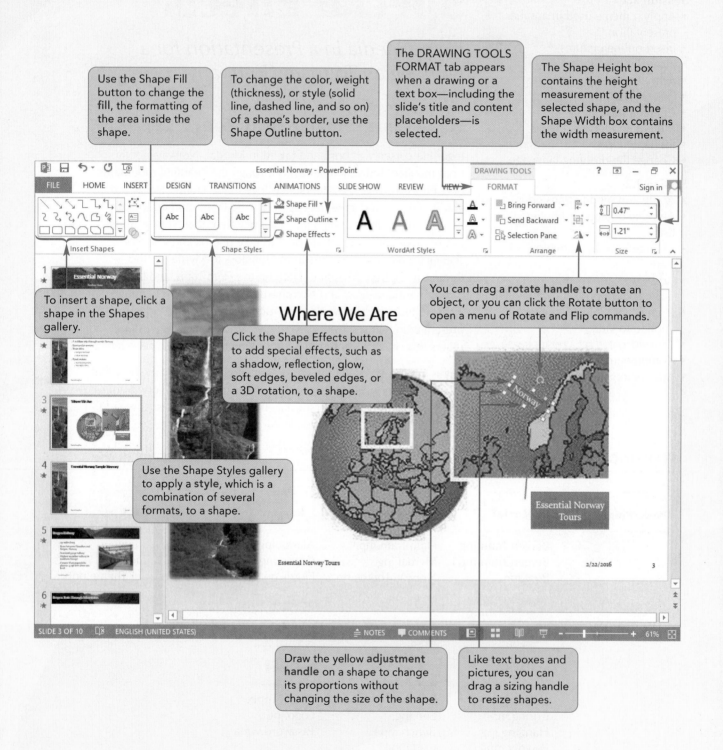

Use the Shape Fill button to change the fill, the formatting of the area inside the shape.

To change the color, weight (thickness), or style (solid line, dashed line, and so on) of a shape's border, use the Shape Outline button.

The DRAWING TOOLS FORMAT tab appears when a drawing or a text box—including the slide's title and content placeholders—is selected.

The Shape Height box contains the height measurement of the selected shape, and the Shape Width box contains the width measurement.

To insert a shape, click a shape in the Shapes gallery.

Click the Shape Effects button to add special effects, such as a shadow, reflection, glow, soft edges, beveled edges, or a 3D rotation, to a shape.

You can drag a rotate handle to rotate an object, or you can click the Rotate button to open a menu of Rotate and Flip commands.

Use the Shape Styles gallery to apply a style, which is a combination of several formats, to a shape.

Draw the yellow adjustment handle on a shape to change its proportions without changing the size of the shape.

Like text boxes and pictures, you can drag a sizing handle to resize shapes.

# Formatting Graphics

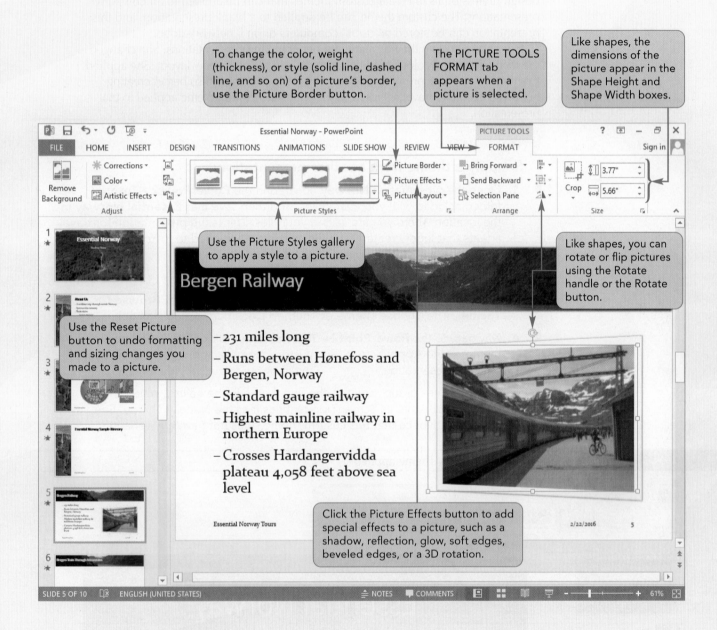

To change the color, weight (thickness), or style (solid line, dashed line, and so on) of a picture's border, use the Picture Border button.

The PICTURE TOOLS FORMAT tab appears when a picture is selected.

Like shapes, the dimensions of the picture appear in the Shape Height and Shape Width boxes.

Use the Picture Styles gallery to apply a style to a picture.

Like shapes, you can rotate or flip pictures using the Rotate handle or the Rotate button.

Use the Reset Picture button to undo formatting and sizing changes you made to a picture.

Click the Picture Effects button to add special effects to a picture, such as a shadow, reflection, glow, soft edges, beveled edges, or a 3D rotation.

# Applying a Theme Used in Another Presentation

As you learned earlier, an installed theme can be applied by clicking one in the Themes group on the DESIGN tab. An installed theme is actually a special type of file that is stored with PowerPoint program files. You can also apply themes that are applied to any other presentation stored on your computer. For example, many companies want to promote their brand through their presentations, so they hire presentation design professionals to create custom themes that can be applied to all company presentations. The custom theme can be applied to a blank presentation, and this presentation can be stored on users' computers or on a network drive.

Inger had a custom theme created for her company's presentations. She changed the theme fonts and colors, modified layouts, and created a new layout. She applied this theme to a blank presentation that she sent to you. Inger also began creating her presentation for travel agents, and she wants the custom theme applied to that presentation.

## To apply a theme from another presentation:

1. Open the presentation **Norway**, located in the **PowerPoint2 ▸ Tutorial** folder included with your Data Files, and then save it as **Essential Norway** in the location where you are saving your files. This is the presentation for travel agents that Inger created. The Office theme is applied to it. You need to apply Inger's custom theme to it.

2. On the ribbon, click the **DESIGN** tab.

3. In the Themes group, click the **More** button, and then click **Browse for Themes**. The Choose Theme or Themed Document dialog box opens.

4. Navigate to the **PowerPoint2 ▸ Tutorial** folder, click **Norway Theme**, and then click the **Apply** button. The custom theme is applied to the Essential Norway presentation.

5. In the Themes group, point to the first theme in the gallery, which is the current theme. Its ScreenTip identifies it as the Norway Theme. See Figure 2-1. Notice that this custom theme does not have any variants.

| Figure 2-1 | Custom Norway Theme applied |
|---|---|

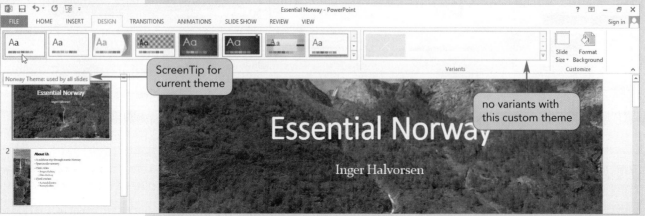

Photos courtesy of S. Scott Zimmerman

6. Click the **HOME** tab, and then on Slide 1 (the title slide), click the title text.

7. In the Font group, click the **Font** arrow. Notice that the theme fonts for the Norway theme are Calibri Light and Constantia. This is different from the Office theme, which uses Calibri for the body text.

8. In the Slides group, click the **Layout** button. The Layout gallery appears. The custom layouts that Inger created are listed in the gallery, as shown in Figure 2-2.

| Figure 2-2 | Custom layouts in the Norway Theme |
| --- | --- |

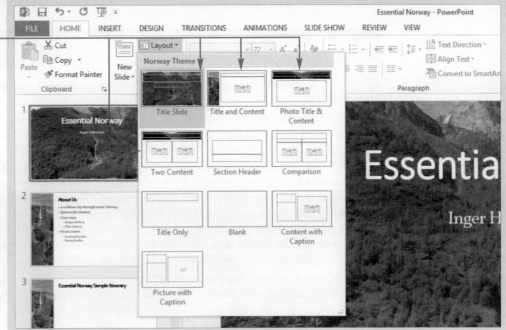

Photos courtesy of S. Scott Zimmerman

Notice the customized Title Slide layout has a photo as a slide background, the Title and Content customized layout has a photo along the left edge of the slide of water running down a cliff, and the customized Two Content layout includes a photo under the slide title. Inger also provided an additional custom layout called Photo Title & Content, which is for a slide with a title and one content placeholder.

9. Press the **Esc** key to close the Layout gallery.

When you applied the custom theme from the Norway Theme presentation, the title slide and the slides with the Title and Content layout and Two Content layout were changed to use the customized versions of these layouts. Slides 4 and 6 have the Two Content layout applied and contain information about the Bergen and Flåm railways. Slides 5 and 7 have the Title and Content layout applied. Currently they only contain a title, but later you will add videos related to the Bergen and Flåm trains to these slides. Inger wants you to change the layout of these two slides to the new Photo Title & Content layout so they better match the slides with the Two Content layouts.

**To apply a custom layout to Slides 5 and 7:**

▶ 1. Display **Slide 5** ("Bergen Train Through Mountains") in the Slide pane.

▶ 2. In the Slides group, click the **Layout** button. The Layout gallery appears.

▶ 3. Click the **Photo Title & Content** layout. The custom layout is applied to Slide 5.

▶ 4. Apply the **Photo Title & Content** layout to Slide 7 ("Flåm Train in Station").

▶ 5. Save your changes.

**INSIGHT**

*Saving a Presentation as a Theme*

If you need to use a custom theme frequently, you can save a presentation file as an Office Theme file. A theme file is a different file type than a presentation file. You can then store this file so that it appears in the Themes gallery on the DESIGN tab. To save a custom theme, click the FILE tab, click Save As in the navigation bar, and then click the Browse button to open the Save As dialog box. To change the file type to Office Theme, click the Save as type arrow, and then click Office Theme. This changes the current folder in the Save As dialog box to the Document Themes folder, which is a folder created on the hard drive when Office is installed and where the installed themes are stored. If you save a custom theme to the Document Themes folder, that theme will be listed in its own row above the installed themes in the Themes gallery. (You need to click the More button in the Themes gallery to see this row.) You can also change the folder location and save the custom theme to any location on your computer or network or to a folder on your SkyDrive. If you do this, the theme will not appear in the Themes gallery, but you can still access it using the Browse for Themes command on the Themes gallery menu.

# Inserting Online Pictures

In addition to adding pictures stored on your computer or network to slides, you can also add pictures stored on websites. To do this, you click the Online Pictures button in a content placeholder or in the Images group on the INSERT tab. When you do this, the Insert Pictures window opens, in which you can choose to search for an image on Office.com or use the Bing search engine to search for images across the Internet. The images stored on Office.com are often called clip art, which are images stored in collections so that you can easily locate and use them.

After selecting where you want to search (Office.com or the Internet using the Bing search engine), click in the Search box next to your choice, and then type keywords. **Keywords** are words or phrases that describe an image. When you use the Bing search engine, you get the same results that you would get if you were to type keywords in the Search box on the Bing home page in your browser.

Images stored on Office.com have keywords directly associated with them. For example, a photo of a train might have the keywords "train" and "engine" associated with it. If the photo is a train going over a bridge, additional keywords might be "bridge" and "trestle." The more keywords you use, the narrower (more specific) your search results will be; conversely, to broaden your search, use fewer keywords.

Inger wants you to add a new Slide 3 to the presentation and then insert a map of Norway. You'll search for an image of this on Office.com.

## To insert a picture of a map from Office.com:

1. Display **Slide 2** ("About Us") in the Slide pane, and then in the Slides group, click the **New Slide** button. A new Slide 3 is inserted with the same layout as Slide 2, Title and Content.

2. Type **Where We Are** as the slide title.

3. In the content placeholder, click the **Online Pictures** button 🖼. The Insert Pictures window opens with the insertion point in the Office.com Clip Art search box. See Figure 2-3.

| Figure 2-3 | **Insert Pictures window** |
|---|---|

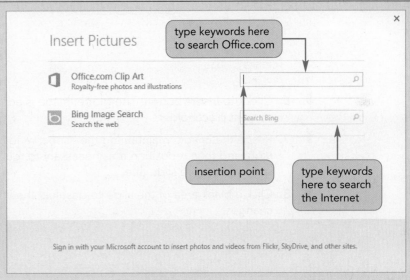

4. In the **Office.com Clip Art** search box, type **Norway map**, and then click the **Search** button 🔍. After a moment, images that match your keywords appear in the window.

5. Click the drawing of a globe with Scandinavia pulled out in a detail map. The keywords associated with the selected image and the image's measurements in pixels are in the bottom-left corner of the window, as shown in Figure 2-4.

| Figure 2-4 | Images found on Office.com in Insert Pictures window |

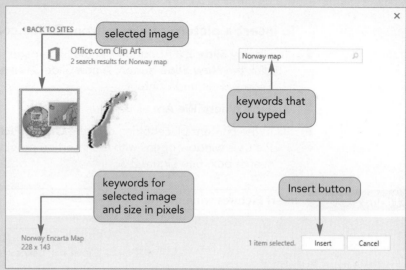

Images used with permission of Microsoft Corporation

▶ **6.** Click the **Insert** button. The globe image is added to the slide in place of the content placeholder.

▶ **7.** Resize the image, maintaining the aspect ratio, so that it is about five inches high, and then reposition it as necessary to roughly center it in the white space below the slide title.

▶ **8.** Click a blank area of the slide to deselect the image, and then save your changes.

## Written Communication: Respecting Intellectual Property

Make sure you understand and abide by copyright laws. If you use someone else's photograph, illustration, video, music, diagram, or chart, or if you use someone else's data to create your own visuals, give proper credit. Students can, for educational purposes only, use copyrighted material on a one-time basis without getting permission from the copyright holder. On the other hand, if you work for a business or nonprofit organization, much stricter copyright laws apply. You must obtain explicit permission from the copyright owner, and in some cases pay a fee to that person or company. You may use all the images on Office.com in your presentations as long as you are not creating the presentation for commercial purposes. If you need to use an image for a commercial purpose, you need to check to see who owns the image. To do this, go to Office.com, search for the image there, point to the image you want to use, and then click View Details. The image appears on a new webpage with information about the image listed on the right. At the top of this list of information, the name of the copyright holder appears, such as Fotalia or iStockphoto. Contact the copyright holder directly for permission to use the image. If there is no copyright holder listed, the image is owned by Microsoft and you cannot use it for commercial purposes. If you use the Bing search engine when you insert an online picture, you should go to the website from which you are copying the photo and determine if you need to get permission to use the image.

# Inserting Shapes

You can add many shapes to a slide, including lines, rectangles, stars, and more. To draw a shape, click the Shapes button in the Illustrations group on the INSERT tab, click a shape in the gallery, and then click and drag to draw the shape in the size you want. Like any object, a shape can be resized after you insert it.

You've already had a little experience with one shape—a text box, which is a shape specifically designed to contain text. You can add additional text boxes to slides using the Text Box shape. You can also add text to any shape you place on a slide.

Inger wants you to add a few labels to the map image. First, she wants you to add a label to identify Norway in the detail map of Scandinavia.

### To insert and position an arrow shape with text on Slide 3:

1. With **Slide 3** ("Where We Are") in the Slide pane, click the **INSERT** tab, and then in the Illustrations group, click the **Shapes** button. The Shapes gallery opens. See Figure 2-5. The gallery is organized into nine categories of shapes, plus the Recently Used Shapes group at the top.

| Figure 2-5 | Shapes gallery |
| --- | --- |

Image used with permission of Microsoft Corporation; Photos courtesy of S. Scott Zimmerman

Make sure you drag the pointer, not just click it. Otherwise the inserted shape will be tiny.

2. Under Block Arrows, click the **Left Arrow** shape ⇦. The gallery closes and the pointer changes to +.

3. On the slide, click above the top-left corner of the pop-out, detail map, and then drag to the right to create an arrow approximately 1¼-inches long and ½-inch high.

   A blue, left-pointing arrow appears. (Don't worry about the exact placement or size of the arrow; you will move it later.) Note that the DRAWING TOOLS FORMAT tab is the active tab on the ribbon.

4. With the shape selected, type **Norway**. The text you type appears in the arrow. It might not all fit on one line and it may be too tall to fit inside the arrow.

5. If necessary, drag the right-middle sizing handle on the end of the arrow to the right to lengthen the arrow until the word "Norway" fits on one line.

6. If necessary, drag the bottom-middle sizing handle down until the arrow is tall enough to display all of the text. Now you need to position the arrow shape on the map. When you drag a shape with text, it is similar to dragging a text box, which means you need to drag a border of the shape or a part of the shape that does not contain text.

7. Position the pointer on the arrow shape so that the pointer changes to ✛⃗, and then drag the arrow shape on top of the map so that it points to the right-lower side of the yellow area in the detail map of Scandinavia. See Figure 2-6.

| Figure 2-6 | Arrow shape with text on Slide 3 |

Image used with permission of Microsoft Corporation; Photos courtesy of S. Scott Zimmerman

Next, Inger wants you to add a shape to point to the part of Norway that she is featuring in the presentation. You'll use a callout shape for this.

**To insert and position a callout shape with text on Slide 3:**

**TIP**

You can also insert a shape using the Shapes gallery in the Drawing group on the HOME tab.

1. On the ribbon, click the **INSERT** tab.

2. In the Illustrations group, click the **Shapes** button. The Shapes gallery opens.

3. Under Callouts, click the **Line Callout 1** shape ⌐□.

4. Below the detail map, drag to create a box approximately two inches wide and one inch high, and then type **Essential Norway Tours**.

5. Resize the square part of the callout shape, if necessary, so that the text "Essential Norway" fits on one line.

6. Save your changes.

# Formatting Objects

Recall that both shapes and pictures, such as photos and clip art, are treated as objects in PowerPoint. The PICTURE TOOLS and DRAWING TOOLS FORMAT tabs contain tools for formatting these objects. For both shapes and pictures, you can use these tools to apply borders or outlines, special effects such as drop shadows and reflections, and styles. You can also resize and rotate or flip these objects. Some formatting tools are available only to one or the other type of object. For example, the Remove Background tool is available only to pictures, and the Fill command is available only to shapes. Refer to the Session 2.1 Visual Overview for more information about the commands on the FORMAT tabs.

## Formatting Shapes

You can modify the fill of a shape by filling it with a color, a gradient (shading in which one color blends into another or varies from one shade to another), a textured pattern, or a picture. When you add a shape to a slide, the default fill is the Accent 1 color from the set of theme colors, and the default outline is a darker shade of that color.

The default blue of the arrow shape blends into the blue color of the image, so you'll change it.

**To change the fill of the arrow and the style of the callout:**

1. Click the **Norway** arrow, and then click the **DRAWING TOOLS FORMAT** tab, if necessary.

2. In the Shape Styles group, click the **Shape Fill button arrow**. The Shape Fill menu opens. See Figure 2-7. You can fill a shape with a color, a picture, a gradient, or a texture, or you can remove the fill by clicking No Fill.

**Figure 2-7** Shape Fill button menu

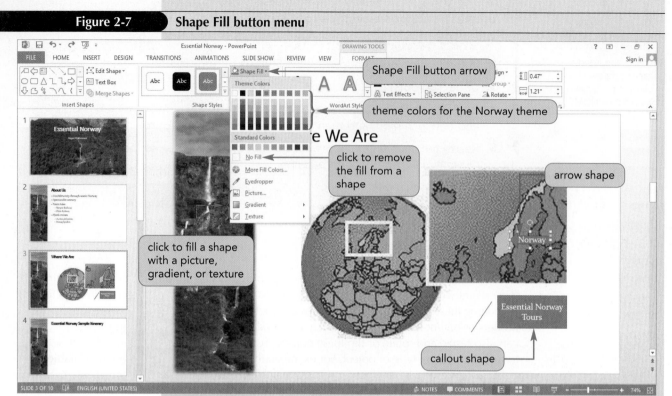

Image used with permission of Microsoft Corporation; Photos courtesy of S. Scott Zimmerman

3. Under Theme Colors, click **Red, Accent 2**. The shape fill of the selected arrow changes to the red color. Next, you'll apply a style to the callout shape.

4. Click the callout shape, and then in the Shape Styles group, click the **More** button. The Shape Styles gallery opens.

5. Click the **Moderate Effect – Red, Accent 2** style. The style, which fills the shape with gradient shades of red and changes the shape outline to the Red, Accent 2 color, is applied to the callout shape.

On some shapes, you can drag the yellow adjustment handle to change the shape's proportions. For instance, if you dragged the adjustment handle on the arrow shape, you would change the size of the arrow head relative to the size of the arrow. The callout shape has two adjustment handles, one on either end of the line that extends out from the part of the shape that contains text. You can drag these adjustment handles to more clearly identify what the callout is pointing to.

You need to position the callout shape and adjust the line so that the line is pointing to the area of Norway highlighted in the presentation.

### To move and adjust the callout shape and change its outline weight:

▶ **1.** Drag the callout shape so that the right edge is aligned with the right side of the map image and there is approximately one-quarter inch space between the callout and the bottom of the detail portion of the map.

▶ **2.** Drag the yellow adjustment handle on the left end of the callout line so that it points to the lower-left portion of Norway on the map. The callout line is hard to see on top of the map, so you will make the shape's outline thicker by changing its weight.

▶ **3.** In the Shape Styles group, click the **Shape Outline button arrow**, point to **Weight**, and then click **3 pt**. Compare your screen to Figure 2-8 and make any adjustments necessary to match the figure.

| Figure 2-8 | Formatted and positioned callout shape |

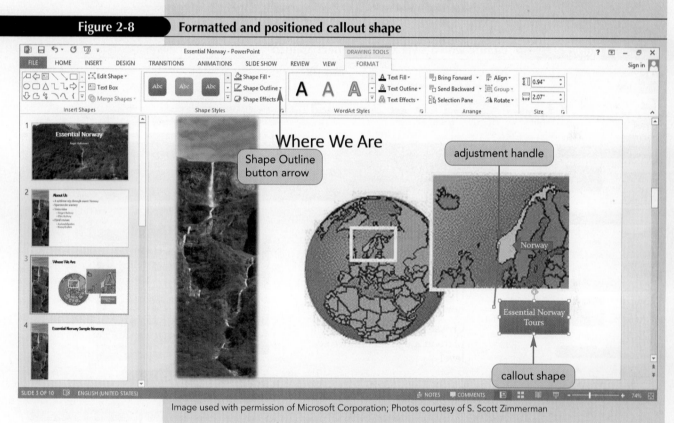

Image used with permission of Microsoft Corporation; Photos courtesy of S. Scott Zimmerman

## Formatting Pictures

You can format photos as well as shapes. To format photos, you use the tools on the PICTURE TOOLS FORMAT tab.

Inger wants you to format the pictures on Slides 5 and 7 by adding a frame and a 3-D effect. To create the frame, you could apply a thick outline, or you can apply one of the styles that includes a frame.

TIP

Click the Reset Picture button in the Adjust group on the PICTURE TOOLS FORMAT tab to remove formatting from a picture or resize the picture to its original size.

## To format the photos on Slides 5 and 7:

1. Display **Slide 5** ("Bergen Railway") in the Slide pane, click the photo of the train, and then click the **PICTURE TOOLS FORMAT** tab.

2. In the Picture Styles group, click the **Beveled Matte, White** style. This style applies a 15-point white border with a slight beveled edge and a slight shadow to the photo. Now you need to add a 3-D rotation to the picture.

3. In the Picture Styles group, click the **Picture Effects** button, and then point to **3-D Rotation**. A gallery of 3-D rotation options opens.

4. Under Perspective, click the **Perspective Left** option. The picture rotates slightly to the left. See Figure 2-9. You need to apply the same formatting to the photo on Slide 7. You can repeat the same formatting steps or you can copy the formatting.

### Figure 2-9    Picture with a style and 3-D effect applied

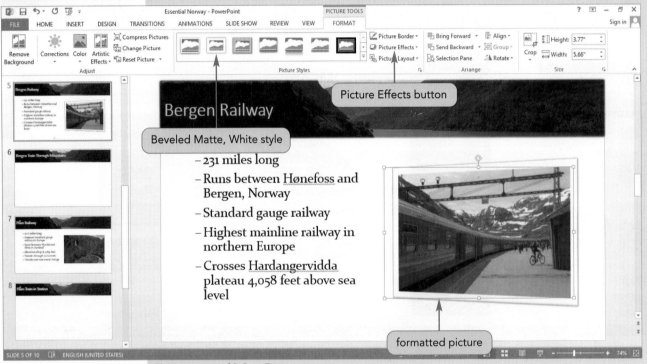

Photos courtesy of S. Scott Zimmerman

5. With the photo on Slide 5 still selected, click the **HOME** tab.

6. In the Clipboard group, click the **Format Painter** button, and then move the pointer to the Slide pane. The pointer changes to ⬓🖌.

7. In the Slides tab, click the **Slide 7** thumbnail, and then in the Slide pane, click the photo next to the bulleted list. The style and 3-D rotation formatting is copied from the photo on Slide 5 and applied to the photo on Slide 7.

8. Save your changes.

# Rotating and Flipping Objects

You can rotate and flip any object on a slide. To flip an object, you use the Flip commands on the Rotate button menu in the Arrange group on the DRAWING TOOLS FORMAT tab. To rotate an object, you can use the Rotate commands on the Rotate button menu to rotate objects in 90-degree increments. You can also drag the Rotate handle that appears above the top-middle sizing handle when the object is selected to rotate it to any position that you want, using the center of the object as a pivot point.

The Norway arrow would look better if it were pointing to the west coast of the country on the map. To correctly position the Norway arrow, you first need to flip it.

## To flip the arrow shape on Slide 3:

1. Display **Slide 3** ("Where We Are") in the Slide pane, and then click the **Norway** arrow.

**TIP**

You can also click the Arrange button in the Drawing group on the HOME tab to access the Rotate and Flip commands.

2. Position the pointer on the Rotate handle ⟳ so that the pointer changes to ↻, and then drag the Rotate handle ⟳ until the Norway arrow is pointing to the right. The arrow is pointing in the correct direction, but the text is upside-down.

3. Undo the rotation, and then click the **DRAWING TOOLS FORMAT** tab.

4. In the Arrange group, click the **Rotate** button. The Rotate menu opens. See Figure 2-10.

| Figure 2-10 | Rotate button menu |
| --- | --- |

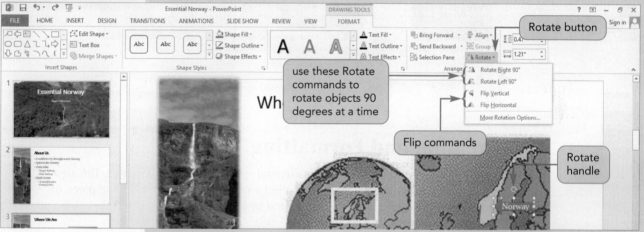

Image used with permission of Microsoft Corporation; Photos courtesy of S. Scott Zimmerman

5. Click **Flip Horizontal**. The arrow flips horizontally and is now pointing right. Unlike when you rotated the arrow so that it pointed right, the text is still right-side up.

Now you need to rotate and reposition the Norway arrow so that it is pointing to the west coast of Norway on the map.

**To rotate the arrow shape and reposition it:**

1. Position the pointer on the Rotate handle ⟳ so that the pointer changes to ↻.

2. Drag the Rotate handle ⟳ to the right to rotate the arrow so that it points down and to the right at approximately a 45-degree angle.

3. Drag the Norway arrow so it is pointing down to approximately the center of Norway's west coast.

4. Click a blank area of the slide to deselect the shape, compare your screen to Figure 2-11, and then make any adjustments needed to match the figure.

| Figure 2-11 | Arrow flipped, rotated, and repositioned on Slide 3 |

Image used with permission of Microsoft Corporation; Photos courtesy of S. Scott Zimmerman

5. Save your changes.

# Creating and Formatting Tables

A **table** is information arranged in horizontal rows and vertical columns. The area where a row and column intersect is called a **cell**. Each cell contains one piece of information. A table's structure is indicated by borders, which are lines that outline the rows and columns.

## Creating and Adding Data to a Table

Inger wants you to add a table to Slide 4 to list a typical tour itinerary. This table will have three columns—one to describe the activity, one to list the time that the activity starts, and one to list notes.

REFERENCE

*Inserting a Table*

- In a content placeholder, click the Insert Table button; or, click the INSERT tab on the ribbon, click the Table button in the Tables group, and then click Insert Table.
- Specify the numbers of columns and rows.
- Click the OK button.

*or*

- On the ribbon, click the INSERT tab, and then in the Tables group, click the Table button to open a grid.
- Click a box in the grid to create a table of that size.

Inger hasn't decided how much data to include in the table, so she asks you to start by creating a table with four rows.

### To add a table to Slide 4:

1. Display **Slide 4** ("Essential Norway Sample Itinerary") in the Slide pane.

2. Click the **INSERT** tab, and then in the Tables group, click the **Table** button. A menu opens with a grid of squares above three commands.

3. Point to the squares on the grid, and without clicking the mouse button, move the pointer down and to the right. As you move the pointer, the label above the grid indicates how large the table will be, and a preview of the table appears on the slide. See Figure 2-12.

| Figure 2-12 | Inserting a 3x4 table on Slide 3 |
| --- | --- |

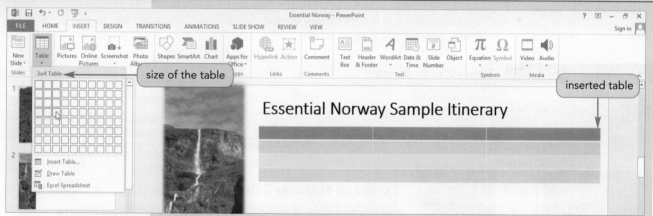

Photos courtesy of S. Scott Zimmerman

4. When the label above the grid indicates 3x4 Table, click to insert a table with three columns and four rows. A selection border appears around the table, and the insertion point is in the first cell in the first row.

Now you're ready to fill the blank cells with the information about the tour. To enter data in a table, you click in the cells in which you want to enter data, and then start typing. You can also use the Tab and arrow keys to move from one cell to another.

### To add data to the table:

1. In the first cell in the first row, type **Activity**. The text you typed appears in the first cell.

2. Press the **Tab** key. The insertion point moves to the second cell in the first row.

3. Type **Time**, press the **Tab** key, type **Notes**, and then press the **Tab** key. The insertion point is in the first cell in the second row.

4. In the first cell in the second row, type **Bergen train from Honefoss**, press the **Tab** key, and then type **8:13 a.m.**

5. Click in the first cell in the third row, type **Arrive Myrdal for lunch, shopping,** press the **Tab** key, and then type **11:41 a.m.**

6. Click in the first cell in the last row, type **Flam train from Myrdal**, press the **Tab** key, and then type **1:11 p.m.**

## Inserting and Deleting Rows and Columns

You can modify the table by adding or deleting rows and columns. You need to add more rows to the table for additional itinerary items. Inger also wants to make the table a little more interesting by adding a new first column in which you will insert pictures related to that part of the itinerary.

### To insert rows in the table:

1. Make sure the insertion point is in the last row in the table.

2. Click the **TABLE TOOLS LAYOUT** tab, and then in the Rows & Columns group, click the **Insert Below** button. A new row is inserted below the current row. See Figure 2-13.

| Figure 2-13 | Table with row inserted |
| --- | --- |

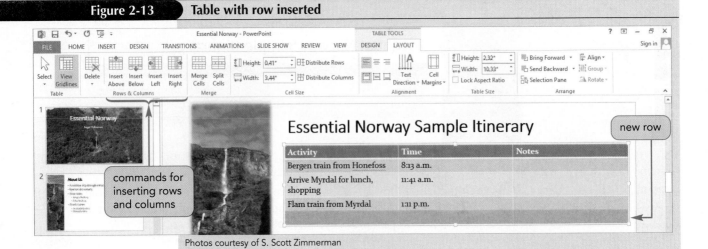

Photos courtesy of S. Scott Zimmerman

3. Click in the first cell in the new last row, type **Arrive Flam**, and then press the **Tab** key.

4. Type **2:05 p.m.**, and then press the **Tab** key. The insertion point is in the last cell in the last row.

5. Press the **Tab** key. A new row is created and the insertion point is in the first cell in the new row.

6. Type **Check in at hotel**, press the **Tab** key, and then type **4:30 p.m.** You need to insert a row above the last row.

7. In the Rows & Columns group, click the **Insert Above** button. A new row is inserted above the current row.

8. Click in the first cell in the new row, type **Fjord cruises from Flam**, press the **Tab** key, and then type **2:20 p.m.**

Inger decided she doesn't want to add notes to the table, so you'll delete the last column. She also decides that the information in the last row in the table about checking into the hotel isn't needed, so you'll delete that row.

### To delete a column and a row in the table:

1. Click in any cell in the last column. This is the column you will delete.

2. On the TABLE TOOLS LAYOUT tab, in the Rows & Columns group, click the **Delete** button. The Delete button menu opens.

3. Click **Delete Columns**. The current column is deleted, and the entire table is selected.

4. Click in any cell in the last row. This is the row you want to delete.

5. In the Rows & Columns group, click the **Delete** button, and then click **Delete Rows.**

6. Click a blank area of the slide to deselect the table. See Figure 2-14.

**Figure 2-14**    **Table after adding and deleting rows and deleting the third column**

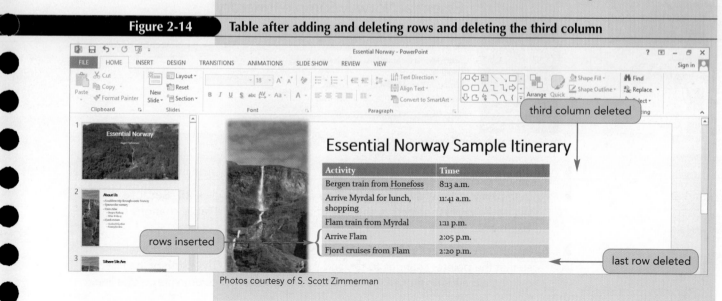

Photos courtesy of S. Scott Zimmerman

# Formatting a Table

After you insert data into a table, you need to think about how the table looks and whether the table will be readable for the audience. As with any text, you can change the font, size, or color, and as with shapes and pictures, you can apply a style to a table. You can also change how the text fits in the table cells by changing the height of rows and the width of columns. You can also customize the formatting of the table by changing the border and fill of table cells.

    You need to make the table text larger so that an audience will be able to read it. You will also increase the width of the Activity column so that it is as wide as the widest entry.

**To change the font size and adjust the column size in the table:**

▶   **1.** Click any cell in the table. You want to change the size of all the text in the table, so you will select the entire table. Notice that a selection border appears around the table. This border appears any time the table is active.

▶   **2.** Click the **TABLE TOOLS LAYOUT** tab, and then in the Table group, click the **Select** button. The Select button menu appears with options to select the entire table, the current column, or the current row.

▶   **3.** Click **Select Table**. The entire table is selected. Because the selection border appears any time the table is active, the only visual cues you have that it is now selected are that the insertion point is no longer blinking in the cell that you clicked in Step 1 and the Select button is gray and unavailable. See Figure 2-15.

| Figure 2-15 | Table selected on Slide 4 |
| --- | --- |

Photos courtesy of S. Scott Zimmerman

▶   **4.** On the ribbon, click the **HOME** tab.

▶   **5.** In the Font group, click the **Font Size** arrow, and then click **28**. Because the entire table is selected, the size of all the text in the table changes to 28 points.

▶   **6.** Position the pointer on the column line between the two columns in the table so that the pointer changes to ┼╟┼, and then double-click. The width of the first column expands so that all the text in each cell in the first column fits on one line.

Inger wants you to change the format of the table so it looks more attractive and so that its colors complement the photo in the slide's layout. You will do this by applying a style to the table. When you apply a style to a table, you can specify whether the header and total rows and the first and last columns are formatted differently from the other rows and columns in the table. You can also specify whether to use banded rows or columns; that is, whether to fill alternating rows or columns with different shading.

### To apply a style to the table:

▶ **1.** Click the **TABLE TOOLS DESIGN** tab on the ribbon, if necessary. In the Table Styles group, the second style, Medium Style 2 – Accent 1, is selected. In the Table Style Options group, the Header Row and Banded Rows check boxes are selected, which means that the header row will be formatted differently than the rest of the rows and that every other row will be filled with shading. See Figure 2-16.

| Figure 2-16 | Default formatting applied to the table |
| --- | --- |

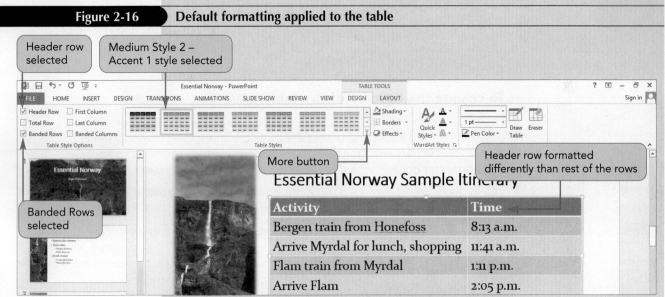

Photos courtesy of S. Scott Zimmerman

▶ **2.** In the Table Styles group, click the **More** button. The Table Styles gallery opens.

▶ **3.** Click the **Medium Style 3 – Accent 3** style, and then click a blank area of the slide to deselect the table.

The color in the first row is a little too bright. You can change the fill of table cells in the same manner that you change the fill of shapes.

## To change the fill of cells in the table:

▶ **1.** In the table, click in the first row, and then click the **LAYOUT** tab.

▶ **2.** In the Table group, click the **Select** button, and then click **Select Row**. The first row in the table is selected.

▶ **3.** Click the **TABLE TOOLS DESIGN** tab.

▶ **4.** In the Table Styles group, click the **Shading button arrow**. The Shading menu is similar to the Shape Fill menu you worked with earlier.

▶ **5.** Click **Olive Green, Accent 3, Darker 50%**. The menu closes and the cells in the first row are shaded with olive green.

In addition, the table might be easier to read if the horizontal borders between the rows were visible. You can add these by using the Borders button arrow and the buttons in the Draw Borders group on the TABLE TOOLS DESIGN tab. When you use the Borders button arrow, you can apply borders to all the selected cells at once. The borders will be the style, weight, and color specified by the Pen Style, Pen Weight, and Pen Color buttons in the Draw Borders group.

## To change the borders of the table:

▶ **1.** Position the pointer to the left of the first cell in the second row so that it changes to ➡, press and hold the mouse button, drag down to the left of the last row, and then release the mouse button. You want to apply a horizontal border between the rows below the header row.

▶ **2.** In the Table Styles group, click the **Borders button arrow**. A menu opens listing borders that you can apply to the selected cells.

▶ **3.** Click **Inside Horizontal Border**. A border appears between each row below the header row. As indicated in the Draw Table group, the borders are solid line borders, one point wide, and black. See Figure 2-17. You can change any of these attributes.

| Figure 2-17 | Table with inside horizontal borders added |
| --- | --- |

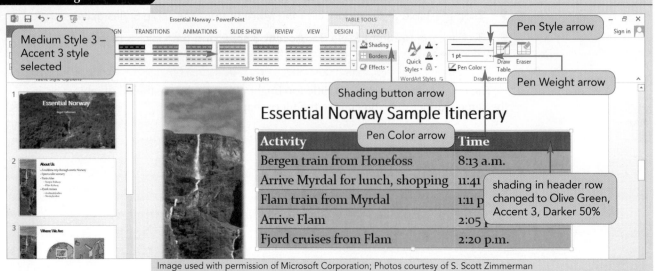

Image used with permission of Microsoft Corporation; Photos courtesy of S. Scott Zimmerman

▶ **4.** In the Draw Borders group, click the **Pen Weight** arrow, and then click **½ pt**. The pointer changes to ⟋. You could drag this pointer along each border to draw them individually. Instead, you will use the Borders button again to apply the new settings to all of the selected cells. Because Inside Horizontal Borders was the last option chosen on the Borders button menu, it is the default option for the Borders button.

▶ **5.** In the Table Styles group, click the **Borders** button. The weight of the borders between each selected row is changed to one-half point.

Inger decides that she wants you to add a picture to each row that is related to that part of the itinerary. Recall that one of the things you can fill a shape with is a picture. You can do the same with cells. First, you'll need to insert a new first column.

### To insert a new column and fill the cells with pictures:

▶ **1.** Click in any cell in the first column, and then click the **LAYOUT** tab.

▶ **2.** In the Rows & Columns group, click the **Insert Left** button. A new column is inserted to the left of the current column.

▶ **3.** Position the pointer on the column line between the new first column and the second column, and then drag left until the column line is approximately below the middle of the "n" in "Essential" in the slide title. The text in each cell in the second column again fits on one line. In the Cell Size group, the measurement in the Width box should be approximately 1.2". See Figure 2-18.

**Figure 2-18**    New column added to table

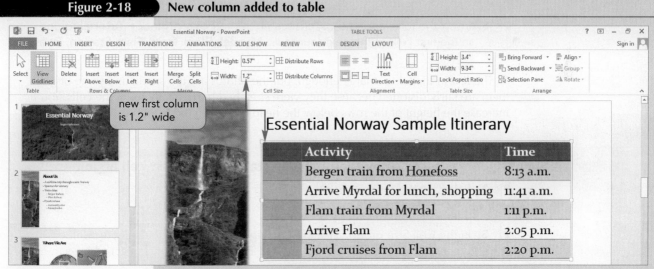

Image used with permission of Microsoft Corporation; Photos courtesy of S. Scott Zimmerman

▶ **4.** Click in the first cell in the second row, and then click the **TABLE TOOLS DESIGN** tab.

▶ **5.** In the Table Styles group, click the **Shading button arrow**, and then click **Picture**. The Insert Pictures window opens. See Figure 2-19.

**Figure 2-19**    **Insert Pictures window with option for locating a file on your computer**

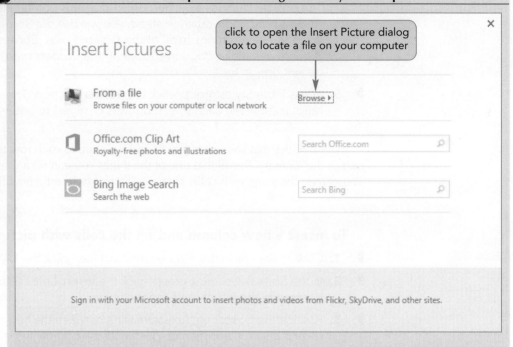

6. Next to From a file, click the **Browse** button. The Insert Picture dialog box opens.

7. Navigate to the **PowerPoint2 ▸ Tutorial** folder, click **Bergen Train**, and then click the **Insert** button. The photo fills the cell.

8. Insert the following photos, all located in the **PowerPoint2 ▸ Tutorial** folder, in the first cells in the next four rows: **Myrdal**, **Flam Train**, **Flam Station**, **Boat**.

The text in the table is large enough, but the photos are too small, and some of them are fairly distorted because they were stretched horizontally to fill the cells. You'll increase the height of the rows below the heading row in the table.

**To increase the row height in the table and adjust cell alignment:**

1. Select all the rows except the heading row.

2. On the ribbon, click the **LAYOUT** tab.

3. In the Cell Size group, click in the **Height** box, delete the selected value, type **1**, and then press the **Enter** key. The height of each selected rows changes to one inch.

Finally, the text in all cells in the table is horizontally left-aligned and vertically aligned at the top of the cells. The headings would look better centered horizontally in the cells, and the text in the other rows would look better vertically aligned in the center of the cells.

You also need to reposition the table on the slide to better fill the space. You move a table the same way you move any other object. The pointer must be positioned on the table border in order to change it to ⊹̇⟵.

## To adjust the alignment of text in cells and reposition the table:

1. Make sure all the rows except the heading row are still selected.

2. In the Alignment group, click the **Center Vertically** button ▤. The text in the selected rows is now centered vertically in the cells.

3. In the first row, drag across the second and third cells to select them.

4. In the Alignment group, click the **Center** button ▤. The headings are now centered horizontally in the cells. Now you will adjust the table's placement on the slide.

5. Position the pointer on the table border so that it changes to ⊹̇⟵, and then drag the table so that its left edge is approximately aligned with the left of the letter "E" in "Essential" in the slide title and vertically centered in the white space below the title. Compare your screen to Figure 2-20.

| Figure 2-20 | Final formatted table |
| --- | --- |

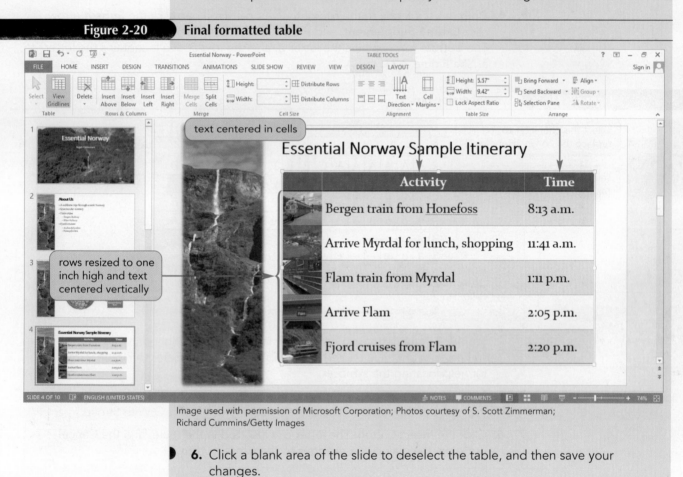

Image used with permission of Microsoft Corporation; Photos courtesy of S. Scott Zimmerman; Richard Cummins/Getty Images

6. Click a blank area of the slide to deselect the table, and then save your changes.

# Inserting Symbols and Characters

The Norwegian alphabet contains three letters that are not in the English alphabet: æ (pronounced like the "a" in "cat"), ø (pronounced like the "u" in "hurt"), and å (pronounced like the "o" in "more"). The city names Flåm and Hønefoss use two of these letters. To insert these letters using a keyboard with only English letters, you can use the Symbol button in the Symbols group on the INSERT tab.

You need to correct the spelling of Flåm and Hønefoss in the table you inserted on Slide 4.

## To insert the special characters:

1. Display **Slide 4** ("Essential Norway Sample Itinerary") in the Slide pane, if necessary.

2. In the row below the table header, click after the "H" in "Honefoss," and then press the **Delete** key to delete the "o."

3. Click the **INSERT** tab, and then in the Symbols group, click the **Symbol** button. The Symbol dialog box opens.

4. Drag the scroll box to the top of the vertical scroll bar, click the **Subset** arrow, click **Latin-1 Supplement**, and then click the **down scroll arrow** four times. The bottom row contains the letter ø, and the row above it contains the letter å. See Figure 2-21.

**Figure 2-21** **Symbol dialog box**

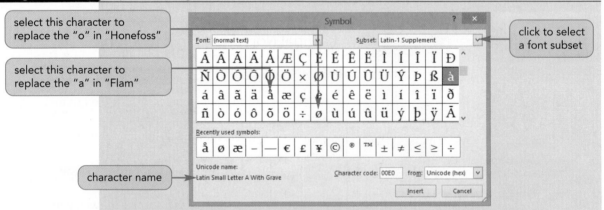

select this character to replace the "o" in "Honefoss"

select this character to replace the "a" in "Flam"

click to select a font subset

character name

Trouble? If the letters do not appear in the rows mentioned in Step 4, someone might have resized the Symbol dialog box. Refer to Figure 2-21 for help locating the symbols.

5. In the bottom row, click **ø**. In the bottom-left corner of the Symbol dialog box, the name of the selected character is "Latin Small Letter O With Stroke."

6. Click the **Insert** button. The letter ø is inserted in the table, and the Cancel button in the dialog box changes to the Close button.

7. Click the **Close** button. The cell below the header "Activity" now contains the text "Bergen train from Hønefoss."

8. In the third row below the header row, click after the "a" in "Flam," and then press the **Backspace** key to delete the "a."

9. In the Symbols group, click the **Symbol** button to open the Symbols dialog box, scroll up one row, and then click **å**, which has the name "Latin Small Letter A With Ring Above."

10. Click the **Insert** button, and then click the **Close** button. The cell now contains the text "Flåm train from Myrdal."

11. Double-click **Flåm**, click the **HOME** tab, and then, in the Clipboard group, click the **Copy** button.

12. In the next row in the table, double-click **Flam**, and then in the Clipboard group, click the **Paste** button.

13. In the last row in the table, replace **Flam** with the text **Flåm** on the Clipboard.

14. Save your changes.

# Changing the Proofing Language

The spell checker can be very helpful, but when it flags words that are spelled correctly, the wavy red lines can be distracting as you work with the presentation. In the Essential Norway presentation, some of the Norwegian city and fjord names have been flagged as misspelled. This is because the proofing language for the presentation is set to English.

You can change the proofing language for the entire presentation or only for specific words to any language supported by Microsoft Office. If the proofing language you specify is not installed on your computer, PowerPoint will stop flagging the words in that language as misspelled, but it will not be able to determine if the foreign language words are spelled correctly. However, if you open the file on a computer that has the other language installed, you can use the spell checker to check the words in that language.

You will set the proofing language of the Norwegian words to Norwegian to help Inger as she reviews the final presentation.

### To set the proofing language for specific words to Norwegian:

1. Display **Slide 4** ("Essential Norway Sample Itinerary") in the Slide pane, if necessary.

2. In the second row of the table, double-click **Hønefoss**. The word is selected.

3. On the status bar, click **ENGLISH (UNITED STATES)**. The Language dialog box opens. See Figure 2-22. The default is for the selected text to be marked as English. The spell check icon next to English indicates that this language is installed.

**Figure 2-22**    Language dialog box

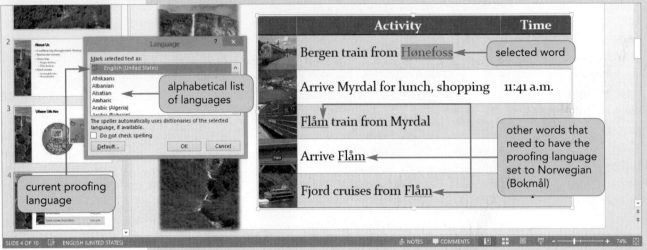

Image used with permission of Microsoft Corporation; Photos courtesy of S. Scott Zimmerman;
Richard Cummins/Getty Images

> **Trouble?** If ENGLISH (UNITED STATES) does not appear on the status bar,
> click the REVIEW tab, click the Language button in the Language group, and
> then click Set Proofing Language.

**4.** Scroll down the alphabetical list until you see **Norwegian (Bokmål)**. There
is no spell check icon next to this language because Microsoft Office sold
in English-speaking countries comes only with English, French, and Spanish
languages installed.

> **Trouble?** If there is a spell check icon next to Norwegian (Bokmål), then that
> language is installed on your computer.

**5.** Click **Norwegian (Bokmål)**, and then click the **OK** button. The wavy red line
under the selected word disappears, and next to the Spelling icon on the
status bar, the language is now Norwegian (Bokmål).

**6.** In the fourth row in the table, double-click **Flåm**. Because specifying the
Norwegian language as the proofing language was the most recent action, a
quicker way to specify it for additional words you select is to use the Repeat
button to repeat that action.

**7.** On the Quick Access Toolbar, click the **Repeat** button ⟳. As indicated on
the status bar, the language for the selected word is changed to Norwegian.

**8.** In the fifth and sixth rows of the table, select **Flåm**, and then set the proofing
language for both instances to **Norwegian (Bokmål)**.

**9.** Save your changes.

You have modified a presentation by applying a theme used in another presentation, inserting and formatting online pictures and shapes, and inserting a table and characters that are not on your keyboard. You also changed the proofing language for Norwegian words. In the next session, you will continue modifying the presentation by applying and modifying transitions and animations, adding and modifying videos, and adding footer and header information.

REVIEW

## Session 2.1 Quick Check

1. What are keywords?
2. Which contextual tab appears on the ribbon when a shape is selected?
3. What is a style?
4. What is a shape's fill?
5. In a table, what is the intersection of a row and column called?
6. How do you know if an entire table is selected and not just active?
7. How do you insert characters that are not on your keyboard?

# Session 2.2 Visual Overview:

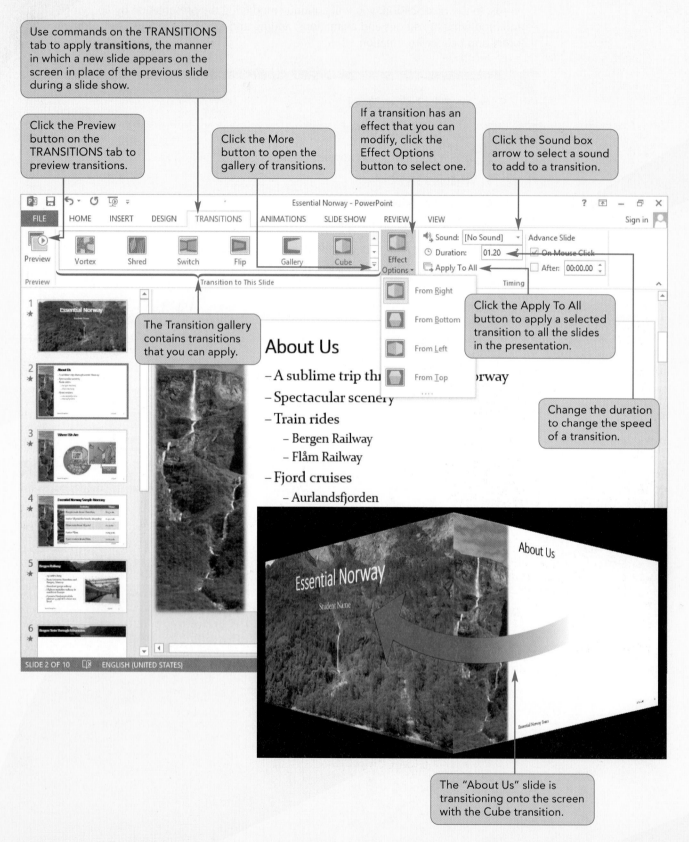

Use commands on the TRANSITIONS tab to apply **transitions**, the manner in which a new slide appears on the screen in place of the previous slide during a slide show.

Click the Preview button on the TRANSITIONS tab to preview transitions.

Click the More button to open the gallery of transitions.

If a transition has an effect that you can modify, click the Effect Options button to select one.

Click the Sound box arrow to select a sound to add to a transition.

The Transition gallery contains transitions that you can apply.

Click the Apply To All button to apply a selected transition to all the slides in the presentation.

Change the duration to change the speed of a transition.

The "About Us" slide is transitioning onto the screen with the Cube transition.

# Using Transitions and Animations

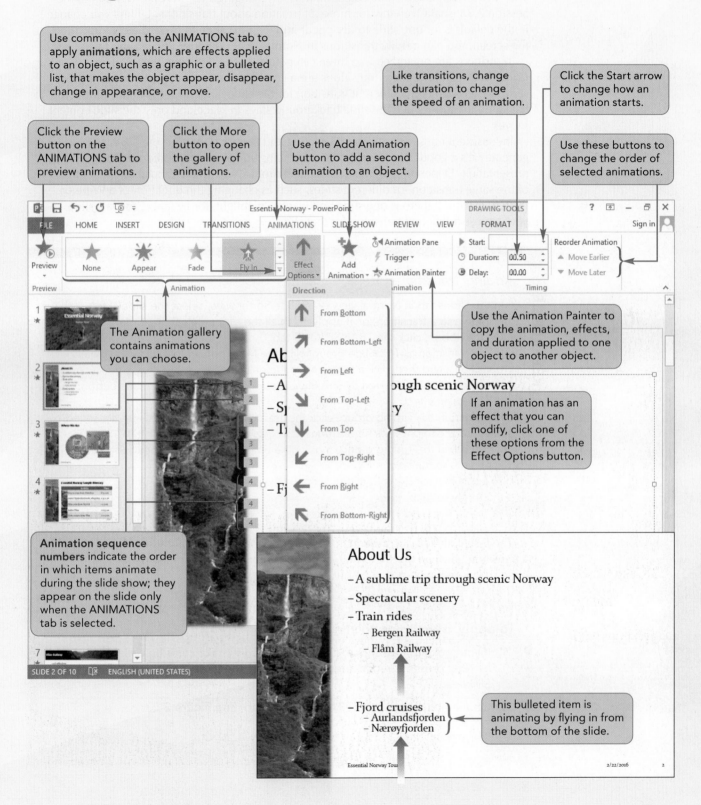

Use commands on the ANIMATIONS tab to apply **animations**, which are effects applied to an object, such as a graphic or a bulleted list, that makes the object appear, disappear, change in appearance, or move.

Like transitions, change the duration to change the speed of an animation.

Click the Start arrow to change how an animation starts.

Click the Preview button on the ANIMATIONS tab to preview animations.

Click the More button to open the gallery of animations.

Use the Add Animation button to add a second animation to an object.

Use these buttons to change the order of selected animations.

The Animation gallery contains animations you can choose.

Use the Animation Painter to copy the animation, effects, and duration applied to one object to another object.

If an animation has an effect that you can modify, click one of these options from the Effect Options button.

**Animation sequence numbers** indicate the order in which items animate during the slide show; they appear on the slide only when the ANIMATIONS tab is selected.

## About Us

– A sublime trip through scenic Norway
– Spectacular scenery
– Train rides
  – Bergen Railway
  – Flåm Railway

– Fjord cruises
  – Aurlandsfjorden
  – Nærøyfjorden

This bulleted item is animating by flying in from the bottom of the slide.

Essential Norway Tour                2/22/2016        2

# Applying Transitions

The TRANSITIONS tab contains commands for changing slide transitions. Refer to the Session 2.2 Visual Overview for more information about transitions. Unless you change it, the default is for one slide to disappear and the next slide to immediately appear on the screen. You can modify transitions in Normal or Slide Sorter view.

Transitions are organized into three categories: Subtle, Exciting, and Dynamic Content. Dynamic Content transitions are a combination of the Fade transition for the slide background and a different transition for the slide content. If slides have the same background, it looks like the slide background stays in place and only the slide content moves.

Inconsistent transitions can be distracting and detract from your message, so generally it's a good idea to apply the same transition to all of the slides in the presentation. Depending on the audience and topic, you might choose different effects of the same transition for different slides, such as changing the direction of a Wipe or Push transition. If there is one slide you want to highlight, for instance, the last slide, you can use a different transition for that slide.

**REFERENCE**

### Adding Transitions

- In the Slides tab in Normal view or in Slide Sorter view, select the slide(s) to which you want to add a transition, or, if applying to all the slides, select any slide.
- On the ribbon, click the TRANSITIONS tab.
- In the Transition to This Slide group, click the More button to display the gallery of transitions, and then click a transition in the gallery.
- If desired, in the Transition to This Slide group, click the Effect Options button, and then click an effect.
- If desired, in the Timing group, click the Transition Sound arrow to insert a sound effect to accompany each transition.
- If desired, in the Timing group, modify the time in the Duration box to modify the speed of the transition.
- To apply the transition to all the slides in the presentation, in the Timing group, click the Apply to All button.

The Essential Norway presentation contains photos of beautiful vistas. Inger wants a transition between the slides that gives the audience a feel for moving through the open spaces in the photos.

### To apply transitions to the slides:

1. If you took a break after the previous session, make sure the Essential Norway presentation is open, and then display **Slide 2** ("About Us") in the Slide pane.

2. On the ribbon, click the **TRANSITIONS** tab. See Figure 2-23.

| Figure 2-23 | Commands on the TRANSITIONS tab |
|---|---|

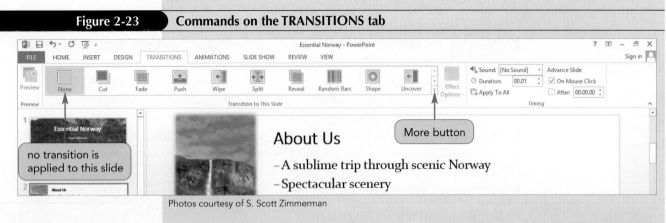

Photos courtesy of S. Scott Zimmerman

▶ **3.** In the Transition to This Slide group, click **Reveal**. The transition previews in the Slide pane as Slide 1 (the title slide) appears, fades away, and then Slide 2 fades in. The Reveal transition is now highlighted in orange in the gallery. In the Slides tab, a star appears next to the Slide 2 thumbnail. If you missed the preview, you can see it again.

▶ **4.** In the Preview group, click the **Preview** button. The transition previews in the Slide pane again.

▶ **5.** In the Transition to This Slide group, click the **More** button. The gallery opens listing all the transitions. See Figure 2-24.

| Figure 2-24 | Transitions gallery |
|---|---|

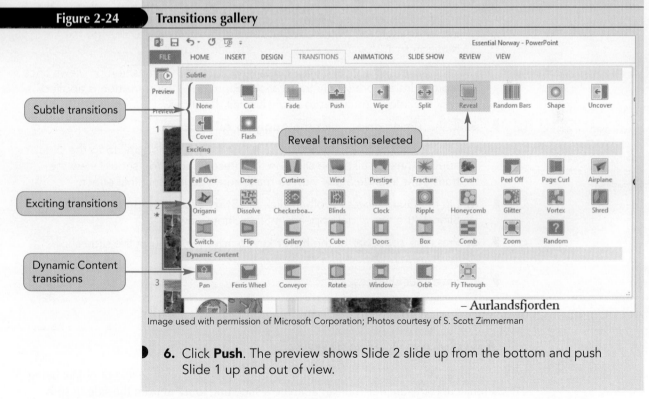

Image used with permission of Microsoft Corporation; Photos courtesy of S. Scott Zimmerman

▶ **6.** Click **Push**. The preview shows Slide 2 slide up from the bottom and push Slide 1 up and out of view.

Most transitions have effects that you can modify. For example, the Peel Off transition can peel from the bottom left or the bottom right corner, and the Wipe transition can wipe from any direction. You'll modify the transition applied to Slide 2.

**To modify the transition effect for Slide 2:**

▶ **1.** In the Transition to This Slide group, click the **Effect Options** button. The effects that you can modify for the Push transition are listed on the menu.

▶ **2.** Click **From Right**. The Push transition previews again, but this time Slide 2 slides from the right to push Slide 1 left. The available effects change depending on the transition selected.

▶ **3.** In the Transition to This Slide group, click **Shape**. The transition previews with Slide 2 appearing in the center of Slide 1 inside a circle that grows to fill the slide.

▶ **4.** Click the **Effect Options** button. The effects that you can modify for the Shape transition are listed.

▶ **5.** Click **Out**. The preview of the transition with this effect displays Slide 2 in the center of Slide 1 inside a rectangle that grows to fill the slide.

Finally, you can also change the duration of a transition. The duration is how long it takes the transition to finish; in other words, the speed of the transition. To make the transition faster, decrease the duration; to slow the transition down, increase the duration. Inger likes the Shape transition, but she thinks it is a little fast, so you will increase the duration. Then you can apply the modified transition to all the slides.

**To change the duration of the transition and apply it to all the slides:**

▶ **1.** In the Timing group, click the **Duration up** arrow twice to change the duration to 1.5".

▶ **2.** In the Preview group, click the **Preview** button. The transition previews once more, a little more slowly than before. Right now, the transition is applied only to Slide 2. You want to apply it to all the slides.

▶ **3.** In the Timing group, click the **Apply To All** button.

In the Slides tab, the star indicating that a transition is applied to the slide appears next to all of the slides in the presentation. You should view the transitions in Slide Show view to make sure you like the final effect.

▶ **4.** On the Quick Access Toolbar, click the **Start From Beginning** 🔲 button. Slide 1 (the title slide) appears in Slide Show view.

▶ **5.** Press the **spacebar** or the **Enter** key to advance through the slide show. The transitions look fine.

▶ **6.** Save your changes.

Make sure you click the Apply To All button or the transition is applied only to the currently selected slide or slides.

# Applying Animations

Animations add interest to a slide show and draw attention to the text or object being animated. For example, you can animate a slide title to fly in from the side or spin around like a pinwheel to draw the audience's attention to that title. Refer to the Session 2.2 Visual Overview for more information about animations.

Animation effects are grouped into four types:

• **Entrance**—Text and objects are not shown on the slide until the animation occurs; one of the most commonly used animation types.

- **Emphasis**—Text and objects on the slide change in appearance or move.
- **Exit**—Text and objects leave the screen before the slide show advances to the next slide.
- **Motion Paths**—Text and objects follow a path on a slide.

## Animating Objects

You can animate any object on a slide, including pictures, shapes, and text boxes. To animate an object you click it, and then select an animation in the Animation group on the ANIMATIONS tab.

**REFERENCE**

### Applying Animations

- In the Slide pane in Normal view, select the object you want to animate.
- On the ribbon, click the ANIMATIONS tab.
- In the Animation group, click the More button to display the gallery of animations, and then click an animation in the gallery.
- If desired, in the Animation group, click the Effect Options button, and then click a direction effect; if the object is a text box, click a sequence effect.
- If desired, in the Timing group, modify the time in the Duration box to modify the speed of the animation.
- If desired, in the Timing group, click the Start arrow, and then click a different start timing.

Slide 9 contains two pictures of fjords, one of Aurlandsfjord and one of Nærøyfjord. Inger wants you to add an animation to the title text on this slide.

### To animate the title on Slide 9:

1. Display **Slide 9** ("Views of the Fjords") in the Slide pane, and then click the **ANIMATIONS** tab on the ribbon. The animations in the Animation group are grayed out, indicating they are not available. This is because nothing is selected on the slide.

2. Click the **Views of the Fjords** title text. The animations in the Animation group darken to indicate that they are now available. See Figure 2-25. All of the animations currently visible in the Animation group are entrance animations.

**Figure 2-25** ▶ Animations available on the ANIMATIONS tab after an object is selected

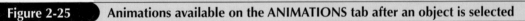

Photos courtesy of S. Scott Zimmerman

3. In the Animation group, click **Fly In**. This entrance animation previews in the Slide pane—the title text disappears and then flies in from the bottom. In the Timing group, the Start box displays On Click, which indicates that this animation will occur when you advance the slide show by clicking the mouse or pressing the spacebar or the Enter key.

Notice the animation sequence number 1 in the box to the left of the title text box, which indicates that this is the first animation that will occur on the slide. You can preview the animation again if you missed it.

4. In the Preview group, click the **Preview** button. The animation previews again.

5. In the Animation group, click the **More** button. The Animation gallery opens. The animation commands are listed by category, and each category appears in a different color. At the bottom are four commands, each of which opens a dialog box listing all the effects in that category. See Figure 2-26. You will try an emphasis animation.

| **Figure 2-26** | **Animations gallery** |
| --- | --- |

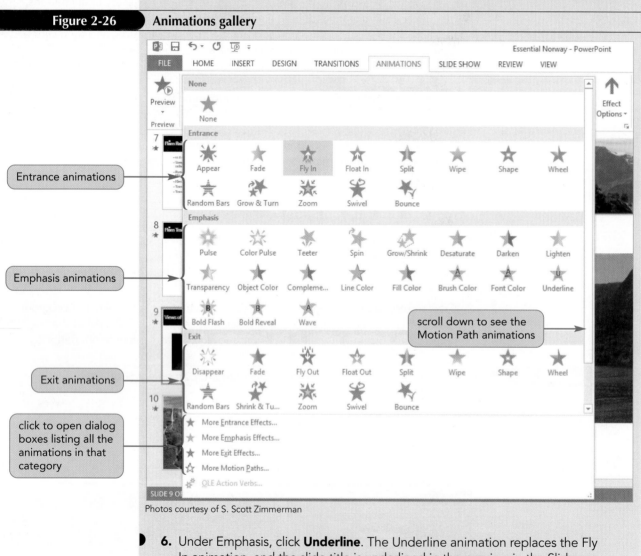

Photos courtesy of S. Scott Zimmerman

6. Under Emphasis, click **Underline**. The Underline animation replaces the Fly In animation, and the slide title is underlined in the preview in the Slide pane. The text did not disappear before the animation started because an emphasis animation causes something to happen to an object already on the slide.

The Underline animation you applied to the slide title is an example of an emphasis animation that is available only to text. You cannot apply that animation to objects such as pictures.

Slide 9 contains photos showing scenic views that customers will see if they book a tour. To focus the audience's attention on one photo at time, you will apply an entrance animation to the photos so that they appear one at a time during the slide show.

**To apply entrance animations to the photos on Slide 9:**

1. With **Slide 9** ("Views of the Fjords") in the Slide pane, click the picture on the right.

2. In the Animation group, click the **More** button. Notice that in the Emphasis section, six of the animations, including the Underline animation you just applied to the slide title, are gray, which means they are not available for this object. These six animations are available only for text.

3. In the Entrance section, click **Split**. The picture fades in starting from the left and right edges and fading into the center. In the Timing group, On Click appears in the Start box, indicating that this animation will occur when you advance the slide show. The animation sequence number to the left of the selected picture is 2, which indicates that this is the second animation that will occur on the slide when you advance the slide show.

Like transitions, animations can be modified by changing the effect or the duration (the speed). You need to change the direction from which this animation appears, and you want to slow it down.

**To change the effect and duration of the animation applied to the photo:**

1. In the Animation group, click the **Effect Options** button. See Figure 2-27. This menu contains Direction options.

**Figure 2-27**    Effect options for the Fly In entrance animation

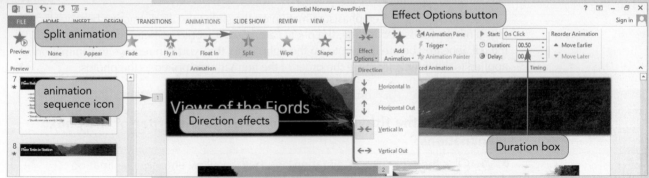

Photos courtesy of S. Scott Zimmerman

2. Click **Vertical Out**. The preview fades the picture in starting from the center and building out to the left and right edges.

3. In the Timing group, click the **Duration up** arrow once. The duration changes from .50 seconds to .75 seconds.

After you have applied and customized the animation for one object, you can use the Animation Painter to copy that animation to other objects. You will copy the Split entrance animation with the Vertical Out effect and a duration of .75 seconds to the other photo on Slide 9.

### To use the Animation Painter to copy the animation on Slide 9:

▶ **1.** Click the photo on the right to select it.

▶ **2.** In the Advanced Animation group, click the **Animation Painter** button, and then move the pointer onto the Slide pane. The pointer changes to ⬚.

▶ **3.** Click the photo on the left. The Split animation with the Vertical Out effect and a duration of .75 seconds is copied to the photo on the left.

After you apply animations, you should watch them in Slide Show, Presenter, or Reading view to see what they will look like during a slide show. Remember that On Click appeared in the Start box for each animation that you applied, which means that to see the animation during the slide show, you need to advance the slide show.

### To view the animations on Slide 9 in Slide Show view:

▶ **1.** Make sure **Slide 9** ("Views of the Fjords") is displayed in the Slide pane.

▶ **2.** On the status bar, click the **Slide Show** button 🖵. Slide 9 appears in Slide Show view. Only the photo that is part of the layout and the title appear on the slide.

▶ **3.** Press the **spacebar** to advance the slide show. The first animation, the emphasis animation that underlines the title, occurs.

▶ **4.** Press the **spacebar** again. The photo on the right fades in starting at the center of the photo and building out to the left and right edges.

▶ **5.** Click anywhere on the screen. The photo on the left fades in with the same animation as the photo on the right.

▶ **6.** Press the **Esc** key. Slide 9 appears in Normal view.

Inger doesn't like the emphasis animation on the slide title. It's distracting because the title is not the focus of this slide, the photos are. Also, it would be better if the photo on the left appeared before the photo on the right. To fix this, you can remove the animation applied to the title and change the order of the animations applied to the photos.

### To remove the title animation and change the order of the photo animations:

▶ **1.** Click the title. In the Animation group, the yellow emphasis animation Underline is selected.

**TIP**

You can also click the animation sequence icon, and then press the Delete key to remove an animation.

▶ **2.** In the Animation group, click the **More** button, and then at the top of the gallery, click **None**. The animation applied to the title is removed, the animation sequence icon no longer appears next to the title text box, and the other two animation sequence icons on the slide are renumbered 1 and 2.

Now you need to select the animation applied to the photo on the left and change it so that it occurs first. You can select the object or the animation sequence icon to modify an animation.

▶ **3.** Next to the left photo, click the animation sequence icon **2**. In the Animation group, the green Split entrance animation is selected. See Figure 2-28.

**Figure 2-28** **Animation selected to change its order**

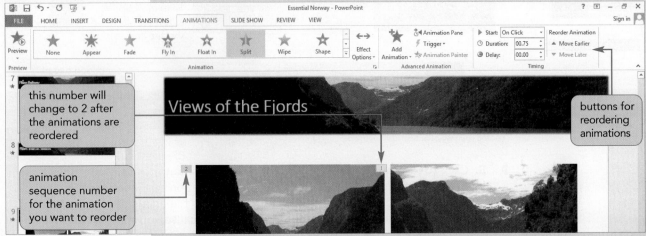

Photos courtesy of S. Scott Zimmerman

▶ **4.** In the Timing group, click the **Move Earlier** button. The animation sequence icon next to the photo on the left changes from 2 to 1, and the animation sequence icon next to the photo on the right changes from 1 to 2.

▶ **5.** In the Preview group, click the **Preview** button. The photo on the left fades in, and then the photo on the right fades in.

## Changing How an Animation Starts

Remember that when you apply an animation, the default is for the object to animate On Click, which means when you advance through the slide show. You can change this so that an animation happens automatically, either at the same time as another animation or when the slide transitions, or after another animation.

Inger wants the photo on the right to appear automatically, without the presenter needing to advance the slide show.

### To change how the animation for the photo on the right starts:

▶ **1.** With **Slide 9** ("Views of the Fjords") displayed in the Slide pane, click the photo on the right. The entrance animation Split is selected in the Animation group, and in the Timing group, On Click appears in the Start box.

▶ **2.** In the Timing group, click the **Start** arrow. The three choices for starting an animation appear. See Figure 2-29.

**Figure 2-29** Options on the Start menu for animations

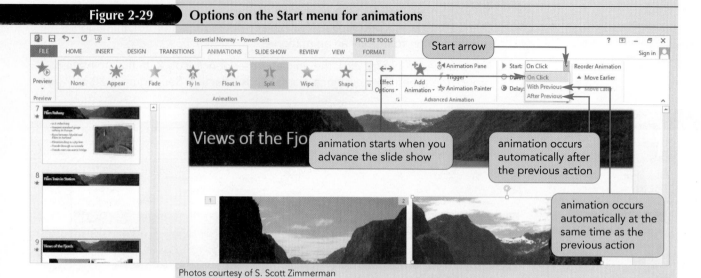

Photos courtesy of S. Scott Zimmerman

> **3.** Click **After Previous**. Now this photo will appear automatically after the photo on the left fades in. Notice that the animation sequence number next to this photo changed to 1, the same number as the animation sequence number next to the photo on the left. This is because you will not need to advance the slide show to make this animation happen.

When you preview an animation, it plays automatically on the slide in the Slide pane, even if the timing setting for the animation is On Click. To make sure the timing settings are correct, you need to watch the animation in a slide show.

**To preview and test the animations:**

> **1.** On the status bar, click the **Slide Show** button 🖵. Slide 9 appears in Slide Show view.

> **2.** Press the **spacebar**. The photo on the left fades in, and then the photo on the right fades in.

> **3.** Press the **Esc** key to end the slide show.

When you set an animation to occur automatically during the slide show, it happens immediately after the previous action. If that is too soon, you can add a pause before the animation. To do this, you increase the time in the Delay box in the Timing group.

To give the audience time to look at the first photo before the second photo appears on Slide 9, you will add a delay to the animation that is applied to the photo on the right.

**To add a delay to the After Previous animation:**

> **1.** Click the photo on the right, if necessary. In the Timing group, 00.00 appears in the Delay box.

> **2.** In the Timing group, click the **Delay up** arrow four times to change the time to one second. This means that after the photo on the left appears (the previous animation), the photo on the right will appear after a delay of one second. You'll view the slide in Slide Show view again to see the change.

3. On the status bar, click the **Slide Show** button 🖵. Slide 9 appears in Slide Show view.

4. Press the **spacebar**. The photo on the left fades in, and then after a one-second delay, the photo on the right fades in.

5. Press the **Esc** key to end the slide show.

## Animating Lists

If you animate a list, the default is for the first-level items to appear one at a time. In other words, each first-level bulleted item is set to animate On Click. This type of animation focuses your audience's attention on each item, without the distraction of items that you haven't discussed yet.

Inger wants you to add an Entrance animation to the bulleted list on the "About Us" slide. She wants each first-level bulleted item to appear on the slide one at a time so that the audience won't be able to read ahead while you are discussing each point.

### To animate the bulleted lists:

1. Display **Slide 2** ("About Us") in the Slide pane, and then click anywhere in the bulleted list to make the text box active.

2. On the ANIMATIONS tab, in the Animation group, click **Fly In**. The animation previews in the Slide pane as the bulleted items fly in from the bottom. When the "Train rides" and "Fjord cruises" items fly in, their subitems fly in with them. After the preview is finished, the numbers 1 through 4 appear next to the bulleted items. Notice that the subitems have the same animation sequence number as their first-level items. This means that the start timing for the subitems is set to With Previous or After Previous. See Figure 2-30.

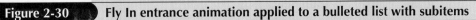

**Figure 2-30**     **Fly In entrance animation applied to a bulleted list with subitems**

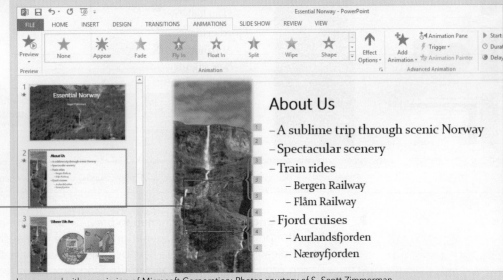

same number indicates that these items will animate at the same time

Image used with permission of Microsoft Corporation; Photos courtesy of S. Scott Zimmerman

3. Next to the Train rides bullet item, click the animation sequence icon **3** to select it. In the Timing group, On Click appears in the Start box.

▶ **4.** Next to the subitem "Bergen Railway," click the animation sequence icon **3**. In the Timing group, With Previous appears in the Start box.

If you wanted to change how the items in the list animate during the slide show, you could change the start timing of each item, or you could change the sequence effect. Sequence options appear on the Effect Options menu in addition to the Direction options when an animation is applied to a text box. The default is for the items to appear By Paragraph. This mean each first-level item animates one at a time, with its subitems if there are any, when you advance the slide show. You can change this so that the entire list animates at once as one object, or so that each first-level item animates at the same time but as separate objects.

**To examine the Sequence options for the animated list:**

▶ **1.** Click in the bulleted list, and then in the Animation group, click the **Effect Options** button. The Sequence options appear at the bottom of the menu, below the Direction options, and By Paragraph is selected. See Figure 2-31.

**Figure 2-31** **Animation effect options for a bulleted list**

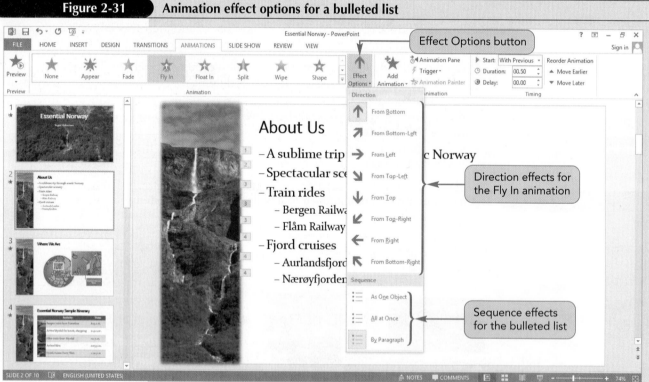

Image used with permission of Microsoft Corporation; Photos courtesy of S. Scott Zimmerman; Richard Cummins/Getty Images

▶ **2.** Click **As One Object**. The animation preview shows the entire text box fly in. After the preview, only one animation sequence icon appears next to the text box, indicating that the entire text box will animate as a single object. In the Timing group, On Click appears in the Start box.

3. In the Animation group, click the **Effect Options** button, and then under Sequence, click **All At Once**. The animation previews again, but this time each of the first-level items fly in as separate objects, although they all fly in at the same time. After the preview, animation sequence icons, all numbered 1, appear next to each bulleted item, indicating that each item will animate separately but you only need to advance the slide show once.

4. Next to the first bulleted item, click the animation sequence icon. In the Timing group, On Click appears in the Start box.

5. Next to the second bulleted item, click the animation sequence icon. In the Timing group, With Previous appears in the Start box.

6. In the Animation group, click the **Effect Options** button, and then click **By Paragraph**. The sequence effect is changed back to its original setting.

7. Save your changes.

**PROSKILLS**

*Decision Making: Just Because You Can Doesn't Mean You Should*

PowerPoint provides you with many tools that enable you to create interesting and creative slide shows. However, you need to give careful thought before deciding to use a tool to enhance the content of your presentation. Just because a tool is available doesn't mean you should use it. For example, the Add or Remove Columns button in the Paragraph group on the HOME tab allows you to create multiple columns in a text box. If you need to include two columns of bullet items on a slide, it is almost always a better choice to use a layout that has two content placeholders. Another example of a tool to use sparingly is a sound effect with transitions. Most of the time you do not need to use sound to highlight the fact that one slide is leaving the screen while another appears.

You will also want to avoid using too many or frivolous animations. It is easy to go overboard with animations, and they can quickly become distracting and make your presentation seem less professional. Before you apply an animation, you should know what you want to emphasize and why you want to use an animation. Remember that animations should always enhance your message. When you are finished giving your presentation, you want your audience to remember your message, not your animations.

# Adding and Modifying Video

You can add video to slides to play during your presentation. PowerPoint supports various file formats, but the most commonly used are the MPEG-4 format, the Windows Media Audio/Video format, and the Audio Visual Interleave format, which appears in Explorer windows as the Video Clip file type. After you insert a video, you can modify it by changing playback options, changing the length of time the video plays, and applying formats and styles to the video.

## Adding Video to Slides

To insert video stored on your computer or network, click the Insert Video button in a content placeholder, and then in the Insert Video window next to "From a file," click Browse to open the Insert Video dialog box. You can also click the Video button in the Media group on the INSERT tab, and then click Video on My PC to open the same Insert Video dialog box.

REFERENCE

## Adding Videos Stored on Your Computer or Network

- In a content placeholder, click the Insert Video button to open the Insert Video window, and then next to "From a file," click Browse to open the Insert Video dialog box; or click the INSERT tab on the ribbon, and then in the Media group, click the Video button, and then click Video on My PC to open the Insert Video dialog box.
- Click the video you want to use, and then click the Insert button.
- If desired, click the VIDEO TOOLS PLAYBACK tab, and then in the Video Options group:
  - Click the Start arrow, and then click Automatically to change how the video starts from On Click.
  - Click the Play Full Screen check box to select it to have the video fill the screen.
  - Click the Rewind after Playing check box to select it to have the poster frame display after the video plays.
  - Click the Volume button, and then click a volume level or click Mute.

Inger has several videos she wants you to add to Slides 6 and 8.

### To add a video to Slide 6 and play it:

1. Display **Slide 6** ("Bergen Train Through Mountains") in the Slide pane, and then in the content placeholder, click the **Insert Video** button 🎬. The Insert Video window opens.

2. Next to "From a file," click **Browse**. The Insert Video dialog box opens.

3. In the **PowerPoint2 ▸ Tutorial** folder, click **Bergen Train**, and then click the **Insert** button. The video is inserted on the slide. The first frame of the video is displayed, and a play bar with controls for playing the video appears below it. See Figure 2-32.

**Figure 2-32**  Video added to Slide 6

Photos courtesy of S. Scott Zimmerman

**Trouble?** Depending on your computer, the video might appear as a black box on the slide. It should still play.

**Trouble?** This video includes sound, so you might want to adjust your speakers if needed to avoid disturbing others when you complete the next step.

4. On the play bar, click the **Play** button ▶. The Play button changes to the Pause button ❚❚ and the video plays. Watch the 14-second video. Next, you'll watch the video in Slide Show view.

5. On the status bar, click the **Slide Show** button 🖳. Slide 6 appears in Slide Show view.

6. Point to the video. The play bar appears, and the pointer changes to 👆. You don't need to click the Play button to play the video in Slide Show view; you can click anywhere on the video to play it as long as the pointer is visible. While the video is playing, you can click it again to pause it.

7. Click anywhere on the video. The video plays.

   **Trouble?** If Slide 7 appeared instead of the video playing, the pointer wasn't visible or you didn't click the video object, so clicking the slide advanced the slide show. Press the Backspace key to return to Slide 6, move the mouse over the video to make the pointer visible, and then click the video.

8. Before the video finishes playing, move the pointer to make it visible, and then click the video again. The video pauses.

9. Move the pointer to make it visible, if necessary, click the video to finish playing it, and then press the **Esc** key to end the slide show.

As you just saw, you clicked the video to play it during the slide show. When you insert a video, its start timing is set to On Click. This start timing means something different for videos than for animations. For animations, On Click means you can do anything to advance the slide show to cause the animation to start. For videos, On Click means you need to click the video object or the Play button on the play bar. If you click somewhere else on the screen or do anything else to advance the slide show, the video will not play. The start timing setting is on the VIDEO TOOLS PLAYBACK tab.

You'll add the video to Slide 8 and then examine the start timing setting.

**To add a video to Slide 8 and examine the start timing:**

1. Display **Slide 8** ("Flåm Train in Station") in the Slide pane, and then click the **INSERT** tab on the ribbon.

2. In the Media group, click the **Video** button, and then click **Video on My PC**. The Insert Video dialog box opens.

3. Click **Flam Train**, and then click the **Insert** button. The video is inserted in the content placeholder.

4. On the play bar, click the **Play** button ▶. Watch the 10-second video.

5. On the ribbon, click the **VIDEO TOOLS PLAYBACK** tab. In the Video Options group, On Click appears in the Start box. See Figure 2-33.

**Figure 2-33**    Options on the VIDEO TOOLS PLAYBACK tab

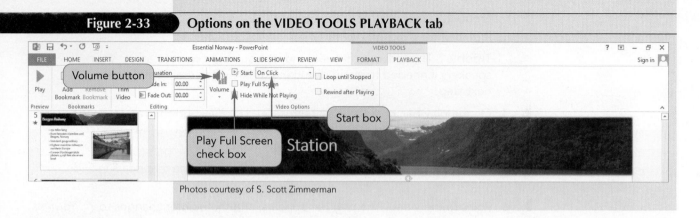

Photos courtesy of S. Scott Zimmerman

## Modifying Video Playback Options

You can change several options for how a video plays. For instance, you can change the start timing so that the video plays automatically when the slide appears during the slide show. The video playback options are listed in Figure 2-34.

**Figure 2-34**    Video playback options

| Video Option | Function |
|---|---|
| Volume | Change the volume of the video from high to medium or low or mute it. |
| Start | Change how the video starts, either when the presenter clicks it or the Play button on the play bar or automatically when the slide appears during the slide show. |
| Play Full Screen | The video fills the screen during the slide show. |
| Hide While Not Playing | The video does not appear on the slide when it is not playing; make sure the video is set to play automatically if this option is selected. |
| Loop until Stopped | The video plays until the next slide appears during the slide show. |
| Rewind after Playing | The video rewinds after it plays so that the first frame or the poster frame appears again. |

© 2014 Cengage Learning

Both videos that you inserted have sound. Inger doesn't want you to mute them, but she would like you to lower the volume. You could adjust this while the videos are playing by using the volume control on the play bar, but she wants you to set the default volume lower so that you don't have to worry about it during the presentation. Inger also wants the video on Slide 8 to fill the screen when it plays, and for it to start automatically when the slide appears during the slide show.

### To modify the playback options of the videos:

1. On **Slide 8** ("Flåm Train in Station"), click the video to select it, if necessary, and make sure the PLAYBACK tab is active on the ribbon. First you'll set the volume to low.

2. In the Video Options group, click the **Volume** button, and then click **Low**. Now you will set the video to play full screen.

3. In the Video Options group, click the **Play Full Screen** check box to select it. Finally, you will set this video to play automatically.

4. Click the **Start** arrow, and then click **Automatically**. Now you need to lower the volume of the video on Slide 6.

5. Display **Slide 6** ("Bergen Train Through Mountains") in the Slide pane, click the video, and then click the **PLAYBACK** tab, if necessary. In the Video Options group, On Click appears in the Start box.

6. Set the volume of the video to **Low**. You'll view the videos again in Slide Show view.

7. On the status bar, click the **Slide Show** button 🖳. Slide 6 appears in Slide Show view.

8. Move the mouse to make the pointer visible, and then click the video. The video plays.

9. After the video finishes playing, press the **spacebar** to advance to Slide 7, and then press the **spacebar** again. Slide 8 ("Flåm Train in Station") briefly appears, and then the Flam Train video fills the screen and plays automatically. When the video is finished playing, Slide 8 appears again.

10. Press the **Esc** key to end the slide show.

## Understanding Animation Effects Applied to Videos

**TIP**

The Media animation category appears only when a media object— either video or audio—is selected on a slide.

When you insert a video (or audio) object, an animation is automatically applied to the video so that you can click anywhere on the video to start and pause it when the slide show is run. This animation is the Pause animation in the Media animation category and it is set to On Click. The Pause animation is what makes it possible to start or pause a video during a slide show by clicking anywhere on the video object. (When you click the video to play it, you are actually "unpausing" it.)

When you change the Start setting of a video on the PLAYBACK tab to Automatically, a second animation, the Play animation in the Media animation category, is applied to the video as well as the Pause animation, and the start timing of the Play animation is set to After Previous. If there are no other objects on the slide set to animate before the video, the Play animation has an animation sequence number of zero, which means that it will play immediately after the slide transition.

To see these animations, click the ANIMATIONS tab on the ribbon, and then select a video object on a slide. The Pause and Play animations appear in the Animation gallery in the Media category.

You'll examine the video animations now.

### To examine the Media animation effects for the videos:

1. Display **Slide 6** ("Bergen Train Through Mountains") in the Slide pane. Remember that the video on this slide is set to play On Click.

2. On the ribbon, click the **ANIMATIONS** tab, and then click the video. See Figure 2-35. The animation sequence icon next to the video contains a lightning bolt instead of a number. In the Animation group, Pause is selected, and in the Timing group, On Click appears in the Start box. This animation is applied automatically to all videos when you add them to slides.

**Figure 2-35**    Pause animation applied to video

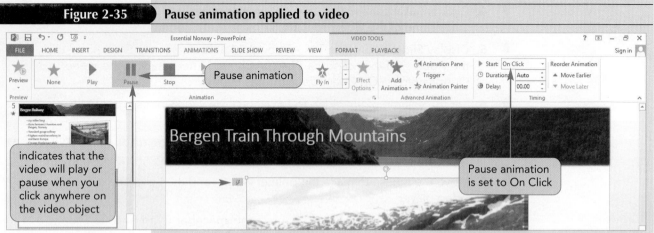

Photos courtesy of S. Scott Zimmerman

3. In the Animation group, click the **More** button. The Media category appears at the top of the Animation gallery because a media object is selected.

4. Press the **Esc** key to close the gallery, display **Slide 8** ("Flåm Train in Station") in the Slide pane, and then click the video. Because you set this video to start automatically, two animation sequence icons appear next to it, one containing a zero and one containing a lightning bolt. In the Animation group, Multiple is selected because two animations are applied to this video.

   When more than one animation is applied to any object, you need to click each animation sequence icon to see which animation is associated with each icon.

5. Click the **lightning bolt** animation sequence icon. In the Animation group, Pause is selected, and in the Timing group, On Click appears in the Start box. This allows you to click the video during a slide show to play or pause it.

6. Click the animation sequence icon **0**. In the Animation group, Play is selected, and in the Timing group, After Previous appears in the Start box. This Play animation was added to this video when you selected Automatically on the PLAYBACK tab. See Figure 2-36.

**Figure 2-36**    Play animation settings for video set to play automatically

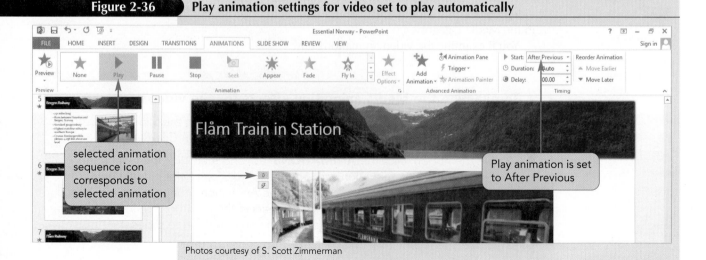

Photos courtesy of S. Scott Zimmerman

## Setting a Poster Frame

The frame that appears when the video is not playing is called the **poster frame**. You can set the poster frame to be any frame in the video or you can set the poster frame to any image stored in a file. The default poster frame for a video is the first frame of the video. You can change this so that any frame from the video or any image stored in a file is the poster frame. The video on Slide 8 is of the Flåm train. To make it clear that this is the Flåm train, you want the poster frame to be the frame in the video in which you can see the train name on the side of the train.

**To set a poster frame for the video on Slide 8:**

▶ 1. With **Slide 8** ("Flåm Train in Station") displayed in the Slide pane, click the video, and then click the **FORMAT** tab.

▶ 2. Point to the **play bar** below the video. A ScreenTip appears identifying the time of the video at that point. See Figure 2-37.

| Figure 2-37 | Setting a poster frame |
| --- | --- |

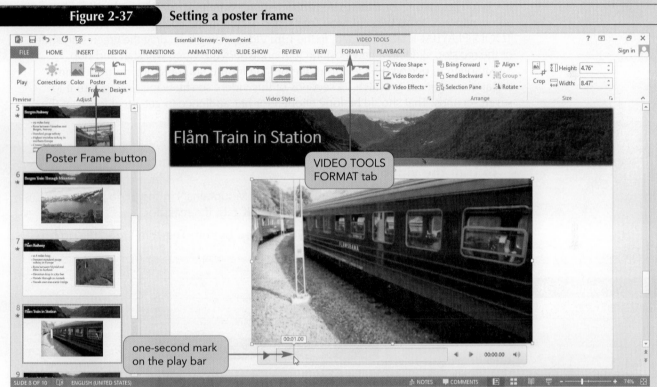

Photos courtesy of S. Scott Zimmerman

▶ 3. On the play bar, click at approximately the **one-second mark**. The video advances to the one-second mark, and the frame showing the car with the name of the train, FLÅMSBANA, appears in the video object.

▶ 4. In the Adjust group, click the **Poster Frame** button. The Poster Frame menu opens.

▶ 5. Click **Current Frame**. The message "Poster Frame Set" appears in the video's play bar, and the frame currently visible in the video object is set as the poster frame.

After you play a video during a slide show, the last frame of the video appears in the video object. You can make the poster frame appear if you set the video to rewind after playing. Inger wants you to do this for the Flåm Train video.

### To set the video on Slide 8 to rewind:

▶ **1.** On **Slide 8** ("Flåm Train in Station"), click the video, if necessary, and then click the **PLAYBACK** tab.

▶ **2.** In the Video Options group, click the **Rewind after Playing** check box to select it.

▶ **3.** On the play bar, click the **Play** button ▶ . The video plays, and then the poster frame appears again.

## Trimming Videos

If a video is too long, or if there are parts you don't want to show during the slide show, you can trim it. To do this, click the Trim Video button in the Editing group on the VIDEO TOOLS PLAYBACK tab, and then, in the Trim Video dialog box, drag the green start slider or the red stop slider to a new position to mark where the video will start and stop.

Although in person the view from the Bergen train is stunning, Inger doesn't think the audience needs to watch 13 seconds of this video, so she wants you to trim it to seven seconds. That should be long enough for her audience to get a feel for what the train ride through the mountains is like.

### To trim the video on Slide 6:

▶ **1.** Display **Slide 6** ("Bergen Train Through Mountains") in the Slide pane, click the video, and then click the **PLAYBACK** tab, if necessary.

▶ **2.** In the Editing group, click the **Trim Video** button. The Trim Video dialog box opens. See Figure 2-38.

**Figure 2-38**　Trim Video dialog box

Photo courtesy of S. Scott Zimmerman

**3.** Drag the red **Stop** tab to the left until the time in the End Time box is approximately seven seconds, and then click the **OK** button.

**4.** On the play bar under the video on the right, click the **Play** button ▶. The video plays, but stops after playing for seven seconds.

**5.** Save your changes.

# Compressing Media

As with pictures, you can compress media files. If you need to send a file via email or you need to upload it, you should compress media files to make the final PowerPoint file smaller. The more you compress files, the smaller the final presentation file will be, but also the lower the quality. For videos, you can compress using the following settings:

- **Presentation Quality**—compresses the videos slightly and maintains the quality of the videos
- **Internet Quality**—compresses the videos to a quality suitable for streaming over the Internet
- **Low Quality**—compresses the videos as small as possible

With all of the settings, any parts of videos that you trimmed off will be deleted, similar to deleting the cropped portions of photos.

After you compress media, you should watch the slides containing the videos using the equipment you will be using when giving your presentation to make sure the reduced quality is acceptable. Usually, if the videos were high quality to start with, the compressed quality will be fine. However, if the original video quality was grainy, the compressed quality might be too low, even for evaluation purposes. If you decide that you don't like the compressed quality, you can undo the compression.

You will compress the media files you inserted. You need to send the presentation to Inger via email, so you will compress the media as much as possible.

### To compress the videos in the presentation:

**1.** Click the **FILE** tab. Backstage view appears displaying the Info screen. See Figure 2-39.

**Figure 2-39** **Info screen in Backstage view**

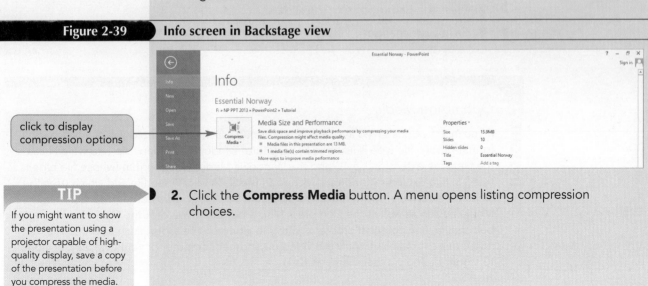

click to display compression options

**TIP**

If you might want to show the presentation using a projector capable of high-quality display, save a copy of the presentation before you compress the media.

**2.** Click the **Compress Media** button. A menu opens listing compression choices.

3. Click **Low Quality**. The Compress Media dialog box opens listing the two video files in the presentation with a progress bar appearing next to each one in the Status column to show you the progress of the compression. After each file is compressed, the progress bar is replaced by a message indicating that compression for the file is complete and stating how much the video file size was reduced. See Figure 2-40.

**Figure 2-40**     **Compress Media dialog box**

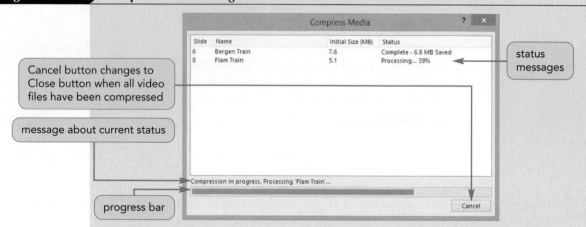

After all the videos have been compressed, a message appears at the bottom of the dialog box stating that the compression is complete and indicating how much the file size of the presentation was reduced.

4. Click the **Close** button. Next to the Compress Media button on the Info screen, the bulleted list states that the presentation's media was compressed to Low Quality and that you can undo the compression if the results are unsatisfactory. Now you need to view the compressed videos.

5. At the top of the navigation bar, click the **Back** button ⊙ to display Slide 6 ("Bergen Train Through Mountains") in the Slide pane.

6. On the status bar, click the **Slide Show** button 🖵 to display the slide in Slide Show view, and then click the video to play it. The quality is lower, but sufficient for Inger to get the general idea after you send it to her via email.

7. Press the **Esc** key to end the slide show.

8. Save your changes.

*Optimizing Media*

INSIGHT

If you insert videos saved in older video formats, such as the Audio Visual Interleave format (whose file type is listed in File Explorer windows as Video Clip and which uses the filename extension ".avi") and the Windows Media Video format (whose file type is listed in File Explorer windows as Windows Media Audio/Video file and which uses the filename extension ".wmv"), the Info screen in Backstage view contains an Optimize Media button as well as the Compress Media button. If you click the Optimize Media button first, any potential problems with the video on the slides, such as problems that might make it difficult to play the video on another computer or would cause the video to stutter during playback, are repaired.

# Adding Footers and Headers

Sometimes it can be helpful to have information on each slide such as the title of the presentation or the company name. This is called a **footer**. It can also be helpful to have the slide number displayed. For example, you might need to distribute handouts that reference slide numbers. And some presentations need the date to appear on each slide, especially if the presentation contains time-sensitive information. You can easily add this information to all the slides. Usually this information is not needed on the title slide, so you can also specify that it not appear on there.

## To add a footer, slide numbers, and the date to slides:

 1. Click the **INSERT** tab on the ribbon, and then in the Text group, click the **Header & Footer** button. The Header and Footer dialog box opens with the Slide tab selected.

 2. Click the **Footer** check box to select it, and then click in the **Footer** box. In the Preview box on the right, the left placeholder on the bottom is filled with black to indicate where the footer will appear on slides. See Figure 2-41. Note that the position of the footer, slide number, and date changes in different themes.

**Figure 2-41**    Slide tab in the Header and Footer dialog box

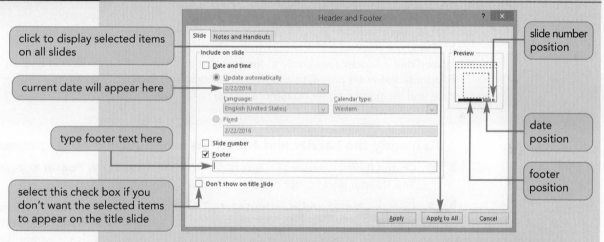

 3. Type **Essential Norway Tours**.

 4. Click the **Slide number** check box to select it. In the Preview box, the box in the bottom-right is filled with black.

 5. Click the **Date and time** check box to select it. The options under this check box darken to indicate that you can use them, and in the Preview box, the box in the middle on the bottom is filled with black.

    You don't want the date in the presentation to update automatically each time the presentation is opened. You want it to show today's date so people will know that the information is current as of that date.

6. Click the **Fixed** option button. Now you want to prevent the footer, slide number, and date from appearing on the title slide.

7. Click the **Don't show on title slide** check box to select it, and then click the **Apply to All** button. On Slide 6, the footer, date, and slide number display. See Figure 2-42.

**Figure 2-42**    **Footer, date, and slide number on Slide 6**

Photos courtesy of S. Scott Zimmerman

In common usage, a footer is any text that appears at the bottom of every page in a document or every slide in a presentation. However, as you saw when you added the footer in the Header and Footer dialog box, in PowerPoint a footer is specifically the text that appears in the Footer box on the Slide tab in that dialog box and in the footer text box on the slides. This text box can appear anywhere on the slide; in some themes the footer appears at the top of slides. This information does not appear on notes pages and handouts. You need to add footers to notes pages and handouts separately.

A **header** is information displayed at the top of every page. Slides do not have headers, but you can add a header to handouts and notes pages. Like a footer, in PowerPoint a header refers only to the text that appears in the Header text box on handouts and notes pages. In addition to headers and footers, you can also display a date and the page number on handouts and notes pages.

## To modify the header and footer on handouts and notes pages:

1. On the INSERT tab, in the Text group, click the **Header & Footer** button. The Header and Footer dialog box opens with the Slide tab selected.

2. Click the **Notes and Handouts** tab. This tab includes a Page number check box and a header box. The Page number check box is selected, and in the Preview, the lower-right rectangle is bold to indicate that this is where the page number will appear.

3. Click the **Header** check box to select it, click in the **Header** box, and then type **Essential Norway Tours**.

4. Click the **Footer** check box to select it, click in the **Footer** box, and then type your name.

5. Click the **Apply to All** button. To see the effect of modifying the handouts and notes pages, you need to look at the print preview.

6. Click the **FILE** tab, and then in the navigation bar, click **Print**.

**7.** Under Settings, click the **Full Page Slides** button, and then click **Notes Pages**. The preview shows Slide 6 as a notes page. The header and footer you typed appear, along with the page number. See Figure 2-43.

**Figure 2-43** **Header and footer on the Slide 6 notes page**

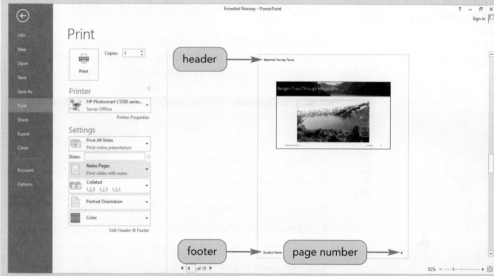

Photos courtesy of S. Scott Zimmerman

**8.** At the top of the navigation bar, click the **Back** button ⊙ to return to Normal view.

**9.** Display **Slide 1** (the title slide) in the Slide pane, replace Inger's name in the subtitle text box with your name, and then save the changes to the presentation.

Now that you have finished working on the presentation, you should view the completed presentation as a slide show.

## To view the completed presentation in Slide Show view:

**1.** On the Quick Access Toolbar, click the **Start From Beginning** button 🖵. Slide 1 appears in Slide Show view.

**2.** Press the **spacebar**. Slide 2 ("About Us") appears in Slide Show view displaying the photo on the slide layout, the slide background, the slide title, and the footer, date, and slide number.

**3.** Press the **spacebar** four times to display all the bulleted items, and then press the **spacebar** again to display Slide 3 ("Where We Are").

**4.** Press the **spacebar** three times to display Slide 4 ("Essential Norway Sample Itinerary"), Slide 5 ("Bergen Railway"), and finally Slide 6 ("Bergen Train Through Mountains").

**5.** Click the video object. The video plays on the slide.

**6.** After the video has finished playing, press the **spacebar** to display Slide 7 ("Flåm Railway"), and then press the **spacebar** to display Slide 8 ("Flåm Train in Station"). Slide 8 briefly appears, and then the video of the train fills the screen and plays automatically. After the video finishes playing, Slide 8 appears again in Slide Show view displaying the poster frame you set.

> 7. Press the **spacebar** to display Slide 9 ("Views of the Fjords"), and then press the **spacebar** again. The photo on the left fades in with the Split animation, and then after a one-second delay, the photo on the right fades in.
>
> 8. Press the **spacebar** to display Slide 10 ("Contact Us"), press the **spacebar** again to display the black slide that appears at the end of a slide show, and then press the **spacebar** once more to return to Normal view.

The final presentation file with transitions, animations, and video is interesting and should enhance the presentation you will give to travel agents in the United States. You can confidently send it to Inger in Norway for a final review.

## Session 2.2 Quick Check

**REVIEW**

1. What is a transition?
2. What are animations?
3. How do you change the speed of a transition or an animation?
4. When you apply an animation to a bulleted list with subitems, how do the first-level items animate? How do the second-level items animate?
5. What does "On Click" mean for a video?
6. What animation is applied to every video that you add to a slide?
7. What is a poster frame?
8. In PowerPoint, what is a footer?

ASSESS

PRACTICE

## Review Assignments

**Data Files needed for the Review Assignments: Alaska.jpg, Cruise.mp4, Fjords.pptx, Gulls.mp4, New Norway Theme.pptx, Norway.jpg**

Travel agents often ask Inger Halvorsen questions about fjords. Inger decided to create a PowerPoint presentation that describes fjords. She also revised the custom theme she created for her company so that it uses a different photo in the background on the title slide, and she created two new custom layouts to show three items on a slide. Complete the following:

1. Open the presentation **Fjords.pptx**, located in the PowerPoint2 ▶ Review folder included with your Data Files, add your name as the subtitle, and then save it as **Information about Fjords** to the drive and folder where you are storing your files.

2. Apply the theme from the presentation **New Norway Theme**, located in the PowerPoint2 ▶ Review folder.

3. Change the layout of Slide 5 ("Fjords in Other Countries") to Three Comparison. Type **Chile** in the text placeholder above the picture on the right. Delete "Chile" in the text box above the content placeholder in the middle, and then type **Alaska**. In the empty content placeholder, insert the photo **Alaska**, located in the PowerPoint2 ▶ Review folder. Apply the Compound Frame, Black style and the Reflection effect "Half Reflection, touching" to the three pictures.

4. Change the layout of Slide 6 ("Norwegian Fjords") to Three Content, insert the photo **Norway**, located in the PowerPoint2 ▶ Review folder in the empty content placeholder, and then apply the Compound Frame, Black style to the three photos.

5. On Slide 2 ("What Is a Fjord?"), insert an online picture from Office.com in the content placeholder using **Norway fjord cliff** as the keywords. Apply the Compound Frame, Black style to the picture, and then apply the Perspective Left 3-D Rotation effect.

6. Click the photo you just inserted, and then compress all the photos in the presentation to 96 ppi.

7. On Slide 3 ("Where Are Fjords Located?"), copy the "North America northwest coast" callout, paste it on the same slide, and then flip the pasted copy horizontally. Position the flipped callout so it points to the red circle on the map, and then delete the red circle. Edit the text of the flipped callout by changing "northwest" to **"northeast."**

8. On Slide 3, add a Left Arrow shape. Type **Norway** in the arrow, and then resize the shape so it just fits the text on one line. Rotate the arrow approximately 45 degrees to the right so that it points up to the left, and then position it so that it points to the area of the map indicated by the top of the red triangle. Change the fill color of the arrow to Orange, Accent 6, and then delete the red triangle.

9. On Slide 4 ("Facts About Countries with Fjords"), insert a 3x6 table. In the first row in the table, type **Location, Famous examples, Flag**.

10. In the first cell in the second row, type **Canada--British Columbia**. (When you press the spacebar after typing "British," AutoCorrect changes the two dashes to an em dash, which is a long dash.)

11. Refer to Figure 2-44 to add the rest of the data to the table. Add a row if needed. (*Hint*: To activate AutoCorrect to change the two dashes after "United States" to an em dash, press the Tab key to move the insertion point to the next cell instead of clicking in the next cell.)

**Figure 2-44**    **Data for table on Slide 4 in the Information about Fjords presentation**

| Location | Famous examples | Flag |
|---|---|---|
| Canada—British Columbia | Howe Sound | |
| Chile | Aisen Fjord | |
| Greenland | Ilulissat Icefjord | |
| Iceland | East Fjords | |
| New Zealand | Milford Sound, Doubtful Sound | |
| United States--Alaska | Kenai Fjords | |

© 2014 Cengage Learning

12. In the table, delete the Flag column. Add a new row above the row containing "United States—Alaska." Type **Norway** in the new cell in the Location column, and then type **Geirangerfjord, Naeroyfjord** in the Famous examples column.

13. In the table, in the "Chile" row, replace the "e" in "Aisen" with **é**. Then in the Norway row, in the word "Naeroyfjord," replace the "ae" with **æ** and replace the first "o" with **ø** so the word is spelled "Nærøyfjord." (All three letters are in the Latin-1 Supplement subset.)

14. In the table, set the proofing language for the two words in the Famous examples column in the Norway row to Norwegian (Bokmål), and then set the proofing language for the two words in the Famous examples column in the Greenland row to Greenlandic.

15. Apply the Light Style 3 - Accent 1 table style, and then change the font size of all of the text in the table to 24 points.

16. Insert a new column to the left of the Location column. Use online pictures on Office.com to fill each cell with a picture of the flag of the country listed in the Location column. To locate each flag, type the keywords listed below in the box next to Office.com in the Insert Pictures dialog box. When more than one result appears, click each result and look at the keywords and measurements in the lower-left corner of the dialog box, and then use the result that has a width measurement of 600 pixels.
    - Canada: type **Canada flag country**
    - Chile: type **Chile flag country**
    - Greenland: type **Greenland flag**
    - Iceland: type **Iceland flag country**
    - New Zealand: type **New Zealand flag**
    - Norway: type **Norway flag country**
    - United States: type **United States flag country**

17. In the table, change the width of the first column so it is 0.8 inches wide, and then make the second and third columns just wide enough to hold the widest entry on one line. Reposition the table so the left edge is approximately aligned with the left edge of the title text and so the table is approximately centered vertically in the space below the title.

18. Apply the Uncover transition. Change the Effect Options to From Top, and then change the duration to .50 seconds. Apply this transition to all of the slides.

19. On Slide 2 ("What Is a Fjord?"), animate the bulleted list using the Fade animation. Change the duration of the animation to .75 seconds.

20. On Slide 5 ("Fjords in Other Countries"), apply the Wipe animation using the From Left effect to the "New Zealand" caption. Apply the same animation to the other two text captions.

21. Apply the Wipe animation with the From Left effect to the photo under "New Zealand," and then change the start timing of that animation to After previous. Move the animation applied to the photo earlier so it has the same animation sequence number as the caption above it (it should be a 1). Apply the same animation using the After previous start timing to the photos under "Alaska" and "Chile," and adjust the animation order so that each photo has the same animation sequence number as the caption above it.

22. On Slide 7, add the video **Cruise**, located in the PowerPoint2 ▶ Review folder, in the content placeholder on the left, and set it to play Automatically and Full Screen and to rewind after playing. (This video has no sound.) Set the poster frame to the frame at approximately the 2.30-second mark.

23. Add the video **Gulls**, located in the PowerPoint2 ▶ Review folder, in the content placeholder on the right. This video should play On Click and Full Screen. Set the volume to Low. Leave the poster frame as the first frame of the video.

24. Trim the Gulls video by adjusting the end time so the video is approximately 10 seconds long.

25. Compress the media to Low Quality.

26. Add **Fjords presented by Essential Norway Tours** as the footer on all the slides except the title slide, and display the slide number on all the slides except the title slide. On the Notes and Handouts, add **Essential Norway Tours** as the header and your name as the footer.

27. Save your changes, and then watch the final presentation in Slide Show view.

## Case Problem 1

APPLY

**Data Files needed for this Case Problem: Group.jpg, Summer.mp4, Theater Theme.pptx, Theater.pptx**

*Ottawa Children's Theatre Workshop*    Adrielle Schlosser is the director of the Ottawa Children's Theatre Workshop in Ontario, Canada. One of her responsibilities is to inform parents, teachers, and volunteers about the organization. She asked you to help her prepare the PowerPoint presentation, which will include photos, a video, and a table to provide details her audience might be interested in knowing. Complete the following steps:

1. Open the file named **Theater**, located in the PowerPoint2 ▶ Case1 folder included with your Data Files, add your name as the subtitle on Slide 1, and then save it as **Children's Theater** to the drive and folder where you are storing your files.

2. Apply the theme from the presentation **Theater Theme**, located in the PowerPoint2 ▶ Case1 folder.

3. Apply the picture style Moderate Frame, White to the pictures on Slides 2, 3, 4, and 5.

4. On Slide 3 ("Eligibility"), animate the bulleted list using the Float In animation with the Float Down effect, and change the duration to .50 seconds. Animate the bulleted list on Slide 5 ("Performances") using the same animation.

5. On Slide 6 ("Recent Summer Performance"), insert the video **Summer**, located in the PowerPoint2 ▶ Case1 folder. Set the movie to play Automatically and to rewind after playing, and set the volume to Low. Trim the video by changing the end time to approximately the 18.5-second mark. Set the poster frame to the frame at approximately the 13-second mark.

6. Compress the media to Low Quality.

7. On Slide 7 ("Classes"), add a new row above the last row with the following data: **Junior Jazzers**, **7th – 9th**, **Rarford Koskosky**, **Tues & Thurs, 4 p.m.** (*Hint*: To activate AutoCorrect to change the "th" after 9 to a superscript, press the Tab key to move to the next cell instead of clicking in the cell.)

8. Change the table style to Medium Style 1 – Accent 1. Select all of the text in the table in the rows below the header row, and then change the font color to Pink, Background 1, Darker 50%. Reposition the table so it is approximately centered vertically in the blank area below the title.

9. On Slide 8, which has the Blank layout applied, draw a rectangle shape so it almost fills the slide but fits inside the purple and pink borders on the slide. (*Hint*: Change the fill color of the rectangle to one of the blue colors in the Theme Colors so that you can more easily see where the rectangle and the purple border lines meet.) After the rectangle is sized to the correct size, fill the shape with the picture **Group**, located in the PowerPoint2 ▶ Case1 folder.

10. On Slide 8, draw another rectangle shape that is one inch high and stretches from the inside of the pink borders on the left and right. Position this rectangle directly below the purple line at the top of the slide. Remove the fill from the shape and remove the outline (that is, change the fill to No Fill and change the outline to No Outline).

11. In the second rectangle, type **See You at the Theater!**. Change the font to Broadway (Headings), and change the font size to 44 points. (If the font color is not White, or if you can't see the text, click the border of the rectangle to select the entire shape, and then change the font color to White.)

12. On Slide 8, animate the text box using the entrance animation Grow & Turn. Set its duration to .50 seconds, set its start timing to After previous, and set a delay of one second.

13. Apply the Drape transition to all the slides using the default Left effect. Then apply the Curtains transition to only Slides 1 and 8. On Slide 8, change the duration of the transition to two seconds.

14. Save your changes, and then watch the slide show in Slide Show view. Remember to wait for the video on Slide 6 ("Recent Summer Performance") to start automatically, and, after the transition to Slide 8, wait for the text box to animate automatically.

## Case Problem 2

CREATE

**Data Files needed for this Case Problem: Coating.pptx, Curing.mp4, Hanging.jpg, Powder.mp4, Touchup.jpg, Wash.mp4, Welding.jpg**

*Powder Coating Power Plus*   Yung Hoang owns Powder Coating Power Plus, a company that uses a process called powder coating to paint metal surfaces. Powder coating results in a high-quality painted metal surface because it bonds with the metal instead of sitting on top of it. His company paints items such as exhaust fans, intake vents, pipes, and bike frames. Potential clients want to know the advantages and the process of powder coating, so Yung decided to create a PowerPoint presentation to provide this information and approximate costs. He started with the Project planning overview presentation template from Office.com and added a custom layout. Complete the following steps:

1. Open the presentation **Coating**, located in the PowerPoint2 ▶ Case2 folder included with your Data Files, add your name as the subtitle, and then save the presentation as **Powder Coating** to the drive and folder where you are storing your files.

2. Change the layout of Slides 3 through 8 to the custom layout Two Content Modified.

3. Refer to Figure 2-45 and insert the pictures and video as shown on Slides 3 through 8. All the files are located in the PowerPoint2 ▶ Case2 folder. Note that none of the videos in the presentation have sound.

**Figure 2-45**     **Slides 3 – 8 in the Powder Coating presentation**

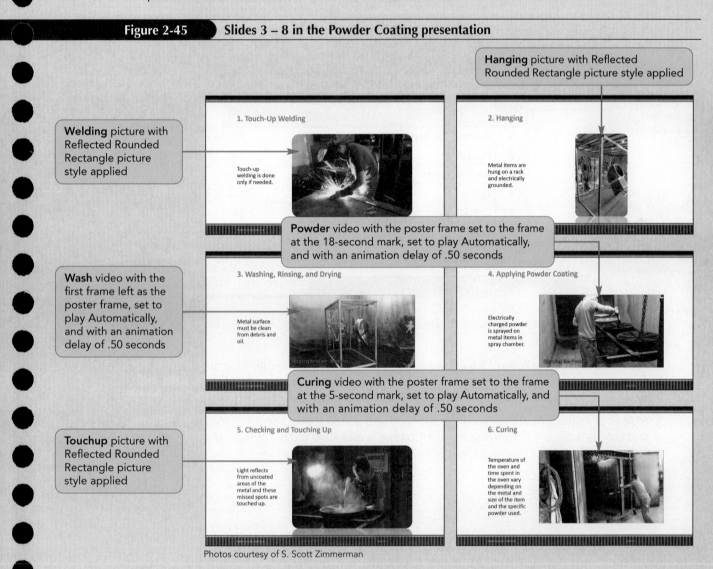

Photos courtesy of S. Scott Zimmerman

4. Compress all the photos to 96 ppi, and compress the media to Low Quality.

5. On Slide 2 ("Why Is Powder Coating Better Than Paint?"), animate the bulleted list to Wipe with the From Top effect.

6. On Slide 9 ("Procedures and Costs"), create the table shown in Figure 2-46, and apply the formatting as described in the figure.

**Figure 2-46** **Table on Slide 9 in the Power Coating presentation**

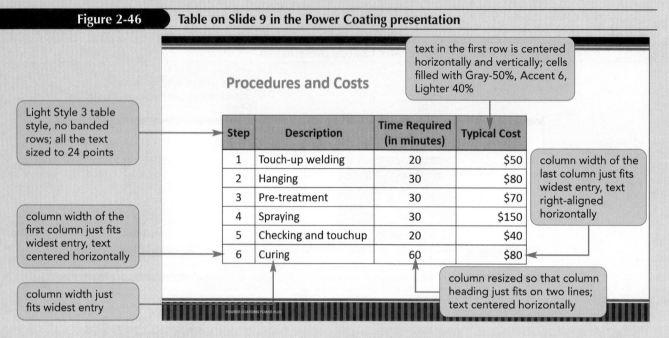

text in the first row is centered horizontally and vertically; cells filled with Gray-50%, Accent 6, Lighter 40%

Light Style 3 table style, no banded rows; all the text sized to 24 points

**Procedures and Costs**

| Step | Description | Time Required (in minutes) | Typical Cost |
|:---:|:---|:---:|---:|
| 1 | Touch-up welding | 20 | $50 |
| 2 | Hanging | 30 | $80 |
| 3 | Pre-treatment | 30 | $70 |
| 4 | Spraying | 30 | $150 |
| 5 | Checking and touchup | 20 | $40 |
| 6 | Curing | 60 | $80 |

column width of the last column just fits widest entry, text right-aligned horizontally

column width of the first column just fits widest entry, text centered horizontally

column width just fits widest entry

column resized so that column heading just fits on two lines; text centered horizontally

POWDER COATINGS POWER PLUS

7. Apply the Fade transition to Slides 1 through 3 and Slides 9 and 10. Apply the Conveyor transition to Slides 4 through 8.

8. Add **Powder Coating Power Plus** as a footer on all slides except the title slide, and display the current date to be updated automatically on all slides except the title slide. On the notes and handouts, display the current date to be updated automatically, and add your name as a header.

9. Save your changes, and then view the slide show. The videos on Slide 5 ("3. Washing, Rinsing, and Drying"), Slide 6 ("Applying Powder Coating"), and Slide 8 ("6. Curing") should play automatically one-half second after the slide appears in the slide show.

APPLY

## Case Problem 3

Data Files needed for this Case Problem: Bench End.jpg, Bench.mp4, Curl.mp4, Gym Theme.pptx, Gym.pptx, Military.mp4

*St. Louis Fitness Consultants*   St. Louis Fitness Consultants provides consulting and training services to gyms, municipal fitness centers, and large companies. Bianca Kocherhans, a personal trainer and sales consultant who works at St. Louis Fitness, realized that many people want the convenience of having a home gym. She approached the company's owners and was given approval to offer consulting to retail stores that sell fitness equipment and to large companies with employees interested in setting up their own home gym. She prepared a PowerPoint presentation with some information on setting up a home gym and doing a few basic weight-lifting exercises. Complete the following steps:

1. Open the presentation named **Gym**, located in the PowerPoint2 ▶ Case3 folder included with your Data Files, add your name as the subtitle, and then save it as **Home Gym** to the drive and folder where you are storing your files.

2. Apply the theme from the presentation **Gym Theme**, located in the PowerPoint2 ▶ Case3 folder.

3. On Slide 10 ("Bench Press Technique"), change the layout to Comparison Three, insert the picture **Bench End** in the content placeholder, and then type **Ending position** in the text placeholder below this photo. Compress this photo to 96 ppi.

4. Apply the Drop Shadow Rectangle picture style to the three photos on Slide 10.

5. On Slide 3 ("Why a Power Cage?"), add the Line Callout 1 shape to the left of the bottom part of the picture. Type **Safety bar to catch barbell** in the shape. Apply the Moderate Effect – Black, Dark 1 shape style, and then change the outline weight to 3 points. Resize the box part of the callout containing the text so that all the text fits on two lines with "Safety bar to" on the first line.

6. Flip the callout shape horizontally, and then drag the end of the callout line to point to the part of the horizontal safety bar in the photo indicated by the red circle shape. Delete the red circle shape.

7. On Slide 4 ("Typical Costs"), insert a 3x6 table. Keep the default style Medium Style 2 – Accent 1 applied to the table. Enter the data shown in Figure 2-47.

**Figure 2-47**    **Data for table on Slide 4 in the Home Gym presentation**

| Item | Cost per Item | Total Cost |
|---|---|---|
| Power cage (1) | $650 | $650 |
| Bench (1) | $200 | $200 |
| Barbell (2) | $50 | $100 |
| Barbell plates (12 pairs) | $30 | $360 |
| Dumbbells (9 pairs) | $20 | $180 |

© 2014 Cengage Learning

8. Add a new bottom row to the table. Type **TOTAL** in the first cell in the new row, and then type **$1,490** in the last cell in the new row.

9. Increase the size of all the text in the table to 24 points. Resize the first column so it is just wide enough to fit the widest entry, and then resize the second and third columns so they are 2.5 inches wide.

10. Horizontally center the text in the first row. Horizontally right-align the dollar values in the second and third columns, and then right-align "TOTAL" in its cell in the last row.

11. Add a Gray-50%, Accent 6, Darker 50%, 3-point horizontal border between the last row and the row above it, and then add a 1-point border using the same color to the top and bottom of the table.

12. On Slide 7 ("Executing the Arm Curl"), insert the video **Curl**, on Slide 9 ("Executing the Military Press"), insert the video **Military**, and on Slide 11 ("Executing the Bench Press"), insert the video **Bench**. All three videos are located in the PowerPoint2 ▸ Case3 folder. (None of the videos in this presentation have sound.) For all three videos, keep the first frame as the poster frame.

13. Trim each video as necessary so that only two repetitions of the exercise are shown.

14. Copy the callout you added on Slide 3 ("Why a Power Cage?") to Slide 11 ("Executing the Bench Press"). Reposition the callout to point to the same location on the safety bar that you pointed to on Slide 3.

15. Animate the bulleted list on Slide 3 ("Why a Power Cage?") with the Appear entrance animation, and then animate the callout on Slide 3 with the same animation.

16. Change the start timing of the animation applied to the callout so that it appears at the same time as the "Safe" bulleted item.

17. Compress the media in the presentation.

18. Add **St. Louis Fitness Consultants** as the footer on all of the slides, including the title slide, and display the slide number on all of the slides. Add your name as a header on the notes and handouts.

19. Apply the Gallery transition to all of the slides except the first one using the default effect options From Right.

20. Save your changes, and then view the slide show.

## Case Problem 4

CHALLENGE

Data Files needed for this Case Problem: Identity.pptx, Logo.jpg, Password.wma

*KeepMeMine ID*   Dudley Zaunbrecher is a regional sales representative for KeepMeMine ID, an insurance and security company headquartered in Fort Smith, Arkansas that protects, monitors, insures, and recovers personal identity. Dudley travels throughout his region meeting with new customers. He wants to use PowerPoint to give a presentation to explain the seriousness of identity theft and how to create strong passwords, and then wrap up by trying to sign up new clients. He has asked you to help him prepare the presentation. Complete the following steps:

1. Open the presentation **Identity**, located in the PowerPoint2 ▸ Case4 folder included with your Data Files, add your name as the subtitle, and then save the presentation as **Identity Theft** to the drive and folder where you are storing your files.

2. Apply the installed Organic theme, and then change the variant to the fourth variant.

3. On Slide 4 ("What Is a Strong Password?"), insert a picture from Office.com. Use the keyword **password**, and insert the picture of asterisks in a password box.

4. On Slide 4, animate the bulleted list using the Wipe animation with the From Left effect.

5. Slide 5 ("Creating a Strong Password") contains four individual text boxes, not the usual bulleted list in one text box. Click the first bulleted item, press and hold the Shift key, click each of the other three items, and then release the Shift key. Apply the entrance animation Appear to the selected text boxes.

✥ **Explore** 6. On Slide 5, select the four animated text boxes, and then modify the Appear animation so that the letters appear one by one. (*Hint*: Use the Animation group Dialog Box Launcher, and then change the setting in the Animate text box on the Effect tab.) Speed up the effect by changing the delay between letters to 0.1 seconds.

✥ **Explore** 7. On Slide 5, insert the audio clip **Password**, located in the PowerPoint2 ▸ Case4 folder included with your Data Files. Position the sound icon to the right of the slide title so that the centers and right edges of the icon object and the title text object are aligned. Point to the sound icon, and then click the Play button. Listen to the recording and notice how it relates to the bulleted items on the slide.

✥ **Explore** 8. Add bookmarks to the play bar for the sound icon to mark four distinct points in the recording at approximately 9, 15, 19, and 32 seconds to correspond to the four text boxes on the slide. (*Hint*: Click the sound icon, and then click the AUDIO TOOLS PLAYBACK tab. Point to the sound icon, click the Play button, and then click the Add Bookmark button in the Bookmarks group on the PLAYBACK tab at the appropriate times, or click the play bar at the point where you want to add the bookmark.)

✥ **Explore** 9. Set the animation of the bulleted list to play automatically as the recording hits each bookmark. (*Hint*: Select each text box, and then use the Trigger button in the Advanced Animation group on the ANIMATIONS tab.)

10. Display Slide 5 in Slide Show view, point to the sound icon, and then click the Play button. Watch as the text in the text boxes animates automatically, one letter at a time, as each bookmark is reached. End the slide show.

11. On Slide 6 ("We Can Help"), insert the picture **Logo**, located in the PowerPoint2 ▸ Case4 folder.

12. Compress all the pictures to 96 ppi, and then compress the media to the lowest quality.

13. Apply the Switch transition to all the slides in the presentation.

14. Save your changes, and then run the slide show.

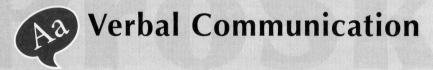

# Verbal Communication

## Rehearsing Your Presentation

The best presentations are planned well in advance of their delivery. Once the content has been created, enhanced, and perfected, it is time to prepare you, the presenter. Presenters who try to stand up and "wing it" in front of a crowd usually reveal this amateur approach the moment they start speaking—by looking down at their notes, rambling off topic, or turning their back on the audience frequently to read from the slides displayed on-screen.

To avoid being seen as an amateur, you need to rehearse your presentation. Even the most knowledgeable speakers rehearse to ensure they know how the topic flows, what the main points are, how much time to spend on each slide, and where to place emphasis. Experienced presenters understand that while practice may not make them perfect, it will certainly make them better.

Where you practice isn't that important. You can talk to a mirror, your family, or a group of friends. If you have a video camera, you can record yourself and then review the video. Watching video evidence of your performance often reveals the weaknesses you don't want your audience to see and that your friends or family may be unwilling or unable to identify. Whatever you choose to do, the bottom line is this: If you practice, you will improve.

As you rehearse, you should remember to focus on the following steps:

- Practice speaking fluently.
- Work on your tone of voice.
- Decide how to involve your audience.
- Become aware of your body language.
- Check your appearance.

## Speaking Fluently

Be sure to speak in an easy, smooth manner, and avoid using nonwords and fillers. Nonwords consist of ums, ahs, hms, and other such breaks in speech. Fillers are phrases that don't add any value yet add length to sentences. Both can dilute a speaker's message because they are not essential to the meaning of what's being spoken. At best, they can make you sound unprofessional. At worst, they can distract your audience and make your message incomprehensible.

## Considering Your Tone of Voice

When delivering your presentation, you usually want to speak passionately, with authority, and with a smile. If you aren't excited about your presentation, how will your audience feel? By projecting your voice with energy, passion, and confidence, your audience will automatically pay more attention to you. Smile and look directly at your audience members and make eye contact. If your message is getting across, they will instinctively affirm what you're saying by returning your gaze, nodding their heads, or smiling. There's something compelling about a confident speaker whose presence commands attention. However, be careful not to overdo it. Speaking too loudly or using an overly confident or arrogant tone will turn off an audience and make them stop listening altogether.

## Involving Your Audience

If you involve your audience in your presentation, they will pay closer attention to what you have to say. When an audience member asks a question, be sure to affirm them before answering. For example, you could respond with "That's a great question. What do the rest of you think?" or "Thanks for asking. Here's what my research revealed." An easy way to get the audience to participate is to start with a question and invite responses, or to stop partway through to discuss a particularly important point.

# Being Aware of Your Body Language

Although the content of your presentation plays a role in your message delivery, it's your voice and body language during the presentation that make or break it. Maintain eye contact to send the message that you want to connect and that you can be trusted. Stand up straight to signal confidence. Conversely, avoid slouching, which can convey laziness, lack of energy, or disinterest, and fidgeting or touching your hair, which can signal nervousness. Resist the temptation to glance at your watch; you don't want to send a signal that you'd rather be someplace else. Finally, be aware of your hand movements. The best position for your hands is to place them comfortably by your side, in a relaxed position. As you talk, it's fine to use hand gestures to help make a point, but be careful not to overdo it.

# Evaluating Your Appearance

Just as a professional appearance makes a good impression during a job interview, an audience's first impression of a speaker is also based on appearance. Before a single word is spoken, the audience sizes up the way the presenter looks. You want to make sure you look professional and competent. Make sure your appearance is neat, clean, and well-coordinated, and dress in appropriate clothing.

As you spend time practicing your presentation, you will naturally develop appropriate body language, tone of voice, and a fluent delivery, ensuring a clear connection with your audience and a professional delivery of your presentation's message.

**PROSKILLS**

## Create and Deliver a Training Presentation

If you hold a job for any length of time, as part of your employment, you might have to train new employees in their work tasks. For example, if you work in a library, you might have to explain how to process returned books, or if you work in a chemistry stockroom at a college, you might have to describe how to make up solutions for the school's chemistry laboratories. A PowerPoint presentation can be an effective way to start the training process. With a presentation, you can give an overview of the job without needing to repeat yourself to explain detailed aspects. Then you can customize the rest of the training to fit the needs of the specific employee.

In this exercise, you'll create a presentation containing information of your choice, using the PowerPoint skills and features presented in Tutorials 1 and 2, and then you will practice techniques for delivering the presentation.

**Note:** Please be sure not to include any personal information of a sensitive nature in the documents you create to be submitted to your instructor for this exercise. Later on, you can update the documents with such information for your own personal use.

1. Create a new PowerPoint presentation and apply an appropriate theme. Make sure you choose a theme that is relevant to the job you are describing and to your audience. Consider using a template from Office.com.
2. On Slide 1, make the presentation title the same as the title of your job or the job for which you are giving the training. Add your name as a subtitle.
3. Create a new slide for each major category of tasks. For example, task categories for a library job might be "Punching In," "Checking in with Your Supervisor," "Gathering Books from Drop-Off Stations," "Scanning Returned Books into the Computer," "Checking Books for Damage or Marks," "Processing Abused Books," "Processing Late Books," "Sorting Books," "Shelving Books," and "Punching Out."
4. On each slide, create a bulleted list to explain the particular task category or to provide the steps required to perform the task, or consider if a graphic, such as a SmartArt diagram or a table, would better illustrate your point.
5. Where applicable, include clip art, photographs, or a video. For example, you might include a photograph of the punch clock (time clock) used by hourly workers in the library, or a photograph of a book with serious damage relative to one with normal wear.

6. On one or more slides, insert a shape, such as a rectangle, triangle, circle, arrow, or star. For example, you might want to place a small colored star next to a particularly important step in carrying out a task.

7. Apply appropriate formatting to the graphics on the slides.

8. Examine your slides. Are you using too many words? Can any of your bulleted lists be replaced with a graphic?

9. Reevaluate the theme you chose. Do you think it is still appropriate? Does it fit the content of your presentation? If not, apply a different theme.

10. Add appropriate transitions and animations. Remember that the goal is to keep your audience engaged without distracting them.

11. Check the spelling of your presentation, and then proofread it to check for errors that would not be caught by the spell check. Save the final presentation.

12. Rehearse the presentation. Consider your appearance, and decide on the appropriate clothing to wear. Practice in front of a mirror and friends or family, and if you can, create a video of yourself. Notice and fine tune your body language, tone of voice, and fluency to fully engage your audience.

# Introduction to Cloud Computing

*Sharing Files and Collaborating with Others Online*

## OBJECTIVES

- Learn about Office 365 and Office on Demand
- Determine if you have a Microsoft account
- Understand the SkyDrive app and the SkyDrive desktop application
- Learn how to upload files to and download files from SkyDrive
- Learn how to share files and folders on SkyDrive
- Learn how to access Office Web Apps to create and edit files

The **cloud** refers to powerful computers called servers connected to the Internet that allow you to store and share files and access data, applications, and resources rather than storing these resources on your own computer. People store files in the cloud so they can access them from any device that has Internet access. Files stored in the cloud are also accessible to others with whom you want to share. **SkyDrive** is free storage provided in the cloud by Microsoft. SkyDrive is like having a personal hard drive in the cloud. You store files on your SkyDrive in folders, similar to the folders on your computer. You can store many types of files on your SkyDrive, including Office documents, photos, and videos. You can also sync files between your SkyDrive and your computer. Software that is stored in the cloud is accessible through a browser from any computer or device that can access the Internet. Examples of software stored in the cloud are **Office Web Apps** (sometimes referred to as **SkyDrive apps** or **Office 365 apps**), which are versions of Microsoft Office applications with basic functionality. Other examples include Google Docs and Zoho.

In this appendix, you will learn about cloud computing. You will also learn how to determine if you have a Microsoft account. Then you will learn about uploading files to and managing files in your storage space in the cloud, and how to use the Office Web Apps and share files with others.

**Note:** SkyDrive and Office Web Apps are dynamic webpages, and might change over time, including the way they are organized and how commands are performed. The information provided in this appendix, including the information about Office 365 subscriptions, was accurate at the time this book was published.

## STARTING DATA FILES

There are no starting data files for this appendix.

# Overview of Office 365 and Office on Demand

**TIP**

The amount of storage space available to you on SkyDrive varies depending on whether you have an Office 365 subscription. You can purchase additional storage space for a fee.

**Office 365** is a subscription to Microsoft cloud services. There are different plans available for home and business users. **Office on Demand** is a benefit of some Office 365 subscription plans. With Office on Demand, you can access Office programs from any computer, even if that computer does not have Office installed. For details on the various subscription plans, go to www.microsoft.com. (Only some of the plans include Office 2013.) Pricing and installation options for each plan differ.

To subscribe to Office 365, you need a Microsoft account. A **Microsoft account** is a free account that you can create that associates your email address and a password with Microsoft cloud services, such as Outlook.com for email, Xbox Live for games, and SkyDrive for file storage.

# Determining If You Have a Microsoft Account

In order to access any of Microsoft's cloud services, you must sign in to your Microsoft account. Even if you think you did not sign up for one, you might already have a Microsoft account. You have a Microsoft account if you have one of the following:

- a subscription to Office 365
- a Hotmail account
- a live.com email account
- a SkyDrive account
- an Xbox account
- a Windows phone
- a Windows 8 user account with a user name that is an email address and that requires a password

If you are not sure if your Windows 8 user account is a Microsoft account, you can check on the PC settings screen. To do this, display the Start screen, display the Charms bar, click the Settings charm, and then click Change PC settings to display the PC settings screen. On the left, click Users to display options for managing Windows 8 user accounts. If you are currently signed in to Windows 8 with a local account, your user name appears as shown in Figure A-1.

**Figure A-1** Users screen showing a local account signed in

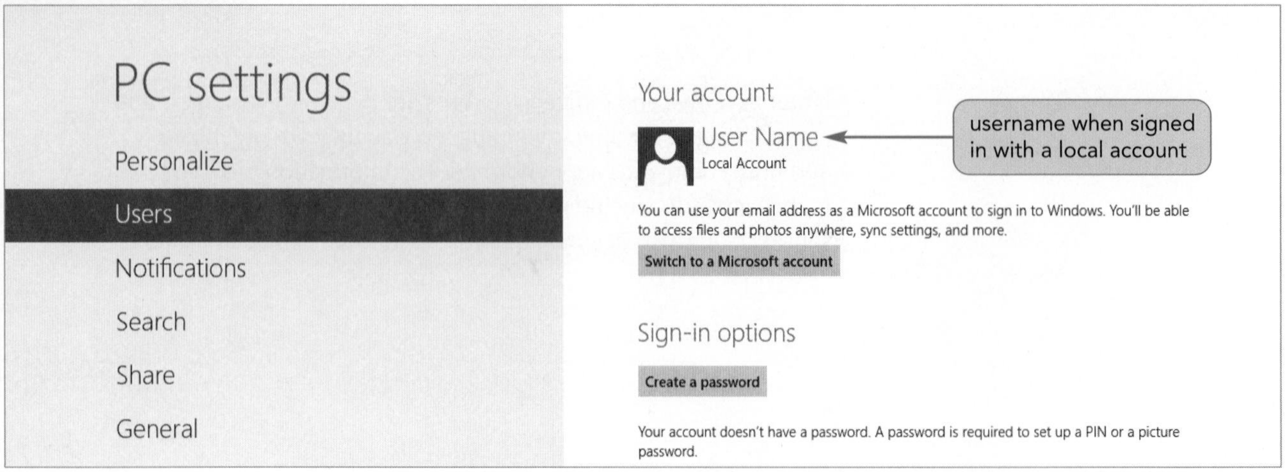

If you are currently signed in to Windows 8 with a Microsoft account, your user name will appear as an email address. See Figure A-2. If your Windows 8 user account is a Microsoft account, every time you use your computer, you are signed into your Microsoft account and you have access to SkyDrive and other Microsoft cloud services.

**Figure A-2**    **Users screen showing a Microsoft account signed in**

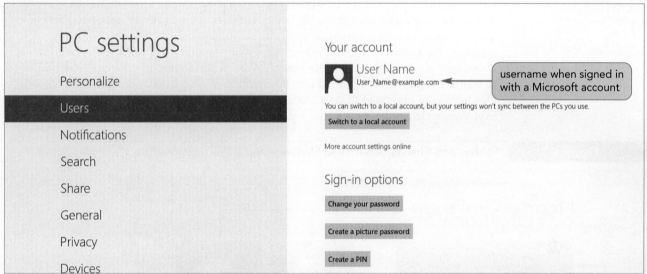

If you do not have a Microsoft account, you will need to create one in order to access SkyDrive and other Microsoft cloud services. When you attempt to access a Microsoft cloud service—for example, when you try to save to SkyDrive from Backstage view in Microsoft Word, Excel, or PowerPoint, or when you try to use an app such as Mail, People, or Messaging—and you are not signed in to a Microsoft account, a screen will appear asking you to sign in or to create a new Microsoft account. Click the Sign up link, and then follow the instructions to create your account.

**INSIGHT**

*How to Determine if You Are Signed In To Your Microsoft Account in an Office Application*

If your Windows 8 account is a Microsoft account, when you start Office 2013 applications, you will be signed in to your Microsoft account. Your user name will appear in the upper-right corner, and you will be able to save to your SkyDrive from Backstage view in Word, Excel, and PowerPoint without signing in again. If your Windows 8 account is not a Microsoft account, you might see a Sign in link in the upper-right corner of the Office applications. You can click this to sign in to your Microsoft account. Or, if you try to save to SkyDrive, you will be prompted to sign in, and then your user name will replace the Sign in link in the upper-right corner.

# Understanding the SkyDrive App and the SkyDrive Desktop Application

The **SkyDrive app** comes with Windows 8 and runs like any other app in Windows 8. The SkyDrive tile appears on the Start screen and you click it to run the app. If you are signed in to your Microsoft account, the folders on your SkyDrive appear. If you are not signed in to a Microsoft account, you will be prompted to sign in. Figure A-3 shows one user's SkyDrive in the SkyDrive app. Using the SkyDrive app, you can click a file to open it in the appropriate app or desktop application on your computer. For example, if you click a photo, the Photo app will start and the photo will appear in the Photo app; if you click a Word document, Word will start and the document will open in Word. You can also download files from your SkyDrive to your computer or upload files from your computer to your SkyDrive. You can also create new folders on your SkyDrive or delete folders from it.

| Figure A-3 | Folders and files on SkyDrive in SkyDrive app |
| --- | --- |

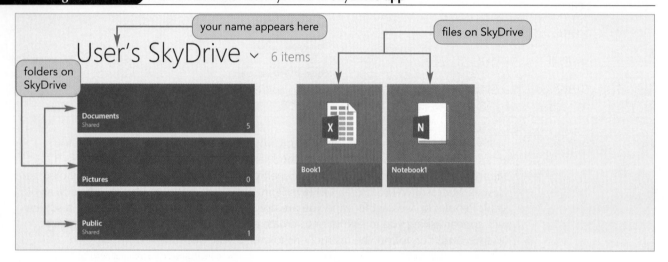

The **SkyDrive desktop application** is available for download from the Windows 8 App Store. (Note that the SkyDrive desktop application is named "Microsoft SkyDrive" in the Windows 8 store.) It runs on the desktop and looks like any other folder in File Explorer. See Figure A-4.

| Figure A-4 | File Explorer window after installing SkyDrive desktop application |
|---|---|

When you install the SkyDrive desktop application, you are asked if you want to sync all the folders on your SkyDrive to your computer. If you do not, you can deselect the folders you do not want to sync. Once the SkyDrive application is installed, any files you place in the SkyDrive folder are automatically uploaded and saved to your SkyDrive. If you edit one of these files on your computer, the edited file is synced with the version on your SkyDrive. If you access the file on your SkyDrive, either through a browser or from another computer, and make changes to it, the changes are automatically synced to the copy on your computer the next time you start your computer.

When you search for SkyDrive from the Start screen, both the SkyDrive app and the SkyDrive desktop application are named "SkyDrive," but the icons are different. Refer to Figure A-5 to see the difference.

**Figure A-5**   SkyDrive app and desktop application on the Apps screen

SkyDrive app

SkyDrive desktop application

## Moving Files Between SkyDrive and Your Computer

Once you are signed in to your Microsoft account, you can store files on your SkyDrive. You can do this from within Word, Excel, or PowerPoint, you can use the SkyDrive app or the SkyDrive desktop application, or you can use your browser to go to www.skydrive.com, log in, and then use the commands on the website. Each file that you upload can be a maximum size of 300 GB if you upload it using a browser or 2 GB if you upload it using the SkyDrive desktop application or SkyDrive app.

**TIP**

You cannot save to SkyDrive from Backstage view in Access.

To upload a file from within Word, Excel, or PowerPoint, display the file in the application window, click the FILE tab to display Backstage view, and then click Save As in the navigation bar. On the Save As screen, click SkyDrive. (Note that your Microsoft account user name will appear before SkyDrive; for example, "John Smith's Skydrive.") Then click the Browse button to open the Save As dialog box with the current location as your SkyDrive. Figure A-6 shows the Save As dialog box open on the Save As screen in Backstage view in Word. The folders on the user's SkyDrive are listed in the dialog box. Double-click a folder to make it the current folder, and then save the file to this folder on your SkyDrive in the same manner that you save files to a folder on your computer.

| Figure A-6 | Save As dialog box open on the Save As screen in Word's Backstage view |
| --- | --- |

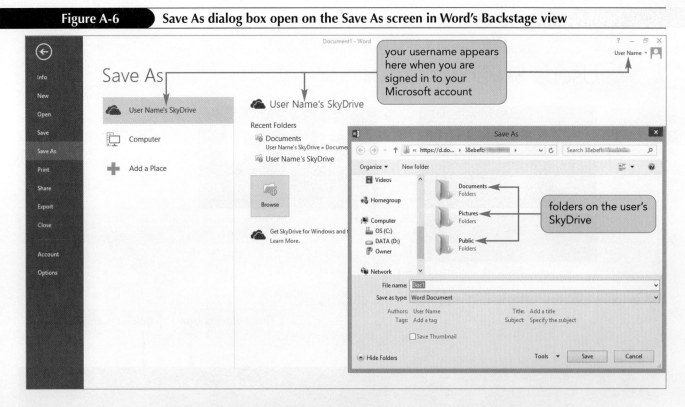

To upload files using the SkyDrive app, start the app from the Start screen. Each of the tiles on the screen represents a folder. Click the folder to which you want to upload the file to open that folder, or right-click anywhere on the screen to display the Apps bar at the bottom of the screen, as shown in Figure A-7 and then use the New Folder button to create a new folder. To upload a file, display the Apps bar, and then click the Upload button. This displays the Files screen, which lists all the files in the current folder (usually the Documents folder). You can select a file in this folder or switch to another folder. After you click a file to select it, click the Add to SkyDrive button at the bottom of the screen. To download files, right-click the file on SkyDrive to select it, and then click the Download button on the Apps bar.

**Figure A-7**   **Apps bar in SkyDrive app**

To upload a file using the SkyDrive desktop application, you either save a file to the SkyDrive folder from within an application, or copy or move a file from another folder to the SkyDrive folder. The file will be automatically synced to your SkyDrive. Likewise, to download a file, simply copy it from the SkyDrive folder to any other folder on your computer.

You can also move files between your SkyDrive and your computer by opening a browser window, going to www.skydrive.com, and signing in to your Microsoft account from that webpage. If your SkyDrive is not the current page, click SkyDrive at the top. Figure A-8 shows a typical SkyDrive page. As in the SkyDrive app, each of the tiles in your SkyDrive window represents a folder. To open a folder, click the folder tile. Then you can use the Upload button at the top of the screen to open the Choose File to Upload dialog box, which is very similar to the Save As dialog box. To download a file, point to it to display a check box in the upper-right corner, and then click the check box to display additional commands at the top of the browser including the Download command.

| Figure A-8 | SkyDrive in Internet Explorer browser |

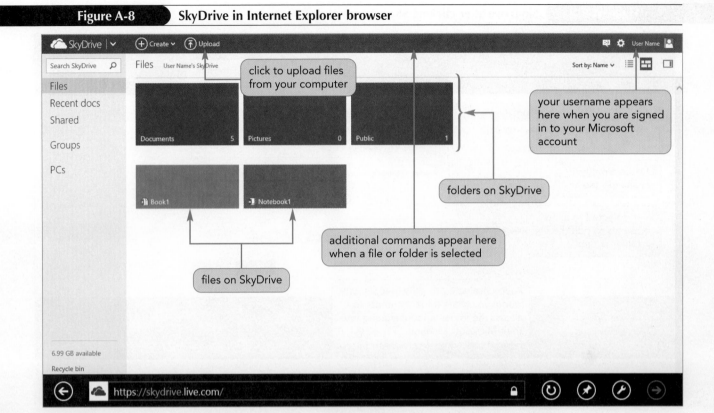

# Sharing Files and Folders on Your SkyDrive

One of the great advantages of working with SkyDrive is that you can share your files with others. Suppose, for example, that you want a colleague to review and edit a presentation you created in PowerPoint. You can upload the PowerPoint file to SkyDrive, and then give your colleague access to the file.

You can choose to share individual files or folders on your SkyDrive. Keep in mind that if you share folders, you are granting permission to whomever you are sharing access to all of the files in that folder.

To share files and folders on your SkyDrive, you need to access your SkyDrive from a browser. To share a single file, point to it to display a check box in the upper-right corner of the file tile, and then click the check box to select the file. When you do this, additional commands appear at the top of the browser screen or window. Click the Sharing command to display a screen similar to the one shown in Figure A-9. You can then send an email to someone, which will include a direct link to the item you are sharing. You can also choose to post the link to one of the social media sites listed, or you can copy the link and paste it anywhere you choose. Finally, you can choose whether the people with whom you are sharing can edit the files or only read them.

| Figure A-9 | SkyDrive after clicking Share command |

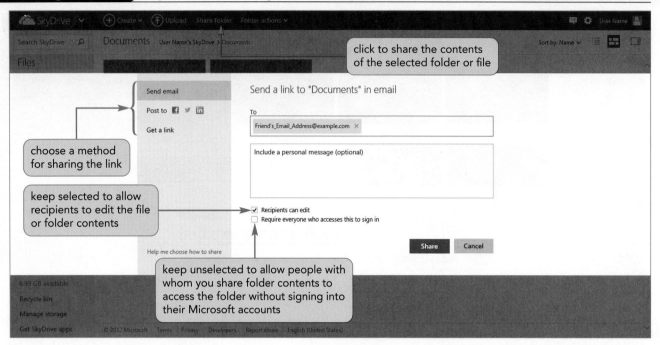

To share a folder, click the folder to open it, and then click the Sharing command at the top of the browser. A warning appears reminding you that you will be sharing all of the contents of the folder. You can choose to continue sharing using the same methods you use to share a file or cancel the sharing request. Note that files stored in the Public folder are viewable by anyone who has the link to them.

Because people with whom you share a file or folder click a direct link to access the file or folder, they do not need to sign in to their Microsoft accounts in order to view or download the files stored in it (unless you require it by selecting that option when you share the file or folder). However, if they want to use the Office Web Apps to edit those files, they do need to sign in to a Microsoft account.

## INSIGHT

### Viewing Photos and Videos on SkyDrive

You can use SkyDrive as a photo viewer and video player. When you click a photo or a video stored in a folder on SkyDrive, the screen changes to show the photo or the video much larger on the screen. At the bottom, thumbnails of the other photos and videos in the folder appear. You can click each thumbnail to display that photo or video on the screen, or move the pointer to display scroll arrows on the left or right edges of the screen, and then click these to scroll through the photos and videos in the folder.

## Using Office Web Apps

When you sign in to your SkyDrive using a browser, you also have access to Office Web Apps. The programs included in Office Web Apps are limited versions of Microsoft Word, Excel, PowerPoint, and **OneNote** (an electronic notebook program). You can use the Office Web Apps from any computer that is connected to the Internet, even if Microsoft Office is not installed on that computer. Although the interface for each Office Web App is similar to the interface of the full-featured program on your computer, only a limited number of commands are available for editing documents using the Office Web App. Figure A-10 shows the Word Web App.

| Figure A-10 | Word Web App |
| --- | --- |

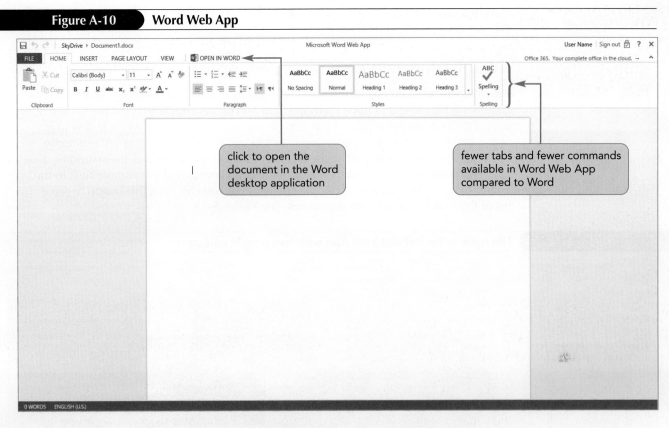

You cannot access Office Web Apps from the SkyDrive App. When you access SkyDrive from the browser, you can choose to open the file in the corresponding Web App, or the corresponding Office desktop application installed on your computer.

To create new files on SkyDrive using an Office Web App, sign in to your SkyDrive in a browser, and then click the Create button at the top of the browser. See Figure A-11. A menu opens allowing you to create a new folder, Word document, Excel workbook, PowerPoint presentation, OneNote notebook, or an Excel survey (an Excel template that allows you to create a survey and collect the responses in an Excel workbook). Select the Office Web App you want to use to open a new file in Edit mode in that Web App.

| Figure A-11 | Create button menu listing Office Web Apps |
| --- | --- |

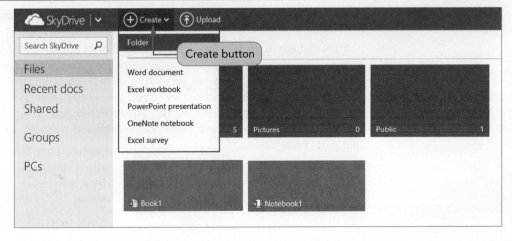

When you work in an Office Web app, you do not need to save your changes. All changes are saved automatically.

## Coauthoring with the Office Web Apps

The ability to work on files at the same time as others is called **coauthoring**. When you coauthor a file using an Office Web App, you and others with whom the file is shared open the file in the appropriate Web App on your own computers. As each new user opens the file, a message appears briefly telling you the Microsoft account username of the person who is now editing the file with you. On the left end of the status bar, a button appears indicating that the file is being coauthored, and the number next to the button indicates the number of people coauthoring. You can click this button to see a list of their Microsoft account usernames. See Figure A-12.

**Figure A-12**    **File open in PowerPoint Web App with two people editing it**

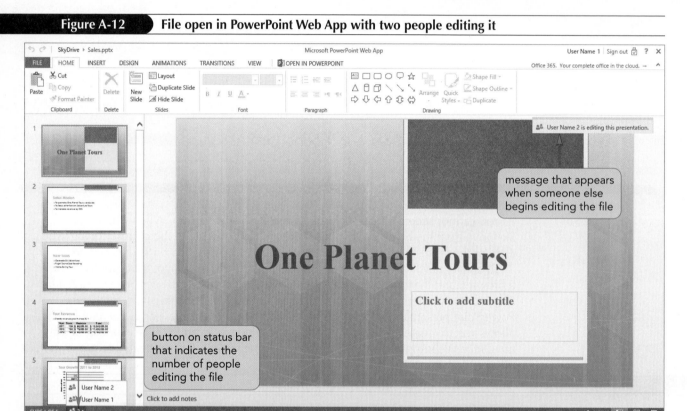

Files that are in the process of being coauthored update every few minutes. The speed of the update depends on the speed of your Internet connection and the size of the file. There can be a delay of up to 10 minutes if the connection is very slow or the files are very large. If two people try to edit the same part of the file at the same time, the edits of the person who started first are accepted and the other user sees a message telling them that his or her edits will not be accepted because another user was editing that part of the file first.

WINDOWS

## OBJECTIVES

**Session 1**
- Start Windows 7 and tour the desktop
- Explore the Start menu
- Run software programs, switch between them, and close them
- Identify and use the controls in windows and dialog boxes

**Session 2**
- Navigate your computer using Windows Explorer and the Computer window
- Change the view of the items in your computer
- Get help with Windows 7 tasks
- Turn off Windows

# Exploring the Basics of Microsoft Windows 7

## Investigating the Windows 7 Operating System

### Case | Back to Work

Back to Work is a nonprofit agency in Minneapolis, Minnesota, that helps people who want to develop skills for the contemporary workforce, such as retirees and parents who are returning to careers after raising a family. Back to Work creates customized plans for people preparing for full- or part-time work. Elena Varney, the director of the agency, coordinates training sessions on developing a wide range of computer skills.

Elena recently hired you to teach some introductory computer classes. Your first class on using the Microsoft Windows 7 operating system meets next week. To help you prepare for your class, Elena offers to walk you through the curriculum, from starting the computer and opening and closing programs to shutting down the computer. In this tutorial, you will start Windows 7 and practice some fundamental computer skills. Then, you'll learn how to navigate using the Computer window and Windows Explorer. Finally, you'll use the Windows 7 Help system and turn off Windows 7.

## STARTING DATA FILES

There are no starting Data Files needed for this tutorial.

# SESSION 1 VISUAL OVERVIEW

The **Recycle Bin** holds deleted items until you remove them permanently.

Recycle Bin

This graphic is part of a **theme**, a set of desktop backgrounds, window colors, sounds, and screen savers.

The **Start button** provides access to Windows 7 programs, documents, and information on the Internet.

Windows 7 provides three default **taskbar buttons**, which are buttons you click to open programs, such as Internet Explorer.

The **taskbar** is a strip that contains buttons to give you quick access to common tools and running programs.

An **icon** is a small picture that represents an object available on your computer.

# THE WINDOWS 7 DESKTOP

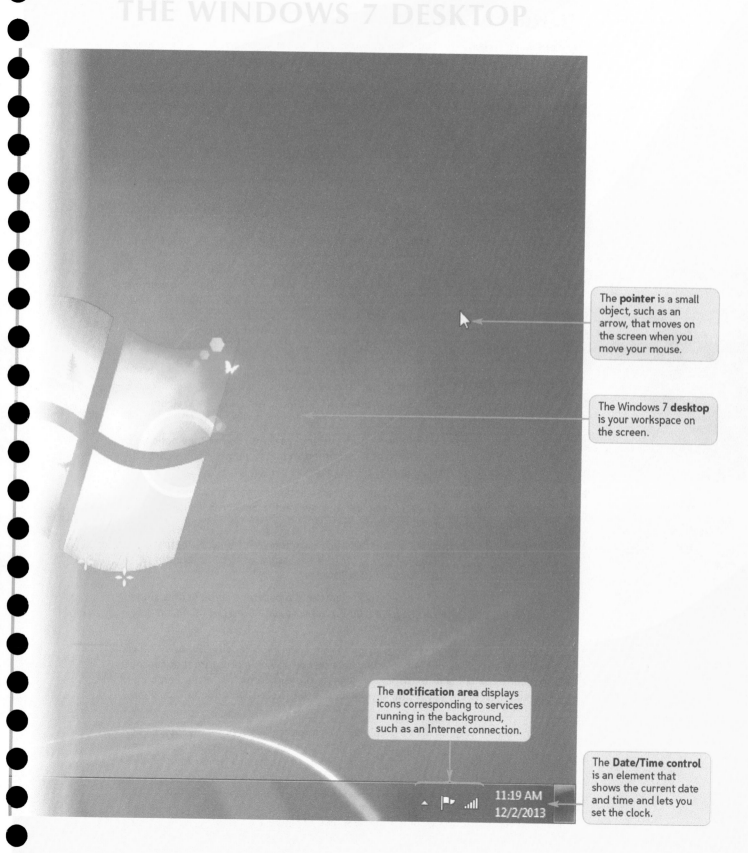

The **pointer** is a small object, such as an arrow, that moves on the screen when you move your mouse.

The Windows 7 **desktop** is your workspace on the screen.

The **notification area** displays icons corresponding to services running in the background, such as an Internet connection.

The **Date/Time control** is an element that shows the current date and time and lets you set the clock.

11:19 AM
12/2/2013

# Starting Windows 7

The **operating system** is software that manages and coordinates activities on the computer and helps the computer perform essential tasks, such as displaying information on the computer screen and saving data on disks. (The term *software* refers to the **programs**, or **applications**, that a computer uses to complete tasks.) Your computer uses the **Microsoft Windows 7** operating system—**Windows 7** for short. *Windows* is the name of the operating system, and *7* indicates the version you are using.

Much of the software created for the Windows 7 operating system shares the same look and works the same way. This similarity in design means that after you learn how to use one Windows 7 program, you are well on your way to understanding how to use others. Windows 7 allows you to use more than one program at a time, so you can easily switch between your word-processing program and your appointment book program, for example. It also makes it easy to access the **Internet**, a worldwide collection of computers connected to one another to enable communication.

Windows 7 starts automatically when you turn on your computer. After completing some necessary start-up tasks, Windows 7 displays a Welcome screen, which lists all the users for the computer. Before you start working with Windows 7, you might need to click your **user name** (a unique name that identifies you to Windows 7) and type a **password** (a confidential series of characters) before you can work with Windows 7. After you provide this information, the Windows 7 desktop appears.

To begin your review of Windows 7, Elena asks you to start Windows 7.

### To start Windows 7:

▶ **1.** Turn on your computer. After a moment, Windows 7 starts and the Welcome screen appears.

Trouble? If you are asked to select an operating system, do not take action. Windows 7 should start automatically after a designated number of seconds. If it does not, ask your instructor or technical support person for help.

▶ **2.** On the Welcome screen, click your user name and enter your password, if necessary. The Windows 7 desktop appears, as shown in the Session 1 Visual Overview. Your desktop might look different.

Trouble? If your user name does not appear on the Welcome screen, first try pressing the Ctrl+Alt+Del keys to enter it. If necessary, ask your instructor or technical support person for further assistance.

Trouble? If you need to enter a user name and a password, type your assigned user name, press the Tab key, type your password, and then click the Continue button or press the Enter key to continue.

Trouble? If a blank screen or an animated design replaces the Windows 7 desktop, your computer might be set to use a **screen saver**, a program that causes a monitor to go blank or to display an animated design after a specified amount of idle time. Press any key or move your mouse to restore the Windows 7 desktop.

The Windows 7 desktop uses a **graphical user interface** (**GUI**, pronounced *gooey*), which uses graphics to represent items stored on your computer, such as programs and files. A computer **file** is a collection of related information; typical types of files include text documents, spreadsheets, digital pictures, and songs. Your computer displays files as icons, which are pictures of familiar objects, such as file folders and documents. Windows 7 gets its name from the rectangular work areas, called windows, that appear on your screen as you work, such as those shown in Figure 1.

| Figure 1 | Two windows open on the desktop |

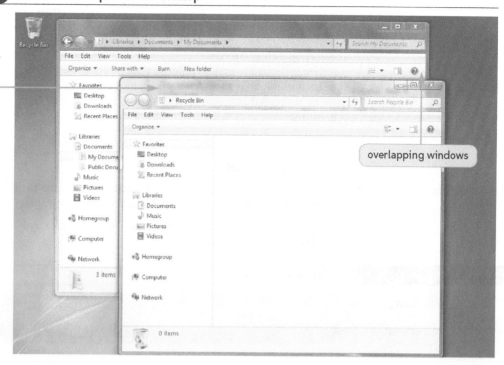

translucent color is characteristic of the Aero experience

overlapping windows

### Windows 7 and the Aero Desktop Experience

Windows 7 provides themes, which are sets of desktop backgrounds, window colors, sounds, and screen savers that allow you to personalize the Aero desktop experience. The themes that take advantage of Aero's rich three-dimensional appearance are called Aero themes. You can use an Aero theme only if your computer hardware and version of Windows 7 support it. (The Microsoft Web site at *www.microsoft.com* provides detailed information about the requirements for using Aero themes.) Otherwise, your computer is set by default to use a desktop theme called Windows 7 Basic, which provides most of the same elements as the enhanced experience, including windows and icons, but not the same graphic effects. In this tutorial, the figures show the Windows 7 Aero theme. If you are using Windows 7 Basic or a high contrast theme, the images on your screen will vary slightly from the figures and some features will not be available. (These are noted throughout the tutorial.)

## Touring the Windows 7 Desktop

In Windows terminology, the desktop is a workspace for projects and the tools that you need to manipulate your projects. When you first start a computer, it uses **default settings**, those Windows 7 has already set. The default desktop you see after you first install Windows 7, for example, displays a blue background with a four-color Windows logo. However, Microsoft designed Windows 7 so that you can easily change the appearance of the desktop. You can, for example, change images or add patterns and text to the desktop.

### Interacting with the Desktop

To interact with the objects on your desktop, you use a **pointing device**. The most common type is called a **mouse**, so this book uses that term. If you are using a different pointing device, such as a trackball or touchpad, substitute that device whenever you see the term *mouse*.

You use a pointing device to move the mouse pointer over objects on the desktop, or to **point** to them. The pointer is usually shaped like an arrow, although it changes shape depending on the pointer's location on the screen and the tasks you are performing. As you move the mouse on a surface, such as a mouse pad, the pointer on the screen moves in a corresponding direction.

When you point to certain objects, such as the icons on the taskbar, a **ScreenTip** appears near the object to tell you the name or purpose of that object.

Elena suggests that you acquaint students with the desktop by viewing a couple of ScreenTips.

### To view ScreenTips:

▶ **1.** Use the mouse to point to the **Start** button 🔵 on the taskbar. After a few seconds, you see a ScreenTip identifying the button, as shown in Figure 2.

> **Trouble?** If you don't see the ScreenTip, make sure you are holding the mouse still for a few seconds.

| Figure 2 | Viewing a ScreenTip |
|---|---|

ScreenTip
pointer

▶ **2.** Point to the time and date displayed at the right side of the taskbar. A ScreenTip showing today's date (or the date to which your computer's calendar is set) appears in a long format, such as Monday, December 2, 2013.

**Clicking** refers to pressing a mouse button and immediately releasing it. Clicking sends a signal to your computer that you want to perform an action on the object you click. In Windows 7, you perform most actions with the left mouse button. If you are told to click an object, position the pointer on that object and click the left mouse button, unless instructed otherwise.

When you click the Start button, the Start menu opens. A **menu** is a group or list of commands, and a **menu command** is text that you can click to complete tasks. If a right-pointing arrow follows a menu command, you can point to the command to open a **submenu**, which is a list of additional choices related to the command. The **Start menu** provides access to programs, documents, and much more.

### To open the Start menu:

▶ **1.** Point to the **Start** button 🔵 on the taskbar.

▶ **2.** Click the left mouse button. The Start menu opens. An arrow ▶ points to the All Programs command on the Start menu, indicating that you can view additional choices by navigating to a submenu.

▶ **3.** Click the **Start** button 🔵 on the taskbar to close the Start menu.

You need to select an item, or object, before you can work with it. To **select** an object in Windows 7, you usually point to and then click that object. Sometimes you can select menu commands simply by pointing to them. Windows 7 shows you which object is selected by highlighting it, usually by changing the object's color, putting a box around it, or making the object appear to be pushed in.

## To select a menu command:

▶ **1.** Click the **Start** button 🌑 on the taskbar.

▶ **2.** Point to **All Programs** on the Start menu. The All Programs command is high-lighted to indicate it is selected. After a short pause, the All Programs list opens. See Figure 3.

---

**Figure 3**   All Programs list

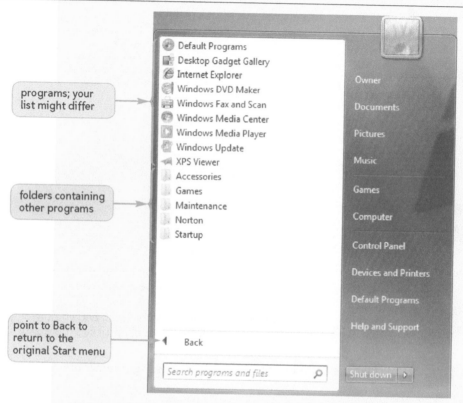

programs; your list might differ

folders containing other programs

point to Back to return to the original Start menu

▶ **3.** Click the **Start** button 🌑 on the taskbar to close the Start menu.

In addition to clicking an object to select it, you can double-click an object to open or start the item associated with it. For example, you can double-click a folder icon to open the folder and see its contents. (A **folder** is a container that helps to organize the contents of your computer, such as files and folders.) Or you can double-click a program icon to start the program. **Double-clicking** means clicking the left mouse button twice in quick succession.

Elena suggests that you have students practice double-clicking by opening the Recycle Bin. The Recycle Bin holds deleted items until you remove them permanently.

## To view the contents of the Recycle Bin:

▶ **1.** Click the **desktop** to clear any selections, and then point to the **Recycle Bin** icon on the desktop. A ScreenTip appears that describes the Recycle Bin.

▶ **2.** Click the left mouse button twice quickly to double-click the **Recycle Bin** icon. The Recycle Bin window opens, as shown in Figure 4.

| Figure 4 | Contents of the Recycle Bin |

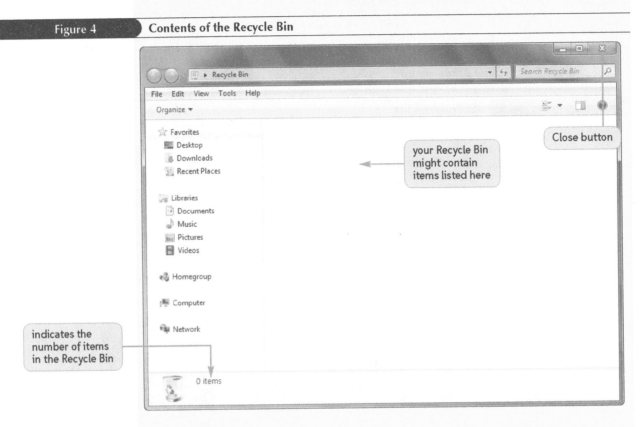

**Trouble?** If the Recycle Bin window does not open, and you see only the Recycle Bin name highlighted below the icon, you double-clicked too slowly. Double-click the icon again more quickly.

▶ 3. Click the **Close** button [ X ] in the upper-right corner of the Recycle Bin window.

You'll learn more about opening and closing windows later in this session.

Your mouse has more than one button. In addition to the left button, the mouse has a right button that you can use to perform certain actions in Windows 7. However, the term *clicking* continues to refer to the left button; clicking an object with the right button is called **right-clicking**.

In Windows 7, right-clicking selects an object and opens its **shortcut menu**, which lists actions you can take with that object. You can right-click practically any object—the Start button, a desktop icon, the taskbar, and even the desktop itself—to view commands associated with that object. Elena reminds you that you clicked the Start button with the left mouse button to open the Start menu. Now you can right-click the Start button to open the shortcut menu for the Start button.

### To right-click an object:

▶ 1. Position the pointer over the **Start** button 🌐 on the taskbar.

▶ 2. Right-click the **Start** button 🌐 to open its shortcut menu. This menu offers a list of actions you can take with the Start button. See Figure 5.

**Figure 5**    **Start button shortcut menu**

right-click the
Start button

Properties
Open Windows Explorer

shortcut menu; yours
might differ

2:35 PM
12/2/2013

**Trouble?** If the shortcut menu does not open and you are using a trackball or a mouse with a wheel, make sure you click the button on the far right, not the one in the middle.

**Trouble?** If your menu looks slightly different from the one in Figure 5, it is still the correct Start button shortcut menu. Its commands often vary by computer.

▶ **3.** Press the **Esc** key to close the shortcut menu.

After opening the Start menu and its shortcut menu, you're ready to explore its contents.

# Exploring the Start Menu

Recall that the Start menu is the central point for accessing programs, documents, and other resources on your computer. The Start menu is organized into two **panes**, which are separate areas of a menu or window. Each pane lists items you can point to or click. See Figure 6.

**Figure 6**    **Start menu**

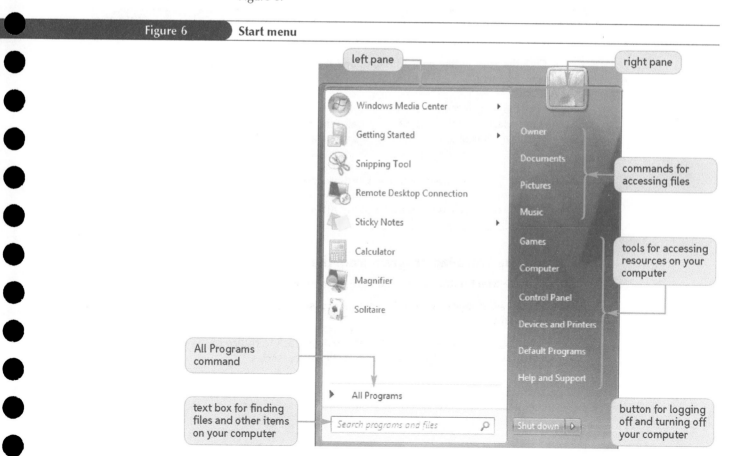

left pane

right pane

Windows Media Center ▶

Getting Started ▶

Snipping Tool

Remote Desktop Connection

Sticky Notes ▶

Calculator

Magnifier

Solitaire

Owner

Documents

Pictures

Music

Games

Computer

Control Panel

Devices and Printers

Default Programs

Help and Support

commands for
accessing files

tools for accessing
resources on your
computer

All Programs
command

All Programs ▶

text box for finding
files and other items
on your computer

Search programs and files

Shut down ▷

button for logging
off and turning off
your computer

The left pane organizes programs for easy access. When you first install Windows 7, the left pane contains a short list of programs on your computer. After you use a program, Windows 7 adds it to this list so you can quickly find it the next time you want to use it. The Start menu can list only a certain number of programs—after that, the programs you have not opened recently are replaced by the programs you used last.

Near the bottom of the left pane is the All Programs command, which you have already used to display the All Programs list. The All Programs list provides access to the programs currently installed on your computer. You'll use the All Programs list shortly to start a program.

The **Search programs and files box** helps you quickly find anything stored on your computer, including programs, documents, pictures, music, videos, Web pages, and e-mail messages. When you want to use the Search programs and files box, you open the Start menu and type one or more words related to what you want to find. For example, if you want to find and play the Happy Birthday song stored on your computer, you could type *birthday* in the Search programs and files box. Windows 7 searches your computer for that song and displays it and any other search results in the Start menu, where you can click the song to play it.

From the right pane of the Start menu, you can access common locations and tools on your computer. For example, the **Computer window** is a tool that you use to view, organize, and access the programs, files, and drives on your computer.

From the bottom section of the right pane, you can open windows that help you effectively work with Windows 7, including the **Control Panel**, which contains specialized tools that help you change the way Windows 7 looks and behaves, and **Help and Support**, which provides articles, video demonstrations, and steps for performing tasks in Windows 7. You also turn off your computer from the Start menu.

## REFERENCE

### Starting a Program

- Click the Start button on the taskbar, and then click the name of the program you want to start.

*or*

- Click the Start button on the taskbar, and then point to All Programs.
- If necessary, click the folder that contains the program you want to start.
- Click the name of the program you want to start.

Windows 7 includes an easy-to-use word-processing program called WordPad, which you can use to write a letter or report. To start WordPad, you open the Start menu and then navigate to the Accessories folder in the All Programs list.

### To start the WordPad program from the Start menu:

▶ **1.** Click the **Start** button ⊙ on the taskbar to open the Start menu.

▶ **2.** Point to **All Programs**, and then click **Accessories**. The Accessories folder opens. See Figure 7.

**Trouble?** If a different folder opens, point to Back to return to the initial Start menu, point to All Programs, and then click Accessories.

| Figure 7 | Accessories folder open on the Start menu |
|---|---|

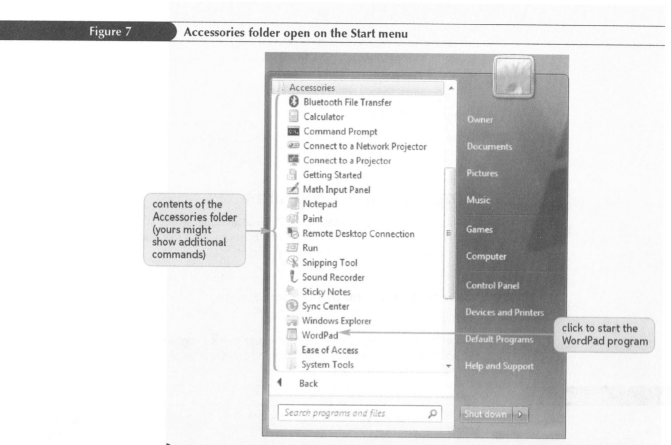

contents of the Accessories folder (yours might show additional commands)

click to start the WordPad program

▶ **3.** Click **WordPad**. The WordPad program window opens, as shown in Figure 8.

| Figure 8 | WordPad program window |
|---|---|

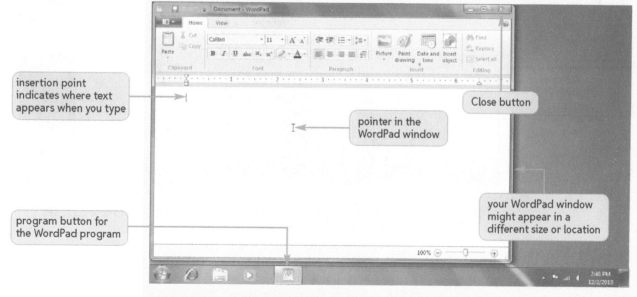

insertion point indicates where text appears when you type

pointer in the WordPad window

Close button

your WordPad window might appear in a different size or location

program button for the WordPad program

**Trouble?** If the WordPad program window fills the entire screen, continue with the next step. You will learn how to manipulate windows shortly.

When a program is started, it is said to be open or running. A **program button** appears on the taskbar for each open program. You can click a program button on the taskbar to switch between open programs. When you are finished using a program, you can click the Close button located in the upper-right corner of the program window to **exit**, or close, that program.

### To exit the WordPad program:

▶ **1.** Click the **Close** button ❌ on the WordPad title bar. The WordPad program closes and you return to the desktop.

## Running Multiple Programs

One of the most useful features of Windows 7 is **multitasking**, which allows you to work on more than one task at a time. To demonstrate, Elena suggests that you start WordPad and leave it running while you start the Paint program.

### To run WordPad and Paint at the same time:

▶ **1.** Start WordPad again.

▶ **2.** Click the **Start** button 🌐 on the taskbar, point to **All Programs**, click **Accessories**, and then click **Paint**. The Paint program window opens, as shown in Figure 9. Now two programs are running at the same time.

| Figure 9 | Two programs open |
| --- | --- |

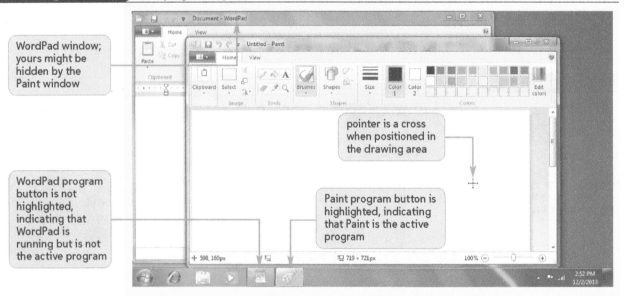

WordPad window; yours might be hidden by the Paint window

pointer is a cross when positioned in the drawing area

WordPad program button is not highlighted, indicating that WordPad is running but is not the active program

Paint program button is highlighted, indicating that Paint is the active program

**Trouble?** If the Paint program fills the entire screen, continue with the next set of steps. You will learn how to manipulate windows shortly.

**TIP**

When more than one window is open, the active program appears on top of all other open windows.

The **active program** is the one you are working with—Windows 7 applies your next keystroke or command to the active program. Paint is the active program because it is the one you are currently using. The WordPad program button is still on the taskbar, indicating that WordPad is still running even if you can't see its program window.

## Switching Between Programs

Because only one program is active at a time, you need to switch between programs if you want to work in one or the other. The easiest way to switch between programs is to use the program buttons on the taskbar.

### To switch between WordPad and Paint:

▶ **1.** Click the **WordPad** program button 🔲 on the taskbar. The WordPad program window moves to the front, and the WordPad program button appears highlighted, indicating that WordPad is the active program.

▶ **2.** Click the **Paint** program button 🔲 on the taskbar to switch to the Paint program. The Paint program is again the active program.

**TIP**

The Windows key displays the Windows logo, which is a curved, four-part window, and is usually located in the lower-left part of the keyboard.

You can also bypass the taskbar and use keyboard shortcuts to switch from one open window to another. A **keyboard shortcut** is a key or combination of keys that perform a command. If you are using an Aero theme, you can press and hold the Windows key and then press the Tab key to activate **Aero Flip 3D** (often shortened to *Flip 3D*), which displays all your open windows in a three-dimensional stack so you can see the windows from the side, the way you view the spine of a book.

### To switch between program windows using Aero Flip 3D:

▶ **1.** Press and hold the **Windows** key and then press the **Tab** key. Windows arranges the Paint and WordPad windows and the desktop in a stack, with the Paint window at the top of the stack. See Figure 10.

**Figure 10**    Aero Flip 3D

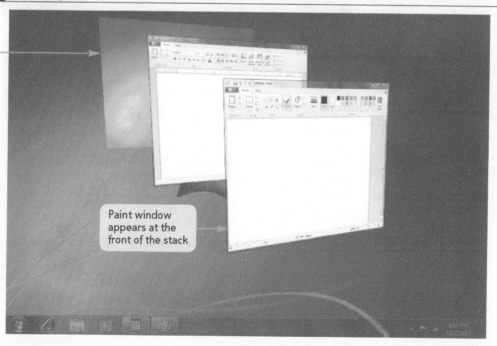

two windows and the desktop image are flipped and stacked

Paint window appears at the front of the stack

> **Trouble?** If a task switcher window displaying generic program icons opens when you press the Windows+Tab keys, you are not using an Aero theme. Click outside the task switcher window and then read, but do not perform, the remaining steps.
>
> ▸ **2.** Press the **Tab** key to flip the WordPad window to the front of the stack. The Paint window moves to the back of the stack.
>
> ▸ **3.** Press the **Tab** key to flip the desktop to the front of the stack, and then press the **Tab** key again to flip the Paint window to the front of the stack.
>
> ▸ **4.** Release the **Windows** key to turn off Flip 3D and make Paint the active program.

You can use another Aero keyboard shortcut called Windows Flip to switch from one window to another. When you hold down the Alt key and press the Tab key once, Windows Flip displays thumbnails (miniature versions) of your open windows. See Figure 11. The thumbnails display the exact contents of the open windows instead of generic icons so you can easily identify the windows. While continuing to hold down the Alt key, you can press the Tab key to select the thumbnail for the program you want; you release the Alt key to close Windows Flip.

**Figure 11**  **Using the task switcher window**

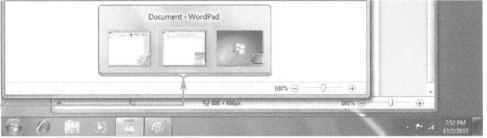

thumbnails of the Paint window, WordPad window, and desktop

In addition to using the taskbar to switch between open programs, you can close programs from the taskbar.

## Closing Programs from the Taskbar

You should always close a program when you are finished using it. Each program uses computer resources, such as memory, so Windows 7 works more efficiently when only the programs you need are open. Elena reminds you that you've already closed an open program using the Close button on the title bar of the program window. You can also close a program, whether active or inactive, by using the shortcut menu associated with the program button on the taskbar.

### To close WordPad and Paint using the program button shortcut menus:

▸ **1.** Right-click the **Paint** program button  on the taskbar. The shortcut menu for the Paint program button opens. See Figure 12.

| Figure 12 | Program button shortcut menu |
|---|---|

shortcut menu opens when you right-click a program button

click to close the selected program

2. Click **Close window** on the shortcut menu. The Paint program closes and its program button no longer appears on the taskbar.

   **Trouble?** If a message appears asking if you want to save changes, click the Don't Save button.

3. Right-click the **WordPad** program button  on the taskbar, and then click **Close window** on the shortcut menu. The WordPad program closes, and its program button no longer appears on the taskbar.

PROSKILLS

*Problem Solving: Working Efficiently on the Desktop*

When you work with Windows and its programs, especially on a complicated project, you often start and run more than one program and open many windows. This can lead to two common problems that affect your productivity: having too many windows open can make it difficult to find the information you need, and running too many programs can slow the performance of your computer.

Deciding how many windows to open and how to arrange them on the desktop depends on your personal preference. Some people like to maximize all their open windows and use the taskbar to switch from one window to another. Other people like to size and arrange each window so it is visible on the desktop, even if that means having some small and overlapping windows. Keep in mind that a clean and organized desktop increases your productivity. Find an arrangement that works for you without cluttering your desktop.

If you find that your computer responds to your keystrokes and mouse actions more slowly than usual, you might have too many programs running at the same time. Closing the programs you are not using frees up system resources, which makes your computer faster and more responsive and can solve performance problems.

## Using Windows and Dialog Boxes

When you run a program in Windows 7, the program appears in a **window**, a rectangular area of the screen that contains a program, text, or other data. A window also contains **controls**, which are graphical or textual objects you use to manipulate the window or use the program. Figure 13 describes the controls you see in most windows.

Figure 13    Window controls

| Control | Description |
| --- | --- |
| Program menu button | Lists commands for common program tasks, such as creating, opening, and saving documents |
| Quick Access Toolbar | Contains buttons for performing tasks, such as saving a document |
| Ribbon | Provides access to the main set of commands organized by task into tabs and groups |
| Sizing button | Lets you enlarge, shrink, or close a window |
| Status bar | Displays information or messages about the task you are performing |
| Tab | Organizes commands on the Ribbon related to similar tasks |
| Title bar | Contains the window title and basic window control buttons |
| Window title | Identifies the program and document contained in the window |
| Workspace | Includes the part of the window where you manipulate your work—enter text, draw pictures, and set up calculations, for example |
| Zoom controls | Magnify or shrink the content displayed in the workspace |

## To look at the window controls in WordPad:

▶ **1.** Start WordPad. On your screen, identify the controls that are labeled in Figure 14.

Figure 14    WordPad window controls

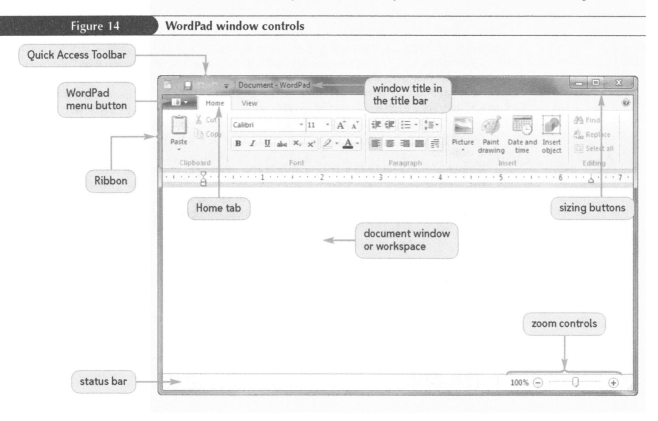

After you open a window, you can manipulate it by changing its size and position.

## Manipulating Windows

In most windows, three buttons appear on the right side of the title bar. The first button is the Minimize button, which hides a window so that only its program button is visible on the taskbar, which means the program is still running. Depending on the status of the window, the middle button either maximizes the window or restores it to a predefined size. You are already familiar with the last button—the Close button.

**To minimize the WordPad window:**

▶ 1. Click the **Minimize** button ⊟ on the WordPad title bar. The WordPad window shrinks so that only the WordPad program button on the taskbar is visible.

  **Trouble?** If the WordPad program window closed, you accidentally clicked the Close button ✕. Use the Start button ⊕ to start WordPad again, and then repeat Step 1. If you accidentally clicked the Maximize button ⬜ or the Restore Down button ⬜, repeat Step 1.

You can redisplay a minimized window by clicking the program's button on the taskbar. When you redisplay a window, it becomes the active window.

**To redisplay the WordPad window:**

▶ 1. Click the **WordPad** program button on the taskbar. The WordPad window is restored to its previous size. You can minimize it by clicking its taskbar button again.

▶ 2. Click the **WordPad** program button on the taskbar again to minimize the window.

▶ 3. Click the **WordPad** program button once more to redisplay the window.

The Maximize button enlarges a window so that it fills the entire screen. Use maximized windows when you need to see more of the program and your data.

**To maximize the WordPad window:**

▶ 1. Click the **Maximize** button ⬜ on the WordPad title bar.

  **Trouble?** If the window is already maximized, it fills the entire screen, and the Maximize button ⬜ does not appear. Instead, you see the Restore Down button ⬜. Skip this step.

The Restore Down button reduces the window so that it is smaller than the entire screen. This feature is useful if you want to see more than one window at a time, move the window to another location on the screen, or change the dimensions of the window.

**To restore a window:**

▶ 1. Click the **Restore Down** button ⬜ on the WordPad title bar. After a window is restored, the Restore Down button ⬜ changes to the Maximize button ⬜.

You can use the mouse to move a window to a new position on the screen. When you click an object and then press and hold down the mouse button while moving the mouse, you are **dragging** the object. If you want to move a window, you drag the window by its title bar. You cannot move a maximized window.

### To drag the restored WordPad window to a new location:

▶ **1.** Position the mouse pointer on the WordPad title bar.

▶ **2.** Press and hold down the left mouse button, and then move the mouse up or down a little to drag the window. The window moves as you move the mouse.

▶ **3.** Position the window anywhere on the desktop, and then release the left mouse button. The WordPad window stays in the new location.

▶ **4.** Drag the WordPad window to the upper-left corner of the desktop.

**Trouble?** If the WordPad window is maximized when you drag it near the upper part of the desktop, click the Restore Down button ⬜ before performing the next steps.

You can also use the mouse to change the size of a window. When you point to an edge or corner of a window, the pointer changes to a double-headed arrow, similar to ⬉. Use this resize pointer to drag an edge or corner of the window and change the size of the window.

## Using the Ribbon

Many Windows 7 programs use a Ribbon to organize the program's features and commands. The **Ribbon** is located at the top of the program window, immediately below the title bar, and is organized into tabs. Each **tab** contains commands that perform a variety of related tasks. For example, the Home tab has commands for tasks you perform frequently, such as changing the appearance of a document. You use the commands on the View tab to change your view of the WordPad window.

To select a command and perform an action, you use a button or other type of control on the Ribbon. Controls for similar types of actions are organized on a tab in **groups**. For example, to enter bold text in a WordPad document, you click the Bold button in the Font group on the Home tab. Figure 15 shows examples of Ribbon controls.

**Figure 15**    **Examples of Ribbon controls**

Figure 16 describes the Ribbon controls.

| Figure 16 | Types of controls on the Ribbon |
| --- | --- |

| Control | How to Use | Example |
| --- | --- | --- |
| Button with arrow | Click the button to display a menu of related commands. | |
| Check box | Click to insert a check mark and select the option, or click to remove the check mark and deselect the option. | √ Ruler |
| Text box | Click the text box and type an entry, or click the arrow button to select an item from the list. | Calibri |
| Toggle button | Click the button to turn on or apply a setting, and then click the button again to turn off the setting. When a toggle button is turned on, it is highlighted. | B  B |
| Two-part button with arrow | If an arrow is displayed on a separate part of the button, click the arrow to display a menu of commands. Click the button itself to apply the current selection. | |

Most Windows 7 programs, including WordPad and Paint, include a **Quick Access Toolbar**, which is a row of buttons on the title bar that let you perform common tasks such as saving a file and undoing an action. You can display the name of each button on the Quick Access Toolbar in a ScreenTip by pointing to the button, just as you do for buttons on the Ribbon. You also can select a button on the Quick Access Toolbar or the Ribbon by clicking the button, which performs the associated command.

### To use buttons on the WordPad Ribbon and Quick Access Toolbar:

1. Click the **Bold** button B in the Font group on the Home tab of the WordPad Ribbon. Now any text you type will appear as bold text.

2. Type your full name in the WordPad window.

3. Click the **Undo** button on the Quick Access Toolbar. WordPad reverses your last action by removing your name from the WordPad window.

## Using List Boxes

As you might guess from the name, a **list box** displays a list of available choices from which you can select one item. For example, to select a font size in WordPad, you use the Font size list box on the Home tab. A list box is helpful because it only includes options that are appropriate for your current task, such as selecting a font size. Some lists might not include every possible option, so you can type the option you want to select. In most cases, the right side of the list box includes an arrow. You can click the list box arrow to view all the options and then select one or type appropriate text.

### To select a new font size in the Font size button list box:

▶ **1.** In the Font group on the Home tab, click the **Font size button arrow** 11 ⌄.

▶ **2.** Click **18**. The Font size list closes, and the font size you selected appears in the list box.

▶ **3.** Type your full name to test the new font size, and then press the **Enter** key.

▶ **4.** Click the **Font size button arrow** 11 ⌄ on the Home tab again, and then click **12**.

▶ **5.** Type your full name again to test this type size. Your name appears in 12-point font.

List boxes sometimes include scroll bars, which appear when the list of available options is too long or wide to fit in the list box. A scroll bar includes arrow buttons and a scroll box that you drag to scroll the list.

## Working with Dialog Boxes

A **dialog box** is a special kind of window in which you enter or choose settings for how you want to perform a task. Dialog boxes can include tabs, option buttons, check boxes, and other controls to collect information about how you want to perform a task.

Besides using buttons on Ribbon tabs, you can also open dialog boxes by selecting a command on the WordPad button menu. You can use the WordPad menu button  to open the Print dialog box, which contains many typical dialog box controls.

### To open the Print dialog box:

▶ **1.** Click the **WordPad menu** button ▣ ⌄ in the upper-left corner of the WordPad window to display a list of commands.

▶ **2.** Click **Print** to open the Print dialog box. See Figure 18.

| Figure 17 | Print dialog box |

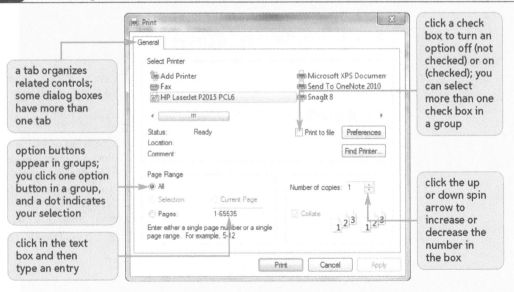

a tab organizes related controls; some dialog boxes have more than one tab

option buttons appear in groups; you click one option button in a group, and a dot indicates your selection

click in the text box and then type an entry

click a check box to turn an option off (not checked) or on (checked); you can select more than one check box in a group

click the up or down spin arrow to increase or decrease the number in the box

Now that you're finished exploring dialog boxes, you can exit WordPad.

**To exit WordPad:**

▶ 1. Click the **Cancel** button to close the Print dialog box.

▶ 2. Click the **WordPad menu** button ▣▾ , and then click **Exit**. A WordPad dialog box opens asking if you want to save the document.

▶ 3. Click the **Don't Save** button to close WordPad without saving the document.

In this session, you started Windows 7 and toured the desktop, learning how to interact with the items on the desktop and on the Start menu. You also started two Windows programs, manipulated windows, and learned how to select options from a Ribbon, toolbar, menu, and dialog box.

**REVIEW**

*Session 1 Quick Check*

1. What does the operating system do for your computer?
2. A(n) _____ is a confidential series of characters.
3. True or False. Your computer represents files with icons, which are pictures of familiar objects, such as file folders and documents.
4. What happens when you point to the Start button with a mouse? What happens when you click the Start button with the left mouse button?
5. In Windows 7, right-clicking selects an object and opens its _____.
6. When more than one window is open, the _____ appears on top of all other open windows.
7. Why should you close each program when you are finished using it?

# SESSION 2 VISUAL OVERVIEW

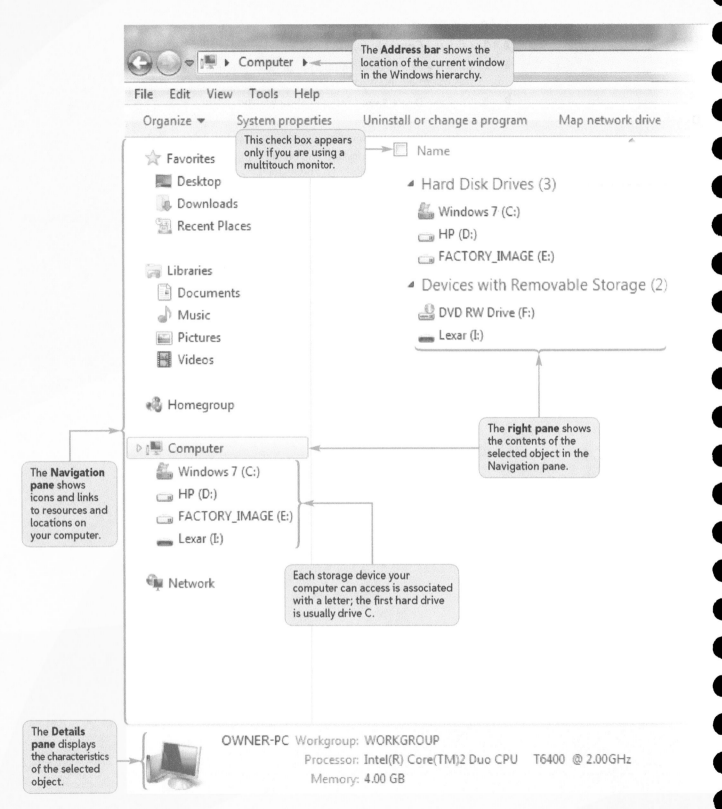

The **Address bar** shows the location of the current window in the Windows hierarchy.

File    Edit    View    Tools    Help

Organize ▾    System properties    Uninstall or change a program    Map network drive

☆ Favorites
   ■ Desktop
   ⬇ Downloads
   ▤ Recent Places

This check box appears only if you are using a multitouch monitor.

▢ Name

📚 Libraries
   ▤ Documents
   ♪ Music
   ▦ Pictures
   ▦ Videos

◢ Hard Disk Drives (3)
   💾 Windows 7 (C:)
   🖴 HP (D:)
   🖴 FACTORY_IMAGE (E:)

◢ Devices with Removable Storage (2)
   💿 DVD RW Drive (F:)
   ▭ Lexar (I:)

🏠 Homegroup

▷ 💻 Computer
   💾 Windows 7 (C:)
   🖴 HP (D:)
   🖴 FACTORY_IMAGE (E:)
   ▭ Lexar (I:)

🖥 Network

The **right pane** shows the contents of the selected object in the Navigation pane.

The **Navigation pane** shows icons and links to resources and locations on your computer.

Each storage device your computer can access is associated with a letter; the first hard drive is usually drive C.

The **Details pane** displays the characteristics of the selected object.

OWNER-PC  Workgroup: WORKGROUP
Processor: Intel(R) Core(TM)2 Duo CPU    T6400  @ 2.00GHz
Memory: 4.00 GB

# THE COMPUTER WINDOW

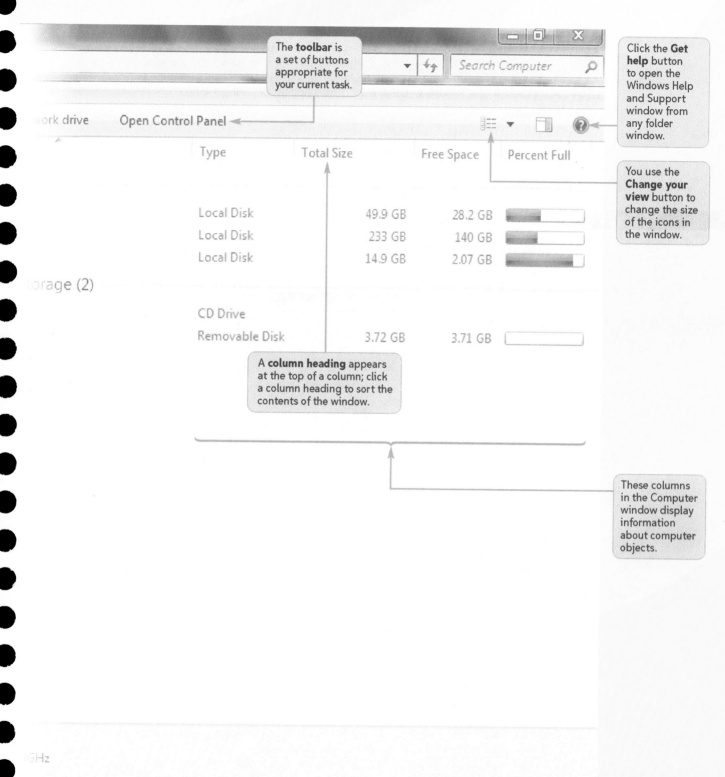

The **toolbar** is a set of buttons appropriate for your current task.

Click the **Get help** button to open the Windows Help and Support window from any folder window.

You use the **Change your view** button to change the size of the icons in the window.

work drive    Open Control Panel

| | Type | Total Size | Free Space | Percent Full |
|---|---|---|---|---|
| | Local Disk | 49.9 GB | 28.2 GB | |
| | Local Disk | 233 GB | 140 GB | |
| | Local Disk | 14.9 GB | 2.07 GB | |
| orage (2) | | | | |
| | CD Drive | | | |
| | Removable Disk | 3.72 GB | 3.71 GB | |

A **column heading** appears at the top of a column; click a column heading to sort the contents of the window.

These columns in the Computer window display information about computer objects.

GHz

# Exploring Your Computer

To discover the contents and resources on your computer, you explore, or navigate, it. **Navigating,** in this context, means to move from one location to another on your computer, such as from one window to another. Windows 7 provides two ways to navigate, view, and work with the contents and resources on your computer—the Computer window (shown in the Session 2 Visual Overview) and Windows Explorer. Both are examples of **folder windows,** which display the contents of your computer.

## Navigating with the Computer Window

The Computer window represents your computer, its storage devices, and other objects. The icons for each of these objects appear in the right pane of the Computer window. See Figure 18.

| Figure 18 | Relationship between your computer and the Computer window |

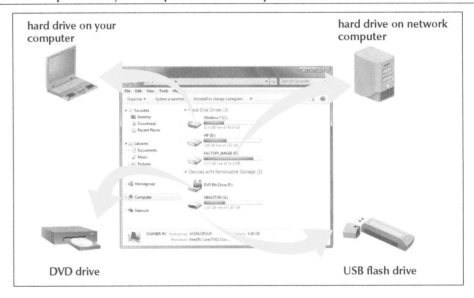

hard drive on your computer

hard drive on network computer

DVD drive

USB flash drive

The Computer window also has a left pane, called the Navigation pane, which shows icons and links to other resources your computer can access. This window also contains a toolbar with buttons that let you perform common tasks, and a Details pane that displays the characteristics of an object you select in the Computer window.

Each storage device you can access on your computer is associated with a letter. The first hard drive is usually drive C (if you add other hard drives, they are usually designated D, E, and so on). If you have a CD or DVD drive or a USB flash drive plugged in to a USB port, it usually has the next letter in the alphabetic sequence. If you can access hard drives on other computers in a network, those drives sometimes (although not always) have letters associated with them as well. In the example shown in Figure 18, the network drive has the drive letter E.

You can use any folder window, including the Computer window, to explore your computer and organize your files. In this session, you explore the contents of your hard disk, which is assumed to be drive C. If you use a different drive on your computer, such as drive E, substitute its letter for C throughout this session.

Elena suggests you explore the Music library, which is a convenient location for storing your music files. (A **library** is a central place to view and organize files and folders stored anywhere that your computer can access, such as those on your hard disk, removable drives, and network.) Even if you store some music files on your hard disk and others on an external drive, such as a digital music player attached to your computer, they are all displayed in the Music library.

The computer Elena provides for you has a multitouch monitor, which lets you interact with objects on the screen using your finger instead of a mouse. If you have a multitouch monitor, a feature in Windows 7 called Windows Touch lets you perform tasks such as selecting icons, opening folders, and starting programs using your finger as a pointing device. To make it easier to select objects and identify which ones are selected, Windows Touch displays a check box next to objects such as files and icons on the desktop and in folder windows. For example, you could touch the check box shown in Figure 19 to select all the folders in the Music library. If you are not using a multitouch monitor, these check boxes do not appear in your folder windows or on the desktop.

### To explore the contents of your computer using the Computer window:

▶ 1. If you took a break after the previous session, make sure that your computer is on and Windows 7 is running.

▶ 2. Click the **Start** button 🔵 on the taskbar, and then click **Computer** in the right pane of the Start menu. The Computer window opens.

▶ 3. In the Navigation pane, click the **Music** link. The right pane displays the contents of the Music library. See Figure 19.

**Figure 19**     Contents of the Music library

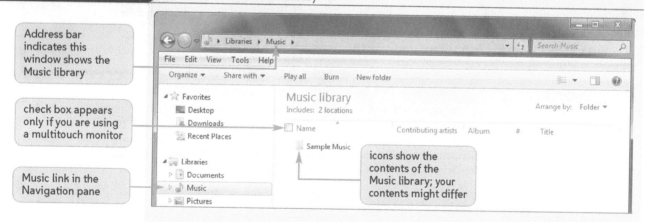

Address bar indicates this window shows the Music library

check box appears only if you are using a multitouch monitor

Music link in the Navigation pane

icons show the contents of the Music library; your contents might differ

**TIP**

The Address bar displays your current location as a series of links separated by arrows. Click a folder name in the Address bar to display the contents of that folder.

**Trouble?** If your window looks different from Figure 19, you can still perform the rest of the steps. For example, your window might contain a different number of folders and files.

▶ 4. In the right pane, double-click the **Sample Music** icon to open the Sample Music folder. The right pane of the window shows the contents of the folder you double-clicked. You can learn more about the contents of a folder by selecting one or more of its files.

▶ 5. Click the first file listed in the Sample Music folder to select it. See Figure 20. (Your files might appear in a different order.)

| Figure 20 | Viewing files in a folder window |
|---|---|

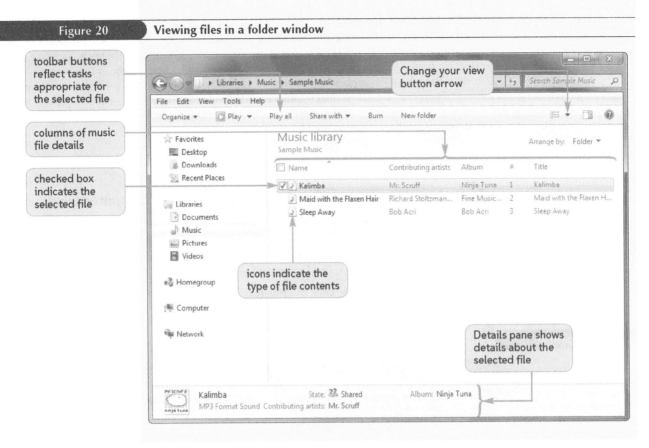

toolbar buttons reflect tasks appropriate for the selected file

columns of music file details

checked box indicates the selected file

Change your view button arrow

icons indicate the type of file contents

Details pane shows details about the selected file

As you open folders and navigate with the Computer window, the contents of the toolbar change so that they are appropriate for your current task. In Figure 20, the toolbar lists actions to take with the selected music file, such as Play all and Burn.

Elena mentions that you can change the appearance of folder windows to suit your preferences, which you'll do next.

## Changing the View

Windows 7 provides at least eight ways to view the contents of a folder—Extra Large Icons, Large Icons, Medium Icons, Small Icons, List, Details, Tiles, and Content. The default view is Details view, which displays a small icon and lists details about each file. The icon provides a visual cue about the file type. Although only Details view lists all file details, such as the contributing artists and album title for music files, you can see these details in any other view by pointing to an icon to display a ScreenTip.

To practice switching from one view to another, Elena says you can display the contents of the Sample Music folder in Tiles view. To do so, you'll use the Change your view button on the toolbar.

### To view files in Tiles view:

▶ 1. In the Sample Music folder window, click the **Change your view button arrow** ▦ ▾ on the toolbar. See Figure 21.

   **Trouble?** If you click the Change your view button ▦ instead of the arrow, you cycle through the views. Click the Change your view button arrow ▦ ▾, and then continue with Step 2.

**Figure 21**    Preparing to change views

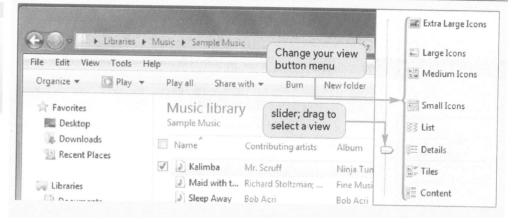

2. Click **Tiles**. The window shows the same files, but with larger icons than in Details view.

3. Click the **Change your view button arrow** on the toolbar, and then click Details to return to **Details** view.

No matter which view you use, you can sort the file list by filename or another detail, such as size, type, or date. If you're viewing music files, you can sort by details such as contributing artists or album title; and if you're viewing picture files, you can sort by details such as date taken or size. Sorting helps you find a particular file in a long file listing. For example, suppose you want to listen to a song on a certain album, but you can't remember the song title. You can sort the music file list in alphabetic order by album to find the song you want.

### To sort the music file list by album:

1. Click the **Album** button at the top of the list of files. The up-pointing arrow in the upper-middle part of the Album button indicates that the files are sorted in ascending (A–Z) alphabetic order by album name.

2. Click the **Album** button again. The down-pointing arrow on the Album button indicates that the sort order is reversed, with the albums listed in descending (Z–A) alphabetic order.

3. Click the **Close** button ❌ to close the Sample Music window.

Now Elena says you can compare the Computer window to Windows Explorer, another navigation tool.

## Navigating with Windows Explorer

Like the Computer window, Windows Explorer also lets you easily navigate the resources on your computer. All of the techniques you use with the Computer window apply to Windows Explorer—and vice versa. Both let you display and work with files and folders. The only difference is the initial view each tool provides. By default, when you open the Computer window, it shows the drives and devices on your computer. When you start Windows Explorer, it displays the Libraries folder, which lets you access resources such as documents, music, pictures, and videos.

Elena mentions that because people use Windows Explorer often, Windows 7 provides its button on the taskbar for easy access.

## To start Windows Explorer:

▶ **1.** Click the **Windows Explorer** button 📁 on the taskbar. The Windows Explorer window opens, displaying the contents of the Libraries folder, as shown in Figure 22.

| Figure 22 | Windows Explorer window |
|---|---|

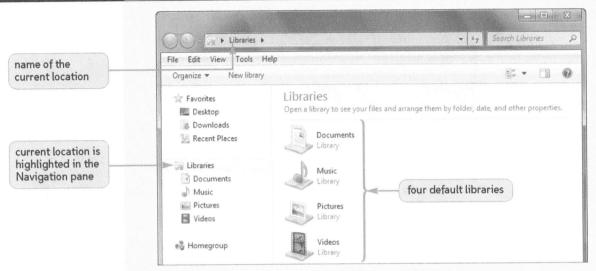

name of the
current location

current location is
highlighted in the
Navigation pane

four default libraries

**Trouble?** If your Windows Explorer window looks slightly different from the one displayed in Figure 22, the configuration of your computer probably differs from the computer used in this figure.

Windows Explorer has the same tools and features you used in the Computer window: the Navigation pane, toolbar, Details pane, and file list in the right pane. The Navigation pane organizes resources into five categories: Favorites (for locations you access frequently), Libraries (for the Windows default libraries), Homegroup (for your shared home network, if any), Computer (for the drives and devices on your computer), and Network (for network locations your computer can access).

When you move the pointer into the Navigation pane, triangles appear next to some icons. An open triangle, or expand icon, ▷ indicates that a folder contains other folders that are not currently displayed in the Navigation pane. Click the triangle to expand the folder and display its subfolders. A filled triangle, or collapse icon, ◢ indicates the folder is expanded, and its subfolders are listed below the folder name. As you saw when working with the Computer window, you can click a folder in the Navigation pane to navigate directly to that folder and display its contents in the right pane.

### Exploring with the Navigation Pane

INSIGHT

Using the Navigation pane to explore your computer usually involves clicking expand icons to expand objects and find the folder you want, and then clicking that folder to display its contents in the right pane. To display a list of all the folders on a drive, expand the Computer icon in the Navigation pane, and then expand the icon for the drive, such as Local Disk (C:). The folders list shows the hierarchy of folders on the drive, so you can use it to find and manage your files and folders.

Now you're ready to use the Navigation pane to find and open a folder people use often—the My Documents folder, which is a convenient place to store your documents and other work. The My Documents folder is stored in the Documents library by default.

### To open the My Documents folder:

▶ **1.** If necessary, click the **expand** icon ▷ next to Libraries in the Navigation pane to display the four built-in library folders for Documents, Music, Pictures, and Videos. (Your computer might include additional library folders.)

**Trouble?** If the expand icon ▷ does not appear next to Libraries in the Navigation pane, the Libraries folder is already expanded. Skip step 1.

▶ **2.** Click the **expand** icon ▷ next to Documents to display the folders in the Documents library. See Figure 23.

| Figure 23 | Folders in the Documents library |

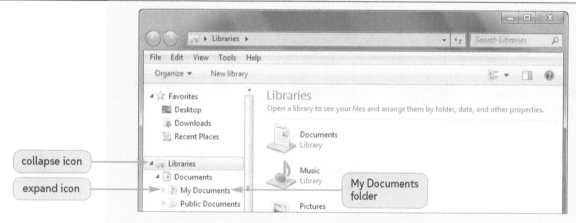

collapse icon
expand icon
My Documents folder

▶ **3.** Click the **My Documents** folder to display its contents in the right pane. (Your My Documents folder might not contain any files or folders.)

▶ **4.** Close the folder window.

## Getting Help

Windows 7 Help and Support provides on-screen information about the program you are using. Click the Start button and then click Help and Support to open the Windows Help and Support window, which gives you access to Help files stored on your computer as well as Help information stored on the Microsoft Web site. If you are not connected to the Web, you only have access to the Help files stored on your computer.

REFERENCE

*Starting Windows Help and Support*

• Click the Start button on the taskbar.
• Click Help and Support.
*or*
• Click the Help button on any folder window.

### To start Windows 7 Help:

▶ **1.** Click the **Start** button 🔘 on the taskbar.

▶ **2.** Click **Help and Support** in the right pane of the Start menu. The home page of Windows Help and Support opens. See Figure 24. The contents of the home page differ depending on whether you are connected to the Internet.

| Figure 24 | Windows Help and Support window |
|---|---|

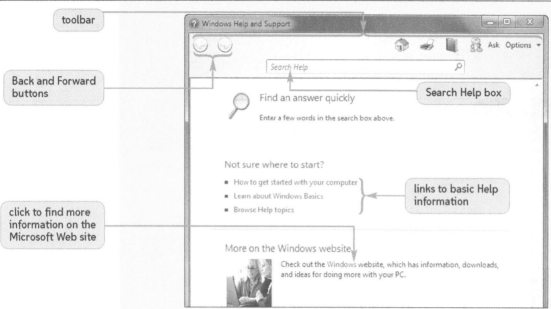

toolbar

Back and Forward buttons

Search Help box

links to basic Help information

click to find more information on the Microsoft Web site

**Trouble?** If the Help and Support window does not display the information shown in Figure 24, click the Home button 🔘 on the toolbar to view Help contents.

The home page in Windows Help and Support provides tools for finding answers and other information about Windows 7. To view popular topics, you click a link in the *Find an answer quickly* section of the Windows Help and Support home page. Click a topic to open an article providing detailed information about that topic or instructions for performing a task. You can also use the toolbar to navigate Windows Help and Support. For example, click the Help and Support home button to return to the home page.

## Viewing Windows Basics Topics

Windows Help and Support includes instructions on using Help itself. You can learn how to find a Help topic by using the *Learn about Windows Basics* link on the Windows Help and Support home page.

**To view Windows Basics topics:**

▶ **1.** Click **Learn about Windows Basics**. A list of topics related to using Windows 7 appears in the Windows Help and Support window.

▶ **2.** Scroll down to the *Help and support* heading, and then click **Getting help**. An article explaining how to get help appears, with the headings in the article listed in the *In this article* section on the right.

▶ **3.** Click **Getting help with dialog boxes and windows**. The Windows Help and Support window scrolls to that heading in the article.

▶ **4.** Click the **Back** button ⊙ on the toolbar. You return to the previous page you visited, which is the Windows Basics: all topics page.

## Selecting a Topic from the Contents List

The Contents list logically organizes all of the topics in Windows Help and Support into topics and categories. In the Contents list, you can click a category to display the titles of related topics. Click a topic to get help about a particular task or feature. For example, you can use the Contents list to learn more about files and folders.

**To find a Help topic using the Contents list:**

▶ **1.** Click the **Help and Support home** button 🔼 on the toolbar to return to the home page for Windows Help and Support.

▶ **2.** Click the **Browse Help** button 🔲 on the toolbar. A list of categories appears in the Windows Help and Support window.

▶ **3.** Click **Files, folders, and libraries** to display the list of topics and other categories related to files, folders, and libraries.

▶ **4.** Click the topic **Working with files and folders**. The Windows Help and Support window displays information about that topic.

▶ **5.** In the first paragraph below the *Working with files and folders* heading, click the word **icons**, which is green by default. A ScreenTip shows the definition of *icons*.

▶ **6.** Click a blank area of the Windows Help and Support window to close the ScreenTip.

## Searching the Help Pages

If you can't find the topic you need by clicking a link or using the toolbar, or if you want to quickly find Help pages related to a particular topic, you can use the Search Help box. Elena provides a typical example. Suppose you want to know how to exit Windows 7, but you don't know if Windows refers to this as exiting, quitting, closing, or shutting down. You can search the Help pages to find just the right topic.

**To search the Help pages for information on exiting Windows 7:**

▶ **1.** Click in the Search Help box. A blinking insertion point appears.

▶ **2.** Type **shut down** and then press the **Enter** key. A list of Help pages containing the words *shut down* appears in the Windows Help and Support window. See Figure 25. (Your results might differ.)

**Figure 25** ▶ **Search Help results**

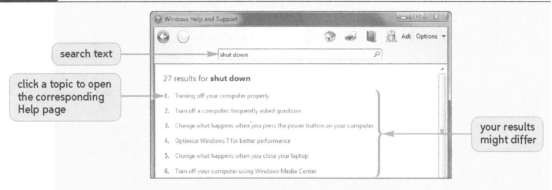

search text

click a topic to open the corresponding Help page

your results might differ

▶ **3.** Click the **Turning off your computer properly** topic. The article appears in the Windows Help and Support window.

**Trouble?** If a *Topic not found* message appears in the Help window, click the Back button 🔙 on the toolbar, and then click a different link in the Windows Help and Support window, such as *Turn off a computer: frequently asked questions*.

If this article did not answer your question, you could click the Ask button on the toolbar. Doing so opens a page listing other ways to get Help information.

▶ **4.** Click the **Close** button 🔲 to close the Windows Help and Support window.

Now that you know how Windows 7 Help works, Elena reminds you to use it when you need to perform a new task or when you forget how to complete a procedure.

# Turning Off Windows 7

You should always shut down Windows 7 before you turn off your computer. Doing so saves energy, preserves your data and settings, and makes sure your computer starts quickly the next time you use it.

You can turn off Windows 7 using the Shut down button at the bottom of the Start menu. When you click the Shut down button, your computer closes all open programs, including Windows itself, and then completely turns off your computer. For greater flexibility, you can click the arrow on the Shut down button to display a menu of shut down options, including Log off and Sleep. If you choose the Sleep option, Windows saves your work and then turns down the power to your monitor and computer. A light on the outside of your computer case blinks or turns yellow to indicate that the computer is sleeping. Because Windows saves your work, you do not need to close your programs or files before putting your computer to sleep. To wake a desktop computer, you press any key or move the mouse. To wake a notebook computer, you might need to press the hardware power button on your computer case instead. After you wake a computer, the screen looks exactly as it did when you turned off your computer.

**TIP**

Shutting down does not automatically save your work, so be sure to save your files before clicking the Shut down button.

### To turn off Windows 7:

▶ **1.** Click the **Start** button 🪟 on the taskbar.

▶ **2.** Click **Shut down**. Windows 7 displays a message that it is shutting down, and then turns off your computer.

**Trouble?** If you are supposed to log off rather than shut down, skip Step 2, click the More Options button ▸ instead, click Log off, and follow your school's logoff procedure.

PROSKILLS

## Decision Making: Log Off, Sleep, or Shut Down?

If you are using a computer on the job, your organization probably has a policy about what to do when you're finished working on the computer. If it does not, deciding on the best approach depends on who uses the computer and how long it will be idle. Keep the following guidelines in mind as you make your decision:

- Log off: This command closes all programs and logs you off of Windows 7 but leaves the computer turned on. If another person might use your computer shortly, log off Windows to protect your data and prepare the computer for someone else to use.
- Sleep: By default, Windows 7 is set to sleep after 15–30 minutes of idle time, depending on whether you are using a notebook or desktop computer. If you will be away from the computer for more than 15 minutes but less than a day, you can generally let the computer go to sleep on its own.
- Shut down: If your computer is plugged in to a power outlet and you don't plan to use the computer for more than a day, you save wear and tear on your electronic components and conserve energy by shutting down, which ends your Windows 7 session and turns off your computer. You should also turn off the computer when it is susceptible to electrical damage, such as during a lightning storm, and when you need to install new hardware or disconnect the computer from a power source. If your notebook computer is running on battery power only and you don't plan to use it for more than a few hours, you should also turn it off to save your battery charge.

In this session, you learned how to start and close programs and use multiple programs at the same time. You worked with windows and the controls they provide, learned how to get help when you need it, and how to turn off Windows 7.

## Session 2 Quick Check

REVIEW

1. The left pane in a folder window is called the _____, which shows icons and links to other resources your computer can access.
2. True or False. The Music library is a convenient location that Windows provides for storing your music files.
3. Describe two ways to change the view in a folder window.
4. In the Windows Explorer window, what appears in the right pane when you click a folder icon in the left pane?
5. How can you view file details, such as size or date modified, in Large Icons view?
6. The _____ list logically organizes all of the topics in Windows Help and Support into books and pages.
7. How can you quickly find Help pages related to a particular topic in the Windows Help and Support window?
8. Describe what happens when you choose the Sleep option on the Shut down button menu.

*Practice the skills
you learned in
the tutorial using
the same case
scenario.*

PRACTICE

## Review Assignments

There are no Data Files needed for the Review Assignments.

The day before your first class teaching Back to Work clients the basics of using Windows 7, Elena Varney offers to observe your tour of the operating system. You'll start working on the Windows 7 desktop, with no windows opened or minimized. Complete the following steps, recording your answers to any questions according to your instructor's preferences:

1. Start Windows 7 and log on, if necessary.
2. Use the mouse to point to each object on your desktop. Record the names and descriptions of each object as they appear in the ScreenTips.
3. Click the Start button. How many menu items or commands are on the Start menu?
4. Start WordPad. How many program buttons are now on the taskbar? (Don't count toolbar buttons, items in the notification area, or the three default taskbar buttons to the right of the Start button.)
5. Start Paint and maximize the Paint window. How many programs are running now?
6. Switch to WordPad. What are two visual cues that tell you that WordPad is the active program?
7. Close WordPad and then click the Restore Down button in the Paint window.
8. Open the Recycle Bin window. Record the number of items it contains. Drag the Recycle Bin window so that you can see it and the Paint window.
9. Close the Paint window from the taskbar. What command did you use?
10. Click the Organize button on the toolbar in the Recycle Bin window. Write down the commands on the menu. Point to Layout, and then click Menu bar to display the menu bar.
11. Use any menu on the Recycle Bin menu bar to open a dialog box. What steps did you perform? What dialog box did you open? For what do you think you use this dialog box? Click Cancel to close the dialog box. Close the Recycle Bin window.
12. Open a folder window, and then open the Public Documents folder from the Navigation pane. Explain how you navigated to this folder.
13. Open a folder in the Videos library and then describe its contents.
14. Change the view of the folder window. What view did you select? Describe the icon(s) in the folder window.
15. Close the folder window, and then open Windows Help and Support.
16. Use the *Learn about Windows Basics* link to learn something new about the Windows 7 desktop. What did you learn? How did you find this topic?
17. Return to the Home page, and then browse Help topics to find information about customizing your computer. How many topics are listed? (*Hint*: Don't include Help categories.) Use the Search Help box to find information about customizing your computer. How many topics are listed?
18. Close Help, and then close any other open windows.
19. Turn off Windows 7 by using the Sleep command, shutting down, or logging off.
20. Submit your answers to the preceding questions to your instructor, either in printed or electronic form, as requested.

*Use your skills to explore the contents of a computer for a small electronics business.*

## Case Problem 1

**There are no Data Files needed for this Case Problem.**

***First Call Electronics***    First Call Electronics is a small business in Atlanta, Georgia, that provides training and repair services for electronic devices, including computers, cell phones, cameras, and portable music players. Antoine Guillaume runs the training department and has hired you to conduct one-on-one training sessions with new computer users. You are preparing for a visit to a client who wants to determine the contents of his new Windows 7 computer, including sample media files and related programs already provided in folders or menus.

Some of the following steps instruct you to list the contents of windows. Refer to the instructions in the ProSkills exercise at the end of this tutorial if you want to print images of these windows instead. Complete the following steps:

1. Start Windows 7 and log on, if necessary.
2. Open a folder window.
3. List the names of the drives on the computer.
4. Click the Pictures link in the Navigation pane. Does the Pictures library contain any folders? If so, what are the names of the folders?
5. In the Navigation pane, expand the hard disk, such as Local Disk (C:), to display its contents. Navigate the folders on your computer to find the folder displayed in the Pictures library. Where is that folder located in the folder structure of your computer?
6. Open any folder in the Pictures library that contains images. View the files as Extra Large Icons.
7. Navigate to a folder that contains other types of media files, such as music, videos, or recorded TV. Point to a file to display the ScreenTip. What type of file did you select? What details are provided in the ScreenTip?
8. Use the Start menu to display the contents of the Accessories folder in the All Programs list, and then click Getting Started. Describe the contents of the Getting Started window.
9. Close all open windows, and then use the Start menu to open a program that you could use with DVDs. What program did you start?
10. Use the Start menu to open any program you might use with music or sound files. What program did you start?
11. Open Windows Help and Support, and then find and read topics that explain how to use a program you started in a previous step. Explain the purpose of one of the programs.
12. Close all open windows.
13. Submit your answers to the preceding questions to your instructor, either in printed or electronic form, as requested.

*Work with Windows 7 on a computer for a catering business.*

APPLY

## Case Problem 2

There are no Data Files needed for this Case Problem.

***East End Catering***    After completing culinary school and working as a sous chef for restaurants in Santa Fe, New Mexico, Felicia Makos started a catering company called East End Catering that specializes in dishes that contain organic, locally grown ingredients. So that she can concentrate on cooking and marketing, she hired you to help her perform office tasks as her business grows. She asks you to start by teaching her the basics of using her computer, which runs Windows 7. She especially wants to know which programs are installed on her computer and what they do.

Some of the following steps instruct you to list the contents of windows and menus. Refer to the instructions in the ProSkills exercise at the end of this tutorial if you want to print images of these windows instead. Complete the following steps:

1. Open the Start menu and write down the programs listed in the left pane.
2. Start one of the programs in the left pane and then describe what it does. Close the program.
3. Open the Start menu, display the All Programs list, and then open the Accessories folder. Examine the list of programs in the Accessories folder and its subfolders, and then close the Start menu.

✦ EXPLORE
4. Click the Start button, and then start typing the name of a program you noted in a previous step. Describe what happens.
5. Use Windows Help and Support to research one of the programs you examined in the previous step, such as Calculator or Notepad. Describe the purpose of the program and how to perform a task using that program.
6. Use the Search Help box in Windows Help and Support to list all the Help topics related to the program you researched in the previous step. How many topics are displayed in the results?

✦ EXPLORE
7. Start the program you researched. Click the Help button on the program's menu bar, and then explore the Help topics. Open and read a Help topic in the program.
8. Find a similar topic in Windows Help and Support, and then read that topic. Compare this topic to the ones you explored in the previous step.
9. Close all open windows.
10. Submit your answers to the preceding questions to your instructor, either in printed or electronic form, as requested.

*Extend what you've learned to customize folder windows.*

**CHALLENGE**

***Friedman Alternatives*** Warren Friedman recently started his own small firm called Friedman Alternatives, which analyzes and recommends sources of alternative energy for various manufacturing businesses. Most of these businesses want to cut their expenses related to energy, and are interested in helping to conserve fuel and preserve the environment. Warren typically uses the Windows Explorer window to work with his files, but suspects he is not taking full advantage of its features. As his new special-projects employee, he asks you to show him around the Windows 7 folder windows and demonstrate how to customize their appearance. Complete the following steps:

1. Start Windows Explorer. Click the Organize button on the Windows Explorer toolbar, and write down any commands that seem related to changing the appearance of the window.

✦ EXPLORE
2. Select a command that lays out the Windows Explorer window so that it displays a single pane for viewing files. What command did you select? Restore the window to its original condition.

3. Navigate to the Pictures library and display its contents. Double-click the Sample Pictures folder to open it. (If your computer does not contain a Sample Pictures folder, open any folder that displays pictures.) Display the icons using Large Icons view.

4. Change the view to Content view. Describe the differences between Large Icons and Content view.

✦ EXPLORE
5. Click the Slide show button on the toolbar. Describe what happens, and then press the Esc key.

6. With the Details pane open, click a picture file. Describe the contents of the Details pane. Also identify the buttons on the toolbar.

✦ EXPLORE
7. Repeatedly click the Change your view button to cycle from one view to another. Describe the changes in the window.

8. Display the window in Details view.

✦ EXPLORE
9. On the Organize button menu, click Folder and search options to open the Folder Options dialog box. Select the option that shows all folders in the Navigation pane, and then click the OK button. Describe the changes in the Sample Pictures window.

✦ EXPLORE
10. Open the Folder Options dialog box again, click the Restore Defaults button, and then click the OK button.

11. Open the Windows Help and Support window and search for information about folder options. Find a topic explaining how to show hidden files. Explain how to do so.

12. Close all open windows.

13. Submit the results of the preceding steps to your instructor, either in printed or electronic form, as requested.

*Use the Internet to provide information to an import/export company.*

**RESEARCH**

## Case Problem 4

**There are no Data Files needed for this Case Problem.**

*Majolica Imports*    After moving from southern France to New York City, Marie and Bruno Tattinger decided to start a company that imports hand-painted French and Italian ceramics. Both Marie and Bruno travel frequently, and they use laptop computers running Windows 7 to manage their business when they are on the move. They have hired you as a consultant to help them use and maintain their computers. Marie asks you to help her research wireless networks so she can set up a wireless network at home and in their office. You suggest starting with Windows Help and Support, and then expanding to the Internet to search for the latest information. Complete the following steps:

1. In Windows Help and Support, find information about the hardware Marie needs to set up a wireless network.
2. Use the Ask button to visit the Microsoft Web site to obtain more information about wireless networks.
3. Choose a topic that describes how to set up a wireless network for a home or small office, and then read the topic thoroughly.
4. On the Microsoft Web site, search for information about adding a Bluetooth device to the network.
5. Write one to two pages for Marie and Bruno explaining what equipment they need to set up a wireless network and the steps they should perform. Also explain how they can add their Bluetooth mobile phones to the network.
6. Submit the results of the preceding steps to your instructor, either in printed or electronic form, as requested.

**ASSESS**

## SAM: Skills Assessment Manager

For current SAM information, including versions and content details, visit SAM Central (http://samcentral.course.com). If you have a SAM user profile, you may have access to hands-on instruction, practice, and assessment of the skills covered in this tutorial. Since various versions of SAM are supported throughtout the life of this text, check with your instructor for the correct instructions and URL/Web site for accessing assignments.

### ENDING DATA FILES

There are no ending Data Files needed for this tutorial.

# Problem Solving

## Gathering Information to Solve Potential Computer Problems

When you solve problems, you work through the following stages to gather information about the problem and its possible solutions:

1. Recognize and define the problem.
2. Determine possible courses of action.
3. Collect information needed to evaluate alternative courses of action.
4. Evaluate each alternative's merits and drawbacks.
5. Select an alternative.
6. Implement the decision.
7. Monitor and evaluate performance to provide feedback and take corrective action.

If you are involved in solving a complex problem with many possible causes, you perform all seven steps in the process. If you are solving a simpler problem or have limited time to explore solutions, you can condense the steps. For example, you might recognize the problem in one step, determine possible actions, evaluate and select an alternative in the next step, and then implement and evaluate your decision in another step.

### Recognize and Define the Problem

A problem is an obstacle that prevents you from reaching a goal. This definition is especially fitting for work with a computer. For example, suppose your goal is to create a report containing text and graphics, but you don't know which program to use. In this case, your lack of familiarity with the programs on your computer is an obstacle preventing you from reaching your goal of efficiently creating a report with text and graphics.

After identifying a simple problem such as which computer program to use, you can focus on solutions. Start by considering any possible solution. For example, start each program on your computer related to text and graphics and examine its features. Next, compare and evaluate those alternatives. Which programs help you meet your goal most effectively? Select the best solution and then try it, observing the results to make sure it actually solves the problem. Can you efficiently create the report with the program you selected? If not, try a different program until you find the best possible solution.

### Anticipate Computer Problems

Even if you are familiar with some features of Windows 7, take some time to explore the basics of Windows 7 on your computer. To solve system problems that might occur later, you should capture and save images of your current desktop, the Start menu, and other resources on your computer. You can save these images for reference if you experience problems with your computer later or want to restore these settings.

To save screen images:

1. Start Paint, and then minimize the program window.
2. Open the window you want to preserve or arrange the desktop as you want it. If you want to capture a window, make sure that window is the active window.

PROSKILLS

3. Hold down the Alt key and press the Print Screen key. (The Print Screen key might be labeled *PrtScn* or something similar on your keyboard.) Pressing this key combination captures an image of the active window. To capture an image of everything shown on the screen, press the Print Screen key without holding down the Alt key.

4. Restore the Paint program window, and then press the Ctrl+V keys to paste the image in the Paint program window.

5. Click the Save button on the Quick Access Toolbar to open the Save As dialog box. By default, Paint saves images in the My Pictures folder in the Pictures library. Use the Navigation pane to navigate to a different folder, if necessary. Type a filename, and then press the Save button to save the screen image.

6. To print the screen images, click the Paint menu button, and then click Print to open the Print dialog box. Select your printer and other settings, and then click the Print button.

7. To open a new window for the next screen image, click the Paint menu button, and then click New.

Now you can explore Windows 7 on your computer and preserve screen images, which will help you solve computer problems:

1. Start Windows 7 and log on, if necessary.

2. Save and print images of your current desktop, the Start menu, the Computer window showing the drives on your computer, and your Documents library.

3. Open a folder in the Documents library that you are likely to use often. Make sure the Navigation pane shows the location of this folder on your computer. Capture and save an image of this window.

4. To learn more about the programs that are included with Windows 7 and how they can help you solve problems, start at least two accessory programs that are new to you. Open a menu in each program, and then capture and save the image of each program window.

5. Using the Ribbon, toolbar, or menu bar in the new programs, find a dialog box in each program that you are likely to use. Capture and save images of the dialog boxes.

6. Explore both programs to determine how they might help you solve problems related to using your computer, completing your school work, or performing on the job.

7. Use Windows Help and Support to find information about a feature in one program that can help you solve problems. Choose an appropriate topic. Print an image of the Windows Help and Support window displaying information about this topic.

8. Close all open windows, and then shut down or log off Windows.

OBJECTIVES

- Develop file management strategies
- Explore files, folders, and libraries
- Create, name, copy, move, and delete folders
- Name, copy, move, and delete files
- Work with compressed files

# Managing Your Files

*Organizing Files and Folders with Windows 7*

## Case | *Distance Learning Company*

The Distance Learning Company specializes in distance-learning courses for people who want to gain new skills and stay competitive in the job market. Distance learning is formalized education that typically takes place using a computer and the Internet, replacing normal classroom interaction with modern communications technology. The head of the Customer Service Department, Shannon Connell, interacts with the Distance Learning Company's clients on the phone and from her computer. Shannon, like all other employees, is required to learn the basics of managing files on her computer.

In this tutorial, you'll work with Shannon to devise a strategy for managing files. You'll learn how Windows 7 organizes files and folders, and you'll examine Windows 7 file management tools. You'll create folders and organize files within them. You'll also explore options for working with compressed files.

## STARTING DATA FILES

| FM → | Tutorial | Review | Case1 |
|---|---|---|---|
| | Flyer.docx | Album.pptx | Art-Agenda.docx |
| | Map.png | Bills.xlsx | Art-Eval.docx |
| | Members.htm | Brochure.docx | Art-Notes.docx |
| | Paris.jpg | Budget.xlsx | Garden.jpg |
| | Proposal.docx | Photo.jpg | Inv01.xlsx |
| | Resume.docx | Plan.xlsx | Inv02.xlsx |
| | Rome.jpg | Receipt.xlsx | Inv03.xlsx |
| | Stationery.docx | Sales.xlsx | Sculpture.jpg |

# VISUAL OVERVIEW

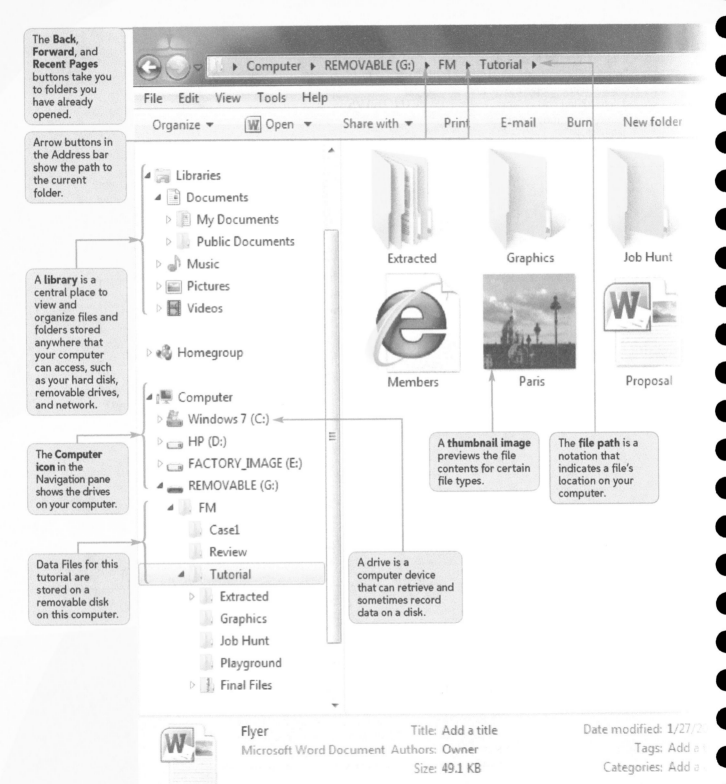

The **Back**, **Forward**, and **Recent Pages** buttons take you to folders you have already opened.

Arrow buttons in the Address bar show the path to the current folder.

A **library** is a central place to view and organize files and folders stored anywhere that your computer can access, such as your hard disk, removable drives, and network.

The **Computer icon** in the Navigation pane shows the drives on your computer.

Data Files for this tutorial are stored on a removable disk on this computer.

A **thumbnail image** previews the file contents for certain file types.

The **file path** is a notation that indicates a file's location on your computer.

A **drive** is a computer device that can retrieve and sometimes record data on a disk.

Computer ▸ REMOVABLE (G:) ▸ FM ▸ Tutorial ▸

File    Edit    View    Tools    Help

Organize ▼    Open ▼    Share with ▼    Print    E-mail    Burn    New folder

▲ Libraries
  ▲ Documents
    ▷ My Documents
    ▷ Public Documents
  ▷ Music
  ▷ Pictures
  ▷ Videos

▷ Homegroup

▲ Computer
  ▷ Windows 7 (C:)
  ▷ HP (D:)
  ▷ FACTORY_IMAGE (E:)
  ▲ REMOVABLE (G:)
    ▲ FM
      Case1
      Review
      ▲ Tutorial
        ▷ Extracted
        Graphics
        Job Hunt
        Playground
        ▷ Final Files

Extracted    Graphics    Job Hunt

Members    Paris    Proposal

Flyer
Microsoft Word Document
Title: Add a title
Authors: Owner
Size: 49.1 KB
Date modified: 1/27/2
Tags: Add a
Categories: Add a

# FILES IN A FOLDER WINDOW

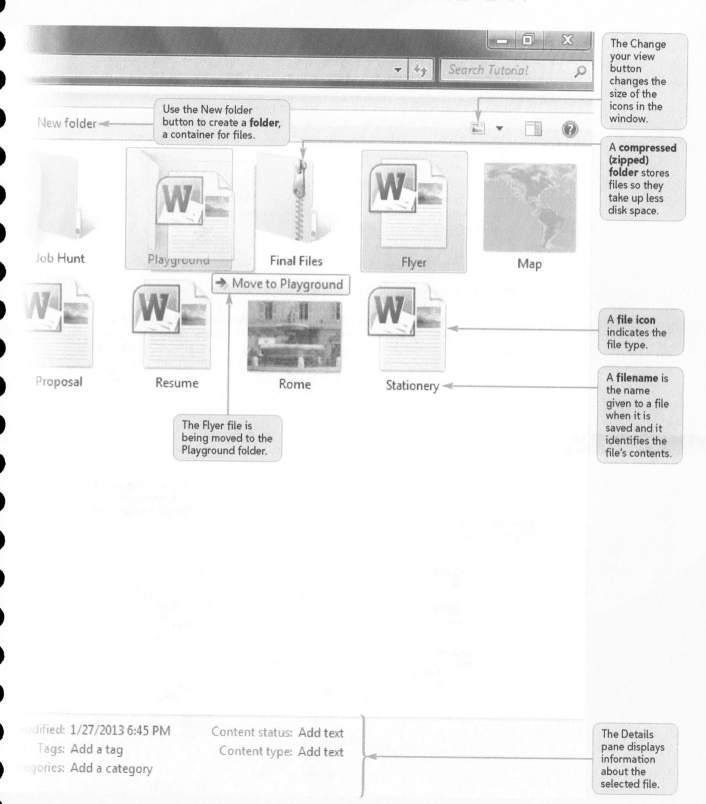

The Change your view button changes the size of the icons in the window.

Use the New folder button to create a **folder**, a container for files.

New folder

A **compressed (zipped) folder** stores files so they take up less disk space.

Job Hunt

Playground

Final Files

Flyer

Map

Move to Playground

A **file icon** indicates the file type.

Proposal

Resume

Rome

Stationery

A **filename** is the name given to a file when it is saved and it identifies the file's contents.

The Flyer file is being moved to the Playground folder.

Modified: 1/27/2013 6:45 PM
Tags: Add a tag
Categories: Add a category

Content status: Add text
Content type: Add text

The Details pane displays information about the selected file.

# Organizing Files and Folders

Knowing how to save, locate, and organize computer files makes you more productive when you are working with a computer. A **file**, often referred to as a document, is a collection of data that has a name and is stored on a computer. After you create a file, you can open it, edit its contents, print it, and save it again—usually using the same program you used to create it. You organize files by storing them in folders. You need to organize files so that you can find them easily and work efficiently.

A computer can store folders and files on different types of disks, ranging from removable media—such as USB drives (also called USB flash drives), compact discs (CDs), and digital video discs (DVDs)—to **hard disks**, or fixed disks, which are permanently stored on a computer. Hard disks are the most popular type of computer storage because they provide an economical way to store many gigabytes of data.

A computer distinguishes one drive from another by assigning each a drive letter. The hard disk is usually assigned to drive C. The remaining drives can have any other letters, but are usually assigned in the order that the drives were installed on the computer—so your USB drive might be drive D or drive G.

## Understanding the Need for Organizing Files and Folders

Windows 7 stores thousands of files in many folders on the hard disk of your computer. These are system files that Windows 7 needs to display the desktop, use drives, and perform other operating system tasks. To ensure system stability and to find files quickly, Windows 7 organizes the folders and files in a hierarchy, or **file system**. At the top of the hierarchy, Windows 7 stores folders and files that it needs when you turn on the computer. This location is called the **root directory**, and is usually drive C (the hard disk). The term *root* refers to a popular metaphor for visualizing a file system—an upside-down tree, which reflects the file hierarchy that Windows 7 uses. In Figure 1, the tree trunk corresponds to the root directory, the branches to the folders, and the leaves to the files.

**Figure 1**   Windows file hierarchy

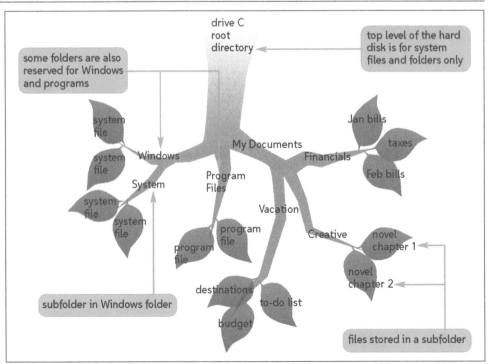

Note that some folders contain other folders. An effectively organized computer contains a few folders in the root directory, and those folders contain other folders, also called **subfolders**.

The root directory, or top level, of the hard disk is for system files and folders only—you should not store your own work here because it could interfere with Windows or a program. (If you are working in a computer lab, you might not be allowed to access the root directory.)

Do not delete or move any files or folders from the root directory of the hard disk—doing so could disrupt the system so that you can't run or start the computer. In fact, you should not reorganize or change any folder that contains installed software because Windows 7 expects to find the files for specific programs within certain folders. If you reorganize or change these folders, Windows 7 cannot locate and start the programs stored in that folder. Likewise, you should not make changes to the folder (usually named Windows) that contains the Windows 7 operating system.

## Developing Strategies for Organizing Files and Folders

The type of disk you use to store files determines how you organize those files. Figure 2 shows how you could organize your files on a hard disk if you were taking a full semester of distance-learning classes. To duplicate this organization, you would open the main folder for your documents, create four folders—one each for the Basic Accounting, Computer Concepts, Management Skills II, and Professional Writing courses—and then store the writing assignments you complete in the Professional Writing folder.

| Figure 2 | Organizing folders and files on a hard disk |

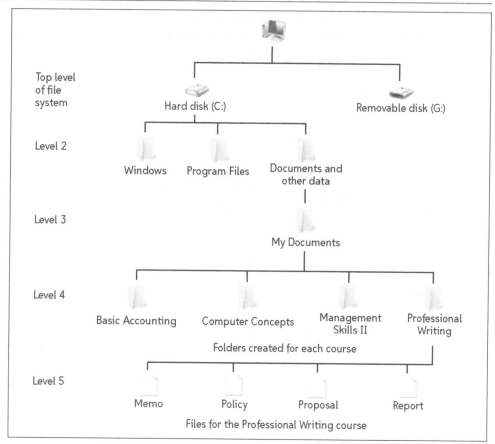

Top level of file system

Hard disk (C:)    Removable disk (G:)

Level 2

Windows    Program Files    Documents and other data

Level 3

My Documents

Level 4

Basic Accounting    Computer Concepts    Management Skills II    Professional Writing

Folders created for each course

Level 5

Memo    Policy    Proposal    Report

Files for the Professional Writing course

If you store your files on removable media, such as a USB drive or rewritable CD, you can use a simpler organization because you do not have to account for system files. In general, the larger the medium, the more levels of folders you should use because large media can store more files, and, therefore, need better organization. For example, if you are organizing your files on a USB drive, you could create folders in the top level of the USB drive for each general category of documents you store—one each for Courses, Creative, Financials, and Vacation. The Courses folder could then include one folder for each course, and each of those folders could contain the appropriate files.

## INSIGHT

### Duplicating Your Folder Organization

If you work on two computers, such as one computer at an office or school and another computer at home, you can duplicate the folders you use on both computers to simplify transferring files from one computer to another. For example, if you have four folders in your My Documents folder on your work computer, you would create these same four folders on your removable medium as well as in the My Documents folder of your home computer. If you change a file on the hard disk of your home computer, you can copy the most recent version of the file to the corresponding folder on your removable disk so the file is available when you are at work. You also then have a **backup**, or duplicate copy, of important files.

## Exploring Files, Folders, and Libraries

Windows 7 provides two tools for exploring the files and folders on your computer—Windows Explorer and the Computer window. Both display the contents of your computer, using icons to represent drives, folders, and files. However, by default, each presents a slightly different view of your computer. **Windows Explorer** opens to show the contents of the Windows default libraries, making it easy to find the files you work with often, such as documents and pictures. The **Computer window** shows the drives on your computer and makes it easy to perform system tasks, such as viewing system information. You can use either tool to open a **folder window** that displays the files and subfolders in a folder.

Folder windows are divided into two sections, called panes. The left pane is the Navigation pane, which contains icons and links to locations you use often. The right pane lists the contents of your folders and other locations. If you select a folder in the Navigation pane, the contents of that folder appear in the right pane. To display the hierarchy of the folders and other locations on your computer, you select the Computer icon in the Navigation pane, and then select the icon for a drive, such as Local Disk (C:) or Removable Disk (G:). You can then open and explore folders on that drive.

**TIP**

Move the mouse pointer into the Navigation pane to display the expand and collapse icons.

If the Navigation pane showed all the folders on your computer at once, it could be a very long list. Instead, you open drives and folders only when you want to see what they contain. If a folder contains undisplayed subfolders, an expand icon ▷ appears to the left of the folder icon. (The same is true for drives.) To view the folders contained in an object, you click the expand icon. A collapse icon ◢ then appears next to the folder icon; click the collapse icon to hide the folder's subfolders. To view the files contained in a folder, you click the folder icon, and the files appear in the right pane. See Figure 3.

**Figure 3**    Viewing files in a folder window

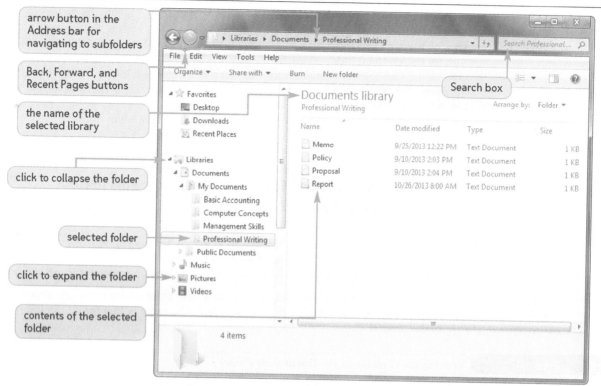

arrow button in the Address bar for navigating to subfolders

Back, Forward, and Recent Pages buttons

the name of the selected library

click to collapse the folder

selected folder

click to expand the folder

contents of the selected folder

Using the Navigation pane helps you explore your computer and orients you to your current location. As you move, copy, delete, and perform other tasks with the files in the right pane of a folder window, you can refer to the Navigation pane to see how your changes affect the overall organization.

In addition to using the Navigation pane, you can use folder windows and many dialog boxes to explore your computer in the following ways:

- Opening drives and folders in the right pane: To view the contents of a drive or folder, double-click the drive or folder icon in the right pane of a folder window.
- Using the Address bar: Use the Address bar to navigate to a different folder. The Address bar displays your current folder as a series of locations separated by arrows. Click a folder name or an arrow button to navigate to a different location.
- Clicking the Back, Forward, and Recent Pages buttons: Use the Back, Forward, and Recent Pages buttons to navigate to other folders you have already opened. After you change folders, use the Back button to return to the original folder or click the Recent Pages button to navigate to a location you've visited recently.
- Using the Search box: To find a file or folder stored in the current folder or its subfolders, type a word or phrase in the Search box. The search begins as soon as you start typing. Windows finds files based on text in the filename, text within the file, and other characteristics of the file, such as tags (descriptive words or phrases you add to your files) or the author.

## Using Libraries and Folders

When you open Windows Explorer, it shows the contents of the Windows built-in libraries by default. A library displays similar types of files together, no matter where they are stored. In contrast, a folder stores files in a specific location, such as in the Professional Writing subfolder of the My Documents folder on the Local Disk (C:) drive. When you want to open the Report file stored in the Professional Writing folder, you must navigate to the Local Disk (C:) drive, then the My Documents folder, and finally the Professional Writing folder. A library makes it easier to access similar types of files. For example, you might store some music files in the My Music folder and others in a folder named Albums on your hard disk. You might also store music files in a Tunes folder on a USB drive. If the USB drive is connected to your computer, the Music library can display all the music files in the My Music, Albums, and Tunes folders. You can then arrange the files to quickly find the ones you want to open and play.

You'll show Shannon how to navigate to the My Documents folder from the Documents library.

## To open the My Documents folder from the Documents library:

▶ **1.** Click the **Windows Explorer** button 🔲 on the taskbar. The Windows Explorer window opens, displaying the contents of the default libraries.

▶ **2.** In the Libraries section of the Navigation pane, click the **expand** icon ▷ next to the Documents icon. The folders in the Documents library appear in the Navigation pane, as shown in Figure 4. The contents of your computer will differ.

   **Trouble?** If your window displays icons in a view different from the one shown in Figure 4, you can still explore files and folders. The same is true for all the figures in this tutorial.

**Figure 4**    **Viewing the contents of the Documents library**

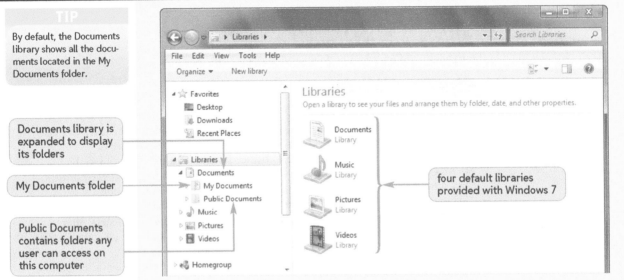

Documents library is expanded to display its folders

My Documents folder

Public Documents contains folders any user can access on this computer

four default libraries provided with Windows 7

▶ **3.** Click the **My Documents** folder in the Navigation pane to display its contents in the right pane.

## Navigating to Your Data Files

To navigate to the files you want, it helps to know the file path, which leads you through the file and folder organization to your file. For example, the Map file is stored in the Tutorial subfolder of the FM folder. If you are working on a USB drive, for example, the path to this file might be as follows:

**G:\FM\Tutorial\Map.png**

This path has four parts, and each part is separated by a backslash ( \ ):

- G: The drive name; for example, drive G might be the name for the USB drive. (If this file were stored on the hard disk, the drive name would be C.)
- FM: The top-level folder on drive G
- Tutorial: A subfolder in the FM folder
- Map.png: The full filename, including the file extension

If someone tells you to find the file G:\FM\Tutorial\Map.png, you know you must navigate to your USB drive, open the FM folder, and then open the Tutorial folder to find the Map file.

You can use any folder window to navigate to the Data Files you need for the rest of this tutorial. In the following steps, the Data Files are stored on drive G, a USB drive. If necessary, substitute the appropriate drive on your system when you perform the steps.

### To navigate to your Data Files:

1. Make sure your computer can access your Data Files for this tutorial. For example, if you are using a USB drive, insert the drive into the USB port.

   Trouble? If you don't have the starting Data Files, you need to get them before you can proceed. Your instructor will either give you the Data Files or ask you to obtain them from a specified location (such as a network drive). In either case, make a backup copy of the Data Files before you start so that you will have the original files available in case you need to start over. If you have any questions about the Data Files, see your instructor or technical support person for assistance.

2. In the open folder window, click the **expand** icon ▷ next to the Computer icon to display the drives on your computer, if necessary.

3. Click the **expand** icon ▷ next to the drive containing your Data Files, such as Removable Disk (G:). A list appears below the drive name showing the folders on that drive.

4. If the list of folders does not include the FM folder, continue clicking the **expand** icon ▷ to navigate to the folder that contains the FM folder.

5. Click the **expand** icon ▷ next to the FM folder, and then click the **FM** folder. Its contents appear in the Navigation pane and in the right pane of the folder window. The FM folder contains the Case1, Review, and Tutorial folders, as shown in Figure 5. The other folders on your system might vary.

| Figure 5 | Navigating to the FM folder |

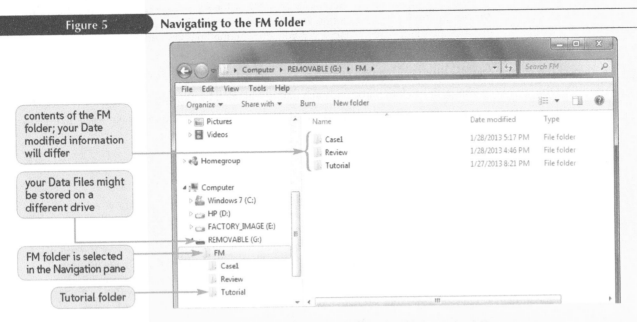

contents of the FM folder; your Date modified information will differ

your Data Files might be stored on a different drive

FM folder is selected in the Navigation pane

Tutorial folder

6. In the Navigation pane, click the **Tutorial** folder. The files it contains appear in the right pane. To view the contents of the graphics files, you can display the files as large icons.

7. If necessary, click the **Change your view button arrow** [≣ ▾] on the toolbar, and then click **Large Icons**. The files appear in Large Icons view in the folder window. See Figure 6.

| Figure 6 | Files in the Tutorial folder in Large Icons view |

TIP
If you change the view of one folder, other folders continue to display files in the default Details view.

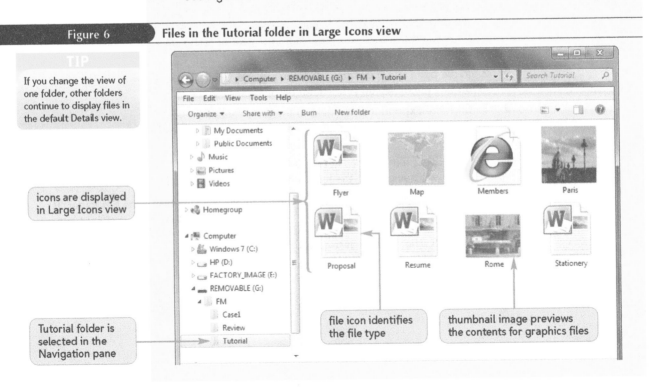

icons are displayed in Large Icons view

Tutorial folder is selected in the Navigation pane

file icon identifies the file type

thumbnail image previews the contents for graphics files

The file icons in your window depend on the programs installed on your computer, so they might be different from the ones shown in Figure 6.

# Managing Folders and Files

After you devise a plan for storing your files, you are ready to get organized by creating folders that will hold your files. For this tutorial, you'll create folders in the Tutorial folder. When you are working on your own computer, you usually create folders within the My Documents folder and other standard folders, such as My Music and My Pictures.

Examine the files shown in Figure 6 again and determine which files seem to belong together. Map, Paris, and Rome are all graphics files containing pictures or photos. The Resume and Stationery files were created for a summer job hunt. The other files were created for a neighborhood association trying to update a playground.

One way to organize these files is to create three folders—one for graphics, one for the job hunt files, and another for the playground files. When you create a folder, you give it a name, preferably one that describes its contents. A folder name can have up to 255 characters, except / \ : * ? " < > or |. Considering these conventions, you could create three folders as follows:

- Graphics folder: Map, Paris, and Rome files
- Job Hunt folder: Resume and Stationery files
- Playground folder: Flyer, Proposal, and Members files

**INSIGHT**

### Guidelines for Creating Folders

- Keep folder names short and familiar: Long names can be cut off in a folder window, so use names that are short but clear. Choose names that will be meaningful later, such as project names or course numbers.
- Develop standards for naming folders: Use a consistent naming scheme that is clear to you, such as one that uses a project name as the name of the main folder, and includes step numbers in each subfolder name, such as 01Plan, 02Approvals, 03Prelim, and so on.
- Create subfolders to organize files: If a file listing in a folder window is so long that you must scroll the window, consider organizing those files into subfolders.

## Creating Folders

You've already seen folder icons in the windows you've examined. Now, you'll show Shannon how to create folders in the Tutorial folder.

**REFERENCE**

### Creating a Folder in a Folder Window

- In the Navigation pane, click the drive or folder in which you want to create a folder.
- Click New folder on the toolbar.
- Type a name for the folder, and then press the Enter key.
*or*
- Right-click a folder in the Navigation pane or right-click a blank area in the folder window, point to New, and then click Folder.
- Type a name for the folder, and then press the Enter key.

You'll create the Graphics, Job Hunt, and Playground folders in your Tutorial folder.

### To create folders in a folder window:

▶ 1. Click the **New folder** button on the toolbar. A folder icon with the label *New folder* appears in the right pane. See Figure 7.

Figure 7    **Creating a folder in the Tutorial folder**

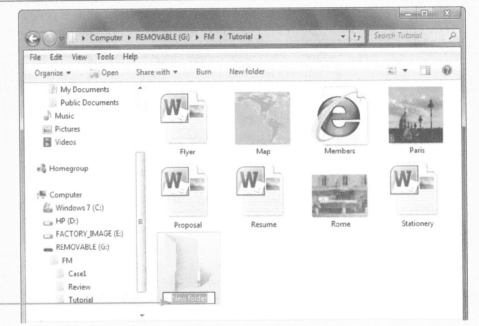

type to replace *New folder* with a folder name

**Trouble?** If the *New folder* name is not selected, right-click the new folder, click Rename, and then continue with Step 2.

Windows 7 uses *New folder* as a placeholder, and selects the text so that you can replace it with the name you want.

▶ 2. Type **Graphics** as the folder name, and then press the **Enter** key. The new folder is named Graphics and is the selected item in the right pane. You'll create a second folder using a shortcut menu.

▶ 3. Right-click a blank area near the Graphics folder, point to **New** on the shortcut menu, and then click **Folder**. A folder icon with the label *New folder* appears in the right pane with the *New folder* text selected.

▶ 4. Type **Job Hunt** as the name of the new folder, and then press the **Enter** key.

▶ 5. Using the toolbar or the shortcut menu, create a folder named **Playground**. The Tutorial folder contains three new subfolders.

## Moving and Copying Files and Folders

If you want to place a file into a folder from another location, you can move the file or copy it. **Moving** a file removes it from its current location and places it in a new location you specify. **Copying** also places the file in a new location that you specify, but does not remove it from its current location. Windows 7 provides several techniques for moving and copying files, which you can also use to move and copy folders.

**REFERENCE**

*Moving a File or Folder in a Folder Window*
- Right-click and drag the file or folder you want to move to the destination folder.
- Click Move here on the shortcut menu.

*or*

- Right-click the file or folder you want to move, and then click Cut on the shortcut menu. (You can also click the file or folder and then press the Ctrl+X keys.)
- Navigate to and right-click the destination folder, and then click Paste on the shortcut menu. (You can also click the destination folder and then press the Ctrl+V keys.)

Next, you'll move the Flyer, Proposal, and Members files to the Playground folder.

**To move a file using the right mouse button:**

1. Point to the **Flyer** file in the right pane, and then press and hold the *right* mouse button.

2. With the right mouse button still pressed down, drag the **Flyer** file to the **Playground** folder. When the *Move to Playground* ScreenTip appears, release the button. A shortcut menu opens.

3. With the left mouse button, click **Move here** on the shortcut menu. The Flyer file is removed from the main Tutorial folder and stored in the Playground subfolder.

   **Trouble?** If you release the mouse button before dragging the Flyer file to the Playground folder, the shortcut menu opens, letting you move the file to a different folder. Press the Esc key to close the shortcut menu without moving the file, and then repeat Steps 1–3.

4. In the right pane, double-click the **Playground** folder. The Flyer file is in the Playground folder.

5. In the left pane, click the **Tutorial** folder to see its contents. The Tutorial folder no longer contains the Flyer file.

The advantage of moving a file or folder by dragging with the right mouse button is that you can efficiently complete your work with one action. However, this technique requires polished mouse skills so that you can drag the file comfortably. Another way to move files and folders is to use the **Clipboard**, a temporary storage area for files and information that you have copied or moved from one place and plan to use somewhere else. You can select a file and use the Cut or Copy commands to temporarily store the file on the Clipboard, and then use the Paste command to insert the file elsewhere. Although using the Clipboard takes more steps, some users find it easier than dragging with the right mouse button.

You'll move the Resume file to the Job Hunt folder next by using the Clipboard.

**To move files using the Clipboard:**

1. Right-click the **Resume** file, and then click **Cut** on the shortcut menu. Although the file icon is still displayed in the folder window, Windows 7 removes the Resume file from the Tutorial folder and stores it on the Clipboard.

2. In the right pane, right-click the **Job Hunt** folder, and then click **Paste** on the shortcut menu. Windows 7 pastes the Resume file from the Clipboard to the Job Hunt folder. The Resume file icon no longer appears in the folder window.

**TIP**

To use keyboard shortcuts to move files, click the file you want to move, press Ctrl+X to cut the file, navigate to a new location, and then press Ctrl+V to paste the file.

3. In the right pane, double-click the **Job Hunt** folder to display its contents. The Job Hunt folder now contains the Resume file.

Next, you'll move the Stationery file from the Tutorial folder to the Job Hunt folder.

4. Click the **Back** button ⬅ on the Address bar to return to the Tutorial folder, right-click the **Stationery** file in the folder window, and then click **Cut** on the shortcut menu.

5. Right-click the **Job Hunt** folder, and then click **Paste** on the shortcut menu.

6. Click the **Forward** button ➡ on the Address bar to return to the Job Hunt folder. It now contains the Resume and Stationery files. See Figure 8.

**Figure 8** **Moving files**

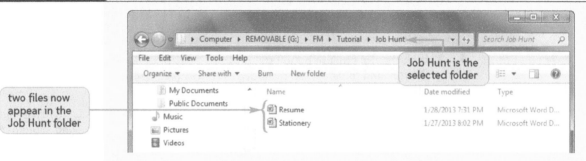

7. Click the **Back** button ⬅ to return to the Tutorial folder.

You can also copy a file using the same techniques as when you move a file—by dragging with the right mouse button or by using the Clipboard. You can copy more than one file at the same time by selecting all the files you want to copy, and then clicking them as a group. To select files that are listed together in a window, click the first file in the list, hold down the Shift key, click the last file in the list, and then release the Shift key. To select files that are not listed together, click one file, hold down the Ctrl key, click the other files, and then release the Ctrl key.

**Copying a File or Folder in a Folder Window**

REFERENCE

- Right-click and drag the file or folder you want to move to the destination folder.
- Click Copy here on the shortcut menu.
or
- Right-click the file or folder you want to copy, and then click Copy on the shortcut menu. (You can also click the file or folder and then press the Ctrl+C keys.)
- Navigate to and right-click the destination folder, and then click Paste on the shortcut menu. (You can also click the destination folder and then press the Ctrl+V keys.)

You'll copy the three graphics files from the Tutorial folder to the Graphics folder now.

## To copy files using the shortcut menu:

▶ **1.** In the Tutorial window, click the **Map** file.

▶ **2.** Hold down the **Ctrl** key, click the **Paris** file, click the **Rome** file, and then release the **Ctrl** key. Three files are selected in the Tutorial window.

▶ **3.** Right-click a selected file, and then click **Copy** on the shortcut menu.

▶ **4.** Right-click the **Graphics** folder, and then click **Paste** on the shortcut menu. Windows copies the three files to the Graphics folder.

Now you can use a different technique to copy the Proposal and Members files to the Playground folder.

## To copy two files by right-dragging:

▶ **1.** Click the background of the folder window to remove the selection from the three files, hold down the **Ctrl** key, click the **Members** file, click the **Proposal** file, and then release the **Ctrl** key. The two files are selected in the Tutorial window.

▶ **2.** Point to a selected file, and then press and hold the *right* mouse button.

▶ **3.** With the right mouse button still pressed down, drag the **Members** and **Proposal** files to the **Playground** folder, and then release the mouse button. A shortcut menu opens.

▶ **4.** With the left mouse button, click **Copy here** on the shortcut menu to copy the files to the Playground subfolder.

You can move and copy folders in the same way that you move and copy files. When you do, you move or copy all the files contained in the folder.

### PROSKILLS

*Decision Making: Determining Where to Store Files*

When you create and save files on your computer's hard disk, you should store them in subfolders. The top level of the hard disk is off-limits for your files because they could interfere with system files. If you are working on your own computer, store your files within the My Documents folder, which is where many programs save your files by default. When you use a computer on the job, your employer might assign a main folder to you for storing your work. In either case, if you simply store all your files in one folder, you will soon have trouble finding the files you want. Instead, you should create subfolders within a main folder to separate files in a way that makes sense for you.

Even if you store most of your files on removable media, such as USB drives, you still need to organize those files into folders and subfolders. Before you start creating folders, whether on a hard disk or removable disk, you need to plan the organization you will use.

## Naming and Renaming Files

As you work with files, pay attention to filenames—they provide important information about the file, including its contents and purpose. A filename such as Car Sales.docx has three parts:

• Main part of the filename: The name you provide when you create a file, and the name you associate with a file

- Dot: The period ( . ) that separates the main part of the filename from the file extension
- File extension: Usually three or four characters that follow the dot in the filename

The main part of a filename can have up to 255 characters—this gives you plenty of room to name your file accurately enough so that you'll know the contents of the file just by looking at the filename. You can use spaces and certain punctuation symbols in your filenames. Like folder names, however, filenames cannot contain the symbols \ / ? : * " < > | because these characters have special meaning in Windows 7.

A filename might display an **extension**—three or more characters following a dot—to help you identify files. For example, in the filename Car Sales.docx, the extension *docx* identifies the file as one created by Microsoft Office Word, a word-processing program. You might also have a file called Car Sales.jpg—the *jpg* extension identifies the file as one created in a graphics program, such as Paint. Though the main parts of these file-names are identical, their extensions distinguish them as different files. You usually do not need to add extensions to your filenames because the program that you use to create the file adds the file extension automatically. Also, although Windows 7 keeps track of extensions, not all computers are set to display them.

Be sure to give your files and folders meaningful names that help you remember their purpose and contents. You can easily rename a file or folder by using the Rename com-mand on the file's shortcut menu.

**INSIGHT**

## Guidelines for Naming Files

The following are a few suggestions for naming your files:
- Use common names: Avoid cryptic names that might make sense now, but could cause confusion later, such as nonstandard abbreviations or imprecise names like Stuff2013.
- Don't change the file extension: When renaming a file, don't change the file extension. If you do, Windows might not be able to find a program that can open it.
- Find a comfortable balance between too short and too long: Use filenames that are long enough to be meaningful, but short enough to read easily on the screen.

Next, you'll rename the Flyer file to give it a more descriptive name.

### To rename the Flyer file:

▶ **1.** In the Tutorial folder window, double-click the **Playground** folder to open it.

▶ **2.** Right-click the **Flyer** file, and then click **Rename** on the shortcut menu. The file-name is highlighted and a box appears around it.

▶ **3.** Type **Raffle Flyer**, and then press the **Enter** key. The file now appears with the new name.

Trouble? If you make a mistake while typing and you haven't pressed the Enter key yet, press the Backspace key until you delete the mistake, and then complete Step 3. If you've already pressed the Enter key, repeat Steps 2 and 3 to rename the file again.

Trouble? If your computer is set to display file extensions, a message might appear asking if you are sure you want to change the file extension. Click the No button, right-click the Flyer file, click Rename on the shortcut menu, type *Raffle Flyer*, and then press the Enter key.

All the files in the Tutorial folder are now stored in appropriate subfolders. You can streamline the organization of the Tutorial folder by deleting the duplicate files you no longer need.

## Deleting Files and Folders

You should periodically delete files and folders you no longer need so that your main folders and disks don't get cluttered. In a folder window, you delete a file or folder by deleting its icon. When you delete a file from a hard disk, Windows 7 removes the file from the folder but stores the file contents in the Recycle Bin. The **Recycle Bin** is an area on your hard disk that holds deleted files until you remove them permanently; an icon on the desktop allows you easy access to the Recycle Bin. When you delete a folder from the hard disk, the folder and all of its files are stored in the Recycle Bin. If you change your mind and want to retrieve a file or folder deleted from your hard disk, you can use the Recycle Bin to recover it and return it to its original location. However, after you empty the Recycle Bin, you can no longer recover the files it contained.

Shannon reminds you that because you copied the Map, Paris, Proposal, Members, and Rome files to the Graphics and Playground folders, you can safely delete the original files in the Tutorial folder. As with moving, copying, and renaming files and folders, you can delete a file or folder in many ways, including using a shortcut menu.

**To delete files in the Tutorial folder:**

&#9654; 1. Use any technique you've learned to navigate to and open the **Tutorial** folder.

&#9654; 2. Click the **first file** in the file list, hold down the **Shift** key, click the **last file** in the file list, and then release the **Shift** key. All the files in the Tutorial folder are now selected. None of the subfolders should be selected.

&#9654; 3. Right-click the selected files, and then click **Delete** on the shortcut menu. Windows 7 asks if you're sure you want to delete these files.

&#9654; 4. Click the **Yes** button to confirm that you want to delete five files.

So far, you've moved, copied, renamed, and deleted files, but you haven't viewed any of their contents. To view file contents, you can preview or open the file. When you double-click a file in a folder window, Windows 7 starts the associated program and opens the file. To preview the file contents, you can select the file in a folder window, and then click the Show the preview pane button 🔲 on the toolbar to open the Preview pane, if necessary.

## Working with Compressed Files

If you transfer files from one location to another, such as from your hard disk to a removable disk or vice versa, or from one computer to another via e-mail, you can store the files in a compressed (zipped) folder so that they take up less disk space. You can then transfer the files more quickly. When you create a compressed folder, Windows 7 displays a zipper on the folder icon.

You compress a folder so that the files it contains use less space on the disk. Compare two folders—a folder named Photos that contains about 8.6 MB of files, and a compressed folder containing the same files but requiring only 6.5 MB of disk space. In this case, the compressed files use about 25 percent less disk space than the uncompressed files.

You can create a compressed folder using the Send to Compressed (zipped) folder command on the shortcut menu of one or more selected files or folders. Then you can compress additional files or folders by dragging them into the compressed folder. You can open a file directly from a compressed folder, although you cannot modify the file. To edit and save a compressed file, you must extract it first. When you **extract** a file, you create an uncompressed copy of the file in a folder you specify. The original file remains in the compressed folder.

If a different compression program, such as WinZip, has been installed on your computer, the Send to Compressed (zipped) folder command might not appear on the shortcut menu. Instead, it might be replaced by the name of your compression program. In this case, refer to your compression program's Help system for instructions on working with compressed files.

Shannon suggests that you compress the files and folders in the Tutorial folder so you can more quickly transfer them to another location.

### To compress the folders and files in the Tutorial folder:

▶ **1.** Select all the folders in the Tutorial folder, right-click the selected folders, point to **Send to**, and then click **Compressed (zipped) folder**. After a few moments, a new compressed folder with a zipper icon appears in the Tutorial window.

  **Trouble?** If the Compressed (zipped) folder command does not appear on the Send to submenu of the shortcut menu, this means that a different compression program is probably installed on your computer. Click a blank area of the Tutorial window to close the shortcut menu, and then read but do not perform the remaining steps.

▶ **2.** Type **Final Files** and then press the **Enter** key to rename the compressed folder. See Figure 9.

  **Trouble?** If the filename is not selected after you create the compressed folder, right-click the compressed folder, click Rename on the shortcut menu, and then complete Step 2.

---

**Figure 9** | **Creating a compressed folder**

When you compress the folders in the Tutorial folder, the original folders remain in the Tutorial folder—only copies are stored in the new compressed folder.

You open a compressed folder by double-clicking it. You can then move and copy files and folders in a compressed folder, although you cannot rename them. When you extract files, Windows 7 uncompresses and copies them to a location that you specify, preserving the files in their folders as appropriate.

## To extract the compressed files:

▶ 1. Right-click the **Final Files** compressed folder, and then click **Extract All** on the shortcut menu. The Extract Compressed (Zipped) Folders dialog box opens.

▶ 2. Press the **End** key to deselect the path in the text box, press the **Backspace** key as many times as necessary to delete *Final Files*, and then type **Extracted**. The final three parts of the path in the text box should be *\FM\Tutorial\Extracted*. See Figure 10.

Figure 10  Extracting compressed files

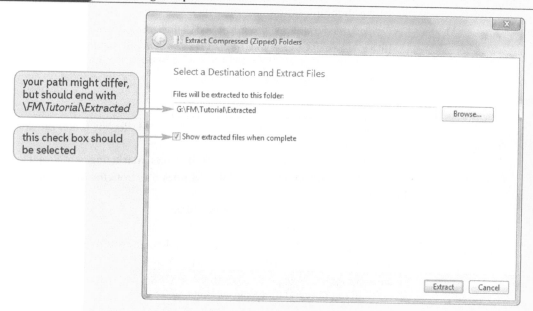

your path might differ, but should end with *\FM\Tutorial\Extracted*

this check box should be selected

▶ 3. Make sure the **Show extracted files when complete** check box is checked, and then click the **Extract** button. The Extracted folder opens, showing the Graphics, Job Hunt, and Playground folders.

▶ 4. Open each folder to make sure it contains the files you worked with in this tutorial.

▶ 5. Close all open windows.

## Quick Check

REVIEW

1. What do you call a named collection of data stored on a disk?
2. The letter C is typically used for the _____ drive of a computer.
3. The term _____ refers to any window that displays the contents of a folder.
4. Describe the difference between the left and right panes of the Windows Explorer window.
5. What does the file path tell you?
6. True or False. The advantage of moving a file or folder by dragging with the right mouse button is that you can efficiently complete your work with one action.
7. What does a filename indicate?
8. Is a file deleted from a compressed folder when you extract it?

*Practice the skills you learned in the tutorial.*

**PRACTICE**

## Review Assignments

For a list of Data Files in the Review folder, see page FM 1.

Complete the following steps, recording your answers to any questions:

1. Use a folder window as necessary to find the following information:
   - Where are you supposed to store the files you use in the Review Assignments for this tutorial?
   - Describe the method you will use to navigate to the location where you save your files for this book.
   - Do you need to follow any special guidelines or conventions when naming the files you save for this book? For example, should all the filenames start with your course number or tutorial number? If so, describe the conventions.
   - When you are instructed to open a file for this book, what location are you supposed to use?
   - Describe the method you will use to navigate to this location.
2. Use a folder window to navigate to and open the **FM\Review folder** provided with your Data Files.
3. In the Review folder, create three folders: **Business**, **Marketing**, and **Project**.
4. Move the **Bills**, **Budget**, **Plan**, **Receipt**, and **Sales** files from the Review folder to the Business folder.
5. Move the **Brochure** file to the Marketing folder.
6. Copy the remaining files to the Project folder.
7. Delete the files in the Review folder (do *not* delete any folders).
8. Rename the Photo file in the Project folder as **Pond**.
9. Create a compressed (zipped) folder in the Review folder named **Final Review** that contains all the files and folders in the Review folder.
10. Extract the contents of the Final Review folder to a new folder named **Extracted**. (*Hint*: The file path will end with \FM\Review\Extracted.)
11. Locate all copies of the Budget file in the subfolders of the Review folder. In which locations did you find this file?
12. Close all open windows.
13. Submit the results of the preceding steps to your instructor, either in printed or electronic form, as requested.

*Use your skills to manage files and folders for an arts organization.*

**APPLY**

## Case Problem 1

For a list of Data Files in the Case1 folder, see page FM 1.

***Jefferson Street Fine Arts Center***    Rae Wysnewski owns the Jefferson Street Fine Arts Center (JSFAC) in Pittsburgh, and offers classes and gallery, studio, and practice space for young artists, musicians, and dancers. Rae opened JSFAC two years ago, and this year the center has a record enrollment in its classes. She hires you to teach a painting class and to show her how to manage her files on her new Windows 7 computer. Complete the following steps:

1. In the FM\Case1 folder in your Data Files, create two folders: **Invoices** and **Art Class**.
2. Move the **Inv01**, **Inv02**, and **Inv03** files from the Case1 folder to the Invoices folder.
3. In the Invoices folder, rename the Inv01 file as **Jan**, the Inv02 file as **Feb**, and the Inv03 file as **March**.
4. Move the three text documents from the Case1 folder to the Art Class folder. Rename the three documents, using shorter but still descriptive names.

5. Copy the remaining files in the Case1 folder to the Art Class folder.
6. Switch to Details view, if necessary, and then answer the following questions:
   - What is the largest file in the Art Class folder?
   - How many files in the Art Class folder are JPEG images?
7. Delete the Garden and Sculpture files from the Case1 folder.
8. Open the Recycle Bin folder by double-clicking the Recycle Bin icon on the desktop. Do the Garden and Sculpture files appear in the Recycle Bin folder? Explain why or why not. Close the Recycle Bin window.
9. Make a copy of the Art Class folder in the Case1 folder. The duplicate folder appears as Art Class – Copy. Rename the Art Class – Copy folder as **Images**.
10. Delete the text files from the Images folder.
11. Delete the Garden and Sculpture files from the Art Class folder.
12. Close all open windows, and then submit the results of the preceding steps to your instructor, either in printed or electronic form, as requested.

*Use your skills to manage files for a social service organization.*

**CHALLENGE**

## Case Problem 2

There are no Data Files needed for this Case Problem.

***First Call Outreach***   Victor Crillo is the director of a social service organization named First Call Outreach in Toledo, Ohio. Its mission is to connect people who need help from local and state agencies to the appropriate service. Victor has a dedicated staff, but they are all relatively new to Windows 7. Because of this, they often have trouble finding files that they have saved on their hard disks. He asks you to demonstrate how to find files in Windows 7. Complete the following:

⊕ **EXPLORE**
1. Windows 7 Help and Support includes topics that explain how to search for files on a disk without looking through all the folders. Click the Start button, click Help and Support, and then use one of the following methods to locate topics on searching for files:
   - In the Windows Help and Support window, click the Learn about Windows Basics link. Click the Working with files and folders link.
   - In the Windows Help and Support window, click the Browse Help topics link. (If necessary, click the Home icon first, and then click the Browse Help topics link.) Click the Files, folders, and libraries link, and then click Working with files and folders.
   - In the Search Help box, type **searching for files**, and then press the Enter key. Click the Working with files and folders link.

⊕ **EXPLORE**
2. In the *In this article* section, click Finding files. Read the topic and click any *See also* or *For more information* links, if necessary, to provide the following information:
   a. Where is the Search box located?
   b. Do you need to type the entire filename to find the file?
   c. What does it mean to filter the view?

⊕ **EXPLORE**
3. Use the Windows 7 Help and Support window to locate topics related to using libraries. Read the topics to answer the following questions:
   a. What are the names of the four default libraries?
   b. When you move, copy, or save files in the Pictures library, in what folder are they actually stored?
   c. What can you click to play all the music files in the Music library?
4. Submit the results of the preceding steps to your instructor, either in printed or electronic form, as requested.

---

## SAM: Skills Assessment Manager

ASSESS

For current SAM information, including versions and content details, visit SAM Central (http://samcentral.course.com). If you have a SAM user profile, you may have access to hands-on instruction, practice, and assessment of the skills covered in this tutorial. Since various versions of SAM are supported throughout the life of this text, check with your instructor for the correct instructions and URL/Web site for accessing assignments.

### ENDING DATA FILES

FM →

**Tutorial**
- Extracted
- Graphics
- Job Hunt
- Playground

Final Files.zip

**Review**
- Business
- Extracted
- Marketing
- Project

Final Review.zip

**Case1**
- Art Class
- Images
- Invoices

 # Decision Making

## Choosing the Most Efficient Organization for Your Computer Files

Decision making is choosing the best option from many possible alternatives. The alternative you select is your decision. When making a decision, you typically complete the following steps:

1. Gather information.
2. Make predictions.
3. Select the best alternative.
4. Prepare an action plan.
5. Perform tasks and monitor results.
6. Verify the accuracy of the decision.

If you are involved in making a complex decision that affects many people, you perform all six steps in the process. If you are making a simpler decision that does not affect many people, you can perform only those steps that relate to your decision.

### Gather Information and Select the Best Alternative

Start by gathering information to identify your alternatives. For example, when organizing your files, you could store most of your work on your computer hard disk or on removable media, such as a USB drive or an external hard drive. Ask questions that quantify information, or use numbers to compare the alternatives. For example, how much space do you need for your files? In how many locations do you need to access the files? How often do you work with your files?

Next, ask questions that compare the qualities of the alternatives. For example, is one alternative easier to perform or maintain than another? After testing each alternative by asking both types of questions, one alternative should emerge as the best choice for you. If one option does not seem like the best alternative, continue comparing alternatives by listing the pros and cons of each.

### Prepare an Action Plan

After you make a decision, prepare an action plan by identifying the steps you need to perform to put the decision into practice. One way to do this is to work backward from your final goal. If you are determining how best to manage your computer files, your final goal might be a set of folders and files organized so that you can find any file quickly. Start by listing the tasks you need to perform to meet your goal. Be as specific as possible to avoid confusion later. For example, instead of listing *Create folders* as a task, identify each folder and subfolder by name and indicate which files or types of files each folder should contain.

Next, estimate how long each task will take, and assign the task to someone. For simple decisions, you assign most tasks to yourself. If you need to use outside resources, include those in the action plan. For example, if you decide to store your files on USB drives, include a step to purchase the drives you need. If someone else needs to approve any of your tasks, be sure to include that step in the action plan. If appropriate, the action plan can also track your budget. For example, you could track expenses for a new hard disk or backup media.

# Complete the Tasks and Monitor the Results

After you prepare an action plan and receive any necessary approvals, perform the tasks outlined in the plan. For example, create or rename the folders you identified in your action plan, and then move existing files into each folder. As you perform each step, mark its status as complete or pending, for example.

When you complete all the tasks in the action plan, monitor the results. For example, after reorganizing your files, did you meet your goal of being able to quickly find any file when you need it? If so, continue to follow your plan as you add files and folders to your computer. If not, return to your plan and determine where you could improve it.

## Organize Your Files

Now that you have reviewed the fundamentals of managing files, organize the files and folders you use for course work or for other projects on your own computer. Be sure to follow the guidelines presented in this tutorial for developing an organization strategy, creating folders, naming files, and moving, copying, deleting, and compressing files. To manage your own files, complete the following tasks:

1. Use a program such as Word, WordPad, or Notepad to create a plan for organizing your files. List the types of files you work with, and then determine whether you want to store them on your hard disk or on removable media. Then sketch the folders and subfolders you will use to manage these files. If you choose a hard disk as your storage medium, make sure you plan to store your work files and folders in a subfolder of the Documents folder.
2. Use Windows Explorer or the Computer window to navigate to your files. Determine which tool you prefer for managing files, if you have a preference.
3. Create or rename the main folders you want to use for your files. Then create or rename the subfolders you will use.
4. Move and copy files to the appropriate folders according to your plan, and rename and delete files as necessary.
5. Create a backup copy of your work files by creating a compressed file and then copying the compressed file to a removable disk, such as a USB flash drive.
6. Submit your finished plan to your instructor, either in printed or electronic form, as requested.

# GLOSSARY/INDEX

Information function, EX 140

**information management software** Software that keeps track of schedules, appointments, contacts, and "to-do" lists. ECC 25

**inkjet printer** A printer that sprays ink onto paper and produces output whose quality is comparable to that of a laser printer. ECC 11

**inline object** An object that behaves as if it were text; like an individual letter, an inline object has a specific location within a line of text, and its position changes as you add or delete text. Compare to a floating object. WD 186

inline picture, WD 52

**input** The data or instructions you type into the computer. ECC 2

**input device** An instrument, such as a keyboard or a mouse, that you use to enter data and issue commands to the computer. ECC 8–10

Insert Address Block dialog box, INT 24

Insert Chart dialog box, EX 213

Insert Citation button, WD 102

Insert Function button, EX 132

Insert Function dialog box
    entering functions, EX 145–149

Insert Greeting Line dialog box, INT 26

Insert Merge Field button, INT 23

INSERT tab
    Chart button, INT 4, WD 209
    Charts group, EX 200
    Cover Page button, WD 164
    Footer button, WD 159
    Header button, WD 159
    Object button arrow, WD 192, WD 193
    Online Picture button, WD 208
    Online Pictures button, PPT 74
    Page Number button, WD 159
    Picture button, PPT 39
    Pictures button, WD 30
    Recommended Chart button, EX 197
    Shapes button, PPT 77, WD 194, WD 195
    Table button, WD 120, WD 128
    Video button, PPT 111, PPT 112

**insertion point** An object on the screen that indicates where text will appear when you start typing, usually appears as a blinking line. AC 13, PPT 7, WD 2
    moving, WD 14

INT function, EX 141

**Integer** The Field Size property that stores whole numbers from -32,768 to 32,767 in two bytes. AC 58

**intellectual property** All creations of the human mind, such as original ideas and creative works

presented in a form that can be shared or that others can recreate, emulate, or manufacture. On a webpage, intellectual property includes the text, images, and videos on the page, as well as the design of the page itself. IB 21–23, PPT 76
    fair use, IB 21–22
    plagiarism, IB 22–23
    public domain, IB 22

**interest** The amount added to the principal by the lender. EX 192

international date format, EX 23

**Internet** A worldwide collection of computer networks that allows people to communicate and exchange information; the largest network in the world. ECC 19–20, IB 4
    connecting to, IB 4

Internet Explorer app, IB 2, IB 11–16
    History list, IB 15–16
    starting, IB 4–5, IB 11–12
    tabbed browsing, IB 13–15

Internet Explorer button, IB 3

Internet Protocol (IP) addresses, IB 5

**Internet service provider (ISP)** A company that provides Internet access by connecting your computer to one of its servers via a telephone or cable modem. IB 4

invisible web. *See* deep web

**IP address** A unique number consisting of four sets of numbers from 0 to 255, separated by periods (such as 216.35.148.4), that identifies the server or computer connected to the Internet. IB 5

IP addresses. *See* Internet Protocol addresses

IPMT function, EX 192, EX 197

ISP. *See* Internet service provider

## J

**join line** In the Relationships window, the line that connects the common field that joins two tables. AC 77

**joining** To relate tables using a common field. AC 98

JPEG file, WD 224

**justified alignment** A type of alignment in which full lines of text are evenly spaced between both the left and the right margins, and no text is ragged. WD 43, WD 44

## K

K. *See* kilobyte

KB. *See* kilobyte

**Key Tip** Label that appears over each tab and command on the ribbon when you press the Alt key that specifies the key or keys to click to access that tab, button, or command. EX 6

**keyboard** The most frequently used input device; consists of three major parts: the main keyboard, the keypads, and the function keys. ECC 2, ECC 8, ECC 9, WIN 4
    Windows and Windows 7 compared, FM 4

**keyboard shortcut** A key or combination of keys you press to access a feature or perform a command more efficiently. AC 79, EX 6, WIN 25

**keyword (Internet)** Specific word or phrase that describes a topic of interest and can be used to search for information on that topic. IB 2, IB 3

**keyword (PowerPoint)** Word or phrase that you can enter in as search box that describes an image that you want to search for. PPT 74

**kilobyte (KB or K)** 1,024 bytes, or approximately one thousand bytes. ECC 13

**kilobytes per second (Kbps)** The measurement used for the data transfer rate for CD and DVD drives. ECC 16

## L

label, ribbon, AC 13

LAN. *See* local area network

**landscape orientation** The orientation where the page is wider than it is tall. AC 206, EX 53, WD 38

language, proofing, PPT 94–97

**laptop computer** A small, lightweight computer designed for portability. Also called notebook computer. ECC 4, ECC 5

Large icons view button, FM 3

**laser printer** A printer that produces high-quality output quickly and efficiently by transferring a temporary laser image onto paper with toner. ECC 11

**layout** The arrangement of placeholders on the slide; in SmartArt, the arrangement of the shapes in the diagram. PPT 11, PPT 24

**Layout view** The Access view in which you can make design changes to a form or report while it is displaying data so that you can immediately see the effects of changing the design. AC 34, AC 181
    modifying form design, AC 185–193
    modifying report design, AC 212–216

**LCD (liquid crystal display)** A display technology that creates images by manipulating light within a layer of liquid crystal. ECC 10

**leader line** A line that connects a data label to its corresponding data marker. EX 207

# TASK REFERENCE

| TASK | PAGE # | RECOMMENDED METHOD |
|---|---|---|
| Absolute reference, create | EX 154 | Type a $ before both the row and column references |
| Access Query results, copy to PowerPoint slide | INT 37 | In query datasheet, click datasheet selector, click HOME tab, in Clipboard group click Copy, on taskbar click PowerPoint button, click in content placeholder, click HOME tab, in Clipboard group click Paste button arrow, click Keep Text Only button |
| Access Query Results, export from Access database to Excel or Word | INT 29 | *See* Reference box: Exporting the Results of an Access Query to Excel or Word |
| Access, start | AC 7 | Click the Access 2013 tile on the Windows Start screen |
| Action, reverse last in WordPad | WIN 21 | Click ↺ on the Quick Access Toolbar |
| Action, undo or redo | EX 19 | Click ↺ or ↻ on the Quick Access Toolbar |
| Aggregate functions, use in a datasheet | AC 162 | Open the table or query in Datasheet view, in Records group on HOME tab click Totals button, click Total field row, click function |
| Aggregate functions, use in a query | AC 163 | Display the query in Design view, click the Totals button in the Show/Hide group on the DESIGN tab |
| Animation Painter, use | PPT 106 | Click animated object, click ANIMATIONS tab, in Advanced Animation group, click Animation Painter, click object to animate |
| Animation, apply | PPT 103 | *See* Reference box: Applying Animations |
| Animation, change order | PPT 106 | Click ANIMATIONS tab, click animation sequence icon, in Timing group click Move Earlier or Move Later |
| Application, close | WIN 27 | Press Alt+F4 |
| Application, start | WIN 13 | *See* Reference box: Starting an Application |
| Apps screen, display | WIN 15 | Right-click a blank area on the Start screen, click All apps |
| AutoCorrect, change | PPT 10 | Click ☰ ▾, click command on menu |
| AutoSum feature, enter function with | EX 37 | Click a cell, click Σ AutoSum ▾ in the Editing group on the HOME tab, click a function, verify the range, press Enter |
| Bibliography, insert | WD 109 | Create citations in the document, click the desired location for the bibliography, click Bibliography button in Citations & Bibliography group on REFERENCES tab, click a bibliography style |
| Bold text, enter in WordPad | WIN 21 | Click **B** in the Font group on the Home tab |
| Border, add to cells | EX 50 | Select a range, click ▦ ▾ in the Font group on the HOME tab, click a border |
| Border, insert around page | WD 226 | Click DESIGN tab, click the Page Borders button in the Page Background group, click the Page Border tab, click Box |
| Border, insert around paragraph | WD 45 | Click in a paragraph, click ▦ ▾ in the Paragraph group on the HOME tab, click a border style |
| Bulleted or numbered item, demote | PPT 14, 16 | Click bullet or number, click ⇥ |
| Bulleted or numbered item, promote | PPT 15, 16 | Click bullet or number, click ⇤ |
| Bullets, add to paragraph | WD 71 | Select paragraphs, click ☷ in the Paragraph group on the HOME tab |
| Calculated field, add to a query | AC 157 | *See* Reference box: Using Expression Builder |

| TASK | PAGE # | RECOMMENDED METHOD |
|------|--------|---------------------|
| Cell, change fill color | EX 76 | Click 🪣 ▾ in the Font group on the HOME tab, click a color |
| Cell, clear contents of | EX 58 | Select a cell, press Delete |
| Cell, delete | EX 46 | Select a cell, range, column, or row; click Delete button in the Cells group on the HOME tab |
| Cell, edit | EX 19 | Double-click a cell, enter changes |
| Cell, go to | EX 10 | Click Find & Select button in the Editing group on the HOME tab, click Go To |
| Cell contents, align within a cell | EX 87 | Click ▤, ▤, or ▤ in the Alignment group on the HOME tab |
| Cell contents, change indent of | EX 88 | Click ▤ or ▤ in the Alignment group on the HOME tab |
| Cell contents, rotate | EX 91 | Click ▧ ▾ in the Alignment group on the HOME tab, click angle |
| Cells, merge and center | EX 90 | Select adjacent cells, click ▦ in the Alignment group on the HOME tab |
| Charms bar, display | WIN 11 | Point to the upper-right or lower-right corner of screen |
| Chart, choose style | EX 204 | Select the chart, click ✎, select a chart style |
| Chart, create | EX 197 | *See* Reference box: Creating a Chart |
| Chart, resize | EX 202 | Select the chart, drag the sizing handle |
| Chart element, format | EX 205 | Double-click the chart element, make changes in the Format pane |
| Chart type, change | EX 214 | Select the chart, click the Change Chart Type button in the Type group on the CHART TOOLS DESIGN tab, click a new chart type |
| Citations, create and edit | WD 103 | *See* Reference box: Creating Citations |
| Clip art, insert | WD 213 | Click INSERT tab, click the Online Pictures button in the Illustrations group, type keywords in the Office.com Clip Art search box, press Enter, click an image, click the Insert button |
| Clipboard task pane, open | WD 76 | In Clipboard group on HOME tab, click the Dialog Box Launcher |
| Column, change width | EX 25 | Drag the right border of the column heading left or right |
| Column, delete from table | WD 136 | Select the column to delete, click the Delete button on the Mini toolbar, click Delete Columns |
| Column, insert in table | WD 135 | Point to the border between two columns, click ⊕ |
| Column, resize width in a datasheet | AC 18 | Double-click ✛ on the right border of the column heading |
| Column, select | EX 26 | Click the column heading |
| Columns, format section in | WD 181 | Click PAGE LAYOUT tab, click Columns button in the Page Setup group, select options, click OK |
| Comments, display and insert | WD 67 | *See* Reference box: Working with Comments |
| Compressed folder, extract all files and folders from | FM 27 | Click the compressed folder, click the Compressed Folder Tools Extract tab, click the Extract all button |
| Compressed folder, open | FM 27 | Double-click the compressed folder |
| Conditional format, apply | EX 108 | *See* Reference box: Highlighting a Cell with a Conditional Format |
| Cover page, delete | WD 164 | Click INSERT tab, click the Cover Page button in the Pages group, click Remove Current Cover Page |
| Cover page, insert | WD 164 | Click INSERT tab, click the Cover Page button in the Pages group, click cover page |
| Data bars, create | EX 242 | *See* Reference Box: Creating Data Bars |

| TASK | PAGE # | RECOMMENDED METHOD |
|---|---|---|
| Data, find | AC 194 | *See* Reference box: Finding Data in a Form or Datasheet |
| Data Type gallery, add fields to a table with | AC 86 | Click the FIELDS tab, click More Fields in the Add & Delete group, click the field or Quick Start selection to add |
| Database, compact and repair | AC 42 | *See* Reference box: Compacting and Repairing a Database |
| Database, create a blank | AC 7 | Start Access, click Blank desktop database, type the database name, select the drive and folder, click OK, click Create |
| Database, open | AC 26 | *See* Reference box: Opening a Database |
| Datasheet view for tables, switch to | AC 75 | In the Views group on the DESIGN tab, click the View button |
| Date, display on slides | PPT 121 | Click INSERT tab, in Text group, click Header & Footer, click Date check box, click Apply to All |
| Date, enter into a cell | EX 23 | Click a cell, type the date, press Enter or Tab |
| Date, insert the current | EX 167 | Enter TODAY() or NOW() function in cell |
| Design view, switch to | AC 73 | In the Views group on the FIELDS tab, click the View button |
| Desktop application, close inactive | WIN 26 | Right-click the application's button on taskbar, click Close window |
| Desktop application, switch to another open | WIN 23 | Click the application's button on taskbar |
| Document, print | WD 25 | Click FILE tab, click Print, click Print button |
| Document, save as a PDF | WD 227 | Click FILE tab, click Export, click the Create PDF/XPS Document button, navigate to the location where you want to save the PDF, click the Publish button |
| Documents library, open | FM 10 | In File Explorer, click ▷ next to Libraries, click ▷ next to Documents |
| Drop cap, insert | WD 200 | Click in paragraph, click the INSERT tab, click the Drop Cap button in the Text group, select options, click OK |
| Endnotes and footnotes, create | WD 150 | *See* Reference box: Inserting a Footnote or an Endnote |
| Envelope, create and save in current document | WD 28 | Click the MAILINGS tab, click the Envelopes button in the Create group, enter return address, if necessary, enter delivery address, click Add to Document |
| Excel chart, embed in Word document | INT 6 | *See* Reference box: Embedding an Excel Chart in a Word Document |
| Excel Table, embed in PowerPoint slide | INT 39 | In worksheet, select cells, click HOME tab, in Clipboard group click Copy, on taskbar click PowerPoint button, click HOME tab, in Clipboard group click Paste button arrow, click Embed |
| Excel worksheet, import data from | AC 81 | Click the EXTERNAL DATA tab, click Excel in the Import & Link group, complete the import dialog boxes |
| Excel worksheet, link to Word document | INT 11 | *See* Reference box: Linking Excel Worksheet Data to a Word Document |
| Excel, start | EX 4 | Click the Excel 2013 title on the Start screen |
| Favorite webpage, delete | IB 19 | Click ☆, click Favorites tab, right-click favorite, click Delete |
| Favorite webpage, save from desktop application | IB 17 | Click ☆, click Favorites tab, click Add to favorites, change name or folder, click Add |
| Field, add to a table | AC 69 | *See* Reference box: Adding a Field Between Two Existing Fields |
| Field, define in a table | AC 59 | *See* Reference box: Defining a Field in Design View |
| Field, delete from a table | AC 87 | *See* Reference box: Deleting a Field from a Table Structure |

| TASK | PAGE # | RECOMMENDED METHOD |
|---|---|---|
| Field, move to a new location in a table | AC 69 | Display the table in Design view, click the field's row selector, drag the field with the pointer |
| Field property change, update | AC 91 | Click [icon], select the option for updating the field property |
| File Explorer, open | FM 10 | Click [icon] on the taskbar |
| File Explorer, return to a previous location | FM 14 | Click [icon] |
| File list, sort | FM 14 | Click the column heading button |
| File, copy | FM 24 | Right-click the file, click Copy, right-click destination, click Paste |
| File, delete | FM 25 | Right-click the file, click Delete |
| File, move | FM 21 | Drag the file to the folder |
| File, open from File Explorer | FM 15 | Right-click the file, point to Open with, click an application |
| File, rename | FM 26 | Right-click the file, click Rename, type the new filename, press Enter |
| File, save with new name in WordPad | FM 18 | Click the File tab, click Save as, enter the filename, click Save |
| Files and folders, compress | FM 27 | Select the files to compress, click the Share tab, click the Zip button in the Send group |
| Files, select multiple | FM 24 | Press and hold the Ctrl key and click the files |
| Files, view in Large Icons view | FM 13 | Click the View tab, click [icon] in the Layout group |
| Fill handle, use | EX 162 | *See Reference box: Copying Formulas and Formats with AutoFill* |
| Filter By Selection, activate | AC 136 | *See Reference box: Using Filter By Selection* |
| Find and replace, text or format | EX 104 | Click Find & Select in the Editing group on the HOME tab, click Replace |
| Flash Fill, apply | EX 49 | Type a few entries in a column to establish a pattern, Flash Fill adds the remaining entries |
| Folder, create | FM 19 | Click the New folder button in the New group on the Home tab |
| Font, change color | EX 73 | Click [icon] in the Font group on the HOME tab, click a color |
| Font, change size | EX 71 | Click the Font Size arrow in the Font group on the HOME tab, click a point size |
| Font, change style | EX 71 | Click [B], [I], or [U] in the Font group on the HOME tab |
| Font, change typeface | EX 71 | Click the Font arrow in the Font group on the HOME tab, click a font |
| Footer, add | WD 160 | Double-click the bottom margin, type footer text, or select a preformatted footer by clicking the Footer button in the Header & Footer group on the DESIGN tab |
| Footer, add to slides | PPT 121 | Click INSERT tab, in Text group, click Header & Footer, click Footer check box, click Footer box, type footer, click Apply to All |
| Footer, don't show on title slide | PPT 122 | Click INSERT tab, in Text group, click Header & Footer, click Don't show in title slide check box, click Apply to All |
| Format Painter, use | PPT 21 | Select formatted text or object, click HOME tab, in Clipboard group click Format Painter, select object to format |
| Form Wizard, activate | AC 182 | Click the CREATE tab, click Form Wizard in the Forms group, choose the table or query for the form, select fields, click Next |

| TASK | PAGE # | RECOMMENDED METHOD |
|---|---|---|
| Formula, enter | EX 32 | Click the cell, type = and then a formula, press Enter or Tab |
| Formulas, display in a worksheet | EX 56 | Press Ctrl+` |
| Function, insert | EX 145 | Click a function category in the Function Library group on the FORMULAS tab, click a function, enter arguments, click OK |
| Goal seek, perform | EX 180 | *See Reference box: Performing What-if Analysis and Goal Seek* |
| Graphic object, resize | WD 50 | Click graphic object, click the FORMAT tab, change the height and width settings in the Size group |
| Graphic object, wrap text around | WD 187 | Click graphic object, click ⬜ next to the graphic object, click a text wrapping option |
| Header and footer, add to notes and handouts | PPT 122 | Click INSERT tab, in Text group, click Header & Footer, click Notes and Handouts, select check boxes for items to display, type information, click Apply to All |
| Header, add | WD 159 | Double-click the top margin, type header text, or select a preformatted header by clicking the Header button in the Header & Footer group on the DESIGN tab |
| Help, search for topic | WIN 29 | On the Help home page, click in the Search box, type word or phrase, press Enter |
| Help, start | WIN 27 | On the Start screen, type help, click Help and Support on the Apps screen |
| Help, use Browse help list | WIN 29 | On the Help home page, click Browse help |
| Help, view Get started topics | WIN 28 | On the Help home page, click Get started link |
| History list, use (desktop application only) | IB 15 | Click ⭐, click History tab, click folder, click webpage |
| Hyperlink, remove | WD 12 | Right-click hyperlink, click Remove Hyperlink |
| Hyphenation, turn on | WD 142 | Click PAGE LAYOUT tab, click the Hyphenation button in the Page Setup group, click Automatic |
| Internet Explorer app, start | IB 4 | On Start screen, click Internet Explorer tile |
| Internet Explorer desktop application, start | IB 11 | On Start screen, click Desktop tile; on taskbar click 🅔 |
| Layout, change | PPT 13 | Click HOME tab, in Slides group click Layout button, click layout |
| Line spacing, change | WD 18 | Select text, click ↕ in the Paragraph group on HOME tab, click a spacing option |
| Linked object, edit | INT 14 | Right-click linked object, point to Linked <Type> Object, click Edit Link, edit linked file |
| Linked object, update | INT 13 | Right-click linked object, click Update Link |
| Link, use | IB 7 | Point to link to see URL in ScreenTip; click link to load page |
| Mail Merge, create merged document | INT 28 | Click MAILINGS tab, in Finish group, click Finish & Merge, click Edit Individual Documents, click All option button, click OK |
| Mail Merge, edit recipient list | INT 22 | Click MAILINGS tab, in Start Mail Merge group, click Edit Recipients, make selections, click OK |
| Mail Merge, insert combined merge fields | INT 24 | Click MAILINGS tab, in Write & Insert Fields group, click Address Block or Greeting Line, make format selections, click OK |
| Mail Merge, insert individual merge fields | INT 23 | Click MAILINGS tab, in Write & Insert Fields group, click Insert Merge Field button arrow, click merge field |

| TASK | PAGE # | RECOMMENDED METHOD |
|---|---|---|
| Mail Merge, preview merged document | INT 27 | Click MAILINGS tab, in Preview Results group, click Preview Results |
| Mail Merge, select existing Access data source | INT 21 | Click MAILINGS tab, in Start Mail Merge group, click Select Recipients, click Use an Existing List, navigate to location, click file, click Open, click table or query, click OK |
| Mail Merge, sort recipient list | INT 22 | Click MAILINGS tab, in Start Mail Merge group, click Edit Recipients, click Sort link, click Sort by arrow, click field name, click Ascending or Descending option button, click OK |
| Mail Merge, start | INT 20 | Click MAILINGS tab, in Start Mail Merge group, click Start Mail Merge, click Letters |
| Margins, change | WD 23 | Click PAGE LAYOUT tab, click the Margins button in the Page Setup group on HOME tab, click a margins option |
| Margins, set | EX 121 | Click the Margins button in the Page Setup group on the PAGE LAYOUT tab, select a margin size |
| Media, compress | PPT 119 | Click FILE tab, on Info screen, click Compress Media, click quality option, click Close |
| Microsoft Access Help, search | AC 41 | Click ? on the title bar, enter the search text in the search box, press Enter |
| Mixed reference, create | EX 154 | Type $ before either the row or column reference |
| My Documents folder, open | FM 10 | In File Explorer, click ▷ next to Libraries, click ▷ next to Documents, click My Documents |
| Number format, apply | EX 82 | Click $, %, ,, or the Number Format arrow in the Number group on the HOME tab |
| Number, enter as text | EX 21 | Type ' and then type the number |
| Numbered list, create | PPT 16 | Select list, click HOME tab, in Paragraph group click 📑 |
| Numbering, add to paragraphs | WD 72 | Select paragraphs, click 📑 in the Paragraph group on HOME tab |
| Object, delete | PPT 48 | Click object, press Delete |
| Object, flip | PPT 83 | Click object, click DRAWING TOOLS FORMAT tab, in Arrange group click Rotate, click Flip option |
| Object, move | PPT 45 | Click object, drag to new position with ⬚ |
| Object, open | AC 22 | Double-click the object in the Navigation Pane |
| Object, rotate | PPT 83 | Click object, drag rotate handle |
| Object, save | AC 20 | Click 💾, type the object name, click OK |
| Online pictures, insert | PPT 75 | In content placeholder click 🖼, type keywords in Office.com Clip Art box, click 🔍, click image, click Insert |
| Page break, insert | WD 108 | Click where you want to insert a page break, click INSERT tab, click the Page Break button in the Pages group |
| Page break, insert or remove | EX 116 | *See* Reference box: Inserting and Removing Page Breaks |
| Page number, insert | WD 98 | Click INSERT tab, click the Page Number button in the Header & Footer group, select options from menu |
| Page orientation, change | WD 38 | Click PAGE LAYOUT tab, click the Orientation button in the Page Setup group, click an orientation |
| Page tab, close | IB 14 | On page tab, click ✖ or ✖ |

| TASK | PAGE # | RECOMMENDED METHOD |
|------|--------|--------------------|
| Page tab, open | IB 13 | *See* Reference box: Opening Tabs for Browsing |
| Paragraph spacing, add or remove default | WD 18 | Click paragraph, click ⬚ in the Paragraph group on HOME tab, click options to add or remove space before or after paragraphs |
| Paragraph spacing, select specific setting | WD 48 | Click paragraph, click PAGE LAYOUT tab, adjust settings in the Spacing Before and After boxes in Paragraph group |
| PDF, open in Word | WD 228 | Click the FILE tab, click Open, navigate to the folder containing the PDF, click the PDF, click the Open button, click the OK button |
| Photo compression options, change | PPT 43 | *See* Reference box: Modifying Photo Compression Settings and Removing Cropped Areas |
| Picture style, apply | WD 51 | Click a picture, click FORMAT tab, click the More button in the Picture Styles group, click a style |
| Picture, apply effect | PPT 82 | Click photo, click PICTURE TOOLS FORMAT tab, in Picture Styles group, click Picture Effects, point to effect type, click effect |
| Picture, apply style | PPT 82 | Click photo, click PICTURE TOOLS FORMAT tab, in Picture Styles group click style |
| Picture, crop | PPT 40 | Click picture, click PICTURE TOOLS FORMAT tab, in Size group, click Crop, drag Crop handles, click Crop |
| Picture, crop | WD 210 | Click a picture, click FORMAT tab, click the Crop button in the Size group, drag picture border to crop, deselect picture |
| Picture, crop to shape | WD 210 | Click picture, click FORMAT tab, click Crop button arrow in Size group, point to Crop to Shape, click shape |
| Picture, insert | WD 49 | Click INSERT tab, click Pictures button in the Illustrations group, select picture file, click Insert button |
| Picture, insert from your computer | PPT 39 | In content placeholder click ⬚, navigate to picture file location, click picture file, click Insert |
| Picture, insert in a form | AC 189 | In Layout view, click the DESIGN tab, click the Logo button in the Header/Footer group, select the picture file, click OK |
| Picture, resize | PPT 46 | Click object, drag a corner sizing handle |
| Pinned tile, unpin from Start screen | IB 20 | On Start screen, right-click pinned tile, click Unpin from Start |
| PowerPoint, exit | PPT 60 | Click ✖ |
| Presentation, close | PPT 30 | Click FILE tab, click Close |
| Presentation, open | PPT 34 | Click FILE tab, click Open, click Computer, click Browse, navigate to location of file, click file, click Open |
| Presentation, print | PPT 57 | Click FILE tab, click Print, select options, click Print |
| Presentation, save changes | PPT 11 | On Quick Access Toolbar, click 💾 |
| Presentation, save for the first time | PPT 9 | On Quick Access Toolbar, click 💾, on Save As screen click Computer, type filename, navigate to location, click Save |
| Presentation, save with a new name | PPT 34 | Click FILE tab, click Save As, on Save As screen click Computer, type filename, navigate to location, click Save |
| Primary key, specify | AC 67 | *See* Reference box: Specifying a Primary Key in Design View |
| Print area, set | EX 115 | Select range, click the Print Area button in the Page Setup group on PAGE LAYOUT tab, click Set Print Area |
| Print dialog box, open in WordPad | WIN 21 | Click the File tab, click Print |

| TASK | PAGE # | RECOMMENDED METHOD |
|---|---|---|
| **Print titles, add** | EX 117 | Click the Print Titles button in the Page Setup group on the PAGE LAYOUT tab, click Rows to repeat at top, select a range, click OK |
| **Proofing language, change for selected word** | PPT 95 | Select text, on status bar click ENGLISH (UNITED STATES), click language, click OK |
| **Property sheet, open** | AC 159 | Make the object current in Design view, click the Property Sheet button in the Show/Hide group on the DESIGN tab |
| **Query, define** | AC 125 | Click the CREATE tab, click the Query Design button in the Queries group |
| **Query, run** | AC 127 | Double-click the query in the Navigation Pane or, in the Results group on the DESIGN tab, click the Run button |
| **Query results, sort** | AC 133 | *See Reference box: Sorting a Query Datasheet* |
| **Quick Start selection, add** | AC 86 | Click the FIELDS tab, click More Fields in the Add & Delete group, click the Quick Start selection |
| **Range, select adjacent** | EX 11 | Click a cell, drag the pointer from the selected cell to the cell in the lower-right corner of the range |
| **Range, select nonadjacent** | EX 12 | Select a cell or an adjacent range, press the Ctrl key as you select additional cells or adjacent ranges |
| **Record, add new** | AC 20 | In the Records group on the HOME tab, click the New button |
| **Record, delete** | AC 122 | *See Reference box: Deleting a Record* |
| **Record, move to first** | AC 30 | Click ⏮ |
| **Record, move to last** | AC 30 | Click ⏭ |
| **Record, move to next** | AC 30 | Click ▶ |
| **Record, move to previous** | AC 30 | Click ◀ |
| **Records, print selected in a form** | AC 199 | Click the FILE tab, click Print in the navigation bar, click Print, click Selected Record(s), click OK |
| **Records, redisplay all after filter** | AC 138 | In Sort & Filter group on HOME tab, click the Toggle Filter button |
| **Recycle Bin, open** | WIN 22 | Double-click the Recycle Bin icon on desktop |
| **Relative reference, create** | EX 150 | Type the cell reference as it appears in the worksheet |
| **Report, print** | AC 39 | *See Reference box: Printing a Report* |
| **Report, print specific pages of** | AC 219 | In the Print group on the PRINT PREVIEW tab, click Print, click Pages, enter number of pages to print in From and To boxes, click OK |
| **Report Wizard, activate** | AC 208 | Click the CREATE tab, click Report Wizard button in Reports group, choose the table or query for the report, select fields, click Next |
| **Ribbon, expand in File Explorer** | FM 13 | Click ⌄ |
| **Row, change height** | EX 29 | Drag the bottom border of the row heading up or down |
| **Row, delete from table** | WD 136 | Select the row to delete, click the Delete button on the Mini toolbar, click Delete Rows |
| **Row, insert in table** | WD 131 | Click a row, click the LAYOUT tab, click the Insert Above or Insert Below button in Rows & Columns group |
| **Row, select** | EX 26 | Click the row heading |
| **Rows, repeat in printout** | EX 118 | Click the Print Titles button in the Page Setup group on the PAGE LAYOUT tab, click Rows to repeat at top, select range, click OK |

| TASK | PAGE # | RECOMMENDED METHOD |
|------|--------|--------------------|
| **Section break, insert in document** | WD 153 | Click where you want to insert a section break, click PAGE LAYOUT tab, click Breaks button in the Page Setup group, click a section break type |
| **Series, create with AutoFill** | EX 162 | Enter the first few entries in a series, drag the fill handle over the adjacent range |
| **Settings menu, open** | WIN 11 | Display the Charms bar, click Settings |
| **Shading, apply to paragraph** | WD 45 | Click in paragraph, click 🖌️▾ in Paragraph group on HOME tab, click color |
| **Shape, apply style** | PPT 80 | Click shape, click DRAWING TOOLS FORMAT tab, in Shape Styles group, click style |
| **Shape, change fill color** | PPT 79 | Click shape, click DRAWING TOOLS FORMAT tab, in Shape Styles group click Shape Fill button arrow, click color |
| **Shape, change outline weight** | PPT 81 | Click shape, click DRAWING TOOLS FORMAT tab, in Shape Styles group click Shape Outline button arrow, point to Weight, click weight |
| **Shape, insert** | PPT 77 | Click INSERT tab, in Illustrations group click Shapes, click shape, drag on slide |
| **Shortcut menu, open** | WIN 15 | Right-click the object |
| **Slide number, display on slides** | PPT 121 | Click INSERT tab, in Text group, click Header & Footer, click Slide number check box, click Apply to All |
| **Slide show, run from current slide** | PPT 53 | On the status bar, click 🖵 |
| **Slide show, run from Slide 1** | PPT 53 | On the Quick Access Toolbar, click 🖵 |
| **Slide show, run in Presenter view** | PPT 54 | In Slide Show view, click ⬤⬤⬤, click Show Presenter View |
| **Slide show, run in Reading view** | PPT 56 | On status bar, click 📖 |
| **Slide, add** | PPT 12 | Click HOME tab, in Slides group click New Slide button arrow, click layout |
| **Slide, delete** | PPT 29 | Right-click slide thumbnail, click Delete Slide |
| **Slide, duplicate** | PPT 28 | Click slide thumbnail, click HOME tab, in Slides group click New Slide button arrow, click Duplicate Selected Slides |
| **Slide, move** | PPT 28 | Drag slide thumbnail to new location |
| **Slide, reset** | INT 36 | Click slide thumbnail, click HOME tab, in Slides group, click Reset |
| **Slides, create from Word outline** | INT 35 | Click HOME tab, in Slides group, click New Slide button arrow, click Slides from Outline, navigate to location, click outline file, click Insert |
| **SmartArt diagram, convert from list** | PPT 24 | *See* Reference box: Converting a Bulleted List into a SmartArt Diagram |
| **SmartArt, create** | WD 152 | Click INSERT tab, click the SmartArt button in the Illustrations group, in the left pane of the Choose a SmartArt Graphic dialog box click a category, in the middle pane click a SmartArt style, click OK, replace placeholder text with new text |
| **Sort, specify ascending in datasheet** | AC 132 | Click a column heading arrow, click Sort A to Z |
| **Sort, specify descending in datasheet** | AC 132 | Click a column heading arrow, click Sort Z to A |
| **Sparklines, create** | EX 239 | *See* Reference box: Creating and Editing Sparklines |
| **Speaker notes, add** | PPT 49 | On status bar click NOTES, click in Notes pane, type note |

| TASK | PAGE # | RECOMMENDED METHOD |
|---|---|---|
| Spelling and grammar, correct for entire document | WD 36 | Click the REVIEW tab, click the Spelling & Grammar button in the Proofing group |
| Spelling, check entire presentation | PPT 51 | Click REVIEW tab, in Proofing group click Spelling |
| Spelling, correct flagged word | PPT 51 | Right-click flagged word, click correct spelling |
| Start PowerPoint | PPT 5 | On Windows Start screen, click the PowerPoint 2013 tile |
| Start screen, scroll | WIN 9 | Move the pointer, drag the scroll bar |
| Start screen, zoom | WIN 2 | Move the pointer, click ▬ on the Start screen |
| Style, apply | WD 85 | Select text, click a style in the Styles group on HOME tab or click ▼ in the Styles group on HOME tab and click a style |
| Switch List, display | WIN 24 | Point to the upper-left corner of the screen, move the pointer down along left edge of the screen |
| Symbols, insert | PPT 94 | Click INSERT tab, in Symbols group click Symbol, click symbol, click Insert, click Close |
| Tab stop, set | WD 143 | *See* Reference box: Setting, Moving, and Clearing Tab Stops |
| Table, add or delete rows and columns | PPT 86 | Click in row or column, click TABLE TOOLS LAYOUT tab, in Rows & Columns group, click option |
| Table, change alignment in cells | PPT 93 | Click cell, click TABLE TOOLS LAYOUT tab, in Alignment group, click option |
| Table, change borders | PPT 90 | Click table, click TABLE TOOLS DESIGN tab, in Draw Borders group select options, in Table Styles group click Borders button arrow, click border |
| Table, change cell fill color | PPT 90 | Click table, click TABLE TOOLS DESIGN tab, in Table Styles group click Shading button arrow, click color |
| Table, change column width | PPT 88 | Point to column border, double-click or drag |
| Table, change row height | PPT 92 | Point to row border, double-click or drag |
| Table, change style | PPT 89 | Click table, click TABLE TOOLS FORMAT tab, in Table styles group, click style |
| Table, create in Datasheet view | AC 11 | *See* Reference box: Creating a Table in Datasheet View |
| Table, fill cell with pictures | PPT 91 | Click cell, click TABLE TOOLS DESIGN tab, in Table Styles group click Shading button arrow, click Picture, navigate to location, click picture file, click Insert |
| Table, insert | WD 124 | Click INSERT tab, click the Table button in the Tables group, move the pointer across the grid to select columns and rows |
| Table, insert on slide | PPT 85 | Click INSERT tab, in Tables group, click Table, click grid |
| Table, open in a database | AC 22 | Double-click the table in the Navigation Pane |
| Table, save in a database | AC 19 | *See* Reference box: Saving a Table |
| Table, sort | WD 133 | *See* Reference box: Sorting the Rows of a Table |
| Text box, insert | WD 188 | *See* Reference box: Inserting a Text Box |
| Text Effects, apply | WD 42 | Select text, click [A ▾] in the Font group on HOME tab, click a text effect |
| Text file, import data from | AC 96 | Click the EXTERNAL DATA tab, click Text File in the Import & Link group, complete the import dialog boxes |
| Text, change format of | PPT 19 | Select text, click HOME tab, in Font group click appropriate button to apply formatting |
| Text, enter into a cell | EX 18 | Click cell, type entry, press Enter or Tab |

| TASK | PAGE # | RECOMMENDED METHOD |
|---|---|---|
| **Text, enter multiple lines in a cell** | EX 28 | Type the first line of the entry, press Alt+Enter, type the next line |
| **Text, move or copy** | PPT 22 | Select text, click HOME tab, in Clipboard group click Cut or Copy, click at new location, in Clipboard group click Paste |
| **Text, wrap within a cell** | EX 28 | Select the cell, click ▦ in the Alignment group on the HOME tab |
| **Theme and theme variant, change** | PPT 36 | Click DESIGN tab, in Themes group click theme |
| **Theme, apply from another presentation** | PPT 72 | Click DESIGN tab, in Themes group click More button, click Browse for Themes, navigate to location, click presentation, click Apply |
| **Theme, apply to a form** | AC 185 | *See* Reference box: Applying a Theme to a Form |
| **Theme, change for workbook** | EX 107 | Click the Themes button in the Themes group on the PAGE LAYOUT tab, click a theme |
| **Theme, select new** | WD 89 | Click DESIGN tab, click Themes button in the Document Formatting group, click a theme |
| **Touch Mode, switch to** | PPT 6 | On Quick Access Toolbar, click ▾, click Touch/Mouse mode if not selected, click 👆, click Touch |
| **Touch mode, turn on** | WD 5 | Click ▾ on the Quick Access toolbar, click Touch/Mouse Mode, click Touch |
| **Transition, change** | PPT 100 | *See* Reference box: Adding Transitions |
| **Unnumbered list, create** | PPT 17 | Select list or placeholder, click HOME tab, in Paragraph group click ▤ or ▤ to deselect it |
| **Video, add to slide** | PPT 112 | *See* Reference box: Adding Videos Stored on Your Computer or Network |
| **Video, set a poster frame** | PPT 117 | On play bar, click time to display frame, click VIDEO TOOLS FORMAT tab, in Adjust group click Poster Frame, click Current Frame |
| **Video, trim** | PPT 118 | Click video, click VIDEO TOOLS PLAYBACK tab, in Editing group, click Trim Video, drag sliders, click OK |
| **View, change in File Explorer** | FM 12 | *See* Reference box: Changing the View in File Explorer |
| **Webpage, pin to Start screen from desktop application** | IB 19 | Click ⚙, click Add site to Start Screen, click Add |
| **Webpage, preview and print from desktop application** | IB 24 | Click ⚙, point to Print, click Print preview, click 🖨 |
| **Webpage, save from desktop application** | IB 26 | Click ⚙, point to File, click Save as, navigate to save location, select Save as type, enter filename, click Save |
| **Webpages, move between with app** | IB 8 | Click ◄ or ◄ and ► or ► |
| **Webpages, move between with desktop application** | IB 12 | Click ◄ or ► |
| **Website, visit** | IB 5 | Click in Address bar, type URL, press Enter |
| **Window, close** | WIN 26 | Click ✕ |
| **Window, maximize** | WIN 19 | Click ▢ |
| **Window, minimize** | WIN 19 | Click ▬ |
| **Window, move** | WIN 19 | Drag the title bar |

| TASK | PAGE # | RECOMMENDED METHOD |
|---|---|---|
| Window, resize | WIN 19 | Drag the edge or the corner of the window |
| Window, restore | WIN 19 | Click ⬜ |
| Windows 8 application, close | WIN 27 | Press Alt+F4 |
| Windows 8 application, snap | WIN 16 | Point to the upper-left corner of the screen, right-click the thumbnail, click Snap left or click Snap right |
| Windows 8 application, start | WIN 13 | Click the application's tile on the Start screen |
| Windows 8 application, switch to another open | WIN 24 | Display the Switch List, click the application's thumbnail |
| Windows 8 application, unsnap | WIN 16 | Drag the separator bar to left or right |
| Windows 8 desktop, display | WIN 2 | Click the Desktop tile on the Start screen |
| Windows 8, start | WIN 8 | Turn on the computer |
| Windows 8, turn off | WIN 30 | Display the Charms bar, click Settings, click Power, click Shut down |
| WordArt, convert text to | WD 204 | Select text, click 🖋, click INSERT tab, click the WordArt button in the Text group, click WordArt style |
| Workbook, close | EX 13 | Click the FILE tab, click Close |
| Workbook, create a new | EX 15 | Click the FILE tab, click New |
| Workbook, open an existing | EX 4 | Click the FILE tab, click Open, select the workbook file |
| Workbook, preview and print | EX 55 | Click the FILE tab, click Print |
| Workbook, save | EX 17 | Click 💾 on the Quick Access Toolbar |
| Worksheet, change orientation | EX 53 | Click the Orientation button in the Page Setup group on the PAGE LAYOUT tab, click Landscape or Portrait |
| Worksheet, change view | EX 52 | Click ▦, ▣, or ⬒ on the status bar |
| Worksheet, copy | EX 16 | Hold down Ctrl and drag a sheet tab to a new location |
| Worksheet, delete | EX 17 | Right-click a sheet tab, click Delete |
| Worksheet, insert | EX 16 | Click ⊕ |
| Worksheet, move | EX 16 | Drag the sheet tab to a new location |
| Worksheet, rename | EX 16 | Double-click the sheet tab, type a new name, press Enter |
| Worksheet, scale for printing | EX 54 | Set the width and height in the Scale to Fit group on the PAGE LAYOUT tab |
| Worksheets, move between | EX 8 | Click a sheet tab or click a tab scrolling button and then click a sheet tab |